THE AUTHOR

Ian Sinclair, born 1932 in Tayport, Fife, was educated at Madras College, St Andrews, and the University of St Andrews, where he read chemistry, mainly because there were no courses in electronic engineering available at the time. He joined the Research Department of the English Electric Valve Co. in 1956, working on electron optics and photoelectric devices and contributing articles to technical magazines. In 1966 he became a lecturer, first at Havering Technical College and subsequently at Braintree College of Further Education, teaching physics and electronics and writing books on these topics. The interest in computing, first aroused by a course in FORTRAN programming in 1964, surfaced again in San Francisco in 1977 when microcomputers became available, and he wrote for several US magazines until microcomputers became available in the UK. He has to date written about 200 books on electronics and computing topics and has been a full-time writer since 1982.

Collins
DICTIONARY
Computing

Collins

DICTIONARY

Computing

THIRD EDITION

Ian Sinclair

HarperCollinsPublishers

HarperCollins Publishers
Westerhill Road, Bishopbriggs, Glasgow G64 2QT

First published 1991

Third edition 2000

Reprint 9 8 7 6 5 4 3 2

© 2000 Ian R. Sinclair

ISBN 0 00 472512 3

Printed in Great Britain by Omnia Books Ltd, Glasgow G64.

PREFACE TO THE THIRD EDITION

Computers are now as much a consumer item as kettles, a normal part of everyday life, yet few other consumer items can have given rise to so many new terms and abbreviations. This has almost amounted to a private language, and the Internet has been responsible for another outbreak of new words and phrases. The *Collins Dictionary of Computing*, Third Edition, is intended firmly for computer users, those for whom the computer is a tool rather than an end in itself. Whether you use the computer in business, in research, in teaching, for the home or as entertainment, you need to know the language that comes as part of the package. The terms therefore relate to the usage of the machine and are defined in lay language rather than in the obscure way that is favoured by so many texts that deal with computer science.

The list of terms is as complete as is possible at a time when new words are being coined daily, and has been extensively revised to include both the most recent 'buzzwords' as well as older terms that arose in the early days of computing and that are now reappearing as the use of computers becomes commonplace rather than exotic. The range of terms covers fundamentals such as bit, byte and bus, languages such as C, FORTRAN, BASIC and Java, and modern software such as desktop publishing, spreadsheets, word processing and computer-aided design, all of which have become commonplace in the computer age. Terms relating to the most recent software packages, and in particular Internet browsers and electronic mail packages, are emphasized.

In addition to the more technical terms that must inevitably be used to describe technical subjects, this dictionary contains a large selection of the less serious words and phrases that add spice to the conversation of computer users. Words such as bug, worm and virus, elastic-banding, digerati and careware, WYSIWYG and gender mender are all fully explained here, making this a unique guide to the words that were once used by only a small coterie and have now become part of our everyday vocabulary.

All aspects of the use of the personal computer are covered, from the virtual reality of games to the abstract work on artificial intelligence, covering all the uses to which these versatile machines are put in everyday life as well as in more academic contexts.

Autumn 1999   Ian Sinclair

A: the A drive, conventionally the FLOPPY DISK drive in a computer with a single floppy drive. See also B:, C:.

A20 handler a memory-resident program (see TSR PROGRAM) that allows a computer using MS-DOS access to the memory addresses above the 640 kilobyte region.

A20 line the ADDRESS BUS line in an IBM CLONE personal computer that controls the high memory area. This line is controlled by the utility called HIMEM.SYS, and any problems will bring up an error message to the effect that the A20 line cannot be used.

abandon to quit a data file without saving it, so that the data is lost.

a-b box a switch that allows a PERIPHERAL such as a printer to be shared by two computers or to allow a computer the use of two printers.

abbreviation a shortened form of a command. For example, the MS-DOS system allows the command CHDIR (change directory) to be abbreviated to CD, and many APPLICATIONS PACKAGE programs also allow commands to be abbreviated to single letters or pairs of letters.

abduction a diagnostic method for explaining faults or developing a plan of action.

abort to stop a RUN (sense 1) or the effect of a COMMAND before it is completed, usually by a deliberate decision when the action is seen to be unsuitable. In general, aborting a program RUN or a DOS command will result in nothing being done so that no files are altered.

aborted (of a RUN, sense 1) being stopped by a fault or other abnormal condition.

ABRD see AUTOMATIC BAUD RATE DETECTION.

ABS a FUNCTION that removes the sign from a number in a cell of a worksheet, or in a program, returning the absolute value. Thus ABS(–22) is 22. One use is to decide whether a given number is close to another. A TEST (sense 1) such as: IF ABS(TARGET – GUESS) < 3 tests for the 'closeness' of TARGET and GUESS to find if they differ by less than 3, irrespective of which is the larger.

abscissa another name for the X-COORDINATE of a graph.

absolute cell reference a CELL REFERENCE in a WORKSHEET that does not change on REPLICATION. Conventionally the DOLLAR SIGN is used to mark the cell letter and number to indicate an absolute reference, and it is also possible to make the row or the column reference absolute on its own. For example, H2 is an absolute reference to cell H2, and $H2 means that the column letter is fixed although the row number can change.

1

absolute instruction an instruction that is complete in itself, requiring no ARGUMENT or further data reference.

absolute maximum rating a value of electrical or mechanical quantity that must not be exceeded, such as input voltage or amount of mechanical shock.

absolute path a PATH (sense 2), the starting point of which is the ROOT DIRECTORY (root folder).

absolute pathname a FILENAME that includes the ABSOLUTE PATH to the file.

absolute tab a TABULATION point, the position of which is measured from the left-hand edge of the paper rather than from the margin line.

absolute value the value of a number, ignoring any sign. For example, the absolute value of –6.7 is 6.7. See also ABS.

abstract data type a DATA TYPE used in OBJECT-ORIENTED programming. An abstract data type is manipulated by actions that do not depend on the format of the data, such as the actions of PUSH and POP on a STACK.

AC (alternating current) the type of electric CURRENT (sense 1) used for power transmission and generated by rotating machines. The current flows in either direction alternately, and the direction reverses typically 100 times a second. This type of current cannot be used directly as a power supply for computer components, so the power supply unit has to convert it to unidirectional current (see RECTIFICATION) and then to steady current (see SMOOTHING, sense 2). Compare DC.

ACAP see APPLICATION CONFIGURATION ACCESS PROTOCOL.

accelerated graphics port see AGP.

acceleration time the time required for a DISK to reach its normal rotating speed when it has been called into action. This particularly affects FLOPPY DISKS, since a HARD DRIVE is normally rotating for as long as a computer is switched on, although small portable machines usually provide for a hard drive to be at rest when not in use.

accelerator a HARDWARE or SOFTWARE device to speed up an action such as GRAPHICS, INTERNET transfers or FLOATING-POINT arithmetic.

accelerator card a CIRCUIT BOARD that contains a MICROPROCESSOR and associated chips. When plugged into an EXPANSION SLOT or replacing the existing microprocessor of the computer, the accelerator board provides faster operation without the need to upgrade to a different computer. Accelerator cards have in the past been used to provide faster GRAPHICS and FLOATING POINT arithmetic actions.

accelerator key a KEY (sense 1) that is used to accomplish an action that otherwise would be done by moving a MOUSE and/or selecting from a MENU. Accelerator keys are often key combinations, consisting of the letter key pressed along with the ALT or CTRL KEY. See also HOT KEY.

accent colour a colour used in a PRESENTATION GRAPHICS program to mark features on a SLIDE or to distinguish different parts of a graph.

accent mark one of the marks that are placed over or under letters in many languages. Typical accent marks are the grave, acute and circumflex. All PC-COMPATIBLE computers and CLONES contain a CHARACTER GENERATOR for these marks, and all DOT-MATRIX, LASER and INKJET printers can produce them on paper. Accented characters can be obtained on the screen of any computer running Windows by using the CHARACTER MAP utility, and these characters can also be printed on paper.

acceptable use policy a set of rules enforced by an Internet provider (ISP) to restrict the uses to which the network may be put, typically to avoid pornography or advertising.

acceptance sample a small sample of a set taken for testing to check that the set is likely to conform to standards.

acceptance testing a scheme for checking that a computer system will perform as intended. A large computer system, the cost of which may amount to many hundreds of thousands of pounds, cannot simply be put in place and switched on. It is extensively tested with the type of program and data that will eventually be used with it. During the time of this testing, the operators of the MACHINE will also undergo training in its use.

access 1. the right of use of a computer and its files. This may require the entry of a PASSWORD if the MACHINE is to be used by a selected number of operators. **2.** to gain connection to SOFTWARE. **3.** to retrieve information from STORAGE. **4.** (**Access**) see MICROSOFT ACCESS.

access code see PASSWORD.

access control a method, such as the use of a PASSWORD, that can be used to ensure that only a selected number of operators can use a computer system. A good access system should be proof against a CRACKER, but many good systems can be rendered useless by carelessness. This includes using the initials of the operator as a password, leaving passwords written on scraps of paper or using numbers like 12345.

access control list the listing of services available to a networked user from the central SERVER.

access field see KEY FIELD.

accessibility options a set of programs packaged with MICROSOFT WINDOWS that makes the use of the KEYBOARD and MOUSE easier for the disabled. For example, two keys that normally need to be struck together can be struck in sequence. Other options allow the use of the keyboard in place of the mouse, provision for larger FONTS and contrasting colours, and visual indications of sounds.

accession number a number that is attached to a RECORD (sense 1) to show the order of entry.

access level a method of enforcing security in a MULTITASKING system that can be running several different programs, all co-existing in memory. Each program is assigned an access level, typically numbered 0 to 3 of which level 0 is the highest PRIVILEGE LEVEL (sense 1). The highest level is usually reserved for vital parts of the operating system (OS), so that no UTILITY program can alter any part of the memory occupied by these bytes unless its access level is also level 0. Access to any program space is granted only to programs with an access level that is either equal to the assigned value or higher.

access method the way in which DATA in MEMORY or in a DISK file is obtained for processing.

access plan a strategy for processing a query to a DATABASE, part of the QUERY LANGUAGE system design.

access point see KEY FIELD.

access time the time that is needed to find data. Access to the memory is fast, with access times measured in NANOSECONDS. Access time is considerably longer for a HARD DRIVE, where it means the time that elapses, on average, between requesting an input and getting the data. The delay in this case is caused mainly (when the disk runs continuously) by the time that is needed to position the disk READ/WRITE HEAD correctly. For a FLOPPY DISK the access time also includes the time that is needed to bring the disk up to operating speed. Average access time for a hard drive is greatly improved by using a disk CACHE memory.

accordion fold see FANFOLD.

account or **accounting file** a log set up for each user on a NETWORK so as to record the use of network resources and, if required, charge for network time.

accounting format the number format that can be used in a SPREAD-SHEET for money quantities for accountancy uses. For example, zero values are show as hyphens and negative values within brackets.

accounting package a software package that deals with money management, replacing the ledgers used in paper accounts. Some accounting packages are very simple, aimed at sole traders or small businesses, and not intended to replace the use of an accountant. Others are much more elaborate and their use demands a good knowledge of accountancy practice. A typical compromise package is QUICKEN-98 for Windows.

accumulator a portion of a MICROPROCESSOR used as a REGISTER (sense 2) for temporary storage, such as for the intermediate results of arithmetic or when transferring data from one location to another. Modern microprocessors have several such registers, but one is usually designated as the main accumulator.

accuracy a measure of how close a measurement is compared to the true value, free from errors in data. For example, in a file dealing with people, accuracy would imply that no one has been recorded as being 190 years old or being 69 feet tall. Accuracy in a data file depends on the correct entry of data by the user, but the programmer can often help by designing a program that checks for ridiculous entries. Do not confuse accuracy with PRECISION OF NUMBER, which could mean that age was recorded to the nearest minute. See also VALIDATION.

ACIA (asynchronous communications interface adapter) a circuit, usually in a single chip, that provides a PORT that can be used for serial communications to and from the computer without the need for a continuous stream of synchronizing signals.

ACK the word used for ASCII character code 6, used as an ACKNOWLEDGEMENT of a message received correctly. See also NAK.

acknowledgement a signal sent to indicate that data or a signal has been received. The ACK signal indicates that the message has been satisfactorily received and NAK (negative acknowledgement) indicates that the message has been corrupted. The NAK would be generated because of a failure in a PARITY or other check on the message bytes.

Acorn™ a computer firm located in Cambridge that manufactured small computers under the BBC brand name for sale to schools. After being bought by Olivetti, Acorn has specialized in RISC processors and developed the Archimedes computer, also sold to schools but incompatible with the PERSONAL COMPUTER or MACINTOSH designs. Later versions have been able to run PC software to some extent, and a more recent development has been a low-cost INTERNET terminal.

acoustic coupler an almost obsolete method of transmitting data over telephone lines or radio links. To transmit computer data over telephone lines, the data must be converted into electrical tone signals and sent at a comparatively low rate. If direct connection of electrical equipment to the telephone system is prohibited, an acoustic coupler converts the electrical signals into musical notes that are sent and received by the normal telephone microphone and earpiece. This is done by placing the hand-piece of the telephone over a pair of rubber cups, one containing a loudspeaker, the other a microphone. Problems of this arrangement include slow speed, interference from other sounds and inefficient coupling, which lead to data errors. Acoustic couplers are used only where a direct connection to the telephone system is impossible, such as in some hotel rooms or in telephone boxes. A direct electrical connection to the telephone system is greatly preferable. See also MODEM.

acoustic hood a sound-muffling cover placed over a noisy piece of mechanism. At one time an acoustic hood would be used for a DAISY-WHEEL printer or, more recently, for an impact DOT-MATRIX printer.

ACPI see ADVANCED CONFIGURATION AND POWER INTERFACE.

Acrobat an application from ADOBE SYSTEMS that allows documents to be written or converted into portable document format (PDF), independent of computer type. Acrobat PDF files are used extensively for documentation transmitted by the INTERNET and are also used in printing along with POSTSCRIPT files.

action frame a screenful (see SCREEN, sense 1) of information that requests or prompts some reply from the user. Action frames are found particularly in computer-assisted learning (CAL) programs in which each frame is designed to advance the user's knowledge of the topic and the response is to a simple question that will check that this part of the topic has been understood.

action query or **bulk update** a form of QUERY action in MICROSOFT ACCESS that allows large amounts of data to be updated in one operation. For example, all cash amounts could be increased by 5 per cent.

action stub see CONDITION STUB.

active area the area of a WORKSHEET that contains data.

active cell or **current cell** the CELL of a WORKSHEET that contains the POINTER (sense 1) or is highlighted (see HIGHLIGHT). See Fig. 1.

active desktop the use of a WEB PAGE as the WALLPAPER for a computer running WINDOWS.

active database the DATABASE file that is currently loaded (see LOAD) and in use.

active file a file that is open and in use. Data programs should be arranged so that a file is active only for as long as it needs to be and that any interruption (see ABORT) should close all active files. Failure to close files properly can cause loss of data and result in disks containing data that cannot be accessed except by an expert programmer.

active loudspeaker a form of loudspeaker that incorporates an amplifier and is powered from the mains supply rather than from the computer, used mainly in sound systems for MULTIMEDIA work.

active low (of an electronic signal) having a valid effect when its voltage level is low. The opposite is *active high*.

active matrix display a form of LCD SCREEN (sense 1) in which each unit is controlled by a separate TRANSISTOR or set of transistors. An active matrix display is more difficult to construct than the older type, but the display is much more controllable, allowing better resolution and contrast, and making colour display possible.

active monitor a routine used in a TOKEN RING NETWORK to check and correct network actions.

active partition a portion of a HARD DRIVE that has been partitioned (see PARTITIONED DRIVE) and contains the MS-DOS operating system. Early versions of MS-DOS (prior to 4.01) could not deal with hard drive storage space of more than 32 megabytes and larger disks had to be partitioned into 32 megabytes (or smaller) portions. Of these, only one could be used to contain the MS-DOS system tracks and be described as active. Later versions of DOS could deal with hard drive sizes up to about 500 megabytes, and hard drives of many gigabytes capacity can now be used along with MICROSOFT WINDOWS. See also FDISK.

active printer the printer in a system that is currently connected to a PORT of the computer. A program may be configured to use more than

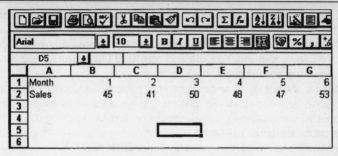

Fig. 1. **Active cell**. The way that Excel marks an active cell is by a thickening of the border of the cell as seen on the screen.

one printer, but only the printer that is connected, either locally or through a NETWORK, can be used.

active sensing a MIDI action that checks for signals on a music CHANNEL (sense 2).

active task list a list of programs that are suspended and that can be switched in and out of use. For small computers TASK SWITCHING is an acceptable substitute for full MULTITASKING, allowing the user to switch from one program to another without loss of data or the need to restart each program. A multitasking system will also maintain an active task list, see ALT-TAB SWITCHING.

active window the window on a SCREEN (sense 1) in which the program is currently running and contains a POINTER (sense 1). In MICROSOFT WINDOWS, other windows may be running programs that are working, but only one window contains the pointer.

Active X a form of programming, created by Microsoft, intended to run on slow INTERNET connections and to produce animated effects. See also JAVA.

activity or **activity ratio** the fraction of the total number of stored DATABASE RECORDS (sense 1) that will be read or written in a RUN (sense 1). A file with low activity might indicate that many records are redundant.

activity light the indicator light for a DISK DRIVE that is lit when the drive is reading (see READ) or writing (see WRITE) data.

activity loading a method of organizing a DATABASE file on a disk so that the RECORDS (sense 1) that are most often used can be most rapidly loaded.

activity ratio see ACTIVITY.

actual argument the ARGUMENT that is used in a call to a FUNCTION, as distinct from the formal argument. For example, a function that is called as POSITION(X,Y), where X and Y are formal arguments, may be executed with numbers 45 and 67 replacing X and Y respectively as the actual arguments.

actual size a SCREEN (sense 1) view of a PAGE (sense 1) in a DTP document that shows the page at the size in which it will be printed. Unless a suitable A4 MONITOR (sense 1) is used, this usually means that only a part of the page can be shown at a time and scrolling (see SCROLL) will be needed to see the remainder. See also PRINT PREVIEW.

actuator a device that uses electrical signals to control mechanical movement. See also HEAD ACTUATOR.

A-D see A TO D.

ADA a comparatively modern HIGH-LEVEL LANGUAGE developed for and used mainly for military computing, in which reliability of software is of primary importance. ADA is named after Ada Augusta, Countess of LOVELACE, who was a friend and colleague of Charles BABBAGE. She employed her mathematical skills to suggest methods of programming Babbage's *difference engine*, the first programmable computer.

adapter a CIRCUIT BOARD that can be inserted into a computer, usually into an EXPANSION SLOT, to provide for some additional action such as better video resolution, the use of a SCANNER (sense 2) or connection to a NETWORK.

adaptive answering a feature of a FAX MODEM that can distinguish between a fax or a voice incoming call.

adaptive channel allocation or **adaptive routing** a system of communications in which communications links are allocated according to demand rather than being fixed.

adaptive digital pulse code modulation (ADPCM) a method of compressing and digitizing (see DIGITIZE) audio data that operates by recording the difference between samples.

adaptive learning an ARTIFICIAL INTELLIGENCE method in which the program adjusts scaling factors so as to produce the correct transformations between input and output.

adaptive routing I. or **dynamic routing** a method of switching signals in a NETWORK so that the quickest route is always used. **2.** see ADAPTIVE CHANNEL ALLOCATION.

adaptive transform acoustic coding (ADTRAC) a method for digitizing (see DIGITIZE) AUDIO signals that achieves compression by ignoring low-amplitude signals that are present at the same time as high-amplitude signals.

ADC see A TO D.

ADCCP see ADVANCED DATA COMMUNICATIONS CONTROL PROTOCOL.

addenda text added to a main document, such as FOOTNOTES, ENDNOTES, TABLE OF CONTENTS and INDEX.

add-in a portion of SOFTWARE that can be called into use by a main program to provide useful ancillary actions. For example, a graph-display program may be added in to a SPREADSHEET so that selected data can be displayed in graphical form. See also DLL.

add-on a HARDWARE board or card that can be plugged into a computer in order to provide additional actions such as the use of a SCANNER (sense 2) or NETWORK.

address 1. a reference number for a byte in the MEMORY. **2.** an INTERNET reference in word form (see also URL). **3.** the name used as a reference for EMAIL.

addressability the degree to which the PIXELS on a graphics SCREEN (sense 1) can be individually controlled. Older graphics systems appear to control small single pixels but in fact deal with pixels in groups. High addressability, as used on VGA systems, requires a very large amount of memory dedicated to graphics use; see VIDEO MEMORY.

address bar the space provided in a BROWSER for typing the INTERNET address for a World Wide Web (WWW) contact.

address book a form of DATABASE containing information on people, particularly names, addresses, telephone numbers and EMAIL addresses. This can be used in conjunction with email and WORD PROCESSOR programs.

address bus the set of connections between the MICROPROCESSOR and the MEMORY and PORTS of a computer. These connections are labelled as A0, A1 and so on, up to A31 for a modern system, and allow the microprocessor to make electronic contact with any location in the computer system.

address resolution the process of converting a coded INTERNET site address into an intelligible and readable form.

ADMA coprocessor a chip that can be used for direct access (see DMA) to MEMORY, particularly intended for older computers that are IBM-COMPATIBLE.

administrative distance a number used as a measure of usefulness of NETWORK routing information.

administrative domain the total content of a NETWORK managed by one authority.

administrator 1. the software that controls a suite of programs. **2.** the human manager of a DATABASE system.

Adobe Systems a SOFTWARE HOUSE (sense 1) located in California, specializing in FONT and printing software. Adobe developed the first page description language (PDL), POSTSCRIPT, and the later PDF document format.

Adobe Pagemaker™ (formerly Aldus PageMaker) or **PageMaker**™ a very well-known DTP and page layout program that allows text and IMAGES (sense 2) to be assembled into pages for book or newspaper publication. PageMaker is one of the leading brands in this type of work. See also MICROSOFT PUBLISHER, VENTURA.

Adobe Type Manager™ (**ATM**) printing software that deals with POSTSCRIPT fonts.

ADTRAC see ADAPTIVE TRANSFORM ACOUSTIC CODING.

ADSL see ASYMMETRIC DIGITAL SUBSCRIBER LINE.

advance to move from one SLIDE to the next in a PRESENTATION GRAPHICS display.

advanced configuration and power interface (ACPI) a standard method for power management for a PERSONAL COMPUTER. Typically this implements systems for shutting down the MONITOR (sense 1) and HARD DRIVE when not required, and for other power-saving actions.

advanced intelligent tape (AIT) a form of tape drive or STREAMER for storing very large amounts of data, with fast data transfer rates.

Advanced Micro Devices Inc. (AMD) a major US manufacturer of MICROPROCESSOR chips and related PERSONAL COMPUTER products. The AMD K6 series of microprocessors are serious rivals to the INTEL Pentium for use in modern PC machines.

advanced power management (AMP) a software program that can reduce the use of power on PORTABLE and other battery-operated computers. This software shuts down parts of the system that are not currently in use, as, for example, a HARD DRIVE motor when disk access is not required. See also ADVANCED CONFIGURATION AND POWER INTERFACE, a more wide-ranging system.

Advanced Research Project Agency Network see ARPANET.

advanced run length limited (ARRL) a way of coding information into magnetic signals on a HARD DRIVE that achieves tighter packing of data and faster operation. See also RLL.

advanced SCSI peripheral interface (ASPI) a set of DLL routines that provides an interface between MICROSOFT WINDOWS and SCSI devices.

advanced technology attachment see ATA.

advanced technology attachment interface with extensions see ATA-2.

adventure game a variety of GAME in which the SCREEN (sense 1) describes situations and the user is challenged to escape and to find some object. This is done by using simple command words and phrases like LOOK LEFT, GO NORTH, PICK UP WAND, etc. The original adventure games were written by Scott Adams for a MAINFRAME computer and consisted of text only. Subsequent adventures have been biased towards mythical kingdoms, with malignant dwarves, trolls and wizards featuring prominently and with graphics that are often animated. Some of the techniques used in the more advanced games have led to VIRTUAL REALITY programs.

aerial view an overall or zoomed out (see ZOOM) view of a drawing, particularly used by CAD programs.

affine infinity an infinite number with a positive or negative sign. See also PROJECTIVE INFINITY.

afterglow or **persistence** the remaining light from the cathode ray tube

(CRT) of a VDU after the scanning beam of electrons has passed. A comparatively long period of afterglow reduces the flicker from the SCREEN (sense 1) but makes the picture blurred when information is changing rapidly. The equivalent of afterglow can be provided for ACTIVE MATRIX DISPLAY screens by using software.

agent software in a networked system that is responsible for locating and transferring information.

aggregate function any FUNCTION of a DATABASE that carries out arithmetical actions (see ARITHMETIC) such as addition, record counting, calculation of averages, etc.

aggregation the grouping, for DATABASE design purposes, of relationships between entities (see ENTITY) along with the entities themselves.

AGP (accelerated graphics port) a type of hardware BUS that allows the use of a fast GRAPHICS ADAPTER on a PERSONAL COMPUTER, replacing the PCI BUS connection formerly used and using a slightly longer EXPANSION SLOT. The use of an AGP connection is essential if THREE-DIMENSIONAL GRAPHICS are required.

AI see ARTIFICIAL INTELLIGENCE.

AIT see ADVANCED INTELLIGENT TAPE.

Aladdin a design of CHIPSET from Acer Laboratories Inc.

alert any form of message, visual or acoustic, that warns of an error or a change in operating conditions.

alert box a MESSAGE BOX that appears on screen to deliver a warning. For example, an alert box will appear if you try to quit a program without saving your data file.

ALGOL (*al*gorithmic-*o*riented *l*anguage) the first HIGH-LEVEL LANGUAGE to break away from mathematical formula processing. See also FORTRAN.

algorithm a plan, routine or sequence of actions for solving a problem. This might be a strategy for playing a game, a method of solving an equation or a way of arranging data. In most common computer applications an algorithmic solution to a problem must be constructed first. It is then converted or coded (see CODE, sense 2) into a program using a PROGRAMMING LANGUAGE. However, computers can solve problems without an algorithm or a program. See NEURAL NETWORK, ANALOGUE COMPUTER.

algorithmic error an error that is incurred in the course of executing an ALGORITHM because of the nature of the algorithm itself, as distinct from a COMPUTATIONAL ERROR.

algorithmic language a PROGRAMMING LANGUAGE that carries out its work by using a set of defined steps rather than by trial and error.

algorithmic-oriented language see ALGOL.

alias 1. a short name that stands in for a longer one and that can be automatically translated into the longer version as required. Microsoft WINDOWS 95 onwards permitted the use of long FILENAMES (up to a total of

255 characters), but when filenames are viewed using MS-DOS, each long name is contracted to a shorter alias, using the MS-DOS 8-3 convention of a maximum of 8 characters in the main part of the name along with an optional extension of up to three characters. The alias is constructed by using the first six letters of the long name, followed by a tilde character (~) and a digit. For example, a Windows file called IANSIN-CLAIR.DOC would appear as IANSIN~1.DOC under MS-DOS. The use of the alias allows the file to be available to older software. CD-R and CD-RW writing drives, using ISO 9660, convert to alias names if needed so as to conform to 8.3 rules. **2.** a shorter version of a name used for a STYLE in MICROSOFT WORD. **3.** a RANGE NAME, as used in a WORKSHEET. **4.** on the INTERNET, any of a set of HOSTNAMES with the same INTERNET ADDRESS.

aliasing 1. or **jaggies** or **sawtooth distortion** the stepped appearance of diagonal lines on a SCREEN (sense 1) caused by a low RESOLUTION display. **2.** errors in a analogue to digital (see A TO D) conversion system caused by trying to convert a signal whose frequency is too high compared with the sampling frequency. See also QUANTIZATION.

alias table a term used in DATABASE design to mean an alternative set of names for data items, allowing different users of the database to use different name references. See also LOCATION TRANSPARENCY.

alien disk a FLOPPY DISK whose FORMAT (sense 3) is for a different type of machine and which therefore cannot be used unless a suitable disk drive and/or software are also available. The PERSONAL COMPUTER, with suitable software, can read some types of disks recorded by a MACINTOSH and can read later types of 3.5-inch disks created by the Amstrad 8256 and 8512 machines.

alife or **A-Life** (artificial life) the simulation of life processes (birth, growth, death) by computer software.

alignment 1. the way in which text in a DTP document is arranged as flush left, ragged right (left alignment), flush right, ragged left (aligned left), centred (each side ragged) or fully justified (see JUSTIFY). **2.** the precision with which the head of a DISK DRIVE is positioned.

alignment character the character, usually a full stop or comma, used by a decimal align (see DECIMAL TAB) action in a WORD PROCESSOR.

allocation 1. the assignment of resources such as memory, disk space, use of printer, etc., to parts of a program, co-existing programs or multiple users of a computing system. **2.** the assignment of financial resources to a business scheme that a suitable program might be able to optimize.

allocation unit or **cluster** the unit of HARD DRIVE storage. For example, a hard drive may use units of 4 kilobytes, so that no smaller portion of the drive can be used. This leads to wasteful use because if a set of files of less than 4 kilobytes are to be saved, each file will occupy one unit, even if this leads to a unit storing only a few bytes.

allophone a unit of sound that makes up a spoken word, used in speech synthesis and voice recognition (see DIRECT VOICE INPUT). All speech can be considered as being made up from a limited number of allophones, making synthesis considerably easier than if voice sounds had to be constructed by using frequency and duration information.

all-points-addressable display (APA) a SCREEN (sense 1) display in which each point (see PIXEL) on the screen can have its colour and brightness controlled by reference to an ADDRESS (sense 1) number.

alphabetical order the order of the letters of the alphabet from A to Z. Computer programs do not necessarily follow a strict alphabetical order when arranging words because the computer ASCII codes distinguish between upper-case and lower-case characters, placing A before Z, and Z before a. For example, in a truly alphabetical index you might find the order *Ambiguous, ASCII, Attack*. The computer would normally arrange these words in the order *ASCII, Ambiguous, Attack* because the upper-case S in *ASCII* is given a position ahead of any lower-case letter. See also DICTIONARY SORT.

alphabetize to put data such as a list of names into ALPHABETICAL ORDER. A *reverse alphabetized list* is a list put into reverse alphabetical order (Z first, A last).

alphanumeric (of a character set, code, file of data, etc.) consisting of a range of characters that includes all the letters (upper- and lower-case) and digits. This excludes PUNCTUATION MARKS and signs such as $ and %.

alpha test the first version of a new program, which is tested by a small number of professional users. This version may not contain the full number of features and is likely also to contain serious BUGS. See also BETA SOFTWARE.

alt on the INTERNET, a NEWSGROUP category that allows the unregulated creation of new groups. Any new group starting with the alt designation can be expected to contain bizarre comments.

Altair 8800 a kit form of computer that was the first put on sale in 1975, creating a new market for personal computers and a new breed of self-educated programmers unfettered by habits of the past. The success of this kit (more than 10,000 units sold) convinced other manufacturers that a HOME COMPUTER was a viable product.

Alta Vista a SEARCH ENGINE for the INTERNET with a vast word index, usually the first choice for any users searching for information.

alternate key a KEY (sense 2) for a DATABASE that is not a PRIMARY KEY.

alternating current see AC.

alternative mode or **alternating mode** a form of MULTI-ACCESS SYSTEM that allows two operators to share a single set of files.

ALT key a KEY (sense 1) used on all PERSONAL COMPUTERS and many other modern computers, usually in conjunction with other keys. See also KEY ASSIGNMENT.

ALT-Tab switching switching from one TASK to another in WINDOWS by using the Alt-Tab key combination. The ALT KEY and TAB KEY are held down to reveal a TASK LIST, and releasing and pressing the Tab key will move from one task to another – the task that is highlighted when the Alt key is released will become the ACTIVE TASK. Windows 95 onwards can use the TASKBAR also for this action.

ALU see ARITHMETIC AND LOGIC UNIT.

AM see AMPLITUDE MODULATION.

ambiguity error error in selection of data caused by ambiguity of file-name or the selection command. This might be caused by the existence of two files with the same name or by using an AMBIGUOUS FILENAME.

ambiguous filename any FILENAME that can refer to more than one file, such as a filename containing a WILD CARD character. For example, the MS-DOS command DEL CHAP*.TXT would delete files CHAP1.TXT, CHAP2.TXT, CHAPTER.TXT, etc.

AMD see ADVANCED MICRO DEVICES INC.

amendment record a RECORD (sense 1) whose data is used to update an existing record in a file, usually by directly replacing the old record.

American Megatrends Inc. (AMI) a manufacturer of BIOS chips for IBM-COMPATIBLE computers.

American National Standards Institute see ANSI.

America Online (AOL) a major US provider of INTERNET services, based in Virginia.

American Standard Code for Information Interchange see ASCII.

AMI see AMERICAN MEGATRENDS INC.

Amiga™ see COMMODORE BUSINESS MACHINES.

Ami Pro a WORD PROCESSOR package that was acquired by LOTUS (now part of IBM) and subsequently named Lotus Word Pro.

AMP see ADVANCED POWER MANAGEMENT.

ampersand the & sign, which is used in some applications with special significance. For example, the ampersand is often used in MAILING LIST programs to surround VARIABLE names.

amplitude the size of a signal, measured from the zero level to one peak. This can apply to an electrical, acoustic or any other signal that is shaped like a wave. The amplitude of a sound signal is a measure of the loudness of the sound that is heard, and the amplitude of a light signal is a measure of the light brightness. Digital signals are of fixed amplitude, with a considerable margin allowed. For example, in a system that uses signals that are nominally zero volts for binary 0 and +5V for binary 1, levels of 0 to +1.2V may be read as binary zero and levels of 3.5V to 5V read as binary 1. See Fig. 2.

amplitude modulation (AM) an old method of coding signals on to a radio wave by varying the amplitude of the CARRIER (sense 2). See also FM; PHASE-SHIFT MODULATION.

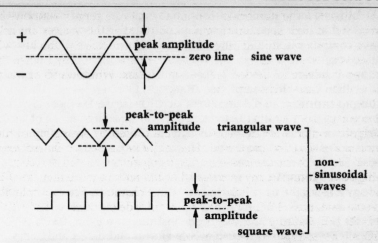

Fig. 2. **Amplitude**. The height of a wave. For the simplest shape of wave, the sine wave, the peak amplitude is measured from the centre (zero) line to either peak. For other shapes it is more usual to measure the peak-to-peak amplitude, as illustrated.

analogical reasoning the use of a computer-modelled (see MODEL BUILD-ING) system to simulate problems and solutions for complex systems such as car and aircraft behaviour.

analogue (of quantities) capable of representation by varying electrical voltage. An input quantity such as temperature, light brightness or sound VOLUME (sense 1) can be represented by an electrical voltage, the amplitude of which is proportional to the amplitude of the input. By contrast, a DIGITAL representation would use a set of BINARY electrical signals to mean a number that measures the amplitude of the input at some instant, with a new number being generated at each instant.

analogue card a printed circuit board PCB that contains circuits for converting changing analogue signals into digital form using AMPLITUDE QUANTIZATION. See also A TO D.

analogue computer a form of computer that deals with ANALOGUE signals of continually varying sizes and the actions of which are conditioned by the HARDWARE connections between units. This type of computer was developed to a working extent before the digital type and is still very useful. A crude example was the bombsight computer of World War II, which used inputs from the bomb-aiming telescope, the air-speed indicator, the altimeter and other measuring units of an aeroplane to operate the bomb-release mechanism. This was done mechanically, but the later analogue computers used electronic methods, making use of a unit called the OPERATIONAL AMPLIFIER. The analogue computer, which does not use a software program, is particularly useful when a

15

system has a large number of continually varying inputs that must be processed at high speed to obtain an output. For this reason, the analogue computer is still favoured for many control tasks. Compare DIGITAL COMPUTER.

analogue device a device whose signals are continuously variable rather than variable in steps. See ANALOGUE, DIGITAL.

analogue monitor an old term for a MONITOR (sense 1) whose signal inputs are ANALOGUE rather than DIGITAL, allowing a large range of shades of colour or monochrome to be displayed. The use of an analogue monitor is now standard, and the term DIGITAL MONITOR is used in a different sense. See also TTL MONITOR.

analogue to digital converter see A TO D.

analogy model the use of costing and time information from a completed SOFTWARE project in order to estimate for a new project.

analyser a measuring and diagnostic instrument for the HARDWARE of a computer system, used to display waveforms and detect anomalies.

analysis the stage in dealing with a problem in which the nature of the problem and its causes are examined in detail so that a solution can be found.

analytical engine the name used by BABBAGE for the calculating machine that he intended to follow his earlier DIFFERENCE ENGINE. A model has now, some 160 years later, been constructed and has been successfully operated.

analytical graphics graphs that are designed to make data easier to understand and interpret. See also PRESENTATION GRAPHICS.

ancestral file an older file in a set of FILE GENERATIONS.

anchor 1. or **lock** a point relative to which the positions of GRAPHICS in a DOCUMENT are located. A graphics object cannot be moved beyond the page on which the anchor is located, but the anchor itself can be dragged to a new position unless it has been locked. An ICON shows the position of the anchor and its locked or unlocked state. See Fig. 3. **2.** a portion of the HYPERTEXT in a WEB PAGE that is either the start of a HYPERLINK or the destination of a hyperlink.

anchor cell a CELL (sense 1) in a WORKSHEET that is the first cell in a range, highlighted or containing the cell POINTER (sense 1).

anchored point a point that is fixed on a SCREEN (sense 1) view of a CAD or DTP document during an action in which other points are moved. For example, drawing a LINE (sense 1) will require the user to mark one point, the *anchor point*, and then move the mouse so as to position the end point of the line. See also ELASTIC BANDING.

AND a LOGIC action that compares two quantities to find if they are both true. In a QUERY in a DATABASE or in a CELL (sense 1) of a WORKSHEET, the AND statement can be used to connect two conditions. For example, the condition statement 'IF Name = "Smith" AND Age <> 40' can be used

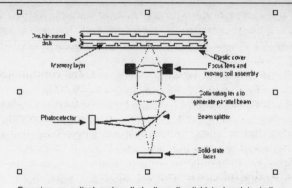

By· using· an· optical· system· that· allows· the· light· to· travel· in· both·
directions·to·and·from·the·disc·surface,·it·is·possible·to·focus·a·reflected·
beam·on·to·a·detector,·and·pick·up·a·signal·when·the·beam·is·reflected·

Fig. 3. **Anchor**. The icon indicates that the graphic image is tied to the text and will
move with the text.

to select RECORDs (sense 1) of one name and a particular age group by
combining two conditions that must both together be true to give a true
answer.

angle the difference in the direction of two straight lines. FUNCTIONs in a
WORKSHEET, such as sin and cos, that take an angle as their ARGUMENT
normally require the angle to be in *radians*. A radian is the angle between
two radii of a circle when the SEGMENT (sense 1) length of the circle
between the ends of the radii is equal to the radius. Some spreadsheets
can work with angles in degrees by using a DEG function. If the DEG
function is not available, then the conversion is 1 radian = 57.295779
degrees or 1 degree = 0.0174532 radians.

angle bracket on the conventional keyboard, either of the characters <
(less than) and > (more than). Books and magazines use a different pair
of characters as angle brackets, and these are embodied in the ISO's
CHARACTER SET.

angry fruit salad a description of a screen GRAPHICS display that uses too
many colours and is tiring on the eye.

ANI see AUTOMATIC NUMBER IDENTIFICATION.

animation making an object appear to move on the SCREEN (sense 1).
This has to be done by drawing the object, waiting, wiping out the diagram and then drawing it in a slightly different position.

animation file a file of GRAPHICS information that can be replayed as an
animated image or VIDEO (sense 2). These files use data that is heavily
COMPRESSED, but even with compression the files can be very large, of
several megabytes each.

annotation a comment made in a document that can be viewed on

SCREEN (sense 1) but not printed. An *annotation mark* in a document is usually a HYPERLINK to the annotation text.

annoyware a form of SHAREWARE that frequently interrupts use to remind the user that the copy is not registered.

annunciator any form of sound or visual warning or reminder used within a program to alert the user to the need for action.

anonymous FTP a form of file transfer protocol (FTP) for which the user needs no PASSWORD other than his/her EMAIL ADDRESS. This gives access to a set of files in a PUBLIC AREA but not to more specialized areas for which rigorous passwording is used.

ANSI (American National Standards Institute) the ANSI CHARACTER SET is a standardized extension of the ASCII set, but most computers and printers use the PC-8 set.

anti-aliasing an effect used to reduce ALIASING (sense 1) of diagonal lines and for creating shades of colour by randomly varying the positions of coloured PIXELs at the edge of lines or throughout a fill colour. See also DITHER.

antistatic mat a mat of made of a material that is an electrical conductor, used to rest CHIPs or circuit cards which are susceptible to ELECTRO-STATIC damage.

anti-tinkle suppression circuitry used in a MODEM that prevents telephones on the same line from sounding briefly when the modem is used for dialling out.

anti-virus program a program designed to search for and remove a VIRUS program. Some versions of anti-virus programs also provide for checking programs during installation to warn of actions that might be associated with INFECTION. Anti-virus programs are a useful safeguard but should not be relied on to catch every virus; in addition, they can issue false virus reports. Rigorous measures to avoid infection are always more useful. An anti-virus program may have to be disabled to allow installation of an upgraded operating system (OS).

antonym a word with the meaning opposite to a selected word. A THE-SAURUS program will usually provide a set of both synonym and antonym words for the word that is being questioned.

anytime algorithm a type of ALGORITHM that is based on repetition and can produce a reasonable answer before it has run to completion.

AOL see AMERICA ONLINE.

APA see ALL-POINTS-ADDRESSABLE DISPLAY.

API see APPLICATION PROGRAM INTERFACE.

Apollo speech system™ a SPEECH SYNTHESIS system for visually impaired computer users that allows typed words to be replayed as speech to headphones or a loudspeaker.

apostrophe or **single quote** the ' sign, ASCII 39, which is used to specify actions in many computer languages. See also SMARTQUOTES.

append to add to existing material; for instance, to add a new RECORD (sense 1) to an existing file. Many WORD PROCESSOR programs allow text to be appended to the CURSOR, meaning that the new text will be inserted at the position in the old text that is indicated by the cursor.

append query a QUERY that is used to add RECORDs (sense 1) from one TABLE to another existing DATABASE table.

Apple™ one of the first and most influential of the microcomputer manufacturers. Founded in 1976 by Steve Jobs and Steve Wozniak, using the family garage as a base and $100 capital, Apple computers were wildly successful. Later types such as Lisa and MACINTOSH have greatly affected the design of other machines and of software; see GUI.

applet 1. a small-scale program, usually distributed along with an operating system (OS) and not available separately. For example, the applets of WORDPAD and PAINT are distributed with MICROSOFT WINDOWS. **2.** a program, usually written in the JAVA language, that can be distributed over the World Wide Web (WWW). The applet is then run by using an INTERPRETER that is part of an INTERNET BROWSER. Browsers allow the user to reject or restrict the use of applets so as to avoid the spread of any computer VIRUS by this means.

application any complete and self-contained PROGRAM that will run on a computer, such as WORD PROCESSOR, ACCOUNTING PACKAGE, SPREADSHEET, etc.

Application Configuration Access Protocol (ACAP) a scheme for setting up data items such as an ADDRESS BOOK for universal access.

application icon a graphics IMAGE (sense 2) that appears when a program has been started in a WINDOWS environment and subsequently minimized. When such an icon appears, the program is suspended (on disk or in memory) and can be resumed at the point where it was minimized earlier, complete with any data it was using. In some cases, the program may continue its tasks while minimized, depending on the nature of the program. Icons are used also on a TOOLBAR, see Fig. 4.

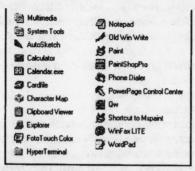

Fig. 4. **Applications icon**. A set of icons for programs as they appear in Windows 95.

application layer the (highest) layer in the ISO/OSI scheme for COMMUNI-CATIONS. This layer deals with the programs that will be distributed over the NETWORK or by EMAIL.

application-oriented language a form of PROGRAMMING LANGUAGE that is specific to some type of application, such as a DATABASE, and is used for creating or controlling such applications. See also VISUAL BASIC.

application program interface (**API**) the set of actions that an operating system (OS) uses to run programs, including SCREEN (sense 1) display, FILE control and management of PERIPHERALS.

application shortcut a KEY (sense 1) or ICON that can be used to launch an application without the need to find the FILE and DOUBLE-CLICK on its name.

application shortcut key a KEY (sense 1) or, more usually, KEY COMBINA-TION that will launch an application in a WINDOWS environment.

applications package or **package** a set of programs that are dedicated to a particular purpose. A WORD PROCESSOR, a SPREADSHEET or a DATABASE are all applications packages. The significance of the word 'package' is that the programs often consist of several sections, and only one may be in the memory of the computer at a given time. A word processor, for example, may consist of a TEXT EDITOR, which deals with the entry of words, their display on the SCREEN (sense 1) and their storage in memory and on disk. The accompanying PRINT FORMATTER is concerned with the formatting (see FORMAT, sense 2) of the text on to paper and with any special codes that must be sent to the printer. Many packages can be modified by the user so as to fit some special purpose, for example by putting in ACCENT MARKS for foreign language use.

application specific integrated circuit (**ASIC**) a form of IC that is manufactured for one particular set of actions, as distinct from the use of general-purpose ICs, often for one computer manufacturer.

application window a SCREEN (sense 1) WINDOW in which an application program runs. Several different applications can appear on the screen, each in its own window. See also CASCADE; TILE.

appointment scheduler a program that performs diary actions, such as noting appointments, maintaining a calendar and using alarm-clock actions.

approximation algorithm an ALGORITHM whose results are usable but not perfect.

approximation error an error caused by ROUNDING a REAL NUMBER. See also PRECISION OF NUMBER.

arbitration selection among competing demands, as when, for example, several users of a NETWORK need to use a printer at the same time.

arc the EXTENSION used for ARCHIVE documents produced by a program that is no longer in use. A few archiving utilities still support the format so that old files can be recovered.

Archie an old-established FILE-SEARCH UTILITY for INTERNET use.

architecture the way in which HARDWARE or SOFTWARE is designed and constructed, either on the overall scale (architecture of a computer system) or in detail (architecture of a microprocessor).

archival backup a system of BACKUP that is intended to retain data over long periods. An archival backup is usually of the whole contents of the HARD DRIVE, including the operating system (OS).

archive any set of data that must be preserved over a long period. The usual system for archiving relies on making several BACKUP copies of disks and tapes. See also FILE GENERATIONS. Archived data may be stored in compressed form (see COMPRESSED FILE) onto disk or tape.

archive attribute an ATTRIBUTE bit that is set to indicate that a file has been altered since it was last recorded (see RECORD, sense 2). This can be used to allow selective BACKUP of files on a HARD DISK.

archived file a file that is intended for long-term storage rather than for frequent use, usually on a removable disk or a tape rather than on the fixed disk. The data may have been compressed (see COMPRESSED FILE) so as to take up less disk space.

archive site a FOLDER on the computer of an INTERNET HOST, used to store files that are available to users.

archiving the action of storing data in a file so as to make BACKUP copies.

ARCnet™ (Attached Resources Computing network) a NETWORK system that is a trademark of Datapoint Corp.

area graph a form of graph in which the area of a bar or other shape is made proportional to the quantity being graphed. An area graph is not so easily interpreted by the eye as a *linear graph* in which a number is represented by a straight-line distance.

area search a search for items of a specified type in a restricted set in a DATABASE, i.e. a search for a number of items that have something in common. The term is used in the context of filing RECORDs (sense 1) – for example, you might want to search through a set of files for the names of all males born in 1945, in which case the area that is searched consists of the items 'male' and '1945'.

argument the data upon which a FUNCTION or COMMAND operates. For example, the SUM command is not valid unless it is followed by a list of items to sum, and these items constitute the arguments for this action. All the arithmetic functions of a SPREADSHEET, such as log, sin, cos, will need a suitable argument, and in many cases the possible range of values is limited. This may make it important to include VALIDATION for these values. The argument of a function is very often enclosed in brackets.

argument separator any character that can be used to separate one ARGUMENT from another. The most common separator is a SPACE, but a comma or a TAB character may be used in DATABASE applications.

arithmetic any action that involves elementary calculation with numbers. The main arithmetic operations are addition, subtraction, multiplication and division. To this is often added the EXPONENTIATION or evolution action (raising to a power).

Arithmetic and Logic Unit (ALU) a part of a MICROPROCESSOR that performs the familiar arithmetic actions of addition, subtraction, multiplication and division (of integer numbers) along with LOGIC (comparison) actions AND, OR, NOT and XOR.

arithmetic capability the ability of a WORD PROCESSOR or any other text-based program to carry out simple arithmetical actions. A word processor with arithmetic capability could, for example, be used to produce a balance sheet. The operator would type the main figures, but the totals would be produced by the computer, under the command of the program. Even a modest amount of arithmetic capability can be of very great use in a word processor because it allows the computer to be used more efficiently. Integrated suites of programs deal with arithmetic by allowing data to be passed from one program to another. A SPREADSHEET might, for example, be used and its output passed to a word processor for incorporation into a report. See also MICROSOFT OFFICE.

arithmetic functions actions, within a SPREADSHEET or DATABASE, on numbers that are more complex than addition, subtraction, division and multiplication. These are programmed by KEYWORDs (sense 2) in combination with an ARGUMENT. Typical arithmetic functions include LOG, SIN, ARCTAN.

arithmetic operations any operations of the type that carry out an action of arithmetic on numbers.

arithmetic operators symbols such as +, −, *, / and words such as DIV and MOD that carry out an arithmetic action.

ARLL see ADVANCED RUN-LENGTH LIMITED.

armour-plated or **bulletproof** (of an ALGORITHM) almost immune to misuse.

ARPANET (Advanced Research Project Agency Network) one of the earliest LONG-HAUL NETWORK applications of the MESH type used in research and defence studies in the USA. This has been the model for the development of the INTERNET.

ARQ an automatic request for data correction. In a signalling system that can detect transmitted data errors, the ARQ signal can be sent back to the transmitter when an error is detected. This signal can be used to force the transmitter to retransmit the dubious character, word or BLOCK (sense 2) of characters.

array 1. or **ring array** a set of OBJECTS (sense 1), copied from a single object and arranged in line or in a ring. Arrays of this type can be created by CAD programs. **2.** a set of related values that can be treated in the same way. For example, a SPREADSHEET may allow the use of an array formula in which several CELL references are used. **3.** a DATA STRUCTURE of numbers or other objects arranged in a matrix of subscripted variables.

array processor a type of computer that uses a large number of linked processors. This allows array data to be manipulated very rapidly, with one processor handling each part of the array.

arrow keys the KEYS (sense 1) used for CURSOR control as an alternative to the use of a MOUSE. Each of the four keys is marked with an arrow (up, down, left or right) to show the direction in which it will move the cursor.

artificial intelligence (AI) the study of methods by which a computer can simulate aspects of human intelligence. One aim of this study is to design a computer that might be able to reason for itself. A more attainable objective of work on AI is the development of systems that can work with NATURAL LANGUAGE, the language that we speak and write as distinct from the artificial languages of programming. Another aspect of AI is the ability of the computer to search KNOWLEDGE in a DATABASE for the best possible reply to a question, because this has strong parallels with the way that we solve problems for ourselves. Another branch is the development of pattern-recognition systems that would allow a computer system a crude form of sight. Work on AI has been more useful for its side effects, particularly on EXPERT SYSTEM research.

artificial life see ALIFE.

artificial neural network an ARTIFICIAL INTELLIGENCE system that consists of a large network of MICROPROCESSORs with memory. These system act like a simple brain and are capable of a form of learning.

asbestos (of any measure) intended to avoid FLAME on INTERNET NEWS-GROUP discussions.

ASC a FUNCTION in a WORKSHEET that finds the ASCII code of a letter or other character.

ascender the part of a printed character that rises above the main body of the character, as in the letters b, d, h, k. Compare DESCENDER.

ASCII (American Standard Code for Information Interchange, pronounced *ass-key*) a number code for letters, digits and other characters that has been standardized for computing use. In general, if a file is recorded (see RECORD, sense 2) as a set of ASCII codes, it can be read by any types of WORD PROCESSOR, TEXT EDITOR or DTP program. The ASCII coding system makes it easy to convert between LOWER-CASE and UPPER-CASE letters, and between the stored form of a number and its ASCII code. The original ASCII codes used only the numbers 32 to 127. However, in a complete byte the numbers 128 to 255 are also available, allowing another set of characters to be encoded. This leads to extended ASCII codes, of which the most used for PC machines is the PC-8 character set, see Fig. 5 (overleaf). See also ANSI.

32		!	"	#	$	%	&	'	(	)	*	+	,	-	.	/	0	1	2	3	4	5	6	7	8	9	:	;
60	<	=	>	?	@	A	B	C	D	E	F	G	H	I	J	K	L	M	N	O	P	Q	R	S	T	U	V	W
88	X	Y	Z	[	\	]	^	_	`	a	b	c	d	e	f	g	h	i	j	k	l	m	n	o	p	q	r	s
116	t	u	v	w	x	y	z	{	|	}	~	□	□	□	,	ƒ	„	…	†	‡	ˆ	‰	Š	‹	Œ	□	□	□
144	□	'	'	"	"	–	—	˜	™	š	›	œ	□	□	Ÿ		¡	¢	£	¤	¥	¦	§	¨	©	ª	«
172	¬	-	®	¯	°	±	²	³	´	µ	¶	·	¸	¹	º	»	¼	½	¾	¿	À	Á	Â	Ã	Ä	Å	Æ	Ç
200	È	É	Ê	Ë	Ì	Í	Î	Ï	Ð	Ñ	Ò	Ó	Ô	Õ	Ö	×	Ø	Ù	Ú	Û	Ü	Ý	Þ	ß	à	á	â	ã
228	ä	å	æ	ç	è	é	ê	ë	ì	í	î	ï	ð	ñ	ò	ó	ô	õ	ö	÷	ø	ù	ú	û	ü	ý	þ	ÿ

Fig. 5. **ASCII**. The extended ASCII set of codes as used by Microsoft Word. The numbers on the left show the code number for the leftmost character in each row.

ASCII art see ASCII GRAPHICS.

ASCIIbetical order a SORT (sense 1) order that follows ASCII number-code order, with all UPPER-CASE letters before LOWER-CASE letters.

ASCII graphics or **ASCII art** the generation of simple drawings using only the ASCII characters, found on some NEWSGROUP communications.

Ashton-Tate Corporation the firm that developed the famous DBASE database program, now owned by Borland International.

ASIC see APPLICATION SPECIFIC INTEGRATED CIRCUIT.

ASK field a FIELD placed in a DOCUMENT that will force the user to enter a name or quantity.

aspect ratio the ratio of width to height for a SCREEN (sense 1), usually the 4:3 ratio of the conventional (not widescreen) TV screen.

assembler a program that converts program instructions in text form into MACHINE CODE to be used by a computer.

assembly language a PROGRAMMING LANGUAGE that uses word ABBREVIATIONs for actions that the microprocessor can carry out. A program in assembly language can be converted by an ASSEMBLER into OPCODES that the microprocessor will obey.

assembly listing a listing of a program in ASSEMBLY LANGUAGE, often with the corresponding machine code and memory addresses printed out. This is the type of listing that is produced by an ASSEMBLER as it operates.

assertion the marking of an item as being true or an action as being permitted or turned on. Used also of a signal to mean that it is in its active state.

ASSIGN an old DOS command that will use a DRIVE DESIGNATOR as a way of gaining access to another drive or to a HARD DRIVE DIRECTORY (sense 1). ASSIGN is no longer part of DOS and must not be used when a computer runs WINDOWS.

assignment the action of making a letter or name (a VARIABLE name or IDENTIFIER) represent a number or a string of characters. For example, a

WORD PROCESSOR may allow you to type the letter *m* (and press the F3 key) to provide the word *Macintosh*, or a SPREADSHEET may allow you to assign a name to a RANGE of CELLS in a WORKSHEET.

associate data the action of linking data tables together in a RELATIONAL DATABASE so that a QUERY will disclose both sets of data.

association the use of a file's EXTENSION letters to RUN (sense 2) a related program and load in that file. In the WINDOWS system, for example, extensions such as TXT and DOC can be associated with a WORD-PROCESSOR program so that clicking (see CLICK, sense 1) on a file with one of these extensions will automatically load the word processor, which in turn will load the text file ready for editing. In MICROSOFT WINDOWS, if the extension is not recognized, clicking on a file will produce a list of programs from which you can select one to use with the file.

associative law a rule about how quantities can be grouped. For example, in simple arithmetic the rules of association are that $(2+3) + (4+5)$ are equivalent to $2+(3+4)+5$, but such a rule would not hold true for vector quantities that have direction as well as size.

associative storage the filing of data so that it can be found by reference to its content rather than by directly using a reference number; see ADDRESS (sense 1).

assumption the term used in Lotus 1-2-3 with the same meaning as SCENARIO in MICROSOFT EXCEL.

asterisk the * symbol, which is used in an operating system (OS) as a WILD-CARD character for any set of characters. The use of *.TXT, for example, means any file with the TXT extension, such as A.TXT or BEFORE.TXT, and using NEW.* would apply to NEW.ABC, NEW.TXT, NEW.WK1, and so on. See also AMBIGUOUS FILENAME. The ? symbol is often used to mean a single ambiguous character.

asymmetrical modulation (of a communications system) allocating more of the available BANDWIDTH to the MODEM that is transmitting the larger amount of information.

asymmetric digital subscriber line (ADSL) a digital connection that allocates more BANDWIDTH for a DOWNLOAD than for an UPLOAD. This is well suited to a connection between a BROWSER and an ISP.

asynchronous communications interface adapter see ACIA.

asynchronous logic a form of LOGIC circuit design in which no CLOCK pulse is used, so that data is output from the stage as soon as it is available.

asynchronous transfer mode (ATM) a communications system that uses a DATA PACKET of fixed size and allocates BANDWIDTH dynamically.

asynchronous transmission the sending of signals from a transmitter to a receiver at irregular intervals rather than at 'clocked' times. To take a simple example, the signals from a keyboard to the computer are asynchronous because the operator presses KEYS (sense 1) at irregular intervals. RS-232 SERIAL communications signals are also asynchronous, but the signals to and from a disk system are normally closely timed SYNCHRONOUS signals, meaning that the time between signals is always the same.

AT (advanced technology) the initials applied by IBM in 1982 to their successor to the original PC-XT machines. This machine used the Intel 80286 chip and was much more capable than the earlier machines. The AT architecture later became the basis of industry standard architecture (ISA).

ATA (advanced technology attachment) a drive interface system for the PERSONAL COMPUTER that is based on the 16-bit bus used on the IBM PC-AT machine. This is used on many PC machines as a low-cost alternative to SCSI for hard drive interfacing. The latest versions are comparable in performance with SCSI but do not allow for as many devices to be connected. The system is also referred to as IDE.

ATA-2 a development of the ATA standard that allows faster data transfer, 32-bit working and the use of DMA. Also referred to as EIDE.

ATA-4 see ULTRA DMA.

AT&T a major US telecommunications firm that is also notable as the origin of the UNIX operating system and the C family of languages.

ATAPI (AT attachment packet interface) software that is incorporated into the EIDE hard drive system to provide additional control commands for devices such as a CD-ROM drive.

AT bus the standard set of signal lines used originally in the IBM PC-AT computer and now widely used by many other COMPATIBLE and CLONE computers. This form of circuit is used on machines with the Intel 80286, 80386, 80486 MICROPROCESSOR chips and is now known as ISA (industry-standard architecture). See also MCA; EISA; PCI BUS; VLB.

AT command set the standard set of letter and number commands used to control a MODEM of the HAYES type. These commands do not need to be used directly because communications software can recognize the modem type and set up a file of commands automatically.

ATE (automatic testing equipment) equipment such as is used for checking electronic components and subassemblies.

Athlon™ a MICROPROCESSOR design from ADVANCED MICRO DEVICES INC., successor to their K2 and K3 designs and a strong challenger for the later PENTIUM processors from INTEL.

AT keyboard a 102-key keyboard with the KEY (sense 1) arrangement that was originally used for the IBM PC-AT machine and is now a standard for all PERSONAL COMPUTERS (sense 1).

ATM 1. abbreviation for automated teller machine, the familiar cash-dispensing machine ('hole in the wall') often found on the outer wall of a bank or building society. **2.** see ASYNCHRONOUS TRANSFER MODE. **3.** see ADOBE TYPE MANAGER.

A to D or **A-D** or **ADC** (analogue to digital converter) an electronic circuit (see ELECTRONICS) that converts an ANALOGUE signal into a DIGITAL signal in the form of a set of 1s and 0s representing a BINARY NUMBER proportional to the input signal amplitude at each sampled instant. Such converters are an essential part of COMPACT DISC recording and of digitization (see DIGITIZER and Fig. 1) of sound and video signals. Once digitized, these signals can be manipulated in any way that can be achieved by a computer.

atom any unit that is irreducible, so that a BIT can be described as the atom of computer numbering. The term is used mainly in DATABASE design to indicate an irreducible unit.

atomic (of an item) that cannot be split; (of an operation) that cannot be interrupted.

atomic domain a set of indivisible units.

at symbol 1. the @ character, which is used as a prefix in some commands. **2.** see COMMERCIAL AT.

attached file a FILE that is transmitted as part of an EMAIL DOCUMENT and can be separately dealt with when an ICON (usually a paperclip shape) is clicked. The result of clicking an attachment may be to see a graphics or text item, or to allow a program file to be saved in a selected folder.

attached processor an auxiliary MICROPROCESSOR in a computer. The attached processor is a separate processor under the control of the main processor and is used for auxiliary actions, usually as a number-cruncher (see MATHS COPROCESSOR). See also COPROCESSOR.

attachment see ADD-IN.

attach note button a facility used in MICROSOFT EXCEL to allow a user to type some notes on a WORKSHEET. The note will be saved along with the worksheet, can be viewed separately if needed and is always available when the worksheet is in use.

attach table a command used in MICROSOFT ACCESS to make use of tables that have been created by another database such as PARADOX.

attention key a KEY (sense 1) that can be pressed to bring up a main menu on the SCREEN (sense 1) or initiate some help action. In practice, this is often the F1 key, the ALT KEY or a combination of keys using ALT or CTRL.

attenuation weakening or thinning. The term is applied to the decrease in AMPLITUDE of a signal as it is transmitted through space or along a cable. If the attenuation is too great, the signal will have to be amplified before it can be used. Attenuation may be important if signals are being transmitted along long lines.

atto- number prefix for 10^{-18}.

ATTRIB a DOS command that allows file ATTRIBUTEs to be displayed and altered.

attribute a coded feature, usually of a FILE, that can be read by an operating system (OS) in order to determine how the file is treated. The term is also applied to the data items in a file, such as name, address, telephone number, etc. See ARCHIVE ATTRIBUTE, HIDDEN ATTRIBUTE, READ-ONLY ATTRIBUTE, SYSTEM ATTRIBUTE.

ATX a form of MOTHERBOARD from INTEL that rationalizes component positions, making it easier to upgrade memory or attachments. The older type of motherboard shape is known as Baby AT. An ATX motherboard must be fitted into an ATX casing.

audio making use of electrical signals that correspond to sounds.

audiographic teleconferencing or **electronic whiteboarding** a TELECONFERENCING system that uses separate audio and data channels.

audio cassette a cassette that is primarily intended for recording sound and which is not suitable for data recordings. Audio cassettes were used in early small computers for data, using slow data rates and MODEM techniques. True digital recordings use tape of video standard; see QIC, DAT.

audio mixer a device that will accept input signals from a variety of audio sources, such as compact disc, tape, vinyl disc, etc., and allow the VOLUME (sense 1) of each to be controlled. The mixed output is then available for amplification. Software can simulate the appearance of a mixer control panel on screen; see VOLUME CONTROL.

audio range the frequency range of about 30 Hz to 20 kHz, which is the range of sound frequencies that can be detected by the human ear. Many communication CHANNELs (sense 1), such as telephones and tape recorders, can deal only with a limited part of this audio range, so that digital signals have to be sent in the form of musical notes in the frequency range of 300 Hz to 2400 Hz, using a MODEM.

audio video interleave see AVI.

audiovisual display a display that shows pictures and plays sounds.

audit trail a method of checking the output of an accounts program by tracing back the steps to the original input. A program that deals with accounts should allow a BACKUP of each file to be retained so that alterations can be traced back by comparing later files with the backup versions.

authentication the cross-checking of identity to ensure that sensitive data can be interchanged safely. Authentication by exchange of codes can be used between computer and user, or between two computers, when it guarantees that the data is genuine and that it is being transmitted to the correct recipient.

authoring the action of creating HYPERTEXT for a WEB PAGE.

authoring language see AUTHOR LANGUAGE.

authorization code a combination of a PASSWORD and identity number that is used to establish the identity of a computer system user.

authorized user a computer user who is allowed to make use of the system. There may be several levels of authorized users, so that some have access to a larger range of files than others, and only a few are allowed to alter and originate files.

author language or **authoring language** a form of PROGRAMMING LANGUAGE used to prepare text that must be in a strictly defined form, such as computer-aided instruction manuals and training systems. An author language is often part of a program for creating MULTIMEDIA displays and HYPERTEXT.

auto advance the ability to move automatically to the next position. Auto advance as used in a SPREADSHEET means that the CURSOR will move to the next CELL when the RETURN or ENTER KEY (sense 1), or any of the cursor-moving keys, is pressed.

auto-answer a MODEM action that allows a COMMUNICATIONS LINK program to answer a caller and RECORD (sense 2) a file transmitted to it.

AutoBackup an option within an application that provides for making a BACKUP copy of data at an interval, typically ten minutes, that can be selected by the user. If a loss of power occurs, the program and its data will be restored when power is re-applied, using the data as it existed at the last backup.

autobaud see AUTOMATIC BAUD RATE DETECTION.

AutoCAD the best-known and most widely used professional CAD package. See also AUTOSKETCH; DXF.

AutoCaption a MICROSOFT WORD action that will supply captions to objects such as drawings or tables. For example, if you specify the use of the title 'Table' for each table that is used in a drawing, AutoCaption will enter 'Table 1', 'Table 2', and so on.

Autocomplete an action used in WINDOWS 98 onwards that detects letters typed into the ADDRESS BAR and attempts to complete the phrase.

AutoCorrect an action of MICROSOFT WORD that will automatically correct words as you type them in. This is done by entering both the incorrect words and the correct versions in a table. For example, you could enter *teh* and *the* so that typing *teh* would always result in *the* being entered.

Autodesk the Californian SOFTWARE company that originated AUTOCAD and AUTOSKETCH.

autodialer see AUTOREDIALER.

AUTOEXEC.BAT a file of the BATCH FILE type that is read by a PERSONAL COMPUTER before any APPLICATIONS PACKAGE programs are loaded. The file can contain instructions, usually to load other programs or data files into memory. For a machine using MICROSOFT WINDOWS this file will have been created already and need not be altered by the user. If DOS programs are not used, the file can be bypassed.

autoexecute macro a MACRO command that is automatically run when a program starts or when a document is opened. This type of macro can be used to release a VIRUS, so it is important to know how to open a document without allowing any autoexecute macro to run.

AutoFill a facility of a SPREADSHEET that allows a set of selected CELLs in a WORKSHEET to be filled automatically, following a pattern established by filling in one or more cells. For example, filling in 2 and 4 in adjacent cells will result in a set of even numbers being entered.

AutoFilter an action of MICROSOFT EXCEL. Using AutoFilter on a COLUMN of a TABLE will reveal all the different items of the table. Clicking on an item will hide all the items that do not use this item. For example, if the word 'Faraday' occurs ten times in a column, clicking on the name in the AutoFilter panel will show only the ten lines that actually include this name.

AutoFit I. an action of MICROSOFT WORD that will adjust the column width and row height in a table so that all the entries fit neatly. **2.** An automatic method of adjusting column width and row height in a TABLE of a SPREADSHEET or a WORD PROCESSOR so that the entries do not need to take an additional line.

autoflow the action in a DTP program in which text that is imported will be placed in successive PAGES (sense 1) as each page is created. In other words, it is not necessary to break up text into units of page size to ensure that text will fit each page perfectly and completely.

AutoForm a BUTTON or WIZARD used in MICROSOFT ACCESS to create a new form for a DATABASE.

AutoFormat I. a facility of MICROSOFT EXCEL that allows data in a WORKSHEET to be formatted (see FORMAT, sense 1) automatically. The formatting applies to number, alignment, font, borders, patterns, column widths and row heights. **2.** an action of MICROSOFT WORD that will format text into headings and body text, numbered or bulleted lists, etc., according to the way that the raw text has been typed.

auto idle a CLOCK rate management system on some INTEL MICROPROCESSORs that reduces the clock rate at times when the processor is waiting for data.

AutoLabel a property used in MICROSOFT ACCESS to provide a label for each text box if the property is on.

automated teller machine see ATM.

automated testing the use of SOFTWARE that will carry out tests on other software without the need for any operator input or assistance.

automatic baud rate detection (ABRD) a feature of a MODEM that can determine the speed and other features of an incoming message and adjust itself for the PROTOCOL (sense 1) that is in use

automatic decimal alignment or **decimal tab** a useful WORD PROCESSOR action that allows columns of numbers to be positioned around a (decimal) tab so that all of the decimal points are aligned. This makes the presentation of items such as balance sheets much easier. The decimal points can, of course, be aligned manually by any word processor system.

automatic error correction a system used for a COMMUNICATIONS LINK in which data is transmitted in batches along with checking codes. At the receiving end, the checking codes are generated again from the data, and if they do not agree with the transmitted checking code, the transmitter is requested to resend the data. This will be repeated until the data is perfect or until there have been several consecutive failures. See also CHECKSUM, CRC.

automatic head parking an action provided on all modern HARD DRIVE types that, at switchoff, places the READ/WRITE HEAD at a TRACK that is normally not used for data. This prevents damage to recorded data when the computer or the drive itself is moved. Automatic head parking is a natural consequence of the use of a VOICE-COIL DRIVE.

automatic hyphenation the action in a DTP program automatically inserting a hyphen into a word that is too long to fit at the end of a line. The position at which a word is broken by the hyphen is determined by an ALGORITHM, and the whole procedure can be overridden if necessary.

automatic letter writing see MAILMERGE.

automatic link the normal OLE action in which altering an object that is linked (see LINK) to one or more documents will result in altering the appearance of the object in these documents.

automatic number identification (ANI) a SOFTWARE system that will find the telephone number of a caller and pass this to the recipient or to the receiving computer.

automatic recalculation the usual default of a WORKSHEET in which altering the contents of a CELL (sense 1) will result in recalculating the values in any other cells that use the value in that cell.

automatic repagination the usual DEFAULT in a WORD PROCESSOR in which editing text on any page will repaginate the document (see REPAGINATION).

automatic repeat request see ARQ.

automation the replacement of human labour with machines, now generally computer-controlled. The positive aspects of automation include elimination of drudgery, raising of standards of workmanship (machineship?) and increased productivity, which should lead to higher living standards. Its undesirable aspects include unemployment, particularly for the lower-skilled, and the feeling that you are 'tied to a machine' if you work in an extensively automated environment.

automaton see ROBOT.

autonomous operation a set of actions determined by HARDWARE, such as driving a disk up to operating speed.

autoplay a feature of Microsoft WINDOWS 95 onwards for a computer that is fitted with a CD-ROM drive. Inserting an audio COMPACT DISC into the drive will play the music from start to finish, with no need to use any form of command. If you need to select tracks you must run the MEDIA PLAYER utility, and you can alter VOLUME (sense 1) by running the VOLUME CONTROL utility.

autoredialer or **autodialer** a feature of a MODEM that allows a telephone number to be redialled at intervals until an answer is obtained. In the UK, the use of an autodialer is subject to BT regulations intended to prevent the repeated dialling of the wrong number, so that any modem featuring this facility must provide for the user to authorize the action.

autorepeat or **keymatic action** the automatic repetition of KEY (sense 1) action. Most modern computers provide autorepeat on all keys, meaning that if any key is held down for more than a fraction of a second, its action repeats. The delay time can be altered to suit the operator.

AutoRoute a MICROSOFT program for finding the optimum road route between towns.

autosave an action that will save a data file at set intervals so as to provide automatic BACKUP in the event of power failure or any other disorderly shutdown. When autosave has been used, the program will be restored along with the last-saved version of the data file when the computer is switched on again.

AUTOSKETCH a CAD program developed from AUTOCAD that offers a smaller set of facilities but is much less costly and is applicable to a very large range of users who are not concerned with industrial design or architecture.

autostart the action of a program that RUNS (sense 2) as soon as it has loaded into memory. This is the normal action of any program running under a standard operating system (OS) such as MS-DOS. For programs running under Microsoft WINDOWS 95 you can DRAG a program name to a STARTUP file to ensure that it is autostarted. You can also opt to start the program in its natural window, MAXIMIZED or MINIMIZED.

AutoText an action of MICROSOFT WORD that will enter text automatically when a letter is followed by pressing the F3 key. The key letters and the full text versions are held in a table. For example, you could arrange it so that typing the letter *m* followed by pressing the F3 key produced the phrase *Macintosh System 7*.

AUX1 or **COM1** a name used for the SERIAL INTERFACE of a computer, allowing this PORT to be treated as if it were a file, with data being passed to and from it. Many computers allow both AUX1 and AUX2, while some use AUX3 and AUX4.

auxiliary battery a battery used in a portable computer that will maintain BACKUP memory (such as CMOS RAM) when the main battery is removed.

auxiliary equipment parts of a computer system that are not directly controlled by the processor. This often refers to PASSIVE (sense 1) objects like copyholders, computer workstands, disk-storage boxes and the like. Equipment that is controlled by the processor is referred to as PERIPHERAL.

auxiliary storage see HARD DRIVE.

availability the fraction of the total active time during which a computer is available to the user. One of the problems of MULTI-ACCESS systems is that the availability may be low for each user. This can lead to each user needing a long time to complete a program RUN (sense 1) or having to wait too long for data to be accessed.

average seek time see HEAD SEEK TIME.

Avery label a label manufactured by the Avery Corporation or using one of the standard Avery sizes. WORD PROCESSORs will usually provide for printing on to the Avery label sizes, but it may be more difficult to make use of other label types.

AVI (audio video interleave) a MICROSOFT WINDOWS standard for MULTIMEDIA video files that use the AVI extension.

AWARD a manufacturer of BIOS chips for IBM-COMPATIBLE computers.

axis (*plural* **axes**) a direction in a GRAPH or chart. The standard axes are the X-AXIS and Y-AXIS, set at right angles to each other.

azerty keyboard the form of keyboard used in France, so named because the first six KEYS (sense 1) of the top row of letters consist of the letters AZERTY rather than the QWERTY used in the UK and in the USA.

B: B drive, conventionally the second FLOPPY DISK drive in a computer with more than one floppy drive. Where only a single floppy drive is used, B: is an alternative designation for that drive. See also A:, C:.

Babbage, Charles (1792–1871) an English engineer who conceived of the general stored program computer, which he called a *difference engine*. His designs were entirely mechanical and the technology of the time was not sufficiently advanced for physical realization of the machine, although a working model has now been constructed and used. Babbage is credited with being the father of modern computing, although in fact his designs were lost and were rediscovered only in the late 1930s. See also ADA.

babble or **crosstalk** interference between two CHANNELs (sense 1) that are transmitting data.

babbling error a NETWORK error that arises on ETHERNET when the default maximum PACKET size of 1500 bytes is exceeded.

BABT (British Approval Board for Telecommunications) a body that determines whether or not equipment can be connected to BT telephone lines. Approved equipment is marked by a green sticker. The use of non-approved equipment can lead to disconnection of the line.

Baby AT the 8.5 x 11-inch version of the old AT MOTHERBOARD (12 x 13-inch) that will fit into the original XT casing. The larger size is obsolete, so that AT and Baby AT now refer to the same size of motherboard. See also ATX.

backbone the common top level circuits of a hierarchical (see HIERARCHY) NETWORK to which all other data-carrying circuits are connected.

back door or **wormhole** an ADDRESS (sense 1) within program code that can be used to circumvent security and permit hacking (see HACKER, senses 1, 3). This also permits maintenance actions, which is why some back doors remain open.

back-end (of routines in software) not obvious to the user, as distinct from FRONT END (sense 2) routines, which provide the interface between the user and the program.

back-end processor the processor in a MULTIPROCESSOR or multicomputer system that handles the bulk of the repetitive processing, as distinct from input/output.

background 1. or **paper** the colour of the parts of the SCREEN (sense 1) that are not occupied by TEXT or GRAPHICS. **2.** the state of a program running non-interactively in a MULTITASKING system. The FOREGROUND program would be the subject of the user's attention, occupying the screen or an ACTIVE WINDOW and being affected by the keyboard use; the background program could be running (perhaps engaged in a calculation or receiving signals through a PORT) but not requiring attention.

background noise the unwanted signals on a line or radio link caused by interference or by natural causes. These should amount to only a small fraction of the AMPLITUDE of the wanted signal, otherwise reception will be poor and liable to error.

background printing see SPOOL.

background processing work that has a low priority, such as sending bytes to a printer. Background processing is used in a TIMESHARING system to allow tasks of lower importance to be carried out at a slower rate than the more important FOREGROUND (sense 2) actions, and the relative time used for foreground and background actions can be allocated, often at a 3:1 ratio.

background recalculation a WORKSHEET action in which each CELL that contains a FORMULA has its value recalculated whenever quantities in PRECEDENT cells are altered. The alternative is MANUAL RECALCULATION, using a command to carry out the recalculation.

background reflectance the relative amount of reflected light from the surface of paper being read by an optical character reader (OCR, sense 1). Too little reflectance will make the characters difficult to read because there will be insufficient contrast between paper and ink.

background repagination the automatic REPAGINATION of a document in a WORD PROCESSOR or DTP program when the content of a page is altered. The alternative is manual repagination, using a command to repaginate the document.

background task a routine in a time-shared system that the computer will execute when there is nothing with a higher priority. For example, the time intervals during the input of data from a keyboard allow for background tasks to be carried out.

backing store a store for data that is not a working part of the computer's memory. Typical examples are a HARD DRIVE or a CD-ROM. A backing store can be used to hold programs and data that can be read and used by the computer during the course of a main program. See also VIRTUAL MEMORY.

backlight a light placed behind an LCD display so that the display can be seen in dim surroundings. Without a backlight, the display may be visible only in a well-lit room. See also ACTIVE MATRIX.

back link a HYPERLINK in a HYPERTEXT DOCUMENT page that reverses the action of a link that led to that page.

backlit display a form of LCD SCREEN (sense 1) that can be lit from behind so as to make it visible in poor lighting conditions.

backoff a short interval of time allowed on a NETWORK following a COLLI-

SION. The randomly selected backoff time makes it less likely that when the data is retransmitted there will be another collision.

backplane see MOTHERBOARD.

back pointer a POINTER (sense 2) to the parent of a NODE. In a TREE data structure, a back pointer is a number that provides the position of the source of a branch, allowing a search to be made backwards to the root.

back quote the single opening inverted comma character (').

backside cache a form of SECONDARY CACHE that can be read directly by the MICROPROCESSOR of the computer system.

backslash the \ sign, which is used by DOS to mean either the ROOT DIRECTORY (sense 1) of a disk, for example, C:\, or as a separator between directory names, as in C:\UTILS\PRINTER. The sign is also used in some SPREADSHEET programs to indicate INTEGER division.

backspace the KEY (sense 1) used to move the CURSOR to the left on the SCREEN (sense 1), usually deleting any character in that position. Sometimes known as the *delete-left key*.

backtracking a type of repetitive ALGORITHM built into the Prolog PROGRAMMING LANGUAGE.

backup a spare copy of a program or data. Storage of data can never be totally trustworthy, and disks are particularly susceptible to damage from high temperatures and magnetic fields. Any valuable program or data should therefore be backed up, and many commercial users maintain two backups, which are renewed at regular intervals, using the FILE GENERATIONS principle. Backups made on disk or tape are often in compressed form (see COMPRESSED FILE) so that a large amount of data can be saved on a small number of disks and tapes. Backups can now also be made on COMPACT DISC or DVD recordable media.

backup job a file used in Microsoft WINDOWS 98 onwards to specify how a BACKUP action will be carried out. The file specifies what folders and files are to be backed up and to what media.

backup utility a program designed to carry out BACKUP actions on selected data automatically. For example, data might be backed up each time it is altered. A backup utility is a normal part of any operating system (OS) and is included with tape STREAMER hardware.

Backus-Naur Form a method of writing PROGRAMMING LANGUAGE commands in general form, extended also to other commands such as MACROS.

backward analysis a PROGRAM planning system that uses the required outputs of a program to indicate what inputs must be made.

backward chaining a method used in ARTIFICIAL INTELLIGENCE to establish a GOAL RULE. The method depends on finding the rules on which the goal rule depends, and the rules in turn on which each of these rules depends, until established data is reached. This is the AI equivalent of REVERSE ENGINEERING.

backward compatibility the ability of a PROGRAM to use data obtained from an earlier version or to write data in a form that an earlier version can use. Also used of a computer that can make use of programs written for earlier machines.

backward recovery a method of recovering original data from a DATA-BASE after a system failure during processing. The partly processed data is used in a routine that reverses the actions of the main program, so that the original data can be calculated and saved.

backward search a WORD PROCESSOR action in which a word or phrase is searched for in reverse. The direction of search is from the starting position in the document towards the start of the document rather than towards the end.

BACS (Bankers Automated Clearance System) a method of settling accounts between banks using computer communications. See also EFT.

bad break a misplaced hyphen, splitting a work awkwardly, encountered when AUTOMATIC HYPHENATION has been used in a WORD PROCESSOR.

bad command or **bad filename** an operating system (OS) message that appears when you have used a COMMAND incorrectly or have specified a FILENAME that does not exist.

badge reader a form of LIGHT PEN or SCANNER (sense 2) that can read characters or marks on a badge, usually for identification of the wearer or to allow particulars such as name and address to be noted in a file.

bad page break a new page position in a WORD PROCESSOR document that splits text badly or splits a table.

bad sector a fault in a FLOPPY DISK or a HARD DRIVE. The bad sector may refuse to be written or may corrupt the data or be unreadable. The operating system (OS) can isolate the sector so that it is not used, or a UTILITY can be used to carry out this action. Most hard disk drives have one or more bad sectors, and these will be notified when the disk is formatted (see FORMAT, sense 3) or tested.

bad track table a table that is created when a HARD DRIVE is formatted (see FORMAT, sense 4). The table lists the tracks that cannot be used because they do not store data correctly.

bag on the side an extension, often hastily written, to a PROGRAM to prolong its usefulness.

BAK an EXTENSION that is used to indicate a BACKUP file, usually when a program creates a backup automatically when a file is altered.

BAK file a file whose EXTENSION consists of the letters BAK, meaning that it is an older (BACKUP) version of a current file of the same main name. For example, the file CHAP1.BAK would be a backup version of a file CHAP1.TXT. Some programs mark backup files with extension names such as $$$ in place of BAK.

balanced computing organization of a computer system so that it is matched to the system organization.

balanced tree a TREE data structure in which each path from a remote branch or leaf to the main root is of the same length.

balloon help a form of HELP (sense 1) that appears in the form of a message when the POINTER (sense 1) is placed over an ICON or MENU item (see Fig. 6). See also SMARTCURSOR.

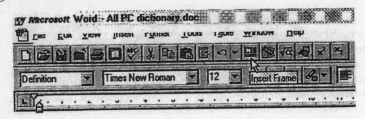

Fig. 6. **Balloon help**. The description of the icon action appears when the pointer is placed over this icon in Microsoft Word 7.

balun (balance-unbalance transformer) a device used in some NETWORK circuits to connect a COAXIAL line to a TWISTED-PAIR CABLE or other twin-line.

band see CYLINDER.

bandwidth the FREQUENCY range of signals. Bandwidths are measured in kilohertz (narrow band) or megahertz (broad band). Data transmission can be carried out on narrow-band channels only by using slow transmission rates; for fast transmissions, broad-band channels must be used. Bandwidth is also important with respect to VDU monitors (see MONITOR, sense 1). The TV-type of video signal that is used for a monitor has a very large bandwidth, and if the monitor cannot make use of this full bandwidth, characters will not be sufficiently clear on an 80-character-per-line display. The typical bandwidth for a monitor can be from 18 MHz to more than 50 MHz, in contrast to the normal 5 MHz for a TV receiver.

banked memory the arrangement of DRAM into groups or *banks*, with a group of bytes spread over the banks. This allows time for refreshing one bank while the processor is reading others, and it allows the use of slower memory chips with a fast processor. For example, a machine that uses 32-bit (4 bytes) groups can use 4 banks of memory with one byte of each set in a bank of its own. Modern machines use memory DIMM EDO units in which the *banking* is implemented on the DIMM unit rather than by requiring multiple DIMM units. Older SIMM memory units had to be used in pairs on Pentium machines.

Bankers Automated Clearance System see BACS.

bank-switching a way of making use of more memory than can normally be addressed. A bank-switching system was used on PERSONAL COMPUTERS using the 8088 or 8086 chips to provide more memory, called

EXPANDED MEMORY. This should not be confused with the use of BANKED MEMORY or EXTENDED MEMORY in modern computers.

banner 1. a PRINTOUT on a long sheet of paper. **2.** a TITLE PAGE for a set of pages in a DOCUMENT.

Banyan a networking company based in Massachusetts that originated the Vines™ network system.

bar chart a form of HISTOGRAM, used in SPREADSHEET programs. A bar chart will display variable names on its X-axis and the associated variable values on the Y-axis.

bar code a method of coding BINARY numbers as a set of thick and thin LINES (sense 1) on paper. The system is used extensively in price and item coding on articles in supermarkets. The code is termed UPC in the USA and EAN in Europe, and the left-hand digit identifies country of origin, with 0=USA and 5=UK. Other digits are used for the manufacturer's code and product number. The codes are repeated in reverse order so that they can be read in either direction and provide a check of one reading against another.

bar-code reader a device for automatically reading BAR CODES in DIGITAL form. The reader generally uses a laser beam that is scanned to and fro over the bar code with a PHOTOCELL reading the number. The software will usually provide for accepting the value that is most frequently found on a number of scans.

bare metal totally new and unprogrammed HARDWARE, such as a newly designed computer with no PROM or BIOS chips so that it cannot be used until these items are designed, created and added.

bar graph or **column graph** a form of GRAPH display in which a changing quantity is represented by the height of a vertical or the length of a horizontal bar.

baroque (of SOFTWARE or HARDWARE) overloaded with features of dubious value.

barrel distortion a MONITOR (sense 1) fault that makes a square appear to have convex sides like the sides of a barrel. See also PINCUSHION DISTORTION.

base or **number base** the number that is represented by the column immediately to the left of the units column of a number system. In the conventional DENARY system, this column represents tens, so that the base of our numbers is ten. In a BINARY system, this column represents 2s, and in octal, 8s. In the HEXADECIMAL system, the column next to the units is the 16s column.

base address a starting address for a BLOCK OF DATA. When a set of items of data is stored in computer memory, it is often convenient to keep the data in order and store it in a set of consecutive addresses. When this is done, the first of these addresses is known as the base address because any other address can be found by adding to this number.

baseband a digital signal that has not been modulated (see MODULATION) and is transmitted in its original form, as in a local area network (LAN).

baseband transmission the direct transmission of DIGITAL signals. A baseband transmission uses a separate electrical voltage to represent each of the two digital signal levels and is not well suited to transmissions over more than a few metres. For longer distances, some form of MODULATION of a CARRIER (sense 2) is required.

base font the FONT that a WORD PROCESSOR or DTP program will use as a DEFAULT at the start of each document. This may be overridden by the selection of a DOCUMENT FONT or a STYLE.

baseline the LINE on which characters of print are arranged, either on paper or on SCREEN (sense 1). Only characters with a DESCENDER will have any portion below the baseline.

base memory see CONVENTIONAL MEMORY.

basename a FILENAME that does not include a PATH (sense 1). See also PATHNAME.

BASIC (Beginners All-purpose Symbolic Instruction Code) a computing language devised originally as a way of teaching computing. BASIC, which is loosely based on FORTRAN, was invented at Dartmouth College, USA. Since that time it has been greatly developed and enhanced to become a powerful and useful language. See also QBASIC; VISUAL BASIC.

Basic Telecommuncations Access Method see BTAM.

BAT an EXTENSION used for an MS-DOS BATCH FILE.

batch file a file of the ASCII text type used in PC CLONE and COMPATIBLE computers to initiate the running of a program under DOS. Instructions can be placed in the batch file, so that a program can be executed by typing a name rather than by typing the full set of instructions. This makes the computer easier to use. Batch files, other than AUTOEXEC.BAT, are not used when the computer is running under MICROSOFT WINDOWS, and even this can be ignored if no MS-DOS program are ever run.

batch parameter a PARAMETER typed on the COMMAND LINE that requires some data to be typed in when running a BATCH FILE under DOS. The parameters are assigned to variables such as %1, %2, etc., within the batch file. For example, a batch file called in the form of COPYIT FILE1 DIR2 might contain the command line COPY %1 %2, which in this example would carry out the action COPY FILE1 DIR2 when the items 'FILE1 DIR2' are typed in by the user following the name COPYIT.

batch processing the processing of data that has been gathered earlier and recorded. Batch processing involves gathering data in the form of magnetic tape or magnetic disks, and operating on all the data in one program RUN (sense 1). For example, if you want to arrange names in alphabetical order, you might enter all the names into a disk file and then use a sorting program on this batch of data. Compare REAL-TIME PROCESSING.

batch total a sum derived from numbers in a batch of data and used as a CHECKSUM to check the integrity of the data numbers.

bathtub curve a description of the usual GRAPH that plots the failure rate of electronics equipment against time. The failure rate is comparatively high at the start of life and drops to almost zero for a long period, rising again at the end of the expected life of the equipment. The problem of high initial failures can be overcome by using a BURN-IN period. See also INFANT MORTALITY.

battery backup a battery, usually a small silver-oxide cell or a lithium battery, used on a MOTHERBOARD to provide a voltage to a CMOS RAM memory so that data held in the RAM will be retained even when the computer is shut down. The REAL-TIME CLOCK is also operated by this battery when the computer is shut down.

baud rate the signal FREQUENCY used for a serial data transmission. The name comes from that of J. M. E. Baudot (1845–1903), the French engineer who pioneered the TELEPRINTER in the 1860s. The rate in terms of data BITS PER SECOND can be higher than the baud rate because each cycle of a wave can convey information on more than one bit of data, but computer users take baud rate to mean the number of bits per second.

bay an empty space in a computer casing, intended to house an extra PERIPHERAL such as a disk drive. See also CARRIER (sense 1).

bboard see BBS.

BBS (bulletin-board system) or **bboard** a computer system connected to telephone lines so that it can be read by anyone who possesses a computer and a MODEM. Bulletin boards are extensively used by hobby computer users as a way of communicating and sharing problems, and are also used by manufacturers of equipment and software as a way of disseminating helpful hints, avoiding the need to keep technical staff tied up answering questions. The functions of the BBS has now been supplanted by the use of WEB SITES.

bcc (blind carbon copy) a method of ensuring that each of several readers of a document copy do not know who else has received a copy. The bcc option is provided for EMAIL as a way of distributing a document without notifying any recipient of the others involved.

BCD (binary-coded decimal) a number system that is used to store, in standardized form, DENARY digits in BINARY form of fixed length. In this system, each digit of a denary number is written as a four-bit binary number rather than converting the entire denary number to its normal binary form. A BCD number always contains a greater number of bits than its true binary equivalent but is convenient for such purposes as calculator displays.

BCS abbreviation for British Computer Society.

beam 1. a set of parallel light rays or a similar set of electromagnetic rays of any FREQUENCY. A LASER is the most suitable light source for generating a tightly parallel beam of light or infrared radiation. **2.** to transfer a document copy electronically, such as by EMAIL.

beep a tone of short duration, used to draw the attention of the operator. See also PROMPT.

beginning of file (BOF) an entry that describes the file content; a form of index to the file.

belief revision a change in the KNOWLEDGE for an ARTIFICIAL INTELLIGENCE system, done in the light of experience.

bell character the ASCII code 7. When the ASCII code was devised, the main printing PERIPHERAL was the TELETYPE, and the ASCII code 7 had the effect of ringing the bell on the teletype. The character has become known as the bell character even although the bell is no longer in use. On many computers, this character produces a BEEP.

bell curve the shape of the NORMAL DISTRIBUTION curve of a set of STATISTICS.

bells and whistles embellishments to a program, often added to justify a new version number. See also CREEPING FEATURISM.

benchmark a short program that is intended to be used as a way of evaluating hardware or software. To be really useful, benchmarking should include a large number of different tests, but it is then misleading to take any kind of average because the test results will often reflect the differing design aims of computers. See also WHETSTONE; DHRYSTONE; LANDMARK.

bending text see WORDART.

Berners-Lee, Tim inventor of the World Wide Web (WWW) during the time when he was employed by CERN (Centre for European Particle Research).

Bernoulli box a form of removable HARD DRIVE used for BACKUP purposes.

best effort (of low-priority telecommunications such as EMAIL) not suffering unduly by being delayed.

best fit an ALGORITHM for finding the best position for new data in a space such as a file.

beta software a version that is the final development stage of a new program almost at the production stage but that may contain some BUGS. By distributing a *beta test* version to several hundred interested users, the last few problems can be discovered and eliminated before production starts. The beta stage can sometimes be very prolonged if users suggest a large number of changes. See also RC.

bezel the front cover surround of any instrument, applied mainly to the front cover of a DISK DRIVE or CD-ROM drive that houses the light that signals drive activity.

Bézier curve a curve whose shape is determined by a relatively simple formula devised by the mathematician Pierre Bézier. Once the basic shape of a Bézier curve has been drawn, it can be altered by dragging HANDLES until the curve is of the desired shape. See also B-SPLINE CURVE.

bible the most authoritative publication referring to or defining a PROGRAMMING LANGUAGE or operating system (OS).

BiCapitalization the use of more than one UPPER-CASE letter within a word, usually a trademark, such as AutoSketch, or an action, such as AutoFormat.

BiCMOS a SEMICONDUCTOR manufacturing process that uses a mixture of techniques to provide low power consumption along with high output current.

bidirectional bus a BUS set of connecting lines on which signals can pass in either direction, although at different times.

bidirectional printing printing in both directions. This is used by many DOT-MATRIX and INKJET printers to achieve extra speed. One line of the text is printed left-to-right, and the next line right-to-left. This requires some memory and a considerable amount of FIRMWARE to be built into the printer.

Big Blue slang for IBM and derived from the appearance of the IBM logo.

big iron see SUPERCOMPUTER.

BIM (beginning of information mark) the name given to a code that marks the start of a stream of data along a connecting line or from a tape or disk.

bin 1. a holder for paper, fitted to a printer, photocopier, etc. **2.** a folder for discarded files; see RECYCLING BIN.

binaries see BINARY FILE.

binary of or relating to any system consisting of only two components. In computing, the term always refers to the number system that uses digits 0 and 1. See BIT.

binary cell a memory unit for one bit that can be SET (sense 2) to 1 or RESET (sense 2) to 0.

binary chop see BINARY SEARCH.

binary-coded decimal see BCD.

binary digit see BIT.

binary file a file, such as a PROGRAM file or a WORKSHEET file, in which the data consists of binary codes using a number range greater than that used for ASCII text. An error in any BIT of a binary file will make the file unusable. See also FILE ATTACHMENT.

binary fraction a fraction that uses powers of 2 rather than powers of 10. For example, the binary fraction 0.101 means one half, no quarters, and one eighth. A REAL NUMBER (not an INTEGER) is stored in the memory of the computer as a binary fraction, and this is the cause of APPROXIMATION ERRORS because binary fractions are seldom exact. See also PRECISION OF NUMBER.

binary number a number that consists of binary digits (BITs). All computer data consists of binary numbers, which are used to convey information of number or STRING quantities.

binary operation an operation on two VARIABLES, such as the addition of two numbers. See also UNARY OPERATION.

binary point the dividing mark between a binary whole number and a binary fraction.

binary search or **binary chop** a fast program method of finding an entry in an ORDERED LIST.

binary-to-denary converter an electronic circuit that for a binary set of inputs will provide outputs that can be used in a scale-of-ten display.

binary tree or **B-tree** a form of TREE (sense 2) structure in which each branching consists of two branches only.

bind to fasten pages of a paper document together for easier reading.

binding constraint see CONSTRAINT.

binding offset the MARGIN used for binding pages into book or magazine form. Many WORD PROCESSOR or DTP programs allow a binding offset to be specified in addition to a normal margin. This binding offset will normally be alternately to right or left, according to the side on which a page is printed.

binoculars icon an ICON that can be clicked to provide a magnified view of the data displayed on the screen in the CURRENT (sense 2) WINDOW. See also ZOOM.

BIOS (Basic Input Output System) a module forming the part of an operating system (OS) that controls the input and output of data to peripherals such as a disk, a keyboard, a monitor, etc. It is stored in ROM on the main MOTHERBOARD. More recently, the BIOS on some motherboards has been stored in writable ROM so that the chip can be upgraded easily, often from a file downloaded from the World Wide Web (WWW). This has led to another way of propagating a VIRUS by reprogramming the BIOS.

BIPS (billions of instructions per second) a measure of computing speed.

BIST (Built in Self-Test) a feature of some INTEL MICROPROCESSOR chips that allows testing to be carried out for consistency of values whenever power is applied to the chip.

bit or **binary digit** either of the two digits 0 or 1, used in BINARY notation. A binary number consists of a collection of bits, often 8, 16 or 32 bits (see also BYTE).

bit block transfer a copying action carried out on a rectangular block of SCREEN (sense 1) PIXELS, either to or from memory.

bit bucket an imaginary holder for data that has in fact been lost.

bit decay see BIT ROT.

bit density the number of BITS recorded per inch of TRACK on a magnetic MEDIUM (sense 1) which can be disk or tape. A high bit density implies that a large amount of data can be recorded in a small physical space. See also BPI.

bit-editing the editing of an image in BITMAP form. The image is displayed magnified so that the individual PIXELS can be seen and their colours altered BIT by bit.

bitfield a portion of a BYTE used for data storage in a DATABASE file. When a large number of data items can each be expressed using just one or two BITS (see BOOLEAN DATA TYPE) it would be wasteful to allocate one complete byte for each data item, so the bits are packed into one or more bytes. Each separate bit in a byte is then a bitfield, carrying its own information.

bit handling the manipulation of individual BITS in a BYTE.

bitmap or **raster graphics** the simplest way of defining a graphics IMAGE (sense 2) in digital terms. A bitmap representation uses a separate BIT or collection of bits to describe each unit or PIXEL of the image. For a simple monochrome image, one bit per pixel can be used, but this is inadequate if shades of grey or colour have to be described. The normal VGA system uses 4 bits per pixel, allowing a range of 16 colours, but SVGA systems can use up to 36 bits per pixel to provide images described as true colour. A bitmap for a whole SCREEN (sense 1) image is a large file, and more compressed forms such as TIFF or PCX are used if possible; see also BMP. See Fig. 7.

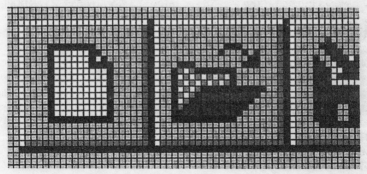

Fig. 7. **Bitmap**. A magnified image of a bimap shows the coarse structure, so that bitmap images should not be magnified – they look best when prepared in a large size and reproduced on a smaller scale.

bitmapped font or **raster font** a file that contains the pattern of PIXEL settings needed to make every character in a FONT. A set of maps must be held for each size of font. See also VECTOR FONT; DTP.

bitmapping see MEMORY MAPPING.

bitonal image any image that consists of two colours only, a BACKGROUND (sense 1) and a FOREGROUND (sense 1) colour.

bit plane memory used in a GRAPHICS ADAPTER to hold an image using one BIT per PIXEL. Graphics software often allows several bit planes to be established so as to provide more image information or to make an image OVERLAY (sense 1).

bit position the position of a BIT in a BYTE. In a byte of 8 bits, each bit is located in its own column when the byte is written as a binary number. The positions are numbered from zero (the units column or LEAST SIG-NIFICANT BIT) to 7 (the 128s column or most significant) bit.

bit rate the speed of transmission of data, expressed as the number of BITS PER SECOND. For computing purposes, this is the same as BAUD RATE.

bit rot or **bit decay** the mythical decay process that causes a PROGRAM to stop working after a period of inactivity.

bit-significant (of a BYTE) using one or more BITs of the byte to convey some meaning other than the number value in binary code. For example, testing bit 6 (see BIT POSITION) of an ASCII-coded letter can distinguish between an upper-case and a lower-case letter.

bits per inch see BPI.

bits per second a measure of the rate of transfer of digital data; see BIT RATE.

bitstream a system for converting digital data into ANALOGUE form, used in COMPACT DISC decoding and other digital systems. Each set of BITs in a digital number is used to generate a voltage that is either posi-tive or negative, and the average of this voltage corresponds to the level of the analogue signal.

bitty box a small primitive computer, particularly a type of MICROCOM-PUTER used before the IBM PERSONAL COMPUTER was developed.

black-and-white see MONOCHROME MONITOR.

black-box testing or **functional testing** a method of testing a program that uses a set of data values that include normal values, values at the extremes of acceptabilit, and non-valid values. The internal structure of the program is not relevant, only the inputs and outputs. Contrast WHITE-BOX TESTING.

black hole the mythical destination of an electronic message that has failed to reach its recipient.

black magic any method, usually in programming, that works despite any clear understanding of its principles.

blank cell a CELL in a WORKSHEET that contains no information, either data or a FORMULA.

blank string or **empty string** a STRING quantity that contains nothing. Some DATABASE programs do not allow you to leave a FIELD (sense 2) empty, but you can insert a blank string.

bleed (originally, in printing) the spreading out of ink from a printed character, a problem in INKJET printers. This makes the outline of the character fuzzy and difficult to read, particularly for optical character readers (OCR, sense 1). Some inkjet printer manufacturers quote two val-ues of dots per inch (DPI), one for ordinary paper on which some bleeding will occur, the other for specially treated paper. The term is also applied in graphics displays to a blob of colour that appears at the point where lines of different colours cross.

Bletchley Park the site of the decoding centre in World War II where the first working electronic computer was designed and constructed by Tommy Flowers (1905–99) in 1943.

blind carbon copy see BCC.

blink to flash on and off, a method of making a POINTER (sense 1), CURSOR, character, word or phrase become prominent on the VDU screen.

blink speed the rate of flashing of a POINTER (sense 1) or CURSOR. This is adjustable so that you can select a rate that is comfortable to your eyes.

bloat see SOFTWARE BLOAT.

bloatware SOFTWARE that has become inflated by SOFTWARE BLOAT.

block 1. a portion of text or graphics that has been selected; see BLOCK OF DATA; SELECTION. **2.** a part of a computer system that carries out one set of actions, such as the memory block or the input/output block.

block copy the action of copying a marked BLOCK OF DATA to another position in a WORD PROCESSOR document or WORKSHEET.

block delete the action of deleting a complete BLOCK OF DATA from a WORD PROCESSOR document or WORKSHEET.

block device a device that deals with data in blocks. For example, a DISK DRIVE may deal with data in 256-BYTE units, so that a complete block of 256 bytes will be used even if the actual data consists of one or two bytes.

block diagram a diagram of a system that shows the main units but no details of any unit. A block diagram is the essential first step towards understanding how any system (not just a computer system) works. See Fig. 8.

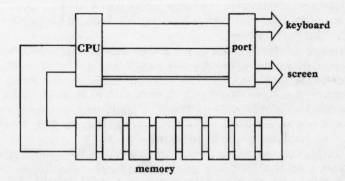

Fig. 8. **Block diagram**. The example shows units of a computer system in the form of blocks, with no details. The aim is to show how parts of a system are connected and how they relate to each other.

blocked records stored data files that have been written as one single unit (on TAPE or on DISK).

block gap see GAP.

block graphics or **character graphics** the use of CHARACTER shapes for creating pictures, now seldom used. Block graphics pictures are of low RESOLUTION because the character shapes consist of several PIXELs each. TELETEXT graphics are of this type.

block header a code or set of codes placed at the start of a BLOCK OF DATA when the data is recorded on tape or on disk. The block header can contain a CHECKSUM, the block length, along with the ADDRESS (sense 1) for the following block (particularly on a disk).

block length the number of characters in a BLOCK OF DATA.

block move the action of cutting a BLOCK OF DATA from one position in a WORD PROCESSOR document or WORKSHEET and pasting it in at another position. See also CUT; PASTE.

block of data a set of data items that belong together. These might, for example, be the items of an ARRAY (sense 2) or a piece of text. A block of data such as this would be stored in a continuous set of memory addresses.

block operation the transfer of a complete set of words of text from one place to another in a WORD PROCESSOR document.

block transfer the movement of a BLOCK OF DATA from one place to another, usually applied to data in memory being copied from one set of memory addresses to another set.

blow an EPROM to program an EPROM with data. Some MODEMS can be modified to the v90 standard by using software that will blow the EPROM, and some MOTHERBOARDS can also have their BIOS information altered in the same way.

blow away to erase, usually unintentionally.

Blue Book one of the reference books for the POSTSCRIPT page description language (PDL), originated by ADOBE SYSTEMS. See also GREEN BOOK, RED BOOK, WHITE BOOK (sense 1).

blue screen of death (BSOD) a SCREEN (sense 1) display of white text on a blue background that appears when MICROSOFT WINDOWS crashes (see CRASH, sense 1).

BMP an extension for BITMAP picture files, such as those created by the Paint program of MICROSOFT WINDOWS.

BNC connector a form of signal plug and socket connector that can be locked so that it cannot be pulled apart accidentally.

BNF see BACKUS-NAUR FORM.

board see CIRCUIT BOARD.

boat anchor a useless piece of HARDWARE or member of staff.

body the main text of a document, excluding headings, captions, header, footer, etc.

BOF see BEGINNING OF FILE.

boilerplate to assemble a document from standard pieces of text held in the memory of a WORD PROCESSOR or from portions held on the HARD DRIVE.

bold a form of TYPEFACE in which the characters print darker and with thicker lines for emphasis.

bomb 1. a concealed fault in a program that has been deliberately planted and can cause a system CRASH (sense 1). **2.** to CRASH (sense 2) with a FATAL ERROR.

bookmark a code that can be placed in word-processed text (see WORD PROCESSOR) to allow the user to locate the place rapidly or to permit cross-referencing.

Boolean (of a data quantity) taking one of only two values that can be described either as 1 and 0 or as TRUE and FALSE, named after George Boole (1815–64) who devised a form of algebra dealing with logical statements.

Boolean algebra a system for dealing with logic problems by writing the logic actions in the form of a set of mathematical equations of sets. Boolean algebra is used in the design of circuits for computing purposes.

Boolean data type or **logical data type** a DATA TYPE that can take only one of two possible values, usually 1 and 0 or TRUE and FALSE.

Boolean operation an action carried out on a BOOLEAN DATA TYPE. The fundamental Boolean operations are NOT, OR and AND, which are used, for instance, in forming a QUERY to a DATABASE.

boot to load in a starting program. Desktop computers require most of the operating system (OS) to be loaded in from disk, and this action is called *booting up*. Some faults can cause this to happen again (a REBOOT), in which case all the data that was in the memory will be lost. Portable computers may contain most of their operating system in ROM and boot from the ROM.

boot block a BOOT program that is located at a fixed position on a DISK, usually the HARD DRIVE, so that the routines in the ROM memory can find it easily.

boot disk a disk that contains the SYSTEM TRACK set of files that are used for the operating system (OS) of the computer. Conventionally, this disk can be used to start the operating system in the event of failure of the main hard drive. MICROSOFT WINDOWS creates a STARTUP DISK that will BOOT into MS-DOS (not Windows) and is used for trouble-shooting when the Windows system cannot be booted from the hard drive.

boot record a file contained on the first SECTOR of a disk that contains information about the disk and its files. Any damage to this file will make the disk virtually unusable.

bootstrap loader a small piece of program code that is loaded into the computer and used to load in the remainder of a program. BOOT is an abbreviation of bootstrap.

boot virus a VIRUS that is placed on the BOOT BLOCK so that it will affect any MS-DOS program run on the computer.

border that part of the video screen display or a WINDOW that surrounds the main portion used for text or graphics.

bot abbreviation of ROBOT, referring to a program that usually carries out a monitoring or assisting action.

bottom margin the blank space at the foot of a page. A WORD PROCESSOR or DTP program will allow the size of the bottom MARGIN to be specified and will also allow some of this space to be used for a FOOTER.

bottom-up model a costing system for writing SOFTWARE that sums the estimated cost of each component.

bottom-up testing a testing scheme that tests the simplest and lowest levels of a system before passing to the more elaborate levels.

bounce the action of an EMAIL message that cannot be delivered, causing an error message to be returned to the sender.

boundary condition a statement of limits for an action. You might, for example, wish to permit a DATABASE program to accept age values of 18 to 90 years only, and these form the boundary conditions for this example.

boundary protection code within a program that prevents reserved parts of the computer memory from being used.

bounding box see FRAME (sense 1).

box tool a drawing aid in a DTP, CAD or PAINT program. When the box tool has been selected, the MOUSE is clicked (see CLICK, sense 1) over the point at which one corner of the box is to be located and the mouse is dragged (see DRAG) so that the CURSOR moves to the opposite corner position – the shape of the box can be seen during this time with the sides ELASTIC BANDING to size. The box shape and size are fixed when the mouse button is clicked again.

box wrap a DTP action in which text being imported to the document will avoid a rectangular area. This area can later be used on the paper for pasting a photograph or it can be filled with a graphics IMAGE (sense 2) in the course of the DTP editing work. See Fig. 9.

BPI (bits per inch) the measurement of recording density.

BPS (bits per second) the measurement of rate of data transmission.

braces the curly bracket characters {}. These are used, for example, in MICROSOFT EXCEL to enclose an ARRAY (sense 2).

brackets or **parentheses** the signs ( ) that enclose words or numbers. Brackets are used in SPREADSHEET programs to enclose the ARGUMENT of a FUNCTION. For example, a CELL in a WORKSHEET might contain SIN(1.7), where 1.7 is the ANGLE in radian measure.

Braille keyboard a computer keyboard designed for the visually

When·you·have·read·all·the·information·on·the·motherboard·and·made· notes· about· anything· you· need· to· watch· out· for,· unpack· the· motherboard.· The· final  wrapping· will·be·of·a·material·that·is slightly· electrically· conducting, and· when· you·take·the·motherboard out·of·this· material· you· should· lay the· board· down· on· this· sheet· of material·to· make· an· inspection. Touch·the· motherboard·only·at·the·edges·at·this·stage,·and·try·to·keep·your·hands· away·from·the·metallic·connections·as·far·as·possible·at·all·times.¶

Fig. 9. **Box wrap**. A box containing a picture is designated for wrapping so that the text in the page will wrap around the box rather than being hidden by it or leaving blank space on each side.

impaired, using 8 KEYS (sense 1) that correspond to the 8-dot code used in the Braille language. See also APOLLO SPEECH SYSTEM; KURZWEIL PERSONAL READER; OPTACON; VERSABRAILLE.

Braille tactile display a computer read-out device for the visually impaired that uses a set of pins that can be felt by the user and the positions of which correspond to the standard Braille language code. The pins are raised and lowered by interfacing circuits from the printer output of the computer. See also APOLLO SPEECH SYSTEM; KURZWEIL PERSONAL READER; OPTACON; VERSABRAILLE.

branch see SUBDIRECTORY.

breadth-first search a method, used in artificial intelligence work, of searching a hierarchical database. In a breadth-first search, the whole of one level will be searched before a lower level is searched. See also depth-first search.

break to stop an action temporarily.

break key a computer KEY (sense 1) that will stop program action.

breakout box a junction box used on a connection to a SERIAL INTERFACE that allows connections to be transposed to suit the equipment being connected. It also allows signal values to be checked by instruments in the event of problems with interfacing.

breakpoint a point at which a program, including a MACRO, will be forced to stop. This can give the programmer time to decide what to do next, or it can be used temporarily for testing.

break tool a TOOLBAR item used in CAD programs to break a line so that a gap is created.

bridge or **transition** a CONNECTOR that allows two different types of NETWORK to interchange information.

bridgeware software that can be used to allow the data of one program to be used by another program, or on a different type of computer, or to allow a program developed on one computer to be used on another.

Briefcase a UTILITY program used in later versions of MICROSOFT WINDOWS, intended to synchronize data files that are kept on two computers that are not permanently networked. Used mainly where a LAPTOP and a DESKTOP COMPUTER need to have identical data files.

bring to front a COMMAND used in PAINT and PRESENTATION GRAPHICS programs to make a selected object appear to be in front of others, partially hiding the other objects.

British Library Method a form of sequential SEARCH.

British Standards Institute see BSI.

British Telecom see BT.

brittle or **fragile** (of SOFTWARE) misbehaving following changes in the operating system (OS) settings or the introduction of other software. See also ROBUST PROGRAM.

broadband (of any method of transmitting information) supporting a wide range of frequencies (see FREQUENCY). A broadband system is ideal for DIGITAL transmissions and can carry many CHANNELS (sense 1) of information.

broadcast a transmission of INFORMATION to a large number of receivers, with no need to specify who can or cannot receive the information.

broadcast network a NETWORK on which a user can transmit a PACKET of data that can be picked up and used by any other computer on the network. Normally, each packet carries an address code so that the packet can be intercepted by one other user.

broadcast quality (of video) conforming to the quality standards of broadcast TV, implying a rate of 25–30 frames per second at 525–625 lines per frame.

brochureware any product, usually SOFTWARE, that is actively promoted to the point of printing and distributing brochures, but which does not exist. This is used as a ploy to hinder the marketing of competitive products.

bromide output or **camera-ready copy** (**CRC**) the master COPY (sense 3) produced by a typesetting machine. A disk produced by the action of a DTP program can be used to prepare master copy on a laser printer, but for high quality reproduction, particularly of GRAPHICS, a typesetting machine must be used. If the disk files use the POSTSCRIPT language, they can be used directly by the typesetter to produce the photographic-quality masters termed *bromides*.

brownout a period of low electrical supply voltage, typically caused by overload and often preceding a total power failure. See UPS.

browse 1. to scan over data before picking one item, allowing data to be cursorily checked but not altered. MICROSOFT WINDOWS uses the term to

mean looking for a disk FOLDER (*directory*) that contains a specified file.
2. to move from one WEB SITE to another following up information; see also SURF.

browser a program that displays HYPERTEXT in readable form on the SCREEN (sense 1), especially on the World Wide Web (WWW). The text can be printed, and the browser controls allow for NAVIGATION from one page to another.

brush a form of tool used in DTP and PAINT programs to simulate the action of a paintbrush on canvas by drawing wide lines, usually in colour.

BSI (British Standards Institute) the body that sets and publishes British Standards for HARDWARE and SOFTWARE along with a host of other items

BSOD see BLUE SCREEN OF DEATH.

b-spline curve a form of curve created by clicking (see CLICK, sense 1) on a set of points that define the shape, used particularly in CAD programs. See also BÉZIER CURVE.

BSRAM see BURST STATIC RANDOM ACCESS MEMORY.

BT (British Telecom) the major UK telecommunications provider, which also offers INTERNET connection (*BTClick*).

BTAM (Basic Telecommunications Access Method) any system for reading from and writing to a remote computer by way of telephone lines.

B-tree see BINARY TREE.

bubble-jet™ trademark of Canon Ltd for a principle used in an INKJET PRINTER. This uses heating of ink in a fine tube to form a bubble that blows the ink from the jet. See also PIEZO-ELECTRIC INKJET.

bubble memory a form of magnetic NON-VOLATILE MEMORY that has been little used because faster but more manageable methods have been developed.

bubble sort a simple but slow way of programming the action of sorting a LIST into order. See also SHELL SORT; QUICKSORT.

bucket a temporary memory store for a batch of data or an ALLOCATION (sense 1) of memory in a DATABASE program to cope with added data so that data belonging together can be kept together.

buffer a piece of memory that is used for temporary STORAGE. A buffer is used in conjunction with a keyboard, so that if several KEYS (sense 1) are pressed in quick succession, all the codes can be dealt with in the correct order. A keyboard that is so equipped is described as having *N*-KEY ROLLOVER. Another use is in TAPE or DISK filing, when data is gathered up in a buffer until it can be transferred. In general, a buffer will be used when a fast-acting part of a system is exchanging data with a slow-acting part or device, and the buffer is used to store data until it can be dealt with. All LASER PRINTERS and many DOT-MATRIX printers contain their own buffers so that their use does not tie up the computer for too long.

buffered write-through a CACHE technique that uses a BUFFER to hold data to be written, so that data can be read at the same time. This is useful only if the main memory is slow compared to the MICROPROCESSOR speed.

buffer overflow the result of attempting to store too much DATA in a BUFFER. This is a programming fault because a well-written program would not accept an amount of data that would overflow the buffer.

bug a fault in a program. The act of removing the fault is called DEBUGGING.

bug-compatible (of a new version of a program) flawed because of the need to maintain COMPATIBILITY with an earlier version that contained a BUG.

bug-fix a program ADD-IN that is devised and used to correct a BUG temporarily. This code will be incorporated into any new version of the program.

bug-fix release a revised version of a major release of a program that cures a BUG in the earlier version without introducing too many new bugs.

build slide or **progressive disclosure slide** a SLIDE on a PRESENTATION GRAPHICS display that is animated so that features appear piece by piece.

built-in font a FONT that is incorporated into a PRINTER so that it can be used as a DEFAULT for text files that contain no font information.

built-in function a FUNCTION in a SPREADSHEET that is available as a COMMAND, such as LOG for logarithm. Actions that cannot be obtained from any built-in function have to be carried out using FORMULAE that in turn must be constructed from built-in functions.

bulk-erase to wipe all signals from a magnetic tape or disk. Tape is normally erased immediately prior to recording, but a *bulk eraser* can clear the whole of a tape without the need to wind the tape past a head. The principle is to set up an intense AC MAGNETIC FIELD around the tape. Valuable disks and BACKUP tapes should be kept well clear of a bulk eraser.

bulk storage a system that allows large amounts of data to be stored, usually with rather slow ACCESS (sense 2) times. The HARD DRIVE and the CD-ROM drive are examples of bulk storage systems; see also BACKING STORE.

bulk update see ACTION QUERY.

bullet a large dot (•). The bullet is used in printed work to draw attention to the start of a paragraph. Since the bullet is not represented in normal ASCII code, DTP programs have to use extended ascii or provide this character specially, along with other symbols such as the dagger.

bulletin board see BBS.

bulletproof see ARMOUR-PLATED.

bump to INCREMENT (sense 1) a number, as in a counter routine.

bumping (of a graphics IMAGE, sense 1) moving to another page. In DTP work, if a graphics image cannot be accommodated on a page because of the presence of another image, it is automatically bumped to the next page.

bundled software SOFTWARE, such as MICROSOFT OFFICE, MICROSOFT WORKS or the LOTUS program set, that is ready-installed on a new computer as an incentive to buy the computer.

bureau or COMPUTER BUREAU an agency selling computing or DTP services. A computing bureau would typically offer data preparation, keying in, rental of hardware and software, systems analysis, consultancy and custom software. A DTP agency would typically offer to prepare master pages from supplied text and graphics, digitization of graphics, preparation of master disks and typesetting from disk.

buried treasure a previously undiscovered piece of poorly designed code in a program.

burn-in a period of use of an electronic circuit or CHIP that is used to weed out any early failures. Units that survive a burn-in period will generally have a very long life. See also BATHTUB CURVE; INFANT MORTALITY.

burst to tear the edgings from TRACTOR-FEED stationer, and also to separate the sheets.

burst EDO (burst extended data output DRAM) a form of DRAM, now extensively used, in which reads and writes are grouped into sets of four in such a way that the bus speed can be considerably higher than the 33 MHz limit of EDO, typically 66 MHz to more than 100 MHz.

burst static random access memory (BSRAM) a form of fast STATIC RAM used for LEVEL 2 CACHE purposes.

bus or **highway** a set of electrical conductors that carry related signals. For example, a DATA BUS carries the set of signals for a character or other data item, and an ADDRESS BUS carries the signals that locate a byte in the memory. See also LOCAL BUS; VLB; PCI BUS.

bus master the HARDWARE device on a MOTHERBOARD that controls the ADDRESS BUS and control bus. Normally the CPU controls the buses by way of bus-mastering software but can relinquish this control to a DMA chip as required.

bus mouse a form of MOUSE that connects directly to a MOTHERBOARD or to an ADAPTER board using a DIN or PS/2 connector. See also SERIAL MOUSE; USB.

bus network a form of NETWORK in which the signals are carried over a BUS and are available to all of the networked computers but are used only by the computer that responds to a unique ADDRESS (sense 1) code. Failure of one computer does not necessarily disrupt the network action for the others, and it is easy to extend the network to include additional computers.

busy signal a signal sent along a control line to indicate that a device cannot be used because it is already working on other data.

button a square shape in a WINDOW. The button is used to implement a simple command or choice such as Go or Yes by placing the POINTER (sense 1) over the button, using the MOUSE and clicking (see CLICK, sense 1) with the mouse button.

button bar see TOOLBAR.

button editor a UTILITY included in MICROSOFT EXCEL and MICROSOFT WORD that allows a button to be altered, using a different ICON or different lettering.

buzzing (of a program) continuing to run without any results appearing.

byline information, such as an author's name, on a WORD PROCESSOR or DTP document.

byte the unit of data or memory that is now universally taken to mean 8 BITS. One important feature of a byte is that a character in ASCII code needs only one byte for storage.

C a HIGH-LEVEL LANGUAGE that is so compact that a few short instruction words and symbols can control a large amount of computing action. C and its later derivative, called C++, are widely used by professionals for writing operating systems (OS), business software and games.

C: C drive, conventionally the main (or only) HARD DRIVE in a computer. The C: drive will normally contain the main or only operating system (OS) if more than one hard drive is fitted.

cable modem a MODEM that connects a computer to the INTERNET by way of a cable TV service. This can allow for faster transfer rates than are achieved with a conventional telephone line modem, but significantly high rates are not necessarily achieved in practice.

cache a form of BUFFER memory. The word 'cache' usually implies that the memory can be randomly accessed (see ACCESS, sense 2) very rapidly, so that the user is unaware of the use of the memory. A cache can be used internally (inside a MICROPROCESSOR), externally (between a microprocessor and memory) or, also externally and using ordinary memory, between the HARD DRIVE and the rest of the system. The effect in all cases is to speed up computing actions by reading from and writing to the fast cache memory as distinct from the ordinary RAM or the hard drive. Unlike a buffer, a cache is read selectively.

cache conflict a problem that arises when two blocks of data require the same CACHE memory space.

cache hit DATA supplied from a CACHE memory rather than directly from the main memory.

cache line or **cache block** the minimum specified amount of DATA that can be transferred between a CACHE memory and the main memory.

cache miss DATA that has to be read from the main memory because it is not present in the CACHE memory.

CAD (computer-aided design) the use of a program that produces precise technical drawings or diagrams, with lists of parts and quantities calculated. The drawings can make use of components that have previously been drawn. Each drawing can be seen on the SCREEN (sense 1) and printed, using a PLOTTER if the dimensional accuracy is particularly important. The drawings are made by dragging (see DRAG) the mouse and using a GRID and GRID SNAPs to ensure precision. CAD programs can be tailored to specific purposes, such as garden planning or furniture layouts, and can be very useful and timesaving. See Fig. 10 (overleaf).

CADCAM (computer-aided design and computer-aided manufacture) a

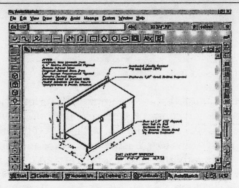

Fig. 10. **CAD**. A typical package (AutoSketch) showing the icons and menus, and with the drawing area in use.

set of programs for integrating the design and the automated production of articles. The design part of the program suite (see CAD) carries out the design actions, producing a disk file that can be converted by the CAM section into a file that can be used to control automated production machines.

caddy a holder for CD-ROM discs in a CD-ROM drive, no longer used.

CAE see COMPUTER-AIDED ENGINEERING.

CAI (computer-aided instruction) a set of programs intended for teachers or instructors to prepare lesson work in an ordered way and to generate tests and other material for assessing rate of learning.

CAL (computer-assisted learning) the term applied to any system in which the computer is used to provide practice, repetitive testing, visual simulations and other aids to learning. The full acceptance of CAL awaits the production of reliable voice recognition devices so that the user can be freed completely from the use of the keyboard. See DIRECT VOICE INPUT.

calculated field or **derived field** a FIELD (sense 2) in a DATABASE whose value arises from a calculation, such as the sum of the values in a set of other fields, that has been calculated by the database program from other values, such as table values. A calculated field cannot be edited and can be changed only by altering the basis of calculation or the data that is used for the calculation. Also found as a WORD PROCESSOR FIELD (sense 1).

calibration the action of comparing a quantity with a known standard so as to correct the value. The simplest example is correction of the REAL-TIME CLOCK in a computer.

callback a SECURITY system in which a user passes a name and PASSWORD to a computer, which then hangs up. The computer then dials the user's number, which is stored as part of a set of authorized user data.

caller ID a MODEM feature that reveals the identity of a caller.

calling the requesting of connection to a remote TERMINAL. A *calling code* is sent to the remote terminal so that it can be activated for the reception of data.

callout text that is used in DTP to identify parts of a drawing. See Fig. 11.

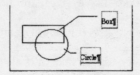

Fig. 11 **Callout**. The callout box contains text and has a pointer to the object that is being illustrated. Callouts can be created by various drawing packages, such as the drawing tool of Microsoft Word.

call scheduling a feature of FAX and MODEM operation that allows outgoing calls to be made when telephone time is less expensive.

CAM 1. computer-aided manufacture (see CADCAM). **2.** computer-aided management. The term is applied to the use of a computer as a management tool by providing information, forecasts, visual simulations and data retrieval. The most important action, however, is usually communication.

Cambridge ring or **ring** a method of passing data round a set of computers. This is a form of local area network (LAN), which, as the full name suggests, was developed in Cambridge and which is widely used in educational applications. See also ETHERNET.

camera-ready suitable for reproduction by printing press. Camera-ready COPY (sense 3) in DTP work is paper copy that can be printed using a photographic process to prepare printing plates, as distinct from work on disk. Camera-ready copy must be of a high standard because of the inevitable losses in reproduction. The use of PDF files of POSTSCRIPT is replacing camera-ready work. See also BROMIDE OUPUT.

cancel to stop a process before it has started or at an early stage in execution.

candlestick chart see HIGH/LOW/CLOSE/OPEN GRAPH.

Canon engine the basic mechanism for a LASER PRINTER, manufactured by Canon Corp. Many of the laser printers that are currently available use the Canon engine, so that replaceable items such as TONER cartridges are common to many makes of printer.

canonical scheme a standard form of outline design for a program that can be applied to any computer and any suitable software because it describes the ends rather than the means. It is often used more broadly to mean obeying a standard way of doing something, such as reading from left to right.

capacitor an electronic component that can store a small amount of electric charge. This is the basis of DRAM.

capability list a LIST of actions that a program can achieve.

capacity as applied to a computer system, the STORAGE space available in the MEMORY or on a DISK, usually in units of BYTES, KILOBYTES (Kbyte) or MEGABYTES (Mbyte). HARD DRIVE sizes are now stated in GIGABYTES (Gbyte).

cap height the unit of FONT size, the height of any UPPER-CASE letter measured in the POINT unit.

capitalization the conversion of text into all UPPER-CASE. Some WORD PROCESSOR designs and most DTP programs allow marked text to be converted in this way, and DTP programs often also provide the option of small capitals (see SMALL CAPS). Some word processors will automatically capitalize the first letter character following a full stop and will remove capitalization from the following letter.

caps or **capital letters** see UPPER-CASE.

caps lock the KEY (sense 1) that can make a keyboard provide either UPPER-CASE letters only or a mixture of upper- and LOWER-CASE. The key has a TOGGLE action (press for caps, press again for lower-case) and should be provided with an indicator light.

capstan the spindle of a tape recorder that drives the tape along past the tapehead of, for example, a TAPE STREAMER. Any dirt deposited, scratching or distortion of the capstan will make the recorder unreliable for BACKUP purposes.

caption the text placed under or to the side of an illustration. Caption text is often in italics and by convention no full stop is placed at the end of a caption.

capture see SCREEN CAPTURE.

carbon copy see CC.

card a CIRCUIT CARD or CIRCUIT BOARD.

cardfile a simple form of data file program. A cardfile program reproduces on SCREEN (sense 1) the appearance of a filing card but with much quicker ACCESS (sense 2) and the ability to specify search criteria. A good example was the CARDFILE program of Microsoft Windows 3.1, later abandoned.

caret the ^ symbol obtained by pressing the SHIFT-6 keys. The caret is often used to mean 'to the power', as in 2^6, meaning 2^6. The caret is also used in some instruction manuals to mean the CTRL KEY, so the ^C key means Ctrl-C.

careware or **charityware** a form of SHAREWARE in which the author requests a donation to a charity rather than (or in addition) to the author.

carpel-tunnel syndrome a form of repetitive strain injury of the wrist that can be attributed to excessive work with a MOUSE.

carriage the printing head portion of an INKJET or DOT-MATRIX printer that needs to be returned to the left-hand side to start a new line of print.

carriage return see CR.

carriage return line feed see CRLF.

carrier 1. a metal framework that is used to hold a DISK DRIVE in a BAY. **2.** a high-FREQUENCY signal whose MODULATION carries signals of lower frequencies, usually for radio transmission but also for cable transmission; see MODEM.

carrier detect a MODEM action used to sense the presence of an incoming signal.

carrier sense multiple access with collision detection see CSMA/CD.

Cartesian coordinates a system of determining position by reference to two axes at right angles to each other. For example, a position on the SCREEN (sense 1) can be referred to as $X = 100$, $Y = 50$, meaning 100 units along from the left-hand side and 50 units down from the top. See also ORIGIN (sense 2).

cartridge 1. a PLUG-IN unit for adding MEMORY or for tape BACKUP. A typical memory cartridge unit would use ROM, which is programmed with data, or RAM as a way of adding RAM to the (usually portable) computer. A tape cartridge would be used along with a TAPE STREAMER drive. A ROM cartridge can be used to provide a program or data for such purposes as printer FONTS, and most LASER PRINTERS provide for the addition of fonts in this way. **2.** a unit that contains ink, or a combination of ink and printing head, for an INKJET PRINTER.

cartridge disk or **disk pack** a disk contained in a removable casing. This is a way of inserting and removing a HARD DRIVE with the disk set itself protected from the atmosphere by being enclosed in its cartridge.

cartridge font a form of ROM in the shape of a plug-in CARTRIDGE (sense 1) for a LASER PRINTER. The cartridge adds one or more fonts to the built-in FONT set of the printer. Cartridge fonts are expensive and are little used now that TRUETYPE fonts are available for WINDOWS programs.

cartridge tape a cartridge containing TAPE, arranged like a CASSETTE (sense 2) and containing digital tape. This is used in tape STREAMERs to back up the entire contents of a HARD DISK or selected portions as required. A BACKUP to a tape streamer is more convenient and often faster than a backup to floppy disks because a single tape cartridge can have a capacity as high as that of the HARD DRIVE. See also QIC; TRAVAN.

cascade or **staggered windows** an arrangement of SCREEN (sense 1) WINDOWS in which each window overlaps another. This allows the MOUSE CURSOR to be clicked on any window without the need to move any of the windows; see Fig. 12 (overleaf). See also TILING.

cascading menu a MENU set in which successive portions are visible on screen, overlapping each other. See also TILING.

cascading windows a set of WINDOWS, each containing a different pro-

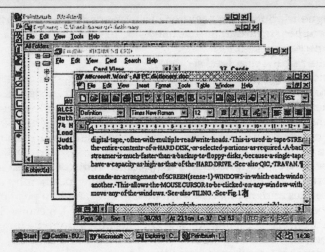

Fig. 12. **Cascade** or staggered windows. The four windows in this illustration are cascaded so that all of one window can be seen and parts of all the others.

gram and overlapping so that at least a TITLE BAR of each is visible. A window can be made active (see ACTIVE WINDOW) by clicking on any visible portion of the window.

CASE see COMPUTER-AIDED SOFTWARE ENGINEERING.

case the classification of an alphabetical letter as UPPER-CASE (capital) or LOWER-CASE. The word originated in printing at a time when lead castings of type were kept in wooden cases whose positioning indicated whether they were capital or ordinary letters.

case-based reasoning an ARTIFICIAL INTELLIGENCE method that sets out to solve problems by examining previous similar examples.

case change a COMMAND, which may be implemented by pressing a key, that will convert from upper- to lower-case or the other way around. Such a command is an essential feature of a WORD PROCESSOR system.

case-sensitive distinguishing between lower- and upper-case in a document. For example, a WORD PROCESSOR SEARCH action can be made case-sensitive, so that a search for 'smith' does not find 'Smith'. Computers running UNIX use FILENAMES that are case-sensitive, so care is needed to use the correct names.

cassette 1. a holder for paper or envelopes in a LASER PRINTER, usually loaded with paper and fitting internally. **2.** a rigid container for TAPE. It consists of two miniature reels that can be wound in either direction and are enclosed in a plastic case. The case also contains TAPE GUIDES and a PRESSURE PAD that will hold the tape against the read/write head of a recorder. See also DAT.

catalogue a set of grouped files, usually for a DATABASE.

catalogue of disk see DIRECTORY (sense 2).

catastrophic error see FATAL ERROR.

catatonic (of a computer) locked up, with no response.

cathode-ray tube see CRT.

cationic cocktail a solution of fabric softener used as an antistatic (see ANTISTATIC MAT) spray.

CAV (constant angular velocity) rotation at a steady speed in terms of the amount of angle covered per second. For example, the old-style vinyl disk gramophone records revolved with a constant angular velocity equivalent to $33^1/_3$ revolutions per minute. Some modern laser disc players (for video) make use of CAV rather than CLV because it makes effects such as picture freeze easier to obtain.

CBM see COMMODORE BUSINESS MACHINES.

CBT see COMPUTER-BASED TRAINING.

cc (carbon copy) the line in an EMAIL editor that specifies the email address to which a copy of the text is to be sent. Compare BCC.

CCD (charge-coupled device) a MATRIX of SEMICONDUCTOR devices that pass electrical charge one to another, used for the light-sensing elements in DIGITAL CAMERAS and SCANNERS.

CCITT protocol a set of standards for MODEMS, using coded descriptions starting with the letter V. For example, a V32 modem is one capable of using the higher speeds of 4800 and 9600 bits per second in addition to the lower speeds used by older modem types.

CD 1. the DOS command, an abbreviation of CHDIR, for logging in to a new DIRECTORY (sense 1). **2.** see COMPACT DISC.

CD-I see COMPACT DISC INTERACTIVE.

CDPD see CELLULAR DIGITAL PACKET DATA.

CD-R a type of blank CD-ROM that can be written once and read as often as needed. The written portion can be erased but cannot be written again, although previously unused parts of the disc can be used in subsequent write operations. The software needs to be able to configure the disc for the expected use because a disc can be configured so that it can be read only by a read/write drive, can be read by any PERSONAL COMPUTER CD-ROM drive or can be read by the CD-ROM drive of any computer (including a MACINTOSH).

CDR file see CORELDRAW.

CD-ROM a method of data STORAGE that makes use of the coding and manufacturing methods of a COMPACT DISC. The main difference is that the digital codes on the conventional CD are intended to be converted to analogue waveforms of sound, those on the CD-ROM are used directly as digital data.

CD-RW a type of blank CD-ROM that can be written, erased and rewritten. These discs are expensive, and some cannot be read in conventional CD-ROM drives.

Ceefax the BBC version of TELETEXT; see also ORACLE (sense 1).

Celeron™ a cut-down form of the INTEL PENTIUM-2, intended for home computers. Some older Celeron types have no LEVEL-2 CACHE and are outperformed by other processors of a similar price.

cell 1. in a SPREADSHEET type of program, a unit position on the SCREEN (sense 1) that will contain a number, a FORMULA or text. Each cell of the spreadsheet is located by numbering its row and lettering its column. **2.** a unit of memory, storing one byte and with a unique ADDRESS (sense 1) number.

cell address see CELL REFERENCE.

cell alignment the ALIGNMENT (sense 1) of text or numbers in a CELL of a WORKSHEET. This is normally either left, right or centred.

cell definition the content of a CELL in a WORKSHEET. This can be a number or STRING, which will be visible on screen, or a FORMULA, which is not.

cell format the way that information will be arranged in a CELL in a WORKSHEET. For example, a number might be formatted with two places of decimals and aligned to the right of the cell, and a STRING might be centred in its cell.

cell pointer the highlighting that appears when a CELL in a WORKSHEET is an ACTIVE CELL.

cell protection a MENU option of a WORKSHEET that prevents the contents of a CELL from being altered. The usual method is to enable protection for all cells and then remove protection from the cells that will be used for entering data.

cell reference the ROWS AND COLUMNS identifiers used to locate a CELL in a WORKSHEET. For example, the cell reference or address D7 means column D and row 7. A cell address may also be assigned to a name, so that cell D7 is referred to as 'CashTotal'.

cellular digital packet data (CDPD) a standard system for data transmission using cellular mobile telephones.

central data access the use of one computer in a NETWORK to control all data processing. This avoids the problems of distributing data among a number of machines with the risk that some users may not be working on updated data or that there will be conflicts of data use.

central processing unit see CPU.

centre alignment the CENTRING of a line of print on a page. Centre alignment is used for some headings. See also JUSTIFICATION.

centre tab a TAB STOP that causes insertion of typed characters at the centre of a page.

centring the placing of a word or phrase in the middle of a printed line during word processing.

Centronics interface a universally accepted INTERFACE for printers. This is the type of interface that is referred to as PARALLEL, meaning that one connecting line is used for each BIT of a BYTE, along with lines for synchronizing signals. The standard was devised by the printer manufacturer Centronics Inc., and it is normal to find that any computer that uses the Centronics interface will be compatible with any printer that uses this interface. See also EXTERNAL PERIPHERAL; IEE 1394.

century meltdown see Y2K.

certificate authority a company that provides proof of identity for INTERNET users. The proof of identity is in the form of a DIGITAL SIGNATURE.

CGA card an ADD-ON card, now obsolete, that was used in an EXPANSION SLOT of a PERSONAL COMPUTER CLONE or COMPATIBLE machine to provide low-resolution colour graphics and poor-quality text displays.

CGI see COMMON GATEWAY INTERFACE.

CGM (computer graphics metafile) a VECTOR form of graphics file that can be used by a wide range of different computer types. See also WMF.

chain printing an action that allows a set of files to be printed in order. The Print Manager of Windows can be used to form a PRINT QUEUE so that files are chain printed, and MICROSOFT WINDOWS offers the option of a SEPARATOR SHEET between files. WORD PROCESSOR programs can also arrange files in a sequence for printing; see MASTER DOCUMENT.

chain search a SEQUENTIAL search through items. This involves items such as RECORDS (sense 1) that can contain POINTERS to other items until the required item or the end of the LIST is reached. A typical example of chain searching is found in information services of the TELETEXT type, so that if you look up 'travel', you will find references to road, rail, sea and air. Looking up 'air' will then produce a list of airports, and so on. Chain searching is acceptable if the computer carries out the search automatically but can be very slow if each item has to be selected manually.

chamfer an action that converts a 90° corner into two 45° angles separated by a short length of line. The chamfer command is an important editing action for a CAD program.

changebar a form of TOOLBAR used in *Serif Page Plus* to alter characteristics of text or graphics in a DTP page.

change-line support a normal facility of a FLOPPY-DISK drive. These drives contain a microswitch that detects the insertion and removal of a disk, so that the operating system (OS) can use this to sense that the directory list needs to be updated. This simple system is often upset by an operating system action that stores the listing in a BUFFER, so that a key (usually F5) has to be pressed to update the display when another disk is inserted.

channel 1. or **stream** a path for the transmission of DATA in a COMMUNICATIONS LINK. **2.** a control path in a MIDI connection between the computer and electronic musical instruments. **3.** an INTERNET system that resembles the structure of TV transmissions, allowing the user to select a set of data of one type and to BROWSE it (sense 2). There is no option for browsing outside the confines of the information in the channel. See also PUSH MEDIA.

character any letter, digit, punctuation mark or graphics symbol that is represented by one ASCII code number in the range 32 to 127, and by extended ASCII (ANSI) codes in the range 128 to 255. This excludes codes for actions, such as LINE FEED or carriage return (CR), which are represented by code numbers in the range 0 to 31.

character block the set of dots that can be used to make up a CHARACTER. A SCREEN (sense 1) display of the usual VDU type uses a dot of light that scans across and down the screen. The shape of a character is obtained by brightening the dot in the required places as it moves across the screen. Each character is therefore built up from dots, and the pattern of dots that is available at each character position is called the character block. This is specified as the number of dots across the character and the number down. A typical block is 15 x 9 dots, but dot-MATRIX PRINTERS often use fewer dots, sometimes only 7 x 5 in draft mode. See Fig. 13.

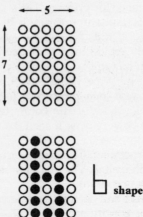

Fig. 13. **Character block**. This consists of the group of dots from which any character shape can be obtained.

character code a number that represents a CHARACTER. Usually the number will be one of the ASCII set, but it can also be one of the extended set like the PC-8 set.

character fill the action of writing an ASCII character into every LOCATION (sense 1) in a specified part of memory. This can be used for testing the memory or as a way of ensuring that any data formerly stored in that part is totally erased. The character fill action is also found in some SPREADSHEET programs as a way of filling a RANGE.

character generator a ROM-based circuit that converts codes. When the input to a character generator is a valid ASCII code, the output will be a set of numbers that will cause the VDU to illuminate the correct pattern of dots in the CHARACTER BLOCK. This is much faster than the process of drawing the character, which is why text-based work can be faster than graphics-based work.

character graphics see BLOCK GRAPHICS.

Character map a MICROSOFT WINDOWS utility that allows characters from different FONT sets to be viewed and inserted into a document. For example, a word-processed document can have Greek characters inserted from the Character map where required. See Fig. 14.

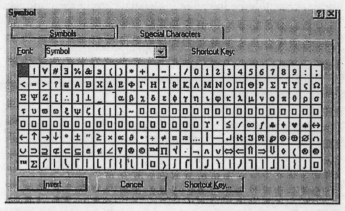

Fig. 14. **Character map**. In this illustration, the Character map shows the Symbol set of characters for mathematical use.

character-mapped display a display that uses a ROM to hold the SCREEN (sense 1) patterns for the range of characters it can use. This allows the screen to be used in CHARACTER MODE.

character mode or **text mode** a SCREEN (sense 1) mode of operation that is used for text or BLOCK GRAPHICS only, not for PIXEL drawing. A video system that uses character mode is very fast-acting, much faster than one that is in GRAPHICS MODE.

character printer a printer that prints one character at a time, such as an INKJET or dot-MATRIX PRINTER, as distinct from a LASER PRINTER which prints a page of type at a time.

character recognition automatic conversion from character shape on paper or as a graphics image to ASCII code. Methods of forming characters that are easily read by computers are unfortunately not easily read by humans, which is why the keyboard remains the main way in which new data can be fed to a computer. The oldest forms of character recognition systems as far as computers are concerned are the magnetic variety, using characters printed with magnetic ink in a FONT that consists of a few straight line patterns. This, although ugly to the eye, is readable. Optical recognition methods are now quite reliable for printed characters, and even handwriting can now be recognized with some reliability. See OCR; GRID; PDA.

character rounding a system of making printed characters look more pleasing by rounding the corners, usable only if the printer has a high RESOLUTION.

character set the complete set of coded CHARACTERs, both text and graphics, that can be printed on the SCREEN (sense 1) by a computer in its CHARACTER MODE. The larger the character set, the more versatile the computer is likely to be in providing visual data in this mode, but with the advent of GUI systems, in which any character shape can be drawn using software, the character set has become less important.

character set identifier (CSID) a number used to identify a particular CHARACTER SET.

characters per inch see CPI.

characters per second see CPS.

character string see STRING.

charge the fundamental electrical property that causes electrostatic attraction or repulsion. The natural unit is the change on one electron, but the SI unit is the Coulomb.

charge-coupled device see CCD.

charityware see CAREWARE.

chart recorder a form of automatic graph-drawing device. A roll of paper is moved at a constant speed, and a pen touching the paper is moved across the width of the paper by an input voltage. See also X-Y PLOTTER. The important difference between the chart recorder and the X-Y plotter is that the computer controls only the up-and-down movement of the pen of a chart recorder; it controls both pen and paper movement in the X-Y plotter.

ChartWizard a WIZARD of MICROSOFT EXCEL that will automatically generate a GRAPH or chart from selected values in a worksheet.

chat system a system that allows a number of users who are logged in to a NETWORK to type conversations that all can read or private messages. Codes and abbreviations are commonly used to save typing time.

chatbot a form of BOT that can take part in a chat conversation.

CHCP a DOS command that is used to set a CODE PAGE.

CHDIR the DOS change DIRECTORY (sense 1) (*folder*) command, usually abbreviated to CD.

cheapernet an ETHERNET system that uses TV-grade COAXIAL CABLE rather than the more expensive specified cable.

check bit a BIT used as a method of error detection. If one bit of a byte (or any other set of bits) is not used for data, it can be used to check that the remaining bits are valid. This is usually done by PARITY checks. The use of a check bit allows each byte to be checked and can be used to signal which byte may contain an error.

check box a selection method in a GUI system. The check box will contain a cross or a tick if an option has been selected, and clicking (see CLICK, sense 1) on the box will reverse the selection.

check digit a CHECKSUM digit added to a set of data in order to allow the integrity of the data to be checked. Check digits are used where it is vitally important to be able to distinguish a number that has been wrongly keyed by an operator, as in a mail-ordering system.

check mark a tick or cross in a box next to a MENU option to show whether that option is enabled or disabled. Clicking (see CLICK, sense 1) on the box will reverse the setting.

checkpoint a method of recovering from a system failure in a DATABASE program. During use, the program periodically saves all RECORDS (sense 1) in memory on to disk or other BACKING STORE and also saves BUFFER contents and a record called *checkpoint* that records the addresses from which data was saved. In the event of a failure, recovering the checkpoint allows data to be correctly replaced in memory, and the checkpoint action ensures that the backing stores are periodically updated.

checksum a system that is used to minimize data errors when data is transferred. The data consists internally of a stream of numbers that are summed. The final total is compared with another total, which is also read in. If the two disagree, there has been a read error, but the method cannot show where. A variation on this is to read data in small BLOCKs (sense 2), with a checksum for each block. In this way, the block that contains the fault can be located. Checksums are particularly important in routines that save and load data on tape or disk and also for data transmission by a MODEM. See also CRC.

Chernobyl packet a data PACKET on a NETWORK that causes the whole network to overload and lock up.

chiclet keyboard the type of rubbery key sets that are used in some calculators and a few hand-held computers, universally detested because they inhibit fast or accurate typing.

child directory a SUBDIRECTORY of any other (PARENT) DIRECTORY. All directories on a hard drive are children of the main ROOT DIRECTORY C:\.

child program a program that is called into action from another program (the PARENT PROGRAM) and remains active in the memory. When the child program has completed its action, any data it has produced can be passed back to the parent program when it resumes. This is the action used for calling the MS-DOS system from MICROSOFT WINDOWS. See also DLL; EXIT.

chip the form of electronic CIRCUIT module used for computer construction, which is an electronic circuit that has been formed on to one small piece of SILICON or other SEMICONDUCTOR crystalline material by photo-

69

graphic printing, etching and the condensation of semiconductor vapours.

chip count the number of integrated circuit (IC) chips used on a CIRCUIT BOARD. A lower chip count can be achieved by using more complex chips, and this can lower costs and improve reliability through the reduction in the number of interconnections between chips.

chipset the set of IC chips, other than the MICROPROCESSOR itself, that are used to form the core of a microcomputer and are placed on the MOTHERBOARD. This would include support chips used for MEMORY MANAGEMENT, CLOCK, BUS control and other functions. See also ALADDIN.

CHK a file EXTENSION used by disk-checking utilities for a file that has been made up from LOST CLUSTERS.

CHKDSK a program formerly distributed along with the MS-DOS operating system (OS) that allows the state of a disk to be examined and any faulty SECTOR to be diagnosed and excluded from use. CHKDSK has now been superseded by SCANDISK.

CHOICE a COMMAND used in a BATCH FILE to implement a MENU choice. CHOICE is used when a computer has to be set up differently for different uses, such as for DOS alone or for DOS with WINDOWS. When CHOICE has been used in the AUTOEXEC.BAT file, the computer will pause during booting (see BOOT) until you choose which option you require.

choke to reject an input.

chord a straight line that connects the ends of an arc drawn by a CAD, PAINT or DTP program.

Christmas tree a commonly used test equipment for RS-232 SERIAL lines that signals the results by using sets of red and green lights.

chroma or **chrominance** the signal component of a MONITOR (sense 1) or TV system that conveys the colour picture information. See also LUMINANCE.

chrome ornamental features of a program, such as three-dimensional coloured icons.

churning pointless disk activity, indicating a program fault or (in WINDOWS systems) insufficient memory so that data continually has to be exchanged between the memory and the hard drive.

cicero a measure of type size. The cicero is used in mainland Europe and is equivalent to about 4.55 mm. Several DTP programs provide for measurements to be made in ciceros. See also DIDOT; PICA; POINT.

cipher a method of altering each CHARACTER in a piece of data so as to make the data unreadable. Each character should be transformed using a different scheme, otherwise the cipher is easily broken. See also ENCRYPTION.

ciphertext the result of ENCRYPTION of text.

circuit the path of an electric current. The circuits of computers are ELEC-

TRONIC circuits in which the current passes through SEMICONDUCTOR devices.

circuit board or **board** a plastic or laminated board that carries a carefully planned network of copper strips. See also CIRCUIT CARD. The printed circuit board (PCB) replaced hand-wired circuits in the 1950s because of its much greater reliability and ease of mass production.

circuit card the insulating board on which an electronics circuit is constructed. A complete circuit card is usually fabricated with a set of EDGE CONNECTORs so that the whole board can be easily plugged into or out of the computer using an EXPANSION SLOT. This makes for easier repairs and also for easier expansion of a computer that has been designed in this form. Memory modules are also made in this form.

circuit switched a communications path between two points along which all data packets will travel. This is the type of system used for telephony before digital systems emerged using a packet switching service (PSS).

circular buffer a form of BUFFER in which the starting address is used following the ending address so that effectively there is no start or finish and old entries are replaced by new ones on the basis of first in, first replaced.

circular file or **ring** a file with no beginning or end, consisting of a LIST of items, each of which contains a POINTER (sense 2) to the next item. The 'last' item in the list carries a pointer to the 'first' item, so that the list can be searched indefinitely from any starting position. The CARDFILE utility of MICROSOFT WINDOWS is arranged as a circular file.

circular reference a WORKSHEET error in which two or more CELLs make references to each other so that a value cannot be determined. For example, if cell B2 contains the reference +D6+2 and cell D6 contains +B2*5 no values can be determined.

Cirrus Logic a well-known manufacturer of GRAPHICS ADAPTER cards for the PERSONAL COMPUTER, along with other interfacing cards.

CISC (complex instruction-set computer) a computer based on a MICROPROCESSOR that has a large and comprehensive set of instructions in code. The use of CISC can make software simpler and shorter but at the expense of longer processing times for each instruction. All PERSONAL COMPUTERS use CISC processors, but some other types of machines have been developed for use with RISC microprocessor chips.

Class A certification the US requirement for a computer that is used in commercial premises, which covers radio frequency interference (RFI) from the computer and also covers the effect on the computer of such interference.

Class B certification the US requirement for a computer that is used in domestic premises, covering radio frequency interference (RFI) from the computer and also the effect on the computer of such interference. The

Class B requirements are more stringent because the computer is likely to be used very close to radio and TV receivers.

class boundaries the items in a class in a DATABASE that outline the limits of that class. If a class of number is defined as the integers 20 to 29, then if the class contains the numbers 20 and 29 these are the class boundaries in that sample.

classic style a form of DESKTOP display in WINDOWS 98 or WINDOWS 2000 that resembles the display used for WINDOWS 95.

class interval the span of values that can be contained in a class in a DATABASE. A class of words might be defined by the interval AARDVARK to ADVANTAGE, a class of numbers as the interval 1 to 65536.

clean 1. to delete files completely from a drive so as to release space. Note that WINDOWS does not delete files that are placed in the RECYCLE BIN, and the hard drive space is not released until the bin has been emptied. **2.** (of a piece of HARDWARE or SOFTWARE) using good design.

clean room a space in which dust has been excluded and air filtered so that materials that are susceptible to pollution can be handled. Clean rooms are used to work on MICROPROCESSOR chips and HARD DRIVE PLATTER assemblies.

clear see DELETE.

clear box testing see WHITE-BOX TESTING.

clear to send (CTS) a signal sent from a MODEM to indicate that a transmission can proceed.

click 1. to press and release a MOUSE button sharply in order to select an item lying under the POINTER (sense 1) or CURSOR; see also DOUBLE-CLICK. **2.** a brief sound caused by a KEY (sense 1) being pressed. A key click is sometimes artificially produced in order to make a silent keyboard more acceptable to a typist.

client a WORKSTATION on a NETWORK that can process data files from a SERVER.

client application an APPLICATION into which an OBJECT can be linked or embedded. See also EMBED; LINK; OLE; SERVER APPLICATION.

client-based application any APPLICATION that is used by one computer but is not available to others on the NETWORK.

client module a TERMINAL on a NETWORK. A client module allows its user ACCESS (sense 2) to files (using the file SERVER) and to printers (using the PRINT SERVER) but only by way of the network – such a module often lacks a HARD DRIVE, and FLOPPY DRIVES are not used because of the risk of introducing a VIRUS.

client server a form of DISTRIBUTED SYSTEM computing, with a CLIENT computer obtaining information from a SERVER.

clip art a file of drawings in a form that can be read by a GRAPHICS or DTP program, allowing the user to edit and make use of drawings that would otherwise take considerable time and talent to create.

clipboard a portion of memory used by MICROSOFT WINDOWS to hold data that has been CUT or copied (see COPY, sense 2) from a text document or a drawing. The data is held until another item is cut or copied or until the clipboard is emptied. Data held on the clipboard can be pasted (see PASTE) into any suitable application that will accept the data. Pasting data does not empty the clipboard.

Clipboard viewer a MICROSOFT WINDOWS utility that allows the contents of the CLIPBOARD to be seen in a screen window. The viewer also allows the clipboard to be cleared if necessary.

clock an electronic circuit that issues signals at regular intervals. Each action of a MICROPROCESSOR is set into motion by an electrical pulse, and the speed of processing depends on the rate of these pulses, called the *clock rate*. The pulses are generated by a circuit which is called the 'clock'. Typical clock speeds for modern small computers range between 166 MHz and 700 MHz, but each new generation of processors uses higher speeds. See also REAL-TIME CLOCK.

clock/calendar board a CIRCUIT BOARD, usually an integral part of a MOTHERBOARD, that maintains a precise time and date that can be used by the computer. See also CMOS RAM; REAL-TIME CLOCK.

clone a computer, microprocessor chip, printer or other device that performs in the same way as the corresponding device from a well-known manufacturer. Many manufacturers make IBM clones, computers that will RUN (sense 2) software intended for the IBM PC-XT or PC-AT, but other types of computers are not cloned. Modern PERSONAL COMPUTERS owe little to the old IBM designs and have developed independently. Software also can be cloned, usually to provide low-cost programs that will behave like better-known examples and use the same data file structure. See also COMPATIBLE; REVERSE ENGINEERING.

close box a WINDOWS box that is used to close a WINDOW. MICROSOFT WINDOWS uses a cross ICON as a close box; older versions required a small box to be double-clicked (see DOUBLE-CLICK) to close a window. Other applications follow the same pattern, although some use a different form of box.

closed architecture the design of a computer that does not permit other manufacturers to manufacture and sell add-on boards. This tends to restrict the selling base of the machine. See OPEN ARCHITECTURE.

closed-box testing see BLACK-BOX TESTING.

closed bus system an old system of computer ARCHITECTURE that does not allow CIRCUIT BOARDs to be plugged into the main BUS. This greatly restricts expansion of the system.

closed user group (**CUG**) a restricted number of intercommunicating computer users. Any computer owner can connect via a MODEM to public telephone lines and hence to any other modems. Database services are available only to users who have paid fees and who have been issued with pass codes. A closed user group is vulnerable to a CRACKER unless the PASSWORD system is a good one or only private lines, as distinct from public telephone lines, are used.

CLS a command used in the MS-DOS operating system (OS) to clear the SCREEN (sense 1).

cluster 1. a set of TERMINALS in a NETWORK that operate together. A system that consists of a central processor with several remote terminals is often arranged so that each terminal will provide an identical display, and this group of terminals constitutes a 'cluster'. **2.** see ALLOCATION UNIT.

clustering the action used in DATABASE design to ensure that data can be rapidly recovered. When a file contains several RECORDS (sense 1) that are associated (such as items sold in one department of a store), these will be held in one BLOCK (sense 2) on the disk or in neighbouring blocks.

CLV (constant linear velocity) rotation of the type used for audio COMPACT DISCS and CD-ROM in which the disk spins faster when the inner part of the track is being read. The speed of the track past the reading beam is constant. Compare CAV.

CMOS (complementary metal-oxide semiconductor) a form of construction for ICs that requires very low power inputs and is now being extensively used both for microprocessors and for memories. See also NMOS; PMOS.

CMOS RAM a small portion of CMOS memory in a PERSONAL COMPUTER that uses a backup battery to provide power while the computer is switched off. This memory is used to store essential information on the video system and disk drives, and also as part of the REAL-TIME CLOCK.

CMY (cyan-magenta-yellow) a colour printing system in which the primary colours are cyan, magenta and yellow used in three successive printing actions to produce a colour picture.

CMYK (cyan-magenta-yellow-black) a development of the CMY colour system that adds black to make outlines and boundaries clearer.

coarse grain see GRANULARITY.

coaxial cable or **coax cable** a cable consisting of one central conductor that is surrounded with an insulator and then with the other conductor. In this way, the outer conductor prevents interference from reaching the inner. Coaxial cable is used for TV signals, including the aerial leads for domestic TV, and also for high speed NETWORK data links.

COBOL (Common Business-Oriented Language) one of the first HIGH-LEVEL LANGUAGES that was not intended for mathematical or scientific use.

cobweb site a page on the World Wide Web (WWW) that is out of date and abandoned.

code 1. the use of one symbol or set of symbols to represent something else. The most important code for microcomputing purposes is ASCII, which uses numbers in the range 32 to 127 to represent characters. **2.** to convert an ALGORITHM into a working computer PROGRAM.

codec a system for compressing (see COMPRESSED FILE) data for audio or video signals. Any MULTIMEDIA system needs to provide for the use of any one of a set of different codecs so as to make use of compressed data.

code conversion the conversion of one code into another. Computers that use INTERNAL CODES for SCREEN (sense 1) displays may carry out conversion from the ASCII codes that are used to store data in memory. The form of an ASCII code may also have to be converted.

coded character set a set of INTEGER numbers used to code characters. The ASCII and UNICODE sets are the most common.

code page a method of coping with foreign languages on a keyboard by setting up codes for KEYBOARD, SCREEN (sense 1) and PRINTER so that all three can use a consistent set of characters. At least one code page needs to be set up for a country in which the computer is used. The system is not needed for the majority of CLONE machines.

coder/decoder HARDWARE that deals with both A TO D and D TO A conversions.

code segment on an older type of INTEL MICROPROCESSOR system, the part of memory used to contain MACHINE CODE that is part of a program being run.

code snippet a short piece of CODE (sense 1), usually activated by clicking (see CLICK, sense 1) on a BUTTON or ICON. See also MACRO; VISUAL BASIC.

cold boot or **cold start** the clearing of computer memory and the starting of the operating system (OS). A cold start is usually performed when a microcomputer is first switched on, and it must allow time to spin the HARD DRIVE up to operating speed before attempting to read program data. If, because of a fault, a cold start is performed during operation, all data and programs in the memory will be lost. Compare WARM BOOT. See also BOOT; REBOOT.

collapse button a BUTTON used to hide text in an OUTLINE view. For example, you can select a heading and click the collapse button, which will hide all the subheadings and BODY text belonging under that heading. See also COLLAPSE DIRECTORY.

collapse directory or **collapse folder** to reduce a display of a DIRECTORY (*folder*) and its subdirectories to that of the directory name alone. In the MICROSOFT WINDOWS system, the [+] sign indicates that subdirectories exist and can be listed by clicking on the symbol. The appearance of the [-] symbol indicates that all the subdirectories are visible and clicking on this symbol will collapse the directory.

collate to put items into order, used of files (merging into a single file) and of pages from a printer. See also DECOLLATE.

collated copy sheets of paper from a printer that are in order even when several copies of the document are to be printed. For example, if you requested three copies of a four-page document, collated copy would consist of the four pages of one set followed by the four pages of the next, and so on. Uncollated copy would consist of the three copies of page 1, followed by the three copies of page 2, and so on.

collision a BROADCAST NETWORK problem that arises when two users put data on to the network at the same time, causing a mixed and corrupted set of signals.

collision detection the reporting of the coincidence of two events. In a BROADCAST NETWORK, collision detection is used to make sure that the shared connecting lines are free when a computer requests to send signals.

colon the : symbol, which is used as a SEPARATOR. For example, the SPREADSHEET MICROSOFT EXCEL uses a colon to separate the parts of a range, as in A7:B10.

Colorado a well-known manufacturer of TAPE BACKUP systems, a division of HEWLETT PACKARD.

Colossus the first programmable computer, designed by Alan Turing and Tommy Flowers in 1943 for code-breaking in World War II. See also BLETCHLEY PARK.

colour coding the number of colours that can be used for one screen PIXEL, often expressed as a number of BITs per pixel. 4-bit colour is equivalent to $2^4 = 16$ colours, and 30-bit colour is equivalent to 2^{30} about 1,000,000,000 colours.

colour look-up table see COLOUR PALETTE.

colour monitor a MONITOR (sense 1) that is fitted with a colour CRT or flat-screen LCD display. The highest RESOLUTION is obtained from a CRT when separate red, green and blue signals can be used, and a monitor with such an input is termed an RGB monitor, as used for VGA and SVGA displays. When the signals are combined into one, cabling is easier but the resolution is poorer. This system, which applies also to video recorders, is called COMPOSITE VIDEO.

colour palette or **colour look-up table** a portion of fast RAM that is filled with data, so allowing numbers that represent colours to be converted into red, green and blue colour signals to a MONITOR. A palette usually contains only a selection of the total number of colours that can be represented.

colour printer a PRINTER that can use three (sometimes four or more) different ink colours to make realistic colour prints.

colour saturation the maximum percentage of a single colour that is possible. Natural colours are all unsaturated, meaning that they are diluted with white. See also HUE, SATURATION, BRIGHTNESS.

colour scheme the range of colours used for a display, such as the colours for a PRESENTATION GRAPHICS SLIDE or the colours used for the constituents of WINDOWS.

colour separation the separation of a colour illustration into its three primary colour constituents. The three images that result can be combined later, during printing, into the reconstituted full-colour illustration.

column a vertical line of data. The VDU screen has character positions which are vertically aligned in columns, usually 80 per screen width. Printers follow the same scheme but can usually select a wider range of column numbers. The position of any character on the screen or on paper can be determined by using the column number and the row number. See also ROWS AND COLUMNS.

column graph see BAR GRAPH.

column guide a LINE (sense 1) that appears on the SCREEN (sense 1) when a DTP program is running to indicate a column position. For many types of page, the left and right margin lines are the only column guides, but where more than one column is used per page, other lines can be used as guides. These lines appear only on screen and are not printed.

column indicator a way of showing the size of a quantity in terms of the length of a bar rather than as, for example, a number or the position of a needle on a scale.

column recalculation a form of WORKSHEET action in which values of FORMULAe are recalculated column by column.

COM1 see AUX1.

Comdex a major computer exhibition held in Atlanta, Georgia, and in Las Vegas, Nevada, USA. Any important new hardware or software will be demonstrated at Comdex.

COM file a form of short program file used in DOS systems. A program with the COM extension (see EXTENDED FILENAME) will load and RUN (sense 2) into 64 kilobytes or less of memory. See also EXE FILE.

comma the symbol , which is used as a SEPARATOR between ARGUMENT items. A SPREADSHEET FUNCTION that requires two arguments will require these arguments to be separated by a comma. A MODEM using the HAYES STANDARDS interprets a comma as meaning a one-second pause while dialling a telephone number.

comma delimited file a file in which a COMMA character is used to separate FIELDS (sense 2) in a RECORD.

command a direct instruction to a computer, often made by way of the keyboard. The word 'command' is normally used to mean a computer instruction that is obeyed at once, as distinct from an instruction or statement in a program that is obeyed when the program is RUN (sense 1).

COMMAND.COM the COMMAND INTERPRETER for MS-DOS. This is the main program of commands for the MS-DOS operating system (OS).

command-driven program a program of the older type in which each action is started by a command word or phrase, followed by pressing the ENTER or RETURN key. DOS itself is of this type, as are UNIX and LINUX.

command interpreter the part of an operating system (OS) that handles typed COMMANDs for immediate execution and the same commands occurring within a program.

command language a form of simplified computing LANGUAGE that is itself part of a PROGRAM. Many programs such as DATABASES, WORD PROCESSORS and SPREADSHEETS require the operator to be able to enter sets of commands that will modify the output of the program. This requires the use of a command language that is specific to the program. A very elaborate command language can make a program very flexible but may also make it difficult to use until the user has had a lot of experience with the program. See also VISUAL BASIC.

command line the LINE (sense 4) used to invoke or RUN (sense 2) a program under an operating system (OS) such as DOS. For most operating systems this line consists of the name of the program and a carriage-return (CR) character.

command line argument one or more items supplied to a program in the COMMAND LINE. These items are placed between the program name and the carriage return (CR), separated by spaces or by other characters. For example, a WORD PROCESSOR called SHRDLU might be RUN (sense 2) and forced to load a file called NEWTXT.DOC by the use of a command line: SHRDLU NEWTXT.DOC. A PAINT program might be specified to run in monochrome by using the command line of PAINTIT /m.

command line option an addition to a COMMAND that is used to modify the action. In MS-DOS, a command option typically consists of a FORWARD SLASH followed by a letter, such as /a.

command processor the DOS program that is used to carry out DOS commands. For MS-DOS the command processor is called COMMAND.COM.

command prompt the indication that DOS is ready for a COMMAND. The usual form of command PROMPT is C:>.

comment a piece of text that is used for viewing only, not affecting a program. Comments are usually marked by symbols such as * or .. or words such as REM.

comment field a space set aside for comments, used in DATABASE programs.

comment out to precede a COMMAND in a program file by a word that ensures it will not be obeyed. Typically, the word REM can be used for this purpose. You would comment out commands in order to find which one was causing problems with a system.

commercial at the @ symbol, which is used in EMAIL addresses to separate the user name from the provider name. See also AT SYMBOL.

committed transaction in a DATABASE an action that reads and updates files and stores the modified versions. The updating cannot be reversed except by repeating the read action and altering the data.

Commodore Business Machines (**CBM**) a manufacturer of calculators and computers whose calculators were the first to be sold in large numbers in the UK. They subsequently manufactured computers, and the PET™ (Personal Electronic Transactor) was the first small computer to appear in the UK. Later outstanding machines included the Commodore 64 and Amiga™, but these were incompatible with the PERSONAL COMPUTER (sense 1).

common carrier a provider of telephone lines and services.

common gateway interface (**CGI**) a specification that defines how programs can be run from a World Wide Web (WWW) SERVER and pass to or from a BROWSER. This is used, for example, when you fill in a form on a WEB PAGE and submit the information to the server.

common storage area a part of RAM memory that is used by more than one program, such as memory used as a CLIPBOARD.

Common User Access see CUA KEYBOARD.

communications the transmission of data over distances other than by using disks. Communications depend on a combination of HARDWARE and SOFTWARE, and both have undergone considerable changes in the short history of computing. Early COMMUNICATIONS LINKs used paper tape as an intermediary, with the tape operating a telegraph transmitter at one end, and received telegraph signals operating a paper tape punch at the receiving end. The rate of transfer was limited to about 50 BITS per second by the mechanical systems, and until PARITY was used the integrity of data was poor. Modern communications are used to allow a computer to use remote PERIPHERALS, to transfer files with perfect accuracy and at high speed, and in some cases to allow terminals of a central computer to be used in REAL-TIME PROCESSING. The improvements in speed have been brought about by using connection of higher quality, first telephone lines and later digital lines, and by the use of MODULATION methods in a MODEM. The improvements in integrity of data have been brought about by using REDUNDANT CODE (adding a CHECKSUM or using CRC methods) with a LOOP CHECK so that an error can trigger the retransmission of a BLOCK (sense 2) of data. Speeds of 28,800 bits per second or more are now common.

communications link a set of HARDWARE (wiring and such devices as a MODEM) along with SOFTWARE (a COMMUNICATIONS PACKAGE) that allows remotely sited computers to interchange data.

communications package a SUITE OF PROGRAMS that allows the use of a MODEM to communicate with other computers.

communications port a connection, usually the SERIAL PORT, used for communications.

communications protocol the collection of settings required for SERIAL communications with a remote system. For example, you might specify a rate of 9600 bits per second, 8 data bits, no parity and one stop bit, and this would be abbreviated to 9600,8,N,1.

communication system an assembly of equipment that allows data to be transferred between two or more places.

comp a detailed dummy publication. In DTP work, the comp is a dummy document produced to show to a client the finished appearance of a project.

COMP a DOS command that will compare two text files and report on differences (up to ten) between them. See also FC.

compact disc (CD) a method of storing DIGITAL data. The form of compact disc that is used for commercial audio, video or digital recording uses a LASER to burn small pits in a metal surface from which plastic discs are moulded. These pits represent digital signals that are used to code the AMPLITUDE of the audio or video signal. This digital recording system is ideal for storing computer data. Such devices, CD-ROMs, are used for permanent storage of data external to the computer in the way that a ROM or PROM would be used internally. The drawback is that ACCESS (sense 2) to data is not as fast as can be obtained from RAM, but large amounts of data can be stored and the rate of transfer can be very high. Data capacity of 650 megabytes and rates of transfer of 20 to 40 times the normal (audio) rate are typical. See also CD-R; CD-RW; LASER DISC.

compact disc interactive (CD-I) a combination of TV and computing systems that uses data on a COMPACT DISC. This allows for interactive games, HYPERTEXT and effective use of the system as a teaching machine.

compacting algorithm or **data compacting** a method of storing data in compressed form. See also ARCHIVING.

companding a combination of COMPRESSING and EXPANDING. The wide range of amplitudes of audio signals, particularly for music, make it difficult to DIGITIZE in a compact way. If the AMPLITUDE range is compressed, the digital signals can use much less storage, and when the signals are reconverted to audio, expansion can be used to restore the original amplitude range. Companding is also used as a noise-reduction system for cassette tapes and for cinema sound tracks, such as the *Dolby* system.

Compaq Computer Corporation the major US manufacturer of PC-compatible computers and a world-wide supplier of computer-related equipment such as ATM (sense 1) machines, SEARCH ENGINES and WEB SITES.

comparator a CIRCUIT that can detect when two or more inputs are identical or when one input is greater than another.

comparing strings the action of determining the relative order of sets of ASCII codes. The comparison can be done by using the ASCII codes for the letters. See also SORT (sense 1).

compatibility the ability of devices to work together. A computer made by one manufacturer may not work with a disk drive made by another manufacturer. Lack of compatibility of this type restricts the user's choice of peripherals and often makes it necessary to replace all the computer equipment when any item is to be upgraded. A particular advantage of the IBM CLONE type of machine is the wide range of compatible devices that can be fitted to it and the ability to run software that was written for older machines of the same type.

compatible (of a computer) able to use the same software as another MACHINE, used mainly of CLONEs for which huge amounts of software are available.

compiled knowledge a specialized term used in ARTIFICIAL INTELLIGENCE studies. KNOWLEDGE is said to be compiled if there is no indication of why the items of knowledge, valid separately, should be valid as a whole.

compiled language a language in which the program instructions are completely converted into MACHINE CODE and stored on disk in that form for use. All commercially sold programs consist of such compiled code. See COMPILER; INTERPRETER; OBJECT CODE.

compiler a program used to convert a HIGH-LEVEL PROGRAM file, usually in ASCII, into MACHINE CODE (OBJECT CODE). See also INTERPRETER.

complement see NEGATION.

complex instruction set computer see CISC.

component density the number of electronics components per unit area of a CIRCUIT BOARD. High component densities require fan cooling to be used to keep the operating temperature low, and can make maintenance and repair difficult.

COM port any SERIAL PORT. The normal PERSONAL COMPUTER serial ports are designated as COM1 and COM2. COM3 and COM4 are also used but with some complications.

compose a method used for the EQUATION EDITOR of MICROSOFT WORD to create characters that are not part of a normal symbol set.

compose sequence a set of characters used, particularly in LOTUS 1-2-3, to generate a character that is not on the keyboard.

composite a colour formed by the overlap of two other colours in a DTP document.

composite page number a page number that consists of two or more parts. For example, a number such as 2.5 might be used to indicate Chapter 2, page 5 in a DTP publication.

composite video video signals that combine both video PIXEL information (monochrome or colour) with the electronic synchronization signals that control the whole screen picture. Most modern monitors work from separated signals; for example, a colour monitor will require, among other things, three separate colour signals (red, green, blue, see RGB) and further lines for synchronization. In contrast, a TV picture arrives as a composite video signal and separation must be carried out within the receiver circuits.

composition the distance between characters and print lines. In a DTP page, the composition of the page refers to the spacing of the characters in each line and between the lines in the page.

compound device a MULTIMEDIA device, such as a MIDI keyboard, that generates sound in response to data files. See also SIMPLE DEVICE.

compound document a document that contains embedded files, for example a MICROSOFT WORD document with embedded picture files. See EMBED; LINK; OLE.

compound key a key (see KEY FIELD) for a DATABASE that consists of more than one key word.

compress disk to subject the contents of a disk to compression (see COMPRESSED FILE). The term was formerly applied to the action now known as DEFRAGMENTATION.

compressed file or **packed file** a file that has been reduced to the smallest possible size. This is done by reducing redundancy, such as repeated characters, or the use of only 7 bits out of 8 for text. A compressed file takes up less space on a disk but it cannot be read as quickly as an uncompressed file because of the time needed for decompression (expansion). See also DRIVESPACE.

compressed print or **condensed type** a print size smaller than the normal 10 or 12 POINT size, usually small enough to print 132 characters per line on screen or on paper.

compressed video data for a video display that has been compressed (see COMPRESSED FILE) to save space.

compressed volume file (CVF) a single file that occupies all or most of a HARD DRIVE or FLOPPY DISK and formerly used by the DRIVESPACE utility of WINDOWS 95 to store compressed data for conventional files.

compressing the packing of anything into a limited space. Data can often be compressed or compacted so as to fit into the minimum possible memory space. See also COMPANDING.

Compuserve a US-based INTERNET information provider, now absorbed by AMERICA ONLINE.

computability the extent to which a problem can be solved by a computer.

computational complexity the number of steps in an ALGORITHM that are needed to solve a problem.

computational error an error caused by arithmetical rounding or problems caused by numbers that are too large or too small to be correctly represented as a BINARY FRACTION.

computation-bound computer speed restriction caused by the MICROPROCESSOR rate. This is particularly apparent in some CAD or SPREADSHEET programs where thousands of calculations need to be performed. The overall speed of a modern computer is more often determined by the HARD DRIVE access rate and the GRAPHICS ADAPTER, so that using a CACHE and a fast graphics board are both more important than processor speed. See also LOCAL BUS.

computer a device that will manipulate data by making use of a program that can be stored in some form. The common features of all computers are input, processing actions and output. See ANALOGUE COMPUTER; DIGITAL COMPUTER; NEURAL NETWORK.

computer-aided design see CAD.

computer-aided engineering (CAE) the use of a program that is intended to analyse a design (manual or computer-generated) and simulate its action.

computer-aided instruction see CAI.

computer-aided software engineering (CASE) the use of a computer program to assist with the design and maintenance of new software.

computer-based training (CBT) the use of a COMPUTER SYSTEM to present questions, explanatory text, illustrations and sounds to assist the user to learn a skill, manual or intellectual.

computer bureau see BUREAU.

computer-generated imagery the production of animated graphics by computer programming for film or TV display.

computer graphics the visual representation of patterns (see GRAPHICS) on the VDU screen. Anything that can be drawn on paper can be drawn on the VDU screen. The difference is that the computer-graphics patterns are programmed, can be erased and changed almost instantly, and can be manipulated in ways, such as flipping (see FLIP), INVERTING and MORPHING, that are impossible with images on paper or on film. Computer graphics are closely associated with computer games, but their more important roles are in simulations (such as flight simulators for pilot training) and in CAD.

computer graphics metafile see CGM.

computer language a set of code numbers, symbols or words that can be used to write a sequence of instructions, or PROGRAM, for a computer. All sequential programs consist of number codes that are read and acted on by the CPU, but these number codes can be prepared by various methods. Languages are described as being of different levels (see LEVEL OF LANGUAGE), with number codes at the lowest level and languages that consist of instructions in English being at the highest (currently available) level. Whatever the level of the PROGRAMMING LANGUAGE, the instructions must be converted into the number codes by an INTERPRETER or COMPILER before they can be used. See also VISUAL BASIC.

computer literacy the understanding of the applications of computers and the ability to use computers. This does not necessarily require knowledge of how computers work or how they are programmed, but it is important to realize how computers can assist human endeavour.

computer program see PROGRAM.

computer security see SECURITY.

computer-supported cooperative work (CSCW) the use of SOFT-WARE (*groupware*) to allow people at different sites to work together. See also WORKGROUP.

computer system a basic set of COMPUTER, MONITOR and KEYBOARD along with PERIPHERALS such as a MOUSE, MODEM, SCANNER, PRINTER, etc.

computer telephony integration (CTI) the use of software that allows a computer to control telephone actions such as making and receiving voice, FAX and data calls. This integration can also replace the need for an external directory enquiries service and can incorporate caller identification (see CALLER ID).

computer virus see VIRUS.

computer vision the use of a computer to capture and process images and to recognize features. An example is the recognition of the finger-print of an approved user.

computing power the relative speed of computing. One computer is described as being more powerful than another if it can handle more work at a faster speed. This, however, is by no means easy to measure because a computer that is fast on one type of task may be slow on another. BENCHMARKS are sometimes used as comparisons, but these are often misleading. For computers of the PERSONAL COMPUTER type, a land-mark number is sometimes used to compare the speed of execution of a computer with that of the original IBM PC/XT or PC/AT machines.

CON (console) a word used in MS-DOS to identify the KEYBOARD and MON-ITOR (sense 1) of a computer system.

concatenation the joining of STRINGS. For example, if one string is HOL-IDAY and another is TIME, then concatenating the strings in that order would give HOLIDAYTIME.

concentrator a digital MULTIPLEXER that allows more than one channel of digital information to be sent along a broadband channel. For example, BT HIGHWAY allows simultaneous use as a telephone line and as a com-puter data link.

conceptual level a programmer's view of a DATABASE that describes what data will be stored and how items of data are related.

conceptual model the description of a DATABASE or other program in terms of data and relationships. The conceptual model need not corre-spond to any existing HARDWARE or SOFTWARE and consists of the DATA MODEL, describing data types. The *process model* defines what is to be done with data, and the *system model* deals with the flow of data from one section to another.

concordance file a file of text consisting of words that are intended to appear in an INDEX and whose position in a document a WORD PROCESSOR PROGRAM will find automatically so that the index can be generated.

concurrency see MULTITASKING.

concurrency control the maintenance of consistency of data in a DATABASE on a NETWORK when several users are updating data at the same time.

concurrent running the use of an operating system (OS) that allows several programs to seem to be running together. This is done by running instructions from each program in sequence, using TIME-SLICING methods. See also MULTITASKING.

condensed type see COMPRESSED PRINT.

conditional anything depending on the result of a TEST (sense 1). A QUERY to a DATABASE can consist of conditional statements that result in the correct data being selected. For example, you might want to find the names of all listed males aged between 30 and 40 with engineering degrees.

conditional expression an expression with two or more possible results, used in a database QUERY. In such an expression, a TEST (sense 1) is made and the action of the expression will depend on the result of the test (TRUE or FALSE).

conditioner see MAINS FILTER.

condition stub or **action stub** the portion of a DECISION TABLE that lists conditions, using one entry for each possible condition.

conference an electronic meeting, using one or more BULLETIN BOARDS or the INTERNET, in which contributors make and read comments. Where the main topic of a conference is technical, the conference is termed a NEWSGROUP. See also MODERATED NEWSGROUP.

conferencing see TELECONFERENCING.

CONFIG.SYS a CONFIGURATION file used in MS-DOS and containing various set-up commands such as MOUSE action, use of disks, keyboard, ports and other actions. Microsoft WINDOWS 95 onwards makes use of a CONFIG.SYS file at startup, but the file does not need to be edited by the user when new devices are added.

configuration the arrangement of some hard or soft feature of the computer system. For example, a SCREEN (sense 1) configuration may be 80 characters per LINE (sense 2) and 25 lines per frame; a DISK DRIVE may use a configuration of 135 tracks, double-sided. Also, the system may be configured, for instance, as a UNIX system or an MS-DOS system.

confirm to indicate acceptance of a COMMAND. An operating system (OS) will normally require the user to confirm the deletion of a file or a set of files. In some cases, the confirmation may be modified so that one confirmation will suffice for a complete set of files.

confirmation message a message that asks the user to CONFIRM that an action is to be carried out. For example, a confirmation message will appear when you start to delete or replace a file.

conflation the action of combining several text files or data files into a single file.

connection the joining of metal conductors in a circuit so that signals can flow from one point to another. See PARALLEL; SERIAL.

connective a symbol used to indicate an action that involves two quantities. In the example, 3 * 2, the sign * is the connective (an OPERATOR) indicating that the two quantities or operands (see ARGUMENT) are to be multiplied together.

connectivity the extent to which a computer can be networked (see NETWORK) so that its resources are shared with others.

connector anything that joins one item to another. In SOFTWARE terms, a connector is a word such as AND, OR, NOT that is used, for instance, to connect conditions in a database QUERY. In HARDWARE terms, a connector means an electrical plug and socket, usually for data transmission. See also FEMALE CONNECTOR; MALE CONNECTOR.

consistency constraints conditions that limit the range of values of data in a DATABASE, such as a credit limit for a customer. Such constraints have to be built into the structure of the database, but it must be possible to make changes to the values, the task of the DATABASE MANAGEMENT SYSTEM.

console an old-fashioned term for a combination of KEYBOARD and MONITOR (sense 1) with no computing action. The term TERMINAL is also used, but this often implies some computing actions as well. See also CON.

consolidation the merging of two or more SPREADSHEET worksheets into a new WORKSHEET. A consolidated worksheet usually consists of values added from the individual worksheets, but subtraction, multiplication and division of corresponding values can also be carried out.

constant a quantity whose value is not changed in the course of a program.

constant angular velocity see CAV.

constant length field a specification of number of characters for data in a DATABASE. When a RANDOM-ACCESS FILE is in use, programming is greatly simplified if each item of data is of a known number of characters. If, for example, all names are of 50 characters and all addresses of 80 characters, then a RECORD (sense 1) that consists of name and address will contain 130 characters, and the start of the next record will be 130 characters beyond the start of the current record. Data items that are shorter than the specified 'field' length can be padded with blanks; items that are longer can be dealt with by TRUNCATION.

constant linear velocity see CLV.

constraint a CELL value in a WORKSHEET whose value or range of values is fixed and will affect values in other cells. Constraint values are used in particular when equations are being solved, so that fixed values can be entered and a limited range of solution values specified.

consumables items such as paper, ribbons, ink cartridges or toner that are used by a printer, or the floppy disks used by the computer.

content-free I. SOFTWARE that is of universal application, as distinct from dedicated software, usually for educational purposes. **2.** (of a communication) having no useful content, such as a chairman's speech or a politician's promise.

contention a conflict caused when two devices are attempting to use a BUS at the same time or to communicate with a remote device at the same time.

contention slot a NETWORK time interval that is the minimum time for transmitting a PACKET that will ensure that no other packet has caused a collision.

content provider a supplier of information on the INTERNET. Typical types of information include news, share prices, entertainment guide or weather conditions.

context-sensitive help a HELP (sense 1) system in which the advice that is obtained depends on the command or menu item that has been chosen and is therefore directed to the immediate problem rather than requiring you to look up a topic in an index. See Fig. 15.

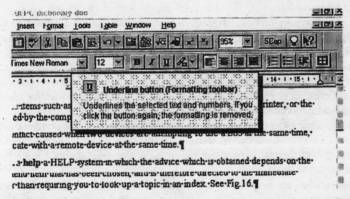

Fig. 15. **Context-sensitive help**. In this illustration, the question-mark icon of Microsoft Word has been clicked, and the pointer moved to the underline icon to obtain the help message illustrated here.

context switching changing from one program to another without shutting down either program. This is achieved by WINDOWS, but in addition, Windows allows the inactive program to continue running in the BACKGROUND.

contiguous touching, as applied to files on disk or in memory, meaning that they are packed close together without intervening portions.

contiguous graphics shapes that touch each other. VDU CHARACTER BLOCKS are arranged so that each text character has a space at one side and underneath. This allows text to be printed on the SCREEN (sense 1) without the letters touching each other. When BLOCK GRAPHICS characters are being used, however, it is usually easier to make satisfactory diagrams if adjacent characters do touch each other. Compare SEPARATED GRAPHICS.

continuation separator a separating line between text and a FOOTNOTE, used when a footnote has been continued to a following page.

continuous stationery paper that consists of a continuous sheet, perforated at lengths of 28 cm (11 inches) or alternatively 30.5 cm (12 inches) and usually tractor-fed (see TRACTOR FEED). The more common alternative to continuous stationery is single sheets, using a sheet feeder mechanism built into or added to the printer. LASER PRINTERS always use single-sheet feeding.

continuous tone a gradual change of shading or colour in a picture, as distinct from a sharp change of shading or colour.

contrast the difference between light and dark. On a VDU screen, the contrast should be made variable so as to allow for differences in the lighting of rooms. Some screens use coloured or neutral-density optical filters to improve contrast, so that the screen looks very dark when the VDU is switched off. Contrast of black lettering on white paper is important when optical character recognition (OCR, sense 2) is being used because low contrast will lead to a large number of errors in character recognition.

control a BUTTON in a GUI form of program that can be clicked (see CLICK, sense 1) to achieve some action.

control character a character whose ASCII code is outside the range of codes that produce shapes on the SCREEN (sense 1). The purpose of a control character is to produce some effect like clearing the screen or moving the CURSOR. These codes, usually in the range 1 to 31, can be used differently by different programs although some, like codes 13, 10, 8, and 9, are standardized.

control code any one of the codes in the ASCII set that is used to control a printer rather than print a character. Control codes are used also by MODEMS; see HAYES COMPATIBLE MODEM.

control key see CTRL.

controlled redundancy the minimum amount of duplication of data permitted in an efficient DATABASE.

controller a circuit that exercises control over some PERIPHERAL, particularly a DISK DRIVE.

control menu a short MENU that appears in MICROSOFT WINDOWS when a small rectangle or ICON at the top left-hand corner of a window is clicked (see CLICK, sense 1). The control bar menu allows the options of close, maximize, minimize, RESTORE, MOVE and size. The menu seldom needs to be used because there are other ways of carrying out these actions.

Microsoft WINDOWS 95 onwards uses a Microsoft icon in place of the box for the control menu.

control panel or **front panel** the set of control switches and indicator lights once used for old-style computers. The phrase is mainly used now to mean a display in a screen WINDOW that looks like a control panel and can be used to select options relating to the computer, such as printer connections, rate of flashing for the CURSOR (*pointer*), and so on.

control token a code or set of codes passed around a local area network (LAN) that will activate the SERVER or one or all of the computers on the network. See also TOKEN-RING NETWORK.

control total a sum of a set of figures, used to check data integrity. When data consists of a set of numbers, the total can be calculated and included in the set. At any time later, perhaps after sending the data through a COMMUNICATIONS LINK or simply retrieving from a disk, the totalling action can be repeated on the data, and the calculated total should agree with the total that is included as part of the data. See also CHECK DIGIT.

conventional memory or **base memory** the MEMORY region, up to 640 kilobytes in the PERSONAL COMPUTER. In order to maintain compatibility with older PC machines, this region of memory is used for all DOS programs, although more modern machines (of the 386, 486 and Pentium types) can use very much more memory; see EXTENDED MEMORY, for WINDOWS programs.

convergence 1. the action of aiming three beams of electrons in a colour cathode ray tube (CRT) of a MONITOR (sense 1) or TV receiver. When convergence is correct, one beam will hit on the red shining portions of the screen, the second beam will hit only the green shining portions, and the third will hit only the blue shining portions. **2.** the use of the same or similar technical methods for computing, TV, recording and telecommunications, leading eventually to devices that combine all these functions.

converter SOFTWARE that converts data from one form to another. Converters are needed to a lesser extent now because the use of WINDOWS makes it easier to transfer data between programs.

cookbook a textbook that contains instructions for assembling SOFTWARE or HARDWARE.

cookie a small file of data that an INTERNET SERVER places on the HARD DRIVE of a user by way of the BROWSER. This information can be passed to the server each time the browser is used, and its purpose is as a way of identifying the user without the need for a PASSWORD. More elaborate cookies can be used to identify preferences (for Internet shopping, for example). Browsers contain options for restricting or eliminating cookie storage.

cookie-cutter slice a sample of a set of WORKSHEETs, meaning that the worksheets can be organized so as to allow a straight slice to be taken of one CELL in each to create another worksheet. See THREE-DIMENSIONAL WORKSHEET.

cooperative multitasking a form of MULTITASKING in which the applications can share all the resources (such as memory) of the system but which allows an application exclusive use of the processor when a task such as saving, loading, searching or calculating is being carried out. This form of multitasking was used for MICROSOFT WINDOWS 3.0 and 3.1, but WINDOWS 95 uses PRE-EMPTIVE MULTITASKING, which allows the processor time to be shared by 32-bit programs.

coordinates systems of defining position by the use of numbers. See CARTESIAN COORDINATES; POLAR COORDINATES.

coprocessor an additional MICROPROCESSOR for auxiliary actions. A very common requirement is for a separate processor that can undertake specialized mathematical work which would otherwise greatly slow down the action of the main processor (see MATHS COPROCESSOR). Another form of coprocessor can be used to deal with display of text and graphics, another with sound. Modern microprocessor chips have mathematical processing incorporated. See also DMA.

copy 1. to make a duplicate of a file on a disk or on backup tape. **2. (COPY)** a COMMAND used in MS-DOS to copy the bytes of a file to another LOCATION (sense 2), such as another disk, a different FILENAME or by appending (see APPEND) to an existing file. The form of the command is 'COPY sourcefile destfile', where *sourcefile* is the file being copied and *destfile* is the file to which the copy is made. The destfile can be a drive letter or directory path if the copy is being made using the same name but a different drive or directory. **3.** text that is ready for a printing company.

copy-fitting determining how a given amount of text can be fitted into a page using a DTP program.

copy protection any system that makes a tape or disk difficult to COPY (sense 1). This inevitably makes it difficult to BACKUP, so making the program risky to use. The distribution of programs on CD-ROM once made the need for copy protection much less, since the CD-ROM can contain files that are too large to place on a floppy disk. Now that CD copying is easily carried out, genuine COMPACT DISCS are identified by a hologram.

copyright notice a warning of copyright vested in a PROGRAM. This takes the form of a statement that is part of a program and is usually printed on the SCREEN (sense 1) at the start of the program. It reminds the user that the program is copyright and that taking copies for any purpose other than for BACKUP is illegal. The user is sometimes asked in addition to sign and return a pledge of observance of copyright. See also PIRACY.

core memory or **internal memory** the internal electronic memory of a DIGITAL COMPUTER. The word 'core' comes from the former use of small magnetic rings, or cores, threaded on to electrical wires and used to store magnetic data that could be read or written by passing signals through the wires.

CorelDraw™ a VECTOR GRAPHICS drawing program whose image files can be used in a very wide range of WORD PROCESSOR and DTP documents.

co-resident program a PROGRAM that shares the memory of a computer with other programs, particularly if the co-resident program can be started and stopped by means of special KEY (sense 1) combinations; see HOT KEY; TSR PROGRAM.

corona an electric discharge through ionized air, used to charge or discharge materials in an ELECTROSTATIC COPIER and in LASER PRINTER technology.

correlation the action of comparing two sets of data in a WORKSHEET to find if any statistical relationship exists. Also called *covariance* in MICROSOFT EXCEL.

corrupted file a file that has been damaged so that its contents are partially or wholly unusable. If a PROGRAM file is corrupted, the program cannot be used, but corruption of a DATA FILE is not always so serious and some data recovery is usually possible.

corruption the unwanted changing of data, either in the memory or during replay from disk or backup tape. If the corruption affects only text that is in ASCII codes, it can be edited out, but corruption of other codes may be impossible to correct. If any part of MEMORY that is used by the operating system (OS) becomes corrupted, the computer may LOCKUP or REBOOT.

counter a VARIABLE that is used to keep a running count of actions or items. Some WORKSHEETS can use a counter in a CELL that will indicate the number of occupied cells in a RANGE, so as to count the number of entered items.

country code a two-letter abbreviation that will identify the country of origin of a WEB SITE. The code *us* is normally omitted, but all other countries and some small islands are identified in this way.

country file a file used by the operating system (OS) to set parameters for a particular country. A country file will establish the type of KEYBOARD and KEY (sense 1) layout, currency sign, use of decimal point or comma, method of printing dates, etc., for the country of use.

courier font the type of FONT used by a simple typewriter in which all letters are equally spaced (see MONOSPACING). Courier is often used for tables, because letters will line up vertically, and is sometimes used to give a typewritten effect.

courseware SOFTWARE that is used for training purposes.

covariance see CORRELATION.

CP/M (control, program, MONITOR, sense 2) CP/M was the first 'universal' disk-based operating system (OS) for microcomputers, devised in 1973. The original CP/M applied only to computers that used the 8080 MICROPROCESSOR chip and was later adapted to the very popular Z-80 microprocessor.

cpi (characters per inch) a measure of the density of printed characters in a line of monospaced (see MONOSPACING) print in terms of the number of characters per inch width. This is not constant when proportional spacing has been used, so that an average figure is used.

cps (characters per second) a measure of the rate of transmission of data, usually in a SERIAL link or in a HARD DRIVE interface. See also BAUD RATE.

CPU (central processing unit) for microcomputers, the CPU is almost invariably a single CHIP, the MICROPROCESSOR. Some computers, however, use more than one microprocessor, such as a MATHS COPROCESSOR or COPROCESSOR that is reserved for mathematical routines. The fundamental speed of the CPU is determined by the CLOCK rate, but for a given clock rate, the speed of CPU actions can be greatly improved by suitable design, such as the use of an onboard CACHE memory.

CR (carriage return) the action of moving the point of printing or display to the left-hand side of a piece of paper or a SCREEN (sense 1). The ASCII code for this action is 13. On a KEYBOARD, the return key is usually marked out by its shape and the arrow symbol; the ENTER key provides the same action.

cracker or **dark-side hacker** as HACKER (sense 3), a malevolent computer user who alters code in other users' files or who inserts a VIRUS. The main interest of the cracker is in defeating SECURITY systems, and these activities have led to considerable efforts to tighten up the security of transmitted data.

crash 1. or **program crash** an undesired end to a program, often brought about by a SOFTWARE fault. Some operating systems (OS) will retain a program unchanged after a crash and allow easy recovery. Others crash very completely, corrupting the RAM, so that the machine must be rebooted (see REBOOT) before it can be used again. A crash can come about as a result of a badly designed program but may also be caused by fluctuations of mains supply voltage, strong radiated signals, the effect of incorrectly connected peripherals or partial failure of memory. See also FATAL ERROR. **2.** to end a program unintentionally.

crawler or **spider** a program that works its way through WEB SITES looking for words to index.

Cray™ one of the world's most powerful computers, of which some 30 are built each year. The Cray is one example of the supercomputer, designed for applications that place a premium on speed and capacity. The most obvious feature is its circular shape, which is intended to reduce the distance over which data signals have to travel. At the computing speeds that are used in this machine, even the time for an electrical signal to cover the distance of one metre (a fraction of a NANOSECOND) is significant.

crayola a computer that provides very high performance at a low price.

CRC 1. (cyclic redundancy check) a method (related to the CHECKSUM) for detecting errors in transmitted data. It is particularly useful for data stored on tape or on disk. CRC methods are also used in the encoding of a COMPACT DISC so as to make this form of reproduction virtually error-free even in the presence of physical damage to the disk surface. **2.** (camera-ready copy) see BROMIDE OUTPUT.

creationism the belief that a new major SOFTWARE can be designed and produced simply by applying enough money and talent. This simplistic belief is the main cause for large and expensive (usually government funded) projects being late in delivery and faulty in execution. All really successful major software has evolved through several generations of collaboration between designers and users.

creeping elegance a feature of later versions of SOFTWARE that concentrate more on appearance than substance. See also CREEPING FEATURISM.

creeping featurism the evolution of a PROGRAM to new versions by the addition of features that are of only marginal utility, often at the expense of speed. See also BELLS AND WHISTLES.

crippled leapfrog test a way of testing the ability of the computer to read and write memory by performing a write and read to a single memory LOCATION (sense 1); see LEAPFROG TEST.

crippleware or **crippled version** a form of demonstration program or SHAREWARE that has an important function (such as saving data) disabled so that the user can try out the program but not employ it for any useful purpose until a fee has been paid and a revised version or a remedial patch installed.

crisp (of LOGIC) precise, distinct from FUZZY.

critical error an error that will stop a program until the cause of the error is corrected. For example, running out of printer paper will cause an error message until the printer is reloaded or the printing operation is abandoned.

critical mass a state of SOFTWARE that results from overloading the specification of the software to the extent that each intended improvement causes new BUGs that make the software unusable.

critical path the route that takes the longest time. In any process that consists of many actions, some actions will take very much more time than others. The critical path is the combination and arrangement of actions that take the longest time, and *critical path analysis* means trying to find this sequence in a scientific way because this will determine the overall time for the project. The main feature of critical path analysis is to try to arrange long tasks so that they can be performed in parallel with other tasks rather than in sequence. This may require substantial redesigning of the tasks themselves.

CRLF (carriage return line feed) the ASCII characters 13 and 10 in sequence. Text that contains only the line feed character without carriage return can cause strange effects when imported into a MICROSOFT WORD document.

crop to trim an image either so as to fit a specified size or to cut out an irrelevant background.

crop mark a MARKER (sense 1) used to show where paper can be trimmed. Many DTP programs, when printing pages on to paper that is larger than the page size, will place crop marks on the paper to act as guides to trimming the paper to the correct dimensions.

cropping the reduction of size of an IMAGE (sense 2) in a DTP SCREEN (sense 1) display by removing part of the image area at the top, bottom or sides. Cropping is used when an image contains only a small portion that is useful, so that the reduction in area removes irrelevant material and focuses the eye better on the important region while leaving more space on the page for text. In many DTP programs, cropping is reversible and the image area can be increased again up to the time when the page data is recorded on disk. See also RESIZING.

cross-assembler an ASSEMBLER program that runs on one type of MICRO-PROCESSOR but produces MACHINE CODE for another type.

cross-compiler a COMPILER program that runs using one type of MICRO-PROCESSOR but produces compiled output to use with a different microprocessor.

cross-hair cursor a CURSOR or POINTER (sense 1) that consists of a large cross formed with thin lines. This is used in CAD programs to make it easier to line up objects that are some distance apart on the screen.

cross-hatching a form of shading that uses criss-cross lines. This is one of the FILL patterns used in a CAD program.

cross-linked files files (usually deleted files) that have become connected so that the data contained in them is garbled. Such files can be cleaned up by using a UTILITY such as SCANDISK.

cross OS operation the use of computers with different operating systems (OS) on a NETWORK. This allows the use of machines such as the MACINTOSH (for graphics and DTP) and the Atari (for sound synthesis) on a network along with PERSONAL COMPUTERS for other business uses.

cross-platform computing the development of programs that can be used on a range of different computer types (such as on the PERSONAL COMPUTER, on the MACINTOSH and on larger machines).

cross-post to send a document to several NEWSGROUPS simultaneously.

cross-reference a reference in a document to material on another page. A cross-reference code can be put in by a WORD PROCESSOR, ensuring that the correct page number will be printed even if the pagination changes.

cross software any software that is designed and produced on one type of computer but intended for use on another type.

CrossTab table an action of earlier versions of MICROSOFT EXCEL, now referred to as a PIVOT TABLE.

crosstalk see BABBLE.

CRT (cathode-ray tube) the display device used in most MONITORs (sense 1) and TV receivers. Alternatives, such as LCD display screens, are used for portable computers and where a flat screen is an advantage, but the CRT still predominates for larger lower-cost displays. It has the particular advantage of being a large bright display that can be used in dark places. Its disadvantages include fragile construction (using glass), large bulk and weight, and the requirement for high electrical voltages. It is also less easy to INTERFACE with computer signals than other devices.

crunching carrying out a set of repetitive actions for a considerable time, hence the name *number cruncher* applied to a MATHS COPROCESSOR. See also FILE COMPRESSION UTILITY.

cryptanalysis the decoding of intercepted encrypted (see ENCRYPTION) messages. See also BLETCHLEY PARK.

cryptography the mathematical science of encoding data so that it cannot be understood by anyone who does not know the ENCRYPTION method. Cryptography has strong links with spying but also has applications in WEB TRADING, allowing personal details such as credit card numbers to be sent to a WEB SITE. There is a continuing legal battle over the legality of encryption systems that do not allow messages to be read by law-enforcement agencies.

crystal or **quartz crystal** the mineral that is used as a timing component for a MICROPROCESSOR. The mechanical vibration of a piezo-electric crystal can be electrically induced and is at a constant FREQUENCY if the crystal temperature is constant. By coating opposite sides of the crystal with thin metal films, the mechanical vibration can be detected as electrical signals, so that this output can be used as a time-controller for a computer, clock or watch. The frequency is determined by the dimensions of the crystal and the circuit in which it is used.

crystal-shutter printer a form of LASER PRINTER in which a powerful light source illuminates an LCD panel which in turn illuminates a photosensitive drum. The printing is done line-by-line rather than in pages.

CSCW see COMPUTER-SUPPORTED COOPERATIVE WORK.

CSID see CHARACTER SET IDENTIFIER.

CSMA/CD (carrier sense multiple access with collision detection) a NETWORK technique designed to avoid COLLISION problems by making two colliding programs wait for random, and hence different, amounts of time.

CTI see COMPUTER TELEPHONY INTEGRATION.

CTRL (control KEY, sense 1) the key that is used to allow the letter keys and each function key of the computer to be used for actions that are determined by the program (see APPLICATIONS PROGRAM) that is running. Many programs allow for these CTRL key actions to be determined by the user; see KEY MACRO.

Ctrl-Alt-Del the KEY (sense 1) combination that will cause a REBOOT when running under MS-DOS or under MICROSOFT WINDOWS.

Ctrl-C the KEY (sense 1) combination that is used in many MS-DOS applications to enforce a pause.

CTS see CLEAR TO SEND.

CTTY an MS-DOS command that allows input to the computer from the KEYBOARD to be replaced by another form of input, usually from the SERIAL PORT.

CUA keyboard a KEYBOARD system using the Common User Access set of keystrokes and commands designed by IBM. This has now become a computer industry standard.

cue card a form of HELP system in which a set of cards appears in turn, each specifying a step in an action. Unlike a WIZARD, the cue card does not carry out the actions, it only specifies what the user should do.

CUG see CLOSED USER GROUP.

curly brackets see BRACES.

currency format the type of currency symbol to be used and how it is placed. Many programs are set up to use the dollar sign for currency as a DEFAULT but can be configured to use others, including the pound and the euro. The currency symbol can be placed ahead of a number or following it.

currency pointer a POINTER (sense 2) to an address on disk, used in a DATABASE to indicate the RECORD (sense 1) that has been most recently accessed (see ACCESS, sense 2). Various currency pointers can be used as references to different types of data.

current 1. flow of electrical CHARGE, unit Ampere (amp). **2.** anything that is being used, in progress, contemporary.

current cell the CELL in a WORKSHEET that is highlighted and is being used.

current cell width the width, in terms of number of characters, of a CELL in a WORKSHEET.

current device the HARDWARE item that is being used.

current directory or **current folder** the DIRECTORY (sense 1) (*folder*) that is currently in use and whose files can be read or written.

current graph the GRAPH that is currently being used in a WORKSHEET. When a print graph command is used, the current graph will be printed.

cursor the SCREEN (sense 1) position indicator, a MARKER (sense 1) or POINTER (sense 1) that is placed on the display screen to show where text will appear when you type when using a WORD PROCESSOR or SPREAD-

SHEET. The cursor often consists of a flashing rectangle or dash. In some systems, such as WINDOWS, one or more pointers may be active at the same time as a cursor.

cursor-control keys the keys that can be used to cause CURSOR movement. These keys are usually marked with arrows that show in which direction the cursor will move when a KEY (sense 1) is pressed. Many modern systems do not use the keyboard for cursor control but make use of the MOUSE instead.

custom dictionary a dictionary used in a SPELLCHECK program that contains specialized words that are not found in the main dictionary. More than one custom dictionary can be created and used. For example, you would create and use a custom dictionary for spellchecking a document with a large number of medical terms.

customize to alter parameters to one's own requirements, used of a program in which various preferences such as SCREEN (sense 1) colours, use of FUNCTION KEYS, etc., can all be tailored by the user.

customizing the action of altering aspects of a program to suit the individual user. For example, you might want to read data files from a folder called C:\MYBOOK or use the Ctrl-X key for inserting a picture.

cut to remove a marked piece of text or graphics from the SCREEN (sense 1) but retaining the data in memory so that it can be pasted (see PASTE) into another document, another part of the same document or into another program.

cut sheet feeder or **bin** a mechanism for handling sheets of paper and feeding one sheet at a time to a printer, particularly a LASER PRINTER.

cut tape to record a MAGNETIC TAPE with data.

CVF see COMPRESSED VOLUME FILE.

cyan-magenta-yellow see CMY.

cyan-magenta-yellow-black see CMYK.

cyber of anything making use of computers or the internet.

cybernetics the study of thought processes. Cybernetics as a study dates from the discovery of the principles of machine control. Machine control systems often mimic in many ways the control action of the brain and nervous system, and the similarities have led to researchers explaining such actions in terms borrowed from electronics. This has been a very fruitful method both for the design of ROBOT mechanisms and for deeper understanding of the action of the human brain. The prefix *cyber-* is often used to refer to actions that have a computing context.

cyberspace see VIRTUAL REALITY.

cycle a set of repeating actions. See also CLOCK.

cycle crunch a situation in which too many users are demanding time on a MULTI-ACCESS system, causing the whole system to slow down to the point of being unusable.

cycle time the time that is needed for a complete cycle of actions.

cyclic redundancy check (**CRC**) or **cyclic check** a method of checking for errors in transmitted code. A number is derived from the code and transmitted along with the code so that it can be compared with a number derived in the same way from the received code. Any discrepancy indicates errors in the transmission. Elaborate forms of CRC can detect the position of the error, but all such methods add to the size of the transmitted code because they are adding redundant information.

cylinder a set of HARD DISK TRACK surfaces all at the same distance from the hub of the disk drive.

Cyrix a manufacturer of MICROPROCESSOR chips for SOCKET-7 use.

D: D drive, a second HARD DRIVE or a CD-ROM drive added to a computer that uses the letter C: for the main hard drive. See also A:, B:.

DAC see D TO A.

daemon a program, such as a print SPOOLING routine, that is called up by selecting an action rather than by explicitly running the program and which runs in the BACKGROUND (sense 2).

dagger a symbol (†) used in DTP work as a bullet character. On programs running under WINDOWS, the dagger is obtained from the extended character set, using the CHARACTER MAP.

daisy-chain a connection that is taken from one destination to another in sequence, used particularly of disk drives. The data has to be coded or the connections made so that the correct device in the daisy-chain will be selected. See also SCSI; USB.

daisywheel the PRINTHEAD of one type of printer mechanism, now obsolete. Type characters are moulded on the end of short flexible stalks that are arranged around a hub like the petals of a daisy. The printer action consists of rotating the daisywheel so as to select the correct character and then hitting the back of the typeblock with a miniature hammer so as to press the type against the ribbon and the paper. Because of the impact action, carbon copies can be made.

dangling pointer a POINTER (sense 2) whose address number is no longer valid because the RECORD (sense 1) or other data to which it pointed has been erased or moved. See also PINNED RECORD.

DAO see DISC AT ONCE.

dark-side hacker see CRACKER.

DAT (digital audio tape) a system for recording sound in the form of digital signals, using a combination of videotape hardware and compact disc signal-processing technology. DAT is ideal for the purpose of making a BACKUP of a HARD DRIVE, since the 8-mm tape can hold a huge amount of data and transfer it with little risk of corruption. DAT back-up systems are now widely available for small computers but are likely to be superseded by writable DVD systems.

data anything that the computer can work with. This could be numbers of any kind, text characters, positions on a diagram, and so on. Whatever the 'raw' data happens to be, it is always converted into BINARY NUMBER form for use by the computer. This causes no problems for TEXT data and INTEGER numbers, but REAL NUMBERS generally have to be stored in the form of a binary approximation because many real numbers cannot be represented as an exact BINARY FRACTION. The computer and program actions depend on valid data being fed in, and ridiculous errors can result if the program does not make some form of check on data that is entered from the keyboard. See also DATA VALIDATION.

data abstraction level a classification of levels at which a DATABASE may be regarded. The lowest abstraction level is the *physical level*, which describes how each item of data is stored in memory and on disk. Above this is the CONCEPTUAL LEVEL, which deals with the types of data and their relationships. The highest level is the *view level*, at which the user operates unaware of the construction of the database, knowing only how to add, alter and use the data. See ISO/OSI.

data acquisition an automatic form of data input, such as from a point-of-sale terminal or from remote sensors.

data administrator the part of a DATABASE program that controls the actions of the program such as entry of new data and ACCESS (sense 1) to existing data.

data area 1. the part of the memory used to store data; see also DATA SEGMENT. **2.** the portion of a disk, hard, floppy or compact disc, that is available for data after formatting (see FORMAT, sense 3).

data bank a collection of data that is similar to that of a DATABASE but contains non-selected information, usually in an indexed form, from which a user may COPY (sense 1) items of interest. A database will contain only items that are specifically required for its purposes.

database a collection of data items in a file that are used by programs that can COPY (sense 1) and alter the items but the actions of which are not restricted by the way in which the items are stored. A database of any size would be kept on a HARD DRIVE, probably on several such drives. For example, a firm might keep a database that consisted of the name, address, phone number and state of account for each customer. This database might then be used extensively each day and be continually updated. The file could be kept in any order, probably in order of adding entries, but the items could be displayed in alphabetical order by a suitable program. Database programs are designed with various forms of QUERY LANGUAGE, which allow them to manipulate the data into a pattern that will be appropriate for the user. The database files are precious, and several copies of each file must be kept in reserve (see FILE GENERATIONS). In addition, the state of the database should be printed out to paper at frequent intervals.

database administrator a manager appointed to maintain a DATABASE. The duties of the administrator will be to ensure that the data is of the correct type, updated and added to regularly, and that ACCESS (sense 1) methods are appropriate, subject to SECURITY. In addition, the data must be documented and MANUALs made available to users.

database language a form of control and PROGRAMMING LANGUAGE specific to one DATABASE program, such as DBASE V, and permitting the actions of the program to be automated.

database machine HARDWARE, such as a specially designed computer, intended specifically for fast DATABASE storing and retrieving actions.

database management system (DBMS) the part of a DATABASE program that maintains the organization of the database, as distinct from the part that carries out input/output and searching through the RECORDs (sense 1). An efficient management system will, for example, organize the data to take up the least amount of space possible on the disk, allow space vacated by deleted records to be reused and allow data records to refer to other records. This prevents duplication of records and of computing activity and ensures, for example, that when an item such as a customer name is deleted from a list, the account number corresponding to that name will also be deleted (if no balances remain outstanding) and the name will be deleted from all actions such as mailing lists. The most important objective of a DBMS is to ensure that data is recorded only once and used by all data-handling programs. The DBMS must also maintain SECURITY of data. If sensitive data such as salary information or medical records can be associated with names, the DBMS must ensure that such ACCESS (sense 1) is granted only to users who need to know the information. Each user will have a PRIVILEGE LEVEL, and information will be graded in such a way that it is available only to certain privilege levels. The DBMS must also allow for the data to be obtained in the form that a user wants, so that anyone looking for a list of left-handed medically qualified women between the ages of 30 and 50 can find such information (if it exists). This requires the use of a QUERY LANGUAGE, which can be used to describe the combination of requirements. In addition, the DBMS must provide a manipulation language that allows records to be added, deleted, modified, arranged into sets or removed from sets and located, and these actions must also be subject to the privilege levels of users; see RELATIONAL DATABASE.

database manager the SOFTWARE within a DATABASE system that is concerned with organization, storage and retrieval of data.

database model the type of design used for a DATABASE. For modern database programs this is usually a RELATIONAL DATABASE model rather than a FLAT DATABASE model.

database query language see QUERY LANGUAGE.

database server a computer designed for fast data manipulation and used in a NETWORK to act as data supplier for the workstations.

database structure the form of the RECORD used in a DATABASE. For example, you might want to design each record to use FIELDS (sense 2) of name, address, age and status.

data bits the number of BITS used for data in a SERIAL communications PROTOCOL (sense 1). This is normally 7 or 8 bits.

data buffer a portion of MEMORY allocated for use by data that is in the course of being transferred to or from a printer, disk drive or other device.

data bus the BUS used to convey data signals to and from the MICRO-PROCESSOR. The data bus for modern microprocessors will transfer 32 bits at a time (the bus is 32-bits wide).

data capture any method that converts raw (not recorded) data into the form of numbers that the computer can use, and includes the keyboard itself, voice input and optical character reader (OCR, sense 1) devices. In computers that are used to control manufacturing processes, the data may be obtained from measuring instruments, using DIGITIZERs to convert to BINARY form. Data capture in such a case is entirely automatic and does not depend on a human operator.

data cleaning the action of removing any errors from data (often manually) before it is entered into the DATABASE program.

data collection the actions of getting data into a computer. These will include gathering the data, checking and transcribing into a form that the computer can use.

data communications equipment see DCE.

data compacting see COMPACTING ALGORITHM.

data compression any system for reducing the number of BYTES in a data file by eliminating REDUNDANCY. This allows more data to be stored on a disk and faster SERIAL COMMUNICATIONS to be made possible. See also ARCHIVE; DRIVESPACE; JPEG; LOSSLESS COMPRESSION; LOSSY COMPRESSION; MPEG.

data compression protocol the standard used for DATA COMPRESSION in a SERIAL link. The V42-bis and MNP-5 standards are commonly used. See CCITT PROTOCOL.

data control the checking of data. Control is needed at all stages in DATA COLLECTION to avoid as far as possible faulty data entering the computer (see GIGO).

data creation the obtaining of data from its source. The basic methods are by retyping documents or by DATA CAPTURE.

data definition language (DDL) a method used by a designer of a DATABASE to express in statements the definitions for a database system. The DDL statements lead to the construction of a *data directory file* that is used to determine how data is read or altered.

data delimiter a number code that is used to indicate the end of a data item or of a data file.

data dependency a restriction on some item of data, such as the condition that a bank balance should not fall below £100.

data dictionary a file maintained by a DATABASE MANAGEMENT SYSTEM. The data dictionary contains descriptions of the data items held in the main database files.

data directory file see DATA DEFINITION LANGUAGE.

data encoding scheme the method of converting data bits into magnetic signals on a disk, used for FLOPPY DISK and HARD DRIVE storage systems. See also ADVANCED RUN-LENGTH LIMITED; MODIFIED FREQUENCY MODULATION; RLL.

data encryption standard an ALGORITHM, which in theory must not be distributed outside the USA, used for ENCRYPTION of data.

data entry the encoding of collected data into digital form to the computer. This will be done using devices such as the KEYBOARD, GRAPHICS TABLET, MOUSE, SCANNER (sense 2) and also by various other DATA CAPTURE methods.

data entry form a SCREEN (sense 1) view that appears for entering data into a DATABASE program. The form can be designed so that all items must be entered, and can force the user to make an entry that follows some pattern, such as three letters and four digits, to reduce incorrect responses. See Fig. 16.

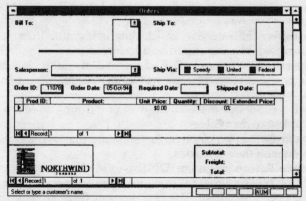

Fig. 16. **Data entry form**. This example shows a typical data entry form created using Microsoft Access database.

data error an error implicit in raw data. This may result from limitations on accuracy of measurements or poor DATA COLLECTION methods.

data field a space that is reserved for entering data. The normal action is to use one field for each different item of data, and the size of the file may be restricted. Data fields can be used in a WORKSHEET, a MAILMERGE program of a WORD PROCESSOR or a DATA ENTRY FORM of a DATABASE.

data file a file that contains only the data generated or used by a program, not any part of the PROGRAM code.

data filtering the selection of data that follows a pattern, such as all names starting with the letters NE or all items dated between 1/9/99 and 1/2/00.

data flow a record of data alterations. As data is processed through a system it may be transformed and reorganized so that knowledge of what has happened to the data is required.

data format the specification for storage or transmission of data.

data fragmentation the splitting of related data items into different BLOCKS (sense 2) on a disk. Excessive fragmentation can lead to delays in recovering data; see ALLOCATION UNIT; BUCKET; DEFRAGMENTATION.

data glove a device for use with VIRTUAL REALITY simulations. The user wears a glove which can detect finger movements that are transmitted to the computer and used to control the image of the glove on the screen and to convey the effects of pushing or pulling.

data hierarchy the TREE (sense 2) structure of data organization. A DATA FILE will consist of a set of RECORDS (sense 1), each record will consist of FIELDS and each field will consist of characters that form the information.

data independence a feature of the design of a DATABASE that makes it easier to gain access to data without knowing where the data is stored. Early designs used an ACCESSION NUMBER for each data item, but modern databases allow search actions on words of data. See STRUCTURED QUERY LANGUAGE.

data integrity the extent to which data is immune from CORRUPTION, particularly while being stored or transferred.

data interchange format (DIF) a method of coding WORKSHEET data into ASCII codes so that different SPREADSHEET programs can interchange data.

data jack a connector placed on a wall or partition so that a computer can be linked to data cables.

data link layer the part of the ISO/OSI standard that is concerned with the flow of data on the NETWORK.

data manipulation language (DML) a form of PROGRAMMING LANGUAGE used in a DATABASE program to allow users to specify the data that is required from a database. The two types of DML are *procedural DML*, which requires the user to state what data is required and how it is to be obtained, and *non-procedural*, which requires only what data is required. A QUERY LANGUAGE is a form of DML that deals with data retrieval only, but the terms are often used interchangeably.

data mask or **field template** a form of FILTER that will accept only the correct type of data (such as Y, a name, a number, etc.).

data model a mathematical description of a DATABASE design.

data modification changes made to data RECORDS, usually by way of a QUERY LANGUAGE.

data name a word used to define data in a DATABASE in which a QUERY LANGUAGE allows data relationships to be specified for the purpose of extracting data.

data packet a unit of data that is transmitted on a NETWORK. The data may be accompanied by a HEADER (sense 1) and also contain error-correction bytes; see ERROR CORRECTION ROUTINE.

data path the size (or width) of a data BUS in terms of the number of bits of data that can be simultaneously transmitted.

data plotter an X-Y PLOTTER used to prepare a graph from data fed to it from a program.

data pointer a stored number contained in a DATABASE that will contain the address of the next data item to be used.

data pollution a method of securing data against a CRACKER or other unapproved user. This applies to a DATABASE that contains both raw statistical data and the statistically processed data (such as standard deviation figures) from which authorized users will extract only the processed statistics. As a method of preventing any unapproved user from extracting raw data that could be related to an individual, data is falsified at random in a way that does not alter the validity of the statistics derived from the data.

data preparation the processing of data, often by manual methods, to ensure that all data input to the computer is as correct as checking can make it. Verification is an essential part of data preparation, and one system that is widely used is to key in data that is then saved to a disk. The information on the disk is then reviewed in a second stage at which corrections can be made. When the computer is used ONLINE, such checking is not easy, and the verification is carried out by displaying the data on the SCREEN (sense 1) after entry, with a message asking the operator to accept or edit the data. In addition, checks are carried out on data that is not entirely new. For example, a customer will be known by both name and account number, so that these two can be checked as belonging together. To this is added the use of a CHECK DIGIT system and a CONTROL TOTAL where appropriate.

data processing (dp) the acquisition, storage, maintenance and arrangement of data. The use of a computer allows data processing to be carried out much more rapidly than by other methods. In addition, much more complex and tedious operations can be carried out, like searching through large amounts of data for given items. The results of data processing actions are only as useful as the validity of the data itself, however. If the data is suspect, the results are not to be trusted. See GARBAGE.

data processing standards a set of statements laying out the methods to be used for communicating, documenting and controlling data. By setting standards that will be adhered to, DATABASE users can avoid the problems that arise when there is uncertainty about the validity of data. If all systems analysts, programmers and users of the database work to the standards that have been laid down, the system can continue to operate when one person leaves and another is appointed. Failure to establish standards causes a considerable waste of time and resources in trying to find out what was done in the past and the reasons for past actions. See also SYSTEMS ANALYSIS.

Data Protection Act the legislation passed in 1984 in the UK that requires any user of a DATABASE of any size to register if the contents of the database contain any information on living persons other than their names and addresses. There are exceptions for certain unincorporated clubs and associations, and all use of databases by government agencies are, of course, exempt. Personal and home computers come within the scope of the Act if they contain software such as databases or mailing lists that deal with any information other than names and addresses.

data rate the speed of transfer of data along a line, measured in units of BITS PER SECOND.

data reduction the process of removing redundant information from data so as to make the remainder more compact.

data redundancy duplication of data in a DATABASE. This is usually undesirable, but it may be used as a way of making the data more secure.

data replication the storage of tables of data with several identical copies stored in different computers in a DISTRIBUTED SYSTEM.

data retrieval the recovery of data from a DATABASE, usually by way of a QUERY. The format of data is not necessarily the same as it was when entered. For example, you might have entered names and addresses but require retrieval based on the first part of the post code.

data security the protection of data against unauthorized use or CORRUPTION. See CRACKER; SECURITY.

data series 1. a set of items placed into a WORKSHEET by a single command that specifies starting value, increment and ending value. For example, you would enter 10, 5, 25 to generate the numbers 10, 15, 20, and 25 in a set of CELLS. **2.** a set of related values in a DATABASE, such as the height and weight of a number of people in a set of medical records.

data set the items contained in a DATA FILE.

data set ready (DSR) a code that is transmitted on a SERIAL link to indicate that a MODEM is ready for signals. The name data set was once used to mean modem.

data striping a system for writing or reading data to multiple disk units so that high writing or reading speeds can be attained.

data structure a set of related data items that the computer can use like one single item. The most common data structure is a RECORD (sense 1). A record for an address-book application might contain data on name, address, age, telephone number and hobbies for each entry. The computer would then manipulate all this data for one entry as one piece rather than as a number of separate items.

data-structure diagram a method of representing the design of a network DATABASE in which boxes represent RECORD (sense 1) types and lines represent links that associate records with each other.

data terminal equipment a HARDWARE device that is a source or destination of data as distinct from an intermediate device such as a MODEM.

data transfer rate the speed in BITS PER SECOND at which data can be transferred along a SERIAL link to or from a DISK DRIVE or from a CD-ROM.

data type the kind of data that can be used, as applied to a DATABASE program. MICROSOFT ACCESS has a typical set of types that include Text, Memo, Number, Date/Time, Currency, Counter, Yes/No and OLE object. The text type allows the entry of up to 255 characters, and the memo type can be text of up to 64,000 characters. Number types can be numbers of any size, and the Date/Time type is self-explanatory, as is Currency. The Counter type is a number that increases by one for each record that is added, and the Yes/No type is a BOOLEAN type. The OLE type (not necessarily available in other databases) allows objects such as digitized (see DIGITIZE) photographs to be used in a database.

data validation a check on entered data. Any data that is entered from a KEYBOARD by a human operator is liable to contain mistakes. These mistakes may be trivial, such as the misspelling of an address. Others may be unimportant for a human operator, who will automatically correct the mistake, but important for the computer. In general, at any point in a program where a keyboard entry is made, the program should contain routines that will check the validity of the entry. Some mistakes, such as a date of 30 February, can easily be trapped and lead to the request for the date to be entered again. Other errors, such as an age of 100 instead of 10, are not so simple to trap. The main problems arise when there is no hard and fast rule that can be applied. In some cases, the only form of validation that can be used is to print the data and ask the user to check it.

data warehouse any DATABASE system that can work with very large amounts of data, allowing fast SEARCH and filtering (see FILTER, sense 1) methods.

DATE a DOS command that allows the current date to be entered. This is needed only when the REAL-TIME CLOCK is being set up for the first time or following a battery change.

date the calendar date, available from a computer's REAL-TIME CLOCK circuits. The date is typically held as the INTEGER part of a number whose limited range requires that dates often start at 1900 or in 1980. The fractional part of the number is used to carry time of day information.

daughterboard a CIRCUIT BOARD that can be plugged into an existing board to add new functions.

dB see DECIBEL.

DB-9 the standard 9-pin connector now used for SERIAL communications.

DB-25 the older RS-232 standard SERIAL connector.

dBase™ the name of a long-established DATABASE program. The program has existed in several versions, most notably dBase 2 and dBase 3. The most important feature is the provision of a specialized PROGRAMMING LANGUAGE that allows the user to create a version of the program for his/her own use. This makes the program very versatile, although difficult to use without help (in the form of guidebooks) and experience. The current version at the time of writing is for WINDOWS, Visual dBase-Pro7 from Borland.

DBLSPACE a form of DATA COMPRESSION for hard and floppy drives used for a short time by MICROSOFT, later replaced by DRIVESPACE and subsequently superseded when low-cost large-capacity hard drives became available.

DBMS see DATABASE MANAGEMENT SYSTEM.

DC (direct current) the form of electrical supply that uses a steady voltage, such as is supplied from a battery. Computer systems require DC supplies at low voltages, typically 12V, 5V and 3V, positive and negative, and a power supply unit is needed to convert the mains AC into this form.

DC-2000 a tape format used for BACKUP (see STREAMER). DC-2000 tape is 0.25 inch wide and contained in a cartridge.

DCE (Data Communications Equipment) a PERIPHERAL connected by a SERIAL INTERFACE. See also DATA TERMINAL EQUIPMENT.

DD see DOUBLE-DENSITY.

DDDS (double-density double-sided) the description of the original IBM PC-XT 360K disk. See also HIGH DENSITY.

DDE see DYNAMIC DATA EXCHANGE.

DDL see DATA DEFINITION LANGUAGE.

DDT any type of SOFTWARE that assists in removing a BUG.

dead or **down** (of HARDWARE) no longer functioning.

dead key a KEY (sense 1) that causes an action, such as CAPS LOCK, rather than typing a character. For example, FUNCTION KEYS are all dead keys.

deadlock 1. the state of a DATABASE system in which a set of incomplete transactions (accesses and updates) exists, with the completion of each transaction depending on another. **2.** or **deadly embrace** a conflict between PROGRAMS. This may occur in a system that allows two programs to run at the same time. A deadlock occurs when both programs require to use a printer, modem or other peripheral at the same time. The operating system (OS) should include a method of avoiding deadlock by assigning PRIORITY.

dead time the time between the end of one action and the start of another, allocated so as to prevent any possible interaction.

dead-tree edition a paper (see HARD COPY) version of a document that also exists in electronic form.

DEBUG the DEBUGGING program formerly supplied along with the MS-DOS operating system (OS). With the adoption of MICROSOFT WINDOWS the use of DEBUG is obsolescent.

debugging the process of removing errors (see BUG) from PROGRAMS. This can be very difficult for large and complicated programs, and most long programs are never made completely bug-free because it is never possible to think of every possible fault that could exist. In addition, the long history of the PERSONAL COMPUTER has lead to a huge range of machines and peripherals being available, making it impossible to test a program with every possible set of variations. A program can be considered as being reasonably debugged if it never crashes (see CRASH, sense 2) or loses data because of an incorrect entry or because of an unusual set of commands. Modern programs are developed by large teams of programmers, and by using extensive ALPHA TEST and BETA SOFTWARE procedures, many bugs can be found and eliminated before commercial release.

DEC (Digital Equipment Corporation) a major manufacturer of MINI-COMPUTER hardware, now involved also in very fast microcomputers.

decade counter any electronic counting circuit that counts or displays in conventional DENARY, scale of ten, units.

decibel (dB) a unit of comparison based on logarithmic ratios so as to correlate with human perception of sound or light. For example, when two amounts of power, P_1 and P_2, are being compared, the decibel ratio is given by $10\log(P_2/P_1)$. A voltage decibel figure is also used to compare voltage ratios, equal to $20\log(V_2/V_1)$. Sound is often measured in decibels relative to the value taken as the threshold of hearing.

decimal a method of writing a fraction, using an unwritten denominator of a power of 10. The decimal 0.3 means $3/10$, the decimal 0.56 means $56/100$, and so on. In this way, the position of each digit indicates its significance, just as it does for numbers greater than 1. See also BINARY FRACTION; DENARY.

decimal point the full-stop character, ASCII 46. Typewriters in the past distinguished the decimal point from the full stop (or *period*) by placing the decimal point higher than the baseline of text, but computer keyboards have always used the full stop for both meanings.

decimal tab a TAB STOP that is used to indicate the position of the decimal point in a list of numbers. When the Tab key is used to move the cursor to the decimal tab of a WORD PROCESSOR, any number that is typed will be positioned so that its decimal point is at the column in which the decimal tab has been placed, provided that the number does not extend to any other tab position.

decision problem any problem that can be formulated so that the answer must be *yes* or *no*.

decision support system an information-providing system that assists in making decisions by presenting rules that allow some options to be discarded and others graded in order of merit.

decision table a two-column tabular display of factors and actions for incorporating into commands of a DATABASE LANGUAGE. For example, the factor AGE > 50 might be entered into one column and the response, 10% REDUCTION, into the other column, so that the database language would be programmed to allow a 10% reduction in insurance rates for drivers aged over 50 years.

decision theory a method of using STATISTICS to assist decision making.

decision tree a method of setting out decisions for a DATABASE LAN-GUAGE, showing each factor with a YES and NO branch, with a different response to each.

decoder a device or SOFTWARE routine that changes data from coded form to clear (or normal) form. A BCD to BINARY decoder, for example, will transform numbers that are stored in BCD form into normal binary form that the computer can use. The term is also used of software that can convert coded material, such as HTML text, into plain form.

decollate to separate into single sheets, applied either to CONTINUOUS STATIONERY to mean splitting off the tractor-feed strips and separating the sheets or to MULTIPART STATIONERY to mean removing the carbons and arranging the sheets into order. See also COLLATE.

decompressing files the action of expanding COMPRESSED FILES, perhaps from a DISTRIBUTION DISK. These files are in a coded form so that more can be stored on a floppy disk, and a decompression program such as EXPAND.EXE can unpack the files and COPY (sense 1) them to the hard drive.

decrement a reduction in the value of a number, usually by one. See also INCREMENT.

decrementing button a BUTTON shaped like an arrowhead that will decrement a number in a small pane each time the button is clicked. Holding the mouse button down when the pointer is over the decrementing button will make the number rapidly decrement. See also INCREMENTING BUTTON and Fig. 26.

decryption the action of applying a cipher to data that has been encrypted (see ENCRYPTION) so as to recover the data in understandable form.

dedicated (of any part of a computer system) designed for one task only. A dedicated WORD PROCESSOR, for example, can be used only for word processing despite the fact that it contains the same circuits as a computer and differs only in FIRMWARE. The PERSONAL COMPUTER has replaced many of the dedicated machines that used to be available. Dedicated SOFTWARE is used for one particular purpose only, such as a DATABASE program tailored to the use of dentists.

dedicated line a cable or telephone line that is used by one user for one purpose only (such as INTERNET use, FAX or data transfers).

dedicated server a computer used as the master in a NETWORK. A dedicated SERVER is used entirely for network control and will possess the main HARD DRIVE and printer. The use of a dedicated server is justified when the number of WORKSTATIONS (sense 1) is large enough – a figure of 6 to 8 is often quoted. For smaller installations, the server may be used to RUN (sense 2) other programs as well as the network; it is not dedicated.

deductive database a form of DATABASE that uses ARTIFICIAL INTELLIGENCE methods to find information from facts and rules.

Deep Blue a SUPERCOMPUTER using PARALLEL PROCESSING, developed by IBM.

de facto standard a product or system that is universally accepted but not formally standardized.

default a decision that is taken or value that is used if not countermanded. Your WORD PROCESSOR program, for example, may set up each document for A4 paper and 2.5 cm. margins. Many programs that allow you a wide choice of actions will also provide sensible default values if you fail to make some or any of the choices, and most programs also allow you to determine for yourself what defaults should be used.

default button a BUTTON on a GUI display that corresponds to the DEFAULT choice or action. The ENTER or RETURN key can normally be used in place of clicking the default button.

default extension an EXTENSION that is placed following a FILENAME by DEFAULT. For example, if you use MICROSOFT WORD to save a file called MYWORK, the extension of DOC will be added.

default font the FONT that will be used for printing or for screen display unless you specify some other font.

default numeric format the normal FORMAT (sense 2) of a CELL in a WORKSHEET if no choices about format are exercised.

default printer the PRINTER that will be used, particularly by WINDOWS, if no change is made to the printer settings.

defect see BUG.

defect analysis a method of improving quality, particularly of SOFTWARE, by identifying and classifying defects.

defect density the ratio of number of defects to program length, a measure of programming quality.

defective sector a HARD DRIVE or FLOPPY DISK fault. A SECTOR may fail to be written, fail to be read or be corrupted between writing and reading. The operating system (OS) will lock out such a sector so that it is not used.

deferral postponing use of a NETWORK until conditions are less busy.

definition see RESOLUTION.

deflate to compress (see COMPRESSED FILE) a file. See also INFLATE.

defragmentation the reorganization of a file from scattered parts of a disk into a set of CONTIGUOUS SECTORS.

defragmentation utility a UTILITY program that will move and rearrange the data stored on a hard drive so that all files are CONTIGUOUS.

The recent version in MICROSOFT WINDOWS will move files in such a way that the most frequently used files are placed where hard drive access is most rapid.

degradation the smoothing out of the shape of a signal's electrical pulses. This form of CORRUPTION makes the number of pulses difficult to count and hinders data interpretation. Degradation inevitably occurs when data is transmitted along cable lines or by radio waves, but it can also be caused by overloading output terminals with too many peripherals.

degrees of freedom the number of specifying COORDINATES that are needed to pinpoint a position. For three dimensions with two coordinates per dimension, this requires six numbers, six degrees of freedom, to position a device such as a ROBOT arm.

DEL see DELETE (sense 2).

delete 1. to remove a character or set of characters from the SCREEN (sense 1), from memory or from a file. In many cases, this action can be reversed (see UNDELETE) by clicking (see CLICK, sense 1) on an undelete icon. **2. (DELETE or DEL)** a COMMAND to the MS-DOS operating system (OS) to delete a file. The FILENAME would be typed with a space separating it from the DEL command. See also ERASE. In MICROSOFT WINDOWS, a file is not totally deleted and is retained in the RECYCLING BIN. It is then recoverable until the action of emptying the bin is carried out.

delete left key see BACKSPACE.

deletion record 1. a DATABASE RECORD (sense 1) that contains new data that will be used to replace older data in a record. **2.** a file containing a list of deleted items that might need to be restored.

deletion tracking a method of restoring deleted files. Deletion of a file is achieved simply by removing the directory POINTER (sense 2), and a deletion tracking file will hold pointers for all files deleted in a session, allowing each to be retrieved provided nothing has been written over the filespace. In MICROSOFT WINDOWS, a 'deleted' file is simply transferred to a special FOLDER (the RECYCLING BIN) and held until it is restored or finally deleted.

delimiter a separating character, usually a PUNCTUATION MARK, that is used to show a boundary between one item and another in a DATABASE or other program in which items are placed in FIELDs. For example, in MICROSOFT WORD, text can be entered using the TAB character as a delimiter, and such text can then be converted into a TABLE.

DEL key the KEY (sense 1) that provides the action of deleting the character that lies under the CURSOR. See also BACKSPACE.

DELOLDOS a DOS command that is used when the new version is installed and that will remove files that had been installed by older versions of DOS.

delta a small change in a quantity.

DELTREE a DOS command that will remove a DIRECTORY (sense 1) and all the files and subdirectories that it contains.

delurk to emerge from LURKING and post messages on a NEWSGROUP.

demand multiplexing a form of MULTIPLEXING in which the percentage of time allocated to one type of signal is not fixed but can be altered to suit the demand.

demand paging a way of using VIRTUAL MEMORY so that PAGES (sense 2) of data are read into memory only when required.

demand processing the processing of data as soon as it is INPUT. The data may be stored in an input BUFFER so that it can be completely assembled, but the only delay will be the time needed to fill the buffer. See also REAL-TIME PROCESSING.

demented (of a program) working badly, such as asking for the same information over and over again or displaying error messages when no error exists.

demigod a distinguished HACKER (sense 1).

demo a program designed to demonstrate the ability of the full version. A demo program is usually a CRIPPLED VERSION so it cannot be fully used.

democratic network a NETWORK in which each connected computer has equal priority on data and resources. Compare DESPOTIC NETWORK.

demodulation the action of decoding a modulated signal, such as the conversion of signals in the form of audio tones back to digital signals, an action carried out by a receiving MODEM.

Demon Internet Ltd a pioneer (1992) UK Internet service provider (ISP).

demote text to reduce the importance of text in an OUTLINE. A Heading 1 could be demoted to Heading 2, for example, or Heading 3 to body text.

demount to disconnect a FLOPPY DISK from the DRIVESPACE utility. When a floppy disk is demounted, a DIRECTORY (sense 2) command will show only one file, the COMPRESSED VOLUME FILE, such as DRVSPACE.000.

demultiplexer a circuit in which a set of combined signals on one or more connecting lines are separated so as to obtain one signal on each of several output lines. Contrast MULTIPLEXER.

denary the scale-of-ten numbering system that we normally use. In this system, the LEAST-SIGNIFICANT DIGIT (see BIT), on the right-hand side of a number, can be 0 to 9. The next column to the left represents tens, the next represents hundreds, and so on. This form of numbering is Arabic in origin and replaced the older Roman system. The same form of arrangement into columns is used by BINARY and HEXADECIMAL scales.

dense index an INDEX structure for a DATABASE in which there is an index RECORD for each KEY (sense 2) that may be searched for. Each record will contain the key value and a POINTER (sense 2) that will lead to the record. See also SPARSE INDEX.

density the degree of the packing of data BITs, particularly on a disk.

depeditating careless typesetting that results in letter DESCENDERs being removed and the 'feet' being cut off the letters.

dependent or **dependant** a CELL in a WORKSHEET that contains a FORMULA that uses values taken from other cells so that the value in this cell depends on the values in the other cells.

dependent variable the VARIABLE, for example in a graph, whose value depends on the value of some key factors, the *independent variables*. For example, the air temperature varies with the time of day, so that the time is an independent variable (it will alter with no intervention from you) and the air temperature is dependent.

dependent worksheet a WORKSHEET that contains data that has been linked (see LINK) in from another SOURCE worksheet.

depth-first search a way of searching (see SEARCH) in a DATABASE HIERARCHY. The first object on a level is checked, followed by the first object on the next lower level before checking any objects on the initial level. See also BREADTH-FIRST SEARCH.

derived field see CALCULATED FIELD.

descender the part of a CHARACTER that lies below the BASE LINE. LOWERCASE characters such as p, q, y and g all have portions that descend below the normal writing line level. These descenders can be printed only if sufficient space is left between lines and the CHARACTER BLOCK is of the correct size. MICROSOFT WINDOWS allows you to choose different character block sizes when you run a DOS program and the smaller blocks distort the shape of descenders. Descenders and ASCENDERs will also be truncated if the line spacing of a WORD PROCESSOR is too small for the size of FONT being used.

descending sort a SORT (sense 1) action on a table of data in which items are to be arranged in descending order, such as from Z to A or from 100 to 1.

descriptor a KEYWORD (sense 1) or identification codeword. This might mean the FILENAME, a program name, an INTEGER number or any word that is used as a code for a file. See also IDENTIFIER.

descriptor table a set of bytes used to hold details of memory addresses for program files, particularly where several programs are running in the same memory. If ACCESS (sense 1) to a program is only by way of the descriptor table, there is no risk of one program corrupting another.

deselection the reversal of a SELECTION action. Selection of a file or set of files is used to allow an action (deletion, copying, renaming) to be carried out, and deselection of a file or set of files will exempt the file or files from the action. Some programs allow you to use the combination of a *select all* command and individual deselection as an alternative to selection.

design element an image in a DTP document. The design element is

114

used both as illustration of ideas and to break up text.

design recovery a form of REVERSE ENGINEERING of a system in order to discover what the system was intended to do.

desk accessory a UTILITY program for business purposes, such as a calendar, calculator, notepad, etc., that would conventionally be in printed form on a desk.

desktop the general SCREEN (sense 1) background appearance while a windows program is being RUN (sense 2). The desktop appearance can be changed by altering border and DESKTOP PATTERN settings.

desktop computer a loose description for a MICROCOMPUTER the main components of which, the KEYBOARD, MONITOR (sense 1) and main processing unit (CPU), will fit on to the top of an ordinary office desk. The larger machines usually require at least one unit to be floor-standing in an elongated box or tower. Compare LAPTOP; PALMTOP COMPUTER; PORTABLE COMPUTER.

desktop pattern a pattern (*wallpaper*) that appears on a WINDOW when the window is not completely filled by a program.

desktop publishing see DTP.

desktop video a MULTIMEDIA effect that allows moving pictures (sometimes very jerkily animated and small) to appear in addition to still images, text and sound.

despool to print out files that have been held in a SPOOL memory.

despotic network a NETWORK in which one computer synchronizes all connections and controls the ACCESS (sense 1) of all the others to data and other resources.

destination the FILE, MEMORY address or LOCATION in a document to which data is to be sent.

destructive cursor a form of CURSOR that deletes the character it is placed over, permitting overtyping; see OVERWRITE.

detect idle time an option in a MULTITASKING system that allows a program to be switched out of use while it is idle, giving preference to another program that is working.

development the process of producing SOFTWARE by analysing the APPLICATION, planning and coding the PROGRAM and subsequent testing and modification of the software.

development software a set of programs that can be used to write other programs of a particular type, usually a DATABASE.

device 1. any active part of a computer system. The name is usually reserved for PERIPHERALS, such as KEYBOARD, SCREEN (sense 1), PRINTER, DISK DRIVE, and so on, that are part of the electronics of the computer system. **2. (DEVICE)** a DOS command that can be used in the CONFIG.SYS file to set up a new HARDWARE item, such as a scanner, sound card, etc. MICROSOFT WINDOWS will carry out this action automatically when new hardware is installed, using the CONTROL PANEL.

device code a number code used to identify and select a particular device such as PRINTER, SCREEN (sense 1), KEYBOARD, etc.

device-dependent being able to function correctly only with some specified device, such as a graphics adapter of one particular type or a specified type of computer.

device driver a short program that allows a device such as a DISK DRIVE or MOUSE to be interfaced to a computer.

DEVICEHIGH a modified version of the DEVICE (sense 2) command that will install DRIVER software into the high memory area (HMA).

device-independent (of a program) able to work with any SCREEN (sense 1) format or PRINTER without the need for CONFIGURATION; being able to function correctly with a wide range of HARDWARE.

device independent bitmap see DIB.

Device Manager a UTILITY in MICROSOFT WINDOWS that is used to check the settings of hardware devices and to report conflicts.

device name the three-letter abbreviation that is used in DOS to refer to devices such as PRINTER (PRN), PARALLEL PORT (LPT), SERIAL PORT (COM), and so on.

DFS (disk-filing system) an older term for an operating system (OS) for managing a disk drive or set of drives for the purposes of data filing. The DFS should make the action of the disk system TRANSPARENT to the user unless a manual action like changing disks is needed. In other words, the user does not have to specify which SECTOR and TRACK of a disk is to be used nor how the data is to be stored on the disk. The modern equivalent is DOS.

Dhrystone a form of BENCHMARK test designed to measure relative processing power in units of MIPS. The figure that is obtained depends on both the speed of the CPU or MICROPROCESSOR and on the speed at which memory can be written and read. A score of about unity is normal for the old (1982) IBM PC-AT machine. See also WHETSTONE.

diagnostic a checking routine or program that allows you to check and report on any faults in the computer or its operating system (OS). Some very large and elaborate programs may contain their own diagnostic system, and many computers are arranged to use a simple diagnostic program (testing RAM) each time the computer is switched on; see POST (sense 3).

Dialler a UTILITY supplied with MICROSOFT WINDOWS that allows telephone numbers to be dialled provided that a MODEM is connected to the computer and correctly installed. The screen appearance of Dialler is of a modern telephone panel with push-buttons and memory settings. See Fig. 17.

dialogue box a small box that appears on SCREEN (sense 1) containing a text message and requiring a reply to be typed into a space in the box. This reply will then be confirmed by ticking an OK BOX. This is done by

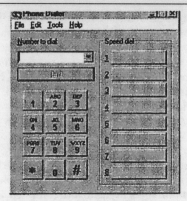

Figure 17. **Dialler**. The Phone Dialler utility of Windows as it appears on the VDU.

using the MOUSE to place the CURSOR over the word OK and then click-ing (see CLICK, sense 1) the mouse BUTTON. The dialogue box is an essen-tial part of GUI program action.

dial-type option an option used in COMMUNICATIONS programs to allow use with either pulse-dialling or tone-dialling telephone systems.

dialup a method of connecting to a remote computer. If the remote com-puter is permanently connected to a MODEM that in turn is permanently plugged into the telephone lines, then the computer can be dialled up just as a telephone can be dialled up. Data on such a system is never totally secure from a CRACKER unless very well-designed PASSWORD sys-tems are used. A useful safeguard is to use a form of RING-BACK system, in which the initial call places the caller's telephone number into mem-ory and prints this out. The caller is then asked to terminate the call, and the remote computer then calls back. In this way, anyone who uses the system has his or her telephone number noted and can be traced later.

Dialup Networking (DUN) a system that is part of MICROSOFT WINDOWS and which allows another computer to be networked (see NETWORK) through telephone lines. A MODEM must be installed and the Dialup Net-working software run so that the remote computer is contacted. The remote computer must also be using Windows for networking purpos-es, but Dialup Networking can also be used for INTERNET connection to any type of computer.

DIB (device independent bitmap) a form of BITMAP for an image in which the arrangement of the PIXEL information is not related to any specific device (monitor or printer).

dictionary a LIST of words in alphabetical order, often in compressed form. This can be used by a WORD PROCESSOR to check the spelling of each word in a document by comparing the word with a dictionary entry. Dictionary files in several languages are available for all the leading word processor programs, and word processors allow the creation of a CUSTOM DICTIONARY for words that are not in common use, such as medical terms.

dictionary sort a method of sorting (see SORT, sense 1) that ignores the CASE of words. For example, a simple ASCII sort, which ranks all upper-case letters ahead of all lower-case letters, would place *DOS* ahead of *damage*, but a dictionary sort would reverse this order.

didot a unit of type size for DTP work, equal to 0.378 mm. See also CICERO; PICA; POINT.

DIF see DATA INTERCHANGE FORMAT.

difference engine a mechanical computer designed by Charles BABBAGE in 1823, intended for producing mathematical tables. The machine was not completed in Babbage's lifetime, but a replica was built in 1991 and is in the Science Museum in London.

differential line a method of using two wires to carry a digital signal that must be as free from noise and interference as possible. One wire carries the signal and the other carries the inverted version of the signal. A differential line is usually implemented using TWISTED PAIR CABLE.

digerati an elite set of people who are knowledgeable about computers and computing.

digest a collection of messages that have been prepared from NEWSGROUP postings. These are often a very useful source of information, and a good example is *Deja News*.

digit literally a 'finger' and denoting a unit of counting. The DENARY counting scale uses ten digits (0 to 9) and the BINARY scale uses only the two digits, 0 and 1. The HEXADECIMAL scale uses 16 digits, with letters A, B, C, D, E and F added to the normal range of 0 to 9.

digital (of quantities) making use of DIGITS. This normally means making use of binary digits (BIT) and refers to any system in which data is coded in the form of BINARY NUMBERS.

digital audio tape see DAT.

digital camera a still camera that uses a CCD device as a light-sensitive detector to record an image on a static memory in the form of a thin card. The image files, which are usually compressed (see JFIF), can be downloaded (see DOWNLOAD) to a computer, processed and printed using a colour INKJET PRINTER of PHOTOGRAPHIC QUALITY.

digital carrier a method of transmitting digital signals that can be classed as BASEBAND or BROADBAND. This corresponds to part of the physical layer in the ISO/OSI model.

digital computer a computer that carries out its tasks by working with numbers in the form of BINARY-coded electrical signals. This distinguishes it from the ANALOGUE COMPUTER, which works with electrical voltages that are not in binary coded form. The data that is manipulated by a digital computer consists of numbers and text, and the binary bits are, for convenience, grouped into BYTE or WORD (sense 2) units. Each character of text can be represented by using an ASCII code that fits into a byte storage area. The actions of the computer consist basically of moving, copying, comparing bits and simple arithmetic, along with shifting bits within a byte, and all program actions are derived by the use of these simple actions. A large number of computing steps are needed to carry out an action, but because the actions can be carried out very quickly and the steps are often repetitive the speed of an program action can be very high. The important feature of any computer is that it is PROGRAMMABLE, and the development of various types of PROGRAM-MING LANGUAGE for digital computers has assisted their rapid development. Another factor is the speed at which miniaturization, particularly using ICs, has made it possible to manufacture digital computers of very large capacity (by historical standards) in a small size. The development of DRAM, in particular, has contributed very greatly to the power of modern small digital computers.

digital logic the use of the AND, NAND, OR, NOR functions on pairs of BITS and the NOT function on single bits so as to produce a result in accordance with the rules for these LOGIC actions. See also BOOLEAN ALGEBRA.

digital monitor a MONITOR (sense 1) that uses ANALOGUE signals but whose control actions for brightness, contrast, etc., are stepwise by way of press-buttons rather than continuous by way of rotating control knobs. The term was formerly used to mean a TTL MONITOR.

digital readout the output of a number directly in readable form on a SCREEN (sense 1) or other display.

Digital Research (DR) a software company that developed the CP/M operating system (OS) and was very influential in the early days of MICROCOMPUTERS.

digital signature a BINARY NUMBER used as an identification code for a device, very often for a ROM but also for video graphics cards, printers and other devices. The signature number can serve also to indicate a fault in the system from which the number is derived.

digital to analogue converter see D TO A.

digital versatile disc see DVD.

digital video interactive (DVI) a system developed by INTEL that uses data compression (see DATA COMPACTING) to store video information that can be played at full speed.

digitize to change into BINARY coded form. Any type of signal can be digitized by measuring the AMPLITUDE of the signal and converting this number into binary form. The process may have to be repeated at frequent intervals if the signal changes amplitude. Digitization is comparatively simple for signals that change comparatively slowly but needs a very high SAMPLING RATE if the signal is a rapidly changing one, such as a VIDEO signal.

digitizer a device that changes information into digital form. A VIDEO digitizer, for example, will change a TV camera image into a set of numbers that can be stored, recalled and used to display and manipulate the image. Digitizers for signals of this type make use of HARDWARE rather than SOFTWARE because of the high operating speeds that are required.

digitizing pad or **tablet** a device that can be used to supplement the MOUSE and KEYBOARD for inputs to the computer. The pad contains a MATRIX of connections that will sense the position of a pen on the surface and translate this position into X-Y coordinates in digital form. This is a useful way of tracing graphics information into the MACHINE.

DIL or **dual in line** a two-line pin arrangement used for connections to many types of ICs.

DIMM (dual inline memory module) a memory board for RAM using 168 pins. This replaces the older SIMM and allows for much larger memory units (currently up to 256 megabytes for each DIMM). A further advantage is that DIMMs, unlike SIMMs, can be used singly rather than in pairs. Modern computers specify fast memory for DIMMS so that they can be used along with a 100 MHz BUS.

DIN (Deutsche Industrie Norm) the German industry standard. In computing, this normally denotes a type of plug and socket that are used for some signal connections. Commonly encountered DIN plugs and sockets can use 3, 5 or 7 pins, and have a 'key and slot' arrangement to ensure that the plug can be inserted only one way round. The sockets were originally used in audio applications and are found only on the smaller sizes of computers. The use of flat-pin connectors with ribbon cable is more common for computer interconnections, but DIN plugs and sockets are often used on SOUND BOARDs. DIN connectors for keyboard and mouse use are now being replaced by USB connectors.

dingbats see ZAPF DINGBATS.

dinosaur any large MAINFRAME computer; see also BIG IRON.

dinosaur pen an air-conditioned computer room for a MAINFRAME machine.

diode a device that carries current in one direction only. Modern diodes are the simplest possible type of SEMICONDUCTOR device.

DIP see DUAL INLINE PACKAGE.

DIR see DIRECTORY.

direct access see DMA.

direct address a number that is part of a file and can be used as a file reference number, e.g. a works number. See also ACCESSION NUMBER; SELF-INDEXING FILE.

direct data entry the entry of data directly into a program from the keyboard, as distinct from indirectly (from a previously prepared and edited file).

direct memory access see DMA.

directory 1. or **folder** a set of files, often related, on a disk. In any modern operating system (OS), provision will be made for more than one directory to exist on a disk, particularly a HARD DRIVE. The main or ROOT DIRECTORY is the one to which ACCESS (sense 2) is gained simply by engaging the disk drive (using a command such as C:\); other directories appear in this directory, and the operating system will include commands such as CHDIR (CD) to make another directory the CURRENT (sense 2) one for use. The DIR command will then LIST all the files contained in the current directory or for any other specified directory. See also PATH; TREE (sense 1). **2.** or **catalogue of disk** a LIST of files on the disk. The form of the list should show the FILENAME, type and approximate length of each file. Under DOS, the catalogue is usually obtained by typing the command word DIR. MICROSOFT WINDOWS shows the (*folder*) list when the WINDOWS EXPLORER application is used.

directory marker the symbols used to indicate current (.) and PARENT (..) directory by using dots. MICROSOFT WINDOWS extends this system to the use of three or more dots.

directory sorting the display of files and subdirectories in some order other than the order of entry. The conventional SORT (sense 1) is by name, ascending, but sorting can be carried out using other features, such as date of creation.

directory tree a display of directories (see DIRECTORY, sense 1) along with subdirectories in a pattern that shows the relationships and PATHs between directories. See Fig. 18.

Fig. 18. **Directory tree**. The screen (sense 1) appearance of a directory (folder) tree as it appears in Windows Explorer. The root is represented by the line farthest left.

direct voice input or **voice input** or **voice recognition** the control of a computer by voice. The enormous variation in human speech patterns makes true direct voice input for anything other than a few control words exceedingly difficult to achieve, so that any system needs a 'training period' to become effective with a new user. Leading software is by IBM and DRAGON. See also SPEECH RECOGNITION; SPEECH SYNTHESIS.

DirectX a MICROSOFT programming system for games, graphics, sound and video, with three-dimensional capabilities.

dirty 1. (of data) having been altered since being loaded from disk into memory. Such data should be resaved before the application that uses it is shut down. **2.** (of an electrical signal) of poor quality because of the presence of noise and other interfering signals.

disable to put some action or device temporarily out of use.

disaster dump the recording of the state of a system, such as memory contents, data locations, etc., to a disk when a power failure or a FATAL ERROR is detected. The speed of modern processors can make it possible to save such information before an event that will end processing has time to take effect. See also UPS.

disc see CD-ROM; COMPACT DISC; DISK.

disc at once (**DAO**) a CD-R/RW writing mode that requires the whole of the data to be written in one uninterrupted session. This is possible only if all the data is initially placed in a single folder on the hard drive. See also PACKET WRITING; TRACK AT ONCE.

disconnect command a COMMAND to disconnect from a NETWORK so that your computer can be used as a standalone machine.

discrete cosine transform a mathematical method for expressing and manipulating WAVEFORMS, used in SIGNAL PROCESSING theory.

discrete Fourier transform a mathematical method used in SIGNAL PROCESSING theory.

discretionary hyphen see SOFT HYPHEN.

disk or **magnetic disk** or **disc** a magnetic method of data storage. See FLOPPY DISK; HARD DRIVE.

disk access the action of writing or reading a disk, requiring the selection of TRACK and SECTOR and the movement of the READ/WRITE HEAD.

disk-bound (of a computer system) limited in performance by a slow HARD DRIVE or INTERFACE. See also LOCAL BUS.

disk capacity the ability of a disk to contain files, in terms of the number of KILOBYTES (FLOPPY DISK) or MEGABYTES (HARD DRIVE) that can be stored. When FILE COMPRESSION is used on a disk, the figure that is used for capacity uses the sizes of the files when uncompressed. See also DRIVESPACE.

DISKCOMP a DOS command that will compare two files and report on any differences between them.

disk compaction see DEFRAGMENTATION.

disk controller a set of circuits on a printed circuit card (PCB) that will control the selection of disk TRACKs and SECTORs so that the disk access commands of the DOS can be used. See also IDE; SCSI.

DISKCOPY a DOS utility that will COPY (sense 1) the contents and arrangement of contents of a FLOPPY DISK to another blank disk of the same type.

disk crash the failure of a disk drive, usually with damage to the disk. A typical disk CRASH might be caused by a speck of grit on a disk, which becomes wedged between the disk head and the surface, causing the disk surface to be scratched. This will remove magnetic coating and result in massive loss of data. If a disk drive crashes with no damage to a disk, it is usually possible to restore normal operation. One common cause of frequent crashes, with no permanent disk damage, is operating a disk drive too close to a video MONITOR (sense 1) or any other device that emits strong magnetic radiation. The steel casing of a disk drive does not protect the drive against magnetic fields, and it can even make the drive more susceptible to such interference. When a crash occurs on a HARD DRIVE, the damage may make the whole disk unusable. Hard disk heads must be parked (see PARK) when the MACHINE is not in use to minimize the risk of damage if the machine is jolted or has to be transported, and all modern hard drives feature SELF-PARKING HEADS.

disk doctor a program that allows you to investigate directly what is stored on a disk. The disk content can be displayed in hex (see HEXA-DECIMAL) on the SCREEN (sense 1) or complete disk SECTORs can be copied into the memory. Several such programs allow you also to modify the content of a disk. This can lead to a disk becoming unreadable in normal use and is the basis of one method of COPY PROTECTION. Disk editing of this kind can also be used to recover data from a disk that has become corrupted. The use of a disk doctor may be the only way of recovering valuable data following a DISK CRASH. This type of action usually requires a program that runs under DOS because WINDOWS programs prohibit direct access to the disk, and only a few programs that run under Windows can achieve this action.

disk drive or **drive** an assembly that contains the mechanisms for spinning a disk and moving a READ/WRITE HEAD over the surface. Disk drives may contain an operating system (see IDE), often with a MICRO-PROCESSOR controller chip of its own, which ensures that the disk spins when required and that the head locates the correct part of the surface.

disk drive controller the CIRCUIT CARD that contains the INTERFACE between the memory of a computer and the DISK DRIVE of the older type of PERSONAL COMPUTER. The controller must convert the digital signals from memory into a form that can be recorded magnetically on a disk. The system has been superseded by the use of the IDE type of drive. See also ADVANCED RUN LENGTH LIMITED; MODIFIED FREQUENCY MODULATION; LOCAL BUS.

disk duplexing or **disk mirroring** the use of more than one HARD DRIVE to contain the same data, providing more security against accidental loss of data. See also RAID.

diskette a term, not common now, once used to distinguish a FLOPPY DISK or other replaceable disk from a fixed or HARD DRIVE.

disk farm a large array of DISK DRIVES. See also RAID.

disk-filing system see DFS.

diskless workstation a computer that contains no DISK DRIVE, hard or floppy, and operates only through a NETWORK. It is impossible to introduce a VIRUS into the network from such a machine.

disk map a LIST of data locations on a disk in terms of TRACK and SECTOR positions.

disk mirroring a technique for protecting against loss of data by writing data to more than one HARD DRIVE. See also RAID.

disk-operating system see DOS.

disk optimizer a UTILITY program for carrying out DEFRAGMENTATION.

disk pack see CARTRIDGE DISK.

display the SCREEN (sense 1) or VDU system that is controlled by circuits on a DISPLAY ADAPTER inside the computer.

display adapter or **display standard** a circuit on a card contained inside the computer that controls the VDU and can determine the RESOLUTION of GRAPHICS displays. See also CGA CARD; EGA; GRAPHICS ADAPTER; SVGA; VGA.

display font a form of FONT, elaborate and flamboyant in design, that is used to gain attention, as used in posters. Display fonts are unsuited to anything other than a few words as they are often tiring to read. See also SWASH.

display standard see DISPLAY ADAPTER.

display terminal see VDU.

distortion a change of the shape of a signal. See DEGRADATION.

distributed database a DATABASE system in which the data is held on several disks on different interconnected computers. One method of implementing such a database is REPLICATION, another is FRAGMENTATION (sense 2), in which parts of the database are stored at different sites. Combinations of replication and fragmentation can also be used.

distributed memory a memory system used for PARALLEL PROCESSING so that each processor can make use of fast memory that is not shared by others. In addition, each processor can use shared memory by way of a controlling NETWORK.

distributed system a collection of devices that use ARTIFICIAL INTELLIGENCE and act as if they were one device.

distributive law the law governing the use of BRACKETS in an EXPRESSION used, for example, in a WORKSHEET. The form of the law is that $A(B+C)=AB + AC$, and it can be applied either in simple arithmetic or in BOOLEAN ALGEBRA.

dither a quantity generated at random and added to another quantity to provide variation, usually applied to a noise signal added to the brightness of each PIXEL of a graphics image. It can provide a better GREY SCALE or improve colour rendering or the overall shape of an image that has been resized (see RESIZING). It is also applied to noise added to the DIGITAL signal of a COMPACT DISC to avoid a form of distortion on small-amplitude signals.

Ditto drive a form of STREAMER (tape drive) for BACKUP purposes, usually connected through the FLOPPY DISK data cable.

DIV an OPERATOR used in some SPREADSHEETs for INTEGER division. The result of using, for example, 7 DIV 2 would be 3, the integer result. Some spreadsheets use the BACKSLASH for this purpose. See also MOD.

DLL (dynamic link library) a set of program routines that can be called into use and then discarded, as required, by other programs. The value of using DLLs is that one routine or set of routines can then be used by a number of programs, correspondingly reducing the size of each of the programs. The risk, however, is that a program will install a DLL for its own use which replaces another of the same name and thus causes some other program to CRASH (sense 2).

DMA (direct memory access) a system for transferring data rapidly between the MEMORY and a PERIPHERAL, such as a disk drive, without requiring each BYTE to be read into the MICROPROCESSOR and then subsequently written. Once a DMA action has been set up by the microprocessor, it proceeds automatically using a DEDICATED DMA chip.

DML see DATA MANIPULATION LANGUAGE.

document a file of text or number data, such as text produced by and read by a WORD PROCESSOR, EDITOR or a DTP program, or a WORKSHEET produced by a SPREADSHEET program.

document architecture the design of a DTP document. This must take account of HEADER (sense 1), FOOTER, the use of HEADINGs and subheadings, FONTs, GRAPHICS and other features of the document so as to produce pages that are pleasing to the eye, avoiding the excessive use of different fonts and STYLEs (sense 2).

document assembly the creation of pages by DTP methods, using either a DTP program or a WORD PROCESSOR. This will involve inserting GRAPHICS into pages, possibly replacing PLACEHOLDERS, adjusting the positions of TEXT and graphics to avoid gaps, or the placing of graphics ahead of the text that refers to them and flowing in text to fill the remaining spaces until the complete document is ready for printing.

documentation the paperwork that accompanies a piece of HARDWARE or SOFTWARE. When this paperwork has been prepared by professional authors, it is clear, comprehensive and allows you to find quickly and easily for yourself what to do in order to get the best from the computer or the program. Only too often, however, the documentation is prepared too early in the course of the design of the project and is written by engineers. As authors, engineers have the advantage of knowing everything about the system but the disadvantage of believing that nothing needs to be explained to the user. Documentation of hardware is often sparse, particularly when a computer is a CLONE of a well-known design, but the documentation for larger computers should be extensive and accompanied by a thorough explanation of any switches, JUMPERs or upgrade sockets used in the machine and illustrations of how the settings should be altered. Even if a machine is a clone, it cannot be assumed that no documentation is needed because even such a simple act as increasing the memory capacity of a machine can be impossible if there is no indication of what alterations are needed on the MOTHER-BOARD. Most users, however, are more concerned with software, and documentation for both operating system (OS) and each APPLICATIONS PACKAGE must be thorough. The documentation should consist of a detailed account of the machine requirements (speed, disk capacity, memory size) along with how the program should be installed, with notes on any difficulties found with some types of machines. This should be followed by an outline of what the program can achieve and an alphabetical list of COMMANDs and their effects.

In the past, software documentation has attempted to teach the user how to use the program, but this is now giving way to the approach outlined above, leaving third party authors to write tutorial books. This reduces the burden of documentation to some extent and allows the manufacturer to concentrate on describing the commands in detail, making the documentation much easier to use as a reference. The most recent undesirable trend is to dispense as far as possible with any printed documentation, forcing the user to rely on HELP (sense 1) pages on the SCREEN (sense 1). This has encouraged the use of inappropriate books bought from the USA and not adapted for use with the UK versions of application programs.

document base font the FONT that is used for most of the text of a DOCUMENT and is the DEFAULT FONT.

document comparison utility a UTILITY program that will compare two DOCUMENT files and report on differences. See also COMP; FC.

document file icon a distinctive ICON that WINDOWS uses to identify DOCUMENT files (as distinct from program files) in a DIRECTORY (sense 1) or FOLDER.

document font a FONT used for a DOCUMENT or part of a document that is not the DEFAULT FONT for the WORD PROCESSOR or DTP program; see BASE FONT. A word processor will normally save a document font along with the document.

document format the arrangement of each page for a DOCUMENT, covering margins, page numbering, headers and footers, use of columns, styles, etc.

document image processing the use of a SCANNER to convert printed or typed pages into WORD PROCESSOR files. This allows the DOCUMENTs to be stored in the more compact form of a file rather than as bulky paper

document reader a method of reading by computer. This is a form of optical character reader (OCR, sense 1) that can deal, often automatically, with complete documents, translating each printed character into ASCII code and transmitting this to the computer. Document readers can never produce ASCII code that is completely free from errors, but, given a good clean manuscript, the results need very little correction, often only a SPELLCHECK.

document window a WINDOW used by a WORD PROCESSOR program to display a DOCUMENT. Most modern word processors allow more than one document to be displayed, each document in its own window.

dollar sign the $ sign, used in a WORKSHEET to indicate an ABSOLUTE CELL REFERENCE.

domain in INTERNET usage, a set of computers that use a common suffix, the DOMAIN NAME, for their HOSTNAME.

domain address the name of an INTERNET HOST.

domain name an IDENTIFIER used on the INTERNET in place of the number system (see ADDRESS, sense 2) that is the true method of location. A domain name consists of three parts, one of which is a COUNTRY CODE and another a TYPE CODE. For example, a government office in the UK would use the codes gov.uk and a university in New Zealand would use ac.nz for these parts of a domain name. The first part of the domain name is intended to act as a mnemonic for the HOST and can consist of more than one part.

dongle a CHIP, CARTRIDGE (sense 1) or other form of circuit that must be plugged into a computer in order to permit a program to be run; a form of protection against PIRACY. The system has almost died out of use because of the unwelcome interactions that were sometimes experienced with other programs along with the constant risk of total loss of data if the dongle ceased to recognize the program correctly.

dongle disk a FLOPPY DISK that must be inserted before some SOFTWARE will run.

doorstop obsolete equipment, particularly early MICROCOMPUTERs, that are shaped suitably, such as the Sinclair Spectrum.

door switch a switch used in a FLOPPY DISK drive to detect when a disk has been inserted and the drive door shut. See also CHANGE-LINE SUPPORT.

dormant code a code used in a WORD PROCESSOR or DTP program. A dormant code normally does nothing but will be converted into active form when the page layout changes.

DOS (disk-operating system) the SOFTWARE that carries out the actions of controlling the DISK DRIVE or drives, selecting correct TRACKs and SECTORs and avoiding accidental CORRUPTION. Disk operating systems such as MS-DOS and LINUX offer a considerable number of 'utilities' in addition to the actions of disk-drive control so that the DOS actions are part of an overall operating system (OS). The use of WINDOWS follows this to a logical conclusion by taking total command of all aspects of the computer system.

DOSHELP a program available from DOS to provide definitions and examples of the use of DOS COMMAND words.

DOSKEY a DOS utility that enhances the use of the KEYBOARD for DOS commands, allowing, for example, a COMMAND to be recalled.

DOS prompt the reminder message, usually the drive letter, such as C:>, used by DOS to mean that the system is waiting for a COMMAND.

DOS-protected mode interface the system incorporated into WINDOWS through the HIMEM.SYS DRIVER that allows a MS-DOS program to run along with Windows.

DOSSHELL a program that was packaged with MS-DOS versions 5.0 to 6.0. DOSSHELL allows DOS programs to be started by clicking (see CLICK, sense 1) and also permits TASK SWITCHING along with easier file commands. It was at one time an alternative to WINDOWS for the user who wished to use only DOS programs and had only the 640 kilobytes of BASE MEMORY installed.

dot command a COMMAND that consists of a full stop followed by alphabetical characters, used in some older types of WORD PROCESSOR programs and EDITORS for EMBEDDED COMMANDS and also for some DATABASE programs. More modern word processor programs use a system of hidden codes, often located at the end of each paragraph.

dot leader a line of dots produced in a WORD PROCESSOR. The dot leader option allows a line of dots to be produced automatically between the end of a word and the next tab position when the TAB KEY is pressed. This is used mainly in contents lists.

dot-matrix a method of making patterns visible, particularly for characters on SCREEN (sense 1) or on paper. A dot-matrix screen display allows a rectangle of closely spaced dots, often 9 across by 15 deep, to be controlled for each character. By lighting a pattern of dots, a character shape is displayed. Screen displays are always of the dot-matrix type, but alternative methods of printing on paper are available. See also CHARACTER BLOCK; INKJET PRINTER; LASER PRINTER; MATRIX PRINTER.

dot-matrix printer see MATRIX PRINTER.

dot notation 1. a way of expressing a FIELD (sense 2) of a RECORD (sense 1). This can be used in a DATABASE program as a way of identifying VARIABLES. For example, the names CUSTOMER.NAME, CUSTOMER.ADDRESS and CUSTOMER.PHONE identify different fields of a record called CUSTOMER. **2.** the method of using four numbers separated by the dot character as an ISP ADDRESS.

dot pitch the distance between two adjacent dots of the same colour on a MONITOR (sense 1) SCREEN. This is usually set at 0.28 mm for 14-inch monitor screens. A smaller dot pitch is desirable if high RESOLUTION displays (such as 1024 x 768) are to be used, although the 0.28-mm dot pitch is very satisfactory for 17-inch and larger screens.

dot prompt a form of PROMPT used in DBASE as an invitation to type a COMMAND.

dots per inch see DPI.

double-click a MOUSE action used for GUI programs. The CURSOR or POINTER (sense 1) is placed over a FILENAME or ICON and the mouse BUTTON is clicked (see CLICK, sense 1) twice in rapid succession to produce an added effect. For example, if the cursor is over a program file, a single click will SELECT the file, but a double-click will RUN (sense 2) the program. The double-click action is used to a much lesser extent in Microsoft WINDOWS 98 onwards because these versions permit the option of selecting by placing the pointer and activation with a single click.

double-density (DD) a disk-recording system for old PC models in which the number of BYTES recorded per SECTOR of disk is double the (old) normal amount, typically 512 bytes per sector in place of 256. Double-density recording obviously doubles the storage capacity of a disk but requires a higher standard of head alignment, cleanliness and smoothness of disk surface. For the PERSONAL COMPUTER, a double-density disk now means a 3.5-inch disk that holds only 720 kilobytes of data as opposed to the 1.4 megabytes stored by a HIGH-DENSITY (HD) disk.

double-density double-sided see DDDS.

double dot see DOUBLE PERIOD.

double-ended queue a form of QUEUE (sense 1) structure in which new data items can be added to either end of the queue.

double period or **double dot** the typed symbol used in MS-DOS to indicate a PARENT DIRECTORY. For example, the command CD.. will change from the current directory to the parent directory, making this parent directory current.

double precision a number that has been stored in a BINARY form and that corresponds to a DENARY precision of 14 significant figures. This is seldom necessary for business calculations, but for important scientific or engineering data used in a WORKSHEET or DATABASE, double precision may be essential. See also SINGLE PRECISION.

double-quote see INVERTED COMMAS.

double-sided disk a disk with usable recording surfaces on each side for disk drives that have two READ/WRITE HEADs, one on each side of the disk. This is the standard form of disk used in PERSONAL COMPUTERS, and single-sided disks are obsolete. See also FLOPPY DISK.

double-sided publication a DTP publication intended to use both sides of each page. This requires more care about the page numbering (odd numbers on the right-hand page) and margins (wide margin to the binding side). See also BIND.

DoubleSpace a MICROSOFT system for compressing data into a disk file, later superseded by DRIVESPACE.

double word or **dword** data that uses 4 BYTES. A WORD (sense 2) means 2 bytes, equal to 16 BITS, hence a double word is 4 bytes, 32 bits. The term is used in particular on 16-bit and 32-bit processors, and the use of dword data is normal with MICROSOFT WINDOWS.

doughnut chart a form of PIE CHART in which more than one set of data can be displayed, each as shading in a ring.

down (of a computer or network system) not working.

download to transfer data to or from a computer along a line, which may be a telephone line, a radio link, a NETWORK or any other type of link. See also MODEM.

downloadable font a FONT that can be transferred to the memory of a PRINTER from a computer rather than being built into the printer or plugged in as a cartridge. See also DTP; TRUETYPE.

download charges fees payable to a WEB SITE for providing files by way of FTP to a remote computer.

downsizing the process of reducing the size of a program so that it can be used on a computer with less memory and disk space than the one for which the program was developed. This is often achieved simply by omitting BELLS AND WHISTLES.

down time the time during which a computer is out of action for repair or maintenance. One of the advantages of MICROCOMPUTERs is that they often have zero down time during their useful life. Another advantage is that a microcomputer is easily replaceable, so that a computer that is down can be replaced by a spare, with little loss of time. For a large computer system, down time can represent an enormous loss of income, and the user will normally maintain both an insurance policy and a maintenance contract to offset these losses.

downward compatibility the ability of a complex system to work along with a simple one. If a large computer in an office can use a program that is also usable by a small portable machine, the program is said to have 'downward compatibility'. This allows data to be handled by both systems and passed between them. Compare UPWARD COMPATIBILITY.

dp see DATA PROCESSING.

dpi (dots per inch) a measure of the RESOLUTION of a PRINTER or SCANNER. Monitors usually quote the overall number of dots, such as 800 x 600, because the same dot structure can be used on MONITOR (sense 1) screens of very different sizes.

DR see DIGITAL RESEARCH.

draft a rough form of a DOCUMENT, applied to a fast DOT-MATRIX printout or to an uncorrected version.

draft mode a PRINTER mode available on dot-MATRIX PRINTERs, both impact and INKJET. This prints faster but with a poor letter shape.

drag to move a MOUSE with the mouse BUTTON held down. This, for many programs, has the effect of allowing a graphics IMAGE (sense 2) to be moved across the SCREEN (sense 1), and the action is also used for RESIZING, moving, cropping, rotating and other graphics actions.

drag-and-drop editing the process of CUT and PASTE, which uses MOUSE dragging (see DRAG). The mouse is dragged over the phrase with the BUTTON held down to select the phrase. Clicking and dragging again then allows the selected portion to be moved to any other part of the DOCUMENT. Some programs will allow drag and drop between two documents in separate windows.

DRAM (dynamic ramdom access memory) the predominant form of RAM memory. This is a form of construction of memory that is very cheap and comparatively simple to manufacture in very large memory sizes. Its disadvantage is that the data is retained for only a very short time unless a 'refreshing' pulse is applied to the memory at intervals of, typically, one thousandth of a second. See also BANKED MEMORY.

draw program a program that allows drawings to be made, usually using VECTOR methods. See also PAINT PROGRAM.

draw tool an ICON or MENU item for drawing a specific shape, such as a straight line, arc, rectangle, etc. The tool is selected, and the shape created by dragging (see DRAG) the MOUSE.

drive see DISK DRIVE.

drive bay the slot within the casing of a computer into which a DISK DRIVE or CD-ROM drive can be inserted.

drive designator or **drive letter** the letter, usually A:, B: or C:, used to indicate a DISK DRIVE. The letters A and B are reserved for FLOPPY DRIVES; C onwards for HARD DRIVE and CD-ROM drives.

drive door the front flap covering a FLOPPY DISK drive. Closing this flap secures the disk in the drive and signals that the disk is ready by way of the DOOR SWITCH. See also CHANGE-LINE SUPPORT.

drive letter see DRIVE DESIGNATOR.

driver a program routine that is used to carry out some interfacing action (see INTERFACE). For example, a PRINTER DRIVER is the routine that is used to control the feeding of signals to a PRINTER. If faulty action of a peripheral is a problem, a new driver may be the answer. The MICROSOFT WINDOWS operating system contains drivers for a very large range of hardware devices, but in some cases the manufacturer of a device may need to supply the driver. See also PNP.

DriveSpace the MICROSOFT system for file compression (see COMPRESSED FILE). When DriveSpace is installed, files are compressed before being saved to the HARD DRIVE and decompressed when being loaded from the drive. Since each file takes up less space on the drive than it would if not compressed, the effective capacity of the drive is increased. Although some files cannot be compressed as much as others, on average, the effective capacity of a drive is doubled in this way. FLOPPY DISKs can also benefit from using DriveSpace. DriveSpace-3, available with the Microsoft-Plus package, increases the compression and allows selected types of files to be more tightly compressed if they are not in frequent use. The availability of low-cost high-capacity hard drives has made the system obsolete.

drop cap an upper-case letter at the start of a paragraph that is larger than normal and extends below the BASE LINE of the first line of text.

drop-down list box a box containing a list of MENU items that drops from a MENU line when the main menu item is clicked (see CLICK, sense 1).

drop-down menu a menu WINDOW that appears over an existing SCREEN (sense 1) view starting at the top of the screen. See also PULL-DOWN MENU.

drop-in a piece of dirt adhering to a disk or tape surface. This will prevent recording on that part of the surface, so corrupting the recording. See also DROPOUT.

dropout a type of failure of magnetic recording MEDIUM (sense 1). A dropout on a tape or disk denotes a small piece of material that does not magnetize correctly. Since no signals can be recorded on a dropout, this can lead to loss of data. Digital tape for BACKUP use is normally certified as being free from dropouts. On disks, if the dropout exists when a disk is new, it will be detected during formatting and the faulty portions will not be used. A dropout that develops later, however, will nearly always lead to loss of data, although recovery is sometimes possible using a DISK-DOCTOR program. The possibility of dropouts makes it important to keep backups of all data and to avoid the use of programs that cannot be backed up because of COPY PROTECTION. See also DROP-IN.

drop shadow a shaded outline placed slightly offset from an image to give the illusion of solidity.

drum the central working part of a LASER PRINTER or photocopier. The drum is made from a photoconductive material, one that conducts electricity when exposed to light. In operation, the revolving drum is charged overall and then selectively discharged by scanning its surface with a LASER beam, making the drum conduct away the charge. The charge pattern remaining will pick up TONER from a cartridge, and this is transferred to paper when the paper is fed through. The toner is then melted on to the paper to fix it in place, the drum is scraped clean, and another page can be printed. On printers that use the HEWLETT-PACKARD engine, the drum and other working parts are part of a toner cartridge, so all important parts that are likely to wear out or become dirty are renewed when the cartridge is renewed.

drunk mouse problem inability to make the screen POINTER (sense 1) move smoothly when the MOUSE is moved. This is caused by dirty rollers in the mouse, less commonly by dirt on the ball of the mouse.

DSR see DATA SET READY.

DTE see DATA TERMINAL EQUIPMENT.

D to A converter HARDWARE that will decode digitized (see DIGITIZE) signals, so that a digital signal at the input will produce a corresponding ANALOGUE signal at the output. This is an essential part of an audio COMPACT DISC player. See also A TO D.

DTP (desktop publishing) a method of producing MASTER PAGES for a book, newspaper or leaflet. The DTP program requires a considerable amount of main memory and disk space, since it will require the use of FONT files that describe the appearance of letters, digits and punctuation marks for use on a LASER PRINTER or INKJET PRINTER. A DTP program was once distinguished from a WORD PROCESSOR by being able to work with a mixture of TEXT and GRAPHICS and the ability to use a wide range of font sizes and types. The distinction, however, is not a static one, and several word processors, notably WORDPERFECT, Lotus AMIPRO and MICROSOFT WORD, have very considerable graphics abilities and can be used to make camera-ready COPY (sense 3). These word processors may even be preferred for setting long documents such as textbooks or novels. When the DTP program is started, text and graphics can be imported from other SOFTWARE or text can be typed directly and graphics imported. It is always an advantage to import text from a good word processor because this allows the use of a SPELLCHECKER and a THESAURUS that will not necessarily be available on the DTP program. The SCREEN (sense 1) arrangement provides, as far as is possible, for a wysiwyg (see WORD PROCESSOR) display, although this generally involves showing the page in a very small scale with the lettering GREEKED. This page can be examined in a magnified view to check text, if necessary, and the page view is enough to show how text and graphics are laid out. Graphics images can be imported from any of the standard packages, using file types such as PCX or TIF, and when the graphics image is placed on the page, text can be forced to flow round the image so that the text does not cover the image nor the image cover the text. The DTP program will provide for RESIZING or CROPPING the image and for moving its position, with the text being rearranged so as to flow around the image. Many DTP packages also provide for a limited graphics capability of their own, such as drawing straight lines, boxes and circles in a range of line thicknesses and styles. When the pages of print have been composed, they can be saved to disk and printed on an inkjet or laser printer. Alternatively, an output file of POSTSCRIPT can be created for use by a printing house.

D-type connector a form of 25-pin connector that was used originally for SERIAL INTERFACE use and is also used for the printer connection of IBM PERSONAL COMPUTERS and their CLONES and COMPATIBLE machines.

dual in line see DIL.

Dual Inline Memory Module see DIMM.

dual-inline package (DIP) a form of packaging used for IC chips, in which the casing is connected by way of two lines of pins.

dual ported (of memory, particularly VIDEO RAM) using two access buses (see BUS) so that it can be written and read simultaneously.

dual-tone multifrequency the touch-tone system of dialling on a telephone by using sound tones.

dual Y-axis graph a form of GRAPH in which two quantities are plotted on the same axes using different scales for the sizes of the quantities.

dumb terminal a TERMINAL with no processing ability. A dumb terminal allows VDU output from a computer and keyboard input but possesses no processing ability apart from the ability to send and receive signals. Compare INTELLIGENT TERMINAL.

dummy text PLACEHOLDER text in a DTP or WORD PROCESSOR document. The dummy text indicates page layout and can be used to print a sample. The text is often in Latin to avoid confusion with the real text.

dump to RECORD (sense 2) a program or data on tape or disk.

dump and restart a procedure for allowing a computer to recover after a CRASH (sense 1). The program is constructed with *dump points* at which the content of memory and the state of peripherals will be saved in a *dump file* on disk. If the program fails, the data in the last-used dump point will be recovered from the disk and used to restore the state of the machine. See also CHECKPOINT.

DUN see DIALUP NETWORKING.

duplex a system of two-way transmission of data. See FULL-DUPLEX; HALF-DUPLEX; SIMPLEX.

duplex printer a PRINTER that can print both sides of a paper sheet. See also RECTO; VERSO.

duplication or **replication** a SPREADSHEET action that copies a FORMULA from one CELL (sense 1) to others, modifying the formula to suit each different cell.

DV cartridge a plug-in CARTRIDGE (sense 1) that is needed to play some types of games.

DVD (digital versatile disc) a development of the COMPACT DISC that allows very much greater storage capacity (up to 17 gigabytes). A DVD drive is now a standard part of a computer system and can read either DVD or conventional compact discs. Read-write DVD drives are more expensive but are capable of storing large quantities of data in times that are short compared to tape-based BACKUP systems. The DVD is also intended as a medium for audio and video recording, with a domestic DVD machine eventually replacing the familiar VCR.

DVI see DIGITAL VIDEO INTERACTIVE.

Dvorak keyboard a non-QWERTY type of KEY (sense 1) arrangement. The normal arrangement of typewriter keys is very inefficient and was originally designed to force typists to operate slowly, so avoiding jamming the type bars of early machines. The reason for the layout has long since disappeared, but because it had become standardized it remains in use despite all its faults. The Dvorak keyboard, like the MALTRON, is an attempt to design a keyboard that is easier and much faster to use, with less training. These keyboards can be specified for a few machines to special order or as a later add-on. See also MICROSOFT NATURAL KEYBOARD.

dword see DOUBLE WORD.

DXF file a standard form of file for interchanging CAD information. The DXF file was originated by AUTODESK and used in AUTOCAD and AUTOS-KETCH, and it can be read by most DTP and WORD-PROCESSOR software.

dye-sublimation printer a form of colour PRINTER that produces bright images of excellent quality (at a high price) using ink vaporization colour-mixing methods.

dynamic allocation the ALLOCATION (sense 1) of memory as and when required. This is a system of allocation of memory for storage of data that does not use fixed memory locations. Dynamic allocation is particularly needed for a MULTITASKING system, when the major part of the memory may be needed for the currently running program and memory has to be re-allocated each time a program is switched.

dynamic data exchange (DDE) a method of exchanging information between files, now superseded by OLE.

dynamic link a system of referring to files so that changes are automatically made. For example, if a picture file is linked into a WORD (sense 1) document in this way, any changes made to the picture when it is edited in a suitable program will appear in the version inside the word document next time the document is opened.

dynamic link library see DLL.

dynamic object any OBJECT that is embedded (see EMBEDDING) or linked (see LINK) into a document and can be edited from within the document, usually by double-clicking (see DOUBLE-CLICK).

dynamic random access memory see DRAM.

dynamic routing see ADAPTIVE ROUTING.

dynaset a collection of data that has resulted from a QUERY. For example, MICROSOFT ACCESS will display a dynaset that is a tabular view of the data that the query has collected. This dynaset can be edited, and changes that are made in this way will alter the data in the tables that have provided the data.

EAN see BAR CODE.

EAPROM (electrically alterable programmable read-only memory) a form of PROM that can be rewritten by altering the electrical voltage applied to a pin and then writing data. This type of PROM was used in 56-kilobyte MODEMS to allow reprogramming to the V90 standard.

EAROM (electrically alterable read-only memory) see EEPROM.

Easter egg a message or image that is coded into a program but which can be viewed only by using some KEY (sense 1) combination that is normally unused.

EASY-PC a program devised and sold in the UK by Number One Systems Ltd that allows electronics printed circuit board (PCB) layouts to be designed. See also COMPUTER-AIDED ENGINEERING.

EBCDIC (extended binary coded decimal interchange) a code that uses all 8 BITS in each BYTE, unlike ASCII which uses only 7 bits. The EBCDIC code can be used for transmitting data from one computer to another. It is not in general use for small computers but is used in some COMMUNICATIONS equipment.

ecash the electronic transfer of money through the INTERNET or by EMAIL. This requires good SECURITY procedures along with the support of banks and shops and has not so far replaced the more common methods of passing on credit card details. The euro is a form of ecash until coins and notes have been distributed.

echo 1. the appearance on the VDU of the character corresponding to the KEY (sense 1) pressed on the keyboard. This sometimes implies that if you are using your computer to communicate with another one, each character that you type will be displayed twice because the remote computer is also echoing back over the line. See ECHO CHECK. **2. (ECHO)** a COMMAND used in MS-DOS BATCH FILES. ECHO OFF is used to suppress the appearance of batch commands on SCREEN (sense 1), and ECHO followed by a phrase will print that phrase on screen when the LINE (sense 4) is executed. Later versions of MS-DOS allow the use of @ECHO OFF to suppress the appearance of even the ECHO OFF command.

echo cancellation a SOFTWARE routine that will remove signal echoes on a telephone or other transmission line.

echo check the checking on SCREEN (sense 1) of the accuracy of data transmission. Each transmitted character is returned ('echoed') to be displayed on the sending terminal so that any CORRUPTION that has been caused by the transmission system will be visible to the sender as well as to the receiver. See ECHO.

ECL (emitter-coupled logic) a method of forming digital circuits that operate at very high speed.

e-commerce or **electronic commerce** the use of NETWORKs, including the INTERNET, as a way of transacting business. This includes buying and selling, mail, conferencing and transfer of funds.

ECP (enhanced capabilities port) a form of parallel (printer) port that allows fast two-way communication, used by printers that are totally controlled by software in the computer. The specification is laid out in the standard IEEE-1284, so that connecting cables for modern printers are often described as IEEE-1284 cables. See also EPP.

edge card a CIRCUIT CARD that is fitted with an EDGE CONNECTOR. An edge card offers a cheap, simple and convenient way of adding facilities (such as additional graphics capabilities, extra memory, communications facilities) to a computer. A computer that can use extra edge cards is almost infinitely expandable and does not readily become out of date. See also MOTHERBOARD; OPEN ARCHITECTURE.

edge connector a way of making contact to an EDGE CARD. The chips of a computer system are mounted on CIRCUIT BOARDs from which connections have to be made to other boards and to the keyboard and other devices. The cheapest way of making these connections is to shape part of the board like a tongue and arrange connecting strips on it, often on each side. A suitable plug can then grip the board and make connection. These connections can be unreliable, are fragile and can break if the plug is disconnected and reconnected too often. A much better method makes use of sockets soldered to the board which can be replaced if they make poor contacts. Edge connectors are satisfactory if they are used for edge cards, which are seldom removed and which can be supported on a MOTHERBOARD.

edge detection a technique used in some advanced graphics programs such as CORELDRAW. Edge detection allows an outline to be produced from a more elaborate BITMAP image, such as a scanned (see SCANNER) photograph, so that photographic images can be converted into line drawings.

EDI see ELECTRONIC DATA INTERCHANGE.

edit to change, delete or amend text. The old LINE EDITING system has now been replaced by SCREEN (sense 1) editing. This is a more versatile system in which anything that appears on the screen can be edited simply by moving the CURSOR to the required place and typing. Typing causes insertion, and a DELETE (sens 1) key is used if text is to be removed. Pressing the RETURN or ENTER key terminates line editing but a MENU command is normally used to terminate screen editing.

edit key a KEY (sense 1), often one of the FUNCTION KEYS, that carries out an editing action or starts an EDITOR program running.

edit mode a mode available in programs to allow the data to be altered.

For example, the contents of a CELL in a WORKSHEET can be changed or the amount of a transaction in an ACCOUNTING PACKAGE.

editor a program that load, edits and saves text files. A WORD PROCESSOR consists of a text editor and a print FORMATTER (sense 2). The editor portion is concerned with the entry, deletion, amendment and repositioning of words in the text. This is the portion of the word processor that is being used until the text is recorded on disk or printed out. Editors for UTILITY use and for use with a PROGRAMMING LANGUAGE can be simpler than the editing portion of a word processor, although some programmers' editors are very comprehensive in their facilities. The usual requirement is to prepare short pieces of text or lines of program commands, and one important requirement is that text shall be recorded on disk in ASCII codes only. Word processors generally add text formatting codes that are unacceptable for text editing work – most word processors permit saving files in text mode, described as *non-document*, ASCII or DOS mode. The programming editor should in addition allow simple insertion, deletion and copying actions, along with BLOCK (sense 2) SEARCH AND REPLACE.

edit window a SCREEN (sense 1) WINDOW that appears with an EDITOR program running in order to carry out an editing action, often while another program is suspended in another window. See also NOTEPAD; WORDPAD; WRITE.

EDO (extended data output) a memory system for use with a PCI BUS structure that allows faster use of DRAM. This type of system is always used along with fast DIMM memory.

EDO DRAM (extended data output dynamic random access memory) a form of DRAM that allows faster access and so can be used with the faster processors that were developed in the late 1990s.

EDP (electronic data processing) the main action of all DIGITAL COMPUTERs. It consists of the fundamental actions of data entry, storage, rearrangement and display.

edutainment SOFTWARE, usually supplied on CD-ROM, that combines education with entertainment.

EEMS (extended expanded memory system) a standard form of memory expansion, now obsolete, for the IBM PC-XT and AT computers and older CLONE or COMPATIBLE machines. This is of the EXPANDED MEMORY type that can be used by some old DOS programs, with memory addressed in 64-kilobyte blocks. Modern WINDOWS programs use EXTENDED MEMORY, which is a different system that addresses the memory as a continuous whole. See also LIM.

EEPROM (electrically erasable programmable read-only memory) a form of PROM that can be erased by an electrical signal rather than by ultraviolet light.

effective time the time for which a piece of equipment operates. This is not necessarily equal to the time for which the equipment is switched on. On computers that are fitted with HARD DRIVES, these drives spin continually but are powered down by power-saving systems when not in use. Where FLOPPY DRIVES are used, the drives spin only when data is being read or written. The effective time might, for example, be recorded by a clock that is driven by the power supply to the disk drives. The reading of time from this clock would then be used to decide when maintenance of the disk drives was needed. Effective time measurement is also used for other mechanical items, such as cooling fans, but not generally for equipment that uses only SEMICONDUCTOR electronics, since their life is indefinite and maintenance negligible.

EFT (electronic funds transfer) the use of computers to transfer cash credits or debits between banks. See also BACS.

EFTPOS (electronic funds transfer at point of sale) the use in a shop of a machine that can debit a customer's account directly, usually by way of a debit card.

EGA (enhanced graphics board) an obsolete form of GRAPHICS ADAPTER that offers higher RESOLUTION and more colours for the PERSONAL COMPUTER than the older CGA CARD. See also VGA.

egosurfing searching the World Wide Web (WWW) for any mention of your own name.

EIA a form of software handshaking (see HANDSHAKE), now superseded by the use of XON and XOFF.

EIDE (extended IDE) a form of IDE controller for a HARD DRIVE that allows faster operation, achieving speeds comparable with SCSI controllers. In addition, EIDE controllers can make use of hard drives of more than 528 megabytes and can handle more than one such drive or CD-ROM drive.

eighty-column screen display a SCREEN (sense 1) display that allows up to 80 characters per screen or printer line. This is the normal display of the older PERSONAL COMPUTER system, although DOS permits the use of commands that will switch to 40-column displays. Much higher resolution figures are now common.

eighty-track disk a disk that has been formatted to use 80 rather than 132 tracks of data (see FORMAT, sense 3). This is the format used for the old DOUBLE-DENSITY 3.5-inch PC disk.

EINO see GIGO.

EISA 1. (extended ISA) an enhanced version of the old AT BUS design, later known as industry-standard architecture (ISA), a form of BUS system for PERSONAL COMPUTERS using the 80386, 80486 and later chips which maintains compatibility with CIRCUIT CARDS using the older AT bus structure. See also MICRO CHANNEL ARCHITECTURE. **2.** abbreviation for Electronics Industry Standards Association.

elastic banding or **rubber banding** the movement of a line drawn from a specified point on the SCREEN (sense 1) to another point. This second point can be moved around the screen by using the CURSOR-CONTROL KEYS or a MOUSE (see DRAG), and the line length will expand or contract as if the line were made of elastic material. This makes the alteration of diagrams very much easier than it would be if lines had to be rubbed out and redrawn, so elastic banding is much used in CAD packages. See Fig. 19.

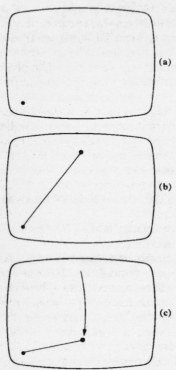

Fig. 19. **Elastic banding**. (a) a point is selected on the screen. (b) when a new point is selected, a line is automatically drawn between this and the first point. (c) as the new point is moved, the line is continually redrawn, giving the appearance of a line that can expand and contract like an elastic band.

elastic buffer a BUFFER that can hold a variable amount of data. Most computer systems use buffers of fixed size, such as 256 or 512 BYTES. The use of an elastic buffer requires an operating system (OS) that can ensure that the buffer does not expand to an extent that will cause overwriting of other data in the memory.

electrically alterable programmable read-only memory see EAPROM.

electrically erasable programmable read-only memory see EEPROM.

electromagnetic compatibility (EMC) a measure of the immunity of

HARDWARE to ELECTROMAGNETIC INTERFERENCE and also of the permitted amount of interference that hardware is permitted to emit during operation.

electromagnetic interference the presence of unwanted ELECTROMAGNETIC RADIATION that can be picked up by circuits in a computer, causing CORRUPTION of data.

electromagnetic radiation a wave of electric and magnetic field that carries energy and can be transmitted through space. All radio waves are of this type, along with visible light, infrared and ultraviolet, X-rays and others.

electromigration movement of atoms within a crystal. This can cause damage to IC chips when they are operated at temperatures exceeding 100°C.

electron the negatively charged (see CHARGE) component of an ATOM, partly or mainly responsible for electric current conduction in metals.

electron gun the part of a CRT in which electrons are released, accelerated and focused into a BEAM (sense 1).

electronic commerce see E-COMMERCE.

electronic data interchange (EDI) a standardized system for exchanging documents in electronic form between computer systems, using telephone or other lines.

electronic data processing see EDP.

electronic funds transfer see EFT.

electronic funds transfer at point of sale see EFTPOS.

electronic magazine or **e-zine** a publication that is sent at regular intervals to subscribers by INTERNET, EMAIL or on DISK. The publication is usually supported by advertising rather than by payment from the subscribers.

electronic mail see EMAIL.

electronic mail address see EMAIL ADDRESS.

electronic point of sale see EPOS.

electronics the science and technology of the development of devices and circuits in which electron flow is directly controlled by electrical signal voltages or currents.

electronic whiteboarding see AUDIOGRAPHIC TELECONFERENCING.

electrostatic operating with the use of electrical voltage to exert force on powders or on electron beams. A LASER PRINTER uses electrostatic principles, but the older types of electrostatic printer are now obsolete.

electrostatic copier a copier system that scans a MASTER PAGE with a light beam and uses the reflected light to alter the conductivity of an electrically charged DRUM. The drum is then coated with an ink TONER, which drops off in uncharged regions, and this is transferred to paper and melted into place to make an exact copy. The same principles are used in the LASER PRINTER.

electrostatic discharge a HARDWARE hazard that can cause IC chips to cease functioning. Hardware is normally protected against electrostatic discharge, but some units are vulnerable if they are not connected into a circuit. Replacement circuit cards, such as a MOTHERBOARD, are usually supplied in a plastic bag that is slightly conductive so as to protect against electrostatic damage.

electrostatic printer a system of printing that uses black paper coated with a thin metal film. The printing head is of the DOT-MATRIX type, using a set of sharp spikes. When a high voltage is placed between the metal coating and a spike, the resulting spark will vaporize the metal, leaving the black paper exposed. The system is simple but suffers from the disadvantages that special paper is needed, only one copy is made, and the paper retains fingerprints and will mark other papers.

electrostatic screen a cover made from conducting material and connected to earth (ground), used to protect sensitive circuits from interference transmitted from signal voltages. An electrostatic screen is also an important way of reducing the emission of electromagnetic waves from a computer.

elegant (of design or construction of HARDWARE or SOFTWARE) simple, efficient and good-looking.

ELF see EXTREMELY LOW FREQUENCY.

elimination factor the fraction of data that is not used. When a DATABASE is searched for specified items, such as the number of red-haired males between 20 and 40, the fraction of the database that does not answer this specification is the elimination factor.

elite a size of monospaced (see MONOSPACING) print that produces 12 characters per inch.

ellipsis a mark consisting of three dots in line (...). This, on a MENU, indicates that there are SUBMENU items present. You might be required to CLICK over the main menu item or keep the POINTER (sense 1) on this item for a short time to reveal the submenu.

em a unit of character spacing used in DTP. Most DTP FONTS use PROPORTIONAL SPACING, so that no fixed PITCH (sense 2) number can be used. The em unit is the width of the letter 'm', and this and other space sizes, such as EN, are used between characters and also between words to justify line lengths. These units are also used for dashes, so that a printer can specify an *en dash* or an *em dash*.

email or **e-mail** a system for delivering messages by downloading (see DOWNLOAD) text from computers along telephone wires. An electronic mailbox consists of a BACKING STORE on a large computer that will store messages until the user requests delivery along the line. An elaborate system of PASSWORDS is needed if the MAILBOX messages are to be secure from a CRACKER. ENCRYPTION can be used for confidential messages, and a DIGITAL SIGNATURE can be applied for verification.

email address a set of characters used to identify the sender or receiver of EMAIL. This consists of a local name and a HOSTNAME separated by the COMMERCIAL AT sign, @. On a local net (INTRANET) only the local name is needed. For example, an email address, jimbo@neverpay.net, consists of the local name, jimbo, and the hostname neverpay.net.

embedded blank see HARD SPACE.

embedded code a code number or set of code numbers placed into a document produced on a WORD PROCESSOR or into a WORKSHEET in order to affect a PRINTER. The embedded codes are usually invisible on the SCREEN (sense 1) display, although they may also control the appearance of the text on the screen.

embedded command a term used in word processing (see WORD PROCESSOR) for coded instructions that allow the text on the SCREEN (sense 1) to be manipulated, for example, centred, printed in bold face or indented. An embedded command consists of codes that will not cause printing but that will be passed to the formatting portion (see FORMAT, sense 2) of the word processor or directly to the PRINTER in order to cause the effects that are needed. For most printers, embedded commands must start with the ASCII ESC code of 27 and be followed by whatever codes that particular printer needs. The problem with embedded codes is that different printers do not use identical codes, so that the code that gives bold type on one printer may cause a new FONT to be taken on another. The type of printer to be used must be set as a DEFAULT for the word processor. All this is made much easier by using MICROSOFT WINDOWS because any program using Windows will automatically make use of the default printer that has been set up for Windows.

embedded object an OBJECT, such as a graphics image, that appears in a document by way of a file that has been created by the appropriate program. This object is stored as part of the document (adding to the file size of the document) and can be edited by double-clicking (see DOUBLE-CLICK), which runs the program that created the object, with the file loaded for use. See also LINKED OBJECT.

embedded system a computer system that is built in as part of a larger system. For example, a LASER PRINTER contains an embedded system (the ENGINE) that is used to guide and control the laser beam. An embedded system often consists of a single-chip MICROCONTROLLER.

embedding the placing of a graphics (or other) OBJECT so that it becomes part of a document file and is saved with the file. An embedded object, however, can be edited by double-clicking (see DOUBLE-CLICK) on it. This will run the program that created the object and allow you to alter the object. See also LINKED OBJECT; PASTE.

embosser a form of DOT-MATRIX PRINTER used for Braille printing.

EMC see ELECTROMAGNETIC COMPATIBILITY.

em dash see EM.

emitter coupled logic see ECL.

EMM386.EXE a DOS program, now obsolescent, that permits EXTENDED MEMORY to be used as if it were the older type of EXPANDED MEMORY and can also be used to allow the use of the upper memory blocks (UMB).

emoticon a crude drawing made using ASCII symbols (particularly brackets, hyphen and colon) to express an emotion such as humour or anger. These are used in EMAIL or NEWSGROUP communications to take the edge off text and to indicate that a verbal message is not to be taken too seriously, too literally or in any offensive way. The best-known emoticon is the smiley face, typed as :-) (tilt your head to the left when you look at it). MICROSOFT WORD can convert such combinations of symbols into a more representative drawing by using its AutoCorrect feature.

emphasis the use in a WORD PROCESSOR of TYPE STYLES such as bold or italic to draw the reader's attention to a word or phrase.

empty string see BLANK STRING.

EMS see EXPANDED MEMORY.

em space the widest spaced character for PROPORTIONAL SPACING, see EM. See also EN.

emulation see EMULATOR.

emulator a program that allows a computer or microprocessor to carry out a set of instructions that are designed for another one. Programs that are termed IBMulators are those that allow a computer of another type to run DOS software, so providing an *emulation* of the IBM machine. Machines used in educational work need to be provided with such emulators so as to offer some opportunity for students to learn about the type of machine they are most likely to use later.

en a unit of character spacing or dash length used in DTP, half the width of the EM.

enable to permit an action or to turn an option on. Contrast DISABLE.

encapsulated PostScript (EPS) a form of coding for GRAPHICS intended for DTP. The file consists of commands that can be used by a POSTSCRIPT interpreter to print the IMAGE (sense 1). The encapsulated form of PostScript can be read and used by a DTP program, but the image cannot usually be shown on SCREEN (sense 1), only in print.

Encarta™ tradename for the Microsoft MULTIMEDIA encyclopaedia.

encode to convert the representation of data as numbers or to encrypt (see ENCRYPTION) data.

encoder a program or system that converts computer data into some code system other than the normal one or any device that converts data into computer-usable form. A *position encoder*, for example, will convert the angular position of a shaft into numbers that can be used by a computer in a control system. See also DECODER; DIGITIZER; OPTICAL DISK.

encrypted database a set of data that has been encrypted (see ENCRYP-

TION) so that it can be read only by the program that created the data, not by a WORD PROCESSOR or a SPREADSHEET.

encryption the transformation of text or other data into coded form, often compressed in addition, making it more secure. Any confidential data that has to be sent over public telephone lines or along radio links should be encrypted. See also DECRYPTION; SCRAMBLING.

en dash see EM.

EnDec (encoder decoder) the circuits that convert from computer data to and from disk signals. The EnDec translator can be placed on the disk controller card or on the disk drive itself (see IDE).

end key a KEY (sense 1) that can be used by programs to move the CUR-SOR to the end of a line or to the end of a BLOCK of text. See also HOME KEY.

endless loop tape a piece of tape that has had its ends spliced together and will return to any position simply by winding in one direction.

endnote a piece of text added to the end of a main document. Several WORD PROCESSOR programs allow endnotes to be typed in the course of preparing the document, and such notes are gathered together and numbered at the end of the document. See also FOOTNOTE.

end of file or **EOF marker** a code byte that indicates where the data of one FILE ends. This marker is usually put in place when a disk file is closed. It will be used when the disk is read to indicate that no more data is to be read from the disk. If the file is left open, no marker is put in, and the file may be impossible to read except with the aid of a DISK DOCTOR. When a file APPEND command can be used, this will delete the end of file mark so that a file can be opened for further writing.

end of text (**EOT**) the character that indicates the end of an ASCII text file, obtained by using CTRL-C.

end user the ultimate user of a device, as distinct from manufacturer, assembler, wholesaler or retailer.

engine the working mechanism of a LASER PRINTER. Only a few different engine types exist, and all laser printers use one of these. See also CANON; HEWLETT-PACKARD.

enhanced capabilities port see ECP.

enhanced IDE see EXTENDED IDE.

enhanced graphics board see EGA.

enhanced keyboard the later type of KEYBOARD for the PERSONAL COM-PUTER. The enhanced keyboard uses 102 keys, with the FUNCTION KEYS set along the top of the keyboard, a NUMBERPAD to the right, and the CURSOR movement keys set between the main keyboard and the number keypad. A 105-key form of keyboard is now available for use with Microsoft Windows.

enhanced parallel port see EPP.

enhanced small device interface see ESDI.

Enigma a mechanical ENCRYPTION machine developed in Germany and used for secret communications during World War II. The team working at BLETCHLEY PARK in the UK found ways of deciphering these messages, first manually and subsequently by mechanical and ultimately electronic computers. See also COLOSSUS.

en space a space character for PROPORTIONAL SPACING, using the same width as the letter 'n' of the same FONT. See also EM.

ENTER an alternative term for the RETURN KEY. The term is a better one in the sense that it often describes the action better than the word 'return'. Keyboards provide an ENTER key as well as the Return key.

entity any data item in a DATABASE, such as a name, address, reference number, and so on.

entity-relationship model a method of modelling a DATABASE by regarding it as split into entities (persons or objects) and relations (actions).

entropy a quantity that measures disorder, used in computing to determine how easily data can be coded.

entry-level system a PC system that uses older technology and lacks RESOURCES such as large MEMORY and HARD-DRIVE space to allow it to be used with the most recent program versions.

envelope printer a specialized printer for envelopes only. This is used only when the number of envelopes to be printed is greater than can be handled by an ordinary LASER PRINTER.

environment 1. a combination of HARDWARE and operating system (OS) required for a program. **2.** a portion of MEMORY set aside by DOS for storing information relating to programs.

environment space the memory used to maintain a RECORD (sense 1) of the additional commands or parameters that are included with the program name when a program is executed.

environment variable a value that is assigned in a COMMAND and made available to any programs that can use it. This is a method used in the PERSONAL COMPUTER to pass data to a program, usually to set up some aspect of the program such as MEMORY use or SCREEN (sense 1) type. See SET COMMAND.

EOF marker see END OF FILE.

EOT see END OF TEXT.

epoch the date and time that corresponds to the zero count of the REAL-TIME CLOCK system of a computer. This ranges from 1904 to 1970, depending on computer operating system (OS).

EPOS (electronic point of sale) a form of computerized till that can debit funds and alter stock control records.

EPP (enhanced parallel port) a form of PARALLEL PORT that can be used to drive peripherals other than a printer. This is not quite the same as ECP, and many CMOS-ROM settings allow a port to be set up as plain, EPP, ECP or both EPP and ECP, according to your requirements.

EPROM (erasable programmable read-only memory) a form of ROM chip that can be programmed with data (including program bytes) by writing the data repeatedly while higher than normal electrical voltages are applied to the chip. See also PROM.

EPS see ENCAPSULATED POSTSCRIPT.

Epson a very well-established make of DOT-MATRIX printer that can print graphics as well as text. Many other makes of dot-MATRIX PRINTERS use the same control codes as the Epson and are said to be 'EPSON-COMPATIBLE'. Epson also manufacture LASER PRINTERS and PIEZO-ELECTRIC INKJET printers that use the Stylus tradename.

Equation Editor an ADD-IN program for MICROSOFT WORD that provides the ability to type mathematical equations of considerable complexity within a document.

erasable programmable read-only memory see EPROM.

erasable storage any STORAGE that can be overwritten (see OVERWRITE). RAM, for example, will store data for as long as power is applied to the memory or until other data is written into the memory. A disk will similarly store data until it is full, after which data can be added only by overwriting older data. Digital tape recorders can overwrite tape, although it is usual to erase a BACKUP tape completely before using it again.

erase to delete errors or data. Erasing a disk often simply involves removing the DIRECTORY (sense 2) entry for a file, and the file data itself is not changed until some other file is recorded in its place; see UNDELETE. Erasing a BACKUP tape means recording a fixed pattern on the tape so that data is completely obliterated (see also BULK ERASE). Erasing text on the SCREEN (sense 1) is done by means of a DELETE or BACKSPACE key, and the action consists of replacing bytes in the screen memory by the ASCII code for a blank space.

eraser tool an erasing method used in a GRAPHICS PAINT program. The selection of the eraser ICON allows a square POINTER (sense 1) to be moved over the graphic. When the MOUSE button is clicked (see CLICK, sense 1), the area within the square will be erased.

ergonomics the science and art of designing machines that humans can use easily.

error a mistake of some kind. A FATAL ERROR will have the effect of stopping a program, often with loss of control so that the computer will have to be rebooted (see REBOOT). As this will cause loss of data, the program should be written in such a way that either fatal errors cannot occur or an ERROR MESSAGE is delivered to the screen before a fatal error can be committed.

error-correcting memory a form of MEMORY that uses ERROR DETECTION. The classic type is the 9-bit memory used in older PERSONAL COMPUTERS, using the ninth bit as a PARITY error bit. In practice, DRAM has

147

proved so reliable that most manufacturers have abandoned the use of the ninth bit.

error correction routine a type of program routine used in COMMUNICATIONS. In a communications link, a detected ERROR in a BLOCK of data will cause the ERROR-CORRECTING ROUTINE to clear the data and request retransmission.

error detection and correction any ALGORITHM that will detect and correct ERRORS, ranging from PARITY methods or cyclic redundancy checking (CRC, sense 1) to more elaborate methods that can correct all but gross errors.

error-handling the routines written into a program that deal with ERRORS. For example, a program might contain an error-handling routine that suspends printing when the printer runs out of paper.

error message a message on the SCREEN (sense 1) that signals an ERROR in the program or in the data. If this is a FATAL ERROR it will always stop the computer from executing the program, and this will usually lead to loss of data, either because data has not been recorded or because disk files are left open. A non-fatal error can be dealt with by programming, which will deal with the error without stopping the program. For example, a misspelling of an entered name is a non-fatal error that is easy to correct. By contrast, pressing the BREAK KEY will cause the computer to stop unless the action of the key has been disabled (as it will be by an applications program).

error trapping a program routine that will detect an error before it can cause other problems. For example, a routine might detect that a zero has been typed and will prevent any attempt to use this number in a division action.

escape key or **Esc** the key that is labelled esc or Escape in some computers. This generates ASCII code 27, and in some programs this code is ignored.

escape sequence the use of the ESCAPE KEY along with another key to produce special effects, such as changes in SCREEN (sense 1) colour.

ESDI (enhanced small device interface) a set of circuits that was formerly used to connect the computer to a DISK SYSTEM, OPTICAL DISK or other PERIPHERAL systems. The system has been superseded for HARD DRIVE uses by IDE.

Ethernet™ a form of local area network (LAN). This is the system that was developed by Rank-Xerox for use with office computers and other equipment.

Eudora a well-established software application for EMAIL use.

euro the common European currency, presently traded electronically because no notes or coins are in circulation.

Eurocard any of a set of standard CIRCUIT BOARD sizes, used for experimental work.

euroconnector see IEC FITTING.

even parity see PARITY.

event an action such as clicking (see CLICK, sense 1) the MOUSE button that can be used to make a program routine run.

event-driven program a program in which selections are made by clicking the MOUSE or by single key actions, as distinct from opening a MENU and selecting an item from the menu.

event handler a program routine that runs in response to an event such as clicking a MOUSE button.

Excel see MICROSOFT EXCEL.

exclamation mark the ! character, ASCII 33.

exclude dictionary or **exclusion dictionary** a SPELLCHECK dictionary in MICROSOFT WORD that contains a list of words that are always to be questioned. For example, if you are in the habit of typing 'inn' rather than 'in', a conventional spelling checker will not query this word because it is a legitimate word. If the word 'inn' is placed in an exclude dictionary it will always be questioned.

exclusive application an APPLICATION that has the exclusive use of the MICROPROCESSOR. An operating system (OS) that permits more than one program to be run at a time normally arranges for TIME-SHARING of the processor, but some applications cannot function if this is done because they require actions to be done at precise time intervals. For such applications, the time-sharing can be suspended so as to provide exclusive use.

exclusive option the option in a MULTITASKING system to RUN (sense 2) a program exclusively, with no other programs running.

executable content a program, such as an APPLET (sense 2), sent by INTERNET from one machine to another. BROWSER software contains options to control whether or not such programs may be run.

executable file a PROGRAM file as distinct from a DATA file.

execute to carry out a PROGRAM. A program will start to execute as soon as it has been loaded from disk into memory.

execution time the time required for a complete MICROPROCESSOR instruction or for a complete PROGRAM.

executive the portion of an operating system (OS) that is memory-resident (see TSR PROGRAM). The executive controls the running of other programs and can call up other parts of the operating system as required.

EXE file a file using the EXE EXTENDED FILENAME on a computer using MS-DOS. This type of program file can be located anywhere in the memory and can use more than 64 kilobytes of memory. See also COM FILE.

exhaustive testing program testing using all possible combinations of inputs.

existence dependency a status of an ENTITY in a DATABASE that is dependent on the existence of another entity. For example, a bank account number is *existence-dependent* on a customer name. If the name is deleted the account number is also deleted.

exit 1. a way out of a program. The word is often used as a verb in a program MENU; for example, 'press 5 to exit program'. **2. (EXIT)** a command used in MS-DOS to leave a CHILD PROGRAM and return to the PARENT PROGRAM.

EXP a number function used in a WORKSHEET for finding a power of the number 'e', the exponential function. The power has to be supplied as an argument to EXP, so that EXP(5) means 'e' to the power 5. The numerical value of 'e' is approximately 2.718.

expanded memory or **EMS** a form of added memory used in old PC-XT or PC-AT machines to allow more than 640 kilobytes of memory to be available to a DOS program. Only specially written programs could make use of such memory. The system is now obsolete.

expanding the restoring of the normal coding arrangement. See COMPANDING.

expansion bus a set of connections on a MOTHERBOARD that allows the computer to be expanded and updated by plugging in cards to a connector, the EXPANSION SLOT.

expansion card a CIRCUIT BOARD that fits into an EXPANSION SLOT on a computer and from then on becomes part of the HARDWARE of that computer.

expansion slot or **slot** a connector that carries all the MICROPROCESSOR signals and that can be used to connect additional boards for the computer. The PERSONAL COMPUTER type of machine features internal expansion slots, 3 to 8 in number, which are 8-BIT on the XT type of machine but a mixture of 16-bit and 32-bit on later machines. These are used to connect in EXPANSION CARDS for SCREEN (sense 1) graphics, disk control and other purposes. Recent machines use only the PCI and AGP type of 32-bit slots. See also VLB.

expert in ARTIFICIAL INTELLIGENCE, one who possesses KNOWLEDGE that is organized or compiled (see COMPILED KNOWLEDGE) so as to be able to perform some designated task more effectively and efficiently.

expert system a program that uses the computer to collect and use human expertise. The study of expert systems is one aspect of ARTIFICIAL INTELLIGENCE (AI) research, aimed at allowing a non-expert to make use of the KNOWLEDGE and strategy of an EXPERT. The combination of both knowledge and expertise distinguishes an expert system from a knowledge-based system, which contains no element of expertise, and a decision support system, which follows a pattern of rules. It is also distinguished from AI in having no form of reasoning. The principle is that if the experience and learning of several humans can be stored in a summarized form in an interactive DATABASE, along with a decision strategy program and a suitable management program, then this expertise can be tapped, made use of and even extended by either expert or non-expert operators. The main applications to date have been to medical diagnosis (mainly preliminary diagnosis to find if a medical practitioner need be involved), in legal work and in car servicing. The reason for the involvement of AI in what might appear to be just a database application is that a lot of human experience and expertise cannot simply be summed into simple rules or examples; unless some attempt at summary is made, the database becomes too bulky to use, and the work that has been done on AI has been applied to this problem.

exploded pie a form of PIE CHART in which one or more segments have been drawn out from the body so that they appear more clearly.

exploit to take advantage of a gap in the SECURITY system of a computer.

extend to add FUNCTIONS to a program, as by use of PLUG-INS.

Explorer or **File Explorer** or **Windows Explorer** the Microsoft WINDOWS 95 onwards replacement for the FILE MANAGER of the earlier WINDOWS versions. Explorer uses a single WINDOW display of folders and files, and file copying can be carried out by dragging or by using a menu of commands obtained when the right-hand mouse button is clicked. See Fig. 20. See also INTERNET EXPLORER.

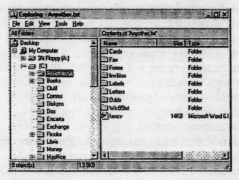

Fig. 20. **Explorer**. The Explorer window, showing a folder (directory) selected on the left and its files on the right.

Explorer bar the left-hand pane of a Windows EXPLORER display, showing folders, FAVOURITES, HISTORY or search action.

exponent the part of a number in STANDARD FORM that represents the power of ten. For example, if a number is written as 2.45E5, then the number 5 is the exponent, the power of ten by which 2.45 is to be multiplied, giving 245000. In BINARY form, the exponent represents a power of 2. See also MANTISSA.

exponentiation the action of raising a number to a power. For instance, 5 raised to the power 4 equals $5 + 5 + 5 + 5 = 125$. Similarly, in common PROGRAMMING LANGUAGES and on hand-calculators, 5E4 is shorthand for

5 multiplied by 10 raised to the power 4, or 5 + 10,000, equal to 50,000. The letter E or command exp is used to indicate this action, so 5E3 or 5exp3 would mean 5 raised to the third power, five cubed, equal to 125.

export to output a data file for use by another program, for example from a DTP to a WORD PROCESSOR program.

export filter a short program that changes the form of a file being exported. A WORD PROCESSOR file that contains formatting codes, for example, might be subject to an export filter that converts it into ASCII format or to a format suitable for another word processor.

express a cut-down version of a large program, often packaged with other applications. For example, Outlook Express is the version of MICROSOFT OUTLOOK that is included in WINDOWS with INTERNET EXPLORER.

expression a FORMULA that is made up from OPERATORS and values so as to define or calculate data. For example, the WORKSHEET expression +5*C1 will cause a value to be placed in its CELL, equal to five times the value in cell C1. The expression >=K in MICROSOFT ACCESS will select items that begin with the letters K to Z inclusive.

extended architecture the CD-ROM drive specification, as described in the GREEN BOOK and WHITE BOOK (sense 2).

extended binary coded decimal interchange code see EBCDIC.

extended capability port see ECP.

extended character set a set of characters that are represented by the numbers 128 to 255, above the normal ASCII set. Unlike the ASCII set, these extended characters are not standardized, so that odd results can be expected if your computer uses one extended character set and your printer uses another. Printers for a PC machine running DOS should be set for the pc-8 character set.

extended data output see EDO.

extended data out dynamic random access memory see EDO DRAM.

extended expanded memory system see EEMS.

extended filename a disk FILENAME that can include disk drive and directory information as well as an extension set of letters that identifies the type of file. For example, the MS-DOS filename of CHKDSK refers to a program that, if it is to execute, must be on the current drive and directory. Typing a name such as C:\WRITING \WORD implies that the program WORD resides in the DIRECTORY (sense 1) called WRITING on the C: disk (the HARD DRIVE) and is being called into use from another drive or directory. The extension letters for programs are COM or EXE. Extension letters such as TXT or DOC can be used to identify text files, so that PARK.COM is a program file and PARK.DOC is a text file. The extension letters COM or EXE do not have to be typed when a program is to be executed but need to be specified if a file is being copied or otherwise worked with.

extended graphics array see XGA.

extended IDE see EIDE.

extended industry-standard architecture see EXTENDED ISA.

extended ISA see EISA (sense 1).

extended memory a form of added MEMORY for later versions of PC-AT machines and clones that allows memory addresses above one megabyte to be used directly. This is intended to be used by an operating system (OS) that is MULTITASKING and cannot generally be used by MS-DOS. The use of WINDOWS requires the presence of a considerable amount of extended memory, and MICROSOFT WINDOWS requires at least 16 megabytes (preferably 64 megabytes for later versions) of extended memory in order to run well – a modified version is installed if too little RAM is available. The older PC-XT machine cannot use extended memory.

extended memory manager see EMM386.

extended parallel port (EPP) a PARALLEL PORT design in which all eight DATA BUS lines can be used as inputs or outputs. An extended parallel port is particularly useful if you use peripherals such as disk drives connected through a parallel port. See also ECP.

extending serial file the adding of data to a SERIAL FILE. A serial file on tape or on disk consists of a LIST of items, one after another. This type of file can normally be amended or extended only by reading it in, making changes or alterations and then recording the whole of the file again. For a large file, this can be very time-consuming, and RANDOM ACCESS filing is greatly preferable.

extensible (of a program) written so as to provide easily for enhancement.

extension the set of up to three characters that can be added to a DOS FILENAME, separated by a dot. The extension is used mainly to convey the type of file, such as DOC for a document. Other operating systems allow extensions of more than three characters to be used if required. See EXTENDED FILENAME.

external command a COMMAND in MS-DOS that is executed by way of loading a program file temporarily from the disk, in contrast to an INTERNAL COMMAND.

external hard drive a HARD DRIVE that is connected to the computer outside the casing, usually by plugging it into the PARALLEL PORT socket. Access to such a drive is slower, but the data is more secure because the drive can be unplugged and taken away after a session.

external modem a MODEM that is in its own case and is connected to the computer through the SERIAL PORT. The advantage of an external modem is that it can easily be switched off to avoid unwanted calls, such as from a HACKER.

external peripheral any PERIPHERAL that is installed outside the computer casing rather than inside. External peripherals usually transfer data by way of the SERIAL PORT or PARALLEL PORT.

external reference a reference in a WORKSHEET to a CELL or RANGE of cells in another worksheet.

extranet a method of access to the World Wide Web (WWW) through a company intranet, generally through a FIREWALL so as to preserve SECURITY.

extrapolation the action of finding a quantity by extending a graph line beyond its measured points or by using proportionality. Extrapolation is justified if the graph line is straight but can be dubious in other circumstances, sometimes amounting to no more than an educated guess. The main problem is that extrapolation assumes that the relationship that has produced known results will continue to be valid for the new results over an extended range. Where data exists as a table of related values in a WORKSHEET, the statistical technique called *regression*, available in a SPREADSHEET program, is used to find the parameters (slope and intercept) from which other points can be calculated, allowing extrapolation. Regression should be used only if there is good reason to believe that there is a valid relationship between pairs of data points.

extremely low frequency (ELF) the FREQUENCY range of about 100 Hz or lower, radiated from all electrical equipment. These frequencies are often blamed for various illnesses, but the evidence is flimsy and often ignores the fact that the predominant emission from a MONITOR (sense 1) is at much higher frequencies.

e-zine see ELECTRONIC MAGAZINE.

face see TYPEFACE.

face time or **face-to-face** live meeting, as distinct from INTERNET or EMAIL contact.

facilitated chat a form of CHAT SYSTEM in which a host (the *facilitator*) acts as a chairperson and keeps order.

facing pages pages in a DOUBLE-SIDED publication. When a book is opened, the facing pages will bear an even number on the left and an odd number on the right.

facsimile transmission see FAX.

fact in ARTIFICIAL INTELLIGENCE, a statement that is always true.

factorial a mathematical FUNCTION of a number that is the product of that number with each other lower number down to unity. For example, factorial 5, written as 5! is 5 x 4 x 3 x 2 x 1 = 120. The function is used mainly in calculations of probability in a WORKSHEET.

fail-safe system or **graceful degradation system** a system that resists human errors. As the name suggests, a fail-safe system is one that will fail in a way that causes least damage to system data. In computing terms, it means that any ERROR that will stop a program should first of all cause a UTILITY program to RUN (sense 2) that will save all data on a disk and close all disk files.

failure-directed testing a method of testing SOFTWARE based on experience of ERRORS in similar software.

failure logging the saving of data and system information in the event of a power failure or a FATAL ERROR.

fallback 1. any system for recovery of data or CPU states in an emergency. **2.** a MODEM feature that allows two modems in contact with each other to use a lower speed because of line noise or CORRUPTION at a higher speed.

fall forward a MODEM feature that allows modems that have fallen back (see FALLBACK, sense 2) to a lower speed to return to a high speed when line conditions improve.

FALSE one of the two BOOLEAN values, the other being TRUE. Boolean values are used in the DATABASE type called Boolean.

false code code that contains impossible values. The normal range of ASCII printing codes is 32 to 127, and some systems are programmed to treat any BYTE outside this range as false code.

fan the air-circulating propeller used to cool a computer, usually located on the power-supply casing. Some manufacturers use the fan to extract air from the casing, others use the fan to blow air into the casing. Modern MICROPROCESSOR chips of the PENTIUM class use a miniature cooling fan mounted over the chip, with a thin film of heat-sink grease to aid heat conductivity.

fanfold or **accordion fold** a continuous strip of paper that is perforated at intervals (usually 28-cm/11-inch intervals) so that it can be folded in alternate directions into a neat pile. Many programs are arranged so that they will not print on the perforated part of the paper, allowing the paper to be separated (see BURST) into separate sheets. Fanfold paper can also be supplied with vertical perforations that allow the SPROCKET HOLE strips to be removed.

FAQ (frequently asked questions) a heading found on HELP (sense 1) pages, on BULLETIN BOARD pages and the INTERNET, used for answers to questions that beginners ask, underlining the point that manuals are written by experts who tend to be unaware of the problems that beginners face.

FAST (Federation Against Software Theft) a body founded in the UK in 1984 to combat illegal copying of software (see PIRACY), particularly by business users of computers.

fast-access (of a computer memory) being capable of reading or writing rapidly. As applied to modern MICROCOMPUTERs, this implies an ACCESS TIME of the order of 60 NANOSECONDs or less.

fast forward an action used in PRESENTATION GRAPHICS or MULTIMEDIA applications in which a sequence is speeded up. For example, you might move quickly from slide 4 to slide 12 or from track 1 on a COMPACT DISC to track 5. The right double-chevron sign (») is used to indicate this action, as used on audio and video recorders.

FASTHELP a DOS command (version 6.0 onwards) that provides help summary pages for each DOS command.

fast key or **keyboard shortcut** or **quick key** a KEY (sense 1) that can be pressed to bypass GUI actions. The use of a fast key allows many otherwise tedious MOUSE, ICON and MENU selection actions to be avoided, making the program as fast and easy to use as one that relies entirely on key actions. A complete set of actions can be programmed as a MACRO and assigned to a fast key.

FASTOPEN a DOS command that can speed up the opening of files by storing file information. FASTOPEN is now obsolete and is not used along with WINDOWS.

fast rewind an action used in PRESENTATION GRAPHICS or MULTIMEDIA applications in which the normal sequence is reversed at high speed. For example, you might move from slide 10 to slide 3 or from track 7 on a COMPACT DISC to track 2. The left double-chevron sign («) is used to indicate this action, as used on audio and video recorders.

fast SCSI a variant of SCSI-2 that runs at a faster transfer rate.

FAT (file allocation table) a table that is prepared (in duplicate) by the computer when a FLOPPY DISK or HARD DRIVE is formatted. This table contains a list of the ADDRESS (sense 1) numbers of all the clusters (see ALLOCATION UNIT) of all the files on the disk. The FAT and DIRECTORY of files are stored on the outer disk TRACK, and a hard drive stores the FAT in duplicate. The starting address for a file is held in the directory, but subsequent addresses for fragmented portions of the file are in the FAT. Older PC operating systems used a 16-bit FAT, but WINDOWS (from the second edition of Windows 95) has used a 32-bit FAT. See also CROSS-LINKED FILES; DEFRAGMENTATION; FRAGMENTATION (sense 1).

FAT32 a later form of FAT using 32-bit numbers, introduced in the second version of WINDOWS 95 and used by subsequent versions.

fatal error or **catastrophic error** an ERROR that stops the execution of a program, with loss of data, possibly causing a REBOOT. See also CRASH (sense 1).

fatal exception a program fault that cannot be handled by the program itself and causes control to return to the operating system (OS), terminating the program. When a fatal exception occurs on a program running in a MULTITASKING system this should not affect other programs that are running concurrently.

father see FILE GENERATIONS.

fault-based testing the use of test data that is arranged to check a range of faults such as missing, incorrect or impossible data entries.

fault tolerance the ability of a COMPUTER SYSTEM to continue operation despite minor HARDWARE faults. For example, if a file SAVE (sense 1) action specifies a floppy disk that is not present, the system should allow a second chance after enough time to insert a disk or the option of abandoning the action rather than shutting down the whole system.

faulty sector a common disk ERROR MESSAGE caused by a defective part of the magnetic surface. If the faulty SECTOR is caused in manufacturing, the FORMAT (sense 2) action will exclude that sector from use. A faulty sector that develops during use may be the result of mishandling and can cause loss of data. Faulty sector messages may be caused by the presence of strong magnetic fields near the disk drive, as, for example, from a VDU. A disk that has a steadily increasing number of faulty sectors should not be used again, and it may be necessary to recover the data with a DISK DOCTOR if no BACKUP disk is available. See also DROP-IN; DROPOUT.

favourites FOLDERS or WEB PAGES that are often used. These can be opened using a single-click action if they are stored in a *favourites folder*.

fax or **facsimile transmission** a method of transmitting documents. Electromechanical systems were in use for many years, particularly in connection with the transmission of photographs to newspapers, but these have been superseded by electronic systems. A *fax card* added to a personal computer will allow the machine to be used for transmitting and receiving messages using disk files and permitting a received fax to be printed on plain paper. This in turn is giving way before the almost universal use of EMAIL.

fax modem a fast MODEM that can transmit and receive at the standard FAX speeds. This must be used with software that can convert a TEXTFILE to and from a BITMAP GRAPHICS FILE in the format that is standardized for fax use. Paper documents need to be scanned (see SCANNER) before use with a fax modem, but documents created with a WORD PROCESSOR can be faxed directly, using the fax modem as if it were a printer.

FC a DOS file comparison utility that will report on all differences between the files, not just the first ten differences as the older COMP command did. See also DISKCOMP.

FCC certification a warranty that the computer or peripheral meets the requirements of the US Federal Communications Commission in respect of electrical safety and acceptably low levels of interference with radio communications.

FDC see FLOPPY DISK CONTROLLER.

FDISK a program that is part of the MS-DOS system, used to perform a LOW-LEVEL FORMAT (sense 2) and partitioning (see PARTITIONED DRIVE) of a HARD DRIVE. At one stage when IDE drives were introduced it seemed that FDISK would no longer be needed, but it has returned to use again with the large-capacity modern hard drives and is an essential preliminary to formatting a new drive. It can still also be used for partitioning a hard drive if, for example, you needed to use a different operating system (OS) in each partition.

feathering 1. a GRAPHICS painting effect in which there is a gradual progression from one colour to another rather than a sharp boundary. **2.** see VERTICAL JUSTIFICATION.

feature any notable action of a program. A new version of a program can be expected to contain a greater number of features (see CREEPING FEATURISM). The term is often also ironically used to mean a BUG.

feature creep see CREEPING FEATURISM.

feature shock the effect on a user when confronted by a new package with a large number of features and no printed manual.

Federation Against Software Theft see FAST.

feedback 1. a form of correction in a system, usually meaning *negative feedback*. A negative feedback signal is a sample of the output of a system, which is used to correct an input. *Positive feedback* reinforces changes and can cause instability. The term has more applicability to analogue computing than to digital computing. **2.** a loose term for ACKNOWLEDGEMENT.

feeder cable a cable for power or signals that is tapped at intervals to provide for terminals.

female connector the socket connector of a cable or the socket on a computer. Compare MALE CONNECTOR.

femto- prefix for 10^{-15}.

fence 1. any form of divider symbol in an equation, such as a bracket, when an equation is being created by the EQUATION EDITOR of MICROSOFT WORD. **2.** a data value or set of values that indicates the boundary between two data items in a file. Programmers who used 9999 or 9/9/99 as a fence did not anticipate that their program might be in use in September 1999.

FEPROM (flash erasable programmable read-only memory) a form of PROM that can be reprogrammed by altering the voltage at one pin and writing data. FEPROM chips are now used as BIOS chips in MOTHERBOARDS so as to allow for upgrading, but unless this process can be disabled by the user it can allow a VIRUS to make changes in the BIOS.

ferrite core memory an early form of NON-VOLATILE MEMORY that uses tiny rings of magnetic material threaded by sensing wires.

ferroelectric RAM (FRAM) a form of RAM that uses for each element a CAPACITOR formed from a material that is permanently charged. This charge can be reversed by an electrical signal, using the same principles as the old FERRITE CORE MEMORY system. The advantages include high speed and memory retention with power off.

FET see FIELD EFFECT TRANSISTOR.

fetch-execute cycle the set of actions that a MICROPROCESSOR performs to carry out a single MACHINE CODE instruction. This includes fetching the instruction code from memory and then executing the instruction.

FF see FORM FEED.

fibre optic a thread of transparent material used to transmit laser light signals that can be used to carry DIGITAL messages.

Fidonet an old-established NETWORK system for BULLETIN BOARD operators, allowing exchange of data over telephone lines.

field 1. a space in a WORD PROCESSOR document into which codes can be inserted. These codes can be simple, such as date and time codes, or complex, such as a data entry space. **2.** a unit of a RECORD (sense 1) in a DATABASE. For example, if your record is of customers, the name would be one field, the address another, and so on. A collection of fields for one data entry constitutes a record. For a RANDOM-ACCESS FILE, you may have to cut or pad each field to a specified length. **3.** see FRAME (sense 2).

field definition the list of items that determine the use and appearance of a FIELD (sense 2) in a DATABASE. For example, a field definition could include the type of data, the maximum number of characters, any DEFAULT entry, a name for the field, and so on.

field effect transistor (FET) a SEMICONDUCTOR device that controls electrical conduction between two points (*source* and *drain*) by altering the electrical voltage at a third, the *gate*. Because it is the electric field rather than current that constitutes the controlling action, the FET can switch significant amounts of current without the need for any measurable amount of current at the gate, so that the power needed to operate the FET is negligible. FETs are used in practically all semiconductor chips intended for computing actions.

fielding the arranging for text or numbers to occupy the correct positions on the SCREEN (sense 1) or on paper.

field name a form of FILENAME used for a FIELD (sense 2) in a DATABASE that allows that field to be uniquely identified. You might, for example, use a field called MONTHTOTAL.

field privilege a data item in a DATABASE that determines what PRIVILEGE LEVEL (sense 1) is required for access. For example, a FIELD (sense 2) might be protected so that only users with the highest privilege level could alter the contents.

field template see DATA MASK.

FIFO (first-in, first-out) the principle of the QUEUE (sense 1).

file a collection of data that can be recorded. A program is one type of file, and the data that it uses is another type of file. The main file types, however, are ASCII and BINARY. The important difference is that a file in ASCII code is much easier to transmit from one computer application to another because ASCII code is a standard for text. Programs such as SPREADSHEETS will use binary-coded files, making it more difficult to interchange files because the coding is not the same for different programs (but see DATA INTERCHANGE FORMAT). Even WORD PROCESSOR files are not easily interchangeable and need a TRANSLATION UTILITY.

file allocation table see FAT.

file attachment a file of text, graphics or sound that is sent along with an EMAIL message. At the receiving end, the existence of an attachment is usually marked by an ICON, usually a paperclip, and clicking this icon will reveal the attachment.

file compression utility or **file crunching** a UTILITY program that will compress a file before saving it and expand it when the file is read again. See ARCHIVE; DRIVESPACE.

file control block a method of storing information about a disk file, used in early PC machines running MS-DOS.

file conversion the transferring of file data from one form to another. You might, for example, want to read an old file from an obsolete type of disk and store it on a modern 1.4-megabyte disk. This will require a file conversion, a program that can read the file from the old type of disk and save on the newer type of disk. If the format of the file is also different, a TRANSLATION UTILITY will be also needed.

file conversion program a UTILITY program that is used to convert one data file format to another. For example, MICROSOFT WORD can read files created by WORDPERFECT by using a conversion program built into Word.

file crunching see FILE COMPRESSION UTILITY.

file descriptor an identifying number that is generated by the operating system (OS) when a FILE is opened and that is used to identify that file until it is closed.

File Explorer see EXPLORER.

file extension see FILENAME EXTENSION.

file format the coding system that is used for a DOCUMENT FILE. The best-known format is as ASCII code, but most programs use their own systems, particularly WORD PROCESSOR and DTP programs that need to add codes for information on margin sizes, font, point size, etc. SPREADSHEET programs also use coding systems other than ASCII, and many file formats also include some DATA COMPRESSION.

file fragmentation splitting a file into sections that are scattered over a disk or drive in NON-CONTIGUOUS SECTORS. This arises when files on a disk or drive have been deleted and other files saved in their place. The file allocation table (FAT) keeps track of the positions of the different file fragments. See also DEFRAGMENTATION.

file generations a BACKUP system of proven reliability. Business users of files normally keep three copies, the *father*, *son* and *grandfather* files. The son file is the most recent copy. After the son file has been in use for some time, a new recording will be made. This will be the new son file, and the old son file will be renamed as father, and the old father file becomes grandfather, with the former grandfather file scrapped. This scheme ensures good file backup and can be easily maintained.

file handle a code number allocated to a saved (see SAVE, sense 1) file in the MS-DOS system. The use of the handle allows information on file LOCATION (sense 2) to be retrieved much faster than was possible using the earlier FILE CONTROL BLOCK system, now obsolete.

file interrogation reading a DATABASE file to verify information. An interrogation does not change the file, and the amount that is read may be limited to a few FIELDS (sense 2).

file locking a system used on a NETWORK to prevent more than one user of a file making alterations at any one time.

file management program a program that makes file deletion, copying, moving and renaming simple by displaying filenames and directories on screen and permitting actions to be carried out using a MOUSE. EXPLORER is the most used system for a modern PERSONAL COMPUTER.

File Manager the FILE MANAGEMENT PROGRAM for MICROSOFT WINDOWS 3.1, replaced by EXPLORER in WINDOWS 95 and subsequent versions.

file merge the action of combining data files in an ordered way, such as preserving ALPHABETICAL ORDER.

filename the reference name that is given to a file when it is recorded. This FILE DESCRIPTOR or identifier allows a disk or tape system to locate the correct file. See also ALIAS (sense 1); EXTENDED FILENAME.

161

filename extension the set of up to three characters used to extend a FILENAME in the MS-DOS operating system. See also ALIAS (sense 1), EXTENDED FILENAME.

file overflow the situation where the growth of a file exceeds its allocated storage space. On a RANDOM ACCESS system, this can be dealt with by designating an overflow area for such a file, from which it can be returned when other files have been deleted and the disk reorganized, usually in the course of making a BACKUP.

file protect tab see WRITE-PROTECT.

file recovery a UTILITY action that will restore the contents of a file following unintentional deletion or damage resulting from FRAGMENTATION and loss of POINTER (sense 2) numbers on parts of the file. File recovery is built into WINDOWS in the form of the RECYCLE BIN. See also UNDELETE.

file-search utility a program that will find the location of a named file on a HARD DRIVE. If the file is found, its DIRECTORY (sense 1) PATH is shown.

file separator the ASCII code 28 character, used to indicate where one file ends and another starts in a continuous sequence of data.

fileserver see SERVER.

file sharing the use of files on a NETWORK by more than one person. When this is done, FILE LOCKING will be needed to prevent simultaneous attempts to alter a file, and some form of ACCESS LEVEL system may have to be used.

file shredding the action of destroying a recorded file on a disk by writing bytes into the space occupied by the file. The normal DELETE action only removes the file from the disk DIRECTORY and does not alter the bytes stored on the disk, allowing a deleted file to be recovered (see UNDELETE). An UNCONDITIONAL FORMAT program will destroy any trace of data on a disk but not selectively.

file signature a number obtained from a mathematical manipulation of the data in a file, used to identify that file and to check for CORRUPTION.

filespec the combination of file PATH, FILENAME and EXTENSION letters for a file. See also EXTENDED FILENAME.

file structure the way in which a DATABASE file is organized into FIELD (sense 2), RECORD (sense 1) and BLOCK (sense 2) units and as a SERIAL, RANDOM-ACCESS or INDEXED file. Random-access files are even more efficient in use when combined with a serial index file (see INDEXED SEQUENTIAL ACCESS METHOD).

file system the method used to arrange, store and refer to files. In general, an operating system (OS) will use its own file system, which is not COMPATIBLE with the methods used by another operating system.

file transfer protocol see FTP.

file transfer utility a UTILITY program used when a file that has been created by one computer type has to be transferred to another type of computer. For example, a WORKSHEET file might need to be transferred from a PERSONAL COMPUTER to a MACINTOSH with the aid of a utility of this type.

file type the format of data stored in a file, usually indicated by the FILE-NAME EXTENSION. See also MIME.

FILL 1. a command used in PAINT programs to fill a closed shape with colour or shading. **2.** a command used in a SPREADSHEET program to fill a RANGE of CELLS with a quantity.

fill colour a colour used for filling outlines, such as bar-graph shapes, on a PRESENTATION GRAPHICS program.

fill-out form a page on a WEB SITE that resembles a paper form and is used to pass information from the user back to the web site. Forms can use typed INPUT, MENU selection or RADIO BUTTONS.

film output the output of a DTP program from a typesetter in transparent film format for printing. See also BROMIDE OUTPUT.

filter or **mask 1.** a form of program, often part of a DATABASE, that selectively removes or alters data. For example, a document that uses mainly ASCII codes can be filtered to remove any non-ASCII codes or to remove any code that is preceded by the ASCII 27 character, or a set of words can be put into ALPHABETICAL ORDER, or an item can be found from a list. **2.** a DOS command that can be interposed between a file command and its ARGUMENT so as to select the data.

finalized disc a CD-R disc that has had its overall LEAD-IN and LEAD-OUT information written, so that no further sessions can be recorded. See also FIXATION.

FIND 1. a MICROSOFT WINDOWS command to find a file on the HARD DRIVE. The FIND command is on the first part of the START MENU. **2.** a form of FILTER (sense 2) command used by DOS to find a specified set of characters in a text file.

find and replace see SEARCH AND REPLACE.

fine grain see GRANULARITY.

fine-tune to make final small adjustments in order to get the best results, used mainly in the context of a TV receiver that needs a fine-tuning adjustment for the optimum display of colour and reception of sound. It is sometimes also used to refer to small adjustments in the final version of a program.

finger a UTILITY used on a NETWORK that provides information on any user who is currently logged in to the network.

firefighting emergency action on a program or system to try to avoid data loss or CORRUPTION.

firewall a set of SECURITY systems intended to separate an INTRANET from the INTERNET so that the intranet cannot be penetrated by a CRACKER. This is usually implemented by a single computer that is connected to both and programmed to avoid connection except where permitted. See also PROXY GATEWAY.

FireWire the name popularly used for the IEEE 1394 fast SERIAL bus. This is similar in action to the USB but operates at speeds up to 2 gigabytes per second using a 6-wire cable. FireWire connectors are fitted on several digital camcorders and other devices that make use of video data. The FireWire system supports plug and play (PNP), and devices can be connected or disconnected (HOT SWAPPING) without the need to switch the computer off.

firmware the SOFTWARE, usually of the BIOS, that is on ROM. Since it is on ROM, which cannot be altered, it is said to be firm. Some BIOS chips, however, allow the contents to be altered by using a UTILITY that activates hardware on the MOTHERBOARD.

first generation computer any of the elite group of pioneering computers using THERMIONIC VALVES and designed before 1950. See also BLETCHLEY PARK; COLOSSUS.

first generation language see MACHINE CODE.

first in, first out see FIFO.

first-line indent a wider MARGIN used for the first line of a paragraph (see INDENT).

fixation the set of actions used at the end of a writing session on a CD-R drive. Fixation writes LEAD-IN and LEAD-OUT information and creates a TABLE OF CONTENTS for the disc so that the disc can be read on a normal CD-ROM drive or audio compact-disc player. If the option of *fixation for append* is used, further sessions can be added to the disc until it is full. See also FINALIZED DISC.

fixed data data, such as a copyright message, that is contained in a program and cannot be deleted easily, or identification data that is written to each and every file created by a program.

fixed disk see HARD DRIVE.

fixed field a FIELD (sense 2) in a RECORD (sense 1) that consists of a fixed number of characters, so allowing a RANDOM-ACCESS FILE to be used. If the number of characters in each field of a record can be fixed, then the number of characters in the whole record is also fixed. This allows any record to be located by counting characters and is the basis of random access to any field of any record.

fixed frequency monitor a MONITOR (sense 1) in which the LINE FREQUENCY and FRAME (sense 2) rates are fixed, making it suitable for only a limited range of GRAPHICS ADAPTER cards. See also MULTISYNC MONITOR.

fixed length field a FIELD (sense 2) in a DATABASE whose length is fixed, regardless of the size of data. For example, a 20-character field might be assigned for a surname, so that the name JONES would leave 15 spaces blank in this field. Contrast VARIABLE LENGTH FIELD.

fixed length record a file RECORD (sense 1) whose length is set to a predetermined limit so that records can be made easily accessible.

fixed-pitch font see MONOSPACING.

fixed point a way of manipulating numbers in which the position of the decimal point is fixed. This has seldom been used on microcomputers except in the form of FIELDING commands for displaying numbers. The alternative system became known as FLOATING POINT.

fixed space character see MONOSPACING.

flag or **status bit** a BIT or BYTE that is used to indicate some event. The term usually denotes a byte in the 'flag' (or status) REGISTER (sense 2) of the MICROPROCESSOR. These flags are used to signal the presence of a carry, a negative number, zero in a register, and so on. The flags are, in fact, bits in the register that may be 1 (*flag set*) or 0 (*flag reset*). In higher-level languages, a *flag variable* may be used to switch different parts of a program into action. Such a flag variable is usually of the BOOLEAN type, which can be either TRUE or FALSE.

flame an insulting message on EMAIL or on a NEWSGROUP, intended to provoke argument.

flame bait a message on EMAIL or on a NEWSGROUP that is intended to cause a FLAME reply.

flame war a series of messages that consist of FLAME comments, often taking up much valuable space to no real effect.

flash erasable programmable read only memory see FEPROM.

flashing the blinking on and off of characters on a VDU SCREEN (sense 1). Many display systems allow characters to be flashed, meaning that they can be displayed in two colours alternating at a fixed interval. This allows programmers to draw the attention of the user to the need for some action, such as replacing a disk. In addition, the MOUSE POINTER (sense 1) of MICROSOFT WORD flashes.

flash memory a form of CMOS memory used in the form of a PCMCIA card on PORTABLE COMPUTERS. This can be used only if the computer supports the Microsoft Flash File System.

flash ROM see FEPROM.

flash session a system for performing UPLOAD or DOWNLOAD actions at specified times, usually as a BACKGROUND (sense 2) task.

flat one-dimensional or limited to one subject.

flat address space see FLAT MEMORY.

flat ASCII ASCII code that uses only 7-bit codes.

flatbed plotter a computer-controlled drawing machine. It consists of a flat plate on which a paper sheet can be laid. A pair of arms attached to a trolley are computer-controlled and can place the trolley at any part of the paper. A pen attached to the trolley can be raised or lowered so as to contact the paper. Then, under computer control, this device can draw pictures. If several pens of different colours can be controlled, then the pictures can be drawn in colour. Plotting is a slow action and, unless very high precision is needed, a printer of the INKJET or LASER type is preferred for such GRAPHICS work.

flatbed scanner a form of SCANNER, such as the HEWLETT-PACKARD Scan-jet, that allows paper to be laid on a flat surface and scanned by a light beam. This allows more precise conversion than a hand-held scanner and is useful for optical character recognition (OCR, sense 2). See also ROLLER-FEED SCANNER.

flat database or **flat file** a DATABASE system in which the data is held in one file or TABLE with no interactions with any other files or tables. See also RELATIONAL DATABASE.

flat memory or **flat address space** a way of using memory that has a single number address for each unit, unlike a SEGMENTED ADDRESSING memory system.

flat panel display a SCREEN (sense 1) display using LCD that is formed as a flat panel rather than in the familiar CRT form. Flat panel displays are essential for all types of PORTABLE COMPUTERS and are coming into greater use for business purposes because of the saving of desk space.

flat thunk see THUNK.

flicker or **screen flicker** a noticeable alternation of light and dark on a SCREEN (sense 1). The standard TV picture flickers at a rate of 50 times a second in Europe, 60 times a second in the USA, and this is not particularly noticeable under normal viewing conditions. On a bright display that is very close to the operator, however, flicker at this rate can be very tiring to the eye, leading to eye irritation and headaches. Displays that use higher repetition rates are not compatible with TV outputs but are much less tiring to use. See also MULTISYNC MONITOR; NON-INTERLACED DISPLAY.

flip a GRAPHICS action that creates a mirror image or inversion of a selected IMAGE (sense 2). A *flip vertical* will turn an image upside down, a *flip horizontal* will reverse it left and right. See Fig. 21.

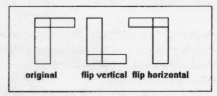

original   flip vertical   flip horizontal

Fig. 21. **Flip**. The effect on a shape when the flip vertical and flip horizontal commands of a graphics program are used.

flippy an obsolete type of FLOPPY DISK that allowed both sides to be used by a drive with one READ/WRITE HEAD by turning the disk over to use the second side.

floating graphic a picture that is part of a document but which can be moved around the page as required. See also ANCHOR.

floating point a system of storing, manipulating and displaying numbers in which the number of figures that follows the decimal point is as many as the quantity needs, subject to the maximum number of digits that the computer will print for a number. This allows the computer, for example, to print results like 2.36 and 5.014 rather than, perhaps, 2.360000 or 5.0142. Most floating-point arithmetic routines will also accept numbers in STANDARD FORM, and the numbers are manipulated in binary standard form, which can lead to ROUNDING errors. See also FIXED POINT; REAL NUMBERS; ZERO COMPRESSION.

floating-point accelerator see MATHS COPROCESSOR.

floating-point unit see MATHS COPROCESSOR.

floating toolbar a form of TOOLBAR that is not fixed in place (for example, at the foot of the screen) but can be moved to any part of the screen so that it does not obscure the document or image that is being edited.

flooding an inefficient method of distributing packets of data on a NETWORK in which each receiving unit distributes the data to each of its neighbours rather than determining the most efficient route.

FLOP a unit of computing time equal to the time needed for one FLOATING-POINT operation. See also MEGAFLOP (sense 1).

floppy disk a thin plastic disc coated with magnetic material and enclosed in a plastic jacket. The standard type of floppy disk is the 3.5-inch type, which in its usual HIGH DENSITY format will store up to 1.4 megabytes of data. See also DISK; HARD DRIVE; WINCHESTER DISK.

floppy disk controller (FDC) the HARDWARE that interfaces the BUS of the computer to the FLOPPY DISK drives, now usually built into a MOTHERBOARD.

floptical disk a form of FLOPPY DISK in which much narrower magnetic tracks can be used because the READ/WRITE HEAD is guided by a LASER tracking system. Typically, a 3.5-inch floptical disk can store around 120 megabytes of data, and much larger amounts are possible. The use of CD-R and CD-RW drives is likely to replace the floptical type.

flow see FLOWING TEXT.

flowchart a method of designing programs that uses standardized shapes to represent computing actions in visual terms. The standard action shapes include terminal, process, in/out, decision and junction, and the flowchart shows the sequence of events in an intended program. The flowcharts for a design are very often constructed with the aid of other visual methods such as a DECISION TREE or DECISION TABLE. Flowcharts were very fashionable many years ago, when computing was taught mainly to those who would become professional programmers, but many programmers always felt that flowcharts were more of a hindrance than a help to good programming.

flow control or **runaround** the use of HANDSHAKE signals in a SERIAL COMMUNICATIONS LINK. For computers joined directly by cables over fairly short distances, HARDWARE flow control makes use of signals along separate wires in the cable that are reserved for the purpose. Where a

MODEM is in use, the flow control takes the form of hardware links between the computer and the modem and uses software flow control signals along the telephone line (see XON and XOFF).

Flowers, Tommy see BLETCHLEY PARK; COLOSSUS.

flowing text or **flow** the action of placing text into a page using DTP or a WORD PROCESSOR. DTP programs deal with text one page at a time, and when the text has been placed in one page, the flow from the SOURCE file is suspended until editing is completed on that page and the following page is selected.

flush to delete any data contained in a BUFFER or other memory space. Flushing a buffer prevents unwanted old data from being mixed with new data.

flush left/right the positioning of text justified (see JUSTIFY) to the left or to the right, respectively.

flutter the rapid fluctuation of tape speed on a BACKUP drive, which may be caused by failure of the speed-controller circuits or by a damaged CAPSTAN spindle. The effect on data recordings is usually to cause CORRUPTION, so that the tape cannot be read. If the flutter exists only on the machine that is being used to read the tape, this can be substituted. If the tape was created with a faulty drive, however, it is very difficult to recover the data. Compare WOW.

flyback or **line flyback** the return of a scanning electron beam on a CRT. A TV picture is built up by a beam of electrons that is focused to a point on the SCREEN (sense 1) and made to SCAN (sense 1) across and down the screen. The rate of scanning across is much greater than the rate of scanning down, so that the beam traces out a pattern of parallel LINES (sense 2). At the end of each line, the beam returns rapidly to its starting position on the left-hand side of the screen. This action is called the *line flyback*. When all the lines of a screen have been scanned, the beam returns to the top of the screen, and this action is called the *field* (or *frame*) *flyback*. During these flyback times, the beam is cut off so that no trace is made on the screen. The importance of flyback is that it occurs at regular intervals. If the ANIMATION of fast graphics is not synchronized to the flyback events, then animation will appear jerky and some parts of the animated pattern will not be visible because they have occurred in a flyback time.

flying head a form of READ/WRITE HEAD for a HARD DRIVE that is shaped so as to be supported on the film of air between itself and the spinning disk.

flyspeck any FONT that is too small to be read without a magnifying glass.

FM (frequency modulation) **1.** an old system of recording data on to a magnetic disk, now used only in modified form. See also ADVANCED RUN LENGTH LIMITED; MODIFIED FREQUENCY MODULATION; RLL. **2.** a method of coding signals on to a radio wave, devised by Edwin Armstrong in 1937.

In this system, the frequency of the CARRIER (sense 2) is modulated rather than, as previously, the AMPLITUDE. See also AMPLITUDE MODULATION; PHASE MODULATION. The system is presently used for high-quality sound broadcasting. This will be superseded by digital sound broadcasting in the lifetime of this book.

FMV see FULL-MOTION VIDEO.

folder see DIRECTORY (sense 1).

follow-up a reply POSTING on a NEWSGROUP.

font or **fount** a set of data that describes letters and numerals of one design and size for printing purposes. Each font is described by the name of its design, a size and a style (for example, Times Roman, 12 POINT and italic). Most printers possess built-in fonts; others can use a font CARTRIDGE (sense 1); some allow the use of a DOWNLOADABLE FONT. See also DTP; TRUETYPE.

font card a CARTRIDGE (sense 1) memory that contains the data for a FONT set for a printer.

font smoothing a system used on some LASER PRINTER designs to smooth jagged lines on large FONTS. See also ALIASING (sense 1).

font substitution the use during printing of FONTS that are different but equivalent to those used on the screen. Substitution is needed mainly when a file is prepared of POSTSCRIPT printer data, and the fonts available at the printer are Adobe (see ADOBE SYSTEMS) fonts, not TRUETYPE fonts.

footer or RUNNING FOOT a piece of text that appears at the foot of each page of printed text. Typical footer items include title, chapter number, page number, etc. See also HEADER.

footnote a note at the foot of a page explaining or enlarging a topic that has been mentioned and marked on that page. See also CONTINUATION SEPARATOR; ENDNOTE.

footprint the amount of space that a computer, plus essential PERIPHERALS, will take up on a desk. A MACHINE with a large footprint may need a desk to itself. The term applies only to microcomputers because larger machines will need floor space rather than desk space.

forbidden character a character that is not allowed in the data produced by a particular program and the appearance of which indicates CORRUPTION.

forbidden operation an action avoided by the operating system (OS) because it will corrupt data or cause a REBOOT. A typical forbidden operation is the use of memory that has already been allocated for some other purpose.

forced page break or **hard page break** a symbol inserted into text in a WORD PROCESSOR that will force the printer to take a new page even although the end of the previous page has not been reached.

force justification a DTP program action. Full justification (see JUSTIFY) normally applies only to lines that would fill more than 80 per cent or so of the allocated line width. When a force justification is used, even a line of only two words will be justified. This is seldom desirable but is sometimes seen in narrow columns of text.

forecasting the use of a WORKSHEET for predicting items such as growth of an amount of money, assuming that the past is a guide to the future. The simplest forecasting uses LINEAR methods, but exponential methods (see EXPONENTIATION) are often more realistic over a short term.

foreground 1. any pattern that is seen on the SCREEN (sense 1). The normal screen colour when the screen is cleared is the BACKGROUND (sense 1) colour. The colour of text or graphics drawn on the screen is foreground. If the two colours are identical, then nothing is visible, so it is possible to draw patterns that cannot be seen until the foreground colour is changed. The significance of this is that drawing can be a slow operation, but change of foreground colour can be very rapid, and this technique can be used for ANIMATION. **2.** a program that is running and producing an output on screen while another program, the BACKGROUND (sense 2) program, is also running at a lower speed, not producing a visual output.

foreign key a DATABASE KEY that performs a cross-reference action.

form a page (sense 1), as used in phrases such as *form length*. See also FORM FEED.

formal methods mathematical methods that assist in the development of HARDWARE and SOFTWARE.

format 1. the CONFIGURATION of a SCREEN (sense 1) display as number of columns and rows. **2.** The set-up of a paragraph for a WORD PROCESSOR or a CELL in the WORKSHEET of a SPREADSHEET or the arrangement of data in a DATABASE program. **3.** the way in which data is organized on a disk in TRACKs and SECTORs. **4.** to prepare a new disk for use by magnetically marking out the surface so that it is divided into TRACKs and SECTORs, with the boundaries indicated. This is accompanied by testing the disk so that bytes are written and read again on all the working surface. Any failure to read a byte correctly will be reported as a formatting error. Some formatting programs will then continually attempt to reformat this sector until successful or until the operator intervenes. A disk that will not format correctly or that formats only after a subsequent attempt should be returned to the manufacturer. Persistent failure to format any disks in a drive indicates a drive fault, although this problem can also be caused by strong magnetic fields such as exist around a VDU MONITOR (sense 1) or TV receiver. **5.** the way in which a GRAPHICS picture is coded into a file.

Format painter a MICROSOFT WORD tool that uses a brush ICON to copy the FORMAT (sense 2) of one paragraph to another or to many others.

formatted output an output that will use specific FORMATs (sense 2). For example, output of text to a printer must be formatted, meaning that it contains codes that will set the printer for the correct margins, font, styles, etc.

formatter 1. a program that will FORMAT (sense 4) a new disk. **2.** see PRINT FORMATTER.

formatting bytes codes used in a WORD PROCESSOR document along with ASCII text to convey the FORMAT (sense 2) of the text, such as font, style, emphasis, page size, margins, etc.

form factor or **form function** a specified shape, such as the AT and ATX MOTHERBOARD designs.

form feed (FF) the form feed, ASCII code 12, that will cause printers to advance the paper to the top of the next fanfold sheet. This is possible only if the paper has been correctly loaded initially and the paper length corresponds to the length setting of the printer.

form letter a standard letter that can be sent out, with small modifications, to a large number of recipients. In word processing (see WORD PROCESSOR), the term denotes a letter of standard text that will need only a name and address to be added. This can be done from the keyboard but is more likely to be carried out using a mailing list. See also BOILER-PLATE.

formula (*plural* **formulae**) a method of arriving at a result through an expression of rules for finding a quantity, usually, but not necessarily, a numerical quantity. A formula would be used in a CELL (sense 1) of a WORKSHEET or as part of a DATABASE QUERY. The items in the formula consist of CONSTANTs and of VARIABLEs, and the formula can be evaluated only when values have been assigned to all the variables. For example, the formula weight x girth / height will produce a number when the amounts of weight, girth and height are entered.

formula bar a type of TOOLBAR used in MICROSOFT EXCEL to build a FORMULA by using an OPERATOR and its associated VARIABLES.

FORTRAN (formula translation) one of the very early high-level programming languages, very popular in the 1950s and 1960s. It is predominantly a language for mathematical, scientific and engineering programs, and its general principles have been absorbed into BASIC. See also VISUAL BASIC.

forty-track disk a DISK that has been formatted (see FORMAT, sense 4) so as to use forty tracks of data. Such disks are no longer used for PC machines. See also EIGHTY-TRACK DISK.

forum or **topic group** a computer meeting place or NEWSGROUP, particularly on the INTERNET, that allows users to exchange views and information.

forward analysis an analysis of program behaviour that arrives at the outputs by examining the inputs and processes. See also BACKWARD ANALYSIS.

forward chaining a way of using rules in ARTIFICIAL INTELLIGENCE work.

Data is used to establish rules that lead to new facts. These rules and facts are then applied to new data, usually leading to new rules and facts, and this process can be repeated until no more new rules are established when data is added, indicating that the system now understands the basis of the data.

forward compatibility the ability of a program or operating system (OS) to be usable by computers not yet in production so that users can be certain of obtaining a long useful life from the software. The forward compatibility of programs for the IBM PERSONAL COMPUTER type of design has been one important factor leading to its dominance.

forward engineering the normal process of engineering design that looks at the overall picture first and moves down to detail later. See also REVERSE ENGINEERING.

forwarding passing on an EMAIL message to one or more recipients.

forward slash the / sign, used to separate sections of an INTERNET URL or to separate a program name from a modifier in an MS-DOS command.

fount see FONT.

fountain fill a GRAPHICS effect used for colour fills in a closed shape. When a fountain fill is specified, the colour shading will alter from one position to another (left to right, start to finish, etc.) rather than being uniform. See also FEATHERING.

fourth generation computer the current type of computer, using IC chips in VLSI form and allowing mass production.

fourth generation language a PROGRAMMING LANGUAGE that is built into an existing application, allowing the user to customize the action of the program. The most usual form is as STRUCTURED QUERY LANGUAGE in a DATABASE program, but to some extent the MACRO LANGUAGE used in packages such as MICROSOFT EXCEL and MICROSOFT WORD is also a form of fourth generation language.

fractal a GRAPHICS image obtained by plotting points from repeated use of an equation such as a MANDELBROT EQUATION or others such as the *Julia set*. The images are always very striking, and, by using suitable starting values, pictures that resemble natural objects such as landscapes, leaves, trees, etc., can be drawn. The strong influence of the starting values makes fractals a useful illustration of chaos theory. The program that generates the images must be terminated by specifying a fixed number of repetitions (see RECURSION) or a limited area in which to plot.

fractal compression a method of compressing (see COMPRESSED FILE) an image by breaking it into FRACTAL pieces.

fragile see BRITTLE.

fragmentation 1. the breaking up of a file so that it is stored in various positions on a disk. When files have been deleted from a disk, the space that they occupy is made available and a new file being recorded can overwrite these spaces. This can cause a file to be stored in fragments all

over the disk. See DEFRAGMENTATION; FAT. **2.** A method used in a DISTRIB-
UTED DATABASE in which parts of a set of data files are located at each of
several locations. See also DATA REPLICATION.

FRAM see FERROELECTRIC RAM.

frame 1. a box drawn by a DTP or WORD PROCESSOR program (a *bounding
box*). The frame, whose outline appears on SCREEN (sense 1), will not necessarily be printed. It is a container for either text (such as a table or a
note) or an image. Text outside the frame will avoid the frame boundaries (see WRAP TEXT) so that the material in the frame is not covered
over. See also MARQUEE (sense 2). **2.** the vertical dimension of the VDU
display. The word *field* is also used in TV technology. The difference arises because a TV display consists of a picture, the frame, built up from
two sets of fields. One field consists of the odd-numbered SCREEN (sense
1) LINES (sense 2), the other of the even-numbered lines. See also INTER-
LACE; RASTER. **3.** in ARTIFICIAL INTELLIGENCE, a network of nodes and relationships that represents an object, situation or topic. **4.** a collection of
data along with error-correction information that is used as a unit for
recording on disk, tape or COMPACT DISC. **5.** a GRAPHICS picture that is part
of a set that forms an animated video.

frame buffer a BUFFER used to store one complete FRAME (sense 2) of a
video image.

frame flyback the point in a TV or MONITOR (sense 1) display at which the
scanning returns to the top left-hand corner of the screen so that a completely new picture is built up. This is done 25 (UK) or 30 (USA) times
per second for TV displays but more frequently on monitors that do not
use interlacing (see INTERLACE). See also FLYBACK; RASTER.

frame grabber a program used in conjunction with a TV camera, camcorder or video recorder to select and DIGITIZE a picture so that it can be
used in a GRAPHICS program.

frame rate the number of FRAMES (sense 2) of a TV display that appear
per second. Higher frame rates produce smoother ANIMATION but
require faster processing.

free-format input any input that is not restrained in size or positioning.
Some DATABASE programs insist that any typed input should be correctly placed and of restricted size while others allow the input to be unre-
stricted subject to terminating with the ENTER key or other recognizable
code.

freeform shape a GRAPHICS editor action that allows a shape to be determined by moving the MOUSE. Such shapes usually need further BIT-EDIT-
ING because the mouse cannot be moved with sufficient precision to
draw with any accuracy. The freeform tool ICON is usually in the shape
of a brush or a pencil.

Freeserve the first high-volume ISP in the UK that offers free INTERNET
services that are supported by commission from the telephone provider

and by advertising. Freeserve was initiated by the Dixons group and has now been floated independently.

free system resources the space available in reserved memory areas by WINDOWS. On older versions, because of the fixed nature of these spaces, it was always possible to run out of system resources even when the total amount of RAM memory was large. Microsoft WINDOWS 95 onwards uses variable memory amounts for system resources and avoids the problems encountered when running programs that make considerable use of resources, such as MICROSOFT WORD.

freeware SOFTWARE that has been placed in the PUBLIC DOMAIN and is therefore free to the user. See also SHAREWARE.

freeze to end the development of SOFTWARE so that it can be released for sale.

freeze-frame video a form of moving picture display in which the picture changes in steps that are at longer intervals than the usual 1/25-second or 1/30-second intervals of a normal video display. Freeze-frame can convey some sense of motion and requires much less BANDWIDTH, memory or disk space. This makes it useful for INTERNET video, and it is used extensively also for security camera systems.

freeze pane an action of MICROSOFT EXCEL and other SPREADSHEET programs. When a view of a WORKSHEET is split into two panes, one of the panes can be frozen so that the information that is displayed does not change when the other pane is scrolled (see SCROLL).

freeze record see LOCK RECORD.

freeze row/title a WORKSHEET action that allows a row or column to be held on screen while other parts of the display are scrolled (see SCROLL). Freezing is usually applied to title rows and/or columns.

frequency the number of times per second that something happens, used to measure the PITCH (sense 1) of a sound, the colour of light or the rate of a CLOCK pulse generator. See also HERTZ.

frequency modulation see FM.

frequency-shift keying see FSK.

frequently asked question see FAQ.

friction feed a method of feeding paper into a printer. The term is applied to a printer action in which unsprocketed paper is gripped between two rollers. This is useful for single sheets and for single-ply paper roll but not for two-ply rolls because the sheets tend to slide sideways over each other, causing unequal margins. See also SPROCKET HOLES.

front end 1. the part of a computer that deals with inputs and outputs. This includes SCREEN (sense 1), KEYBOARD and PERIPHERALS like DISK DRIVES, that pass data to and from the processor stage of the computer. All the actions of the front end of the computer are slow. **2.** an operating system (OS), such as WINDOWS, that makes use of another operating system, such as MS-DOS, with the object of making the system more USER-FRIENDLY.

front panel see CONTROL PANEL.

frozen row or **frozen column** a row or column of a WORKSHEET that does not SCROLL with the rest of the worksheet and that cannot be changed. This allows titles to remain on the SCREEN (sense 1) when the rest of a worksheet scrolls.

FSK (frequency-shift keying) a COMMUNICATIONS system in which a number is represented by a tone, used in telephone dialling (replacing the older pulse system) and in the MODEM.

FTP (file transfer protocol) a set of rules, using CLIENT-SERVER protocol, for transferring files from one computer to another over a NETWORK, particularly the INTERNET. See also ANONYMOUS FTP.

FTP server a NETWORK SERVER that is used for running FTP software. This will have a WEB SITE whose name starts with FTP so as to identify it as an FTP server.

full backup or **global backup** or **system backup** a BACKUP that saves not only all data files on a HARD DRIVE but the operating system (OS) and setup information. For modern hard drives, a full backup requires some form of TAPE STREAMER or removable hard drive rather than FLOPPY DISKS.

full duplex or **local echo** a type of COMMUNICATIONS link in which two-way communications can be effected simultaneously. In a full-duplex system, one machine will often send data that is received by the second machine and immediately retransmitted as a verification. What is seen on the SCREEN (sense 1) of the first machine is therefore the text retransmitted from the remote machine. See also HALF-DUPLEX; SIMPLEX.

full justification the use of variable spacing between words in a line of text so that all lines (except the last) are of the same length. See also JUSTIFY.

full-motion video a display of moving pictures with sound that uses the normal rate of picture change, typically 25 (UK) or 30 (USA) frames per second. Compression (see COMPRESSED FILE) is used so that the data can be stored on CD-ROM or obtained from the INTERNET. Full-motion video is very demanding of storage space and processor speed, and unless a specialized video COPROCESSOR is used can be achieved only in small WINDOWS rather than full-screen. See also MPEG.

full-page display 1. or **print preview** an option in a WORD PROCESSOR or DTP program that will show a view of a complete page. Because of the limited RESOLUTION of the usual MONITOR (sense 1) the lettering of the page will be GREEKED. **2.** or **full-size display** a monitor that is of the shape and size of the paper on which a document will be printed, for example, A4. Such monitors are very expensive but are essential for purposes such as newspaper or magazine production by DTP methods.

full-screen application a program whose display makes use of the full-screen rather than a reduced WINDOW. Some DOS programs cannot be run within a window, and most programs are much easier to use when they occupy the whole of the screen.

full-screen editing an editing system, now universal, that shows text on the whole screen rather than a selected line. Compare LINE EDITING; see also EDIT.

full-size display see FULL-PAGE DISPLAY (sense 2).

full stop or **period** the dot character that is placed at the end of a sentence of text or used as a separator between the main part of a FILENAME and the EXTENSION.

fully populated (of a MEMORY BOARD) with all the sockets for memory chips or sockets for DIMM or SIMM strips occupied.

fully qualified domain name the full name of an INTERNET site, including the COUNTRY CODE and any other letters (such as com, co, edu, ac, etc.). This name is converted into the number code for the site by the BROWSER software. See Fig. 22.

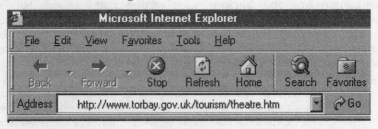

Fig. 22. **Fully qualified domain name**. An Internet site reference is shown as a readable name rather than as a number code.

function a computer action, used in a WORKSHEET, that works on data (see ARGUMENT) to produce other data. A number function will act on a number to produce another number. For example, the EXPRESSION INT(24.6) will produce 24, the INTEGER part of 24.6.

functional specification the initial documentary specification for an APPLICATIONS PACKAGE that describes what the application is intended to do but without details of how the program is to be written.

functional testing see BLACK-BOX TESTING.

functional unit a part of the computer system that carries out a clearly defined task.

function code a code that controls an action rather than causing a character to appear on SCREEN (sense 1) or in print. See also EMBEDDED CODE.

function key one of a set of ten or twelve keys situated above the main letter/number keys on a computer KEYBOARD. These keys are used to provide command actions and can be used either alone, along with the shift key, or along with the CTRL or ALT KEYS (allowing 40 commands to be assigned from a set of ten function keys). Many programs provide for these keys to execute a KEY MACRO instruction.

fuse or **fuze** a method of preventing electrical overload by providing an easily melted link in the circuit. Most microcomputers and peripherals should be protected by a 3-amp fuse rather than by the 13-amp type that is commonly supplied in plugs. In addition to the fuse in the plug, equipment will also use fuses on the low-voltage supplies. These fuses will be internal, located on the printed circuit boards of the computer, usually in the power supply unit (PSU). Any fuse failure should be investigated. Because fuses do not wear out in normal use, their failure is normally the result of either the failure of another part of the circuit or of overloading.

fuzzy anything in computing that is indeterminate. Many DATABASE or QUERY programs allow you to make a *fuzzy search* or *fuzzy specification*. This would permit you, for example, to specify a word like SMITH and get answers on SMYTHE as well because the search allows similar sounding names to be checked. *Fuzzy action*, which deals in similarities and probabilities, is very difficult to program but is an essential part of ARTIFICIAL INTELLIGENCE because human beings can make considerable use of this type of logic. *Fuzzy logic* actions are now used in camera control systems and in a wide range of software.

G

gain access to be allowed to work with a file, as by using a PASSWORD.

game a computer program intended for entertainment. Some games call for manual skill, such as flight simulation games; some for strategy, such as chess; others for devious thinking, such as ADVENTURE GAMES.

games paddle see PADDLE.

gamma a constant for a colour or monochrome MONITOR (sense 1) that expresses the relationship of light intensity to signal voltage. The usual value is around 2.5, depending on which primary colour is being used and the design of the monitor.

gamma correction a compensating system that allows for the value of gamma for a monitor, so that the light output will be proportional to the signal voltage. Gamma correction is usually handled by the GRAPHICS ADAPTER.

gamut the range of colours that can be displayed by a MONITOR (sense 1), sometimes used with the same meaning as PALETTE.

gap or **block gap** or **interblock gap** a space between groups of data, usually applied to tape backup systems in which the data is grouped into BLOCKS (sense 2). Each block starts with a HEADER (sense 2) that contains the FILENAME and some information on the block, such as the number of bytes in the block. A short part of the tape is then left unrecorded between blocks, and this is referred to as the *gap* or *interblock gap*. The presence of this gap allows time for the computer to check the block data and to stop the tape if an error is found. The tape can then be rewound to the previous gap so that another read can be attempted.

garbage meaningless computing data. No matter how well written a program may be, unless the data is valid, the program cannot produce useful results. The motto of all computer users is 'garbage in, garbage out' (GIGO). The name is also applied to bytes that appear in RAM memory at switch on. These bytes are caused by random switching of the memory units and are meaningless. The initializing actions of the computer will clear this form of garbage (see INITIALIZE). Garbage may also be left in memory when one program has replaced another.

garbage collection the action of releasing memory that has been allocated for temporary use. If this system fails, a *low memory* warning may be triggered.

garage in, garbage out see GARBAGE; GIGO.

gas plasma display or **plasma screen** a form of display, now seldom used, for LAPTOP computers that allows a FLAT SCREEN (sense 1) to be constructed. The light is emitted by glowing gas that is ionized by the electrical voltage between metal electrodes. See also ACTIVE MATRIX SCREEN; LCD.

gateway a device, consisting of SOFTWARE that responds to a code, that can be used to connect two NETWORKs of dissimilar type.

gbps (gigabits per second) a fast rate of data transfer of 10^9 BITS PER SECOND.

GDI (graphics device interface) software used to control the display of GRAPHICS on the SCREEN (sense 1) and on the PRINTER.

gender changer a double plug or double socket intended to change the connector at the end of a cable from MALE CONNECTOR to FEMALE CONNECTOR or female to male.

gender mender or **sex changer** a connector for RS-232 serial cables to allow either two MALE CONNECTORs or two FEMALE CONNECTORs to be joined.

general format the DEFAULT FORMAT (sense 2) that a WORKSHEET will use for numbers.

general MIDI a standardized form of MIDI file that will work with any synthesizer.

general protection fault see GPF.

generate to produce a document automatically, as of an INDEX or TABLE OF CONTENTS.

generator a program that will itself generate programs under the instructions of the user. The most common generator programs are for GAME programs (which is why so many look alike) and for DATABASE programs.

generic (of a common standard) interchangeable, applied to HARDWARE (sometimes unbranded) and particularly to SOFTWARE that behaves like well-known examples and generates COMPATIBLE files.

generic mark-up the addition of coded information to ASCII text so as to indicate layout of items such as paragraphs, headers, footers, notes, and so on. See also HTML.

generic thunk a program routine that allows a 16-bit application from an older WINDOWS package to call subroutines from a 32-bit library (see DLL). See also THUNK.

genlock a system for synchronizing video signals so that images from different sources can be edited and combined.

geostationery (of a satellite that has the same angular rotation as the Earth) appearing to hover over one spot. This allows broadcasting over the whole area under the satellite. See also LOW EARTH ORBIT.

GFLOPS (gigaflops per second) a speed of a thousand million FLOATING POINT operations per second.

ghost a faint permanent image, such as can be caused by displaying the same picture on a MONITOR (sense 1) for too long a time (*burning in* the image). See also SCREEN SAVER.

ghost cursor a second CURSOR or POINTER (sense 1), often controlled by the MOUSE, that appears in a program and can be used for selecting commands while the main cursor is used for marking the position of text or numbers.

Ghostscript™ a SHAREWARE interpreter for POSTSCRIPT files that allows these files to be edited and viewed as they will appear in print.

gid see GLOBAL INDEX.

GIF (graphics interchange format) an image file of the BITMAP type that can be saved in a very compressed form. This makes GIF files particularly suitable for transmission over telephone lines using a MODEM. See also JPG.

giga- a prefix denoting a thousand million or US billion.

gigabyte 1024 MEGABYTES.

gigaflops per second see GFLOPS.

GIGO (garbage in, garbage out) expressing the point that the results from a computer are only as valid as the information fed into it (see GARBAGE). A more modern version applied to ARTIFICIAL INTELLIGENCE is EINO, everything in, nothing out.

glass-box testing see WHITE-BOX TESTING.

glitch any disturbance, often a surge in a power supply, that leads to a program failing (usually in the form of a LOCKUP) or causing a computer to REBOOT.

global of or relating to anything in computing that extends over the whole system. For example, a global SEARCH AND REPLACE using a WORD PROCESSOR means that every occurrence of a word will be found and the word will be replaced by another specified word. The alternative is a selective action, in which the operator is notified each time the search word is found and asked if it is to be replaced.

global backup see FULL BACKUP.

global format a FORMAT (sense 2) applied to a WORKSHEET that will affect each and every CELL in the worksheet.

global index a form of file using the GID EXTENSION and used in WINDOWS help files for indexing HELP files and holding information on user preferences for the help window appearance.

global search a WORD PROCESSOR search action for a word or phrase that extends over a whole document.

glossary a list of words or phrases that can be placed into a WORD PROCESSOR document by using a KEY COMBINATION for each word or phrase. For example, you might use the letter *h* followed by pressing the F3 key to print HarperCollins.

goal rule in ARTIFICIAL INTELLIGENCE, a rule that is to be established if possible.

goal seeking a method of solving an EQUATION used by MICROSOFT EXCEL. One CELL, the set cell, contains a FORMULA using values that are referred to in other cells. The desired value for the set cell, the result of the formula, is entered into another cell, and a third cell contains a value that is used in the formula and will change. When the goal-seeking action is complete, the value in the changed cell will be the required amount that will produce the set cell value. For example, you can enter a formula for money growth and find how many years it will take for £100 to grow to £180. The action is equivalent to algebraic methods of changing the subject of an equation.

Gopher an INTERNET utility for finding documents of any type, now overtaken by the use of more modern SEARCH ENGINEs on the World Wide Web (WWW).

gorilla arm a painful arm cramp caused by the use of a TOUCH SCREEN rather than a KEYBOARD.

GPF (general protection fault) a problem arising in MICROSOFT WINDOWS 3.1 in which a program tries to make use of memory that is protected because it is being used by another program. Usually the only option is to close down Windows. See also UAE.

GPIB see IEEE-488.

grabber a hand-shaped ICON in a DTP or GRAPHICS program. This is used to seize and move (DRAG) a marked piece of text or an IMAGE (sense 2) from one place to another.

graceful degradation system see FAIL-SAFE SYSTEM.

Graffiti an operating system (OS) for PALMTOP COMPUTERs that deals with handwriting recognition.

grain see GRANULARITY.

grammar checker a program devised to carry out GRAMMAR CHECKING and analysis of style of a document. Grammar checkers are of very little use unless you already understand the grammatical structure of the language.

grammar checking an action available in a WORD PROCESSOR that will carry out a check for grammatical syntax, such as incorrect plurals, verb tense, etc. The GRAMMAR CHECKER is usually configurable so that it can be set to trap the most likely type of faults. Grammar checkers in general are not so useful as spelling checkers (see SPELLCHECK) because even the best grammar checkers are likely to report faults that are not grammatical faults and also to pass over glaring errors of grammar. The problems are caused by the irregular nature of English grammar rather than the design of the checker.

grandfather see FILE GENERATIONS.

granularity the mesh size of a GRID pattern used to force the CURSOR to move only to set positions (grid intersections).

graph a method of displaying number relationships visually. This is usually done by plotting distances that are proportional to numbers. One number is plotted horizontally (X-AXIS) and the other vertically (Y-AXIS) so that the intersection is a dot on the SCREEN (sense 1) or the paper. The data can thus be displayed as a set of points that can be joined to form a graph LINE (sense 1).

graphic boundary a dotted line appearing around a GRAPHICS image in a DTP, WORD PROCESSOR or GRAPHICS program. This enclosure indicates that the image is selected and can be deleted, moved or copied. See also FRAME (sense 1). See Fig. 23.

Fig. 23. **Graphic boundary**. In this illustration, the frame of dotted lines has been drawn by dragging the arrow icon, forming a graphic boundary. The images enclosed by this boundary can now be dragged to a new position, deleted, re-coloured, etc.

graphic placeholder a rectangular FRAME (sense 1) in a DTP or WORD PROCESSOR page. This frame will hold a place for an IMAGE (sense 2) to be added later, and text will be forced to flow round the PLACEHOLDER as it would flow around an image. The image may be imported into the DTP program or pasted on the paper (as a photograph, for example).

graphics diagrams that are produced on the SCREEN (sense 1), can be saved as a file and also printed. Graphics programs are almost always designed to use high-resolution graphics in which the detail of the diagrams can be considerably finer than was possible in early systems. The VGA graphics card used on practically all personal computers allows a reasonable standard of graphics drawing, and higher resolution and/or a larger range of colours can be obtained by using one of the SVGA systems. Matching colour printers can now be obtained, and the INKJET types can produce acceptable colour renderings at comparatively low prices.

graphics accelerator board an ADD-ON CIRCUIT CARD that uses a COPROCESSOR to speed up the handling of GRAPHICS by relieving the main processor of this task. A graphics accelerator board is almost essential for efficient use of WINDOWS programs and is incorporated into the graphics adapter card for modern machines. See also AGP.

graphics adapter or DISPLAY ADAPTER a CIRCUIT CARD used in IBM PERSONAL COMPUTER CLONE and COMPATIBLE machines. The original IBM PC machine did not provide for a graphics display, and graphics were added by way of circuit cards that were plugged into an EXPANSION SLOT. The system has persisted, although some modern machines incorporate a graphics card on to the MOTHERBOARD. For fast graphics actions, a graphics card should be connected to a LOCAL BUS. See also CGA CARD; EGA; HERCULES CARD; PCI BUS; VGA; VLB.

graphics character a shape such as a short line, corner or other pattern that can be typed on the SCREEN (sense 1) as if it were a text character. Graphics characters can be allocated to ASCII codes 128 to 255 and are present in the character set of the old IBM PERSONAL COMPUTER and CLONE machines.

graphics converter a program that will convert a GRAPHICS FILE in one graphics format to another format, such as TIF to PCX or PCX to EPS. One of the best-known programs of this type in the UK is Paint Shop Pro.

graphics coprocessor a chip that is designed to control the SCREEN (sense 1) display independently of the main processor, allowing much faster operation.

graphics device interface see GDI.

graphics file the file produced by a GRAPHICS program, either of the CAD or PAINT type. The most commonly used files are those bearing the extension letters of TIF, PCX or EPS (ENCAPSULATED POSTSCRIPT) but many others exist, all incompatible with each other and requiring a GRAPHICS CONVERTER program if files have to be used with a variety of software.

graphics file format the method used to code a picture into a file. There is no standard method, and this makes the use of conversion utilities important.

graphics interchange format see GIF.

graphics mode the use of a SCREEN (sense 1) or PRINTER to draw each shape of character or other image by specifying each PIXEL colour. Older DOS programs often made use of TEXT MODE in which one code represents a ready-made character. This is faster but less flexible, and only graphics mode is used by WINDOWS. See also GUI.

graphics pad see GRAPHICS TABLET.

graphics primitive an elementary shape, such as a straight line, circle, arc, rectangle, etc., from which a picture can be made up. The term is used mainly in connection with drawing, using VECTOR methods.

graphics scanner a form of SCANNER that delivers its output as a file in some recognized picture format, such as TIF. In fact, all scanners obtain data in picture form, and most can be set to produce a picture file or to use OCR (sense 2) methods on text to produce a text file.

graphics tablet or **graphics pad** a method of digitizing (see DIGITIZE) a diagram through a network of contacts or tiny pressure switches that INTERFACE to the computer. A piece of paper that carries a diagram is placed on the tablet, and a pen or stylus is used to press on the lines of the diagram, tracing out these lines. As the pen presses on the tablet, the lines appear on the SCREEN (sense 1). The SOFTWARE that allows the tablet to operate is usually devised so that the position COORDINATES of each point can be memorized, allowing the pattern to be reproduced. Once the tracing is complete, the drawing can be saved as a file and further edited in a suitable PAINT or CAD program.

graphics user interface see GUI.

graphics workstation a computer, which may be part of a NETWORK, that is configured for GRAPHICS work using a fast processor and a HIGH-RESOLUTION display with appropriate software for both BITMAP and VECTOR graphics manipulation.

graph plotter see PLOTTER.

greater than operator the sign >, meaning that the quantity on the left-hand side is greater than that on the right-hand side, used in, for example, a DATABASE QUERY. The same sign is also used in MS-DOS for REDIRECTION.

Green Book one of a set of documents, now replaced by WHITE BOOK (sense 2), that defines one of the formats for the CD-ROM. The term is also used for other defining documents, such as for POSTSCRIPT.

green monitor any MONITOR (sense 1) that uses the ADVANCED POWER MANAGEMENT system.

greeked (of text or graphics seen on SCREEN, sense 1, in a DTP program) having the page size displayed on screen too small to show the detail of text, particularly in the small FONT sizes. Greeked text consists of meaningless line patterns that show the spacing and arrangement of text but are not readable. Very small graphics images can also appear greeked.

green PC a PERSONAL COMPUTER designed to save energy. The principle is that devices that consume energy, such as hard drives and monitors, will be shut down if they have not been used for some set interval and reactivated when a key is pressed or the mouse moved. The saving is significant only if several hundred machines in an office are being used every day.

grey scale the number of discernible shades of grey between black and white on a VDU SCREEN (sense 1). The larger the grey scale, the better the picture quality. A good grey scale is important in computer use if graphics are to be used on a MONOCHROME screen or printed in monochrome.

grey-scale image an image that represents colours by shades of grey. This is possible only if the MONITOR (sense 1) uses ANALOGUE signal inputs; monitors using TTL inputs cannot display a grey scale. Some GRAPHICS programs simulate grey shades by patterns (see DITHER), but these often look unsatisfactory, and the best grey-scale rendering on a LASER PRINTER is obtained by altering the density of the dot pattern. In this respect, 600-DPI printers produce much better results than 300-dpi printers, and typesetters using 2400 dpi can provide images of almost photographic quality.

grey-scale monitor a MONITOR (sense 1) that will display shades of grey rather than colours, such as a monochrome VGA monitor.

grid 1. a mesh of intersecting lines used in CAD, PAINT program and DTP APPLICATIONS PACKAGES as a way of guiding the drawing and placement of images. See also GRID SNAP. **2.** a pattern that can be used for gauging shape and size. In character readers, the shape of a character can be assessed by placing a grid (or matrix) over it and measuring the intensity of print in each part of the grid. See also OCR (sense 1).

gridlines dotted or dashed lines used in a MICROSOFT EXCEL graph display to make it easier to assess values.

grid snap or **snap** an action used in CAD programs in which the GRID (sense 1) pattern that is drawn on SCREEN (sense 1) also defines the only points to which the POINTER (sense 1) can be moved. This ensures that the movements of the MOUSE can be translated into exact positions on the screen, so that lines which are intended to meet at a point will do so perfectly rather than just being close.

group 1. a set of objects in a DTP program. A group can consist of a mixture of text and graphics defined by a boundary line. All objects in the group can then be manipulated (moved, copied, deleted, rotated) together. **2.** to collect a set of objects together so that they can be manipulated as one object. For example, four separate lines making up a square can be grouped so that actions such as COPY (sense 2) or MOVE affect the whole square rather than individual lines. **3.** a set of programs in MICROSOFT WINDOWS 3. Any program in a group can be RUN (sense 2) by double-clicking (see DOUBLE-CLICK) on its FILENAME. Groups are not used as such in Microsoft WINDOWS 95 onwards, but programs are gathered into sets that correspond to the groups of Windows 3.1.

group icon an ICON used in MICROSOFT WINDOWS 3.1 to denote a group of programs. Using a DOUBLE-CLICK on the group icon revealed the separate icons for the programs in the group. Groups are not used (as such) in WINDOWS 95 onwards.

group separator the ASCII character code 29.

groupware see COMPUTER-SUPPORTED COOPERATIVE WORK.

group window a WINDOW of MICROSOFT WINDOWS 3.1 containing the ICONS for the programs in a GROUP (sense 3).

group work area a portion of memory allocated for users of a NETWORK to share.

guest a level of ACCESS (sense 1) in a NETWORK that allows the user to work with a remote computer without providing a PASSWORD.

GUI (graphics user interface) a name for a system developed by Xerox and first used commercially in the Apple MACINTOSH that utilizes the high-resolution graphics screen for programs that use ICONs and the MOUSE. Microsoft Windows is a GUI system for PERSONAL COMPUTERS.

guides thin straight lines drawn on a DTP page but not printed. The guides are used to position text and/or graphics precisely and are visible only on SCREEN (sense 1), although they are recorded with the page file.

guru a computing expert who is prepared to advise beginners in an understandable way, particularly over the INTERNET.

gutter the space between text columns in a multiple-column document produced by a WORD PROCESSOR or DTP program.

GW-BASIC a form of BASIC language INTERPRETER formerly supplied along with MS-DOS for PERSONAL COMPUTERS. The GW was an abbreviation of Gee Whiz. GW-BASIC has been replaced by the more structured QBASIC Interpreter on MS-DOS 5.0 and subsequent versions. See also VISUAL BASIC.

hacker 1. originally, a very skilled programmer, particularly one skilled in MACHINE CODE and with a good knowledge of the MACHINE and its operating system (OS). The name arose from the fact that a good programmer could always 'hack' an unsatisfactory system around until it worked. **2.** a programmer who creates programs quickly and shoddily. **3.** see CRACKER.

hairline rule a horizontal line of as thin a LINE WEIGHT as can be achieved. A DTP program will provide for a hairline rule in addition to the more usual sizes measured in the POINT scale. The actual thickness of the rule depends on what the PRINTER can achieve, and it will not be correctly represented on the SCREEN (sense 1).

half-duplex a COMMUNICATIONS link that has two separate lines, one for each direction, but which transmits messages in one direction only at a given time rather than in both directions simultaneously; see DUPLEX; FULL DUPLEX; SIMPLEX.

half-height drive the standard height of 5.5-inch DISK DRIVE used in PERSONAL COMPUTERS, approximately 42 mm at the front panel, 38 mm internally. This now applies mainly to CD-ROM drives, and the standard 3.5-inch disk drives are of a smaller height.

halftone a method of processing a photograph so that shades of grey are changed into areas of small dots whose density produces the illusion of grey shades. Halftone methods have been used for processing photographs for newspapers for more than a century and can be adapted to printing shading on a LASER PRINTER. Unfortunately, the half-toning looks very coarse at the usual 300 or 600 dots per inch of a laser printer, and the appearance becomes reasonable only at very high resolutions such as 2400 dots per inch.

Hall-effect switch a system used for some KEYBOARDS for switching a circuit on and off without using mechanical contacts. A SEMICONDUCTOR is made to change conduction as a magnet approaches it, making use of an effect discovered (for metals) in the late 19th century.

Hamming code a method of detecting and correcting transmission errors in data. Named after its inventor, the code uses CHECK BITS and CHECKSUMS to detect errors in data that has been transmitted. The system is complex and is used mainly in TELETEXT systems.

hamster a MOUSE with infrared beam communication so that no lead (*mouse tail*) is needed.

Han character a set of picture characters used in Chinese, Japanese and Korean text.

hand-held computer see PALMTOP COMPUTER.

handler a part of the operating system (OS) designed to control the action of a PERIPHERAL like a tape or disk drive. The SCREEN (sense 1), printer and keyboard also have handlers. See also DRIVER.

handles the small black squares that appear at corners and at midpoints of the SELECTION BOX around a graphics OBJECT or a FRAME (sense 1). Clicking (see CLICK, sense 1) and dragging (see DRAG) on a handle will alter the shape and size of the box and its contents. If a corner handle is dragged, the ASPECT RATIO of the box is preserved, but dragging the other handles will change the shape of the box. See Fig. 24.

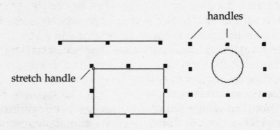

Fig. 24. **Handles**. The small squares can be clicked and dragged to alter the size and/or shape of the image.

handouts paper sheets with a COPY (sense 3) of text and illustrations used on a PRESENTATION GRAPHICS SLIDE. These provide the viewer with a more permanent record of the presentation, making it unnecessary to make notes on the content of the presentation.

hand-roll to install a program manually because the normal automatic system has failed.

handshake a method used in data transmission for stopping data from being sent or received until it can be processed. This is particularly true if data is being sent to a slow-acting device like a printer or a modem. A handshake signal, carried on a separate connecting line, is one that is used to signal ready or not ready for data. When the printer has no BUFFER memory or no SPOOL action is used, this may mean that a computer is unavailable for use until the whole of a printing run has been completed. On longer-distance connections, particularly using a MODEM over telephone lines, handshaking cannot make use of additional wire connections and must be carried out by way of signals. One scheme widely used on small computers is XON and XOFF, using ASCII codes 17 and 19, which are not found in text documents; see FLOW CONTROL (sense 1).

hands-on (of experience) gained by practice and trial and error as distinct from theoretical knowledge.

hanging indent a negative (left) indentation of DTP text. A normal indent uses a larger margin than the remainder of the text; a hanging indent uses a smaller margin, with the remaining text at a larger margin.

hang-up see LOCKUP.

hang-up command a command to a MODEM that will cause it to close the open telephone line ('hang up the phone') and so terminate a communications link.

hard (of a part of a computer system) being in visible and solid form, as distinct from program instructions, which are SOFT or *firm*. See FIRMWARE; HARDWARE; SOFTWARE.

hard boot a REBOOT that starts the system from scratch, with all unsaved data lost. See also SOFT BOOT.

hard character a fixed DTP or WORD PROCESSOR character, such as a space, tab, page break, etc. The hard character will not be altered when text is rearranged, unlike a SOFT CHARACTER.

hard-coded (of DATA) embedded into program code and not alterable by the user.

hard copy a document on paper as distinct from on the SCREEN (sense 1). For older types of commercial DATABASE programs, all outputs are hard copy, with the screen used only for messages to the operator.

hard drive (HD) or **fixed disk** a set of PLATTERS that are made of rigid material, such as aluminium, coated with a magnetic material and normally permanently encased. This construction allows the platters to work in a dust-free space, spinning at high speed, with a magnetic READ/WRITE HEAD placed very close to each disk surface. A drive of this type can offer very large amounts of storage, typically 6 to 30 GIGABYTES, and very fast ACCESS (sense 2). The problem of BACKUP is dealt with by backing on to other hard disks, to FLOPPY DISKS or to various forms of tape STREAMER, but total irrevocable data loss from a hard disk is rare, although data recovery may not be easy when a disk breaks down. The older name of this type of drive is *Winchester drive*, named after the location of the IBM factory that first manufactured such drives.

hard drive assembly see HDA.

hard error a fault in the chips, wiring or other interconnections of a circuit, as distinct from a fault in the SOFTWARE.

hard hyphen a hyphen in a WORD PROCESSOR document that is present at all times and is used within a hyphenated word. See also SOFT HYPHEN.

hard page break a PAGE BREAK that is inserted manually in a WORD PROCESSOR document and will always remain at the same place until moved. A hard page break can be used when a page must end at a particular place, such as the end of a book chapter. See also SOFT PAGE BREAK.

hard sectoring a system of permanent SECTOR allocation, not used for PC disk drives. This is a system of disk formatting (see FORMAT, sense 4) in which disks can be supplied ready-formatted with the sectors always marked out mechanically in the same way. The marking is done by a set of holes near the hub of the disk, with each hole marking the start of a sector. Each hole can be detected in the drive by passing a beam of light through the hole to a PHOTOSENSOR. Compare SOFT SECTORING.

hard space or **embedded blank** or **intelligent space** or **non-break space** or **pad character** a space code used in a WORD PROCESSOR document that will be treated as a character, so that the words separated by the hard space will not be split across a line or a page.

hardware the mechanically visible parts of the computer, such as the KEYBOARD; printed circuit board (PCB); CHIPS; CONNECTORs, etc. See also FIRMWARE; SOFTWARE.

hardware compatibility the construction of a computer so that it can use the SOFTWARE designed for another type of machine without modification or the use of an EMULATOR. An important feature of the IBM PERSONAL COMPUTER has been extraordinary hardware COMPATIBILITY that allows the latest machine to be able to RUN (sense 2) software intended for the earliest versions.

hardware-dependent (of a program) able to be used only on the computer system it was designed for.

hardware handshaking the use of separate control signal lines to control flow of data on data lines. For RS-232 serial signals, the REQUEST TO SEND (RTS) and CLEAR TO SEND (CTS) lines implement hardware handshaking. See also SOFTWARE HANDSHAKING.

hardware interrupt an INTERRUPT signal that is delivered to a processor by way of wiring, usually from a PERIPHERAL, as distinct from an interrupt generated by SOFTWARE.

hardware platform a particular form of computer design. In general, programs designed for one hardware platform, such as the personal computer, will not run on another, such as the mac.

hard wiring connection with wires rather than by using metal strips on (printed-circuit) boards. Hard wiring implies that the connections are made by hand, although automated methods are normally used. In computers, hard wiring is found mainly on connections between units. Hard wiring may also be needed to carry out modifications to a circuit.

hash code see HASHING.

hash collision a problem of HASHING when two items of data produce the same hash code.

hashed key a KEY FIELD number that has been subjected to HASHING to generate a new number. Hashing is used on key field numbers where the natural key number would lead to an uneven distribution of disk records over the available disk tracks.

hashing a method for extracting a reference code number for data in a RANDOM-ACCESS DATABASE. For example, a set of names could be *hash coded* by adding up the ASCII codes for the first three letters of each name.

The resulting number is then used as a reference for locating the name in a file. In any reasonably simple hash-code system, different names may give the same hash codes. This *collision* problem is dealt with by storing the names in sequence at the next available LOCATION (sense 2). In general, a database that uses a hashing system of filing data can reduce the time that is needed to find a given entry.

hashing algorithm a procedure for obtaining an address number from data in order to store the data in a way that makes it easy to retrieve.

hash mark the # mark, used in the USA as a symbol for number and found as a KEY (sense 1) on the keyboard. In US manuals this is sometimes, confusingly, called the pound sign.

hat the circumflex (^) character, ASCII 94, sometimes used to indicate the power of a number. For example, 2^5 can be written as 2^5 and spoken as '2 hat 5'.

Hayes-compatible modem a MODEM that makes use of the control codes originally devised by the HAYES CORPORATION. Virtually all modern modems are of this type.

Hayes Corporation a leading manufacturer of MODEMs, located in Georgia, USA.

Hayes standards the standard MODEM commands established by the HAYES CORPORATION and used almost universally.

HCLO chart (high, close, low, open chart) a form of chart used for stock market prices and showing the maximum, minimum, opening and closing prices of a stock.

HD see HARD DRIVE; HIGH DENSITY.

HDA (hard drive assembly) meaning the PLATTER and head assemblies.

HDAM see HIERARCHICAL DIRECT-ACCESS METHOD.

head see READ/WRITE HEAD.

head actuator the mechanism that moves the READ/WRITE HEAD of a disk drive across the tracks. See also STEPPING MOTOR; VOICE-COIL DRIVE.

head arm a rigid rod that holds each READ/WRITE HEAD of a disk drive.

head crash the contact of disk head and disk surface on a hard drive, causing the disk surfaces to be scratched and made useless.

header 1. or **running head** a piece of text, such as a book or chapter title, or an image, placed in the top margin of each page of a published work. The header for a book page, for example, is usually the book or chapter title. The headers in this dictionary show the first or last defined word in the page. This can be done automatically by a DTP or WORD PROCESSOR program. **2.** a set of signals at the start of the recording of a file on BACKUP TAPE. The header usually contains the FILENAME and numbers for the file length and its position in memory at the time of recording. The header can also contain bytes that assist in protection systems. On replay, the header allows the program to be identified and placed correctly in memory. See also GAP.

heading a classification of text according to importance. A level-1 heading, for example, might be used at the start of a chapter, with level-2 headings for sections in the chapter and level-3 headings for lesser divisions. These heading levels can be determined in a DTP or WORD PROCESSOR programs and used to assign STYLES. Heading levels are also used in OUTLINER programs.

headline a title for a piece of text. The headline is usually distinguished by a larger FONT.

head-mounted display a pair of miniature CRT or LCD displays that are arranged to be worn like goggles, used to provide 3-D effects (*stereoscopy*) in connection with VIRTUAL REALITY displays. See also DATA GLOVE.

head number the number allocated for each head of a hard disk. A six-head drive, for example, will use numbers 0 to 5.

head parking the action of locating the heads of a HARD DRIVE on an unused TRACK so that jolting the drive will not cause damage to data. See VOICE-COIL DRIVE.

head-seek time the average time in units of milliseconds needed for the READ/WRITE HEAD of a disk drive to be positioned on a specified TRACK.

head slot the opening in the casing of a FLOPPY DISK through which the READ/WRITE HEAD makes contact with the disk surface.

heap an area of memory used to store important SYSTEM data while a program runs. See also SYSTEM RESOURCES.

heartbeat any repetitive signal, such as a CLOCK, a SYNCHRONIZATION signal or an indicator (such as a flashing text message), to show that SOFTWARE is working on a lengthy task.

heat sink a massive piece of metal, usually finned, for dissipating the heat from a SEMICONDUCTOR chip. For modern MICROPROCESSORs, the heat sink usually has a fan built in to increase the rate of heat dissipation.

Hello World! a phrase used as a test. A beginner's first venture in PROGRAMMING is traditionally to write a program that will produce this phrase on the screen. Some programming languages may require a page of commands to perform this simple action.

help 1. a program action that provides textual information about a MENU choice or action, usually in response to pressing a KEY (sense 1) such as the F1 key. See also CONTEXT-SENSITIVE HELP; ONLINE HELP. **2. (HELP)** a DOS command that will produce help pages relating to DOS commands. See also DOSHELP.

help online see ONLINE HELP.

Helvetica a widely used SANS-SERIF font, available under a variety of names (such as Arial) and widely packaged as a built-in font for laser printers.

Hercules card a GRAPHICS ADAPTER card, now obsolete, devised by the Hercules Corporation, which for several years set the standard for high-resolution monochrome displays on the PC-XT type of machine. Graphics cards manufactured now by the Hercules Corporation are to VGA and SVGA standards.

hertz (Hz) the unit of FREQUENCY. A frequency of one hertz means that the action is carried out once per second. The units of hertz are therefore 1/seconds, the same as cycles per second, and written as s^{-1}. For the rates that are used in computing, the units of kilohertz (kHz), equal to one thousand hertz, and megahertz (MHz), equal to one million hertz, are more appropriate.

heuristic (of learning) being based on experience, particularly by trial and error. A heuristic program is one that can 'learn' from the response of a user, meaning that the program can modify itself. The subject is of particular importance in the study of ARTIFICIAL INTELLIGENCE. For example, a SPELLCHECK program may learn which of a set of words is the most appropriate for a particular misspelling. See also NEURAL NETWORK.

Hewlett Packard (HP) a very influential manufacturer of computers, plotters, LASER PRINTERS and scanners. The company was set up following World War II as a manufacturer of electronic instruments and has remained in the forefront of instrumentation and measurement ever since.

Hewlett Packard graphics language (HPGL) a form of page description language (PDL) that is used by the HEWLETT PACKARD Laserjet and Deskjet printer range and also by many other printers. See also POST-SCRIPT.

Hewlett Packard printer control language (HPPCL) the CONTROL CODE set first introduced for the Laserjet printer and developed through several versions of laser and inkjet printers to become a standard for these machines.

hexadecimal or **hex** a number system that uses 16 as a base. The digits 0 to 9 have to be supplemented by letters A to F to represent the numbers 10 to 15. In this scale, a number like 2A means 2 x 16 + 10 = 42 in DENARY. The system is used extensively by programmers because one byte can be represented by just two hex digits.

hex dump a display, usually on the SCREEN (sense 1), of the bytes of a program or BLOCK (sense 2) of data, in HEXADECIMAL code, for use by a programmer in tracing errors.

hex pad a HEXADECIMAL keyboard that contains digits 0 to 9 and letters A to F. Early microcomputers used a hex pad in place of a full KEYBOARD because the machines were intended to be programmed only in MACHINE CODE.

HIDAM see HIERARCHICAL INDEXED DIRECT-ACCESS METHOD.

hidden attribute a code bit used to prevent a file from appearing in a directory display using MS-DOS. See ARCHIVE ATTRIBUTE; ATTRIBUTE; READ-ONLY ATTRIBUTE; SYSTEM ATTRIBUTE.

hidden code codes in a WORD PROCESSOR file that do not appear on SCREEN (sense 1) or in print. Hidden codes are used to carry formatting information (characters per line, lines per page, page size, etc.) and to ensure that the printer is used correctly.

hidden file a file that does not appear in a DIRECTORY (sense 2) list of files because of a HIDDEN ATTRIBUTE.

hidden lines 1. lines of a diagram that are intentionally invisible, such as guidelines. **2.** in perspective drawing, lines that are part of a three-dimensional drawing but which cannot be seen because they are masked by the near surface of the drawn object. Graphics programs can often be arranged to draw in these lines in dotted form. **3.** lines that have been drawn on the SCREEN (sense 1) in BACKGROUND (sense 1) colour and will not become visible until the colours are switched.

hidden text text in a WORD PROCESSOR document that is not printed and can optionally be hidden or revealed on screen. Hidden text can be used for notes and other reminders.

hierarchical classification an arrangement of data in the order of importance. The classification starts with the most important headings, each of which can lead to a number of less important headings, and so on. The important feature of this TREE (sense 2) structure (family tree rather than the botanical variety) is that the order is of relative importance, rather than by features such as alphabetical order, numerical size, etc.

hierarchical direct-access method (HDAM) a DATABASE system for obtaining records by using HASHING on root entries, followed by a TREE (sense 2) structure for the entries under each main heading.

hierarchical indexed direct-access method (HIDAM) a system of retrieving data from a DATABASE that uses an INDEX to find main records that contain POINTERS (sense 2) to related records.

hierarchical index-sequential access method (HISAM) a DATABASE retrieval system that uses an INDEX file to find main items and a TREE (sense 2) structure for related items.

hierarchy a form of organization arranged in different levels of importance. A strict hierarchy is modelled as a family TREE (sense 2), with a single root NODE at the top and many branch nodes at lower levels. A *tangled hierarchy* is one in which one branch can lead to more than one level of lower branch.

high bit the most significant (see SIGNIFICANCE) bit in a byte, normally written at the left-hand side.

high, close, low, open chart see HCLO CHART.

high density (HD) tightly packed storage on a disk. The term usually denotes the packing of stored data bits on a disk, measured in terms of bits per linear inch of track. The standard 3.5-inch disk used by PERSONAL COMPUTERS is high density, permitting a storage capacity of 1.4 megabytes. See also DOUBLE-DENSITY; QUAD DENSITY.

high-end applied to the most expensive and most fully featured in a manufacturer's range of products.

high frequency a fast rate of repetition of signal waveforms; see FREQUENCY.

high-level format the format of a HARD DRIVE so that data can be recorded. This type of format, corresponding to the format of a FLOPPY DISK, cannot be performed until after a LOW-LEVEL FORMAT has been carried out using FDISK. A high-level format will appear to wipe all the files from the drive, although it may be possible to recover files after a format if nothing else has been saved since the format. A set of BACKUP disks or tapes should be prepared before formatting a disk that contains data. Normally, a high-level format would be used only on a new hard drive, but sometimes a reformat is needed to wipe out all possible traces of a VIRUS.

high-level language a language that allows you to program without having to know about the MICROPROCESSOR actions that actually carry out the program actions. LOW-LEVEL LANGUAGES such as MACHINE CODE and ASSEMBLER require considerable knowledge of the microprocessor and how it is connected into the computer, along with other details of the computer ARCHITECTURE.

high-level recovery the recovery of data following a program CRASH (sense 1) by the use of BACKUP files rather than by (low-level) methods such as reading the contents of the computer's memory.

highlight the emphasis of a character, word or phrase by using such methods as a change of colour or brightness on SCREEN (sense 1) or the use of bold print or underlining on paper. Also used to mean the indication of selection of a MENU item by placing it on a bright or coloured BACKGROUND (sense 1).

highlighter an action of later versions of MICROSOFT WORD that places a yellow background behind a selected word or phrase, analogous to the use of a highlighter on printed documents.

high/low/close/open graph (HLCO) a specialized form of GRAPH that is used to display stock market high, low, closing and opening prices for commodities.

high memory area see HMA.

high performance serial bus (HPSB) see FIREWIRE.

high-resolution graphics (HRG) GRAPHICS that permit the use of advanced drawing and painting packages. The use of a SCREEN (sense 1) for text demands at most 80 columns and up to 30 rows, corresponding to 2400 screen positions at most, enabling only very coarse diagrams to be made. In a high-resolution graphics system, the number of controllable points is greatly increased. In general, a number of controllable points greater than 300,000 can be taken as corresponding to HRG. See also SVGA; VGA.

Highway a digital connection provided by BT in the UK. This offers the use of twin channels that can be used separately (one for voice messages, the other for computer signals at 64 kilobits per second) or combined as a 128 kilobits per second connection. The cost is appreciably higher than that of using a V90 MODEM.

highway see BUS.

HIMEM.SYS the DRIVER program that is used in DOS to permit the use of extended memory by WINDOWS.

hinting a process used to print small FONTS in which the thickness (LINE WEIGHT) of the characters is reduced to avoid blurring.

HISAM see HIERARCHICAL INDEX-SEQUENTIAL ACCESS METHOD.

histogram a form of data display showing sizes of quantities represented as areas of bars. The similar BAR CHART uses the *length* of a bar to represent the quantity. Its merit is that its meaning is obvious and clear, but it becomes unusable if the ratio between the largest and the smallest quantities is too great.

history a log of previous use, such as the INTERNET sites visited in a previous session.

hit 1. a success in matching data. When a DATABASE is being searched for an item, a hit occurs when an item answering to the description is found. **2.** in the use of a CACHE memory, a hit occurs when the data that is needed is found in the cache. If the data is not present, this is a miss, and the HARD DRIVE will need to be read to find the data and refresh the cache contents.

hit rate the percentage of HITs (sense 2) made in a CACHE memory.

HLCO see HIGH/LOW/CLOSE/OPEN GRAPH.

hlp the EXTENSION letters for a WINDOWS help file.

HMA (high memory area) the memory region of 64 kilobytes in the PERSONAL COMPUTER that lies immediately above 1 megabyte. Because of a quirk in the design of older INTEL processors, this part of memory can be used by DOS without any need for additional software. See also UPPER MEMORY BLOCK.

holding current the minimum amount of electric current that must be supplied to a CMOS memory to ensure that it retains data. For some memory types, the holding current can be so small that it can be supplied for long periods by a battery, so allowing data to be retained while the machine is switched off.

Hollerith, Herman (1860–1929) a founder of modern computer systems who used punched cards to analyse the 1880 US census returns. He later founded the Tabulating Machine Company which ultimately became part of IBM.

holy war any dispute in which fact is totally obscured by fantasy or superstition.

home a starting point on the SCREEN (sense 1). In most text and graphics systems, the 'home' position of the CURSOR is taken as being at the top left-hand corner of the screen.

home computer a computer intended mainly for games and entertainment use and sold as such, as distinct from a PERSONAL COMPUTER (PC) which is intended for serious purposes at work or in the home.

Home key the KEY (sense 1) that can be used, depending on program design, to move a CURSOR to the start of a line or of a BLOCK of text. Like the END KEY, the action is not standardized, and some programs make quite different use of the keys.

home page the first WEB PAGE that a BROWSER will display on a WEB SITE. Other pages are usually indexed from this page.

homophone error the incorrect use of a word because it sounds similar to the correct word, such as 'two' and 'too'. Homophone errors are not corrected by a SPELLCHECK program but can be picked up by a good GRAMMAR CHECKER.

horizontal application an APPLICATION, such as a WORD PROCESSOR, that can be used for a variety of tasks. See also VERTICAL APPLICATION.

horizontal scan rate the number of SCANNING (sense 2) lines that a MONITOR (sense 1) can display per second. UK TV uses 625 lines, but computer monitors employ higher rates, particularly for SVGA displays.

host a large computer used as a SERVER in a wide area network (WAN), the main computer in a DISTRIBUTED SYSTEM.

hostname an identifying name or string of characters. A hostname can be used on a LAN to identify a computer, and on the INTERNET the hostname consists of a LOCAL NAME and a DOMAIN NAME.

host number or **network number** the portion of an INTERNET ADDRESS that identifies the HOSTNAME.

HotBot one of several well-known INTERNET SEARCH ENGINES.

hot key a KEY (sense 1) or, more usually, KEY COMBINATION that is assigned to some purpose, such as starting a program that lies in memory, particularly on the PERSONAL COMPUTER. See also RESIDENT SOFTWARE; TSR PROGRAM.

hot link an active link; see LINKED OBJECT.

hotlist a WEB PAGE that contains a number of links to other pages, so acting as an INDEX.

hot spot a part of a WEB PAGE display that can be clicked (see CLICK, sense 1), usually to move to another page on the same site or to another WEB SITE.

hot swapping the ability to connect or disconnect hardware without the need to switch off the computer. This is normal for USB and FIREWIRE connections, for example.

hot zone the space between the margins of a document in a WORD PROCESSOR.

hourglass icon the ICON that appears on screen when a WINDOWS program is working and cannot be interrupted. This applies particularly to Windows 3.0 and 3.1 because Microsoft WINDOWS 95 onwards uses a different system (see PRE-EMPTIVE MULTITASKING).

housekeeping the actions that the computer must take to keep data intact and carry out program actions correctly. Housekeeping involves such items as correctly allocating memory space, ensuring that there is enough memory for a program to RUN (sense 2), maintaining the SCREEN (sense 1) display, keyboard, disk drive, and so on. This forms a part of the operating system (OS) of the computer that must be used independently of the use of a program. All housekeeping actions are TRANSPARENT to the user.

HP-compatible a printer that uses the same CONTROL CODE set as a HEWLETT PACKARD Laserjet or Deskjet.

HPGL see HEWLETT PACKARD GRAPHICS LANGUAGE.

HPPCL see HEWLETT PACKARD PRINTER CONTROL LANGUAGE.

HRG see HIGH-RESOLUTION GRAPHICS.

HSB see HUE, SATURATION, BRIGHTNESS.

HSRA attribute set the ATTRIBUTE set of Hidden, Secret, Read-only and Archive, used in MS-DOS files.

HTML (Hypertext Mark-up Language) a standardized format for documents that will be stored in WEB SITES. This uses ASCII characters to embed commands or formatting instructions (see TAG) so that the text will display well on the screen and in print.

HTTP (Hypertext Transfer Protocol) the form of CLIENT-SERVER rules for exchanging information over the World Wide Web (WWW). All WEB SITE names therefore start with the characters http://.

hub 1. the central part of a FLOPPY DISK. A disk must be gripped at the centre, or hub, by the DISK DRIVE so that it can be spun at the correct speed. Floppy disks use hubs that are reinforced to reduce the risk of tearing the thin plastic at this point. **2.** The SERVER machine in a NETWORK of the STAR type.

hue one of the specifiers for a coloured light. The hue measures the precise colour that corresponds to the frequency of the light waves. See also CMY; HUE, SATURATION, BRIGHTNESS; RGB.

hue, saturation, brightness (HSB) one of the ways that a colour can be defined in terms of light wavelength (hue), percentage of colour (saturation) and brightness. See also CMY; RGB.

huff to compress (see COMPRESSED FILE) data using HUFFMAN CODING.

Huffman coding a method of coding digital data, using error-correction bits, that has a very high immunity to error and is used for COMPACT DISC systems, both audio and CD-ROM.

hung system a computer system that does not respond to commands. The only remedy is to switch off, losing any unsaved data.

hyperlink a link from one place in a document to another place in the same document or in another document. A hyperlink is usually emphasized in a BROWSER display by blue text and underlining.

hypermedia the MULTIMEDIA equivalent of HYPERTEXT.

Hyperterminal a COMMUNICATIONS PACKAGE that is part of Microsoft WINDOWS 95 onwards. This, along with a MODEM, allows the user to communicate with any other computer that uses a modem, irrespective of the size or operating system (OS) used by the other computer. Microsoft recommends that connections between computers that both use Windows should be made using DIAL-UP NETWORKING.

hypertext a text document (or series of documents) that can be read in any order, using hidden BUTTON CONTROLS. Clicking (see CLICK, sense 1)) on a highlighted word, for example, takes the user to another piece of text – a form of cross-referencing. A hypertext document might appear initially as a contents list for which clicking on any item would lead to an entry for that item, which itself would contain other highlighted words. The HELP (sense 1) system of MICROSOFT WINDOWS is an example of such a system. Extended versions of hypertext are used in MULTIMEDIA publications, such as the Microsoft Encarta encyclopedia, that cover text, pictures (still and animated) and sounds. The disadvantage of hypertext is that it is too easy for the user to be distracted by cross-references and to become lost, so that it is difficult to regain the original place in the document. The main differences between hypertext and normal text are that:

(a) the text can be used in a more flexible way, moving from one topic to another much more quickly than would be possible in the text of a book;

(b) the text can appear in small sections, each in its own WINDOW, avoiding the intimidating appearance of a large amount of text on a screen.

Hypertext Mark-up Language see HTML.

Hypertext Transfer Protocol see HTTP.

hyphenation the insertion of hyphens into words, usually to allow line lengths in a document to be made more even or to JUSTIFY the lines correctly. Many WORD PROCESSOR programs will carry out hyphenation automatically, following a set of rules. See also HARD HYPHEN; SOFT HYPHEN.

hyphenation zone the portion of a line in a WORD PROCESSOR document in which automatic HYPHENATION may be used to split a word.

hyphen ladder or **hyphen stack** the visually disturbing appearance of a set of hyphens occurring in the same column on a set of adjacent lines.

I-beam a form of CURSOR or POINTER (sense 1) shape. The I-beam cursor is used for text in WORD PROCESSOR and TEXT EDITOR programs to distinguish the text cursor from the MOUSE pointer.

IBM (International Business Machines) the largest and most influential computer manufacturer in the world. IBM also manufactures a large range of other office equipment. The firm was a latecomer to MICRO-COMPUTERS, since most of its computing business is in the manufacture of MAINFRAMES. The IBM PERSONAL COMPUTER, although not technically very innovative, set standards in 1980 that other manufacturers have adopted, and it used an OPEN ARCHITECTURE that has spawned a huge industry in CLONE machines, so that the term personal computer is now used as a description of any computer based on the principles of the IBM computer, particularly the AT type of machine.

IBM-compatible computer any PERSONAL COMPUTER that follows the design principles of the IBM PC-AT machine of 1982. The ARCHITECTURE has been developed and refined and is now known as industry standard architecture (ISA). The later IBM PS/2 machines used a different architecture that has not been cloned (see CLONE). See also EISA (sense 1).

IC (integrated circuit) a complete circuit in miniature that has been constructed on a small chip of SILICON. The result is an electronic circuit in miniature form in which all the connections between components have already been made in the manufacturing process. Since interconnections are generally the least reliable portions of electronic circuits, this approach has led to much improved reliability. The development of ICs,

Fig. 25. **IC**. A typical small IC chip of the type used for early microprocessors. Modern microprocessor chips are square, with up to 248 pins, but the smaller types are still used for other types.

intended to improve the reliability of electronic equipment for space use, has made the manufacture of microcomputers possible. See Fig. 25.

icon a small image on the SCREEN (sense 1) that is used to select an action. For example, the image might be of a dustbin. If you have selected a file, then moving the CURSOR to this icon and clicking (see CLICK, sense 1) has the effect of deleting the file. Icons are used in conjunction with a MOUSE and WINDOWS in computers that offer GUI operation. The aim of these systems is either to provide the operating system (OS) of the machine or to supplement it in ways that make the system more USER-FRIENDLY. The use of icons and GUI methods was pioneered by the Xerox corporation and adopted by Apple in the design of the Lisa computer followed by the very successful macintosh range. The success of the MACINTOSH spurred other manufacturers to explore the use of new operating systems and add-ons to existing operating systems to include the use of icons along with windows and mouse use. The MICROSOFT WINDOWS system is the standard GUI for PC machines.

ID or **identification** some disk systems insist on an identification code of a few letters being supplied when a disk is formatted (see FORMAT, sense 3). The purpose of this is to prevent CORRUPTION of the disk when copying is carried out because the system is arranged to prevent a disk being copied to another disk with the same ID mark.

IDE (integrated device electronics) used for a HARD DRIVE for the modern ISA type of machine. In this system, the hard drive itself contains all the electronics of a hard drive so that only a very simple INTERFACE to the main computer is needed. See also EIDE; SCSI.

identification see ID.

identifier a name or set of characters used to identify a number or a STRING in a DATABASE or a named RANGE in a WORKSHEET. See also DESCRIPTOR.

identity hacking the act of posting (see POST, sense 1) messages (to a NEWSGROUP, for example) using a pseudonym or the name of someone else.

idle character a 'do nothing' code, denoting a byte that is sent repeatedly down a connecting line in a SYNCHRONOUS TRANSMISSION to inform the receiver that there is no data to be sent.

idle time the time during which a machine is switched on but not in use.

IE (Internet Explorer) the BROWSER developed by MICROSOFT and included in later versions of WINDOWS. Windows 98 contained the IE5 version.

IEC fitting or **euroconnector** a mains connector that uses shrouded rectangular pins. The mains cable uses the IEC socket so that live pins cannot be touched, and the same form of plug and socket is used to allow a monitor (sense 1) to be powered from the main computer, so that a separate mains switch is not needed.

IEE (Institution of Electrical Engineers) the old-established registration and control body for electrical and now also for electronics engineers in the UK. The US equivalent is the IEEE.

IEEE-488 or **GPIB** (general-purpose interface bus) a standard for interface connections drawn up by the (American) Institute of Electrical and Electronic Engineers. Only data and HANDSHAKE signals are used, and the system is intended in particular for interfacing computers to measuring instruments. Most microcomputers can, however, be connected by means of interfaces to peripherals that provide IEEE-488 inputs and outputs.

IEEE 1394 see FIREWIRE.

ignore all a SPELLCHECK program instruction that allows a word to be ignored throughout a document. This prevents items such as proper names or specialized terms from being queried each time they occur.

ill-behaved (of SOFTWARE) taking shortcuts, misusing the operating system (OS) or directly controlling the HARDWARE so that it is COMPATIBLE with only a limited number of machines.

illegal character a code that does not correspond to a valid character. The standard ASCII codes used for printer characters extend from 32 to 127. Any code in an ASCII file outside the 32 to 127 range is illegal.

illegal operation any action that the operating system (OS) of the computer will not permit it to perform. This might, for example, be a command that would corrupt the memory, misuse the printer, corrupt a disk, etc.

illustration program a drawing program that contains all the features required by a professional illustrator, such as HATCHING and filling, CALLOUT boxes, outline tracing, etc. CORELDRAW is the best-known program of this type.

image 1. a copy of the pattern of each bit in a part of memory See also BITMAP. **2.** a picture or scene that is in digital form or can be converted into digital form by way of a video camera, SCANNER, DIGITIZING PAD or other equipment.

image area part of a DTP or WORD PROCESSOR page. The image area is the space between the margins in which text and graphics will normally be placed, and it is likely to be marked out by the use of a FRAME (sense 1).

image compression the processing of image data into a COMPRESSED FILE. This can be done in several ways, but the highest compression factors are achieved by using LOSSY COMPRESSION methods. See also ARCHIVE; LOSSLESS COMPRESSION.

image format any method of storing an IMAGE (sense 2) as a digital file. Popular formats are BMP, JPEG, TIF and PCX.

image map a screen image that is part of a HYPERTEXT document and contains HOT SPOTS that can be clicked for further information.

image processing the conversion of an image into DIGITAL data and its subsequent processing (see DIGITIZE). Once a TV type of image has been digitized into BINARY data, the computer can process this data in any way that the user wishes. This can be used to enhance the contrast of an image, to blend images, change colours, change shapes, and so on. See also DIGITAL CAMERA.

image processor any electronic system, such as a TV camera, video recorder, etc., used to obtain an IMAGE (sense 2) in electronic signal form and to manipulate this image.

image recognition a branch of ARTIFICIAL INTELLIGENCE that deals with interpreting shapes in an image by computer means. An example is fingerprint analysis by computer.

image sensor a device such as a photocell that provides an electrical signal output proportional to the amount of light falling on a sensitive surface. Image sensing is usually carried out by an array of individual PHOTOSENSORS.

imagesetter or **phototypesetter** a typesetting machine such as the Linotronic that can work with POSTSCRIPT files and produce high-resolution documents on paper or film. Resolution figures of 1200 to 2400 are normal and are better suited to HALFTONE work.

imaging the creation of DIGITAL image files from images, using a camera or a SCANNER.

IMAP see INTERNET MESSAGE ACCESS PROTOCOL.

immediate processing the processing of data as it becomes available, as distinct from gathering the data for BATCH PROCESSING. See also REAL-TIME PROCESSING.

immunizing program see VACCINE.

impact printer any type of printer whose action involves mechanically striking the paper. ELECTROSTATIC and THERMAL PRINTERS use special papers and do not strike the paper. Similarly, the INKJET and LASER PRINTERS rely on depositing material on the paper without direct contact. Impact printers, however, rely on the principle of needles or type shapes being hammered against inked ribbons that strike the paper. These printer types are comparatively noisy and slow, but they have the considerable advantage that they can be used with ordinary paper and also with several sheets of interleaved carbons if copies are needed.

import to read a file of text or graphics, particularly to a DTP or WORD PROCESSOR program, using a file prepared with another program.

imported style a page arrangement for DTP or WORD PROCESSOR use that is read in as part of a file. The DTP program may have been set up to use a format such as A4, Times FONT, 12-point BODY text and 16-point HEADLINE sizes, etc., but a page read in as a file may change the settings to those of the file, importing these styles to the document.

import filter a program used to alter the characteristics of a file used for IMPORT purposes. A text program prepared using WORDPERFECT might be converted to ASCII or to the native format of the WORD PROCESSOR that is importing the file. A graphics file saved in the PCX format may be converted to a BITMAP format to be used in a graphics editor.

improper argument an error in the use of a FUNCTION in a WORKSHEET. When this phrase appears in an error message, you should look for a function whose ARGUMENT is an impossible one. For example, you cannot take the square root of a negative number nor find an angle whose sine or cosine exceeds 1.

inactive window a WINDOW that is available but is not currently in use. The window may be hidden by others and be visible in a CASCADE or TILE view.

Inbox the folder that is used by an EMAIL program to store incoming email or NEWSGROUP messages until they are read. This is indicated by an ICON that appears on the desktop of MICROSOFT WINDOWS and which is used to start MICROSOFT OUTLOOK. See also MAILBOX; OUTBOX.

inbuilt or **integral** (of any device or facility) provided as part of a hardware or software system rather than having to be added.

inches per second see IPS.

include to duplicate an original message in a NEWSGROUP reply so as to avoid the need to open and examine a separate file.

incoming traffic the signals received by a computer COMMUNICATIONS LINK and directed to the computer.

incompatible unable to work with established equipment, applied in particular to computers that do not follow the IBM PERSONAL COMPUTER standard and therefore cannot use the vast range of equipment and software designed for that system.

increment 1. an increase, usually by one, applied to a count. **2.** the distance between markings on the RULER of a DTP or WORD PROCESSOR page display.

incremental backup a BACKUP system in which only altered data is backed up. If a FULL BACKUP has previously been used, the incremental backup is useful for saving data that has changed since the full backup. Note that new files are not necessarily backed up in an incremental backup, only files that were backed up previously and altered since.

incremental data data that represents only the change from previous data, such as the updated position of a vehicle on a road or a change in a set of files that are to be backed up.

incremental plotter a form of PLOTTER in which each LINE (sense 1) is drawn as a series of small strokes, each corresponding to a unit of data input.

incremental writing or **packet writing** a method of writing data to a CD-R or CD-RW disc in which several sets of data can be written in each track. This reduces the effect of the OVERHEAD (sense 2) of 150 recorded blocks (see BLOCK OF DATA) used for RUN-IN, RUN-OUT and LINKING. See also TRACK AT ONCE.

incrementing button a BUTTON shaped like an arrowhead that will increment a number in a small pane each time the button is clicked. Holding the mouse button down when the pointer is over the incrementing button will make the number rapidly increment. The incrementing button is usually placed next to a DECREMENTING BUTTON. See Fig. 26.

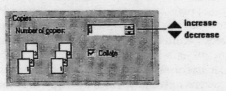

Fig. 26. **Incrementing button**. Clicking on this button will increase (by 1) the number of items – in this example, copies to be printed. The decrementing button has the opposite effect.

indent a space between the normal margin position and the start or end of a line of text. In a WORD PROCESSOR, the term is used to describe the action of leaving a larger than normal left-hand margin. A word may be indented, for example, to mark the start of a new paragraph. A single indent at the left is often used to mark the start of a paragraph, and an indent at both left and right is used to emphasize a paragraph, particularly a paragraph that is a quotation. See FIRST-LINE INDENT; HANGING indent; PARAGRAPH INDENT.

indentation the arrangement of lines in an OUTLINER or OUTLINE view to indicate HIERARCHY of headings by using larger indents for less significant lines.

independent variables see DEPENDENT VARIABLE.

indeterminate (of data or the state of a system) not predictable, such as the content of memory after switching on a computer.

index a method of keeping track of an item in a large set. In text work, an index is a list of key words in ALPHABETICAL ORDER with page or reference numbers.

indexed file a file in which each entry can be located by reference to a much shorter INDEX file.

indexed sequential access method (ISAM) a disk filing method that is a compromise between SERIAL and RANDOM ACCESS. This method uses a second, serial, file as a form of INDEX to the items in the main file. When an item is required, the subsidiary file is searched and the result used to gain rapid access to the correct part of the main file.

index hole the small hole near the hub of a FLOPPY DISK of the older type which is used to locate the start of the first sector. Modern 3.5-inch floppy disks use a slot cut into the hub as a method of locating position.

indicator light a small light (usually LED) which is a method of indicating power on, disk drive active or the state of a toggling KEY (sense 1).

indirection using an ADDRESS (sense 1) number, a POINTER (sense 2) to work with data that has its first byte at that address.

industry standard architecture see ISA.

industry-standard user interface see CUA KEYBOARD.

inequality operator a sign used to indicate that two quantities are not equal. The symbol pairs of != or <> are generally used in DATABASE QUERY LANGUAGES.

infant mortality failure of hardware in the first few hours of use. See also BATHTUB CURVE; BURN-IN.

infection the occurrence of a VIRUS in a computer system.

inference the generation of new rules by using established rules, used in ARTIFICIAL INTELLIGENCE.

inference engine the set of procedures used to deduce an answer from the KNOWLEDGE base of an EXPERT SYSTEM.

infinite retry an option for printer use in which the computer will endlessly try to send data to a printer that is not responding. See also PRINTER TIMEOUT.

infix notation the normal way of expressing arithmetic. This uses operator signs between numbers, unlike REVERSE POLISH NOTATION. For example, the expression 5*4= in infix is, in RPN, written as 5 4*=.

inflate to decompress a compressed file (see COMPRESSED FILE). See also DEFLATE.

infobahn see INFORMATION SUPERHIGHWAY.

informatics the science of information handling and processing.

information any data that is arranged and organized so that it has a meaning to a human user.

information island a set of data files that are not available on a NETWORK.

information management the control of the uses of information technology (IT) within an organization.

information retrieval any method of obtaining stored information. Information can be stored in a DATABASE and retrieved by the request of the user. To retrieve information, the user has to provide the database program with some item from which the DATABASE MANAGEMENT SYSTEM can either calculate the LOCATION (sense 2) of the data or carry out a systematic search. The key item that has to be provided may simply be a reference number or it can be a feature of the data, such as a surname. The system should be able to cope with items that are logically linked (all females of ages 21 to 35, secretarial experience, computer-literate) and often with FUZZY specifications.

information superhighway the global network of fast communications services, particularly those using FIBRE OPTIC or radio (including satellite) links.

information system any computer system that can represent, store, manipulate and transform data.

information technology see IT.

information theory a mathematical basis for treating information. This covers methods of coding data and the most efficient ways of transmitting data.

Infoseek net search a popular SEARCH ENGINE on the World Wide Web (WWW).

infrared (IR) the band of ELECTROMAGNETIC RADIATION whose WAVELENGTH is greater than that of red light so that it is not visible. IR links are used for many forms of remote control and short distance data communications systems.

inheritance the passing of information to a lower level of a HIERARCHY.

inherited error an error in data that is the result of a previous program, action or process.

inhibit to prevent an action, HARDWARE or SOFTWARE. An inhibit signal can be applied to a pin of an IC to prevent it from responding to other signals; an *inhibit bit* in a REGISTER (sense 2) can be used to prevent data being read or written.

INI file a file type used by MICROSOFT WINDOWS 3.1 to hold details of the state of the Windows system and any data required to run programs. WINDOWS 95 onwards uses the REGISTRY file to hold this information for 32-bit applications but retains the use of INI files for the older programs.

initial base font the DEFAULT FONT for a WORD PROCESSOR program.

initialization the preparation of a computer, software or program variables for use with a set of starting values. A computer runs through an initialization routine when it is switched on. In many cases this consists of clearing, and perhaps testing, the memory and then reading a set of data from the ROM into RAM. Similarly, when a program starts running, some variables may have to be allocated with values, and this step is described as an *initializing step*. Large and elaborate programs may require many variables to be initialized by the user, and in this case it is usual for the program to supply DEFAULT values that the user can then change if needed.

initialization file a file of settings used in connection with a program, such as the WINDOWS INI FILE.

inkjet printer a form of NON-IMPACT PRINTER that uses a matrix of fine jets to squirt ink at the paper (older designs used a single jet that was guided by electrostatic forces). The ink cartridge and the set of jets are usually made as one cartridge so that clogging of the jets is avoided by changing the jets along with the ink cartridge. The advantages include fairly high speed, silent operation, high resolution (600–1200 or more dots per inch) and the ability to form any character shape and to execute HIGH-RESOLUTION GRAPHICS. In addition, colour inkjet printers can be made at little more initial cost than the monochrome version, although running costs are higher.

inner join or **join** a DATABASE action in which values in a column of one table are automatically copied to a column in another table.

input an item of data that is entered into a computer. This may be from the KEYBOARD, from a tape or from a disk. The input can also be obtained directly from a DIGITIZER, GRAPHICS TABLET, BAR-CODE READER and other devices. An input may be of as little as a single BYTE or it may consist of a long stream of bytes. Large input items are normally broken into sections of up to 255 bytes by the action of the programs that carry out input. The input material will be saved as a file.

input-bound (of a computer action) limited in speed because the speed of input of information is the main factor that determines the speed of the whole program. The usual cause of a program being input-bound is excessive requirement for keyboard entry. Compare OUTPUT-BOUND.

input device any device that can supply an INPUT to the computer. This includes the KEYBOARD, DISK DRIVE, tape unit and any other PERIPHERALS that supply input signals.

input/output controller a form of INTERFACE found on the larger computers that controls the PATHS between the computer and its PERIPHERALS. This allows the peripherals to be used more efficiently and speeds up the action of the main computer. Some types of input/output controller incorporate both memory and a separate MICROPROCESSOR. They can therefore prevent the main processor from being INPUT-BOUND or OUTPUT-BOUND by carrying out input or output steps while the main processor is performing other tasks. See also DMA.

input/output redirection a SOFTWARE-controlled shift of the normal route of INPUT or OUTPUT for a computer. For example, the input of information might be redirected from the keyboard to a file, and the output might be redirected from the monitor to a printer.

insertion point the position in a document marked by the CURSOR.

insertion sort an ALGORITHM for sorting (see SORT, sense 1) data that compares each new entry with existing entries until it finds the appropriate position for insertion.

insert mode the placing of characters between existing items. Editing often requires characters to be inserted, and many editing systems will insert by DEFAULT (see EDIT). This means that when the CURSOR is placed over a letter, any character that is typed will be inserted between this character and the previous one. Insertion is an essential feature of the editing system of a WORD PROCESSOR. The alternative process is to use OVERTYPE MODE.

inside margin the MARGIN that will lie along the bound edge of a DTP or WORD PROCESSOR page. This will be the left margin of an odd-numbered page or the right margin of an even-numbered page.

installed user base see USER BASE.

installer a program, often a WIZARD, that installs a larger program with the minimum of effort from the user. An UNINSTALLER is often provided also so that the large program can be removed cleanly.

install program or **setup program** a program used to place the file of a complete suite of programs on to a disk. An install program will usually create a DIRECTORY (sense 1) or folder on the HARD DRIVE, read files from a FLOPPY DISK (often in compressed form), decrypt (see DECRYPTION) these files if necessary and place them on the hard drive. Many install programs will require the user to answer questions on the nature of the equipment or on preferences (SCREEN, sense 1, colours, use of sound, etc.) so as to CUSTOMIZE the program. The install program can usually be used again when some change has occurred in the system (a different video system, new printer, etc.). Some setup programs use files that are supplied in compressed form, so that a large program can be supplied on a reasonable number of floppy disks (although some use 30 or more floppies). Compression is not needed when the setup program and its files are supplied on CD-ROM, as is more usual now.

instance a set of information stored in a DATABASE at some particular instant – a SNAPSHOT (sense 2) of the database.

Institution of Electrical Engineers see IEE.

integer a whole number (no fractions), usually of a limited range. The use of data in integer form allows for faster actions on such data as compared to the use of REAL NUMBER data. See also PRECISION OF NUMBER.

integer division the division of whole numbers to give a whole number result, ignoring all fractions. For example, using integer division, $7/5 =$ 1. SPREADSHEETS can use integer division and remainder functions (see FUNCTION; MOD) to handle working with integers.

integral see INBUILT.

integrated circuit see IC.

integrated database 1. a DATABASE that can supply data for several different requirements but with the minimum of redundant information. **2.** a DATABASE program that is combined with other data handling programs.

integrated device a device that is incorporated in another device. PORTABLE COMPUTERs are supplied with integrated disk drives, displays and keyboards. The main advantage is that no connecting cables are needed, but the user is deprived of the choice of how the equipment should be arranged. See also IDE.

integrated device electronics see IDE.

integrated services digital network see ISDN.

integrated software a set of programs that are designed to run together with shared resources. Examples include MICROSOFT Office for Windows and Lotus SmartSuite.

integrity reliability of data. Preservation of the integrity of disk files means that files have not been corrupted. Integrity of data has been maintained in an operation if none of the data has been corrupted or changed (made DIRTY) in the course of the operation.

Intel the corporation that developed the first successful MICROPROCESSOR (the 4004) and has subsequently developed the types that are used in IBM machines and their CLONE and COMPATIBLE rivals. The original IBM PC-AT machine used the Intel 8088 chip, and the faster 8086 has been used in many clones and compatibles. The later PC-AT machine used the 80286 chip, and the 32-bit 80386, 80486 and PENTIUM chips have replaced these earlier designs for applications that call for high speed and MULTI-TASKING. The original Pentium design has been followed by Pentium II, Pentium III, XEON and CELERON designs.

intellectual property the ownership and control over ideas. This is an important aspect of copyright on SOFTWARE and DOCUMENTs in electronic form. See also LOOK-AND-FEEL.

intelligent buffer a form of BUFFER memory used in a NETWORK that can transfer its contents to the correct destination.

intelligent database a form of DATABASE that carries out DATA VALIDATION actions without the need for separate validation programs.

intelligent space see HARD SPACE.

intelligent terminal or **smart terminal** an assembly of KEYBOARD and SCREEN (sense 1) that also includes some computing circuits. An intelligent terminal can DOWNLOAD data from a main computer and carry out some processing work, thus decreasing the load on the main system. MICROCOMPUTERS can often be used as intelligent terminals for MAINFRAME computers. Compare DUMP TERMINAL.

intelligent till a shop till that is a computer terminal, allowing BAR CODE pricings to be read and recorded, and also allowing stock RECORDS (sense 1) to be altered each time an item is sold.

Intelsat abbreviation for International Satellite Agency.

interactive (of a program) allowing the user to respond to the computer and vice versa, unlike the use of a prepared file of input data that is fed in (see BATCH FILE). Most modern software is of this type.

interactive graphics graphics SCREEN (sense 1) displays that are under the control of the user, as for a CAD drawing or a BITMAP painting program and also in GAME programs.

interactive video a combination of computer and video-disk or video-tape player that uses the computer to control the video display, used particularly in CAI systems so that the picture seen is a direct result of the answer a student has given to a question.

interactive video disk a CD-ROM or DVD disk that can be used along with a supporting program to provide HYPERMEDIA information. This is particularly useful for instructional work; see CAI.

interblock gap see GAP.

interface a circuit that allows otherwise incompatible items to be connected. For HARDWARE items this process is called *matching*. For example, a computer may work at a CLOCK rate of 4 million pulses per second and a printer at 20 characters per second. An interface is therefore needed to feed signals from the computer to the printer at the correct speed, and in the correct form, to allow the printer to operate. Interfaces are needed to connect the computer to almost any other device, and in many cases, interfacing problems are the most intractable that a user can suffer. Many engineers believe that incompatibility is the natural state of all systems and that correct interfacing is the exception rather than the rule. Some interfacing can be done entirely in software (see FILTER). Interfacing problems are mainly concerned with speed differences and with code conversions. Large differences in speed between systems, such as the example above, can be dealt with by using a BUFFER into which the computer places data that the slow device can use at a slow rate. In addition, an INTERRUPT signal can be sent by the slow device to trigger a short routine that will feed out a character of data as and when requested. The same techniques can be used when a slow device is feeding data into the computer. Conversions are needed if the signals from or to the slow device are not electrically compatible with those of the computer (now generally 0 V or +5V for logic 0 and logic 1 respectively).

interface analysis a test using SOFTWARE to check that interfaces are operating correctly.

interior gateway protocol a PROTOCOL used on the INTERNET to pass on routing information (see GATEWAY; ROUTER).

interlace a method used for TV and for computer MONITORs (sense 1) that provides higher VERTICAL RESOLUTION with lower BANDWIDTH. In an interlaced system, one vertical scan of the electron beam covers the odd-numbered lines and the next vertical scan deals with the even-numbered lines, so that two vertical scans (*fields*) are used in each frame. See Fig. 27 (overleaf). Although the technique is useful for television, it is now almost obsolete for monitors because it produces a flickering effect on bright images. Contrast NON-INTERLACED DISPLAY.

interleaved memory a method of using DRAM that overcomes the problem of the time needed for REFRESH. The chips are used in banks with consecutive bytes of data stored in different banks. This allows for refreshing one bank while another is being used, and it also allows the use of memory with a comparatively slow ACCESS TIME to be used. See BANKED MEMORY.

interleaving 1. anything in computing acting on slices of items alternately. For example, two programs can appear to be running simultaneously if the computer runs a small piece of each program alternately. See also TIMESHARING. **2.** a method of working with a slow hard drive, now

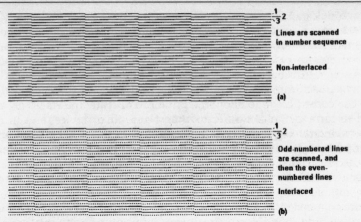

Fig. 27. **Interlace**. A non-interlaced scan traces out all the lines in order, from top to bottom. An interlaced scan traces the odd-numbered lines in one pass, and then the even-numbered lines, thus using two passes (*fields*) to one complete frame.

obsolete. On an interleaved drive, data that occurs in two adjacent sectors is read from one sector on one revolution of the disk, and from the next sector on the next revolution, to allow time for processing.

INTERLNK a data transfer program of MS-DOS 6.0. This uses the SERIAL or PARALLEL PORTS of two computers to connect the machines so that disk drives and printers can be shared. This is by far the simplest way of achieving a limited form of networking (see NETWORK) between two machines. The linked machines can use DOS or WINDOWS programs.

interlock a form of security device. In computing, it refers to a PASSWORD system that is part of a LOG-ON procedure and is intended to prevent unauthorized use.

intermediate storage see TEMPORARY STORAGE.

internal cache a portion of CACHE memory that is formed as part of a MICROPROCESSOR chip, used in 80486, Pentium and later chip designs. See also LEVEL 1 CACHE.

internal codes number codes other than ASCII for characters used in the operating system (OS) but not transmitted externally.

internal command a command in MS-DOS that is part of the operating system (OS) and can be executed without the need to load any other files because it is held in MEMORY, unlike an EXTERNAL COMMAND held on the HARD DRIVE.

internal hard drive the normal arrangement of a HARD DRIVE inside the casing of the computer and permanently connected to the MOTHER-BOARD. See also EXTERNAL HARD DRIVE; PARALLEL-PORT DEVICE.

internal memory see CORE MEMORY.

internal modem a MODEM on a CIRCUIT CARD that is inserted into an

EXPANSION SLOT on the MOTHERBOARD of a computer. Contrast EXTERNAL MODEM.

International Business Machines see IBM.

international data encryption algorithm an ALGORITHM devised in 1992 for secure messages. See PRETTY GOOD PRIVACY.

internationalization the methods used to allow an application program to be configured by a user for different languages, weights and measures, currency units, date formats and time zones.

International Organization for Standardization (ISO) the body that sets and maintains international standards for computer and communications technology.

International Standards Organization Open System Interconnection see ISO/OSI.

Internet a set of linked computers world-wide, using telephone and satellite communications. At its best, it can be a valuable way of exchanging information; at its worst it rivals Citizens' Band radio for banality and trivia. The Internet is unregulated, and the international transmissions are paid for by governments and by universities, a situation that is unlikely to continue and which arose because of the roots of the Internet in military requirements for a system that was too widespread to be crippled by bombing. The main problem of using the Internet (apart from the high cost in the UK of all telephone contacts) is the time needed to gain access to anything useful, although several utility programs are now available to speed up this process. See also EMAIL; WWW.

Internet access provider see ISP.

Internet address a 32-bit number that identifies an Internet HOST. This number is usually written in decimal form in four groups separated by dots, for example, 195.147.216.26. This number is seldom used directly because a BROWSER can find the Internet address number from the DOMAIN NAME.

Internet assigned numbers authority a central registration bureau for number codes relating to INTERNET use.

Internet backbone the fast NETWORKs that carry long-distance INTERNET information. These include FIBRE OPTIC and satellite links.

Internet Explorer see IE.

Internet message access protocol (IMAP) a PROTOCOL for EMAIL that allows the user access to a remote MAILBOX to work with stored messages. See also SMTP.

Internet number see INTERNET ADDRESS.

Internet relay chat (IRC) a world-wide NETWORK of message services allowing a CHAT SYSTEM to be set up between users.

Internet service provider see ISP.

Internet Society a professional organization dedicated to the maintenance and improvement of the INTERNET and education of prospective users.

Internet telephony the use of the INTERNET to carry digitized (see DIGITIZE) voice messages. This avoids costly telephone charges for international calls and is not subject to the regulations that affect normal telephone use. Telephony requires the use of a VOICE MODEM or an ISDN line.

interoperability the ability to communicate data from one set of SOFTWARE and HARDWARE to another.

inter-packet gap a time delay between consecutive data PACKETs on a NETWORK.

interpolation the action of finding a quantity from a set of known values by proportion or by reading from a graph. The quantity to be found must lie within the existing range; if not, the action is EXTRAPOLATION, which is a much less reliable process.

interpreted language a language such as QBASIC or JAVA that is implemented by an INTERPRETER.

interpreter a program for running a language such as BASIC step by step. An interpreter reads an instruction from a program text, locates a set of machine code bytes that will carry out the action and then executes the instruction before reading the next instruction. This can be a comparatively slow process because it means that each instruction word has to be analysed each time it is encountered. See also COMPILER; JAVA; VISUAL BASIC.

interprocess communication (IPC) the transmission of data between programs that are running simultaneously, as in WINDOWS. See also DDE; OLE.

interrupt an electrical signal to the MICROPROCESSOR that will cause the processor to complete its current instruction, save the data it is working on and then attend to the device that has caused the interruption. After running a program, the *service routine*, which attends to the device, the microprocessor will recover its data and resume executing the program.

interrupt handler or **interrupt service routine** a routine that deals with an INTERRUPT and restores the action that the computer was engaged on when the interrupt occurred.

interrupt mask or **maskable interrupt** a code bit that inhibits the processing of an INTERRUPT. Microprocessors make provision for two types of interrupt, the maskable type, which can be inhibited in this way, and the non-maskable, which cannot and must not be interrupted.

interrupt request (IRQ) a hardware or software signal into a MICROPROCESSOR that causes an INTERRUPT to be executed whenever possible.

interrupt service routine see INTERRUPT HANDLER.

intranet a NETWORK that operates in a way similar to the INTERNET but which is confined to a single organization or set of organizations. An intranet need not be connected to the Internet, but when such a connection is made it is through a FIREWALL so that a VIRUS cannot be transmitted from the Internet to the intranet.

intrinsic function a FUNCTION that is built into an operating system (OS) or a program such as a SPREADSHEET. The use of an intrinsic function will not require a separate disk file to be read to carry out the action.

invalid parameter an ERROR MESSAGE that is triggered when a DOS command word has been followed by incorrect data. For example, using DIR K: when no drive labelled as K: exists would trigger this message.

inverse video or **reverse video** a display that uses black text on white BACKGROUND (sense 1) when the normal display consists of white text on a black background. The name denotes any display that interchanges the normal background and foreground colours.

inverted commas or **double-quotes** the " " signs used in some DATABASE programs or in QUERY LANGUAGE to mark a STRING.

inverting the interchanging of bits 0 and 1. Inverting the byte 11110000, for example, would give the byte 00001111. See also COMPLEMENT; NEGATION; TWOS COMPLEMENT.

invoking add-in the action of running an ADD-IN program.

I/O see INPUT/OUTPUT.

IO-bound used of a system in which slow INPUT and output routines limit the speed of programs.

Iomega Corporation a major manufacturer of BACKUP HARDWARE such as tape drives (see STREAMER).

I/O redirection see REDIRECTION.

IO.SYS the FILENAME for one of the two HIDDEN and SYSTEM FILES of the MS-DOS operating system (OS). The IO.SYS file links the operating system to the routines that are held in the BIOS ROM for ACCESS (sense 2) to inputs and outputs. See also MS-DOS.

IPC see INTERPROCESS COMMUNICATION.

ips (inches per second) the measure of tape speed on a BACKUP system.

IR see INFRARED.

Iron Age the years from 1961 to 1971 when computers were large, bulky, made to order and programmed to order. The Iron Age ended when the first MICROPROCESSORS became available.

IRC see INTERNET RELAY CHAT.

IRQ (interrupt request) a code passed to a MICROPROCESSOR that initiates an INTERRUPT.

irrational number a number that cannot be expressed by the ratio of two integers. A well-known example is the ratio of circumference to diameter of a circle, pi (π).

irregular case a document fault that can be corrected by a SPELLCHECK or a GRAMMAR CHECKER of a WORD PROCESSOR. This will detect such misuses as the word 'THat' and alter it to 'That'.

ISA (industry standard architecture) the use of design and construction methods that are based on the IBM PC-AT and are followed by virtually all PERSONAL COMPUTER manufacturers (although not necessarily by IBM itself). See also CLONE; EISA (sense 1); IBM COMPATIBLE.

ISAM see INDEXED SEQUENTIAL ACCESS METHOD.

ISDN (integrated services digital network) a communications system that uses DIGITAL methods for audio, video and data signals. The basis of ISDN is FIBRE OPTIC lines overland along with satellite communications for longer haul communications. The use of ISDN will eventually supersede the older type of telephone lines.

ISO see INTERNATIONAL ORGANIZATION FOR STANDARDIZATION.

ISO 9660 the standard for the CD-ROM file system.

ISO Latin I the ISO 8859 standard set of 8-bit codes for European languages. This is the normal set used in place of ASCII for WORD PROCESSORS and other SOFTWARE in Europe.

ISO/OSI (International Standards Organization Open System Interconnection) a standard design for a NETWORK that defines seven levels or layers of actions, each layer making use of the layers below it.

ISP (Internet service provider) an organization that administers a large computer system that deals with access to the INTERNET for users. Most ISPs also provide other services, such as EMAIL, WEB SITES for users, news and advertising.

IT (information technology) a loose term that encompasses virtually all aspects of computing, data recording, TV, video and communications. IT means any modern electronic technology that deals with information and its use.

italic a slanting form of type used for emphasis. All WORD PROCESSOR and DTP programs will provide for use of italic letters in each FONT. See also OBLIQUE.

item a single unit of data. An item may be represented by one BIT, one BYTE or a large number of bytes, depending on the complexity of the item.

item size the number of BYTES needed to represent an item.

iteration a method of solving problems by the repeated application of a routine. Mathematical solutions that use iteration are particularly suited to solution by computing methods, and several SPREADSHEET FUNCTIONS use such methods.

jacket the cardboard or plastic cover for a FLOPPY DISK. This has holes and slots cut into it so as to expose the HUB and also to allow the READ/WRITE HEADS access to the disk. The older type of floppy disks, now obsolete, in the 8-inch and 5.25-inch sizes used stiff plastic or cardboard jackets with glued or crimped seams. The smaller 3.5-inch disks use rigid plastic envelopes, with spring-loaded sliding metal shutters to protect the disk surface from being accidentally touched. This makes for greater INTEGRITY of data.

jack plug a form of audio connector of the COAXIAL CABLE type that is used on a sound card for inputs and outputs, particularly from a microphone and to an amplifier. A *jack socket* is also used on a CD-ROM drive so that audio compact discs can be played.

jaggies see ALIASING.

jam see LOCKUP.

JANET (joint academic network) a long-haul NETWORK that is used to link university computer systems in the UK.

jar a sharp knock that will cause hardware damage, particularly to a HARD DRIVE. See also PARK.

Java a simple INTERPRETED programming language developed by Sun Microsystems and used for creating APPLETS (sense 2) to be downloaded with INTERNET files and run on the user's computer.

Jaz™ drive a form of BACKUP system from IOMEGA CORPORATION that uses removable HARD DRIVE cartridges.

JCL see JOB CONTROL LANGUAGE.

jewel case the transparent hard plastic case used for a CD-ROM.

JFIF (JPEG File Interchange Format) a GRAPHICS file format that is used for DIGITAL CAMERAS. Each image is converted to this format and stored in the memory of the camera to be eventually downloaded (see DOWNLOAD) to the computer.

jitter a display fault on the SCREEN (sense 1). A displayed picture is said to jitter if it can be seen to be rapidly moving up and down by a short distance. This is very unpleasant to watch and is usually caused by faulty SYNCHRONIZATION of the video field (vertical) signals. This can be because of the MONITOR (sense 1) itself or, more likely, the video signals from the computer.

job a complete piece of work, usually involving many processes on a large amount of data. A job may require one or more program RUNs (sense 1) and may also require more than one program to be used.

job control language (JCL) a form of programming language that controls the use of applications programs and the data that is fed to such programs. The MS-DOS form is the BATCH FILE, and the UNIX form is the SHELL procedure or shell script. See also MACRO.

job control program a program written in the JOB CONTROL LANGUAGE to carry out a defined series of tasks. For MS-DOS this is called a BATCH FILE.

job queue a list of tasks that will be carried out in order.

join see INNER JOIN.

join command an old MS-DOS command to assign a drive, not used now. For example, the command JOIN B: C:\SUBDIR will make the contents of the disk in drive B part of the SUBDIR DIRECTORY. This directory must be empty before JOIN is used. The command must not be used when the Windows system is being run.

Joint Photographic Expert Group see JPEG.

journal or **log file** a list of actions such as changes to a file or messages in and out of a terminal.

journalling maintaining a log of all messages sent or received on a computer system.

joystick a miniature version of the aircraft control stick, which can generate electrical signals. On computers that contain a joystick PORT, this allows position control of a cursor or a graphics character if a suitable DRIVER program is running. The use of joysticks is by no means confined to games, and the principle of control without the use of the keyboard has been extended via the TRACKERBALL to the MOUSE.

JPEG (Joint Photographic Expert Group) the committee that devised a standard form of image file format and compression (see COMPRESSED FILE) method. Files saved in JPEG format can be surprisingly small, but the format uses LOSSY COMPRESSION, so that such files should not be edited and resaved. A form of JPEG called JFIF is often used as a file compression method for DIGITAL CAMERA storage systems.

jpg the file EXTENSION that identifies a JPEG image file.

jukebox a multiple drive that allows a set of CD-ROM discs to be used.

jump the action of moving from one WEB PAGE to another.

jumper a connector that can be placed over a set of pins on a circuit board so as to set some feature of the action of the board. Many boards require a set of jumpers or switches to be set so that the correct functions can be activated (see MULTIFUNCTION CARD). The use of plug and play (PNP) devices should make the use of jumpers obsolete on cards for modern computers, although some jumpers may need to be set on the MOTHERBOARD.

jump term an underlined or shaded word in a Help document. Clicking (see CLICK, sense 1) on the jump term will cause a cross-reference page to appear. See also HYPERTEXT.

junction box a box containing a terminal strip where several connectors are joined.

junk 1. out of data information or hardware. **2.** to scrap a file or a piece of hardware.

junk email undesired and unsolicited EMAIL that advertises unwanted goods. See also SPAM.

justify to line up text by adjusting the spaces between the words. Text is normally left-justified, meaning that each line starts at the same position relative to the left-hand side of a page, with the exception of new paragraphs and other indented material (see INDENT). If only LEFT JUSTIFICATION is used, the right-hand side of the text will appear irregular. When RIGHT JUSTIFICATION is used, the last character in each line is placed at a specified position relative to the right-hand side of the paper. Text can also be fully justified so that each line, which would occupy at least 80 per cent of the available width, will be spaced out to fill the width of a page exactly. The other justification system is CENTRING, in which each line is exactly centred between the margins. All these justification actions can be carried out by any DTP program or a good WORD PROCESSOR program.

K

K (computing kilo) in computing, the upper-case K is used to mean the number 1024, which is two to the power ten (2^{10}). This is the unit that is implied in words such as KILOBYTE.

k or **kilo** one thousand, as in kilohertz.

K56flex™ a standard system for fast MODEMS (56,000 bits per second) developed by Rockwell. This and the rival X2™ system have now been merged into a single V90 standard.

K6 a processor comparable with the PENTIUM in performance, manufactured by ADVANCED MICRO DEVICES (AMD). Although the INTEL Pentium II and Pentium III and CELERON now use a slot fitting, the AMD K6 processors have retained the smaller Socket-7 fitting. There have been several versions of the K6, labelled as 1, 2 and 3. See also ATHLON.

kanji the Japanese form of HAN CHARACTER. Kanji characters exist in UNICODE but not in ASCII.

Kansas City standard an old-established standard of data recording. This was drawn up in the late 1970s in the USA to pave the way for exchange of data on audio cassettes. It is still used in some industrial applications of data storage.

kbps (kilobits per second) a measure of data transfer rate.

Kbyte see KILOBYTE.

keep lines together an instruction relating to the formatting (see FORMAT, sense 2) of a paragraph in a WORD PROCESSOR. By using this option, the lines of a paragraph will not be split by a page break, a table or a graphics FRAME (sense 1).

keep with next an instruction relating to the formatting (see FORMAT, sense 2) of a paragraph in a WORD PROCESSOR. When this option is used, the paragraph will be kept with the following paragraph and cannot be separated by a page break, a table or a graphics FRAME (sense 1).

KERMIT a COMMUNICATIONS PACKAGE system that allows files to be sent through a SERIAL INTERFACE with a checking system that prevents a corrupted file from being received, used mainly in the USA by colleges.

kernel the fundamental part of an operating system (OS) that provides routines for interfacing (see INTERFACE) with the HARDWARE.

kerning or **pair-kerning** the adjustment of spacing between printed characters. True PROPORTIONAL SPACING applied to large sizes of lettering results in some pairs of letters such as To, We, Tw, etc., being spaced wider apart than is pleasing, and kerning is the process of reducing these spacings, usually automatically. Many WORD PROCESSOR and all DTP programs allow the kerning limit DEFAULT to be set by the user. This decides what minimum size of FONT will be kerned. For example, you might set the lower limit of kerning to 18-point, so that smaller sizes are not kerned.

key 1. a touch-controlled BUTTON or an unlocking device. The keys of the KEYBOARD of a computer are buttons, each of which operates a miniature electrical switch. **2.** see KEY FIELD. **3.** a set of characters used in the ENCRYPTION and DECRYPTION of data.

key assignment the action produced when a KEY (sense 1) is pressed. All the keys on a KEYBOARD are programmable, but the standard assignment of letters, numerals and punctuation marks is normally used. Programs that allow different key assignments usually require the CTRL or ALT KEYS to be used along with ALPHANUMERIC keys.

KEYB a DRIVER program used in MS-DOS to ensure that the KEYBOARD is suited to the language being used. The program uses an information file that contains language-specific information, so that the instruction KEYB UK will be found in the AUTOEXEC.BAT file for UK computers.

keyboard the assembly of KEYS (sense 1) by which we communicate with the computer. Since the keyboard is the most used part of the computer, a good keyboard is an essential part of any computer that will be used for business purposes. This generally implies keys with a reasonable range of movement, as on a typewriter. Various mechanisms are used, and all can be made to provide good positive action if well constructed. Since the feel of a keyboard is a matter of individual preference, it is important to try out a keyboard before buying one. Keyboards for the PC type of computer are of standardized forms and are readily available for replacement purposes.

keyboard buffer a portion of memory used to hold the codes generated from pressing KEYS (sense 1). This allows the computer to suspend reading the KEYBOARD for short periods (such as when access to a DISK DRIVE is needed) without losing typed information.

keyboard layout the standardized position of keys. In English-speaking countries, the standard layout is described as QWERTY, from the characters on the top half-line of keys. In several continental European countries, the AZERTY layout is followed. See also DVORAK; MALTRON; MICROSOFT NATURAL KEYBOARD.

keyboard overlay see KEYBOARD TEMPLATE.

keyboard plaque the layer of greasy dirt that builds up on a much used KEYBOARD. Plaque can be removed by using cleaning sprays.

keyboard processor a MICROPROCESSOR that is part of the KEYBOARD circuits, used to detect key closure and generate the appropriate codes. This relieves the main processor of the work and therefore speeds computing actions.

keyboard scan the process by which the depression of a key is detected.

Signals are sent in turn to the row lines of the KEYBOARD MATRIX, and any output from the column lines is detected and used to form the KEY NUMBER code. On most modern computers, this set of actions is carried out by an independent KEYBOARD PROCESSOR in the keyboard.

keyboard shortcut see FAST KEY.

keyboard template or **key overlay** or **keystrip** a paper or plastic printed strip that can be placed on the KEYBOARD, usually between the function keys and the main key set. The template is a reminder of how a program makes use of keys, and templates are available for WORD PROCESSOR, SPREADSHEET, DATABASE, CAD and other programs.

key click the sound made by a key being pressed. On some keyboards that are silent, the sound can be generated by software with an output to the small loudspeaker of the PC machine. See also CLICK (sense 2).

key code number the internal code for a key. This is the internal code number that is returned to the memory of the computer when a given key is pressed. The internal code number is not usually the same as the ASCII code number.

key combination the use of more than one KEY (sense 1) to provide an action. The combination can be of two ALPHANUMERIC keys or of the CTRL or ALT KEYS along with an alphanumeric key. In some cases, a key combination can use keys pressed in sequence rather than together, and this latter method is particularly useful for disabled keyboard users. See also STICKY KEY ACTION.

key disk a form of COPY-PROTECTION scheme, now obsolete, that requires a FLOPPY DISK to be inserted before a program can be started.

keyed-hashing message authentication a method of applying a DIGITAL SIGNATURE to a message, using HASHING.

key field or **key** or **access field** or **access point** the FIELD (sense 2) in a RECORD (sense 1) of a data file that is used for indexing and retrieving the data. The key field contains an ALPHANUMERIC 'word' (the *key*), which is unique to that record.

key frame a drawing that is one FRAME (sense 5) of a set used in an ANIMATION. The key frame is the one that has been drawn manually; the others are computer-generated.

key macro a set of instructions that are executed when a KEY (sense 1) or KEY COMBINATION is used, usually involving the FUNCTION KEYS, the CTRL key or the ALT KEY. By using key macros, the control of a program can be tailored to suit the user. Key macros are commonly available in WORD PROCESSOR and SPREADSHEET programs in order to automate processes that would otherwise require a considerable number of key actions.

keymatic action see AUTOREPEAT.

key matrix a way of wiring key switches. Each KEY (sense 1) on the KEYBOARD operates a small on/off switch. To avoid a mass of wiring, the key switches are connected in groups so that they can be accessed by COOR-

DINATES (rows, column numbers). This is known as a *matrix connection*, and it can sometimes cause odd effects, like finding that holding down three keys can simulate the action of another key. The computer operating system (OS) must contain routines that will interpret the matrix numbers and find the correct ASCII codes.

key overlay see KEYBOARD TEMPLATE.

keypad an auxiliary set of keys, usually numeric and used for entry of numbers.

key redefinition the action of reprogramming each KEY ASSIGNMENT so that pressing a KEY (sense 1) produces some other character or action.

key rollover or **N-key rollover** a system that allows fast typing. Simple types of KEYBOARDS respond to one key at a time and may give nothing if two or more keys are pressed in rapid succession. Key rollover is a system that makes use of a BUFFER memory to hold the result of keystrokes that are made almost simultaneously. The buffer is read by the computer in the brief intervals when keys are not being pressed.

key status indicator a light that reminds the user of the state of LOCK KEYS, such as CAPS LOCK and NUM LOCK.

keystrip see KEYBOARD TEMPLATE.

keystroke the action of pressing a single KEY (sense 1).

key to disk a system of direct disk entry. When a KEY (sense 1) is struck on the KEYBOARD, the ASCII code for the character is stored directly on a disk rather than being held in the memory of the computer. In practice, what is done is that the codes are entered into a BUFFER and transferred to the disk only when the buffer is full.

key variable a constant quantity placed in a CELL of a WORKSHEET, preferably a PROTECTED CELL, and referred to in other cells. For example, the rate of VAT could be placed in a cell and used in each cell that required a VAT calculation.

keyword a word that is part of a name or description used to identify a RECORD (sense 1) in a DATABASE. In a phrase such as 'description of transformer action', the keyword is 'transformer' since none of the other words is significant. In a phrase such as 'history of steam locomotives', the words 'history', 'steam' and 'locomotive(s)' might all be used as keywords although not necessarily of equal importance.

Khornerstone one of several BENCHMARK programs that attempt to measure several aspects of computer performance. See also DHRYSTONE; WHETSTONE.

killer application a program that is available for a specific machine and which is so desirable that users will buy the hardware simply to obtain the software. The first SPREADSHEET program was a killer application for the Apple-2 computer.

kill file to delete a file.

kilo see K.

kilobaud a speed of 1000 BAUD.

kilobyte or **Kbyte** the term for 1024 bytes. This is two to the power ten (2^{10}). See also MEGABYTE.

Kilostream™ a point-to-point communications line for speech or data provided by BT. Kilostream offers transmission speeds of 2.4 kilobits per second to 64 kilobits per second, and no MODEM is needed to make use of the line. See also MEGASTREAM.

KISS (acronym of keep it simple, stupid) a reminder to avoid excessive complication, such as CREEPING FEATURISM.

kludge 1. an unsatisfactory mock-up. **2.** a connection of items that are not intended to work together and do not do so satisfactorily. **3.** any trick used as an expedient.

knowbie one who is skilled in networking (see NETWORK).

knowbot a form of SEARCH program used over a NETWORK.

knowledge in ARTIFICIAL INTELLIGENCE, belief backed up by sufficient evidence to amount to certainty.

knowledge acquisition the process of adding some KNOWLEDGE to the DATABASE portion of a KNOWLEDGE SYSTEM.

knowledge base the data held in a KNOWLEDGE SYSTEM that can be used in ARTIFICIAL INTELLIGENCE by way of the INFERENCE ENGINE.

knowledge domain the field of application for which an EXPERT SYSTEM can be useful.

knowledge system a system for solving problems that makes use of the methods of ARTIFICIAL INTELLIGENCE. The first-generation systems use only a set of rules that are generally agreed, along with relevant data. Second-generation systems contain knowledge along with reasoning coded as OBJECTS.

Kurzweil personal reader™ a document reading system with voice output, used for the visually impaired.

L1 cache see LEVEL 1 CACHE.

L2 cache see LEVEL 2 CACHE.

label a name that can be applied when a disk is formatted (see FORMAT, sense 4) or subsequently, and used as an identifier for that disk. MS-DOS also generates and records a identifying number for each disk that is formatted.

label alignment the arrangement of text in a CELL of a WORKSHEET. The DEFAULT is usually right alignment but this can be changed. It is usually possible to define different default alignments for text and for numbers.

label prefix a PUNCTUATION MARK, such as a single quote, caret, double quote or slash, that can be placed ahead of text to determine its alignment in a CELL of a WORKSHEET. The use of a prefix in this way overrides the default LABEL ALIGNMENT. The SLASH MARK usually causes the label to be repeated to fill the cell width.

label printer a specialized PRINTER for use with continuous reels of labels.

lag the period of AFTERGLOW or persistence of the phosphor of a CRT. Too long a lag makes it impossible to see rapidly changing displays.

LAN (local area NETWORK) a cable system that can be used to link suitable computers together. This allows, for example, one computer to be connected to disk drives and printers, and the other computers on the network to make use of these peripherals. A LAN is a very useful way of providing computing power among a group of users without needing to multiply the number of disk drives and printers in use. The drawback is that with a large number of users working together, the speed of computing for each user may become unacceptably slow. LANs have become very popular in educational computing, where resources are necessarily limited. The use of a LAN is possible only if suitable HARDWARE, in terms of interface circuitry on each computer, is available. For some computers, this may have to be added externally. Special SOFTWARE is also required so that conflicting demands by different computers in the network can be resolved. A local network may be connected to external networks through the telephone lines. See also DIAL-UP NETWORKING; WAN.

LAN-aware program a program that has been written so that it can be used within a NETWORK. Such a program must provide for the use of ACCESS LEVEL passwords and all the other measures needed to prevent CORRUPTION of files when several users can work on files.

LAN backup program a program that will perform a FULL BACKUP on the SERVER of a local area network (LAN), usually at scheduled times.

landing zone a TRACK on a HARD DRIVE set of PLATTERS that can safely be allowed to come into contact with the head; see HEAD PARKING.

landline a connection made by cable, including telephone line, excluding any form of radio link.

Landmark a form of BENCHMARK test specifically intended for PERSONAL COMPUTERS of the IBM XT or AT type and their CLONE or COMPATIBLE equivalents. The test performs standard instruction routines and compares the speed of processing to that of a standard 4.7 MHz XT machine or of a 6 MHz AT machine, whichever is the more appropriate. Most manufacturers quote speed relative to the XT speed because this produces higher figures. See also DHRYSTONE; MIPS; WHETSTONE.

landscape one of the two possible orientation positions of paper. A WORD PROCESSOR or DTP program can be arranged to print on paper held with shorter side horizontal (PORTRAIT) or longer side horizontal (landscape).

language see PROGRAMMING LANGUAGE.

language support environment programs, often of the UTILITY type, designed to assist with programming in some particular language or making use of a GUI.

language translator any program that permits conversion between languages (meaning natural languages, not programming languages). Several translation programs are available and are suitable for some purposes, although for colloquial phrases their output should be checked by someone who knows both languages well.

LAN server see SERVER.

laptop a portable folding computer that is intended to be used while travelling and featuring a low-energy flat SCREEN (sense 1) – almost always LCD – of reasonable size and resolution (usually 800 x 600), ROM used to supplement the operating system, and often battery-backed RAM as well as a HARD DRIVE and a floppy drive. The laptop can be operated from batteries, although it is often more desirable to use mains power when it is available. A laptop machine can be expected to cost at least twice as much as a desktop machine of equivalent power and is usually impossible to upgrade.

laser (light amplification by stimulated emission of radiation) a source of *coherent* light. Normal light sources emit light waves that are not coherent, meaning that the light waves are emitted in bursts that do not behave like portions of a continuous wave. This lack of coherence prevents light from normal sources from exhibiting the obvious physical features of a wave. A laser forces light waves to be emitted in step, of one single wavelength, so that it behaves in a way that accords with wave theory. The laser therefore makes it possible to generate very small diameter beams of light that are almost perfectly parallel, with no measurable divergence. The lasers used in computing are based on semi-conductors and are of very low power.

laser disc a disc that is digitally recorded using methods essentially similar to those of a COMPACT DISC. The distinction is that laser disc usually refers to a larger disc carrying video data, such as a feature film. The modern equivalent is the DVD.

laser perforated see MICROPERFORATED.

laser printer a form of printer that depends on the use of LASER light. The laser printer uses the principle of XEROGRAPHY and is technically more like an office copier than a conventional printer. Laser printers are more expensive than impact DOT-MATRIX or INKJET PRINTERS, but they have considerable advantages over the dot-matrix type. Laser printers are quieter and faster in operation than impact dot-matrix types. Prices have fallen to a level that is equivalent to that of the more expensive dot-matrix types, and although running costs are relatively high (mainly TONER and DRUM costs) the paper can be less expensive than the tractor-feed type used by dot-matrix printers. Many laser printers come with a small number of built-in FONTS, but if the memory of the printer is sufficient, it is possible to DOWNLOAD other fonts (SOFT FONTS), and the TRUETYPE fonts of WINDOWS can also be used. For printing graphics, the RAM memory within the printer must be of the order of two megabytes, since a whole page of information has to be held before a page can be printed. The printing speed is generally quoted for multiple copies, ignoring the time needed to set up the page IMAGE (sense 1) in the memory. A more recent development is the windows printer, in which the laser engine uses the memory of a computer running MICROSOFT WINDOWS, allowing the printer to be sold at a price much lower than the traditional type of laser printer and comparable with the prices of inkjet printers.

laser scanner a method of reading a BAR CODE. The SCANNER moves a LASER beam to and fro over the bar codes, reading the reflected light pulses and converting them into digital form. Since the codes are read many times and only the most frequently obtained answer is used, this gives more reliable readings than hand scanners.

lasso an outline drawn by dragging (see DRAG) the MOUSE around text or picture objects so that these items are selected. Unlike a SELECTION BOX or FRAME (sense 1), a lasso can be of irregular shape.

LASTDRIVE a DOS command that will define the range of letters that can be used to denote DISK DRIVES.

last in first out see PUSHDOWN LIST.

latency computer waiting time. The latency of a program is the amount of time that is taken up in getting data from a HARD DISK or other store.

lateral reversal the exchange of left for right in a picture, making it look like the reflected image in a mirror.

Latin I see ISO LATIN 1.

launch to start a program running.

layer a system used in CAD and other VECTOR drawing programs that allows drawings to be made as if they occupied different layers of the SCREEN (sense 1), 64 or more, and maintained independently. This allows layers to be separately deleted, printed or merged with others.

layering the use of separate LAYERS for text and for graphics in a DTP program.

layout the arrangement of text and graphics on a printed page, in particular when shown on a SCREEN (sense 1) using a DTP system.

layout grid the design plan for a DTP page. This consists of the GUIDE lines of columns, margins and ruler guides, all of which appear on the SCREEN (sense 1) but do not print.

LBA see LOGICAL BLOCK ADDRESSING.

LCD (liquid crystal display) a form of display using a material that can be changed from transparent to opaque or back by applying an electrical voltage across it. The display emits no light of its own and depends for visibility on light from other sources. This makes it an ideal method of display for well-lit places in which the conventional luminous type of display is less suitable. The very low power consumption of the LCD SCREEN (sense 1) also makes it very useful for portable battery-operated computers. Colour LCD displays are now in production, mainly for small-screen TV use, and large-screen LCD is likely to replace the CRT as the predominant technology for TV and MONITOR (sense 1) use in the 21st century. For desktop computers and TV applications, the screens are brightly illuminated from behind (see BACKLIGHT).

leader 1. a line, often dotted (see DOT LEADER), between items separated by a TAB spacing in a WORD PROCESSOR document. Also a line indicating a feature of a drawing or indicating dimensions in a CAD drawing. **2.** a section preceding a document in a WORD PROCESSOR in which details such as font, print size, page length, line width, etc., may be specified. **3.** the first FIELD (sense 2) of the RECORD (sense 1) that carries information about that record.

lead-in a section of all CD-ROM or music discs, pre-recorded, CD-R or CD-RW, that contains information on the data or music contents. The lead-in area immediately precedes the recorded area. For a fully recorded disc, the lead-in contains the TABLE OF CONTENTS (sense 2). See also LEAD-OUT; PCA; PMA.

leading (pronounced 'ledding') the spacing between lines in a DTP or WORD PROCESSOR document. The leading size is measured using the same POINT scale as FONT size, and the normal leading size is 120 per cent of font size.

leading zero a zero placed before the first significant figure (see SIGNIFICANCE) of a number, such as 05 or 02.66. Most number displays suppress these zeros unless they are required to fill a provided space, such as in a date written as, for example, 08-06-01.

leadless chip carrier a form of PACKAGE (sense 2) for a CHIP that makes contact to metallized edge connections on the chip. This is common on the square packages of 300 pins or more that are used for MICROPROCESSOR and other large chips.

lead-out a section of all pre-recorded COMPACT DISCS that follows the recorded area (on the outer rim of a fully recorded disc). On the CD-R or CD-RW discs, the lead-out is not created until the disc is declared as fully recorded (preventing further recording). With no lead-out, the disc cannot be replayed on music players, and some older CD-ROM drives may not accept it. See also LEAD-IN; PCA; PMA.

leaf site a computer that serves news and EMAIL but does not relay other communications.

leapfrog attack a CRACKER action using stolen name and password information to download confidential files.

leapfrog test a test of memory that involves writing and subsequent reading of many locations in memory taken at random. See also CRIPPLED LEAPFROG TEST.

learn an action that can be selected in a MACRO system to allow the computer to store in code form each action that is selected while the learn feature is switched on. These codes can be stored in a named file and used to duplicate the actions by running the macro. See also VISUAL PROGRAMMING.

learning curve the diagram of the rate of acquiring experience. Anyone learning a new WORD PROCESSOR program or any other new system will work slowly at first, referring to the MANUAL. As experience is obtained, the manual has to be consulted less often, mistakes are fewer and the speed of using the program or system improves. Finally, the ultimate speed of use is achieved. If the effectiveness of use, as measured by speed of error-free output, is plotted against the time for which the program or system has been used, the curve shape always conforms to the same pattern, which is called the learning curve. This can be applied to predict how soon a new system can start to become effective in the hands of inexperienced operators. One advantage of a standard operating system such as MICROSOFT WINDOWS is that the learning period for a new application can be reduced because the system is familiar. See Fig. 28 (overleaf).

least recently used algorithm an ALGORITHM for determining which data in a CACHE memory has been least used so that it can be replaced by other data.

least significant the digit in a number that denotes the lowest value. By convention, this is the digit at the extreme right-hand side of a number. See also SIGNIFICANCE.

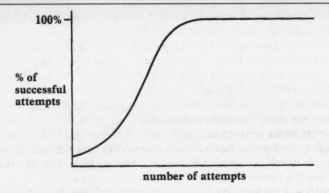

Fig. 28. **Learning curve**. This shows a rate of progress that starts as slow, becomes rapid ('got the hang of it now') and slows again as the system is almost completely understood.

least significant bit the BIT in a digital number that is in the LEAST-SIG-NIFICANT position.

least significant byte the BYTE in a multibyte MACHINE WORD that is in the LEAST-SIGNIFICANT position.

least significant digit the digit in a number that contributes least to the value, such as the units digit of an INTEGER or the final digit of a decimal fraction. See also SIGNIFICANCE.

leaving files open a phrase indicating that no close instruction (see CLOSE BOX) has been used for a FILE, particularly before switching the machine off. This will leave data in the BUFFER and no END OF FILE marker on the disk. The file will be unusable, and data will be lost as far as the conventional reading system of the computer is concerned. Some data may be readable from a disk by using a DISK DOCTOR, but data that was not recorded from the buffer cannot be recovered unless the buffer can be read before switching the computer off. Any good data-handling system should close all files when the program ends and also when a fault stops the program prematurely.

LED (light-emitting diode) a miniature low-voltage light source that has now replaced filament bulbs and neons for such purposes as INDICATOR LIGHTs. The LED is a semiconductor device, and the light is emitted with no significant amount of heat.

LED printer a form of LASER PRINTER that uses a row of tiny LED light sources in place of a LASER. This type of printer needs only a modest amount of memory as compared to the laser-beam type and is accordingly lower in price.

left brace or **left curly bracket** the { character, ASCII 123. See also RIGHT BRACE.

left bracket or **left parenthesis** the (character, ASCII 40. See also RIGHT BRACKET.

left curly bracket see LEFT BRACE.

left indent the amount by which the left side of a paragraph is moved in from the left MARGIN (see INDENT).

left justification the starting of each line of text at the left-hand MARGIN, with an irregular right margin. This is normal for typewritten work, but a WORD PROCESSOR can JUSTIFY text fully.

left parenthesis see LEFT BRACKET.

left-shift a CURSOR-CONTROL KEY that causes the CURSOR to be moved to the left and is usually marked with a left-pointing arrow. Modern programs often use the MOUSE for this purpose, but see NUDGE.

left square bracket the [character, ASCII 91. See also RIGHT SQUARE BRACKET.

left tab a TAB STOP at whose position the first character of a set will be placed, with the following characters on the right of the stop position.

legacy code or **legacy software** a program that is out of date but is still in use, usually because the cost of redesigning it would be too high but sometimes because no modern equivalent exists. Legacy software is useful only if it runs on modern HARDWARE.

legacy system HARDWARE that uses an outdated processor, inadequate MEMORY and a small HARD DRIVE, suitable only for use with MS-DOS and possibly the early WINDOWS versions.

legend a portion of text used to explain the use of colours or patterns in a display. For example, a BAR GRAPH might be accompanied by legends that describe the quantity depicted in each bar.

length of filename the number of characters in a FILENAME. MS-DOS has always limited the length of a filename to eight characters, excluding spaces, and with an optional EXTENSION of up to three characters – the 8+3 system. A system that accepts longer filenames and spaces is much easier to work with because it is then possible to use filenames that describe the data better. A filename such as NAMES OF FRIENDS is much more useful than NAMFRN, for example. Microsoft WINDOWS 95 onwards will permit the use of long filenames that include spaces and long extensions, up to a total maximum of 255 characters (including any path). See also ALIAS (sense 1).

LEO (Lyons Electronic Office) the first digital computer system designed for business use in the UK.

less than operator the < sign, used in WORKSHEET FORMULAE and in DATABASE QUERY statements to indicate that the quantity on the left of the symbol is less than the quantity on the right. The sign is also used as a REDIRECTION sign in MS-DOS, meaning that an input is to be redirected.

letterbomb an EMAIL that contains a form of VIRUS. This may be in the form of a HYPERLINK or as an ATTACHED FILE that can be run by clicking an icon.

LetterPerfect see WORDPERFECT.

letter quality a print quality that is suitable for office letter use. The output of a simple DOT-MATRIX printer is acceptable for draft work but can make the text of business documents hard to read. For business purposes, dot-MATRIX PRINTERS using 24-pin heads can provide letter quality, but the use of a LASER PRINTER or INKJET PRINTER is even better.

level 1 cache or **primary cache** a small CACHE memory that is implemented as part of a MICROPROCESSOR chip or connected very close to it. This has the effect of considerably improving performance. Level 1 cache sizes can range from as small as 16 kilobytes to around 250 kilobytes, and the cost of a processor will be very high when a large level 1 cache is present on the processor chip.

level 2 cache or **secondary cache** a CACHE that is used between the processor and the main memory, usually placed on the MOTHERBOARD. This cache can be larger and slower than the LEVEL 1 CACHE, and sizes of 512 kilobytes to 1 megabyte are common.

level of directory applied to MS-DOS to mean the relative distance, in terms of number of branches, of a DIRECTORY from the main or ROOT directory.

level of language classification of a PROGRAMMING LANGUAGE as *low* (close to MACHINE CODE) or *high* (machine-independent).

LF see LINE FEED.

LHN see LONG HAUL NETWORK.

library a disk-filing term. In some disk-operating systems, a letter can be designated as a *library letter*. Files that use this letter as their directory entry are normally program or subprogram files. These files will be given priority in any disk search for programs or routines. The DOLLAR SIGN is very often the DEFAULT library letter. See also DLL.

library function a program FUNCTION that is supplied separately in a set of functions in a file and included into a program by using its name (see DLL).

life cycle the set of stages in SOFTWARE development.

LIFO see PUSHDOWN LIST.

ligature a set of characters that are run together, required in some languages. The most common ligatures, such as 'æ', are obtained in the CHARACTER MAP display of WINDOWS.

light-emitting diode see LED.

light pen a device that detects light, usually from the SCREEN (sense 1), and can send signals to the computer. The light pen is normally a very simple device, and it sends a digital 1 signal to indicate the presence of light and digital 0 to report the absence of light. The sensitivity of the device is usually adjusted so that ambient lighting has no effect on it.

Since the pen is a simple light sensor, a program must be operated to make it useful. If a suitable program is used, a light pen can be used to create diagrams on the screen or to make MENU choices.

light pipe see FIBRE OPTIC.

LIM (Lotus-Intel-Microsoft) the three corporations that agreed a standard for the use of EXPANDED MEMORY for the older types of PC machines. The LIM 4.0 standard is almost identical to the EEMS standard (see also EMS). The system is now obsolete.

line 1. in GRAPHICS, a mark made on the SCREEN (sense 1) or on paper joining a set of points. The line may be straight or curved, and its thickness depends on the RESOLUTION of the DISPLAY. **2.** one single trace of the cathode-ray beam across the MONITOR (sense 1) or TV SCREEN (sense 1). **3.** a connection, such as a telephone line or FIBRE-OPTIC cable, used to communicate data over long distances.

line adapter any type of electronic circuit that converts signals from one form to another, such as a MODEM.

linear address space a MEMORY that is organized so that each portion can be addressed (see ADDRESS, sense 1) using a single number, unlike a SEGMENTED ADDRESSING memory system.

linear graph see AREA GRAPH.

linear function a mathematical function that, when plotted as a graph, yields a straight line. The most general type of linear function is represented in the equation $Y = mX + C$, where m and C are each constants. This is the basis of linear regression (see EXTRAPOLATION) in a WORKSHEET.

linear list a list of data items with no gaps.

linear network a form of NETWORK in which signals from the main computer will be input to each computer in turn on the network until accepted. Contrast RING NETWORK.

linear programming a specialized mathematical method used to find an optimum solution for a system that uses a number of variables.

linear search a SEARCH through a LIST, starting at the first item and working through each item in turn until the wanted item is found. If the list is sorted into order, the much faster BINARY SEARCH method can be used.

line art any drawing made using lines only, without shading, hatching or colouring.

line-busy tone the tone placed on a telephone line to indicate that the line is engaged. This can be detected by a MODEM and used to activate an AUTOREDIALER system (where the use of such a system is permitted).

line chart or **line graph** a GRAPH that uses a line, either in straight sections or curved, to connect the plotted points.

line driver a circuit, usually in IC form, that is used to transmit pulses down a long line (as opposed to the BUS lines within a computer).

line editing a text editing system, now obsolete, that requires the user to specify a line of text for alteration. See EDIT.

line feed (LF) or **newline character** the selection of a new line. On the SCREEN (sense 1), this implies moving the CURSOR down to the next screen line; on a printer, feeding the paper up by one line spacing. In either case, a *line feed code*, normally ASCII code 10, is sent to the operating system (OS). Most printers can be switched so that they line feed on the LF character, ASCII 10, only or also when the carriage return (CR) code (13) is received.

line flyback see FLYBACK.

line frequency the rate of repetition at which the horizontal lines are scanned on the face of a MONITOR (sense 1) CRT. Some graphics cards, notably VGA, require a higher line frequency than the older types such as CGA CARD.

line graph see LINE CHART.

line graphics a simple provision for drawing used in DTP and WORD PROCESSOR programs. This permits straight lines, boxes and circles to be drawn and sometimes also for filling with colour or shading. Such drawings cannot generally be rotated or manipulated in the ways that are possible with graphics imported (see IMPORT) from a specialized package.

line length the number of characters in each printed line produced by a WORD PROCESSOR.

line noise meaningless electrical interference on a LINE (sense 3) that can cause unwanted characters to appear or other CORRUPTION of messages.

line printer a type of mechanical printer, now used only for very high-volume printing, that prints one complete line at a time. The name lives on in the designation LPT1 for the PRINTER PORT.

line probing a MODEM action that adjusts the rate of communication to suit the quality of the LINE (sense 3) that is being used.

line spacing the gap between printed lines, usually single or double, produced by a WORD PROCESSOR.

lines per minute (lpm) a measure of printing speed for text.

line style the type of line used in a DTP or WORD PROCESSOR document. Lines can be solid, dotted, dashed or use combinations of dots and dashes, and DTP programs allow several (typically 6 to 9) different such styles to be used.

line transient a pulse of interference carried along the mains power supply line and capable of causing problems in a computer. Line FILTERS (sense 3) can be bought to suppress such TRANSIENTs and create 'cleaner' power.

line weight or **weight** the thickness of a line. The term, used in DTP, is borrowed from printing. Since a line was originally printed by using a line of lead, the thickness was proportional to weight. Line weight is measured using the POINT unit or in millimetres.

link a joining of two devices or two items of software so that signals or characters can be passed from one to another.

linked files files that have some relationship to each other and are used by the same program. See also DLL; RELATIONAL DATABASE.

linked object an OBJECT that is viewed in a document but whose file information is stored separately. The file size of the object is not added to that of the document, and the object can be edited by double-clicking (see DOUBLE-CLICK) on it. In addition, changing the object and saving the altered file will result in the object in the document being changed when the document is opened. See also EMBEDDED OBJECT; OLE.

link rot loss of LINKS (sense 2) in a WEB PAGE because of changes in the TARGET (sense 1) of each link.

Linotronic™ a high-resolution printing machine that can make use of DTP files. See also IMAGESETTER.

Linux a form of UNIX, written by Linus Torvalds and used extensively on SERVER machines, particularly for the INTERNET. The Linux operating system (OS) is free and is available on CD-ROM together with APPLICATIONS, the whole comprising a *Linux distribution*. Linux is a MULTI-ACCESS system and is MULTITASKING, and is pre-installed on several major computer systems. Because the system is directed more to experienced users, a Windows-like FRONT END is now available to increase its appeal to the non-professional user.

Linux documentation project an organization of voluntary writers devoted to providing documentation for LINUX.

liquid crystal display see LCD.

list a set of items in some order. This could refer to a set of characters in a word, words in a sentence, sentences in a book, and it could also refer to items in a disk file.

list box a box that appears in a WINDOW to provide a choice of items that can be selected by clicking (see CLICK, sense 1).

listing paper paper, usually continuous, made specifically for printing program instruction lines, often music-lined with a five-line pattern.

list processing actions on lists of data. The action of a WORD PROCESSOR, for example, is almost entirely list processing.

literal 1. a printing error where one character is substituted for another. **2.** a CONTROL CHARACTER in a WORD PROCESSOR program.

lite version a version of a program that omits important functions or is otherwise crippled and is sold at a cut price or distributed free with a magazine.

liveware human programmers and operators, sometimes referred to as the weakest link in a computer system. The term started as a joke but has been taken up seriously to refer to the most essential 'ware' of computing, which is often the most difficult to replace.

LN a mathematical function. The term is used in some SPREADSHEET programs to mean natural (or Napierian) logarithm, as distinct from the conventional base-10 logarithm, although the log function is used by a few spreadsheets for the same action.

load to transfer a program from disk into the memory of the computer. In MS-DOS this is done by typing the program name and pressing the return or enter key. WINDOWS will load and run a program when you CLICK (sense 1) on the program name or on the name of a shortcut to the program in Microsoft Windows 95 onwards.

load and run the normal program action for DOS or other COMMAND-LINE operating systems (OS) such as UNIX or LINUX, in which typing the name of a program file will have the effect of loading the program into memory and running it.

loader a program that loads another program. The term usually denotes a very short program, often held in ROM, that is used to load the rest of a program, often an operating system. The MS-DOS system, for example, uses a loader in ROM to load in the rest of the system from disk. The name is also used for a program that will load in a large program from several sections held on a set of disks.

loadhigh a command first used in MS-DOS 5.0 to load a short program into the high memory area (HMA) of the PC machine.

local connected directly to the user's computer, as distinct from REMOTE, accessed by way of a NETWORK.

local area network see LAN.

local bus a set of BUS connections that allow high-speed transfer of data between the MICROPROCESSOR and other circuit cards. The standard form of bus runs at a very low speed, fixed by the rate used in the early IBM PC-AT computer. The use of a local bus for the hard drive interface and the graphics card greatly speeds up computer actions. See also AGP; PCI BUS; VLB.

local drive a DISK DRIVE that is directly connected to the user's computer, as distinct from a REMOTE DRIVE on a NETWORK.

local echo see FULL DUPLEX.

local loop the line connecting your telephone to an exchange.

local loopback address the INTERNET ADDRESS 127.0.0.1, which allows an Internet HOST system to send messages to itself for testing purposes.

local name the portion of a URL that is local, as distinct from the DOMAIN NAME.

local printer a PRINTER that is connected to the user's computer, as distinct from a REMOTE PRINTER on a NETWORK.

location 1. the position or ADDRESS (sense 1) of a BYTE in memory. **2.** the position of a BYTE of data in terms of TRACKS and SECTORS on a disk.

location transparency a system used in a DISTRIBUTED DATABASE in which each user will be unaware of how the data is scattered around the system. This is done by replacing names that might include a location reference by other names (*alias* names) which are translated within the system.

lock see ANCHOR (sense 1).

locked document a WORD PROCESSOR document file that cannot be altered. This might be a form of template, which can be copied and used rather than being used directly, or a document that is networked (see NETWORK) and has been circulated for comments rather than for amendments.

locked file a FILE that is inaccessible for writing. Many disk operating systems allow a file to be 'locked', meaning that it cannot be altered and no other file of the same name will be accepted. This deters accidental alteration or erasure of a file in a system. Locking in this way is a software protection, applied by writing a code byte into the disk directory, and can be released by deleting the locking byte. This form of local 'write prevention', which is applicable to a floppy or a HARD DRIVE, should not be confused with the use of a WRITE-PROTECT tab on a floppy disk, which protects the whole disk surface and cannot be released by software instructions.

lock guide a DTP action to preserve GUIDE positions. Locking a guide prevents the guide from being dragged out of position by careless use of the MOUSE.

lock-in being tied to something that cannot be changed, usually of a standard such as the keyboard layout or an operating system (OS).

lock keys the KEYS (sense 1) used to TOGGLE actions such as CAPS LOCK and NUM LOCK.

lock record or **freeze record** a DATABASE action that is used when the database is shared by several users on a NETWORK. When one user locks a record, other users cannot edit the record.

lockup or **hang-up** or **jam** an inactive KEYBOARD and/or SCREEN (sense 1), the state in which the computer ceases to respond to keys and sometimes displays no further information on the screen. An unintentional lockup is usually caused by CORRUPTION of the operating system (OS) or of some RAM that is used by the operating system. Lockup is also deliberately built into the operating system. Most systems will lock up the keyboard and screen during a disk load or save operation, and also during any processing that does not require an INPUT. See also INTERRUPT.

log or **logarithm** usually meaning the base-10 logarithm.

logarithmic graph a GRAPH in which one or more quantities are plotted as logarithms. For example, instead of plotting 10, 100, 1000, the graph would plot 1, 2, 3, the logarithms of these numbers. Logarithmic graphs are particularly useful when a large range of quantities must be plotted.

log file or **journal** a file that maintains a record of other files. Where many files have been archived (see ARCHIVE), for example, a log file could be used to maintain an ASCII list of filenames. An operating system will often maintain log files of some actions, such as the number of times a computer is booted or the actions that are carried out on each boot.

logic a system for deducing a result from two or more items of data. In electronics and computing, the inputs to a logic device will consist of bit signals, 0 or 1, and the output will also be the bit 0 or 1. All logic actions, no matter how complicated, can be built up from a few fundamental actions, originally described by George Boole in 1836. These actions are the LOGICAL OPERATORS AND, OR and NOT.

logical block addressing (LBA) the system used for locating data on a HARD DRIVE. This system replaced the earlier FILE CONTROL BLOCK system so as to allow the use of large hard drives, increasing the maximum addressable size from 528 megabytes to 8.4 gigabytes. Larger drives can now be accommodated.

logical data type see BOOLEAN DATA TYPE.

logical drive a drive designated by a letter. The letter need not correspond to a physically present DISK DRIVE; it may be a RAM drive, refer to a part of a hard drive (see PARTITIONED DRIVE) or refer to a drive on another machine in a NETWORK.

logical error an ERROR of design in a program, as distinct from an error of implementation.

logical operator a symbol for the AND, NOT and or logic action, used in programs such as a DATABASE or in actions such as searching (see SEARCH) in a WORD PROCESSOR document or a WORKSHEET.

logical record a RECORD (sense 1) as it would be presented on SCREEN (sense 1) or on paper, stripped of control codes and other information that would be used in the disk file.

logical testing see WHITE-BOX TESTING.

logic bomb see BOMB (sense 1).

log in see LOG ON.

logo a corporate emblem. Many WORD PROCESSOR and all DTP programs allow for a logo to be added to text by importing (see IMPORT) a graphics file.

log on/off the procedure for starting or ending use of a COMPUTER SYSTEM. Several systems, particularly networked systems (see NETWORK), demand that a user should go through an elaborate procedure of providing passwords, the date, names of files, and so on, before being granted ACCESS (sense 1) to the system. This is called *logging on*. Similarly, it is sometimes necessary to go through a routine of providing answers to questions in order to stop using a system, and this is called *logging off*. Log on and off procedures are also used when one computer is shared by several users, each of which can specify his/her preferred setup.

long-haul network (LHN) a computer NETWORK that consists of NODES that are at least several kilometres apart, requiring the use of MODEMS.

long-persistence phosphor see AFTERGLOW.

look-and-feel a description of how a program appears to a user. Many accusations of plagiarism hinge on one program looking and feeling like another, and these accusations have been made since the first SPREAD-SHEET program, VISICALC, was introduced, followed by other spread-sheets that are now well established.

look-up table a method of storing data directly in a program to save cal-culation and thus ensure quick ACCESS (sense 2). The data is kept in some ordered form, such as twin lists, in consecutive cells, and a FORMULA that uses these cell addresses can be used to carry out actions such as look-ing for a quantity in one list and substituting the quantity in a parallel list. The use of a look-up table is often quicker than the use of a formu-la for many computing purposes but requires more memory. Several SPREADSHEET programs allow you to construct look-up tables for your own data.

loop a program action that allows a section of a program to be repeated until a condition is fulfilled. A typical condition is that a variable reach-es some pre-set value (often zero).

loop check a method of checking the action of a COMMUNICATIONS LINK using a MODEM by having the remote terminal return messages that can be compared with the original to detect CORRUPTION.

lossless compression a form of COMPRESSED FILE structure that allows the retrieved file to be identical to that saved file, with no loss of infor-mation because of the compression.

lossy compression a form of COMPRESSED FILE structure that achieves greater compression by omitting some data, such as by using a smaller range of colours and reducing resolution. The loss is not noticeable when the file is retrieved, but if a file is retrieved and resaved several times in succession, the effects of the loss of data will become noticeable. Lossy compression should be used only when a file has been fully edit-ed and will not be changed again. See also JPEG.

lost allocation unit see LOST CLUSTER.

lost chain a portion of a file, usually a deleted file, that is not listed in the DIRECTORY (sense 2) but which has a non-zero entry in the file allocation table (FAT) of a DISK DRIVE. Such fragments occupy disk space, causing other files to be fragmented (see FRAGMENTATION, sense 1). UTILITY pro-grams such as SCANDISK will collect these fragments and either delete them or create files from them.

lost cluster or **lost allocation unit** a cluster or ALLOCATION UNIT that contains part of a file but has lost its identification bits which allow the file to be recovered.

lost in the noise (of a signal) that cannot be understood because its AMPLITUDE is less than the NOISE that accompanies it. See also SIGNAL/NOISE RATIO.

Lotus 1–2–3™ a well-known SPREADSHEET program that also includes DATABASE actions, graph drawing and display actions. Versions 2.0 on are suitable for use in any PC machine, but Version 3.0 on can be used only on the later types of PC machine using the 80286, 80386 or 80486 chips. Version 4 for WINDOWS includes many advanced features, and later versions are integrated into the SmartSuite set.

Lotus-Intel-Microsoft see LIM.

loudspeaker a device that converts electrical signals in the range of 20 Hz to 20 kHz into audible sound. A built-in loudspeaker is a useful warning device on a computer or a MODEM, and if the computer contains a sound card and uses MULTIMEDIA the loudspeaker is an essential part of the sound system. See also ACTIVE LOUDSPEAKER.

Lovelace, Ada Augusta (1818–52) the Countess of Lovelace and daughter of Lord Byron who, as a friend and colleague of Charles BABBAGE, developed a method of programming his computing machine. She is often referred to as the first programmer and her name has been given to the programming language ADA.

low-bandwidth (of a lecture or document) carrying little information.

low earth orbit the path of a satellite used for communications. A low earth orbit satellite constantly circles the Earth (unlike the GEOSTATIONARY type), so that several low earth orbit satellites are needed to cover the whole earth.

low end applied to the least expensive and least featured in a manufacturer's range of products.

lower-case of or relating to the 'small' as distinct from 'capital' letters. Compare UPPER-CASE.

low-level format a process that was formerly carried out during the installation of a HARD DRIVE, enabling a HIGH LEVEL FORMAT to be carried out later. On the older versions of MS-DOS, the FDISK program was used to carry out low-level formatting and to partition the disk before high-level formatting (see PARTITIONED DRIVE). Low-level formatting is neither necessary nor desirable when modern IDE or EIDE drives are used.

low-level language a PROGRAMMING LANGUAGE that is written for direct programming of the MICROPROCESSOR. Each CPU or microprocessor design needs its own low-level language, but some families of microprocessors, such as the Intel set, share a large part of their low-level language instructions. See HIGH-LEVEL LANGUAGE.

low resolution (of an image) constructed with a low number of PIXELS per inch. A RESOLUTION of, for example, 15 dots per inch can be classed as low, just as 300 dots per inch is high, but the terms are relative, and the boundary between low and high resolution is flexible.

lpm see LINES PER MINUTE.

LPT1 the code word for the parallel printer output on PERSONAL COMPUTERS. The word PRN: is also used, but LPT has the advantage that it can be used with a reference number, allowing more than one printer to be connected if more than one parallel port is installed.

luggable (of a computer) alleged to be PORTABLE but the weight and/or bulk of which makes it difficult to carry.

luminance the portion of an electrical signal used by a MONITOR (sense 1) or TV system to convey the brightness of a portion of a picture. See also CHROMA (chrominance).

lurking reading the postings (see POST, sense 1) of a NEWSGROUP but not contributing significantly. A *lurker* will learn the etiquette of a group in this way.

Lycos a SEARCH ENGINE and vast index to the World Wide Web (WWW) maintained by Carnegie Mellon University, USA.

Lyons Electronic Office see LEO.

LZH a COMPRESSED FILE system devised by Lempel-Ziv and Haruyasu.

LZW a COMPRESSED FILE system devised by Lempel-Ziv and Welch.

M (Mega) meaning one million.

m (milli) one thousandth.

Mac™ see MACINTOSH.

machinable see MACHINE-READABLE.

machine an alternative, informal term for computer.

machine code or **machine language** a number-code system for MICRO-PROCESSOR programming. Programming in machine code requires a detailed knowledge of the microprocessor and of how the computer has been designed. Such programming also requires considerably more planning than is needed for a program in a HIGH-LEVEL LANGUAGE.

machine cycle one cycle of the machine CLOCK. The processing speed of the MICROPROCESSOR is governed primarily by the clock pulses. The time between two clock pulses is referred to as a machine cycle because any of the actions of the microprocessor can be timed in terms of an integral number of machine cycles. An instruction set for a microprocessor will contain timings for all the microprocessor's actions in terms of the machine cycle. In this way, therefore, if the clock pulse timing is known, the time required for any instruction or set of instructions can be calculated.

machine dependency the reliance of a program on the ARCHITECTURE of a particular computer so that the software will run only on some specified hardware.

machine language see MACHINE CODE.

machine learning a form of artificial intelligence that allows a machine to improve its performance by experience.

machine-oriented language a PROGRAMMING LANGUAGE that is closely related to the way that the MICROPROCESSOR works, hence less oriented to the way that a programmer thinks.

machine-readable capable of being read directly by the computer. This applies mainly to storage forms like disks and cassettes. If, for example, an author is required to provide work in machine-readable form, this implies that a WORD PROCESSOR should be used, with the output in ASCII code form or other agreed form on disks. These disks can be read directly into another computer, unlike printed text, and set directly into print by computer.

machine word the unit of data used in a computer, ranging on PERSONAL COMPUTERS from one byte to a double-word of four bytes. Modern PCs use a 32-bit DOUBLE WORD data unit and are capable of running 32-

bit software under Microsoft WINDOWS 95 onwards. Some video GRAPH-
ICS ADAPTER cards work in 64-bit or 128-bit units.

Macintosh™ or **Mac**™ a trend-setting product by APPLE. The Macintosh
used the GUI principles initially developed by Xerox Corp. for the first
time on a lower-priced machine and has introduced other ideas that
have been widely imitated although no CLONEs of the machine itself
have ever been tolerated. In Europe, a policy of high price maintenance
once made the Macintosh a comparatively rare machine, but it was and
is extensively used for professional DTP work, and prices started to drop
in the 1990s. The advent of WINDOWS on PERSONAL COMPUTERS has less-
ened the attraction of the Macintosh for many users, and the uncertainty following a proposed takeover of Apple by IBM also had an effect on
sales. The Macintosh is, however, extensively used by publishers and
graphics designers, and some of its most significant software (such as
WORD and EXCEL) is available also on the PC clone type of machine,
allowing for interchange of files.

macro a compound statement of commands that can be stored as a unit
and inserted into several different places in a program. Macros are a
useful way of making a program, such as a SPREADSHEET or WORD PROCES-
SOR, PROGRAMMABLE, carrying out a set of actions when some KEY COMBI-
NATION is used. A macro can be created by a form of recording method.
This involves using a start command and then carrying out manually
the set of commands that the macro is intended to automate, then using
a stop command. The macro can then be assigned to a MENU, a HOT KEY
or an ICON. The other option is to write directly the command lines of
text that make up the macro, but this requires some programming experience.

macro command a single letter or word that is used to run a MACRO and
therefore carry out a set of instructions so as to simplify the use of a program and customize it.

macro language the structure of the PROGRAMMING LANGUAGE used to
write a MACRO, in particular the steps needed to create a macro and the
way in which a macro is invoked (such as using the ALT KEY along with
a letter or choosing a name from a menu). For example, VISUAL BASIC is
the macro language for many Microsoft products.

magnetic card a storage system for small amounts of data. The magnetic card, as exemplified by credit cards and cash cards, uses a strip of
magnetic material to store data. The card is written by automatic
processes that can control the rate at which the magnetic strip is pulled
past the head of a recorder. Reading can be equally well controlled, as
used in automatic cash tills, but is sometimes done by pulling the card
by hand past a reading head. The chance of errors is greatly increased
when hand operation is used because the speed of movement cannot be
kept constant, but the use of error-detection and correction software

makes errors very rare, so that the data is either read perfectly or not at all.

magnetic cell the unit of magnetic storage, meaning a particle of magnetic material that can be magnetized in one direction or the other.

magnetic disk see DISK.

magnetic domain the smallest possible magnetic cell (of atomic dimensions) in a magnetic material, corresponding to the minimum possible amount that can be magnetized. A material is fully magnetized when all its domains are aligned in the same direction.

magnetic field the magnetic effect in the space around a magnet. Anywhere around a magnet, magnetic materials will experience a force caused by the magnet, and the strength of the magnetic force in such a region is a measure of magnetic field. Strong magnetic fields are generated at TAPEHEADS and disk READ/WRITE HEADs so that magnetic materials can be magnetized. Equally strong fields elsewhere can demagnetize tapes or disks, causing CORRUPTION of data. Alternating magnetic fields, in which the magnetism changes to an opposite direction many times per second, are particularly destructive. Disks and tapes must therefore be kept clear of magnets (such as the magnets of loudspeakers) and from any apparatus that generates alternating magnetic fields, including monitors, TV receivers and electric motors.

magnetic head see READ/WRITE HEAD.

magnetic ink a form of ink that contains magnetic powder. An ink that is made using fine particles of iron oxide will be magnetic. It is therefore possible for the ink to carry magnetic messages in addition to any visible text. The system has been widely used for the numbering of cheques, using digit shapes whose magnetic fields can be recognized by a set of reading heads.

magnetic ink character recognition (MICR) the reading of characters formed in MAGNETIC INK.

magnetic medium any form of recording medium that depends on magnetic material, such as magnetic tape or disks. See also MAGNETO-OPTICAL RECORDING.

magnetic screen a material such as mu-metal that can be used to enclose any part of a circuit that might be affected by MAGNETIC FIELDs.

magnetic tape see TAPE.

magnetic tape drive see STREAMER.

magneto-optical drive (MOD) a form of writable CD-ROM drive that makes use of a LASER beam to affect a magnetic layer. The resulting data can be read using the same methods as are used for CD-ROM, and the disk can be erased and reused, making the system very useful for large scale BACKUP, typically 1.5 gigabytes and more.

magneto-optical recording a system of recording on a material using magnetic signals for writing and reading the disk by a LASER beam, as used in the WORM type of drive. Recording systems for COMPACT DISCS have become available and are now at low prices, and rewritable OPTICAL DISKS use a combination of magnetic storage with optical reading. See also CD-R; CD-RW; DVD; FLOPTICAL DISK.

mail see EMAIL.

mail-bomb to send large numbers of EMAIL messages to a single recipient in the hope of causing a CRASH of the computer that is at the receiving end.

mailbox a folder that is used to store EMAIL messages until they have been processed. Emails that have been sent are moved to a Sent box and incoming emails that have been read are placed in the Deleted mail box. See also INBOX; OUTBOX.

mail bridge a form of GATEWAY that relays EMAIL between different networks.

mail exploder the part of an EMAIL program that attends to the delivery of a single message to multiple recipients.

mail filter the part of an EMAIL program that selects email according to the user's preferences. This allows mail to be refused if it comes from certain senders, contains certain phrases or is directed to certain recipients. The mail filter is commonly used to avoid advertising letters or pornographic circulars.

mailing list a form of DATABASE program that is used to keep a list of names and addresses in the style that will be used on envelopes or on form letter documents. The use of a mailing list along with a WORD PROCESSOR allows form letters to be created and printed.

mailmerge or **automatic letter writing** a WORD PROCESSOR action that allows one file containing a standard document and another file containing a mailing list to be merged so that a set of letters are addressed to each name on the mailing list, usually with individual features in each letter.

mail server a SERVER that handles EMAIL. Available servers are described as POP3, IMAP (INTERNET MESSAGE ACCESS PROTOCOL) or HTTP, according to the PROTOCOL used. No mail can be received until the mail server provided by the ISP is entered into your email program.

mainframe a term for the largest types of computers. These will usually take up a complete room or suite of rooms, require air-conditioned surroundings, use fast STATIC RAM storage along with replaceable HARD DRIVE units and be capable of dealing with very large amounts of data at very high speeds (see MEGAFLOP).

main memory see RANDOM ACCESS MEMORY.

mains the national electrical supply available from wall sockets. Sudden changes of mains voltages (SURGES or SPIKES, sense 2) can cause a REBOOT and loss of data. See also MAINS FILTER; UPS.

mains filter or **conditioner** electronic equipment that will remove

245

SURGES or SPIKES (sense 2) from a MAINS supply, so protecting computer systems connected through the filter.

maintenance changes in SOFTWARE, usually to correct BUGs. See also SERVICE RELEASE.

maintenance release a program UPDATE that is intended to fix a BUG or add a FEATURE to a MAJOR RELEASE. A maintenance release is (or ought to be) marked by digits following a decimal point, so that release 4.1 would be the first maintenance release following version 4.0.

major release a new version of a program, rewritten and incorporating many new features and all the corrections used in each earlier MAINTENANCE RELEASE. A major release carries a whole-number identifier, such as 4.0, 5.0, and so on.

male connector the plug connector of a cable. Compare FEMALE CONNECTOR.

malfunction routine a software UTILITY used to detect the cause of a persistent hardware error such as failure of a machine to recognize a port or to be able to use added memory.

Maltron keyboard a non-QWERTY KEYBOARD. The Maltron keyboard is one of the three main systems (the others being DVORAK and the MICROSOFT NATURAL KEYBOARD) that places the keys in a logical order and/or position, ensuring that both hands are equally occupied and that typing speed and accuracy are greatly increased.

Manchester encoding any of several systems for coding DIGITAL BIT DATA that makes it easy for the receiver to synchronize (see SYNCHRONIZATION) with the transmitter.

Mandelbrot equation or **Mandelbrot set** a deceptively simple equation that can be used recursively (see RECURSION) to generate a set of values for FRACTAL graphics. The equation was the first to be discovered whose graphical forms create patterns like those found naturally.

manipulation any action on data, including moving, copying, deletion, addition or alteration.

mantissa the part of a number in STANDARD FORM that contains the significant figures (see SIGNIFICANCE). For example, in the number 1.23E6, the mantissa is 1.23. When a number is written in binary standard form, the mantissa is always fractional. See also EXPONENT.

manual the instruction book for a computer or for computer SOFTWARE. This is often very brief for modern IBM CLONE machines, although the IBM manuals themselves are very comprehensive. The best manuals are reference books for the setting up and use of the computer, but most users find that it is necessary to purchase more specialized texts, preferably written around the version of the software (US or European) that is being used. The trend now is to minimize the use of manuals, relying instead on HELP (sense 1) pages within the software. See also DOCUMENTATION.

manual entry the entry of data from the KEYBOARD. In many systems for which the computer is used, the data is obtained from measurements that are made by machines. These measurements can be digitized (see DIGITIZE) and entered directly into the computer through PORTs, eliminating the mistakes that a human operator can make.

manual link an option for a LINKED OBJECT in which changes made to the OBJECT file do not appear in the version linked to a document until a menu option is used or a link button is clicked (see CLICK, sense 1).

manual recalculation a SPREADSHEET option in which CELL FORMULAE are not recalculated until a MENU option to recalculate is used. Most modern spreadsheets will carry out recalculation automatically when any cell value that affects formulae is altered.

manual testing SOFTWARE testing that requires manual assistance for input or to interpret the test results.

map a schematic diagram, such as of the computer's MEMORY. A memory map for a computer shows the memory in ranges of ADDRESS (sense 1) number, with the use of each range noted. See also MEMORY MAPPING.

MAPI (messaging application programming interface) the design of software INTERFACE for handling EMAIL and similar documents.

mapping function a FUNCTION that provides a translation of data. For example, a LOCATION address for data might be found by multiplying a number (see KEY FIELD) by one hundred and adding ten; this would then be the mapping function for that key.

margin the blank paper around the edges of a DTP page. DTP, WORD PROCESSOR and GRAPHICS programs allow the sizes of top, bottom, left and right margins to be defined, although this can be overridden by the requirements of the printer.

margin guide a faint line drawn in the page view of a DTP or WORD PROCESSOR display to show the position of the right or left MARGIN.

marker a shape such as a white block that marks the start and end of a piece of text in a WORD PROCESSOR or a code inserted into text to mark the position of a FOOTNOTE or ENDNOTE. See also BOOKMARK.

mark-up coding that indicates how ASCII text is to be laid out and formatted. Mark-up systems are used by WORD PROCESSORs, but the universal form is the hypertext mark-up language (HTML) used on the World Wide Web (WWW).

marquee 1. a moving-message form of SCREEN SAVER used in MICROSOFT WINDOWS. **2.** A dotted outline placed around selected cells in MICROSOFT EXCEL; see also GRAPHIC BOUNDARY; LASSO.

mask see FILTER.

maskable interrupt see INTERRUPT MASK.

masked ROM a mass-produced pre-programmed and unalterable ROM, as distinct from a PROM.

masquerading rewriting details of data (such as the From portion) in a message when the message is sent. This avoids revealing internal details to the recipient.

mass storage the large-scale storage of data, such as on a HARD DRIVE or on CD-ROM, possibly on BACKUP tape.

master clock the main source of timing CLOCK pulses in a computer to which all the units are synchronized.

master disk see SYSTEM DISK.

master document a MICROSOFT WORD term for a file that consists of codes that will insert subdocuments (see NESTING DOCUMENTS) into the master. The master document is a comparatively short file, but when it is opened, the nesting documents are linked in so as to form a very large document. This allows SEARCH AND REPLACE actions to be carried out over the whole document, and for page numbering and indexing to be simplified. When the master document is saved, the constituent documents are also saved in updated form. If required, the subdocuments can be permanently incorporated into the master, deleted or split as required.

master file a file created by a program that needs to be RUN (sense 2) each time the program is run in order to establish the format of the program and to supply any data that is required throughout the use of the program.

master items any items that form part of a MASTER PAGE for DTP or WORD PROCESSOR documents. Examples are running heads (see HEADER), RULES and GUIDES.

master page or **template** a method of ensuring consistency in a DTP or WORD PROCESSOR document. The master page(s) will contain layouts for left- and right-hand pages of ordinary text, and for start of chapter text. By copying the layout from a master page, each new page of a document will use the correct layout. See also STYLESHEET. Note that the term 'master' is used with a different meaning in MICROSOFT WORD (see MASTER DOCUMENT).

matching the connecting of systems correctly together. See INTERFACE.

mathematical model a set of equations that represent the action of a system.

maths chipset see MATHS COPROCESSOR.

maths coprocessor or **floating-point unit** a COPROCESSOR chip designed to speed up the handling of FLOATING-POINT calculations by early INTEL processors. Later processor types have included a floating-point unit on the same chip.

matrix an arrangement of rows and columns, such as pins on a DOT-MATRIX printer or data, usually numbers, in the mathematical meaning of the term.

matrix math extensions see MMX.

matrix printer or **dot-matrix printer** any type of printer that 'draws' a character from a set of dots. The impact form of DOT-MATRIX printer uses a vertical line of tiny needles to mark the paper. Each character is formed by shooting some of the needles against the inked ribbon, so that each needle prints a dot on the paper. The head is then moved slightly and other needles fired until the character shape is built up. Early printer designs used seven needles and shifted the head in five steps to print a character. This design is known as a 7 x 5 PRINTHEAD, and although UPPER-CASE letters are printed reasonably well, it distorts the shapes of any LOWER-CASE letters that have DESCENDERS. These are letters such as y, g and p, which have descending tails. More modern designs use a larger number of needles, from 9 to 24, and make more steps across the paper for each character. This makes for better character shapes but at the expense of slower printing speed. Several types allow the choice of high-speed printing for a draft copy, and NLQ (near letter quality) slow printing for other office uses. The highest print quality of matrix printing, however, is obtained from the non-impact INKJET PRINT-ERS.

matrix rotation the mathematical action of interchanging rows and columns in a MATRIX.

maximized window a WINDOW whose size is as large as can be accommodated by the SCREEN (sense 1). See also MINIMIZING WINDOW.

maximum seek time the time, measured in milliseconds, needed for a HARD DRIVE head to carry out a SEEK action over all the tracks of each PLATTER. This is used to compute the performance for critical applications that require a continuous data flow.

maximum transmission unit (MTU) the largest PACKET of data that can be handled on a NETWORK. For BROWSERS, this is usually set at 512 bytes, but it can be advantageous to increase this size. Utilities for the World Wide Web (WWW) are available to check and optimize the MTU size.

mbps see MEGABITS PER SECOND.

Mbyte see MEGABYTE.

MCA see MICRO CHANNEL ARCHITECTURE.

MCGA (multicolor graphics array) a graphics card used on some PS/2 machines but not emulated by others.

MCI see MEDIA CONTROL INTERFACE.

MD see MDIR.

MDA see MONOCHROME DISPLAY ADAPTER.

MDAS rule see PRECEDENCE.

MDIR (MD) the DOS command to create a DIRECTORY (sense 1) branching from the current directory. The MD command must be followed by a name for the new directory. See also CHDIR; RMDIR.

mean time before failure see MTBF.

mean time to recovery a measure of how quickly a self-resetting device can be expected to return to service after (non-fatal) failure.

mechanical an old term for a complete set of DTP pages. These will have been filled with text and graphics, checked and are ready for reproduction. See also CAMERA-READY.

media (*plural of* MEDIUM) disks, backup tapes, paper and any other methods for retaining data.

media control interface (MCI) or **multimedia extensions** the set of DRIVERS that are used to add MULTIMEDIA capabilities to WINDOWS.

media conversion the copying of data from one MEDIUM to another. Old data stored on tape might, for example, be copied to HARD DRIVE, or data on old 5.25-inch disks copied to modern 3.5-inch disks.

media error an ERROR MESSAGE indicating a disk fault.

Media Player a WINDOWS utility that is used to control the playing of music from an audio COMPACT DISC. You can, for example, see a display of music titles and artists (if these have been coded on the CD or on the HARD DRIVE) and decide what tracks to play and in what order.

medium (*plural* MEDIA) anything that stores computer output, such as a disk or backup tape.

mega see M.

megabits per second (mbps) a measure of data flow speed.

megabyte or **Mbyte** literally one million bytes, but in computing the term generally denotes 1,048,576 bytes. The reason is that a KILOBYTE is taken as meaning 1024 bytes, two to the power ten, so that a megabyte then means 1024 kilobytes, two to the power 20.

megaflop 1. a measure of processing power in terms of the FLOP time. One megaflop means that a million FLOATING-POINT actions can be carried out per second. The megaflop has been used as a measure of speed for MAINFRAME machines for some time but only recently applied to MICROCOMPUTERS. **2.** a colossal failure!

megahertz (MHz) millions of cycles of electrical voltage or current per second, used to measure CLOCK speeds and BUS speeds.

Megastream™ a BT data line service that provides for communication at 2 MEGABITS PER SECOND or 8 megabits per second, using interfacing equipment obtained from BT. See also KILOSTREAM.

meltdown total failure, usually of a NETWORK.

MEM the DOS command for providing information on the amount of memory installed on a computer and how it is used.

membrane keyboard a form of KEYBOARD in which the contacts are made through metallized strips on plastic sheets. The term is also (incorrectly) used to mean keyboards that are covered by clear plastic sheeting to allow use in wet or dirty environments.

MEMMAKER a DOS program that will configure a computer system for the optimum use of DOS memory, particularly with WINDOWS 3.1. The Memmaker program was not supplied with later versions of Windows.

memory a method of storing data in an organized way. Any physical effect that can be switched in one of two ways can be used to create a memory system. Microcomputers use dynamic RAM (DRAM) memory, in which microscopically small components either store electric charge or do not, so signalling the storage of BINARY 1 or 0. The alternative and faster method is to use elements that either pass or do not pass electric current (see ROM; STATIC RAM). Memory can be VOLATILE or NON-VOLATILE, read/write (RAM) or read-only (ROM). The action of a computer depends on the use of both ROM and RAM types of memory, and an important factor is the speed with which memory can be read because this determines how fast the computer can operate in practical programming terms. Since RAM is generally faster than ROM, many computer designs copy firmware from ROM to RAM at BOOT time; see SHADOWING.

memory access time the time that elapses between sending out the pulses that address the memory and receiving the data from the memory, usually of the order of 60 ns (see NANOSECOND) or less.

memory bank a set of memory chips connected together to make a memory unit. Memory chips are usually organized to store 1 BIT (sometimes 4 bits) per chip, so that for a conventional 32-megabyte memory bank on a personal computer, a set of 8 4-megabyte. chips would be used. See also BANKED MEMORY; EDO.

memory board a board or card added to a computer to increase the total memory, as distinct from plugging more memory chips into the MOTHERBOARD. See DIMM; SIMM.

memory cache see CACHE.

memory cell the unit of bit memory, which is a small capacitor for a dynamic RAM (DRAM) or a flip-flop circuit for a STATIC RAM.

memory diagnostic a UTILITY program that will check memory by repeatedly writing and reading, reporting on any problems. The MEM program of MS-DOS is of this type. See also LEAPFROG TEST.

memory dump a printout on SCREEN (sense 1) or paper of the contents of each ADDRESS (sense 1) in a section of memory, usually in HEXADECIMAL, used for fault-finding.

memory edit the process of looking at and changing computer memory contents, used for fault-finding.

memory location the position of a unit of memory, usually a BYTE, expressed as a number, and its ADDRESS (sense 1). For a BLOCK OF DATA in memory, the starting byte and the number of bytes are used as a reference.

memory management the software, usually part of the operating system (OS), that controls the use of memory and prevents conflicts when more than one program is in use. The management software is used to allocate memory such as VIRTUAL MEMORY, PAGE ADDRESSING and SWAP FILE use. See EMM386.EXE; HIMEM.SYS.

memory management program any program, such as MEMMAKER, that allows optimum use of DOS memory by placing DRIVER programs into upper memory blocks (UMB) so as to release the greatest possible amount of base memory (see CONVENTIONAL MEMORY).

memory management unit (MMU) HARDWARE that translates ADDRESS (sense 1) numbers provided by the processor into numbers that can be used to address data. This allows real MEMORY or VIRTUAL MEMORY to be used as required.

memory map a diagram that shows how memory address numbers are used for ROM and RAM. See also MAP; MEMORY MAPPING.

memory mapped I/O the use of ADDRESS (sense 1) numbers similar to memory address numbers to refer to inputs and outputs rather than the use of a separate I/O bus.

memory mapping or **bitmapping** the correspondence between data character position and memory ADDRESS (sense 1). One example is the system in which each position on a SCREEN (sense 1) corresponds to an address in memory. What is contained in that memory will then affect what is seen at that part of the screen. This system allows for both the shape and the colour of a point on the screen to be controlled by the content of memory. The simplest memory-mapping systems use the ASCII code for a character to provide the shape of the character on the screen. For graphics work, much more elaborate memory-mapping systems are in use in which the brightness and colour of each point on a screen, or produced by a printer, are controlled by bits stored in memory addresses of the computer, so that the shape of a character may be controlled by bits taken from several bytes located at widely differing addresses. Whatever system of memory mapping is used, both software in the form of machine code programs and hardware in the form of specialized CRT signal generators are needed to convert the stored numbers into signals that can cause a shape to appear on the screen.

memory optimizer a program such as the MS-DOS MEMMAKER or the Quarterdeck QEMM series that is designed to release as much of the lower 640 kilobytes of PERSONAL COMPUTER memory as possible by placing DRIVERs and other short RESIDENT programs into the upper memory area (see UMB).

memory page a unit of memory, typically 4 kilobytes, used for CACHE memory purposes or for addressing VIRTUAL MEMORY.

memory protection any system that prevents an APPLICATION from encroaching on the memory used by another. See GPF; unrecoverable application error (UAE).

memory-resident program see TSR PROGRAM.

menu a set of choices that the user can take in a program. Menus are often set out with the different choices numbered or named. The user can then select by typing the chosen number or name or, more usually, by clicking (see CLICK, sense 1) the MOUSE over the number or name. In modern programs, menus are supplemented or replaced by ICONs.

menu bar a strip along the top of a window that lists the MENUs that are available.

menu-driven (of a program) operating by making use of choices from a MENU. Such a program is usually easy for a user to follow and can be easy to alter or extend. It can, however, be time-consuming in use, particularly if one menu leads to another (a SUBMENU).

merge the action of combining files, usually maintaining some order (such as ALPHABETICAL ORDER). Contrast APPEND.

mesh network a way of making connections. A NETWORK of connections is described as being a mesh if there are two or more connections between each pair of items in the network.

message box a box that appears, in WINDOWS, with text containing notes or other messages to the user.

message header information that is placed at the start of an EMAIL message to show the author's name, name(s) of recipient(s), subject and date of sending.

message slot a set of digital bits used to carry messages around a NETWORK.

messaging application programming interface see MAPI.

metabit or **tag bit** an extra BIT assigned to each memory unit (BYTE or WORD, sense 2) and used for identification.

metafile a FORMAT (sense 5) for image files that allows the file to be read and used by a large variety of devices. The best-known example is the Windows metafile, using the WMF extension.

metal-oxide semiconductor see MOS.

metal-oxide-semiconductor field effect transistor see MOSFET.

metaphone a text ALGORITHM that ensures that words that sound similar will provide the same index code. This can be used, for example, in a SPELLCHECK program to provide a list of suggested words that is not confined to those with similar spelling.

metaprogram a program that can create or modify other programs.

MFM see MODIFIED FREQUENCY MODULATION.

MHz see MEGAHERTZ.

mickey a unit of MOUSE movement, approximately 1/200 inch.

Mickey Mouse program any program that is considered trivial. See also HELLO WORLD!

MICR see MAGNETIC INK CHARACTER RECOGNITION.

microcentury a time of 52.6 minutes, almost an hour.

microchannel architecture (MCA) a BUS system, used by IBM in the PS/2 machines and intended to replace the PC-AT bus, that makes such machines incompatible with expansion cards used on older machines. Unlike the earlier system, micro channel architecture has not been widely adopted by other manufacturers, and its use has been challenged by the EISA bus, which maintains COMPATIBILITY with earlier designs. In addition, new LOCAL BUS designs such as VLB and PCI have made the MCA design obsolescent.

microcode a set of coded instructions built into a MICROPROCESSOR to enable the processor to respond to EXTERNAL COMMAND codes.

Microcom network protocol see MNP.

microcomputer a computer that has been designed to be as compact as possible. Microcomputers can be loosely subdivided into PALMTOP, NOTEBOOK, LAPTOP, PORTABLE and DESKTOP sizes. The CPU is a single-chip MICROPROCESSOR, the MEMORY consisting of a small number of SEMICONDUCTOR memory chips and the whole electronics system held in a casing that in some examples is little bigger than the keyboard. This type of machine has been available since the early part of the 1970s and has been responsible for the enormous upsurge of interest in, and the more widespread use of, computers for all purposes. Most early microcomputers were designed to be programmed by the user, but later machines, since 1980, have concentrated on running APPLICATIONS PROGRAMS (OFF-THE-SHELF) rather than custom-written programs. The types of machine that have come to dominate the market completely are typified by the IBM PERSONAL COMPUTER and its CLONE and COMPATIBLE machines, and the APPLE MACINTOSH, all of them general-purpose machines for which an immense number of applications programs are available.

microcontroller a MICROPROCESSOR and associated components, including ROM, used in a circuit for control of a device. Such a microcontroller is DEDICATED, meaning that it cannot be easily converted for any other function. For example, a microcontroller intended for a toaster cannot be used in a washing machine even if the same microprocessor has been used.

microelectronics a development of ELECTRONICS that reduces the number of faults in a system by increased use of chips, thus eliminating large numbers of connections. Before the advent of microelectronics, electronics systems depended on assembling large numbers of components that had to be connected by means of copper wire or strip and soldered joints. These connections were always the least reliable part of any system. Work by G. R. Dummer in the UK in 1954 led to experiments in which several transistors and other components were formed along with interconnections on one small wafer of SEMICONDUCTOR material. The technology developed rapidly in the 1960s, mainly because of the demand for ultra-reliable systems for space technology, and by the early 1970s it was possible to fabricate several thousand devices and all their interconnections on one piece of SILICON. By the end of the 1970s, several hundred thousand devices could be put on one chip. Although the reliability of these units was the main reason for the widespread adoption of microelectronics, the very small size of each chip led to the possibility of making computers that were very much smaller than any previously imagined. The technology also led to such items as calculators, digital watches, miniature TV receivers and video cassette recorders, electronic typewriters and a host of other consumer goods. Modern production technology now allows the fabrication of millions of devices on a single chip.

microfloppy an old name for a miniature disk, referring to the 3.5-inch disks that are now a standard for small computers.

microinstruction a set of steps that are permanently coded within a MICROPROCESSOR which carries out part of the action of a software instruction. See also MICROPROGRAM.

micron a unit of length, equal to a millionth of a metre, used mainly to describe the sizes of units and connections in ICs.

microperforated or **laser-perforated** (of paper) divided into sheets or sections that are finely perforated to allow them to be separated or divided without leaving ragged edges. For example, fairly thick paper can be microperforated into business cards so that an A4 page of connected cards can be printed and the individual cards separated.

microprocessor the central processing unit (CPU) of a MICROCOMPUTER. Any computer can be thought of as consisting of MEMORY, INPUT/OUTPUT and processor. In this division, the processor is the part that carries out actions such as ARITHMETIC and LOGIC, which are the basis of all computing. The microcomputer was made possible by the creation of processors in one-CHIP form, with all the units built in and interconnected. The type of design also permitted the actions of the microprocessor to be controlled by electrical signals, so that the whole chip was programmable. Early microprocessors could deal with only four binary digits at a time, but by the middle of the 1970s, 8-bit chips were available, and by the end of the 1970s the first 16-bit chips were in production. All manufacturers are now turning out 32-bit chips, and the operating systems (OS) to make use of such chips effectively have also been developed. At the time of writing, 64-bit microprocessors are already being used, particularly in advanced GRAPHICS ADAPTER cards. Outside the realm of computing, microprocessors, particularly the 4-bit and 8-bit types, are being extensively used in machine-control applications; see MICROCONTROLLER.

microprogram a program used within a MICROPROCESSOR. In order for a single number-code instruction to cause an action such as addition, the microprocessor has to execute several steps, such as reading, addition and storage. These individual steps are controlled by a built-in program, the microprogram, which has been devised by the manufacturer. This program cannot be changed, patched or avoided in any way because it exists in the form of permanent connections inside the SILICON of the microprocessor.

microsecond (μs) a time interval equal to one millionth of a second, used for intervals such as TIME-SLICING periods. See also MILLISECOND; NANOSECOND.

Microsoft™ a very influential software HOUSE (sense 1). Founded by Bill Gates, Microsoft wrote the basic interpreters for most of the early microcomputers, such as the Commodore PET and Tandy TRS-80. Microsoft later developed the MS-DOS operating system (OS), which was the basis of most of the 16-BIT machines subsequently developed. Latterly, Microsoft developed the WINDOWS system as a FRONT END (sense 2) for MS-DOS and the OS/2 operating system for the PS/2 machines made by IBM. With the introduction of 32-bit machines and Microsoft WINDOWS 95, the dominance of Microsoft on software became greater, and the use of techniques such as plug and play (PNP) has extended this dominance to affect HARDWARE design.

Microsoft Access a RELATIONAL DATABASE that runs under WINDOWS. Access is provided with WIZARDs to guide the user through the creation of forms and reports that make use of data tables, so providing methods of inputting and organizing the data. Access is provided as part of the MICROSOFT OFFICE set of programs, with the latest version revised for use with Microsoft WINDOWS 2000.

Microsoft Certified System Engineer a certification awarded by MICROSOFT to those who satisfactorily complete an approved training course.

Microsoft Diagnostics (MSD) a program that can be run by any computer using MS-DOS or WINDOWS and that will provide information on the HARDWARE and SOFTWARE of the computer system. MSD can, if required, generate a disk file that can be sent to Microsoft or others so that a fault condition can be diagnosed.

Microsoft Excel a large and very capable SPREADSHEET program that runs under WINDOWS and can be used with the other components of MICROSOFT OFFICE.

Microsoft Exchange the facility in Microsoft WINDOWS 95 for dealing with EMAIL and FAX messages. Exchange allows you access to online services and makes it easy to organize and share such information. See also MICROSOFT OUTLOOK.

Microsoft mouse see BUS MOUSE.

Microsoft Network (MSN) an INTERNET provider that has been more successful in the USA than in the UK, partly because of the attraction of free Internet providers in the UK.

Microsoft natural keyboard a form of KEYBOARD that is not straight but shaped so that the keys can be reached with the minimum movement of the hands. See also DVORAK; MALTRON.

Microsoft Office a set of programs that are closely integrated, particularly in the later Office 2000 version. The basic set is composed of

Microsoft Word, Excel, Query and PowerPoint, and the professional package also contains Access.

Microsoft Outlook a program for managing EMAIL and NEWSGROUPs. It is now part of the MICROSOFT OFFICE 2000 suite and in EXPRESS form is also part of the INTERNET EXPLORER BROWSER that is incorporated into later versions of WINDOWS.

Microsoft Plus see SYSTEM AGENT.

Microsoft Publisher one of the three leading DTP and page layout program brands. The other two are ADOBE PAGEMAKER and VENTURA PUBLISHER.

Microsoft Windows or **Windows** a GUI program used on PERSONAL COMPUTERS (sense 2) as a FRONT END (sense 2) to MS-DOS. Windows, originally developed for the 80286 machines, allows MULTITASKING on 386 (and later) machines, with full cut and paste facilities between programs that have been written to use the system. Version 3.1 was outstandingly successful in persuading computer users, particularly commercial users, of the advantages of the GUI, and the later versions, Microsoft WINDOWS 95 onwards, have greatly expanded the facilities of the system, using 32-bit coding and successfully hiding the underlying DOS.

Microsoft Windows 95 see WINDOWS 95.

Microsoft Windows 98 see WINDOWS 98.

Microsoft Windows 2000 see WINDOWS 2000.

Microsoft Word or **Word** a very large and capable WORD PROCESSOR program, now regarded as an industry standard, particularly for publishers and for science and engineering users. The capabilities of Word match or exceed those of many DTP programs, so it can be used for typesetting work as well as for traditional word processing actions such as preparation of documents, spell checking (see SPELLCHECK), MAILMERGE, EMAIL, TABLE construction, columnar work, equation editing, graphics insertion, and so on. Version 7.0 of Word was released along with Microsoft WINDOWS 95, and new versions were released along with WINDOWS 97 and WINDOWS 2000.

MIDI (musical instrument digital interface) a system for connecting electronic musical instruments to each other and to a computer so as to allow the computer or one instrument to control all the others.

migration a change from an older version of software or hardware to a newer version, such as from MICROSOFT WINDOWS 3.1 to WINDOWS 95.

milk disk a disk that is used to gather data from a small machine (such as a LAPTOP) with a view to processing the data in a larger machine later.

milking machine a computer that can read data from various disks and transfer the data to a larger machine, usually a MAINFRAME.

milli see M.

millions of instructions per second see MIPS.

millisecond (ms) a time interval equal to one thousandth of a second, used for timing mechanical actions such as the movement of a READ/WRITE HEAD. See also MICROSECOND; NANOSECOND.

MIME (multipurpose Internet mail extensions) a standard file FORMAT (sense 5) for files that contain graphics and/or sound data in addition to text, transmitted over the INTERNET.

MIME type a registered identification for a MIME file transmitted over the INTERNET.

mimencode a form of coding for EMAIL and NEWSGROUP messages, intended to replace UUENCODE.

minicomputer an intermediate stage between the MAINFRAME and the MICROCOMPUTER that makes use of the electronics technology of the micro but has a memory capacity and speed that take it closer to the mainframe in capability. A mini consists of several cabinets of equipment, but these do not take up nearly as much space, nor require the elaborate cooling, that is needed by a mainframe. Fast-acting SEMICONDUCTOR memory is used as the main store, and several HARD DRIVES as the backing store. The keyboard and video monitor units are generally remote from the main processor unit, often connected by serial links. There is often provision for MULTI-ACCESS connections and NETWORK use.

Mini Disc a form of miniature COMPACT DISC pioneered by Sony Corporation. This is expected to replace the tape cassette as a way of distributing popular music, but since it uses a coding method that omits bits that make only a small contribution to the sound, it is unlikely to replace the standard CD for serious music, and it has not been used as a data storage device.

minimal tree a TREE (sense 2) structure in which the branching has been arranged in the most efficient possible way.

minimax an ALGORITHM for selecting an appropriate move in a board game for two players.

minimized reduced to an ICON. The WINDOWS SHELL system will minimize a running program to an icon, suspending activity but retaining data. The existence of the program is indicated by the presence of its icon at the foot of the SCREEN (sense 1).

minimizing window the action of reducing a WINDOW to an ICON. The icon can be clicked to restore the original window size.

minimum seek time the time, measured in MILLISECONDs, needed to move the READ/WRITE HEAD of a DISK DRIVE from one TRACK to the next. This indicates how fast the drive will be for gathered data.

minmax a method of deciding between two possibilities by allocating points for and against each, used in ARTIFICIAL INTELLIGENCE.

minus the – sign that is available in a WORD PROCESSOR but is usually replaced by the hyphen (-) in other applications.

MIPS (millions of instructions per second) another measure of computing power. See also MEGAFLOP.

mirror 1. A mirror-imaging action in a GRAPHICS editing program. **2.** the use of extra HARD DRIVES on a system to hold copies of data on other drives, minimizing the risk of loss. See also RAID.

mirroring the rotating of a graphics display by 180 degrees in a plane at right angles to the picture plane in order to produce the sort of image that you would see reflected in a mirror. See also FLIP.

mirror margins a setting for a WORD PROCESSOR page in which both left- and right-hand pages use the same size of INSIDE MARGIN and also the same size of OUTSIDE MARGIN.

mirror site a site on the World Wide Web (WWW) that contains a copy of a set of files at another site. This reduces the amount of long-distance communications by making the files easily available to local users.

misfeature a program feature arising from an apparently reasonable decision that has subsequently become undesirable, such as the use of two digits to indicate the year. See also Y2K.

mission critical any piece of SOFTWARE that is indispensable to the user.

mixed cell reference a WORKSHEET CELL reference in which one portion is constant (an ABSOLUTE CELL REFERENCE) and the other variable. For example, the cell reference C$5 uses a fixed row number and a variable column number. See also DUPLICATION.

MMU see MEMORY MANAGEMENT UNIT.

MMX (matrix math extensions or multimedia extensions) additional instructions built into MICROCODE in the later PENTIUM chips so as to allow fast digital signal processing, particularly for MULTIMEDIA uses. The system has also been used in processor chips from other suppliers, notably ADVANCED MICRO DEVICES.

mnemonic a reminder of KEY (sense 1) action. A letter in a MENU that is underlined indicates that the letter can be used to produce the menu action, usually when the letter key is pressed along with the CTRL or ALT KEY.

mnemonics abbreviated names for assembly language instructions, used when programming in machine code.

MNP (Microcom network protocol) a system for error detection and correction in a MODEM, devised by Microcom Inc. and used as a standard on communications equipment.

mockingbird communications interception software used by a CRACKER to steal confidential data by simulating the actions of a legitimate contact.

MOD 1. a number FUNCTION used in a WORKSHEET that gives the remainder after INTEGER division. For example, 8 MOD 3 gives 2, the remainder after 8 has been divided by 3. **2.** see MAGNETO-OPTICAL DRIVE.

mode one of a number of optional systems of operation. For example, a computer may offer several SCREEN (sense 1) modes that allow different degrees of RESOLUTION and require different amounts of video RAM. A very common choice for text is the choice of 40 or 80 characters per line. MS-DOS uses a mode command for configuring aspect of printer, screen and keyboard use.

mode indicator a screen message, often on a STATUS LINE, that indicates what mode is being used. For example, a mode indicator can show whether INSERT MODE or OVERTYPE MODE is being used in a WORD PROCESSOR.

model a simplified description of a system that can be used to predict and simulate system behaviour.

model building the construction of a system that simulates a process in the real world, from the running of a business to a flood prevention scheme. The model is a mathematical model, with each feature of the real system represented by an equation. If the equations are simplified, the programming will be simpler and the answers will be obtained more quickly, but their validity may be suspect. If the equations are complex, the programming will be difficult and the action will be slow. The usual compromise is to make as many simplifying assumptions as seem possible and reasonable, and to test the working of the model against the real-life system. This is not always easy, and one simple test is to run the model in reverse to try to calculate past conditions from present conditions. If this action (sometimes called *postdicting*) is not successful, it gives little confidence in the ability of the model to predict into the future, as was intended. In many examples, however, a simplified model will give results that compare reasonably with real-life results, and where the divergence can be explained, some of the relationships can be made more precise without the need to remove all the simplification.

modem (modulator/demodulator) a device that allows computers to communicate along telephone lines – see MODULATOR (sense 2), DEMODULATION (sense 1). Telephone lines are useful only for signals that change comparatively slowly, up to a few thousand changes per second. The normal signal change rates of computers are several millions of changes per second, so a program (the terminal program) must be used to change the computer signals into signals that can be sent over telephone lines. The modem does part of this and also performs the conversion from telephone line signals to computer signals. In the UK any modem must be type-approved by BT. See also AT-COMMAND SET; BULLETIN BOARD; CCITT PROTOCOL; COMMUNICATIONS LINK; HAYES STANDARDS; V-SERIES.

modem mantra or **whale song** the screeching sounds that can be heard from a MODEM with a loudspeaker (or connected to a SOUND CARD) while the modem connects to another modem.

moderated newsgroup a NEWSGROUP for which an editor will ensure that messages are to the point and that reasoned argument does not deteriorate into personal abuse.

moderator a committee or person responsible for monitoring a NEWS-GROUP to ensure that abusive postings are not published, so avoiding a FLAME WAR.

modified frequency modulation (MFM) a method of coding digital signals into magnetic signals that can be recorded on a HARD DRIVE or FLOPPY DISK. The MFM system is fairly old, and hard drives more usually employ the ADVANCED RUN-LENGTH LIMITED system.

modifier a subcommand that modifies the effect of an MS-DOS main command. In MS-DOS, a modifier is typically a character following a slash sign, such as /o.

MO drive see MAGNETO-OPTICAL DRIVE.

MODULA-2™ a comparatively modern PROGRAMMING LANGUAGE developed from PASCAL.

modular accounting an accounting system for large-scale users that consists of several interacting programs which reflect the traditional divisions of accounting (daybook, accounts receivable, accounts payable, etc.).

modularization the design of programs from established routines, leading to greater reliability and freedom from BUGS.

modulation a system that modifies some characteristic of a radio or light wave so as to carry messages. The oldest form of modulation is the starting and stopping of a radio wave in the form of Morse code. Signals at sound-wave FREQUENCY, as from a microphone, can be modulated on to a radio CARRIER (sense 2) wave by using the signals to alter either the AMPLITUDE or the frequency of the radio wave, providing AMPLITUDE MODULATION (AM) or frequency modulation (FM) respectively. The opposite action, which recovers the original signal, is called DEMODULATION (sense 2). In computing, modulation generally refers to a system that codes a digital 0 as one audio tone and digital 1 as another tone. This system, used in a MODEM, allows the tone-coded signals to be recorded on audio tapes or cassettes and transmitted over telephone lines. These tones can, in turn, be modulated on to radio waves to be transmitted by radio.

modulation protocol the standards used by a MODEM to send and receive messages.

modulator 1. any device that carries out the MODULATION of a signal on to a higher-frequency carrier. **2.** in computing, a device that converts digital signals into audio frequency tones, part of the action of a MODEM.

modulator/demodulator see MODEM.

module a self-contained unit which can be HARDWARE or SOFTWARE. A software module means a piece of program code that can accept data and output data but acts sufficiently independently to avoid conflicts with the main program or with other modules.

modulo the BASE of a number system.

261

moiré effect a coarse hatching and flickering effect caused by viewing two grid patterns superimposed, or by interaction between a grid pattern and the scanning lines of a MONITOR (sense 1).

molly-guard a cover for a switch to prevent a system being accidentally switched off or reset.

monitor 1. a display unit that can make direct use of the computer's video signals. A monitor is constructed so that the computer (or video recorder) signals can be connected directly, so providing much better RESOLUTION than can be obtained when a MODULATOR (sense 1) is used in conjunction with a TV receiver. This latter method is often used in conjunction with PRESENTATION GRAPHICS so as to allow a larger audience to see pictures on a large-screen TV. See also COLOUR MONITOR; MONOCHROME MONITOR. **2.** a MACHINE CODE program that allows a programmer to trace what a computer is doing when a program is running. A monitor should allow the user to read what is stored in any part of the memory and to change anything that is stored in RAM. It should also allow analysis of the action of a machine code program, even to the extent of reading the data within the MICROPROCESSOR.

monochrome display adapter (MDA) the form of text display unit used in the original IBM PERSONAL COMPUTER. This allowed the display of 80 high-quality characters in 25 lines on the MONITOR (sense 1) but did not provide for GRAPHICS other than a few box shapes.

monochrome monitor or **black-and-white monitor** a MONITOR (sense 1) whose display is in one colour only. The traditional monochrome means white text on a dark SCREEN (sense 1), but colours such as green or amber are considered more restful to the eye. See also COLOUR MONITOR.

monospacing or **fixed-pitch font** or **fixed space character** the allocation of a fixed space to each printed character, as is done by a typewriter. This is essential for columnar work, but printed text looks much better when PROPORTIONAL SPACING is used. A WORD PROCESSOR that uses proportionally spaced FONTS will usually provide for tables to be constructed using special commands that ensure correct column alignment even for such fonts.

Monte Carlo method a method of analysing statistics in a WORKSHEET that makes use of random selections.

MORE a DOS FILTER program that will break up a text document into screen-sized pages. For example, the command TYPE *textfile* | MORE will display the file called *textfile* on the screen 20 lines at a time, with the message 'More' appearing on the bottom line. Pressing any key will display the next page.

morphing the action of changing one image into another in a set of gradual steps so that when performed rapidly it appears like a continuous change.

Morse code a form of BINARY code invented by Samuel Morse (1791–1872) for sending signals over telegraph lines, used also in the early days of radio transmissions and still useful for emergency signalling. The characters of the alphabet, along with digits, are codes as a set of short (dot) and long (dash) tones.

MOS (metal-oxide semiconductor) the sandwich of materials used in the construction of ICs and some types of TRANSISTOR.

MOSFET (metal-oxide-semiconductor field effect transistor) the type of TRANSISTOR formed using MOS methods.

most significant bit see MSB.

most significant byte the BYTE in a multibyte MACHINE WORD that is in the MOST SIGNIFICANT position.

most significant digit the digit in a number that denotes the highest value. By convention, this is the digit at the extreme left-hand side of a number. See also SIGNIFICANCE.

motherboard or **backplane** a main CIRCUIT BOARD or baseboard for a computer circuit. Almost all desktop computers make use of a motherboard construction. This means that the main part of the computer is constructed with a number of SILICON chip circuits soldered or plugged into a main connecting board. This motherboard is also provided with connectors into which other boards can be plugged. In this way, the capabilities of the computer can be greatly extended because the supplementary boards can contain extra memory, GRAPHICS ADAPTER board, PORTS, SOUND BOARD, INTERFACEs to PERIPHERALs, communications circuits or any new equipment that is developed. Replacing a motherboard is an essential step in upgrading a computer. See also LOCAL BUS.

motion picture expert group see MPEG.

Motorola™ the manufacturer of the 68000 series of MICROPROCESSORs, the main rivals to the INTEL type of chips for computing use. Motorola chips are used in the APPLE machines and are not cloned (see CLONE) in the way that Intel chips are.

mount to make a file set available, used of the MICROSOFT compression system called DRIVESPACE, for which a disk had to be *mounted* so that it could be written or read.

mouse a device for computer operation that dispenses with the use of the KEYBOARD for issuing commands to the computer. The mouse is a miniature trolley that can be moved about on a desk surface. As the mouse is moved, a POINTER (sense 1) on the VDU SCREEN (sense 1) moves and can be made to point at various symbols, the ICONs or to items on a conventional MENU. Pressing a BUTTON on the mouse will then initiate the action related to that symbol or phrase. See also GUI.

mouse droppings small dots on a picture in a GRAPHICS program that appear when the mouse has been moved. These usually disappear before the picture is saved or printed.

mouse mat a sheet of material (rubber or plastic) with a matte surface on which a MOUSE can be moved easily without any tendency for the ball to skid.

mouse pointer see POINTER (sense 1).

mouse trails an option for WINDOWS that allows the MOUSE movement to leave a trail on the screen. This is particularly useful for PORTABLE COMPUTERS with an LCD display on which the normal mouse movement makes the POINTER (sense 1) invisible while it is moving.

mouse wrist a form of repetitive strain injury caused by resting the weight of the arm on the wrist while using a MOUSE.

M out of N code a code system that uses REDUNDANCY to achieve error-checking and correction. In 8 out of 14 code, for example, as used on CD-ROM, each 14-bit code must contain 8 1s in a valid number.

MOVE an operating system (OS) command to move files. Moving a file implies copying to another drive and/or directory and deleting the original version.

movie a form of PRESENTATION GRAPHICS in which the each SLIDE is shown in rapid sequence like the frames of a movie film.

Moving Pictures Experts Group see MPEG.

MPEG (Motion or Moving Pictures Experts Group) a committee that sets standards for file FORMATs (sense 5) and compression methods for video and audio digitized signals. The MPEG standard for video files is a LOSSY COMPRESSION file system for animated images. See also JPEG.

ms see MILLISECOND.

msb (most significant bit) the BIT in a BYTE that is in the MOST SIGNIFICANT position. The most significant bit of a BINARY number is often used to convey the sign (positive or negative) of the number.

MSCDEX the driver needed by DOS and WINDOWS to deal with MULTIMEDIA programs.

MSD see MICROSOFT DIAGNOSTICS.

MS-DOS™ an operating system (OS) that was designed by the MICROSOFT Corporation for use with 16-BIT computers, notably the machines like the IBM PERSONAL COMPUTER. Early versions resembled the CP/M system that was used on 8-bit computers, but in later versions MS-DOS expanded, taking on new commands that owed much to the influence of UNIX and XENIX (a Microsoft derivative of UNIX). MS-DOS was conceived as a single-user, single-task operating system, and its use in machines that achieve MULTITASKING and MULTI-ACCESS actions is because of the addition of other software that makes use of MS-DOS. File commands are generally simpler to remember than those of UNIX, and a few examples are illustrated in this book. Later versions of MS-DOS featured the PIPE, FILTER (sense 1) and REDIRECTION actions of UNIX while retaining the very compact nature of MS-DOS, although Version 4.0 was considered by many users as too large and later versions were shorter. Version 5.0

allowed a considerable portion of code to be accommodated in the higher memory addresses of AT computers, releasing more of the useful memory in the first 640K of the machine, and this was reinforced in Versions 6.0 to 6.22. The introduction of Microsoft WINDOWS 95, although it still made use of MS-DOS, makes the separate use of DOS commands obsolescent other than for a few disk reader programs, and later Windows versions have become less reliant on DOS. See also CLS; COMPACT DISC; COPY (sense 2); DELETE (sense 2); DIRECTORY (sense 1); REN; TYPE.

MSN see MICROSOFT NETWORK.

MTBF (mean time before failure) a measure of reliability.

MTU see MAXIMUM TRANSMISSION UNIT.

mugtrap see VALIDATION.

multi-access system or **multi-user system** a system in which several users of one computer all have ACCESS (sense 1) to a computing system by way of a TERMINAL, each linked to the main computer by either direct cables or by telephone lines by way of a MODEM. The terminals can range from cash registers sending data on sales to INTELLIGENT TERMINALS with their own computing actions. Such a system can be used running a single program suite, as is often the case for an in-store unit, or it can allow the user of each terminal to RUN (sense 2) a program independent of all other users. Multi-access is an essential part of REAL-TIME PROCESSING, used in booking office (travel, theatre, cinema) and banking applications. The larger the system, the more likely are delays because of the amount of processing and the effect of busy lines, so the more the processing that can be carried out at each terminal the better. The whole scheme works by TIMESHARING the main computer, and when this machine approaches the fully loaded condition, annoying delays are likely to develop.

multibus system a system that uses one main BUS between the MICROPROCESSOR and MEMORY and other buses linking other components, sometimes running at different speeds. The AT BUS system, for example, makes use of five address buses and four data buses. See also LOCAL BUS.

multicolor graphics array see MCGA.

multidrop network a linear NETWORK in which machines are linked in a chain from a master.

multifunction card a card designed to fit into an EXPANSION SLOT that can carry out several actions, such as PARALLEL PORT, SERIAL PORT and games port, or a combination of video graphics and parallel port. Switches or jumper connectors are used to switch functions on or off and to assign ports as LPT1, LPT2, COM1 (AUX1), COM2, etc.

multilayer PCB a PCB whose conductors are formed on several layers of insulating material, allowing considerably more complex circuits to be constructed. Modern MOTHERBOARD designs invariably use this form of construction.

multilevel display a GRAPH display that contains information from more than one data table. For example, three data tables might be used to create a BAR CHART in which three different bar shadings are used to distinguish the data sets.

multilevel sort a SORT (sense 1) action in which sorting is carried out more than once, used mainly in DATABASE programs. For example, a list of names might be sorted in order of surname, and then a second-level sort would sort in order of occupation, so that for all the entries for the name *Smith*, the names would be put in alphabetical order from *Archery consultant* to *Zero-defect consultant*.

multimedia a combination of text, still and moving images and sounds that provides more information than can be obtained from text alone. The use of multimedia can greatly enhance works such as an encyclopedia, and the use of CD-ROM can make such a work very compact, one disc replacing 30 volumes or more of printed material. See Fig. 29. A computer is equipped for multimedia if it contains a CD-ROM drive or DVD drive and a SOUND BOARD with loudspeakers. The machine should preferably be fast and have a large memory capacity.

Fig. 29. **Multimedia**. A page of Microsoft Encarta encyclopedia, showing text and graphics. Clicking on the loudspeaker icon will produce a sound.

multimedia extensions see MEDIA CONTROL INTERFACE; MMX.

multipart stationery paper that consists of a top sheet with one or more copy sheets separated by carbons. This requires an IMPACT PRINTER.

multiple DOS configuration a PERSONAL COMPUTER system in which the user can specify at BOOT time how the computer will be used, so that the appropriate CONFIGURATION can be selected.

multiple selection the selection of more than one RANGE of CELLS in a

WORKSHEET. The older form of selecting a range permitted only one rectangular block of cells to be selected.

multiplexer (MUX) a circuit that can accept inputs from several lines and combine the signals (or some number less than the number of inputs) into one output. See also TIME DIVISION MULTIPLEX.

multiprocessing the use of more than one main processor in a computer, as distinct from the use of a COPROCESSOR.

multiprocessor system a system in which more than one microprocessor can take command of the BUS connections. The use of a COPROCESSOR is the most common example.

multiprogramming see MULTITASKING.

multipurpose internet mail extensions see MIME.

multiread a standard for COMPACT DISC drives that allows all types of COMPACT DISC media to be read, including the CD-RW type that reflects much less of the LASER beam than the stamped-out pre-recorded discs or the CD-R types.

multiscan monitor see MULTISYNC MONITOR.

multisession referring to a CD-ROM that can be recorded more than once, adding new material on the subsequent recording. All CD-ROM drives should be capable of playing COMPACT DISCs recorded in this way. See also CD-R; CD-RW; PHOTO-CD.

multisession disc a CD-R or CD-RW disc that is partly recorded and is not a finalized disc. FIXATION, by contrast, does not prevent an additional session from being recorded.

multisync monitor or **multiscan monitor** a monitor, following the layout of a design by NEC, that allows a variety of high-resolution graphics cards to be used and automatically adapts to the type of signal from each card.

multitasking an action that allows a MICROPROCESSOR to appear to be running several programs simultaneously. This is done by TIMESHARING, so that the microprocessor carries out several steps of one program then switches to the next in sequence. The main problem of multitasking is ensuring that programs do not interfere with each other, and this is done by restricting the way that the microprocessor can gain ACCESS (sense 2) to programs.

multithreading the action of processing more than one task simultaneously in the course of a program.

multi-user system see MULTI-ACCESS SYSTEM.

music chip a specialized IC used on a SOUND BOARD that can be programmed to synthesize ANALOGUE signals, which, when amplified and fed to a loudspeaker, will produce sound.

musical instrument digital interface see MIDI.

MUX see MULTIPLEXER.

My Computer an ICON that appears on the DESKTOP of a computer running Microsoft WINDOWS 95 onwards. By double-clicking (see DOUBLE-CLICK) this icon, the user will see a WINDOW that is an overview of the computer system, allowing access to all drives and to other features such as the RECYCLE BIN. See Fig. 30.

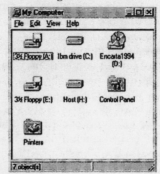

Fig. 30. **My Computer**. When the My Computer icon is double-clicked, this panel will appear, allowing access to all the disk drives, including CD-ROM, the control panel and the printer.

Mylar™ a form of polyester material made by the Du Pont Corporation and used for FLOPPY DISKS. The Mylar disc is coated with magnetic material and encased in a paper. The modern 3.5-inch disks use a smaller Mylar disc encased in a rigid plastic casing.

N

naive user a user of a computer program, particularly a DATABASE, who is unaware of the ARCHITECTURE of the program but can use one or more features to carry out limited tasks such as updating accounts.

nagware a form of SHAREWARE that displays frequent reminders of the desirability of registering with the author.

NAK (negative acknowledgement) a code used by a remote TERMINAL to indicate that data has not been correctly received and should be retransmitted. See also ACK.

name a title that represents data. Quantities that are being processed, whether numbers, letters or words, are often represented by names or identifiers. Any action that is to be carried out on a number or other quantity can therefore be programmed in terms of the name. A WORKSHEET RANGE, for example, can be named, as can a DATABASE QUERY or an INTERNET FAVOURITE.

name resolution the interpretation of a name into an INTERNET ADDRESS number.

NAND a LOGIC action equivalent to the AND action followed by the NOT action. For example A NAND B means that there will be a zero output when both A and B are 1, but a 1 output for all other input conditions. This is equivalent to NOT A OR NOT B.

nano- prefix meaning one thousandth of a millionth and also used to mean microscopic scale. For example, NANOTECHNOLOGY refers to engineering with components that are so small in size that their dimensions are stated in *nanometres*, such as the proposed ROBOT that can move along human blood vessels.

nanosecond (ns) a unit of time equal to one thousandth of a millionth of a second, that is 1E-9 seconds. For most modern computers, the time to carry out an instruction may be much less than a millionth of a second (a microsecond) and is therefore expressed in nanoseconds. The time needed to ACCESS (sense 3) memory is usually 70 ns or less.

nanotechnology a proposed construction technology that would work with individual atoms to create objects smaller than any previously possible. This would make it possible to fabricate extremely small processor units.

nastygram see LETTERBOMB.

national characters accented characters that are not used in English. See also ACCENT MARK.

National Television Standards Committee see NTSC.

native format the built-in or DEFAULT format of a program. A DATABASE program, for example, might use an entry form that was built-in until modified, and a WORD PROCESSOR might set up a page with 66 lines of 64 characters per line, each being an example of the native format for that particular program.

natural constant a number that is determined by natural causes, such as the value of PI, the exponential constant e, or the amount of charge on an electron.

natural language the language that is spoken and written by human beings, as distinct from computer PROGRAMMING LANGUAGES. Natural languages are much more complex than computing languages and are full of ambiguities, whereas a computing language must be simple and unambiguous. The closer a programming language comes to natural language, the higher the level of the programming language. See also TRANSLATE UTILITY.

natural language processing programming that allows a computer to work with NATURAL LANGUAGE. This is extensively used in SPEECH RECOGNITION programs.

natural number any of the whole number set 0, 1, 2, 3, etc.

natural recalculation a method of recalculation of FORMULAE in a WORKSHEET that carries out the recalculations in the order required by the formulae. For example, if a formula contains references to other CELLS that in turn contain formulae, these cells are recalculated first, regardless of their position in the worksheet.

navigation the act of moving from one WEB SITE to another using a BROWSER, from one DIRECTORY (sense 1) or folder to another or, in a DATABASE, of moving between displays of tables, queries, records and reports.

Navigator see NETSCAPE NAVIGATOR.

NC see NUMERICAL CONTROL.

NCR (National Cash Register) the company that introduced NCR paper, the 'no carbon required' copying paper.

near letter quality see NLQ.

NEAT chipset (New Extended AT chipset) now obsolescent, used of a set of chips for the early PC-AT type of computer.

NEC (Nippon Electric Company) the company that developed the MULTISYNC MONITOR.

needle drop a short extract from a recording, used of MULTIMEDIA sound clips.

needles the printing elements of a DOT-MATRIX printer.

negation or **complement** the inversion of a BINARY digit. Negating binary 1 gives binary 0, negating binary 0 gives binary 1.

negative conventionally, a number that is less than zero. In DENARY, a negative number is represented by a special sign, the negative (or minus) sign, written as –. In binary code, there is no negative sign, and one BIT of each number (the MSB) is used to convey sign. This is done by using a 1 to mean negative and a 0 to mean positive.

negative acknowledgement see NAK.

negative logic the use of a low voltage as level 1 and a higher voltage for level 0, the inverse of the more normal POSITIVE LOGIC arrangement. See LOGIC.

nested indent a form of INDENT used in outlining (see OUTLINE). Each new subtopic is indented further, using both left and right indents, to emphasize the structure of the text.

nesting arrangement into a HIERARCHY. For example, MICROSOFT ACCESS allows you to group records and to nest these groups so that the groups are shown indented by a distance that corresponds to their nesting level, with the highest level to the left.

nesting documents documents that form part of a MASTER DOCUMENT of MICROSOFT WORD. Each nesting document can be edited independently or as a portion of the master document.

net see INTERNET; NETWORK.

NetBIOS a part of DOS that allows the computer to make use of NETWORK HARDWARE and SOFTWARE.

Net computer a computer designed for INTERNET NAVIGATION rather than for other purposes. Such a machine can use a processor that is no longer fashionable, together with a specification of an older design, possibly with an output to a TV receiver rather than a monitor. Such machines can be made at such low cost that they can be given away in exchange for a contract with an ISP or a telephone service.

netiquette a set of good behaviour rules intended to make INTERNET communications, particularly NEWSGROUP postings, more friendly and to avoid offending users who seem determined to be offended.

netlag a delay caused by heavy traffic on the INTERNET.

NetNanny a utility that can be run to deter children from using a BROWS-ER to view pornographic WEB SITES.

Netscape Navigator a BROWSER designed by Netscape Communications Corporation.

net surfing see SURFING.

Net Watcher a feature of Microsoft WINDOWS 95 onwards that allows the use of a NETWORK to be monitored. For example, you can find who is currently using resources on your computer, and you can control the sharing of files and disconnect other users.

network a system of interconnections between computers that allows them to share facilities, typically HARD DRIVES and PRINTERS. A network also allows different users to communicate and to pass data to and from each other. Networking can greatly increase the utility of a system by allowing different users to contribute data. The snag is that the use of a network can sometimes cause an unacceptable reduction in the speed of computing and can introduce operating complications that require professional help to resolve.

network address the first portion of an address number that identifies the ISP.

network analysis a mathematical study of the routes, message lengths and frequency of route use with a view to improving the performance of a NETWORK.

network architecture the arrangement of each NODE and the connections between nodes in a NETWORK system. There are five main architectures used, with names that are descriptive of the arrangement. The *fully connected network architecture* (or MESH) contains links between each pair of nodes so that the number of links is very large for a large number of nodes. The *partially connected architecture* contains links only between selected nodes. The *tree architecture* has one root node linked to two others, each of which is in turn linked to two others. *Star architecture* uses a central node linked to each other node, and *ring architecture* has all the nodes linked in a chain that is joined at the ends to form a ring.

network card see NETWORK INTERFACE CARD.

network diagram a method of representing the connections of a NETWORK. It is also used to describe the LOGIC of a set of interdependent commands.

network drive a DISK DRIVE that is not physically present on the computer you are using but is on another computer on the NETWORK. See also LOCAL DRIVE.

network interface card a plug-in CARD that provides the connections for NETWORK cables.

network layer one of the ISO/OSI levels of action in a NETWORK system.

network management the COMPUTER SYSTEM of routines that controls a NETWORK and keeps it working efficiently. This includes keeping a file of registered users, controlling the COMMUNICATIONS LINKs through the network, testing the network and analysing performance.

network number see HOST NUMBER.

network operating system the operating system (OS) that controls a NETWORK, allowing computers to be linked and operated together.

network printer a PRINTER that is not connected directly to your computer but is available through the network.

network protocol the SOFTWARE methods that are used to ensure that a NETWORK operates smoothly with no collision problems.

network redundancy the provision of more connections between each NODE in a NETWORK so as to make the possibility of failure less likely to occur.

network server see SERVER.

network topology the geometrical design of a NETWORK in terms of NODEs and connections. The network topology can be centralized, such as the *star network*, or decentralized, like a *ring network* (see NETWORK ARCHITECTURE).

network transparency the ability to gain access to files and resources (such as printers) without needing to know if the file or resource is local or at some other point in the NETWORK.

neural network a software or hardware system that is capable of learning. Inputs and outputs are subjected to a learning process with known data so as to teach the system some rules. This is then used to request outputs from new sets of inputs. The idea is to emulate part of the process that the brain uses in learning. The system thus, effectively, develops its own method of solving problems, with no software program written for the solution, which simply 'exists' in the neural network. A program must, however, be written to allow the network to carry out inputs, to process data and provide outputs.

NEW a command used in many text and graphics programs to clear a program file from the memory. The command is used in some WORD PROCESSOR and DTP applications to close an existing file so that a new file can be opened.

New Extended AT chipset see NEAT CHIPSET.

newline character see LINE FEED.

newsgroup or **forum** a set of users with a common interest in a topic who contribute (see POST, sense 1) messages and read others to create a discussion that can be informative but which can easily descend into abuse (see FLAME WAR). See also MODERATOR; NETIQUETTE.

newsletter a document file published at intervals over the World Wide Web (WWW) containing information of use to a limited number of subscribers.

newspaper columns or **snaking columns** multiple columns on a page in which text is read down the left-hand column and is continued on the next column to the right until the end of the page. See also TABULAR COLUMNS.

news reader a program, usually part of a BROWSER, that allows the user to DOWNLOAD NEWSGROUP names, select some for subscription and read from and POST (sense 1) to the selected groups.

new technology see NT.

Newton a model of personal digital assistant (PDA) developed by the APPLE Corporation.

nibble four BITS, half a BYTE.

1900 date system the standard date system used by most SPREADSHEET programs in which the days are numbered in sequence, starting at 1 January 1900. The year 1904 is sometimes used instead.

N-key rollover see KEY ROLLOVER.

NLQ (near letter quality) an attribute of a DOT-MATRIX printer that has been designed to produce characters of similar print quality to that of a

DAISYWHEEL. See also MATRIX PRINTER. This is now described as *normal* (as distinct from *draft*) mode for an INKJET PRINTER.

NMOS (n-type metal-oxide semiconductor) a form of FIELD EFFECT TRANSISTOR construction that is used for fabricating MICROPROCESSORS and memory chips. See also CMOS; PMOS.

noddy (of a program) trivial. See HELLO WORLD!; MICKEY MOUSE PROGRAM.

node a point where connecting lines join or a place where NETWORK signals are switched. A node in a communications system may also need to store signals before retransmitting them.

noise unwanted electrical signals, such as those that radiate from fluorescent lights or electric motors. If a lot of electrical noise is present in a mains supplies or is radiated, then computers may have to be shielded (see SHIELD). The COMPUTER SYSTEM itself radiates electrical noise that can interfere with radio reception, particularly on VHF bands, and with MODEM signals.

noise immunity the ability of signals to resist corruption by noise, either because of shielding (see SHIELD) or because of the amplitude or timing of the signals.

nomenclature any system of allocating names.

nonaligned out of position, as of a DISK reading head that is not positioned correctly on a TRACK.

non-break space see HARD SPACE.

non-contiguous sectors disk SECTORs that are not adjacent to each other on a disk. Data in contiguous (touching) sectors can be read and written faster than data in non-contiguous sectors, hence the importance of DEFRAGMENTATION programs.

non-dedicated server a NETWORK server that is also used to RUN (sense 2) other programs. Compare DEDICATED SERVER.

nondestructive causing no erasure. For example, a nondestructive CURSOR is one that can be moved around the SCREEN (sense 1) without erasing any characters over which it passes.

nondisclosure agreement any agreement regarding secrecy made with computer manufacturers, journalists and others who have access to new products before the official release date.

non-impact printer one using a printing method in which paper is not mechanically struck. Non-impact printers are quiet but cannot produce carbon copies. See ELECTROSTATIC PRINTER; INKJET PRINTER; LASER PRINTER; THERMAL PRINTER.

non-interlaced monitor a MONITOR (sense 2) that does not use interlace actions, so that each LINE is scanned (see SCAN, sense 1) in turn and one set of consecutive line scans makes up a complete frame. Absence of interlacing is a feature of a MULTISYNC MONITOR.

nonintrusive testing a testing system for SOFTWARE that does not interfere with the normal running of the software.

nonlinear any system whose output is not proportional to input. A nonlinear system is less predictable than a linear one (see LINEAR FUNCTION).

non-optimal solution any solution to a problem that is demonstrably not the best solution but that is better than a wild guess.

non-preemptive multitasking a system of MULTITASKING in which the operating system cannot hold back one task so as to process another task but timeshares (see TIMESHARING) the tasks. The WINDOWS system uses this form of multitasking.

non-printing codes ASCII code numbers, usually in the range 1 to 31, that do not represent a character but an action like clearing the SCREEN (sense 1), taking a new line, switching the printer on and off, and so on.

non-printing items SCREEN (sense 1) patterns in a DTP or WORD PROCESSOR program that do not appear in print. Typical non-printing items are column and margin guides.

non-return to zero see NRZ.

non-return to zero inverted (NRZI) a recording system used for magnetic tapes.

non-scrollable (of a portion of SCREEN, sense 1, usually top or bottom) not capable of being scrolled (see SCROLL) along with the rest of the screen and can be used for instructions and reminders. This system is often used in a SPREADSHEET program; see FROZEN ROW OR COLUMN.

non-transactional application a program used on a NETWORK whose output does not need to be shared with other users.

non-volatile memory or **permanent memory** or **persistent memory** any MEMORY that retains its contents when electrical power to the machine is switched off. The normal RAM of the computer loses all data within a millisecond of being switched off, and a different memory system must be used for any data that has to be retained. This is usually provided by ROM, but machines also use CMOS RAM, which is connected to a small backup battery and which will then retain data after the main power supply has been switched off. The CMOS RAM is maintained by a battery and is used to retain essential settings (such as for HARD DRIVES).

non-volatile random access memory (NVRAM) a form of STATIC RAM that has a battery permanently connected to maintain data, or a type of EEPROM that can retain data without applied power.

non-Windows application an MS-DOS program that can be run under MS-DOS or optionally using WINDOWS. A Windows application cannot normally be run under MS-DOS, but this facility is provided when Microsoft WINDOWS 95 onwards is used as the main operating system.

no parity digital communication that does not use PARITY for error-checking.

no proofing option an option applied to a MICROSOFT WORD document in which a selected portion of text will be omitted when actions such as spell checking (see SPELLCHECK) and GRAMMAR CHECKING are carried out. This is particularly useful if the selected text is a table or contains a large number of words, such as proper names, that are not contained in the spelling dictionary.

NOR a LOGIC action that is the result of using the NOT action followed by OR. For example, A NOR B is true only when both A and B are false.

normal distribution the GRAPH of a quantity plotted against the number of examples of that size (*frequency distribution*). This gives a BELL CURVE for many natural examples, such as the weight of a species of fish.

normal range the expected range of a number, such as the range 1 to 31 for dates, used to check the validity of data since any number outside such a range must be incorrect.

normalize to operate on numerical data in which each item has to be adjusted so as to make the data fit a specified pattern. A common example is the normalization of examination marks so that the average is 50 per cent and the standard deviation (the average difference from the average mark) about 15 per cent. Normalization of marks in this way compensates for the fact that some examinations may be difficult and others easy, but it can be criticized on the grounds that it makes absolute comparisons, particularly from year to year, impossible. In programs that produce graphs or bar charts, quantities may be *range-normalized*. This means that the range of values is compressed or expanded to fit the graph scales so that the maximum value will correspond to the highest point on the graph or the longest bar, and the smallest value to the lowest graph point or a single unit of bar.

NOT the word that is used in DATABASE QUERY and other languages to mean NEGATION.

not-action see ONES COMPLEMENT.

notator a program that will convert musical notes played on the MIDI system into written musical notation which can be printed.

notebook or **scratchpad** (US) a feature of office management programs that allows you to make notes which are then stored on a separate file. The notes are usually arranged to appear in a SCREEN (sense 1) WINDOW rather than on the main part of the screen.

notebook computer a computer whose size is about that of an A4 page, smaller than a LAPTOP but larger than a personal digital assistant (PDA). A computer in this class is now expected to provide features such as colour display, a HARD DRIVE and the use of WINDOWS.

Notepad a simple TEXT EDITOR supplied with WINDOWS. See also WORD-PAD.

notice board a form of BULLETIN BOARD used in an EMAIL system that is intended to be read by all users.

Novell™ a leading maker of NETWORK systems. The Novell net is extremely comprehensive, requires a large SERVER and is expensive. It is more suited to the large-scale user than the small office and for situations where skilled installation and suitable training are available.

NRZ (non-return to zero) a method of recording on magnetic media in which a 0 bit is represented by magnetization in one direction and a 1 bit by magnetization in the opposite direction. See also MODIFIED FREQUENCY MODULATION.

NRZI (non-return to zero inverted) a variant of the NRZ system.

ns see NANOSECOND.

NT™ (new technology) an operating system (OS) for the larger desktop computers and MINICOMPUTERS that uses the same Intel chip architecture as desktop machines. The system makes no use of MS-DOS other than as a start-up system and is designed to take full advantage of 32-bit software but excluding software written for the older Windows versions. The facilities and requirements of NT and of MICROSOFT WINDOWS converge in Windows 2000 which is also NT 5.

NTFS (NT filing system) the form of disk filing system used by Windows NT, and present in Windows 2000 Professional. The user can opt to use this in place of the FAT-32 system used for Windows 95 and Windows 98, and the existing files can be converted to this format.

NTSC the original colour television system developed in 1952 by Radio Corporation of America and named after the National Television Standards Committee. The system is used in the USA and Japan, but not in Europe where the more technically advanced PAL and SECAM systems have been adopted. The three systems are incompatible, so that videos cannot run interchangeably.

nudging an action of MICROSOFT WORD and some graphics programs that allows a selected graphics object or part of the Equation Editor to be moved in steps of one PIXEL by using the CURSOR-CONTROL KEYS.

NUL a name used like a DEVICE (sense 1) in DOS commands. Unlike PRN (the printer) or CON (the screen), NUL will cause any data sent to it to vanish. Using a REDIRECTION to NUL, for example, is a good way of removing unwanted text, such as notices about software installation.

nuke to delete totally and intentionally a complete set of files.

null the zero (0) character.

null modem a connection from one SERIAL PORT to another without the use of a MODEM. The cable used for this purpose must have connections that are reversed at one plug so that the sending pin of one port is connected to the receiving pin of the other.

number base see BASE.

number cruncher see MATHS COPROCESSOR.

number format the way that a number is displayed in a CELL of a WORKSHEET or other applications. For example, the format may determine the number of decimal places, the use of points or commas, or the way that negative numbers are printed. See also PRECEDENT.

numberpad see NUMERIC KEYPAD.

numeric of or relating to numbers, as distinct from CHARACTER data.

numerical control (NC) the control of machines by digital data.

numeric character the characters 0 to 9 and A to F. The letters are included to take account of HEXADECIMAL numbers and also to allow the use of E to indicate a power of ten, as in 2.16E5.

numeric coprocessor see MATHS COPROCESSOR.

numeric keypad or **numberpad** a separate set of KEYS (sense 1) or buttons for entering numbers, usually placed on the right-hand side of the KEYBOARD and therefore useless to left-handed operators.

num lock the KEY (sense 1) that will TOGGLE the use of the NUMERIC KEYPAD on a standard personal computer keyboard. With num lock on, the keypad keys produce numerals; with the lock off, these keys produce CURSOR movement actions.

NVRAM see NON-VOLATILE RANDOM ACCESS MEMORY.

Nyquist theorem a theorem concerning digitization (see DIGITIZE) of a sound or other ANALOGUE wave. This states that the SAMPLING RATE must be at least twice the frequency of the highest signal frequency.

object 1. an item of data to be manipulated in a program. For example, a graphics picture or a worksheet table can be inserted as an object into a WORD PROCESSOR document; see EMBED; LINK. **2.** in ARTIFICIAL INTELLIGENCE, the encapsulation of a set of attributes with or without methods of using these attributes. In AI, a FRAME (sense 3) is an object, and a KNOWLEDGE BASE will usually consist of a HIERARCHY of objects.

object code the BINARY (MACHINE CODE) output of a COMPILER.

object computer the computer for which a program has been specifically written.

object linking and embedding see OLE.

object-oriented using objects that consist of both data and procedures. A picture, for example, becomes an object that consists of the drawing data for the picture and also the methods used to process the data.

object-oriented architecture a software structure in which all files, inputs and outputs are considered as objects, with the program subroutines that deal with these items also taken to be part of the objects.

object-oriented database a form of DATABASE in which an item of data is stored and manipulated as an OBJECT. This has advantages, notably in speed of SEARCH actions and the use of MULTIMEDIA, as compared to the conventional RELATIONAL DATABASE.

object-oriented drawing see VECTOR GRAPHICS.

object-oriented programming programming in a language with OBJECT-ORIENTED ARCHITECTURE. This implies that each data structure will be contained completely in one program MODULE. This ensures that changes to the design of a data structure and the actions carried out on it will be localized, making this form of programming particularly useful for team efforts. Any ACCESS (sense 2) to the data has to be obtained by using the module. Programming in this way is referred to as *OOPS* (object-oriented programming system). See also ABSTRACT DATA TYPE; DATA ENCAPSULATION.

object-specific graphics see VECTOR GRAPHICS.

oblique any form of slanting type such as ITALIC. Italic generally implies a slope to the right, oblique is often used of a slope to the left.

oblique stroke see SLASH.

OCCAM a HIGH-LEVEL LANGUAGE designed to run parallel computers such as the TRANSPUTER (see PARALLEL PROCESSING).

Occam's razor a logical rule that the fewer the number of unprovable assumptions or dogmatic beliefs that have to be made in trying to explain anything, the better the explanation. Another form is the KISS principle.

OCR 1. (optical character reader) software that will convert a BITMAP picture of a document into ASCII-coded signals that can be saved and used in a WORD PROCESSOR. OCR software is used in conjunction with a SCANNER, preferably the flatbed or roller type of scanner, in order to reduce paper documentation by making file copies of paperwork. **2.** (optical character recognition) the process of using an optical character reader to capture text or a graphic.

octal a number in BASE 8, used in programming at one time. In octal, digits 0 to 7 are used, and decimal 8 is represented by 10.

octave a set of 8 notes (counting inclusively) which is the basis of Western music. The term is also used in computing to describe any set of 8 objects.

ODBC see OPEN DATABASE CONNECTIVITY.

odd parity see PARITY.

OEM see ORIGINAL EQUIPMENT MANUFACTURER.

Office or **Microsoft Office** a SUITE OF PROGRAMS that together implement all the functions that a small office might need. The versions are numbered by year, so that Office 95, Office 97 and Office 2000 are all in use.

offline (of a PERIPHERAL) not connected to the computer.

offline favourite a WEB PAGE that has been stored locally so that it can be viewed without going ONLINE (sense 2). Such pages can be updated each time the computer is online.

offline reading viewing a WEB PAGE without making an INTERNET connection because the data has been stored locally.

off-the-shelf (of HARDWARE or SOFTWARE) available to be bought and used, as distinct from being designed and installed to order. One of the distinguishing features of MICROCOMPUTER use as compared to MAINFRAME machines is the extensive use of off-the-shelf software.

OK a SCREEN (sense 1) PROMPT that is used by some operating systems in place of a message such as READY.

OK box a box appearing within a WINDOW in a GUI program and used to signify acceptance by moving the MOUSE cursor to the box and clicking (see CLICK, sense 1) on the mouse button.

OLE (object linking and embedding) a set of methods used in WINDOWS for making an OBJECT, such as a drawing, appear in a document, such as a page in a WORD PROCESSOR. An EMBEDDED OBJECT will be saved along with the document and adds to the size of the document. Clicking (see CLICK, sense 1) on the drawing in the document will run the program that created the drawing with the image in place so that the image can be edited. When an image file is linked (see LINKED OBJECT), only a code (a form of POINTER, sense 2) is inserted into the document so that the size of the document file is not appreciably increased. If the image file is edited using the application that created the drawing, the image in the document will also change, and the image will change also in any other documents that are linked to that image.

onboard contained on an internal board (see MOTHERBOARD) of a computer, as distinct from being added by way of an EXPANSION SLOT or connected externally through a PORT.

on-chip contained as part of a CHIP rather than having to be supplied by connection to another chip. For example, the 80486DX and Pentium chips contain the mathematical COPROCESSOR actions on-chip and therefore require no separate FLOATING-POINT processor.

ones complement or **not-action** the inversion of each digit in a binary number, exchanging each 0 for 1 and each 1 for 0. The ones complement of 00001111 is 11110000, for example.

one-to-one relationship a connection between each entity in a DATABASE so that one entity is associated with only one other, such as one name to one address.

onion-skin architecture the design of a system in separate layers, from the MICROPROCESSOR as the central layer or kernel to the operating system (OS), which can be followed by the PROGRAMMING LANGUAGE. See also ISO/OSI.

online I. (of a PERIPHERAL) being connected to the computer. **2.** (of a user) connected to a NETWORK, particularly the INTERNET.

online form a form that exists as a file and can be displayed on the SCREEN (sense 1). Data can be entered into the reply spaces of the form, which can then be sent to its destination by EMAIL.

online help or **help online** a help system that can be consulted while using a program, with the help text appearing in a separate WINDOW. See also CONTEXT-SENSITIVE HELP.

online registration a system that allows the purchase and installation of SOFTWARE to be registered with the manufacturer. If a MODEM is installed, the user need only fill in some details on a form on screen and click a BUTTON to register.

online service a provider of INTERNET access and information.

online tutorial a system of context-sensitive instruction. This is similar to ONLINE HELP but with a more thorough explanation of each topic made available by pressing a KEY (sense 1), such as F1, when a MENU choice has been made.

on-screen formatting see PRINT PREVIEW.

OOPS see OBJECT-ORIENTED PROGRAMMING.

opamp see OPERATIONAL AMPLIFIER.

opcodes or **operation codes** numbers that represent MACHINE CODE instructions which a MICROPROCESSOR can interpret and execute directly. All programs must be converted into this form before they can be run, and this is the main action of a COMPILER.

open architecture the design of a COMPUTER SYSTEM that is published so that other manufacturers can design ADD-ON cards.

open-box testing see WHITE-BOX TESTING.

open bus system a BUS in a computer that is connected to sockets into which expansion cards can be plugged. See also AGP; ISA; LOCAL BUS; PCI BUS.

open database connectivity (**ODBC**) a set of standardized routines that translate DATABASE data into a FORMAT (sense 2) that another database can use.

open document architecture the ISO 8613 standard that allows easy interchange of text and graphics between different computer systems.

open file the action of preparing a file for reading or writing.

open-system interconnection see OSI.

open wire a cable link that uses an uninsulated wire or wires supported on insulators. A telephone line is a typical open wire and is also *open* in the sense of allowing easy tapping.

operand see ARGUMENT.

operating system see OS.

operational amplifier or **opamp** a unit of an ANALOGUE COMPUTER whose behaviour can be altered by connecting electronic components to two terminals. When a waveform whose shape corresponds to a mathematical expression is applied as an input to such an amplifier, the output waveform represents the effect of a mathematical operation on the input. For example, if the opamp is arranged to carry out summation, the amplitude of the output waveform will be proportional to the sum of amplitudes of the waves at the inputs.

operational database any DATABASE whose data is maintained regularly, so is up to date. A database, for example, that uses data from a CD-ROM is not in this class.

operational research a method of analysing a system. The method is usually applied to large organizations with a view to producing a computer simulation of the organization. Working on the computer simulation can then suggest methods of improving the organization itself.

operation codes see OPCODES.

operator a symbol that represents an action on a number or character. Numerical operators of addition, subtraction, multiplication and division are represented by symbols such as +, −, * and /. Operations on characters and STRINGS of characters are not so standardized. Operators are used in SPREADSHEET FORMULA writing and also in DATABASE QUERY expressions.

operator precedence mathematical operations in computing, which are always carried out in a set order. This order is, in general, raising to a power (EXPONENTIATION), multiplication or division, addition or subtraction. For example, if you type, as a WORKSHEET FORMULA, for example: A+B*C^D, then C will be raised to the power D, the result multiplied by B, and then A added. The order of action is not the same as the order of writing the commands. Many computers transform the order of expressions internally into REVERSE POLISH NOTATION as part of their processing action. The order of precedence can be altered by the use of BRACKETS. Any expression that is contained within brackets will be carried out before actions that lie outside the brackets.

Optacon™ a text-reading device for visually impaired users that uses a miniature TV camera to read text. Its output is to a BRAILLE TACTILE DISPLAY, allowing the user to read printed text.

optical character reader and **optical character recognition** see OCR.

optical data link a connection between computers (or other digital machines) using a light beam either in air or carried by a FIBRE OPTIC cable.

optical disk any form of storage system that is read using a LASER beam. This includes the CD-ROM, FLOPTICAL DISK and the read/write type of system that uses magnetic signals for writing along with an optical reading system. See also CD-R; CD-RW.

optical fibre a thin thread of glass. By using a coaxial system, with one type of glass enclosed by another, these fibres can be constructed so that a light beam will pass down the length of the fibre with very little loss of energy. This can be used for information transmission because light is a waveform similar in nature to radio waves but with a much higher FREQUENCY. Optical fibres are generally used in conjunction with LASERs.

optical font a printing FONT that is designed to be particularly easy for an OCR (sense 1) to recognize.

optical mark reader a miniature, often pen-size, SCANNER that is used to read reply marks such as ticks or crosses on forms.

optical transmission a system of data communication using LASERs and OPTICAL FIBRES.

optimization the process of transforming code so that it runs faster and/or takes up less space.

optimizer a program that will adapt another program to RUN (sense 2) more efficiently or to make more efficient use of MEMORY.

option a choice that can be made from a MENU. In some programs options can be set so as to configure the program to the user's requirements.

option button a small square ICON used in a MENU choice. In a GUI SCREEN (sense 1), each option of a menu will be represented by its own option button, and the option is selected by placing the CURSOR over the button and clicking (see CLICK, sense 1) the MOUSE button.

OR a LOGIC action that compares two quantities to find if either one or both is true. In a DATABASE QUERY, the OR statement can be used to connect two conditions. For example, the statement 'IF Name = "Smith" OR

Age < 40' can be used to select RECORDS (sense 1) of one name and a particular age group by combining two conditions, and will give a TRUE answer if either one condition or the other or both is true. These comparisons are described as BOOLEAN, meaning that either condition can be described as being true or FALSE. See also AND; NAND; NOR; NOT.

Oracle see TELETEXT.

ordered list a list of items in some order such as alphabetical or numerical order.

order of precedence the order in which arithmetical actions are processed (see OPERATOR PRECEDENCE).

ordinate the vertical direction on a GRAPH, normally the Y-COORDINATE AXIS. See also ABSCISSA.

organization chart a hierarchical display (see HIERARCHY) of an organization. Organization charts can be generated and edited by PRESENTATION GRAPHICS packages.

orientation the positioning of a printed page, as tall (PORTRAIT) or wide (LANDSCAPE).

origin 1. a reference point. **2.** in graphics, the point that is picked to be the zero of each axis. All COORDINATE positions in subsequent graphics instructions are measured from this point.

original equipment manufacturer (OEM) a firm that manufactures an item of hardware or software, as distinct from one that simply resells equipment made elsewhere.

orphan in DTP work, a first line of a paragraph that occurs as the last line on a page. Contrast WIDOW.

OS (operating system) the MACHINE CODE program, sometimes in ROM, that controls all the main actions of the computer, such as the use of the KEYBOARD, SCREEN (sense 1), disk system, and so on, and in addition controls the actions of other programs, which are said to RUN (sense 2) *under* the operating system, meaning under its control. The operating system in particular looks after the details of such actions as disk ACCESS (sense 2), which would otherwise require very tedious programming on the part of writers of APPLICATIONS programs and which might result in incompatibilities. If a computer is designed to make use of an established operating system, it will run any program that has been designed to run under that system unless the program deliberately bypasses the system (see BADLY BEHAVED PROGRAM). No two operating systems are COMPATIBLE, and programs cannot be run unless they are designed to be used under the operating system for the computer. PALMTOP machines use an operating system in ROM to avoid the need for using disks for their operating system.

OS/2™ an operating system first developed by MICROSOFT for the IBM PS/2 machines. At the time, the system required vastly greater memory resources than MS-DOS or WINDOWS, and its adoption was not encouraging. A later development by IBM, known as OS/2 Warp, was released just prior to Microsoft WINDOWS 95.

OSI (open-system interconnection) a standardized form of NETWORK connection system (see ISO/OSI).

outage an interval of time when a COMPUTER SYSTEM is out of use because of servicing or maintenance.

outbox a folder used by an EMAIL program to store messages that will be sent when the MAIL SERVER is activated.

outline a set of short lines or paragraphs forming a synopsis, often numbered and arranged with subordinate parts indented.

outline font a FONT whose character shapes are drawn in outline using VECTOR methods, with the printer filling in the closed shapes.

outliner a WORD PROCESSOR action that will prepare a document summary in outline form, using headings of different weightings and BODY text. Such an outline can then be expanded into a full document, but editing can be carried out on the outline view, so that subheadings along with their body text can be moved around without the body text being visible. See Fig. 31.

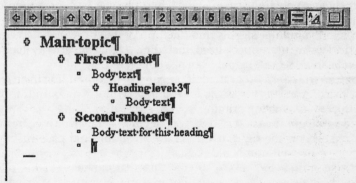

Fig. 31. **Outliner**. An outline being typed using Microsoft Word. The arrow icons allow movement from one level to another, and the cross or dot icons indicate whether a line is heading or body text. Once an outline is created, the text can be expanded so as to produce a full-sized document.

outlining toolbar a TOOLBAR that appears when the OUTLINER action of a WORD PROCESSOR is selected. These toolbar ICONs can be clicked (see CLICK, sense 1), using the MOUSE as an alternative to using a MENU for commands.

Outlook see MICROSOFT OUTLOOK.

out of range an ERROR MESSAGE that means that a number is unusable. This might refer to an INTEGER that has been incremented or decremented (see INCREMENT, sense 1; DECREMENT) to an unacceptable value, or to a number used as a coordinate that has reached a value that corresponds to a position off the SCREEN (sense 1).

output any signal or data that is passed out of a system. The term has to be used with care because the signal that is the output of one system is often the input of another system. Typical computer outputs include the PRINTER, DISK system, MONITOR (sense 2), NETWORK and MODEM outputs.

output-bound (of a COMPUTER SYSTEM) restricted in speed because of an output. The term mainly denotes a program that makes extensive use of a printer for output. Unless the printer is fitted with a large BUFFER, the computer will be forced to hang up (see LOCKUP) during the time while the printer is operating. This makes the speed of computing as slow as the speed of printing. A useful method of dealing with the problem, apart from the use of a printer buffer, is to SPOOL the output. Compare INPUT-BOUND.

output devices the PERIPHERALS that convert computer signals into forms that can be understood by human beings or used to produce data that can be used by other machines. The VDU is the most used output device as far as modern computers are concerned. PRINTERS are used extensively to obtain HARD COPY which can be checked more thoroughly than VDU output. For specialized CAD use, a pen PLOTTER can be used to convert computer signals into the form of line drawings. Other output devices are more specialized, including D TO A converters which will provide an ANALOGUE signal from a set of DIGITAL signals.

output formatter a program that prepares data for sending to an external device. A WORD PROCESSOR, for example, will use an output formatted to prepare data for printing.

outside margin the MARGIN of a DTP page that is farther away from the binding. This is the right margin of an odd-numbered page or the left margin of an even-numbered page.

overdrive chip a PROCESSOR ADD-ON chip that enhances CLOCK rate to make the processor work faster. For example, the Intel DX2 and DX4 chips will operate the 80486 processor at double or four times (respectively) the normal clock rate. There are also overdrive chips that will add PENTIUM capabilities to 80486 chips and others that upgrade older Pentium designs to more modern specifications.

overflow the result of a number becoming OUT OF RANGE. The term usually denotes the result of a number becoming too large to store in the number of bytes allocated to it.

overflow file a file used by a WORD PROCESSOR to contain part of a document. The use of an overflow file allows part of the document to be held in memory and the rest on the disk, allowing long documents to be dealt with and maintained backed up. The penalty is a time delay in moving from the start to the end of a long document. See also MASTER DOCUMENT.

overhead 1. a display of text and/or graphics on a transparent sheet suitable for use in an overhead projector. Overheads can be generated by a PRESENTATION GRAPHICS display, along with a LASER PRINTER using suitable transparent sheets. **2.** the cost in terms of memory space or in response time that is incurred in the performance of a process because of the need to organize data in the memory. For example, when a file is loaded from the HARD DRIVE, there is a time overhead incurred in finding the file that is additional to the time needed to transfer the bytes of data. When a file is stored on a disk, some part of the disk must be used for a DIRECTORY (sense 2) entry for the file, so that there is a storage overhead.

overhead bit a BIT that is used for PARITY checking.

overlaid window a WINDOW that covers another, partially or completely. See also CASCADE; TILE.

overlay 1. a pattern laid on top of something else. **2.** a pattern superimposed on the normal SCREEN (sense 1) display which, for example, might show a scale (a *screen overlay*). **3.** or **program overlay** a program that can be called up from a disk and RUN (sense 2) in order to provide variable values that the main program can use.

override a type specification in a DTP page that replaces the DEFAULT specification either permanently or temporarily.

overrun data loss because of data arriving at a PORT faster than it can be processed.

overstrike 1. a DOT-MATRIX printer action. Overstriking means printing a character, shifting the paper or PRINTHEAD slightly and then printing again. The effect is to emphasize the character, as if bold type had been used. Overstrike is a method of producing better character quality from dot-MATRIX PRINTERs because by this method the gaps between dots can be filled in. A similar scheme, under various brand names, can be used to improve the quality of graphics for an INKJET PRINTER. **2.** see OVERWRITE.

overtype mode a typing mode in which each character that is typed will replace the character at the CURSOR. See also INSERT MODE.

overwrite or **overstrike** to replace a character by another on the SCREEN (sense 1) or in MEMORY. Overwriting on the screen means that one character that is typed will replace any other character in that space. This is the normal action of the screen, but when a WORD PROCESSOR is used this is changed to an INSERT action. Some computers allow *non-erasing overwrite* action, in which a typed character is added to the character that is already present. This can be used to form special characters and to add accent marks to characters on the screen. To *overwrite memory* means that when a byte is stored in a memory address, it replaces any byte that was formerly stored at that address.

package I. see APPLICATIONS PACKAGE. **2.** The form of the casing and pin layout for a CHIP.

packed decimal a way of coding a DENARY number using four BITs for each denary digit and the last bit to code the SIGN.

packed encoding rules (PER) a 1994 PROTOCOL for encoding data into a very compact form.

packed file see COMPRESSED FILE.

packed format any compressed method of representing data.

packet a set of data BITs. The term usually denotes a set of bits that is sent over a NETWORK or along a connecting line. The data bits are accompanied by error check bits and also by codes that signal the start of the packet and the end of the packet.

packet assembler/disassembler or **packet driver** SOFTWARE that will divide a stream of data into PACKETs for onward transmission and can also reassamble packets into a continuous data stream. See also PSS.

packet Internet groper see PING.

packet radio a communication system that uses amateur radio transmitters operating along with computers to relay data.

packet sniffing illegal interception of PACKETs of data being relayed on the INTERNET.

packet switching service see PSS.

packet switch node a computer used purely for relaying PACKETs as part of a NETWORK.

packet writing see INCREMENTAL WRITING.

packing density the number of BYTEs of data that can be stored in a unit length of disk TRACK.

pad see GRAPHICS TABLET.

pad character see HARD SPACE.

padding to length the adding of blanks to data. This is done automatically in a DATABASE that uses a fixed size of FIELD (sense 2) so that data which takes up less space is padded to fill the field.

paddle or **games paddle** a form of JOYSTICK, a controller that is held in the hand and used to control the position of an object, such as a CURSOR, on the SCREEN (sense 1). It was used mainly in games at one time but is now superseded by the joystick. See also MOUSE; TRACKERBALL.

page I. a form of division into GROUPs (sense 1). *Screen paging* means that a full SCREEN (sense 1) of information is presented to the user, and a new screenful will appear when a PAGE UP/PAGE DOWN key is pressed. *Print* *paging* implies the division of text so that it will fit into separate sheets of paper. In DTP applications, the page is the unit of a document that is built up (paper) page by page. **2.** a set of BYTES in memory, very often 512 bytes, 1, 2 or 4 kilobytes, used as a way of organizing memory for fast access.

page addressing a MEMORY MANAGEMENT system that divides the available RAM into PAGES (sense 2) and allocates an ADDRESS (sense 1) number to each page. The size of page is determined by the designer, 4 kilobytes being typical. A block of code using this amount of memory is often used for a considerable time so that very efficient use of memory can be made by storing a program in pages on the HARD DRIVE and using one page at a time in the memory. The ACCESS TIME for consecutive bytes of data within the same page can be much lower than can be achieved using the same RAM chips conventionally. See also VIRTUAL STORAGE.

page break a command code in a WORD PROCESSOR document, usually an EMBEDDED COMMAND, that will cause the printer to take a new page. This means that any FOOTER will be printed on the current page and the paper rolled out. When continuous paper, such as FANFOLD, is used, the page-break action must ensure that the perforation between pages lies between the footer of one page and the HEADER (sense 1) of the next. When single manually fed sheets are used, the page-break action must stop the printer and the computer and deliver a signal to the operator so that a new sheet can be fed in. If a single-sheet feeder is in use, this action can be made automatic, and printing will resume at once when the new sheet is fed in. A page break can be automatic (*soft*) or manual (*hard*). The position of an automatic page break will change as a document is edited because this position is determined by the word processor software. A manual page break is put in using a KEY COMBINATION and remains in place no matter how a document is changed. It can be used, for example, to separate the last page of one chapter from the first page of the next chapter.

page definition file see PDF.

page description language see PDL.

page fault a request for access to data that does not exist in any stored page (see PAGE ADDRESSING) so that data has to be fetched from the SWAP FILE on the HARD DRIVE or a fault reported.

page icon an ICON that is used in DTP to show each MASTER PAGE and each page number in a document.

page-in the act of reading data from the HARD DRIVE to a page (see PAGE ADDRESSING) in RAM. See also MEMORY MANAGEMENT UNIT.

page layout an important set of options in a WORD PROCESSOR or DTP program. The page layout menu will determine dimensions such as paper size, MARGIN sizes, use of COLUMNS, position of HEADER (sense 1) and FOOTER, etc.

page layout program any program, such as a DTP program or an advanced WORD PROCESSOR, that will compose a page on screen, displaying GRAPHICS, columns, tables and other text features.

PageMaker see ADOBE PAGEMAKER.

page-mode RAM a method of using dynamic ram (DRAM) in PAGE (sense 2) units, reading the entire page into CACHE memory so that access can be much faster than is normally possible.

page-out the act of copying data from RAM to the HARD DRIVE (see SWAP FILE). See also MEMORY MANAGEMENT UNIT.

pager bar an ICON used in a DTP program. The pager bar can be selected with the MOUSE to create a new page or to select any page number that has already been created.

page setup the specification for a DTP or WORD PROCESSOR page, including paper size, MARGINS, ORIENTATION, FONT, etc.

page status area part of the SCREEN (sense 1) display of a DTP program. The page status area shows information about the page, such as size, FONT, line and column position, current selection, etc.

page up/page down keys the keys on the CURSOR movement portion of a standard KEYBOARD that can be programmed to move up or down a SCREEN PAGE. Different programs can assign these keys in different ways, and some WORD PROCESSOR programs use the keys to move up or down a paper page, which is not the same as a screen page.

page view a SCREEN (sense 1) view of a complete DTP or WORD PROCESSOR page or pair of facing pages. On this scale, text will be GREEKED and only the arrangement of text and graphics can be seen.

pagination the process of dividing a document into pages that correspond to printed pages and are usually numbered. This process has to be repeated if editing work alters the content of pages; see BACKGROUND REPAGINATION.

paging see PAGE ADDRESSING.

Paintbrush the GRAPHICS PAINT PROGRAM packaged with MICROSOFT WINDOWS. The version supplied with WINDOWS 95 is highly valued because it allows the pointer to be moved one PIXEL at a time by using the arrow keys and also can write the popular PCX type of files. Later versions have removed these useful facilities.

paint program a program PACKAGE that allows BITMAP drawing, usually in colour, to be done on the SCREEN (sense 1) and the result printed (either in monochrome or in colour, depending on the printer). The RESOLUTION of a drawing is determined by the resolution of the screen rather than by the resolution of the printer, unlike a CAD package. See Fig. 32.

paired bar graph a form of BAR GRAPH that has two different X-AXIS scales. Contrast DUAL Y-AXIS GRAPH.

pair-kerning see KERNING.

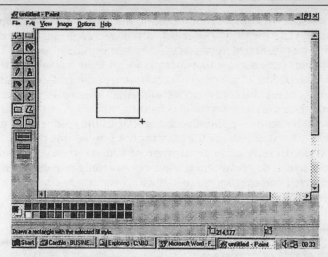

Fig. 32. **Paint program**. The screen appearance of the Paint program of Windows 95, a typical example of this type of program.

palette see COLOUR PALETTE.

palmtop computer or **hand-held computer** the smallest size of PORTABLE COMPUTER, which can be held in the palm of a hand. Although considerable computing capacity can be obtained, these machines require the use of very small keys, which can make their use difficult. The best-known palmtop computers in the UK are manufactured by Psion. Some palmtop designs dispense with any form of keyboard and rely on writing or speech input.

PAL TV system the colour TV system used in the UK, Germany and many other European countries. This is incompatible with the NTSC colour system used in the USA and Japan, and the SECAM system used in France, the former French colonies and Eastern Europe.

pan to alter the view of a GRAPHICS display as if by shifting a camera sideways. By *panning* across a drawing, the centre of the SCREEN (sense 1) can be used to show the left or right edge of the drawing, or any part between these extremes. See also ZOOM.

pane or **panel** a small WINDOW or portion of a window.

panning see PAN.

Pantone™ a system of coding colours for colour printing from GRAPHICS files.

paper see BACKGROUND (sense 1).

paper advance transport of paper through a PRINTER. The two main methods of feeding the paper through the printer are SPROCKET FEED and FRICTION FEED. The sprocket feed method uses paper in continuous roll

291

or FANFOLD form with a set of rectangular holes down each side. A pair of sprockets on the printer engages with these holes, and this allows the paper to be positioned very precisely by turning the sprockets. The friction system uses a roller that extends for at least the full width of the paper. The paper, which can be a continuous roll or cut sheets, is sandwiched between this main roller and a set of smaller rollers and is moved when the roller turns. This feeding method is not so positive for a dot-MATRIX PRINTER as the sprocket feed. Friction feed is not a problem on a LASER PRINTER because the paper is not printed line by line. Friction feed is particularly unsuitable when MULTIPART STATIONERY (sheets of paper with carbons between) is used, because only one sheet is held reasonably well and the others are likely to slip sideways. Most dot-matrix printers are fitted with sprocket feed as standard and friction feed is optional. INKJET and laser printers use friction feed from a PAPER TRAY or CASSETTE (sense 1).

paper handling the method or methods available on a PRINTER for feeding paper. Many printers permit the use of TRACTOR FEED, plain paper roll or cut sheets, but most LASER PRINTER and INKJET types can use only cut sheets.

paperless office a postulated future office in which all data is stored on disk or in memory. In practice, the more computers are used in offices, the greater is the consumption of paper, but the increasing use of OCR (sense 2) and CD-R may change this situation.

paper-out switch a switch fitted inside a printer that makes contact when no paper is present, allowing printing to be suspended when CONTINUOUS STATIONERY runs out. For a printer using a sheet-feeder, the switch detects when no paper is present and causes printing to be suspended.

paper tray the tray on a printer, usually a LASER PRINTER, from which paper is fed to the printer. An enclosed internal paper tray is termed a CASSETTE (sense 1); either type can be referred to as a BIN.

paper-white monitor a monochrome MONITOR (sense 2) that displays black print on a white SCREEN (sense 1) and is used for laying out type. Some monitors of this type, now rarely seen, are arranged in the exact shape and size of the paper to be used; see A4 MONITOR.

Paradox™ a well-known RELATIONAL DATABASE that runs under MICROSOFT WINDOWS.

paragraph in WORD PROCESSOR or DTP work, any section of text terminated by a carriage-return (CR) character. See also PARAGRAPH-ORIENTED.

paragraph indent an INDENT that persists for the duration of a DTP or WORD PROCESSOR PARAGRAPH. The paragraph indent is often symmetrical, being indented both at left and right.

paragraph mark the ¶ mark that appears optionally in a screen view of MICROSOFT WORD and other WORD PROCESSOR programs to show where a

PARAGRAPH ends. This is important because there are codes stored at this position in a document that control the formatting (see FORMAT, sense 2) of the paragraph. Deleting a paragraph mark will have the effect of making the formatting of that paragraph identical to that of the *following* paragraph.

paragraph-oriented (of a WORD PROCESSOR) designed so that changes that are made to the format of a document (such as FONT, MARGINs, style of type, etc.) will hold only for the PARAGRAPH in which the changes are made. Permanent changes are made by changing the STYLE (sense 2) used for normal paragraphs. MICROSOFT WORD is a well-known example of a paragraph-oriented word processor.

parallel changeover a form of multiconnection switch. For example, parallel changeover switches with sufficient contacts can be used in printer-sharing applications to switch a computer to one of several printers or one of several computers to one printer.

parallel connections the use of several side-by-side connections so that several signals can be transmitted simultaneously using one connecting line for each signal. A PARALLEL PRINTER connection, for example, uses eight signal wires, one for each BIT in a BYTE (so allowing for extended ASCII codes), and several control signal wires, as distinct from a SERIAL connection in which each bit is sent one at a time along a single wire.

parallel port an INTERFACE for parallel signals. The parallel port, generally a single chip, is connected to the BUSes of the MICROPROCESSOR and can pass signals from the microprocessor to external PERIPHERALS, such as a printer or disk drives. The port also includes handshaking signals (see HANDSHAKE), so that the microprocessor action can be controlled by the speed of the peripheral. This means that the microprocessor can be held waiting until a printer, for example, has dealt with a character code and is ready to process another. If the printer contains a BUFFER, the character codes can be fed very quickly through the port until the buffer is full. When the 'buffer full' signal is received at the port, the microprocessor is again forced to wait. The use of the port therefore requires both HARDWARE connections and SOFTWARE programming.

parallel-port device any device, such as a HARD DRIVE, a SCANNER or a TAPE STREAMER, that is connected through the parallel (printer) port rather than as a card inserted into the computer. This makes it easier to remove peripherals for reasons of security or for moving from one machine to another. See also ECP; EPP.

parallel printer a PRINTER that makes use of parallel signals. This implies that the connecting cable will use eight data lines. The CENTRONICS standard of PARALLEL CONNECTION requires the use of eleven active lines, although a number of additional 'ground' lines are often added to the connector. Because of the general use of the Centronics standard, a parallel printer can be connected to a computer that provides a PARALLEL

PORT with reasonable certainty that printing will be achieved. The system has now been standardized as IEEE 1394.

parallel processing a method of increasing processing speed. The traditional design of computer uses SERIAL PROCESSING, which means that instructions are carried out one after another. Parallel processing is a system, currently used mainly in MAINFRAME machines, in which several instructions can be carried out simultaneously, although the use of a COPROCESSOR is a simple example of parallel processing. See also OCCAM; TRANSPUTER.

parallel signals several signals sent along a set of wires at the same time (see PARALLEL CONNECTIONS).

parameter a quantity that takes a value for some time, after which the value can be changed. Sometimes jokingly defined as a 'variable constant', a parameter can be assigned with a value, but that value remains assigned only until it is changed.

parent the predecessor of a son or daughter in a TREE (sense 2) diagram.

parent directory any DIRECTORY (sense 1) or folder on a drive that has at least one SUBDIRECTORY. The subdirectory is then a CHILD DIRECTORY.

parentheses see BRACKETS; see also BRACES.

parent message an EMAIL or NEWSGROUP message that starts one or more follow-up messages.

parent node the NODE above the current node, nearer to the ROOT in a HIERARCHY.

parent page a page of information that contains an index that allows the user to select another page, used particularly of TELETEXT systems.

parent program a program that can be halted while another program, the CHILD PROGRAM, is loaded and RUN (sense 2). The parent program can be resumed after the child program has finished. See also EXIT.

parity the numerical quality of a count being even or odd. When data is transmitted over a COMMUNICATIONS LINK or fetched from CORE MEMORY, each BYTE involved contains either an even or an odd number of 1s (or 0s). This can form the basis of an ERROR check. For instance, an extra bit can be added to each byte, which may be a 1 if the actual parity of the byte is even, say. After receipt of the byte and its extra parity bit, the actual parity of the byte can be checked against the parity bit. Any discrepancy implies an error.

parity error a mismatch of a PARITY bit with data parity that indicates an ERROR in transmitted or stored data.

park to place the heads of a HARD DRIVE over an unused CYLINDER. See HEAD PARK; LANDING ZONE.

parse data or **parsing** a SPREADSHEET action that will convert text taken from, for example, a WORD PROCESSOR and process it to a form suitable for a WORKSHEET entry.

partitioned drive a HARD DRIVE used under older versions of MS-DOS that could not work with drive capacities greater than 32 megabytes. A drive of more than 32 megabytes could be partitioned into a set of LOGICAL DRIVE units, each with its own drive letter and each with a capacity of 32 megabytes or less. The limit was later raised to 512 megabytes, then to 2 gigabytes and is currently 2048 gigabytes for the FAT32 system.

partition table a portion of a partitioned (see PARTITIONED DRIVE) HARD DRIVE that carries information on the partitioning.

Pascal™ a language invented by Niklaus Wirth and much used in teaching programming principles.

pass the execution of an action or set of actions.

passive I. relating to anything in computing not requiring power. **2.** relating to an electronic component that has no power-amplifying action.

passive-matrix screen a form of LCD display that is controlled by using a TRANSISTOR to drive each row and column (as distinct from each cell). This is cheaper and easier to manufacture than the ACTIVE-MATRIX screen type, but the performance is inferior. See also TFT.

passphrase an extended PASSWORD that can ensure much greater SECURITY because of the larger number of characters.

password or **access code** a set of characters that can be used as an ACCESS (sense 1) code to a COMPUTER SYSTEM or DATABASE. The exploits of CRACKERS have driven home the point that simple passwords based on initial letters of names or on simple number sequences like a date of birth are completely inadequate as safeguards. A particularly simple way of generating a password that is easy to remember yet meaningless to outsiders is to use the first letter of each word in the first line of a song.

paste to COPY (sense 1) data from memory into a document or graphics page, particularly temporarily stored data that has been CUT from another place. See also CLIPBOARD.

pasteboard an area of SCREEN (sense 1) used for composing print. In a DTP program, the area outside the page can be used for arranging text and graphics that will later be shifted into the page.

patch a piece of BINARY code that can be inserted into an existing program to remedy a BUG or to extend the usefulness of the program. When a patch is very large it may be termed a SERVICE RELEASE.

patch space a deliberate gap in a program left so that a PATCH can later be inserted.

path I. a LIST of DIRECTORY (sense 1) steps from the ROOT DIRECTORY to a desired file, such as C:\WORD\BOOKS\COMPDICT.TXT. **2. (PATH)** a command in MS-DOS used to establish a set of path routes that the computer will use to try to locate program files.

pathname or **pathspec** the portion of a FILENAME that represents the PATH (sense 1) from the ROOT DIRECTORY.

pathname separator the BACKSLASH character used in MS-DOS and WINDOWS FILENAMES to separate the sections of a PATH (sense 1). Other operating systems use the FORWARD SLASH for this purpose.

pathspec see PATHNAME.

PATH statement a command line in DOS that determines where the computer will search for data files.

pattern generator a circuit or program that can generate signals that produce SCREEN (sense 1) patterns, used normally for checking the performance of a MONITOR (sense 2) or TV receiver.

pattern recognition a form of computer 'sight'. Pattern recognition systems use a matrix of PHOTOSENSORS. This can be connected to a computer and, by means of suitable software, can compare a pattern of light and dark on the sensors with predetermined patterns that are held as coded numbers in the program memory. This allows some patterns to be clearly recognized and is the basis of a SCANNER. Pattern recognition is also a vital part of ROBOTICS because it provides a robot with a limited form of sight. It also has considerable uses in medical diagnostic programs, automatic inspection of manufactured components and in image enhancement. Pattern recognition is a vital part of ARTIFICIAL INTELLIGENCE studies.

pause 1. a short delay in a program. The pause may be for a fixed time, or can be interruptible, meaning that pressing a KEY (sense 1) will end the pause. **2. (PAUSE)** a DOS command that will display a 'press any key' message on the SCREEN (sense 1) and suspend actions until a key is pressed.

payware commercial SOFTWARE as distinct from SHAREWARE or FREEWARE.

PC see PERSONAL COMPUTER.

PCA (Program Calibration Area) the portion of a CD-R disc that is used for making a trial recording to calibrate the LASER intensity needed for the disc that is being used. This allows for differences in disc materials, particularly between CD-R and CD-RW discs.

PCB (printed circuit board) the plastic board that carries the chips and the interconnections of a unit of a COMPUTER SYSTEM. The smaller computers can be constructed on a single board, but larger machines normally use a set of boards with interconnections. See also EDGE CARD; MOTHERBOARD.

PC Card see PCMCIA.

PC-DOS a DOS, now obsolete, written and marketed by IBM as an alternative to MS-DOS.

pc-8 an extended character set that uses the ASCII set along with a set of symbols that provide for other languages and for technical symbols.

PCI bus (peripheral component interconnect bus) the BUS that has replaced older bus types such as ISA or VLB for connections between the MICROPROCESSOR and the EXPANSION CARDS. The PCI bus runs faster (up to

33 MHz) and is 32-bits wide. Modern MOTHERBOARDS now use PCI and AGP bus slots only, dispensing with the ISA type.

PCL see PRINTER CONTROL LANGUAGE.

PCM see PULSE-CODE MODULATION.

PCMCIA (Personal Computer Memory Card International Association) a standardizing agency whose initials are used for memory storage cards initially designed for plugging into LAPTOP COMPUTERS and now also used on some DIGITAL CAMERAS. Other plug-in devices such as MODEMS and HARD DRIVES can be manufactured to make use of the same connecting system.

PCMCIA slot a flat socket on a PORTABLE COMPUTER used to plug in a 68-pin memory cartridge or other adapter.

PCX a file EXTENSION denoting that the file is of a graphics IMAGE (sense 2) created by one of the popular PC GRAPHICS programs such as PC Paintbrush. The PCX type of file has become a standard because of its compact nature, and most DTP and WORD PROCESSOR packages are able to read and display such files. The Paint utility of Microsoft WINDOWS 95 onwards can read PCX files but cannot save files in this form. See also BMP; JPG; TIF; WMF.

PDA (personal digital assistant) a small hand-held computer, usually of the PEN-BASED COMPUTER type. A feature of most PDA designs is a (limited) ability to recognize handwriting.

PDF (page definition file) a standard type of file for formatted documents (including graphics) devised by ADOBE SYSTEMS and used in conjunction with POSTSCRIPT to create a file structure that can be used by a variety of computer and typography machines. See also ACROBAT.

PDL (page description language) a form of PROGRAMMING LANGUAGE in which instructions are used to describe the layout of a complete page of text and graphics, including FONT styles and sizes, and picture shapes and positions. See ADOBE SYSTEMS; ADOBE TYPE MANAGER; POSTSCRIPT.

peer to peer communication between systems using devices at the same layer level (see ISO/OSI).

peer-to-peer network a form of NETWORK that does not use a SERVER. All computers on the network are equal partners, and each user can decide what files will be available on the network.

pel see PIXEL.

pen-based computer a small PORTABLE COMPUTER that can recognize neat uniform handwriting on its SCREEN (sense 1), using a form of LIGHT PEN.

pen recorder a method of plotting changes in a quantity by using a pen whose position is moved by changes in the quantity. The paper is moved past the pen at a steady rate so that the resulting chart is a graph showing how the quantity has changed with time. A familiar example is the use for making charts of temperature and pressure.

Pentium™ the successor to the 80486 processor in the INTEL design series. The Pentium contains a built-in CACHE (see LEVEL-1 CACHE) and is significantly faster than its predecessor at the same CLOCK speed. The name was used because a number designation such as 80586 could not be trademarked. See also ATHLON.

Pentium™ II or **Pentium™ 2** the INTEL chip that has replaced the PENTIUM PRO and has in turn been replaced by PENTIUM 3. A simpler version named CELERON™ is intended for HOME COMPUTERS, and a faster version with a larger CACHE, the Xeon™, was for professional use.

Pentium™ 3 or **Pentium™ III** a development of the PENTIUM II Xeon™ design intended for professional use and featuring a large CACHE and high CLOCK speeds.

Pentium™ Pro a development of the original PENTIUM chip design that used a two-chip arrangement of CPU and CACHE on a DAUGHTERBOARD that plugged into a slot on the MOTHERBOARD. Because of this slot fitting, the later Pentium chips cannot be fitted on the same motherboard as the earlier (Socket-7) types.

PER see PACKED ENCODING RULES.

percent sign the % character, used in a DOS BATCH FILE to refer to a file, such as %1.

performance the relative score attained by a computer in a TEST (sense 2), such as a BENCHMARK test.

period 1. see FULL STOP. **2.** the full-stop sign used in the DOS CD command (see CHDIR) to mean the CURRENT (sense 2) directory, with the DOUBLE-PERIOD meaning the PARENT DIRECTORY.

peripheral a device that is not part of the KEYBOARD-computer-SCREEN (sense 1) system but is connected to it separately and can exchange signals with it. Typical peripherals are an external DISK DRIVE, a MODEM, a PRINTER and possibly a LIGHT PEN or SCANNER. For each peripheral, HARDWARE in the form of PORTs and suitable connectors is needed. SOFTWARE is also needed to allow the peripheral to operate. In some cases, such as printers and disk drives, the computer's operating system (OS) will almost certainly contain the necessary software. For less standardized peripherals, software on disk or in ROM form must be added.

peripheral component interconnect see PCI BUS.

peripheral interface adapter see PIA.

peripheral memory memory devices such as HARD DRIVES that are not part of the main addressable memory of the computer. This formerly applied to any memory on a MAINFRAME machine that was not part of the CORE MEMORY. It is now sometimes applied to mean memory contained in a peripheral such as a laser printer.

peripheral sharing the action of using a NETWORK to allow a PERIPHERAL such as a printer or a disk drive to be used by all the computers in the network.

peripheral-bound slowed by the use of a peripheral. Unless MULTITASK-ING can be used, or a printer BUFFER, printing a document will make the computer unavailable for other actions. The machine is similarly locked out from other uses during disk ACCESS (sense 2) and SERIAL communications.

permanent file a file that is not wiped after completing a RUN (sense 1). This does not necessarily imply that the file is recorded on disk. Compare SCRATCHFILE.

permanent memory see NON-VOLATILE MEMORY.

permanent swap file a SWAP FILE used by Windows and permanently in place on the HARD DRIVE. Microsoft WINDOWS 95 onwards can make use of a permanent swap file on a compressed drive (see DRIVESPACE).

permission the specification of access to a secure DATABASE. Users on a NETWORK can be allocated different levels of permission, according to whether they can, for example, view data only, alter existing data or enter new data.

persistence see AFTERGLOW.

persistent memory see NON-VOLATILE MEMORY.

personal computer (PC) 1. any computer that will RUN (sense 2) SOFT-WARE intended for the IBM PC, hence any machine that uses the INTEL processors and runs under MS-DOS or OS/2. The term is now taken to mean an industry-standard computer, one that will run MS-DOS and Windows. **2.** originally, a computer that is used by one person, as distinct from a shared MAINFRAME machine. The distinction is rather like that between the owner-driver of a car and the user of a pooled chauffeur-driven car. The term PC implies a MICROCOMPUTER and at one time was synonymous with 'HOME COMPUTER'. The term PC later came to mean a machine that was primarily for business use but with the additional facilities that had been pioneered by the home computer manufacturers.

personal digital assistant see PDA.

personal identification number see PIN.

personal information manager see PIM.

PET™ see COMMODORE BUSINESS MACHINES.

peta- prefix for 1015.

PGP (Pretty Good Privacy) a method of encrypting (see ENCRYPTION) a document and adding a method of identifying the sender so as to ensure confidentiality without the need to use secure communications methods.

phage a form of VIRUS that acts by modifying another program.

phase modulation see PHASE-SHIFT MODULATION.

phase shift an alteration of a signal wave that advances or retards its timing relative to a standard. Shifting phase is a way of modulating a wave in a MODEM.

phase-shift modulation a method of transmitting digital signals by using a CARRIER (sense 2) wave whose phase is altered in one way for a digital 1 and in the opposite way for a digital 0. See also AMPLITUDE MODULATION; FREQUENCY MODULATION.

Philips the international electronics group, based in Eindhoven in the Netherlands, that jointly with Sony developed the COMPACT DISC system and subsequently the standards for CD-R and CD-RW.

Phoenix a manufacturer of BIOS chips for personal computers. See also AMERICAN MEGATRENDS INC.; AWARD.

phone mail see VOICE MAIL.

phoneme a sound unit of language. Any spoken word or phrase can be broken up into a set of basic phonemes and reconstructed by sounding the same phonemes in the correct order and with the correct timing. The analysis of sound into phonemes and its reconstruction are important in computer SPEECH SYNTHESIS and also in DIRECT VOICE INPUT.

phono plug a push-in connector for audio signals, using one plug per channel and found mainly on US equipment. European equipment tends to use DIN plugs.

phosphor the light-emitting coating on the SCREEN (sense 1) of a CRT. Despite the name, there is no phosphorus present; the materials used are complex zinc-cadmium sulphides or silicates.

phosphor fatigue the reduction in brightness caused by extended use of a MONITOR (sense 1). This can cause a static pattern to appear if the monitor shows the same picture for a prolonged period (several weeks) and is the usually quoted reason for using a SCREEN SAVER.

Photo CD a Kodak system for recording and replaying photographic images on a COMPACT DISC. The modern MULTISESSION format allows a CD-ROM to be recorded in stages until it is filled with images.

photocell a device that is sensitive to light and will generate a voltage or pass electric current when illuminated.

Photodraw a GRAPHICS program from MICROSOFT, incorporated into the OFFICE 2000 package. The unique feature of Photodraw is that it can deal with mixtures of BITMAP and VECTOR graphics.

Photoenhancer a GRAPHICS program often packaged with DIGITAL CAMERAS and intended for manipulating digital images.

photographic quality a GRAPHICS quality that is equivalent to that of a good photograph. This requires a RESOLUTION of at least 300 dots per inch (DPI) and the use of 30-bit COLOUR CODING.

photorealism the use of high RESOLUTION and COLOUR CODING of 30 bits or more to produce images that can appear as good as a photograph when printed by a suitable printer, such as a DYE-SUBLIMATION PRINTER.

photosensor any device that is sensitive to light. See PHOTOCELL.

Photoshop a well-known PHOTOREALISM graphics program from ADOBE SYSTEMS.

phototypesetter see IMAGESETTER.

physical drive the HARDWARE of a DISK DRIVE, as distinct from LOGICAL DRIVE. A physical drive in the form of a HARD DRIVE might be partitioned (see PARTITIONED DRIVE) into two or more logical drives, using letters C:, D:, and so on. The physical drive will be referred to by a number such as 0 or 1 rather than by a letter.

physical file the stored form of a file, such as the magnetized disk tracks. A single data or program file may be stored as several physical files, making use of parts of the disk where other files have been deleted.

physical layer the lowest layer in the ISO/OSI model, referring to the hardware of the NETWORK system.

physical memory the RAM memory installed in the computer, as distinct from the VIRTUAL MEMORY obtained by using the HARD DRIVE as additional memory.

physical page the content of a printed page, as distinct from a SCREEN (sense 1) page.

PIA (peripheral interface adapter) a unit that will allow signals to be passed out from and into PARALLEL PORTs, along with control and HAND-SHAKE signals.

PIC a filename EXTENSION used by LOTUS 1-2-3 for graph files.

pica a unit of print size used in DTP and WORD PROCESSOR work. The pica is 12 POINTs, equal to 1/72 inch.

pico- prefix denoting one millionth of a millionth, that is, 1E-12 (10^{-12}).

picture element see PIXEL.

picture quality scale (PQS) a method of assessing image quality that attempts to mimic the effect of an image on the eye rather than by using the SIGNAL/NOISE RATIO.

pie chart a form of data display that shows a circle divided into sectors to represent the relative contributions of various factors to a whole, such as how the profits of subsidiary companies contribute to the profit of a group of companies.

piezo-electric inkjet a principle used for the Epson Stylus printers in which a narrow-bore tube containing ink is formed partly from a piezo-electric material that will constrict when a voltage pulse is applied to it. This has the effect of ejecting a microscopic drop of ink. See also BUBBLE-JET.

PIF (program information file) a file formerly used in MULTITASKING applications such as WINDOWS 3.1 and the SHELL for MS-DOS 5. The PIF describes for a program the memory it requires and the way that it makes use of the KEYBOARD, SCREEN (sense 1) and SERIAL PORT. This information can be read by the computer and used to determine what needs to be done when the program is swapped in and out of use with others.

piggyback (of a unit) fitting over the top of another. It is often possible to improve the performance of a computer by adding a faster MICRO-

PROCESSOR that fits on a *piggyback board* over the existing processor. The memory of a LASER PRINTER can be upgraded by fitting another memory board in piggyback fashion over the existing board.

pilot error any malfunction that is caused by the user's misunderstanding rather than by a BUG.

PIM (personal information manager) a form of DATABASE for the type of information that is often scattered, such as names and addresses, telephone numbers, notes and memos, appointments, to-do lists. The database actions are supplemented by a rudimentary WORD PROCESSOR to make the program more useful.

PIN (personal identification number) a security device to ensure that a computer user is authorized to gain ACCESS (sense 1) to the system; also used of bank cards along with an ATM (sense 1).

pinchwheel the wheel, made of synthetic rubber, that on a tape backup system holds the tape firmly against the CAPSTAN spindle so that the tape can be moved at a constant speed. Any dirt on this wheel will cause speed error problems such as FLUTTER and WOW.

pin-compatible (of a CHIP) capable of being plugged into a socket intended for another make of chip.

pincushion distortion a form of SCREEN (sense 1) display distortion in which a rectangular shape appears to have concave sides. This is the reverse of BARREL DISTORTION.

pinfeed see SPROCKET FEED.

ping (packet Internet groper) a program that is used for testing INTERNET destinations by sending a request for a signal to be returned.

pinned record a DATABASE record whose address is held in the form of a POINTER (sense 1) in another RECORD. A pinned record must not be deleted (see DANGLING POINTER) until the pointer in the other record has been deleted.

pin-out the table of connections to each pin of a CHIP.

pipe a method used in an operating system (OS) such as MS-DOS or UNIX to make the output of one program become the input of another without any intermediate step. For example, in the MS-DOS system, the command TYPE will place a text file on the SCREEN (sense 1), scrolling rapidly. The FILTER (sense 1) program MORE will arrange screen output into 24-line sets, moving on to a new set when any KEY (sense 1) is pressed. By using a command such as TYPE TXTFILE | MORE, the contents of TXTFILE are placed on screen in 24-line sets by piping the output of TYPE into the filter MORE. See also REDIRECTION.

pipeline burst cache a form of fast CACHE memory using PIPELINING along with STATIC RAM.

pipelining a method of increasing processing speed. The principle is to reduce the difficulties that are caused by an INPUT-BOUND system by having inputs arrive at a time when nothing else is happening. The word applies particularly to the MICROPROCESSOR action. For example, the input of a 2-byte address from memory to a single-byte (8-bit) microprocessor is a time-wasting process because nothing can be done until the second byte has been read. In a pipelined 8-bit processor, two-phase CLOCK pulses are used and data is read on one phase of the clock, with all processing being carried out on the other phase. In this way, there is always a byte or word being read and one 'in the pipeline'. Pipelining is used on the later 32-bit INTEL processors, along with internal CACHE memory to speed up processing.

piracy or **software piracy** unlawful copying, particularly of SOFTWARE. Because magnetic recording methods are not totally reliable, computers are designed so as to make it easy to prepare backups of software. This, however, means that it is easy to make illegal copies of a program for sale. This has been possible because the law of copyright was formed at a time when magnetic recording was unknown, and suitable changes in the law should ensure better copyright protection. Piracy has had the effect in the past of forcing COPY PROTECTION on some software suppliers, particularly of games. Distribution of programs on CD-ROM, using files that are too long to save on a disk, has reduced amateur piracy, but professional pirates are prepared to copy CD-ROM in order to make profits. The possession and use of pirated software is an offence, and the main offenders seem to be large commercial institutions.

pitch 1. the effect on the ear of the FREQUENCY of a note of sound. **2.** the number of characters per inch in a WORD PROCESSOR or DTP document that uses MONOSPACING.

pivot table a table derived from a WORKSHEET and used to analyse data. For example, if a worksheet contains data on items sold and their values, a pivot table could be created to show the total amount of one type of item sold in the first six months of a year, along with the value of the items.

pixel or **pel** or **picture element** a unit of SCREEN (sense 1) display. A pixel is the smallest size of spot on the screen that can be independently controlled by the computer. Many TEXT characters are built from a 9 x 15 matrix of pixels, and in HIGH-RESOLUTION GRAPHICS each pixel has to be manipulated separately, requiring a large amount of RAM to be dedicated for this purpose, particularly if the colour of each pixel is to be determined. The number of pixels used for any type of display can be found by multiplying the horizontal and vertical resolution figures. For example, the standard VGA graphics screen uses 640 x 480 pixels, equal to 307,200 pixels. This is usually a smaller number than the number of pixels a CRT can display.

PKlite a well-known compression program (see COMPRESSED FILE) from PKWARE Inc. that runs under MS-DOS.

PKzip a well-known compression and decompression program (see COM-

PRESSED FILE) from PKWARE Inc. that exists in both MS-DOS and WINDOWS forms and incorporates the PKUNZIP decompressing utility. See also ARCHIVE.

placeholder any piece of text or graphics that is used to represent the final version that will occupy the same space on a page. Placeholders are used on DTP pages and on PRESENTATION GRAPHICS SLIDES to show how a page or slide will appear. A rectangle or cross can act as a placeholder for a photograph that will be pasted on to the paper or for an IMAGE (sense 2) that will be read from a file. Placeholder text, often in Latin to distinguish it from the intended text, shows the FORMAT (sense 2) of the document without the need to put in the final version of the text.

plain text document a DOCUMENT that uses no printer effects and whose file contains only ASCII codes.

planner a SOFTWARE form of diary that allows appointment times to be displayed, copied, edited or moved, along with comments, in order to make efficient use of limited time. See also PIM.

plasma screen see GAS PLASMA DISPLAY.

plastic bubble keyboard a form of KEYBOARD in which pressure on a KEY (sense 1) makes a plastic bubble collapse, joining two metal coatings. These keys have the advantage of being less susceptible to damage from moisture than conventional switches, but the keyboard has an unsatisfactory feel and is not ideal for fast touch-typing.

platen the part of an IMPACT PRINTER that supports the paper at the point where the paper is struck.

platform a computer system for which some application is specifically intended.

platform independence the ability to work with different types of computer, applied mainly to a NETWORK.

platter an aluminium disc that is coated with magnetic materials and used in a HARD DRIVE. See Fig. 33.

play symbol the > symbol that is used on a control BUTTON to indicate the play action for MULTIMEDIA, as on a video display or an audio recorder. See also FAST FORWARD; FAST REWIND.

PLC see PROGRAMMABLE LOGIC CONTROLLER.

PLCC package a way of encapsulating a CHIP into a square holder using thin pins for connections.

plenum cable a cable, usually for a NETWORK, that will not emit hazardous fumes at high temperature so it can be installed in the space (the *plenum*) between a ceiling and the floor above.

plesiochronous almost synchronized, of signals that can be used despite not being in perfect synchronism.

plot to find the position of a GRAPH point from its COORDINATES. The graphing action of a SPREADSHEET will use values in a RANGE of CELLS to plot points.

Fig. 33. **Platter**. A hard drive showing the stack of platters.

plotter a graphics PERIPHERAL that draws lines under computer control with a CAD program running. See also PRINTER-PLOTTER; X-Y PLOTTER.

plotter font a FONT whose characters are drawn stroke by stroke and particularly suitable for use with a PLOTTER.

plug a connection that makes use of projecting pins to fit into a matching SOCKET. Mains voltage should never be connected to a plug unless it is quite impossible to touch the pins.

plug and play see PNP.

plug-compatible (of a HARDWARE device, such as an external MODEM) capable of being plugged in to replace another make of such device and which will then work in the same way. Of all peripherals, PARALLEL PRINTERS are the most plug-compatible.

plug-in a SOFTWARE extension to a program, usually in the form of a file of data. Unlike an APPLET (sense 2), a plug-in is PASSIVE and carries no VIRUS risk.

plug-in card a PCB card that is equipped with an EDGE CONNECTOR to allow it to be inserted into a SOCKET, usually on a computer MOTHER-BOARD.

plug'n'play see PNP.

PMA (program memory area) the portion of a CD-R or CD-RW disc that contains a table of TRACK numbers along with start and stop data positions for each track.

PMOS (p-type metal-oxide semiconductor) a variety of FIELD EFFECT TRANSISTOR construction used for ICs. See also CMOS; NMOS.

PNP (plug'n'play or plug and play) a standard for HARDWARE that allows an added hardware device to be recognized and installed automatically. This requires a suitable BIOS in the computer, a ROM inside the hardware device and the use of Microsoft WINDOWS 95 or any other operating system (OS) that permits the use of plug'n'play. See also HOT SWAPPING.

point the DTP and WORD PROCESSOR unit of FONT size, equal to 1/72 inch. For example, 12-point type means that all the upper-case letters of a font are 1/6 inch high. Graphics programs are more likely to use millimetre units for type size. See also CICERO; PICA.

point of presence see POP.

pointer 1. a form of CURSOR, often an arrow shape, that is moved by a MOUSE and used to select a MENU item or an ICON, or to draw an object in a graphics program. In WINDOWS programs, the shape of a pointer usually indicates the action that is being carried out, such as copying files. **2.** a number that is stored in memory and gives the memory ADDRESS (sense 1) of data.

pointing a MOUSE selection action. The arrow on the SCREEN (sense 1) is moved by moving the mouse and can be pointed to an item that can then be selected by pressing the mouse BUTTON.

pointing device any HARDWARE that can move a screen pointer. This is usually a MOUSE, but it can also be a TRACKERBALL, DIGITIZING PAD, LIGHT PEN or a more exotic device such as a DATA GLOVE.

point of sale terminal the combination of computer, cash till and BAR-CODE reader used at supermarket checkouts and other shops.

point-to-point protocol see PPP.

polar coordinates a system for specifying position that uses the distance from an ORIGIN (sense 1) and the angle measured to a fixed direction. An alternative to CARTESIAN COORDINATES, which are better suited to some forms of data. Conversion formulas for Cartesian to polar and polar to Cartesian are available.

polarity 1. the sense of an electrical voltage, plus or minus. **2.** The shape of a PLUG and SOCKET that allows insertion one way round only. **3.** The use of black and white, with positive meaning black characters on white background and *negative polarity* the opposite.

polarized plug a PLUG whose pins are arranged, or which is fitted with a keyway slot, so that it can be inserted in only one way into a matching SOCKET.

polling the checking of a part of computer system at intervals. For example, the operating system (OS) of a computer may poll the KEYBOARD at intervals while a program is running. This allows the machine to check if the BREAK KEY or ESCAPE KEY is pressed. The alternative to polling is the use of INTERRUPTS. Polling is also used in communications systems in which a central terminal will poll others for data. This avoids any conflicts that might be caused if several remote terminals tried to interrupt the central terminal simultaneously.

polyline a drawing OBJECT that consists of a set of joined lines. When a polyline is completed, the resulting figure will be closed and the last closing line will be drawn automatically if it is not specifically drawn. Some CAD programs use a polyline method to draw a thick line.

Pong a very early (1972) computer GAME based on table tennis.

POP or **PULL** the action of reading a data RECORD (sense 1) from a STACK. See also PUSH.

PoP (point of presence) an INTERNET dialling site, allowing access to local subscribers whose calls are then routed through to the main site.

POP server a computer that is permanently connected to the INTERNET, usually by a fast link such as a FIBRE-OPTIC cable, and used for storing and transmitting EMAIL using the Post Office Protocol system. The current PROTOCOL version is POP3, which is not COMPATIBLE with earlier versions. See also SMTP.

pop-up menu see PULL-DOWN MENU.

port a circuit, usually in single CHIP form, that is used to connect the signals of the computer to other devices. A port is very often used to connect the KEYBOARD and the SCREEN (sense 1), and for disk and cassette signals also. The port is usually a very complex chip, second only in complication to the MICROPROCESSOR itself, and PROGRAMMABLE to some extent. See also PARALLEL PORT.

portability the independence of a PROGRAMMING LANGUAGE from a particular type of computer. A portable language would allow a program to be written on one type of computer and used on a different computer type without errors. The most portable programming languages are the most strictly defined.

portable computer a computer that can be folded up and moved easily. The form of a portable computer is of a small case, the lid of which contains the LCD SCREEN (sense 1) and the body the DISK DRIVE and KEYBOARD along with the circuitry and batteries. Smaller machines are referred to as LAPTOP or NOTEBOOK types.

portable document format see PDF.

porting adapting SOFTWARE developed for one system so that it can be used on a different computer or operating system (OS).

portrait orientation positioning of paper with the lines of print along the short side (see LANDSCAPE ORIENTATION; ORIENTATION).

positive logic the conventional scheme that uses a low voltage to represent level 0 and a higher voltage to represent level 1. Contrast NEGATIVE LOGIC.

post I. to send a message to a NEWSGROUP, usually to all members of the group rather than to a few named members. **2.** to enter data into a RECORD (sense 1) of a data file. **3. (POST)** (power-on self test) the action of many modern computers that check memory and chip actions before loading the operating system ready to RUN (sense 2) a program.

postcardware a form of SHAREWARE in which the author requests the user to send a postcard in lieu of payment.

postdicting see MODEL BUILDING.

post-fix notation see REVERSE POLISH NOTATION.

post-formatted arranged into order during printing. The term is usually applied to WORD PROCESSOR commands that FORMAT (sense 2) the text at the printer rather than on the SCREEN (sense 1).

postmaster the person responsible for maintaining EMAIL facilities at an INTERNET site. See also WEBMASTER.

post-mortem routine a program that can be RUN (sense 2) after failure of software to find possible causes.

Post Office Protocol see POP SERVER.

post-processor 1. anything that follows a processing RUN (sense 1). **2.** a separate MICROPROCESSOR that deals with data that has been already processed by another CHIP. **3.** a program that carries out a second processing of data following an earlier processing run. Compare PRE-PROCESSOR.

PostScript™ a page description language (PDL) developed by the ADOBE SYSTEMS Corp. and used extensively in DTP work. A LASER PRINTER that contains a PostScript INTERPRETER can make use of files in PostScript that have been produced by computers, allowing easier use of different sizes of FONT and of high-resolution drawings. Because PostScript can be used by typesetting machines with a resolution of 2400 dots per inch (DPI) it is a useful method of saving documents that may have to be printed professionally.

posture the direction of slant in a FONT. See ITALIC; OBLIQUE.

pound the £ sign that appears on UK keyboards. This is sometimes referred to as a HASHMARK in US manuals, causing considerable confusion.

POWER a DOS command applicable to computers, such as a PORTABLE COMPUTER, that use power management systems. The POWER command (using the POWER.EXE driver program) allows the power-saving features to be turned on or off.

power down to switch off.

power line filter an electronic circuit that will smooth out voltage fluctuations in a supply line. This is desirable if the fluctuations are serious and are affecting computers, but the electricity supplier should be consulted first as they have a statutory duty to supply a steady value of AC voltage.

power on reset the action of clearing all the memory locations in a MICROPROCESSOR whenever power is applied – the alternative is to allow each memory location to take a value of 0 or 1 at random, resulting in the memory containing GARBAGE.

power on self-test see POST (sense 3).

PowerPoint a PRESENTATION GRAPHICS package from Microsoft that is also part of the MICROSOFT OFFICE set of programs. See Fig. 34.

power save mode an energy-saving system that reduces power consumption by switching off devices such as the DISPLAY, HARD DRIVE or

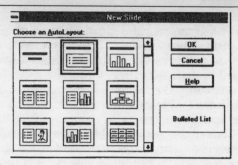

Fig. 34. **PowerPoint**. A typical screen view in which a slide layout can be selected.

other units when the computer is not active. A power save mode is particularly important for LAPTOP and other portable machines, but it can also significantly reduce heat dissipation and energy waste in large offices when applied to DESKTOP COMPUTERS.

power supply unit see PSU.

power surge a sudden and transient large increase in supply voltage that can often cause damage to the power supply unit (PSU) of a computer.

power take-off a SOCKET on the computer that allows a limited supply of low-voltage power to be used for other units, such as the disk drive. Most systems use separate power supplies for each peripheral with a mains-voltage socket to supply power for a monitor.

PPP (point to point PROTOCOL) the standard method used for transmitting PACKETS of information over INTERNET serial connections. PPP has replaced the older SLIP protocol.

PQS see PICTURE QUALITY SCALE.

precedence the order in which mathematical actions are performed if no BRACKETS are used for guidance. This is important for a FORMULA in a WORKSHEET and is expressed by the MDAS rule – multiplication and division, then addition and subtraction. Raising a number to a power has the highest precedence, but if brackets are present in an EXPRESSION the action within brackets is performed first. Thus the expression 5 + 2 * 3 means that 2 is multiplied by 3 to give 6 and 5 is added, making 11, rather than adding 5 to 2 to give 7 and then multiplying to give 21. Precedence means that mathematical expressions in conventional form cannot be treated in left-to-right order. See also REVERSE POLISH NOTATION.

precedent a CELL in a WORKSHEET whose value is used in a FORMULA contained in another cell. See also DEPENDENT.

precision of number the extent to which a number can be stored or expressed in exact form. Numbers can be stored as INTEGERS, as BINARY FRACTIONS or in binary-coded decimal (BCD) form. Of these, the integer form is always exact but of limited range. The BCD form is exact, providing that a specified number of decimal places is not exceeded. The binary fraction form, however, which is used on many computers to store FLOATING-POINT numbers, almost always stores numbers in approximate form, called EXPONENT-MANTISSA form. The exceptions are numbers that are powers of 2. The reason is that the floating-point number is stored in the form of a binary fraction multiplied by a power of 2. Unless a number happens to be an exact power of 2, its binary fraction form will not terminate, and no matter how many places of binary fraction are used, the stored form will never be exact. The approximations are disguised by ROUNDING when the numbers are displayed, but the numbers are not rounded while they are stored. This can lead to rounding errors.

pre-emptive multitasking or **time-slice multitasking** a form of MULTITASKING in which each task is allocated a fraction (a *time-slice*) of processor time. At the end of a time-slice for a task, another task is run. This allows tasks to seem to run simultaneously, with the processor dividing its time among them. Microsoft WINDOWS 95 uses this form of multitasking for 32-bit software, and it is possible to make use of a 32-bit program while a 16-bit program is working and displaying the HOURGLASS ICON. See also COOPERATIVE MULTITASKING.

prefix a letter or set of letters used to indicate a power of ten, such as M meaning 10^6.

pre-order search a method of searching DATABASE RECORDS (sense 1) in a TREE (sense 2) system that starts at the root and moves to the next set of branches from left to right, searching the leftmost branch of each branch, and so on, until the end of branching is encountered (at a leaf).

pre-processor of any action carried out on data before processing. Compare POST-PROCESSOR.

presentation graphics a program that combines text editing with GRAPHICS to create the electronic equivalent of a slide show. The program can be used with a MONITOR (sense 2) display to create film slides or to create overhead projector transparencies with the option for paper handout sheets.

presentation layer part of a standard ISO/OSI NETWORK control program that determines how connections are made and broken.

press any key a message that can be printed on the SCREEN (sense 1) when a pause action is being used. The pause continues until a KEY (sense 1) is pressed, and then the computer resumes normal action. Despite the message, pressing some keys may have no effect, and a BREAK or ESCAPE KEY may allow you to break out of the program completely.

pressure pad a form of contact switch. A pressure pad will allow electrical contacts to close when pressure is applied to the unit. A form of miniature pressure pad can be used for a rather unsatisfactory type of KEYBOARD. Pressure pads are also used in burglar alarm systems and as limit switches on mechanical devices such as printers.

Pretty Good Privacy see PGP.

preview see PRINT PREVIEW.

PRF (PULSE repetition frequency) the number of pulses completed per second, used as a measure of CLOCK speed.

primary cache see LEVEL 1 CACHE.

primary key a code that identifies one RECORD (sense 1) in a DATABASE in a unique way. This could be a social security number, for example, since such numbers are always unique.

primary partition the portion of a PARTITIONED DRIVE that contains the operating system (OS) and from which the computer will BOOT up.

primary storage the main RAM memory of the computer.

prime attribute the most important feature of a MACHINE or a piece of SOFTWARE.

primer an elementary instruction MANUAL. Many computers and peripherals used to come with a primer and also with a guide suitable for experienced programmers but nothing of intermediate level. The use of brief Help files is now more common. This gap is generally filled by books from independent publishers, who very often also publish more USER-FRIENDLY primers. Some care is needed to ensure that a software primer deals with the version of software (for example, US or UK) that is being used – you cannot expect a US primer to tell you how to print a £ sign or to cater for UK accountancy methods, for example.

print control character a NON-PRINTING CODE whose action controls some aspect of the printer, such as selecting a FONT or taking a new page. Most printing control characters are sequences of characters that start with the ESCAPE KEY code, ASCII 27.

printed circuit board see PCB.

print engine the working heart of a LASER PRINTER. Only a few types of print engines are manufactured, each used by several manufacturers of laser printers.

printer a device that will print text on paper, producing HARD COPY. For personal computers, the choice is between IMPACT or NON-IMPACT PRINTERS. Of the non-impact printers, only the INKJET and LASER types will be considered for commercial work, although THERMAL PRINTERS are often used as built-in devices in computer-controlled equipment. Among impact printers, the DOT-MATRIX is the only contender; the older DAISY-WHEEL machine is now obsolete. See also NLQ; PRINTER-PLOTTER.

printer control language (PCL) a set of codes, based on ASCII, that are used to control a PRINTER. The most widely used printer control languages are the EPSON and HEWLETT PACKARD varieties. See also HEWLETT PACKARD PRINTER CONTROL LANGUAGE.

printer driver a type of DRIVER program that is run to allow the use of a specific model of printer.

printer emulation the ability of a PRINTER to behave like a different make or model by making use of the PRINTER CONTROL LANGUAGE of the other printer. The usual models for emulation are EPSON and HEWLETT PACKARD.

printer font a FONT that is built into a PRINTER but may not be available on the SCREEN (sense 1) of the computer. The use of fonts such as TRUE-TYPE has ended the old problems of screen and printer fonts that do not match.

printer memory MEMORY used within a printer as a BUFFER or to arrange a bitmapped image (see BITMAP). Laser printers in particular must possess enough memory for the images that they will be printing and for the use of a formatting language interpreter such as POSTSCRIPT.

printer-plotter a form of combined printer and plotter. The mechanism consists of a penholder that can be moved under computer control in a horizontal plane and a friction drive for paper that allows the paper to be moved in either vertical direction, also under computer control. The machine is primarily a PLOTTER, allowing diagrams to be drawn by simultaneous movement of both paper and pen. Many printer-plotters can use several pens, allowing coloured lines to be drawn, with the colour also under computer control. In addition, the ROM of the machine allows ASCII codes to be accepted, causing a character to be 'printed'. The character is in fact drawn, rather than printed, by movement of pen and paper. In the small sizes, such printer-plotters can be remarkably low-priced and can provide very useful effects that are almost impossible by other means except at much greater cost. The snag is that the action is very slow so that a CAD drawing can take an hour or more to produce.

printer port the connector, usually the Centronics parallel type (see CENTRONICS INTERFACE), used to connect to a PRINTER. Serial ports are less common now, but later machines use the USB type of connection for printers and most other relatively slow peripherals. See also ECP; EPP.

printer timeout an error caused by failure of a PRINTER to accept data. The computer can be set to allow a time, such as 45 seconds, during which it will try to send data. After this time has expired a TIMEOUT message will be displayed to draw the attention of the user to a potential problem, such as a jammed printer.

print formatter or **text formatter** a program that is normally a part of a WORD PROCESSOR. A print formatter arranges for printing to be carried out with the correct MARGIN position, indentation, words per line, lines per page, HEADER (sense 1), FOOTER, etc. It is, in other words, concerned with how a continuous piece of text can be broken up into sections for printing. Some word-processing programs require the print-formatting decisions to be taken before the text is entered while others can leave this step until just before the file is saved. The formatting instructions are saved with the text. Text can also be 'printed' to a file, meaning that codes for a specified printer and format are saved on disk, allowing the document to be printed by way of another computer connected to the specified printer.

printhead the active portion of a DOT-MATRIX type of PRINTER that produces the characters on paper.

print manager a program that organizes the printing of documents as a BACKGROUND (sense 2) task. This allows documents to be queued and printed while the computer is working on other tasks, since printing requires very little of the time of the computer. See also SPOOL.

print modifiers coded instructions that modify the way that printing is carried out (see MODIFIER).

printout see HARD COPY.

print pause an EMBEDDED COMMAND in text, produced by a WORD PROCESSOR, that stops the PRINTER in order that a ribbon or ink colour can be changed.

print preview or **preview** or **on-screen formatting** a facility used in a WORD PROCESSOR, DTP, CAD or GRAPHICS program to display on SCREEN (sense 1) the appearance of a final printed document. A preview facility is useful to look at layout, particularly when a document contains graphics. Because screen size is usually smaller than paper size, the appearance of text may be GREEKED and graphics can seem to have missing lines. See Fig. 35.

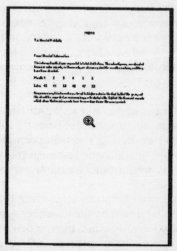

Fig. 35. **Print preview**. A typical print preview, showing greeked text, with the magnifier pointer that can be used to show detail where necessary.

print queue a list of document files awaiting printing, making use of a SPOOL action.

Print Screen key or **PrtSc key** the KEY (sense 1) that when pressed will print or save the screen image. Under DOS, the effect of the Print Screen key is to print the screen image on the printer. Under WINDOWS, the effect is to save the file on the CLIPBOARD so that it can be pasted into a GRAPHICS program.

print server a computer on a NETWORK that is connected to a PRINTER. Document files from any of the computers on the network will pass through the print server machine to be printed. The print server is usually a MULTITASKING machine and will be working on other actions as well as printing.

print spooling see SPOOL.

printwheel the printing part of a DAISYWHEEL printer.

priority the order of importance. In a NETWORK a method of assigning priority must be used to avoid clashes when two computers try to use the network together. The operating system (OS) of any machine must also determine priorities in the use of MEMORY.

priority scheduler a program that will arrange tasks into an order that ensures the fastest possible processing.

privacy enhanced mail any EMAIL system, such as PGP, that makes messages inaccessible other than to the sender and recipient and also provides proof of the sender's identity.

private work area a non-shared area on a NETWORK. Each computer can be allocated workspace that is private to that machine and not shared along the network.

privilege level 1. the status of a user as far as ACCESS (sense 1) to shared files is concerned. **2.** the status of MEMORY space. In the later INTEL microprocessors, a privilege level number is allocated to a program to ensure that it cannot unintentionally violate the memory space assigned to another program.

PRN: see LPT1.

problem-oriented language a PROGRAMMING LANGUAGE that is designed to solve a specific type of problem.

process a program that is running and using computer resources.

process control the application of computers to AUTOMATION so that a manufacturing process is controlled by the software of a computer system.

processor the processing unit of a computer; see MICROPROCESSOR.

processor-bound slowed down by the excessive use of the main PROCESSOR. The term is applied mainly when the CPU is used for FLOATING-POINT calculations, as in CAD or SPREADSHEET use. A considerable increase of speed can be achieved by using a floating-point COPROCESSOR for such work, leaving the main CPU free.

profile a form of control file of data that can be used to tailor the settings for a program to the user's own preferences. This is applied particularly to WINDOWS in a MULTI-ACCESS system, in which each user will see the customized version of Windows that he/she has set up. See also PLUG-IN.

program a set of instructions to a COMPUTER that will be carried out in order to produce the desired effects. See also ALGORITHM; APPLICATIONS PACKAGE; CODE (sense 2); COMPILER; HIGH-LEVEL LANGUAGE; INTERPRETER; LOW-LEVEL LANGUAGE.

program calibration area see PCA.

program crash see CRASH (sense 1).

program editor see TEXT EDITOR.

program generator a PROGRAM that will generate another program. This is usually applied to a DATABASE program that will generate another database for some specific purpose (medical records, store stocktaking, newspaper deliveries, etc.). Program generators are also used to create GAMES programs.

program icon the WINDOWS ICON that represents a PROGRAM.

program information file see PIF.

programmable capable of being programmed. The MICROPROCESSOR is a programmable device, hence its use in MICROCOMPUTERS. Some other chips, notably PORTS, SOUND CHIPS and VIDEO-controlling chips, are also programmable to a lesser extent.

programmable key or **soft key** a key such as a FUNCTION KEY whose action can be changed by a command or program instruction. Most modern software allows a large range of key combinations to be programmed.

programmable logic controller (PLC) a form of MICROCOMPUTER used for machine control. The number of commands that can be used is very small compared to the types of MICROPROCESSOR used in PC machines, but the PLC features a very large number of inputs and outputs.

programmable read-only memory see PROM.

program maintenance the updating and amending of a PROGRAM in response to the remarks made by users.

Program Manager the main TASK MANAGER part of WINDOWS 3.1 which attends to starting and running programs. See also START MENU.

programmed halt an interruption in a PROGRAM that is brought about by a software instruction, used in testing.

program memory area see PMA.

programmer one who programs a computer. For MAINFRAME computers, the operator will have coded and typed the PROGRAM, the programmer will have written the program, and the systems analyst will have produced the ALGORITHM. These distinctions are less clear when MICRO-COMPUTERS are used, and very often all the work of SYSTEMS ANALYSIS,

PROGRAMMING and operation will have been done by one team, possibly even by one person.

programming the creation of instruction codes that will act as instructions to the computer. The computer is totally dependent on its programming, and even the simplest tasks require quite large amounts of code. The preparation of a program therefore requires the problem to be thoroughly understood so that the instructions for solving the problem, whether of a mathematical equation or arranging a book index, can be written in detail and in the correct order.

programming language or **language** any method of generating a program of instructions for a computer other than by the direct input of number codes. A programming language is a way of generating the number codes that can be interpreted by the operating system (OS) or fed directly to the MICROPROCESSOR so as to cause a program to RUN (sense 2). In general, the use of a programming language implies typing instructions that are in order or that can be put into order. Languages are classed as LOW-LEVEL or HIGH-LEVEL, with high-level meaning that the instructions are closer to NATURAL LANGUAGE. Whatever the level, the purpose of a language is to produce a PROGRAM file, a set of instruction codes in BINARY that the machine can use. See also ASSEMBLER; ASSEMBLY LANGUAGE; BASIC; COMPILER; INTERPRETER; MACHINE CODE; PASCAL.

program overlay see OVERLAY (sense 3).

progressive coding a method of transmitting an IMAGE that starts with a LOW RESOLUTION image and adds detail. This allows the image to be visible earlier than would be possible if it had been transmitted in PIXEL order.

progressive disclosure slide see BUILD SLIDE.

projective infinity the representation of an infinitely large number with no sign BIT; contrast AFFINE INFINITY.

PROM (programmable read-only memory) a CHIP that will retain data but which can be written on by suitable circuits. An erasable version should be entitled EPROM, but 'PROM' is now often used to refer to either variety. A PROM is a very useful way of putting a PROGRAM into permanent form without making it completely impossible to change.

promote text to alter the importance of a section of text in an OUTLINER or a PRESENTATION GRAPHICS program. For example, a level-3 heading might be promoted to level 2 and other subheadings at level 3 added under it.

prompt or **system prompt** a message on the SCREEN (sense 1) for the benefit of the operator, usually a reminder that some action is needed. A prompt can also take the form of a BEEP. For business programs in which most of the output is to the printer, the screen will mainly be used only for prompts and for input ECHO CHECK.

propagated error an ERROR that has occurred in one program or routine and that affects other programs or routines. It is also applied to an error in one CELL of a WORKSHEET that causes an error in other cells.

propagation delay the time needed for a signal leaving a transmitter to reach a receiver or for a PULSE to move from one CHIP to another.

property as applied to a DATABASE, a feature of a RECORD. For example, a record may have a *field size property* of 20, meaning that the FIELD will hold up to 20 characters, or a *required property*, meaning that data must be entered in that field.

proportional leading a method of LEADING used in DTP work. In a proportional leading system, two-thirds of the leading space is above the BASE LINE of the text and one-third is below the base line.

proportional spacing a system used in a WORD PROCESSOR or a DTP program that allocates different sized spaces between letters, as distinct from the fixed space size that a typewriter uses. This produces better-looking COPY (sense 3), but both PRINTER and word processor must be correctly matched (with the correct DRIVER in use) in order to take full advantage of the facility. See also KERNING.

proposition a statement that is BOOLEAN, with a TRUE or FALSE answer.

proprietary software SOFTWARE that is not released to the public because it is specific to one device or commissioned by one manufacturer.

protected cell a CELL in a WORKSHEET that has been given protected status so that its contents cannot be altered.

protected location a piece of MEMORY that cannot normally be used. For example, the operating system (OS) must make some use of RAM during the time when a program is running. This part of RAM must be protected against an OVERWRITE because any CORRUPTION of the data stored in it would cause the program to CRASH (sense 2). The part of memory that is used is protected by software methods, by placing the address of the start of the protected area in memory, and forcing the computer to check at each memory-storage step that none of the protected addresses is being used. This protection system operates normally for any HIGH-LEVEL LANGUAGE but can be circumvented by the use of a LOW-LEVEL LANGUAGE.

protected mode a method of running a MICROPROCESSOR chip of the INTEL type so that it can timeshare (see MULTITASKING) a number of programs while preventing any interaction between the programs.

protection a system that is designed to make a tape or disk secure from copying. See COPY PROTECTION.

protocol 1. a set of computing rules. The term is usually applied to SERIAL transmission of data, which requires the receiver to be set up in exactly the same way as the transmitter. For example, a transmission might use the protocols of 7-BIT code, no PARITY, one START BIT and two STOP BITS, 9600 BAUD. This set of protocols would have to be obeyed by the receiver also. The need for protocols in serial printer use makes serial printers much more difficult to use for a range of different computers than parallel printers. **2.** in ARTIFICIAL INTELLIGENCE, the set of messages to which an OBJECT can respond or a set of descriptions provided by an EXPERT during the solution of a problem.

prototype an early version of a system. The prototype of a hardware or software system is intended to allow evaluation and is often designed as a simplified version, carrying out less than will eventually be possible. See also ALPHA TEST.

proxy gateway see FIREWALL.

proxy server an INTERNET SERVER that maintains a large number of WEB PAGES in a CACHE, allowing fast access to those items.

PrtSc key see PRINT SCREEN KEY.

prune and graft the set of actions that allows a complete subdirectory and all of its files to be transferred to another part of the main directory TREE (sense 1).

pseudo a false name for a user of EMAIL or NEWSGROUP postings.

pseudo-random (of numbers) appearing to be random but actually consisting of a very long repeated sequence. Also, a computer can generate numbers that appear to be random numbers but, because everything in a computer is programmed, these numbers do not satisfy strict statistical tests of randomness and are described as being pseudo-random.

PSS (packet switching service) a method of grouping data into PACKET units for transmission over lines by the fastest possible route. This is more efficient than devoting a line to one stream of data because it is possible to interleave packets and to send consecutive packets of a transmission by different routes.

PSU (power supply unit) the source of DC power for the computer. Computers generally use low-voltage DC supplies, typically of 3V, 5V and 12V, and draw currents of several amperes. The power-supply section is designed to provide steady and stable low-voltage supplies, using the mains 240V AC as a source. The PSU is a sealed unit and is the only part of the main computer in which dangerous voltages exist. Small PORTABLE COMPUTERS can use battery power, but if mechanical devices such as disk drives are incorporated, battery life is likely to be short.

p-type metal-oxide semiconductor see PMOS.

public area a set of folders maintained by a SERVER that can be used by outsiders for both downloading and uploading data from the World Wide Web (WWW). See also FTP.

public domain common ownership of a PROGRAM, so that the program can be distributed free of all charges other than those associated with copying a disk. See also SHAREWARE.

public domain software SOFTWARE that has no copyright and can be copied and altered by anyone. See also FREEWARE; POSTCARDWARE; SHARE-WARE.

public-key encryption a security system for EMAIL messages that makes use of two KEYS (sense 1) for each user. One key is the *public key* and is easily available, and the other is a *private key* which is maintained confidentially. There is no need for the recipient to know the private key of the sender because although a message is encrypted using the public key it can be decrypted only by using the private key of the recipient. See also PGP.

PULL see POP.

pull-down menu or **pop-up menu** a MENU that appears, often in a WINDOW, when a particular KEY (sense 1) or KEY COMBINATION is used, allowing choices of action to be made. The menu window will appear over anything else displayed on the SCREEN (sense 1), and the window disappears when the selection has been made. See also GUI. See Fig. 36.

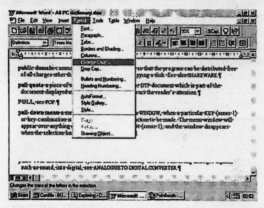

Fig. 36. **Pull-down menu**. The screen appearance of Microsoft Word with one of the menus pulled down.

pull media the normal INTERNET system in which the user requests the data that he/she wants.

pull quote a piece of text in a WORD PROCESSOR or DTP document that is part of the document displayed in larger type and used to attract the reader's attention.

pulse a sharp rise of electrical voltage followed by a fall to the previous level. Pulses are used as the signals on MICROPROCESSOR BUS-connecting lines and in all DIGITAL systems.

pulse-code modulation (PCM) a method of transforming ANALOGUE waveforms into a serial stream of DIGITAL data in real time (see REAL-TIME PROCESSING). These BASEBAND data may themselves then be used to modulate (see MODULATION) a carrier for transmission over a telecommunications line. PCM is used to transform audio signals into digital data that is recorded on a COMPACT DISC.

pulse repetition frequency see PRF.

punctuation marks the marks such as comma, semicolon, full stop and others that are used for punctuating NATURAL LANGUAGE. In computing languages, and also on some WORKSHEET and DATABASE applications, these marks are used as SEPARATORS or MODIFIERS.

purge to remove unwanted data.

PUSH the action of storing a data RECORD (sense 1) on a STACK. See also POP.

push button a button shape in a DIALOGUE BOX of WINDOWS that can be clicked (see CLICK, sense 1) to carry out some action.

pushdown list a LIST in which the last item that was added is at the top of the list. This is a form of LIFO (last in first out) memory or STACK.

push media an INTERNET distribution system in which a server determines the data being sent, like a broadcasting station. The user can select a CHANNEL (sense 3) to receive some specified type of data such as news or sport.

push-up list a LIST in which the last item added is at the bottom of the list. This corresponds to the operation of a QUEUE (sense 1).

QBASIC a form of DOS BASIC from Microsoft. QBASIC was distributed in INTERPRETER form along with MS-DOS versions 5.0 to 6.0 and also separately as a COMPILER. See also VISUAL BASIC.

QBE (query by example) a method of generating a database QUERY by filling in criteria on a DATABASE table. For example, MICROSOFT ACCESS allows you to generate a query by dragging fields from a list into a grid.

QEMM™ (Quarterdeck extended memory manager) a program that allowed a computer of the PC-AT type to make the most efficient possible use of its EXTENDED MEMORY.

QEMM386 a program developed by Quarterdeck and designed to free up MEMORY space in the first megabyte of memory for machines using the 80386 or 80486 chips, making both DOS and WINDOWS operation faster with fewer 'out of memory' messages.

QIC (quarter-inch cartridge) a standard form of TAPE CARTRIDGE used in tape STREAMER systems. The letters are also used as the extension for a BACKUP file used by the BACKUP program of Microsoft WINDOWS 95 onwards.

QL see QUERY LANGUAGE.

quad density the highest density of conventional FLOPPY DISK recording, equal to four times normal DENSITY. See also FLOPTICAL DISK.

quantization the process of sampling a varying (ANALOGUE) quantity at closely spaced time intervals and recording the size (AMPLITUDE) of the quantity at each interval. The amplitude sizes are rounded off to a whole number of units, so that a quantity whose variation with time can be represented by a sloping line is *quantized* into a set of steps. If the step size is very small, the approximation is unnoticed. Amplitude quantization is the basis of a DIGITIZER such as is used in COMPACT DISC technology.

Quarterdeck extended memory manager see QEMM.

quarter-inch cartridge see QIC.

quartz crystal see CRYSTAL.

QUEL a commercially used QUERY LANGUAGE that involves a different internal system from those used in STRUCTURED QUERY LANGUAGE or QBE.

query a data TABLE obtained from a larger set of data entries by defining the range of data. For example, you might want to find the amount of sales of an item in June 1995, broken down into the colours that were requested.

query by example see QBE.

query language (QL) a form of a PROGRAMMING LANGUAGE used to formulate the requirements for data to be obtained from a DATABASE. See QBE; QUEL; QUERY; STRUCTURED QUERY LANGUAGE.

question mark the ? sign, used as a WILD CARD. The ? mark is used to mean any single character, unlike the * symbol.

queue 1. a data type in which added data is placed behind existing data in order of time of arrival, and the earliest-arriving data is processed first. See FIFO. **2.** a set of instructions awaiting execution, as in the internal CACHE memory of a MICROPROCESSOR.

Quicken™ a UK accounts program for WINDOWS that is particularly suitable for small-business and private users.

quickformat or **safe format** a method of formatting (see FORMAT, sense 4) a FLOPPY DISK that does not destroy information, so that it is possible to use an UNFORMAT UTILITY to recover data from a disk that has been formatted in this way by mistake. See also UNCONDITIONAL FORMAT.

quickkey see FASTKEY.

quicklist a short list of recently used files that appears on a file MENU. This allows you to gain access to one of these files quickly without needing to BROWSE (sense 1) among the full set of files and folders.

quicksort an ALGORITHM for rapid data sorting. The quicksort is advantageous only when the number of items in the list is fairly large (i.e. several hundred or more). See also BUBBLE SORT; SHELL SORT.

QuickView a utility of Microsoft WINDOWS 95 onwards that allows the text of a document to be viewed without the need to run the program that created the document. This can speed up the action of finding a document file.

quit a MENU choice that causes the end of a program.

quotes see INVERTED COMMAS.

QWERTY keyboard a KEYBOARD laid out in conventional typewriter style, with the top line consisting of the QWERTYUIOP keys. This layout was devised in the 1880s to ensure that typists could not type too fast for the machines. Various attempts to produce a better layout (DVORAK, MALTRON) have had little effect because the QWERTY layout is so widely used and entrenched. This is often quoted as a warning of the dangers of standardizing anything at an early stage in technical development.

radar chart a form of display that is useful to show relative amounts of constituent parts. The name is derived from the form of the radar plan-position display, in which the direction of a line shows the bearing of a target and the distance from the centre of the screen shows the range.

radian see ANGLE.

radio button an ICON of BUTTON shape that can be used to trigger an action by placing the POINTER over the button and clicking (see CLICK, sense 1) the MOUSE button. In a set of radio buttons, only one can be selected, shown as a dot appearing in the button. See Fig. 37.

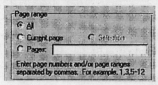

FIG. 37. **Radio button**. In this portion of a window for printing a document, the radio buttons each present a choice that excludes the other choices.

radio frequency see RF.

radio frequency interference see RFI.

radix a number BASE. For example, the ordinary numbers we use have a radix of ten.

ragged margin the right MARGIN of a document in a WORD PROCESSOR when only the left-hand side is justified (see JUSTIFY). It can also apply to the left-hand side of text when right justification is used, but this is rare.

RAID (random array of independent disks) a method of increasing the reliability of HARD DRIVE storage for a NETWORK. Several hard drives are connected so that the data they hold is duplicated and the total failure of one drive will not bring down the whole system.

rain dance any action performed more in hope than in realistic expectation. Examples include reinstalling a program that has crashed, and removing and reinserting the data plug on a printer that is not working.

RAM (random access memory) a type of MEMORY in which any part of the memory can be read or written as required without the need to read or write all the memory. In the early days of microcomputing, some memory systems operated in SERIAL form, with data being put in at one end and eventually emerging from the other. It was then impossible to gain ACCESS (sense 2) to a given piece of data without reading all the rest of the stored data that had been recorded earlier. Random access is ensured by assigning a number, the ADDRESS (sense 1), to each BYTE of data so that the use of an address number allows one unique byte to be written or read. The memory is VOLATILE, so that any data that must remain stored after switching off must be retained in a BACKING STORE, which is usually a HARD DRIVE system. One variety of RAM, CMOS, allows data to be retained providing a low-voltage battery is connected. The drain on the battery is very small, and data can be stored for several years in this way until rewritten. This form of RAM is used on PC-AT and subsequent machines to maintain the real-time clock system and also to hold details of set-up (number and type of floppy drives, type of hard disk, etc.). See also DRAM; STATIC RAM.

RAM cram the problem of running large programs in the limited memory space of a 1-megabyte DOS machine.

RAMdisk or **silicon disk** or **virtual drive** a portion of RAM organized so as to store data in the way that a disk does and to be treated as a LOGICAL DRIVE with a letter identification such as D: or E:. Unlike a real disk, the RAMdisk will lose all data when the computer is switched off, and its main advantage is speed. The use of RAMdisk is now almost obsolete, as it has no advantages when compared with the use of the same amount of memory as a CACHE memory. The modern exception is the use of a temporary RAM drive by the START-UP disk of a WINDOWS computer when a hard drive failure makes it impossible to store large files.

RAM refresh a signal or set of signals applied to a dynamic ram (see dram) in order to maintain the level 1 voltage in each CELL (sense 2). Refresh is needed about one thousand times per second, and the use of memory in banks (see BANKED MEMORY) ensures that this process does not disrupt processing.

random (of numbers) having no pattern, such as the numbers obtained from throwing unbiased dice. A set of truly random numbers will not favour any particular number or set of numbers and no sequence will be repeated. If a large set of truly random numbers is generated, using a fixed range like 1 to 10, then each number in the range should be picked an equal number of times. A truly random choice like this is very difficult to arrange using only software. Compare PSEUDO-RANDOM.

random-access file a method of storing files on disk so that any one RECORD can be read, written or changed without having to read or rewrite all the others. This can be done by allocating equal amounts of space to each record and is possible only if the disk operating system (OS) allows some way of specifying at what part of the disk a set of items can be stored. See also FIXED FIELD; INDEXED SEQUENTIAL ACCESS METHOD.

random access memory see RAM.

random array of independent disks see RAID.

range a selection of CELLS in a WORKSHEET. At one time, only a rectangular range could be selected, but modern spreadsheets allow you to select ranges that consist of several rectangles that may or may not overlap.

range expression an EXPRESSION that gives the ROWS AND COLUMNS references for the upper-left and lower-right corners of a RANGE in a WORKSHEET. For example, MICROSOFT EXCEL uses an expression such as A5:G10 and LOTUS 1-2-3 uses A5..G10 to describe a typical rectangular range. If a range is not rectangular, it must be named; see RANGE NAME.

range left to align text at the left-hand side of a page. See LEFT JUSTIFICATION.

range name a name, like a FILENAME, used to refer to a RANGE in a WORKSHEET. The advantages of naming a range are that the name can help to remind you of what the range contains (like SUMCASH) and the name can still be used even if the range has been moved to another set of cells. A named range in Excel need not be rectangular.

range of cells a set of WORKSHEET CELLS (sense 1) that form a rectangle on the screen and can be marked in some way. This allows these cells to be treated as one unit for the purposes of deleting, moving, copying or other actions. Modern SPREADSHEET programs such as MICROSOFT EXCEL allow you to create a RANGE that consists of several rectangular shapes, not necessarily touching.

range of number the limiting extents of numbers which can be represented in a particular way. If integers are represented in two bytes, for example, the range is from −32768 to +32767.

rank the order of any sorted quantity; its place in a LIST.

raster the pattern of lines on a blank TV or VDU screen. The action that produces a picture on a cathode ray tube (CRT) is called SCANNING (sense 2). The electron beam sweeps across the face of the tube, starting at the top left-hand corner. At the same time, the electron beam is being deflected downwards at a much lower rate so that when the beam has swept or scanned from left to right, it will be slightly farther down the tube face when it returns (in the FLYBACK) to the left-hand side. At the end of a complete FRAME (sense 2), every part of the screen has been covered with this pattern of horizontal parallel lines. For a TV picture, the frame consists of two interlacing *fields*, with each field consisting of lines at double the normal spacing. This is done in order to economize in the rate at which video information must be fed to the receiver and is not essential for a MONITOR (sense 2) so that most modern monitors dispense with interlacing (see NON-INTERLACED DISPLAY). Normally, the line structure is invisible because the electron beam is cut off or is at a very low current during scanning. The picture is created by increasing the beam current, so making part of the screen surface bright, at various places in the scan. If no picture (VIDEO) information is used to brighten the beam, the screen remains dark. The pattern of lines is known as the 'raster', and it can be made visible by advancing the brightness control of the TV receiver or monitor. Making the raster visible is one way of checking for the presence of JITTER.

raster burn a permanent pattern on a SCREEN (sense 1), caused by exposure of the phosphor to a still bright picture. See also SCREEN SAVER.

raster font see BITMAPPED FONT.

raster graphics see BITMAP.

rational number a number that can be expressed as a ratio of any two whole numbers. Numbers such as 2 or 1.5 are rational – one is 4/2, the other is 3/2 – but the value of π (*pi*) is not rational. Although we use the approximation of 22/7, there is no ratio of whole numbers that truly represents pi.

raw data data that has not been processed in any way. This generally refers to data as it has been entered at the KEYBOARD or obtained from DIGITIZERS or other input devices. Some programs are arranged so that raw data is recorded for later processing. This is particularly necessary if the amount of the data is likely to be more than the memory of the computer can hold. The recording of raw data is also useful in the event of a CRASH (sense 1) shutting down the system because it avoids the necessity of entering all the data again.

ray tracing a system, used main in THREE-DIMENSIONAL GRAPHICS, that calculates the path of light rays from an imaginary source so that drawn objects can be shown with realistic shadows.

rc (release candidate) a term used by MICROSOFT to mean a piece of software that has been beta tested (see BETA SOFTWARE) but is not yet regarded as in its final version.

RD see RMDIR.

read to COPY (sense 2) a file from a disk or other stored form into memory or to copy from memory to the screen.

read-back check a method of ensuring that data has been correctly received at a remote terminal by reading back the data from the terminal and comparing it with the original.

reader a device that can convert data from paper copy into electrical signals (see SCANNER).

Readme file a text file that accompanies SOFTWARE and is used to point out information that is not in the manual or Help pages or that needs to be emphasized.

read-only attribute an ATTRIBUTE bit that, when set, makes a file read-only so that the file cannot be altered by any normal methods. See also ARCHIVE ATTRIBUTE; HIDDEN ATTRIBUTE; SYSTEM ATTRIBUTE.

read-only memory see ROM.

readout or **soft copy** the display of data on the SCREEN (sense 1), as distinct from paper output, which is HARD COPY. To be legible, a readout should be paged (see PAGE, sense 1), with the paging controlled by pressing a KEY (sense 1).

read/write head the magnetic head of a tape or disk recorder. This is the data reading or writing device, an assembly of wire coils and shaped metal that will convert electrical signals into magnetic signals and vice versa. When electrical signals are applied to the head of a disk drive and the magnetic disk is spun in close contact with the head, the disk will be magnetized in a pattern that represents the coding of the electrical signals. Conversely, if a magnetized disk track is spun close to the head, the coils will have electrical signals generated in them that correspond to the magnetic signals on the disk. The same head can therefore be used both for recording (writing) data signals on the disk and for reading back these signals. The form of coding is not simply the on or off DIGITAL type of signals because this does not record satisfactorily, and systems described as MODIFIED FREQUENCY MODULATION or RLL are used to ensure greater reliability.

reality check any simple test of SOFTWARE or HARDWARE, such as checking that a computer will BOOT up or that a program will run.

real mode the mode of operation used by DOS and by the earlier INTEL microprocessor chips. Older versions of WINDOWS also supported real-mode running, using only 1 megabyte or less of memory. Intel chips from the 80286 onwards have all been capable of using much larger amounts of EXTENDED MEMORY, but the need to maintain compatibility with older software has been a handicap to full exploitation of the capabilities of these processors. See also PROTECTED MODE.

real number a number that can take values which are positive or negative, whole or fractional or a mixture of integer and fraction. Many applications of computers (such as WORD PROCESSOR or GRAPHICS displays) require only INTEGERs, but for working with the numbers that are used in engineering, science or finance, real numbers are necessary. A real number is stored in the form of a BINARY FRACTION, which can cause APPROXIMATION ERRORS. See also FLOATING POINT; PRECISION OF NUMBER.

real-time application any application with a fast response so that it can produce an output from an input before the next input arrives.

real-time clock a circuit that generates a set of signals that can be used to indicate time, as distinct from the SYSTEM CLOCK. The presence of real-time clock signals allows the computer to keep time and to indicate the time of creation of files. The real-time clock circuits can be maintained by a battery backup when the computer is switched off.

real-time processing computer processing 'as it happens'. Computing can be carried out on data that has been gathered in the past, like working with census data, or it may be required on data that is being typed at that moment, like hotel reservation requests. When the computer is working with data that is being typed or otherwise freshly input and is expected to process that data and give a rapid reply, then the computer is said to be working in 'real time'. Compare BATCH PROCESSING.

reboot to start again as if just switched on (see BOOT). In a reboot, the computer starts afresh, which usually implies loss of data and usually also loss of program unless the program is in ROM form. Every effort must be taken in the design of a program to prevent accidental rebooting, and a program that resists such rebooting is known as a ROBUST PROGRAM.

recalculation the reworking of a FORMULA in a CELL in a WORKSHEET when data has been changed.

recalculation order the order in which CELL FORMULAE in a WORKSHEET are recalculated when data is changed. See COLUMN RECALCULATION; NATURAL RECALCULATION; ROW RECALCULATION.

receive to accept data from an external source, usually a remote source.

receive-only (RO) terminal a TERMINAL with no KEYBOARD that cannot transmit messages. In this sense, the domestic TV receiver is a receive-only terminal.

recognition logic SOFTWARE for use with an OCR (sense 1).

reconfiguration alteration in the way that a program presents data or to its DEFAULTs. Reconfiguration may be needed when a different video graphics system is to be used, or a printer has been changed, or simply because some feature of the program, such as screen colours, needs to be changed.

reconstituting file a set of actions that results in a file being restored to its former state after being damaged in a program CRASH (sense 1).

record 1. a unit of a FILE. A file consists of a collection of records that are themselves made up of FIELDs. For example, in a file of names and addresses, one record would consist of the name (one field) and address (also one field) of one person. **2.** to save on disk or tape.

record count the number of RECORDs in a complete data file. DATABASE programs usually show a record number in a STATUS LINE.

record gap see GAP.

recording density the number of data bits recorded per linear inch of recording MEDIUM (sense 1). See BPI; DOUBLE-DENSITY; QUAD DENSITY.

record pointer a DATABASE status message that indicates the accession number of a RECORD.

record separator the ASCII character 30, used as a way of separating one DATABASE RECORD from the next or previous.

record sequencing number see RSN.

recoverable error any type of ERROR that is not a FATAL ERROR and allows a program to be resumed. An example is trying to write to a write-protected floppy disk – the write action can be retried when the write-protection has been removed.

recovery system a method of CRASH (sense 1) investigation, a program, used mainly in MAINFRAMES, that keeps records of steps in a main program so that in the event of a crash the cause can be traced.

rectification the conversion of alternating current (AC) into current flowing in one direction. This is normally followed by SMOOTHING (sense 2) so that the resulting supply can be used to power ELECTRONICS equipment.

recto the right-hand page in a set of document pages. This will conventionally be a page that carries an odd number. See also VERSO.

recursion the action of a routine calling itself. For example, if a formula uses a variable quantity x and provides a number y, then substituting y for x and repeating the action is *recursive use*, with each repetition yielding a different answer.

Recycle Bin or **trash can** or **bin** an ICON placed on the DESKTOP of Microsoft WINDOWS 95 onwards. A file can be deleted by dragging it to the Recycle Bin, and when a file is deleted by using the Delete key, it is also transferred to the Recycle Bin. Files deleted in this way can be resurrected from the Recycle Bin and are only truly deleted, releasing HARD DRIVE space, when the bin is emptied. See Fig. 38.

Recycle Bin

| Open |
| Explore |
| Empty Recycle Bin |
| Paste |
| Create Shortcut |
| Properties |

Fig. 38. **Recycle Bin**. The appearance of this Windows 95 icon and its menu, which allows the bin to be emptied or files recovered.

Red Book 1. one of the POSTSCRIPT reference books. The others are the BLUE BOOK, GREEN BOOK and WHITE BOOK (sense 1). **2.** a specification of the use of a COMPACT DISC for 16-bit audio signals.

redefine key to alter the action of a PROGRAMMABLE key so as to provide some desired action when it is pressed.

red-green-blue see RGB.

Red Hat one well-known assembly of LINUX programs and utilities.

redirection or **I/O redirection** the re-routing of data from one DEVICE (sense 1) to another, such as to a FILE instead of a PRINTER or to the SCREEN (sense 1) instead of to a file. An operating system (OS) such as MS-DOS or UNIX will provide for redirection by a symbol such as > so that the MS-DOS command TYPE FILE > PRN, for example, will display a file on the printer rather than on the screen, the normal destination for the type command. See also FILTER (sense 1); PIPE.

redlining a method of marking text in a WORD PROCESSOR, used when more than one editor is working on a document. Despite the name, the colour need not be red, and the text may be marked by lines drawn in the margin. The text that is added or changed does not become a part of the completed document until the results of the editing are confirmed. See also HIGHLIGHTER.

redo command or **repeat command** a command used in WORD PROCESSOR, GRAPHICS and DTP programs that will reverse the effect of an UNDO COMMAND.

redraw action an action in a CAD program that allows a set of lines to be redrawn after editing work has made some lines appear incomplete.

reduced instruction set computer see RISC.

redundancy the provision of excess capacity in a COMPUTER SYSTEM. The use of 'redundancy' means that a system is organized so that at least two units are always available to carry out any task. In the event of failure or non-availability of one unit, the other can take over. Redundancy in a transmitted message applies to characters that can be omitted without losing the meaning of the message. Redundancy is an important topic in SPEECH SYNTHESIS, visual recognition and ARTIFICIAL INTELLIGENCE.

redundant code a method of error checking (see PARITY).

Reed-Solomon a form of coding system for digital data that allows for a large amount of error detection and correction. Reed-Solomon coding is used for COMPACT DISC and DAT coding and also in some MODEM communications packages.

reformat to repeat the magnetic 'marking out' of a disk. This can totally remove any data that was stored on the disk and rechecks the material for DROPOUTS and other failures. Old disks should have their data backed up so that they can be reformatted at intervals. See also FORMAT (sense 4); QUICKFORMAT; UNCONDITIONAL FORMAT.

refresh 1. a command to reread disk files. Many SHELL programs, including WINDOWS, maintain a DIRECTORY of each disk in memory but do not alter the memory each time files are altered. The refresh command (often pressing the F5 key) allows the disk to be reread, updating the file information. **2.** to refresh a dynamic memory bank (see RAM).

refresh CRT or **refresh rate** to maintain a display of data on the SCREEN (sense 1). A CRT display exhibits a picture that is built up from a line pattern by brightening the beam at selected places. This picture is transient because the glowing material (the phosphor) on the tube face glows only for a very short time after the electron beam has struck it. The process must be repeated at a rate of 25 times per second if the picture is to be shown continuously. This action is termed *refreshing* and is part of the task of the video processor or whatever circuits are used to carry out the task of controlling the video display. The earlier types of LCD screens also required refreshing, so that large displays suffered from FLICKER. Later types used LCD systems that required no external refreshing. See also RASTER.

register 1. to put the three colour images (red, green, blue) into alignment in, for example, colour printing or a colour TV tube. **2.** a form of RAM storage that is built into a MICROPROCESSOR and used for data processing.

registration mark a small cross or + mark (usually one of a set) in the MARGIN of a DTP page that allows pages to be aligned, particularly for colour registration when colour separation pages are being printed, or to show the extents of a printed page. See also CROP MARK.

registry a form of DATABASE used by Microsoft WINDOWS 95 onwards to store information on the HARDWARE and SOFTWARE in a COMPUTER SYSTEM. Registry CORRUPTION will cause Windows to crash, and in the later versions (WINDOWS 98 on) elaborate BACKUP systems are used to safeguard the registry. The registry can be edited using a program called REGEDIT.EXE, but in normal use this is unnecessary, and in unskilled hands any attempt to alter the registry files can cause misfunctioning of the system. Registry files first appeared in Windows 3.11 and are intended to replace the older INI FILES for 32-bit software. The older INI files are still used by 16-bit applications.

regression see EXTRAPOLATION.

relation a mathematical term that corresponds in a DATABASE design to a table of corresponding values, not to be confused with RELATIONSHIP.

relational database a collection of data in which item groups are related in some way. The aim of a relational database is to allow large amounts of data to be held and manipulated without the need for excessive duplication, with the data grouped into separate lists or tables of which the user may need to operate with only one at a time. Suppose, for example, that a bookseller keeps a DATABASE that works with book titles and publishers and also with sales information. It would be unnecessary duplication if, each time a sale was recorded, the full name of the book, author and publisher had to be recorded too since this information is already held. A relational type of database can hold two sets of files in this example, one containing records for title, author and publisher along with a reference number. The other list will contain the reference number along with details of data, number sold and any other relevant information, such as discount rate or stock situation. In this simple example, the relation between the files is the reference number for each book, and this is the only element of duplication. The database can usually be programmed using its QUERY LANGUAGE so that a user, subject to ACCESS LEVEL, can look up all the information on a book without requiring to use the files separately. See also MICROSOFT ACCESS.

relational files files that consist of tables, each table containing one set of items that is common to another table. See RELATIONAL DATABASE.

relational operator a comparison symbol (i.e. the mathematical signs such as =, > <) that is used to establish or TEST (sense 1) relationships between quantities.

relationship an association between entities in a DATABASE design. For example, a bank account is a relationship that associates a customer with a sum of money.

relative cell reference a CELL REFERENCE in a WORKSHEET whose values will change when an EXPRESSION containing the reference is copied. For example, the cell reference C6 placed in cell C2 will change to D6 when cell C2 is copied to D2. This automatic change can be prevented by using an ABSOLUTE CELL REFERENCE or modified by using a MIXED CELL REFERENCE.

relative coordinates a set of COORDINATES that uses the current position of the CURSOR as an ORIGIN (sense 1) rather than having a fixed origin at one place (such as the bottom left-hand corner). This can be very useful for GRAPHICS and also in the use of a WORKSHEET.

relative error a difference between a displayed number and its stored value or its correct value. This would be caused by using a small number of decimal places for display (such as in a WORKSHEET) or by ROUNDING the number at some stage.

relative pathname a PATH that branches off from the current folder.

release candidate see RC.

release number an incremental change in a VERSION NUMBER for software, such as from version 4.2 to 4.3.

relevance how closely a search for an item matches the desired item, particularly when a SEARCH ENGINE is used in the World Wide Web (WWW).

religious issues disputes, often about SOFTWARE or HARDWARE, that seem vastly important to participants but are regarded as pointless by outsiders.

relocatable program a PROGRAM that is written so that it can be loaded and run in any set of consecutive memory addresses. The PERSONAL COMPUTER distinguishes such programs with the EXE EXTENSION letters, and during loading, address numbers within the program will be changed to suit the memory locations being used.

relocation the shifting of a program or other data from one set of memory ADDRESSes to another. See also BLOCK TRANSFER.

relocator a PROGRAM used in RELOCATION of another program. This loads the program data into memory, starting at any of a range of selected ADDRESSes. It then corrects each address in the program that refers to another address within the program so that the program can run.

REM a statement used in a BATCH FILE and also in some PROGRAMMING LANGUAGES to mark a REMARK line. A line that starts with REM in a program or batch file will be ignored and can thus be used as a documentation remark. This can be a very convenient way of temporarily disabling a command for testing purposes. For example, if you suspect that a NETWORK-loading command is causing trouble, it is possible to 'REM it out' by adding the word REM at the start of the line in the AUTOEXEC.BAT file and rebooting.

remark text within a program LINE (sense 4) that is ignored by the computer. See also REM.

remote (of a computer) at some distance away and connected by a link such as a SERIAL link or a NETWORK.

remote administration an option of NET WATCHER that allows a user to monitor the resources that are shared by another computer over a NETWORK.

remote control any device that allows something in computing to be operated at a distance, usually without connecting wires. Remote controls for TV receivers use infrared signals, and a few computers use remote-control KEYBOARDS that are linked to the main processor by infrared signals. Similarly, a MOUSE can be linked to the main system in this way because the ability to control a mouse free of connecting cables is much more important than being able to move a keyboard around while typing.

remote control program a UTILITY that allows one of two computers linked by a NETWORK or through a MODEM to control the other.

remote drive a DISK DRIVE that is used over a NETWORK rather than directly, as a LOCAL DRIVE would be.

remote echo a return of data to sender in a COMMUNICATIONS LINK as a way of confirming that the data has been received. Remote echo is useful only for text data because any other form of data would need to be interpreted by a program.

remote login making a connection to a remote computer so that it can be used as if it were local. See also TELNET.

remote printer a PRINTER that is used over a NETWORK rather than directly, as a LOCAL PRINTER would be.

remote server a NETWORK file-SERVER that is ONLINE (sense 2) by way of a MODEM.

remote user anyone who connects to a NETWORK by way of a MODEM and telephone lines or an ISDN link.

removable disk any disk, other than a FLOPPY DISK, that can be taken out and replaced. This allows for quick upgrading of HARD DRIVE capacity, simple BACKUP and easy movement of files from one machine to another.

removable hard drive a form of HARD DRIVE in which the drive is enclosed in a casing that can be removed from the framework of the drive. This type of drive can be used for BACKUP or as a SECURITY measure, allowing valuable data to be stored in a quite separate location, for example, a bank vault.

REN the MS-DOS command to RENAME a file. The form of the command is REN *Oldname Newname*.

rename an action that can be used to alter the FILENAME of a file.

rendering creating a three-dimensional image from a set of mathematical equations or conversion of a LINE ART drawing into a three-dimensional drawing by the addition of shading and colouring. See also RAY TRACING.

repagination the action of rearranging a document in a DTP program or a WORD PROCESSOR into pages following editing or after altering the proposed page size. The repagination action is normally automatic (*background repagination*), but it can be altered to manual repagination as an option.

repeat command see REDO COMMAND.

repeater an amplifier for signals that are being transmitted along a long line. The repeater will restore signal shapes that have become distorted because of the effect of the line.

repeating field a fault in the design of a DATABASE that requires the user to type the same material more than once.

repeating label character a WORKSHEET facility that allows a label to be created by repeating a character or set of characters. LOTUS 1-2-3 uses the BACKSLASH (\) character for this, so that using \> will result in the CELL being filled with >>>>>>>>>.

repeat key any KEY (sense 1) that will repeat its action when held down. On modern KEYBOARDS, all character keys will repeat; see TYPEMATIC ACTION.

repetitive algorithm a form of ALGORITHM in which a set of actions has to be repeated on data in order to obtain a result – usually the result from one run is used as the initial data for the next. The actions are repeated until the output of a run is almost identical to the input. See also ITERATION.

replication see DUPLICATION.

reply see FOLLOWUP.

report printed output from a DATABASE QUERY or a business application program. A simple report can be viewed on screen, but HARD COPY is more usual because of the amount of information that is likely to be contained.

report generator a program, which can be part of another program such as a DATABASE, that arranges data into a printable REPORT for display purposes.

report program a form of UTILITY that prints out information on a data file. This is usually quicker than any method that makes use of the main DATABASE handling program.

request to send (RTS) a signal used in RS-232 serial signalling to indicate to a REMOTE terminal that there is data to be sent to it.

requirements analysis the document that specifies what is expected of a SOFTWARE system.

rerun a repeat of a program run. A rerun is usually carried out to check data or to TEST (sense 2) for a fault in the program.

rescue dump a recording of data on to a disk when a CRASH (sense 1) occurs. If this can be programmed to take place automatically, then a crash of any type will not result in the loss of data. Large machines are often organized so that a rescue dump will be carried out if the main power supply fails or if the machine is switched off during operation.

reserved memory see UPPER MEMORY BLOCK.

reserved sector a SECTOR of a disk that is used for HOUSEKEEPING purposes, such as the disk DIRECTORY (sense 2). DOS will maintain such sectors, often located on the first track or first pair of tracks on the disk.

reserved word a word that is used in the operating system (OS) as a command and therefore cannot be used for other purposes, for example as a FILENAME or an IDENTIFIER.

reset 1. to restore anything in computing to its original state. **2.** to put the machine system into its normal or default CONFIGURATION. This can result in loss of data from a program.

reset button a BUTTON that, when used, applies a PULSE to the MICRO-PROCESSOR to cause a RESET (sense 2). This is sometimes referred to as a *hardware reset*, as distinct from a *software reset*, obtained by using a combination of keys (such as Ctrl-Alt-Del) or by an instruction within a program. The use of a hardware reset button is now out of favour with manufacturers.

resident always present in computing memory as distinct from having to be loaded in from tape or disk. For example, a portable machine may be described as having a 'resident' operating system (OS). See also TSR PROGRAM.

resident routine a program that remains in memory and can be run either continuously or at intervals. The operating system (OS) depends on such routines; see also TSR PROGRAM.

resident software software that is held permanently in memory. This may be in ROM or in CMOS RAM, which is permanently connected to the machine. The smallest sizes of portable machines use software that is resident, including the operating system (OS).

resistor an electronic component that has resistance to the flow of electric current, used to dissipate energy.

resizing the alteration of scale of a GRAPHICS image. Images that are drawn by VECTOR GRAPHICS methods can be resized indefinitely without loss of detail, but BITMAP images cannot. When images are resized for the purposes of a DTP page, the amount of resizing is usually fairly small and the limitations of the bitmap representation are not so severe. In some DTP programs, a KEY COMBINATION can be held down while resizing to ensure that the RESOLUTION of the picture is as high as possible – this allows only certain suitable sizes to be used.

resolution or **definition** a measure of the fineness of detail that can be seen on a screen, often quoted in terms of the number of PIXELs that can be controlled. These are specified in two numbers, of which one represents the number across the screen and the other is the number down the screen. For example, 640 across by 480 down represents the standard resolution VGA display. This figure means that a total of 640 x 480 = 307,200 pixels can be controlled. If a two-colour system (see FORE-GROUND, sense 1, BACKGROUND, sense 1) is used, one BIT will be needed to control each pixel, and with 8 bits per BYTE this will require 38,400 bytes of memory. If 24-bit colour (3 bytes per pixel) is being used, the memory requirement for a full screen becomes 921,600 bytes. See Fig. 39.

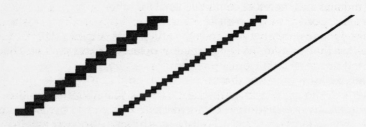

Fig. 39. **Resolution**. A good test of resolution is to draw a diagonal line. Low-resolution displays make such a line too jagged, and only high-definition displays will produce a line that looks smooth.

resolver a set of software routines that are used to guide conversion of a HOSTNAME to an INTERNET ADDRESS.

resource any part of memory, drives, programs or linked files that can be used in the course of running a program (see DLL).

response the reply made to any interrogation of a DATABASE or any reply message on the screen following an entry from the keyboard.

response time the time that is needed for a system to respond to some stimulus, normally used of systems that include a mechanical action because the response times for electronic systems are very rapid.

restart see WARM BOOT.

RESTORE a DOS program used for recovering data that has been backed up by the DOS BACKUP program. The WINDOWS versions of the backup program do not use a separate restore program; you CLICK (sense 1) either the backup button or the restore button for the action you want to use.

restricted data access a SECURITY scheme for a DATABASE or a NETWORK. Data is classed in degrees of security, and users are allocated an ACCESS LEVEL number that will determine which degree of data they can use. Very often, only users with the highest levels of ACCESS (sense 1) are permitted to alter data.

retrieval the recovery of data from storage, particularly in a DATABASE.

Return key the key that is marked with a bent arrow and is used to terminate any DOS COMMAND or to enter typed data. The key marked *Enter* on the NUMBERPAD carries out the same action.

reverse alphabetized list see ALPHABETIZE.

reverse engineering analysis of a program in order to discover the principles that it uses. Reverse engineering is used generally so as to create a CLONE program that will present the same appearance and working principles as another program, and its use can lead to a legal action if the resulting product is too similar (see LOOK AND FEEL) to the original. In some cases, reverse engineering is necessary even when a program is innovative because it must of necessity conform to certain presentation standards such as MICROSOFT WINDOWS.

reverse polish notation (RPN) or **post-fix notation** a system of arranging instructions and data in which the data is listed first. In a calculator that uses the RPN system, for example, the more familiar command sequence of 3 x 2 = would be replaced by 3 2 x.

reverse video see INVERSE VIDEO.

revert the action of using an earlier version. Several DTP and other programs allow for *reversion* to the last recorded file or the most recent backup in the event that a document is changed too drastically to re-edit.

revision a minor release of software that incorporates some new features.

rewind to wind a backup tape back to its start – this is normally automatic.

RF (radio frequency) an old term for any frequency of electromagnetic wave that could be broadcast from an aerial. This is usually taken to refer to any frequency above 100 kHz.

RFI (radio frequency interference) the unwanted noise signals generated by a computer that interfere with radio and TV reception. Conversely, the interference produced from some radios and TV receivers may cause computer malfunction.

RF modulator see MODULATOR (sense 1).

RGB (red-green-blue) one of the methods of specifying a colour in terms of the relative amounts of three primary colours of light. A suitable mix of all three provides white light. A MONITOR (sense 2) that requires separate R, G and B signals is called an *RGB monitor* and cannot be used with a COMPOSITE VIDEO signal (such as from a video recorder) unless a separate composite input socket is present. The RGB system is used to obtain the highest possible resolution from a monitor. See also CMY; HUE, SATURATION, BRIGHTNESS.

ribbon cable a cable with a large number of connecting wires that are laid flat rather than being compacted into a circular form. The flat form reduces interference between signals.

rich text format see RTF.

right brace or **right curly bracket** the } character, ASCII 125. See also LEFT BRACE.

right bracket or **right parenthesis** the) character, ASCII 41. See also LEFT BRACKET.

right click the action of clicking (see CLICK, sense 1) the right-hand (secondary) MOUSE button. A few programs use this BUTTON for special actions, but Microsoft WINDOWS 95 onwards has standardized the use of a right-button click to make a MENU appear. The nature of the menu depends on the position of the mouse POINTER (sense 1) at the time when the button is clicked.

right curly bracket see RIGHT BRACE.

right justification the arrangement of text so that the right-hand edge is aligned, used for placing an address over to the right-hand side of a document. See also JUSTIFY.

right parenthesis see RIGHT BRACKET.

rights the actions that are available to a NETWORK user as a result of his/her PRIVILEGE LEVEL.

right shift a CURSOR-CONTROL key that causes the CURSOR to be moved to the right and is usually marked with a right-pointing arrow. Modern programs often use the MOUSE for this purpose, but see NUDGE.

right square bracket the] character, ASCII 93. See also LEFT SQUARE BRACKET.

right tab a TAB STOP placed at the right-hand side of a page. Typing characters at a right tab will insert each character so that the typed phrase is ranged right against the stop position.

ring see CAMBRIDGE RING; CIRCULAR FILE.

ring array see ARRAY (sense 1).

ring-back system a method of contacting a REMOTE computer. This method is used by some BULLETIN BOARDs and also for enforcing SECURITY. In the example of a bulletin board, you first ring the number and let it ring twice. You then hang up, prepare the MODEM and ring again. This time you will get the tone that indicates that a computer is ONLINE. This system is used in particular by a number of part-time bulletin board operators so as to distinguish calls that need to ACCESS (sense 2) the bulletin board from ordinary telephone calls on the same number. When used as a security method, it is the remote computer operator who rings back a number that has been supplied by the originator of the call. This discourages hacking unless the HACKER (sense 3) has managed to re-route calls through another number. See also PASSWORD.

ring indicator a signal that shows that an incoming call to a MODEM is being received.

ring network a form of NETWORK in which each TERMINAL is connected to two others in a ring. See also STAR NETWORK.

ripple-through the effect in a WORKSHEET of making one change to a CELL that affects a large number of other cells. For example, a change that causes the contents of a cell to become zero can cause an ERROR MESSAGE (ERR) to appear in cells that contain FORMULAE using the contents of the cell as a divisor.

RISC (reduced instruction set computer) a computer designed around a MICROPROCESSOR CHIP with a very limited range of instruction codes The set contains only the most used instructions, which are arranged to be performed very rapidly, and more complex actions are obtained by using software at the cost of comparatively slower execution. The advantage as compared to the more usual complex instruction set computer (CISC) is speed, but if programming requires a large number of complex actions, the speed advantage of the RISC can be eroded.

river a fault in document editing that lines up blank spaces so that they appear to form a column. See also HYPHEN LADDER.

RLE (run-length encoding) a well-established method of compressing files (see COMPRESSED FILE) that contain long sequences of repeated characters, particularly GRAPHICS files. Each run of repeated characters can be replaced by a single character and the number of repetitions.

RLL (run-length limited) a form of DISK DRIVE recording system used for a HARD DRIVE that permits tighter packing of data than the MODIFIED FREQUENCY MODULATION system. See also ADVANCED RUN LENGTH LIMITED.

RMDIR (RD) the DOS command that is used to delete a DIRECTORY (sense 1). The directory must not be CURRENT (sense 2) and must not contain any SUBDIRECTORY. The later DOS command DELTREE will delete a directory that contains subdirectories.

RO see RECEIVE-ONLY TERMINAL.

robot any device that can be programmed, possesses some sensing functions and carries out mechanical actions.

robotics the study of ROBOT systems, incorporating many of the systems that are also of interest in ARTIFICIAL INTELLIGENCE.

robust program a program or a system with the ability to resist a CRASH (sense 1). A robust program is one that you can use with confidence, knowing that if your little finger accidentally brushes against the BREAK or ESCAPE KEY, you won't lose either the program or your data. A robust program is particularly important for inexperienced operators and in educational use. The most robust programs require that the operating system and the program itself be in ROM form, but this is now rare.

rogue value see TERMINATOR (sense 1).

role indicator a specialized code in data retrieval for the type of data that is to be recovered, allowing the data to be recovered selectively.

roller-feed scanner a type of SCANNER, typified by the *Logitech PowerPage*, that rolls a sheet of paper through a small rectangular box of page width. This system can permit precise scanning for OCR (sense 2) or

GRAPHICS illustration purposes, and can be used as a photocopier and FAX machine if the other hardware is present (PRINTER and FAX MODEM).

rollover see KEY ROLLOVER.

ROM (read-only memory) a type of MEMORY CHIP whose contents are permanent and cannot be altered by writing data nor by switching off power. ROM is used for storing essential code, such as the BIOS for DOS, so that the code can be run at the instant when the machine is switched on. The advantage of using ROM is that its contents are incorruptible; the disadvantage is that any errors cannot be changed except by plugging in a new ROM. See also MASKED ROM; PROM.

roman (of a FONT) containing letters of unemphasized normal type, as distinct from BOLD or ITALIC.

root directory the main DIRECTORY (sense 1) of a HARD DRIVE or FLOPPY DISK, which contains both data or program files and any subdirectory files. See also TREE (sense 2).

root name the main part of a DOS FILENAME, consisting of up to eight characters. This can be preceded by a PATHNAME and ended with an EXTENSION.

roping a MONITOR (sense 2) fault in which straight lines appear twisted.

rot-13 a simple ENCRYPTION method in which each character is replaced by one that is 13 places farther on in the ASCII number set (allowing the number 33 to follow the number 127 in a circular sequence), used in INTERNET communications to conceal text that some viewers might prefer not to see.

rotated-bar graph a form of BAR GRAPH that has been rotated so that the bars and the Y-AXIS are horizontal.

rotated type text in a WORD PROCESSOR, DTP or GRAPHICS program that has been rotated from its normal horizontal orientation.

rotation the revolving of text or an IMAGE (sense 2) in a GRAPHICS or DTP program. This is often slow unless a very fast processor is used. See also MATRIX ROTATION.

rotation tool the ICON in a GRAPHICS program that allows an OBJECT to be rotated. The amount of rotation can be controlled by dragging (see DRAG) the MOUSE or by typing a number of degrees of angle.

RO terminal see RECEIVE-ONLY TERMINAL.

roughs preliminary sketches or prints for a DTP layout.

rounding the adjusting of a number to a value that contains fewer places of decimals. This is done by adding or subtracting a very small fraction. For example, 4.9999999 can be rounded to 5.0 or 4.000000001 to 4.0. Rounding has to be carried out automatically when a REAL NUMBER has been stored because such storage is always in an approximate form. See also PRECISION OF NUMBER.

round-trip time the time for a PACKET to be sent to and returned from a remote HOST, using PING.

router a connecting device for NETWORKS that passes signals between networks only when the networks use identical PROTOCOLS.

routine a part of a program that carries out some complete action. A complete program can be built up from a number of linked but separate routines, in which case the program is said to be *modular*.

row recalculation a form of WORKSHEET action in which values of FOR-MULAE are recalculated row by row. See also COLUMN RECALCULATION.

rows and columns an arrangement of text displayed on the screen. The row number is the number of the line of text, starting from the top of the screen. The column number indicates the position of a character along from the left-hand side of the screen. Similar numbering is used for GRAPHICS, but the row number is then usually called the Y-COORDINATE and the column number the X-COORDINATE. For graphics, some applications use Y-coordinates, starting at the bottom of the screen (like a conventional graph), but most use a starting position at the top of the screen.

RPN see REVERSE POLISH NOTATION.

RS-232 the old-established system that is used for ASYNCHRONOUS SERIAL transmission of data. The connections and signals are standardized, but few manufacturers of the smaller computers pay much attention to the standards, with the result that few microcomputing RS-232 devices can be connected with any degree of confidence. The RS-232 signal consists of a START BIT, which is used to signal the start of a BYTE of data, followed by 7 or 8 BITS of data and then by one or two STOP BITS. If only ASCII codes are used for data, with no PARITY checking, then 7 data bits can be used. The precise number of bits of data and of stop bits forms part of the PRO-TOCOL (sense 1) for the transmission. See also BAUD RATE; RS-422/423/449.

RS-422/423/449 varieties of SERIAL interface standards for distances up to 1000 feet. The RS-449 is the recommended standard for future serial ports and incorporates the methods of RS-422 and RS-423.

RSN (record sequencing number) a number allocated to each RECORD of a DATABASE in the sequence of entry.

RTF (rich text format) a form of WORD PROCESSOR file that contains only ASCII codes but conveys all the commands that would be contained in a coded file with FORMATTING BYTES. RTF is useful for passing formatted files between different computer types and for SERIAL communicated documents but is being superseded by HTML.

RTS see REQUEST TO SEND.

rubber banding see ELASTIC BANDING.

rule or **ruler** or **ruler guide** a scale marked with character positions for WORD PROCESSOR or DTP use. The scale shows the position of each character in a line and is normally displayed at the top of the screen. Some word processor programs allow a selection of rules, with each one used to display different information about the text as well as indicating positions.

ruler, ruler guide see RULE.

run 1. one complete execution of a program. **2.** to command the execution of a program.

runaround see FLOW CONTROL.

run-length encoding see RLE.

run-length limited see RLL.

running foot see FOOTER.

running head see HEADER (sense 1).

run-time environment a set of library routines (see LIBRARY FUNCTION) that provide the most frequently used actions that a program needs when running.

run-time error a programming ERROR that becomes obvious only when the program is run and cannot be detected beforehand.

run-time system a program that must be present in the memory in order to allow another program to run (sometimes used of a partial system, in the sense that a demonstration may be supplied in a limited form which cannot be used for any other purpose).

R/W video disc a form of COMPACT DISC that can be written by the computer as well as read by it. This normally uses MAGNETO-OPTICAL RECORDING methods. See also WORM.

S

safe format see QUICKFORMAT.

safety-critical system any system whose failure can have catastrophic results.

safety net an emergency provision. This usually denotes a system that will save data in the event of a system CRASH (sense 1). See also RECOVERY SYSTEM; RESCUE DUMP; RERUN.

Sage a Newcastle-based SOFTWARE HOUSE specializing in bookkeeping and accounts programs.

sampling rate the rate of digitizing information (see DIGITIZE) by measuring the AMPLITUDE, or other characteristic of a signal, many times per second. Each measurement is converted into BINARY number form, and this set of numbers comprises the digitized data. For example, high-quality sound is digitized by sampling at around 44,000 times per second.

sans serif a FONT design in which the characters lack SERIF (sense 1) embellishments.

satellite a TERMINAL or NODE connected to the SERVER in a NETWORK.

saturation an attribute of colour. The saturation of a colour is defined as the percentage of pure HUE in a colour, since natural colours are never pure but diluted with white. Strong colours are more saturated than pale colours. See also LUMINANCE.

save 1. the action of recording a file on to a disk or to a backup tape. A file that has not been saved and which exists only in the memory will be lost when the machine is switched off. **2. (SAVE)** a command used by many programs that will cause a file to be recorded on disk. The use of SAVE implies that a FILENAME has already been supplied (see SAVE AS). Some programs require a separate CLOSE command to remove the file from memory.

Save All a MICROSOFT WORD command that will save all active documents and also their TEMPLATE files.

SAVE AS a file command used in many APPLICATIONS PROGRAMS to specify a name to use when saving a new file or to save an existing file under a new name. Some programs do not require a FILENAME to be supplied initially, and a SAVE AS command is used by DEFAULT.

save generic a WORD PROCESSOR command to save a file in ASCII form with no hidden codes. Most word processors provide SAVE (sense 1) and SAVE AS commands that allow a choice of file form.

sawtooth distortion see ALIASING (sense 1).

scaleable font a FONT that can be used in any of its range of sizes without distortion either on SCREEN (sense 1) or on the PRINTER. The most common form for WINDOWS use is TRUETYPE. See also BITMAPPED FONT; OUTLINE FONT.

scaling 1. an adjustment to the size of an OBJECT in a GRAPHICS program or an object embedded in a WORD PROCESSOR document or DTP page. **2.** the increase or reduction in size of an IMAGE (sense 2) by a factor, the *scaling factor*. Scaling will be uniform if the scaling factor is the same in each direction, but if the X-scaling factor is not the same as the Y-scaling factor the image will be distorted. **3.** an adjustment to a GRAPH range so that a set of figures in a table will make use of all of the permitted area of the graph. Scaling can be used by SPREADSHEET and PRESENTATION GRAPHICS programs.

scan 1. to move an electron beam over the face of a CRT or to operate LCD cells in turn on an LCD screen. See also RASTER. **2.** to check each item of data in a DATABASE to find if it belongs to a set that is to be accessed. **3.** to use a SCANNER on a paper document so that it is converted into a document file. **4.** to check connections to a KEYBOARD, using software, to find which KEY (sense 1) is pressed.

scan code the number code that is generated when a KEY (sense 1) on the KEYBOARD is pressed. The BIOS program will convert this scan code into ASCII code.

ScanDisk a UTILITY that is part of Microsoft WINDOWS 95 onwards and was also used in earlier versions of Windows. ScanDisk will test the HARD DRIVE (or a FLOPPY DISK) to check that the medium is capable of recording and holding data and will lock out any portions that are unsuitable. The ScanDisk utility can be run automatically as part of other actions, such as SYSTEM AGENT or DRIVESPACE.

scan line the line traced out on a SCREEN (sense 1) by a single horizontal SCAN (sense 1).

scanner a device that will convert an image on paper into DIGITAL signals that can be stored and manipulated in a computer. Small hand-held scanners have to be pulled down or across the image while larger roller types allow a page to be fed in, and flatbed machines allow the scanning of sheets or book pages. The FAX machine uses a roller scanner system to DIGITIZE an image, and scanners are also an important part of a DTP system in order to produce images to print. Colour scanners with resolution figures up to 1200 DPI are now available, permitting a very high standard of reproduction of images but requiring large resources of MEMORY and HARD DRIVE space.

scanning 1. the action of using a SCANNER on a page of paper. **2.** the action of drawing a picture on the face of a CRT or LCD SCREEN (sense 1). The electron beam produces a small spot of light, and this is moved from left to right (*horizontal scanning*) and from top to bottom (*vertical* *scanning*) at speeds that are high enough to provide an illusion of a completely lit screen or RASTER.

SCART a form of connector found mainly on TV receivers, satellite decoders and video recorders to allow interconnection, and for connections to and from computer and laser-disc players. The SCART connector uses a standard format and carries stereo sound signals as well as the video signals.

scattered file a file whose bytes are held in disk SECTORs at various parts of a disk which are not CONTIGUOUS.

scatter graph a GRAPH in which each pair of COORDINATES is plotted as a point, with no attempt to draw lines between points. The interpretation of the graph depends on how the points appear – they may be arranged in one or more clusters or in a nearly straight line, for example.

scenario a set of WORKSHEETs that shows the results of different assumptions obtained by using different values in one set of CELLs. For example, a scenario might show worst case, average and best case assumptions for a business plan.

schedule a LIST of order of execution of tasks.

schema a summary of all the stored items of data in a DATABASE.

scientific notation a method of expressing a number in MANTISSA EXPONENT form. For example, the number 213,000 can be expressed as 2.13E5 or 2.13 x 105, meaning 2.13 multiplied by ten to the power 5.

scissoring cropping an image by enclosing the wanted portion in a SELECTION BOX or LASSO. The name comes from the ICON of a pair of scissors that usually appears in the TOOLBOX for this action. See also GRAPHIC BOUNDARY.

scissors tool a method of SELECTION used in PAINT and DTP programs. Selecting the scissors tool allows a SELECTION BOX to be drawn, and the objects within the box can be cut, deleted or copied.

SCO Unix a form of the UNIX operating system (OS) originating in the Santa Cruz Operation branch of MICROSOFT.

scrambling the encoding of data so that it is difficult for an unauthorized person to decode. The term originally denoted sound signals, in which frequency ranges were inverted so as to make the sounds unintelligible and now usually denotes methods of coding and regrouping data bits into unintelligible bytes.

scrap a portion of a DOCUMENT that can be saved as a separate file. In Microsoft WINDOWS 95 onwards a scrap is created when some text in a document is selected and then dragged (see DRAG) to the DESKTOP. The scrap can then be dragged to other programs or documents.

scratch to wipe out anything. The term is used in the disk systems of computers to mean deletion of a file.

scratchfile a temporary file on disk. This will usually be deleted after use or by the recording of the next scratchfile. Compare PERMANENT FILE.

scratchpad see NOTEBOOK.

screen 1. the viewed surface of a CRT or LCD unit that displays text and graphics. **2.** a printing process for reproducing HALFTONE images. The image is photographed through a glass screen that is etched with lines so that the image is broken up into tiny dots. The printing process will render all these dots as black (or FOREGROUND, sense 1, colour), but varying the sizes of the dots and the number of black dots in each group produces the effect of shading. The process is satisfactory only if the number of dots per linear inch is 1200 or more.

screen capture or **capture** the action of creating and saving a file of the current SCREEN (sense 1) image. This is a useful way of obtaining illustrations for a manual dealing with software. When WINDOWS is being used, the PRINT SCREEN KEY acts as a screen capture method, but a GRAPHICS program is needed to read the image from the CLIPBOARD and to save it as a file.

screen dump the copying of the image on a screen to a printer or to a file, accomplished by a screen-dump program that is memory-resident (see TSR PROGRAM) and can be called into action using a HOT KEY.

screen editing an editing system that allows you to load a file and alter anything that is visible on the screen before saving the file again. See EDIT; FULL-SCREEN EDITING.

screen editor an EDITOR program that presents the lines of text on the full screen or in a WINDOW, as distinct from LINE EDITING.

screen elements the portions of a WINDOWS display, such as scroll bars, message boxes, borders, buttons, etc.

screen flicker see FLICKER.

screen font a FONT as displayed on the SCREEN (sense 1). At one time all screen fonts were bitmapped (see BITMAPPED FONT) so that the appearance of text on screen did not match the appearance of printed output. The use of TRUETYPE fonts (an OUTLINE FONT system) ensures that screen fonts are a perfect match for printer fonts.

screen memory MEMORY that is used to store data for the screen display. On PC computers, this is separate from the main RAM of the computer and is placed on the GRAPHICS ADAPTER board. The amount of RAM can range from a minimum of 250 kilobytes to more than 8 megabytes, depending on the RESOLUTION that can be used and the number of BITS used for colour information.

screen page the page of about 25 lines (depending on FONT size) that can be displayed on the SCREEN (sense 1). This is smaller than the number of lines (40 to 60) that can be printed on a page of paper. See also PAGE UP/PAGE DOWN KEYS.

screen reader a UTILITY that converts text (sometimes only ASCII text) on screen (sense 1) into audible speech (sometimes with a *Dalek* accent).

screen saver a UTILITY program that comes into operation after a selected time interval and displays a moving image on the screen. This avoids burning a permanent static image on to the screen. See also MARQUEE (sense 1).

script 1. a form of type that resembles handwriting. **2.** a file of instructions in text (ASCII) form that can be used to automate a task such as making a connection with a REMOTE computer over telephone lines using a MODEM.

scripting language a form of PROGRAMMING LANGUAGE, such as MS-DOS BATCH FILE language, that is used to create a SCRIPT (sense 2) that will modify the action of a running program rather than be used for writing programs that can stand alone.

scroll to shift lines of text up the screen so that a new line always appears at the foot. When the screen is clear, commands that print text will normally place text on the top line of the screen, taking a new line down as each line fills. When the screen is filled with text, the scroll action moves each line up the screen so that the top line is lost and the most recent line appears at the bottom. TEXT EDITOR and WORD PROCESSOR programs allow this scroll action to be controlled easily by the user and also provide for *inverse scrolling* so that lines of text scrolled out of sight can be recovered. Very rapid scrolling can make text unreadable so that paging is needed (see PAGE, sense 1). Some applications permit *horizontal scrolling* as well as *vertical scrolling*.

scroll arrow an arrow or, more usually, arrowhead that can be clicked (see CLICK, sense 1) to make the screen SCROLL in the direction of the arrow.

scroll bar a bar shape at the side and/or foot of the SCREEN (sense 1) that contains a MARKER box. Movement of the marker by dragging (see DRAG) the MOUSE will SCROLL the screen.

scroll box or **scroll handle** the small black box in a SCROLL BAR that can be dragged to SCROLL the SCREEN (sense 1).

scrub to delete, remove or wipe out data.

SCSI (small computer systems interface) a system for connecting the computer to disk drives and other peripherals. The SCSI system allows for very fast data transfer between a variety of peripherals and the main computer. See also EIDE; IDE.

SCSI ID the number used to identify a SCSI device in a chain, typically a number between 0 and 31 on a modern system. Number 7 is reserved for the computer (the SCSI *host*). Other devices have their ID number set using switches.

SDRAM (synchronous dynamic random access memory) a type of fast DRAM that uses a separate CLOCK signal in addition to the normal control signals.

Seagate Technology a well-known manufacturer of HARD DRIVES and other storage and BACKUP peripherals.

search to look through text for a given letter, word or phrase (see SEARCH AND REPLACE) or (in programming) to check a LIST of data items to find an item that corresponds to a description. See also SORT (sense 1).

search and replace or **find and replace** or **selective search** an action common in TEXT EDITORS and WORD PROCESSORS that allows a letter, word or phrase to be found in a text and replaced with something else. This has to be used with care – it's easy to command that each 'smith' should be replaced by 'jones', but when you find words like 'blackjones' appearing you realize that the computer carries out these actions in a completely unthinking way. Most word processors allow the action to be *global* or *selective*. A *global search and replace* will find each occurrence of a word and replace it by the specified word. A *selective search and replace* will find each occurrence as before but will prompt the user to make a Yes or No decision on replacement.

search engine a program running on a large computer that allows searches for words and phrases over the INTERNET. One of the best known is ALTA VISTA.

search path the directory PATH designated for a SEARCH action. An operating system (OS) will usually allow a FILENAME or a piece of text to be searched for along a specific path, since this is much faster than searching the whole of a HARD DISK.

search string the set of characters that are to be found in a SEARCH action.

SECAM system the system of encoding colour information invented by Henri de France and used for colour TV systems in France, French colonies and Eastern Europe. See also NTSC; PAL-TV SYSTEM.

secondary cache see SECOND LEVEL CACHE.

secondary storage any form of STORAGE that is not directly addressed by the CPU. This includes HARD DRIVE, FLOPPY DISK, CD-ROM and any other PERIPHERAL storage. See also PRIMARY STORAGE.

second generation computer a computer, usually dated between 1955 and 1965, that uses TRANSISTORS and magnetic ring CORE MEMORY, with tape used for the BACKING STORE.

second level cache or **level 2 cache** a CACHE that is larger and slower then the LEVEL 1 CACHE and usually placed on the MOTHERBOARD.

second source an alternative supplier for a product.

section a portion of text in a WORD PROCESSOR that can be treated separately from other text. For example, text might be placed into a separate section so that it could be formatted (see FORMAT, sense 2) differently, using a different page size or page numbering style.

sector a portion of a disk TRACK. A disk track is a circle on the disk surface, and the circle is magnetically divided into a number of sectors, ten or more sectors per track. Each sector will then store a set number of bytes, usually 512. Programs or items of data that need less than a sector will nevertheless use the complete sector because the disk system does not work in units of less than one sector. The sector size of a HARD DRIVE is the same as that of a floppy, but sectors are grouped into CLUSTERs.

sectoring hole a method of locating the first SECTOR of all the TRACKs on the old 5.25-inch type of FLOPPY DISK. The sectoring hole is a small-diameter hole that is punched in the disk and also in the jacket. This hole is located at a distance from the HUB, which is clear of the innermost track on the disk. As the disk rotates, these holes will line up at some point. By passing a beam of light through the hole, detected by a PHOTOCELL, the drive can sense the position of this hole and establish the position of the first sector. The more modern 3.5-inch disks use no sectoring holes because the hub locates in a fixed position because of a flat portion, allowing the sectoring position to be a fixed point on the hub shaft of the drive. See HARD SECTORING; SOFT SECTORING.

sector interleaving see INTERLEAVING (sense 2).

secure connection a link to a site on the World Wide Web (WWW) that uses ENCRYPTION to ensure that personal data is not available to unauthorized persons. Your BROWSER will usually notify you when you are entering or leaving a secure connection.

security the safeguarding of computer systems against damage to HARDWARE, program software or data software. The risks to hardware are the usual hazards of fire, flood and malicious damage. For large computers, an air-conditioning system must be present to ensure that temperature, humidity and dust are all controlled, and any failure of this system can also cause damage to the COMPUTER SYSTEM. The program software is also vulnerable to the same hazards as the hardware and in addition to several others. Software for small machines is generally OFF-THE-SHELF and comparatively easy to replace, but it should nevertheless be backed up by copies unless it has been supplied on CD-ROM. If a program, the cost of which is a substantial fraction of the price of the hardware, cannot be backed up or can be backed up only to a limited extent, it should not be used. Promises by the manufacturers that damaged software can be replaced in 24 hours should be disregarded. Several backup copies of important software and data must be kept, but they need to be accessible. Although out-of-date data is better than nothing, it could represent a lot of effort if it had all to be updated following the loss of disks, particularly if the paperwork from which the data was derived had also been lost, as it often is in the course of a fire. The other hazard for data software is interference resulting in the CORRUPTION or copying of data. Corruption can sometimes be accidental, a result of a program fault, but malicious damage is more usual. For small systems, a considerable improvement in security results from using machines with no built-in FLOPPY-DISK drives. These can be networked to a file SERVER that can be fitted with a removable floppy drive, to be used only when new software is loaded. Where a computer makes extensive use of public telephone lines, the COMMUNICATIONS LINK should be a secure one, demanding a PASSWORD of every REMOTE user and restricting full file access to a few users only. Perfect security is impossible, but many computer users do not take even the most elementary precautions, treating their system as so many treat a car, leaving it unlocked and with the ignition keys inside. Even the most elementary precautions are useful, and concentrating on the fact that most computer fraud is internal should make it easier to direct attention to the most obvious points.

seek to move the head of a DISK DRIVE from one TRACK to another.

seek area a restricted portion of a file, a disk or a part of memory that is to be searched for specified data.

seek time 1. the time required to find specified data. **2.** the time needed for the READ/WRITE HEAD of a HARD DRIVE to find the correct TRACK on a disk to read or write data.

segment 1. a portion of straight line created by a GRAPHICS editor that is a separate OBJECT so that it can be moved or resized independently of other line segments. For example, a square might be drawn as a square, which is a single object, or as four line segments that can be moved independently. **2.** a 64-kilobyte unit of memory used by the INTEL microprocessors in order to maintain COMPATIBILITY with older designs.

segmentation fault an error that results in a program making use of memory that is allocated to another program, causing a CRASH.

segmented addressing the system used on early INTEL processors such as the 8088 and available on later types for the sake of COMPATIBILITY. Segmenting uses memory in 64-kilobyte SEGMENTs (sense 2) rather than as one continuous range.

select to mark out a piece of text or graphics for some action. In a WORD PROCESSOR, CAD, PAINT or DTP program, *selecting* can be used to choose text or graphics for deletion, moving, copying or other actions.

selectable of any option that can be chosen. *Hardware-selectable* implies that a choice can be made by setting switches or JUMPERs; *software-selectable* implies that selection can be made by way of menus or commands within a program.

selection the marking out of a piece of data in a WORD PROCESSOR, a RANGE in a WORKSHEET or a set of records in a DATABASE so that the complete BLOCK (sense 2) can be deleted, copied or moved. See also LASSO; RANGE OF CELLS; SCISSORS TOOL.

selection box a rectangle that marks out a selection. The selection box is usually dotted or coloured to distinguish it from a box that might be a graphics IMAGE (sense 2).

selective search see SEARCH AND REPLACE.

selective sort a method of sorting large files on disk. The program picks out items in the order of the sort (numerical order, ASCII code order, etc.)

and places the data into another file. This second file will be in the correct sorted order. The speed of sorting is slow because the process is INPUT-BOUND and OUTPUT-BOUND by the speed of disk ACCESS (sense 2). For very large amounts of data, however, that could not be held in RAM, this is a preferred method.

self-checking code a set of bytes of a program or of data that contains redundant bytes that are used for checking the integrity of the code. This is a more elaborate form of PARITY.

self-extracting archive a type of COMPRESSED FILE that can be extracted by clicking its WINDOWS FILENAME.

self-indexing file a file that contains reference numbers that can be used as an index to a main file.

self-learning (of an EXPERT SYSTEM) capable of adding new information to its data bank automatically when a question to the user results in a reply that illustrates a new rule or an extension of KNOWLEDGE.

self-parking heads a system used in all modern HARD DRIVES in which the heads PARK automatically when power is switched off. See also STEPPING MOTOR; VOICE-COIL DRIVE.

self-relocating code code for a program that can be loaded into any part of the memory and which can then change any ADDRESS (sense 1) numbers that form part of the code so as to refer to the correct range of memory. The program files that carry the EXTENSION of EXE for the IBM PC type of computer are self-relocating.

self-test a system of testing equipment by using signals and checking the response, applied in particular to a MODEM.

semantic pertaining to meaning, used particularly in ARTIFICIAL INTELLIGENCE.

semantic error an ERROR caused by the use of an incorrect symbol in an instruction.

semantic network a type of GRAPH diagram that represents data and the connections between data items.

semi-automatic text flow a DTP method of placing text one paragraph at a time. The text will be entered starting at the CURSOR position and will flow into its column space until all the paragraph has been entered. The next paragraph must be entered by moving the cursor and clicking (see CLICK, sense 1) the MOUSE button again.

semicolon the ; PUNCTUATION MARK that can used as a SEPARATOR between FIELDS or items that are to be placed in a TABLE. See also TEXT TO TABLE.

semiconductor a type of material whose electrical characteristics can be controlled by the addition of very small amounts of impurities. The intense study of semiconductors by the Bell Laboratories in the USA in the 1920s and 1930s led to the invention of the transistor in 1948, and this in turn led to the development of ICs. Currently, the most favoured semiconductor material is the element SILICON.

semiconductor laser a miniature and low-power form of LASER. This makes use of the same principle as the LED. Semiconductor lasers are particularly suited as laser sources to be used with FIBRE OPTICS and are found in COMPACT DISC players and CD-ROM drives.

semi-processed data data entered into a computer that is not totally RAW DATA but has been sorted or checked in some way.

Send To an option in the File menu of Microsoft WINDOWS 95 onwards. When Send To is clicked, a selected document is routed to a destination, with the DEFAULT being the floppy drive. By configuring this option, MICROSOFT OUTLOOK can be used to route the current document to any destination that makes use of EMAIL.

send to back a GRAPHICS action that will hide an OBJECT behind other objects that overlap its position. See also BRING TO FRONT.

sense to detect the state of a hardware switch or connection or a software BIT or BYTE.

sensor an electronic device that can detect a physical quantity such as temperature, humidity, vibration, strain, etc., giving an electrical output related to the amount of the quantity being detected.

sensor glove an image that appears in VIRTUAL REALITY displays to represent the user's hand.

sentinel a flag or MARKER (sense 1) that can be sensed by a program.

separated graphics GRAPHICS characters with spaces between them. Graphics characters drawn on a character block that is smaller than the allowable size, such as using 7 x 7 instead of 8 x 8, will be printed with a space at one side and at the top or bottom. When a set of such characters is printed in adjacent screen positions, the spaces will separate the graphics characters just as they normally separate text characters. Compare CONTIGUOUS GRAPHICS.

separator any character, typically a COMMA or TAB CHARACTER, used to separate data of different types in a LIST.

separator sheet a blank sheet of paper ejected from a printer in order to separate documents that are being printed in sequence.

SEQUEL see STRUCTURED QUERY LANGUAGE.

sequence an arrangement of items that ensures that the items are dealt with in order. A SORT (sense 1) is a method that is employed to put data into a sequence of ascending or descending value.

sequencer a program used to edit MIDI files so that notes can be rearranged or played.

sequential of or relating to anything following a sequence; one by one.

sequential access allowing ACCESS (sense 2) to a number of items one by one in order. See SERIAL FILE.

sequential file a file that is arranged so that it can be read in a specified order.

sequential processing see SERIAL PROCESSING.

serial of or relating to anything using one BIT at a time in data transmission. For instance, many serial transmissions use the RS-232 system, and a set of PROTOCOLs (sense 1) must be specified. For example, an 8-bit BYTE might be transmitted using 11 bits, with 1 bit to indicate the start, then 8 bits of the byte and 2 bits to indicate the end. The protocol will also specify whether or not PARITY is used and, if so, whether even or odd. Serial RS-232 communication is possible only if both transmitter and receiver are using the same protocols.

serial file a file on tape or on disk in which the items are recorded one after the other with one FILENAME. When this file is read, the whole file must be replayed because there is no method of obtaining any one item separate from the others. Disk systems permit some form of RANDOM ACCESS FILE to be used in addition to serial filing. Although serial files are simple to set up and use, altering such a file is time-consuming. To add, delete or change an item, the file must be read, amended and saved again. The use of serial files makes a computer program INPUT-BOUND and OUTPUT-BOUND.

serial input/output (SIO) the action of a SERIAL PORT that can transmit serial signals in either direction.

serial interface an INTERFACE for transmitting and receiving SERIAL signals. Such an interface would normally be of the RS-232 type, but a few manufacturers use other systems. The main merits of a serial interface are that it uses fewer connections. A serial interface is used to connect between a computer and a MODEM, to connect the KEYBOARD to the main computer on PERSONAL COMPUTERs and for a small number of PRINTER types.

serial line wire connecting SERIAL PORTs and carrying SERIAL FILE data.

serial line internet protocol see SLIP.

serial mouse a type of MOUSE that can be plugged into a SERIAL PORT rather than into a DEDICATED port (see BUS MOUSE).

serial port the computer INTERFACE that allows the use of SERIAL signals as inputs or outputs. See also COM.

serial printer a PRINTER that uses a SERIAL INTERFACE, now unusual.

serial processing or **sequential processing** the conventional system of running a program from start to end using a single CPU, as distinct from MULTITASKING or PARALLEL PROCESSING.

serial to parallel converter a hardware converter that will convert a stream of signals from SERIAL form into PARALLEL form. Such converters were used when some computers provided only for serial output.

serif 1. an ornamental tail to the shape of a letter, used in several familiar FONT designs for DTP use, such as Times, Centurion or Bodoni. Letters that are unadorned are termed SANS SERIF, such as Helvetica, Futura or Univers. **2.** a SOFTWARE HOUSE specializing in DTP programs.

server a computer, usually possessing a fast processor, large memory and large-capacity HARD DRIVE, used in a NETWORK to pass files to other machines on the network and therefore referred to as a *network server* or *LAN server*. See also PRINTER SERVER.

server application a program that creates an OBJECT that can then be linked (see LINK) or EMBEDDED into another document (the CLIENT APPLICATION) See also OLE.

service any action that can be done (or offered) by a SERVER, such as sending data.

service bureau see BUREAU.

service provider any organization that supplies a service using the telephone system. See also ISP.

service release (SR) a form of PATCH, sometimes very large, that fixes BUGS in a program as an interim measure before the next MAJOR RELEASE (which will have different bugs).

session a recording made on CD-R or CD-RW that can consist of from one to 99 tracks. A session is preceded by a LEAD-IN and ended by a LEAD-OUT, and a MULTISESSION DISC is one that can be recorded at different times, writing a complete session on each occasion, with all the data readable.

session layer one of the layers in the ISO/OSI NETWORK scheme, responsible for maintaining communication during a file transfer session.

set 1. a group of related items. The pieces on a chess board constitute a set, as do the months of the year, the days of the week, and so on. Each part of a set is an *element*. **2.** to make a BINARY NUMBER equal to 1; contrast RESET.

SET command a variable-assigning command of MS-DOS. By using SET in a form such as SET TEMP=C:\TEMP, a word can be assigned with a meaning for use within any program that is subsequently run. In this example, the word TEMP means the disk directory C:\TEMP. This type of variable is termed an ENVIRONMENTAL VARIABLE.

set theory a branch of mathematics that deals with operations on sets and elements. Set theory makes use of relationship OPERATORs such as 'includes' and 'member of'. Many set actions closely parallel those of BOOLEAN ALGEBRA.

SETUP a FILENAME commonly used for an INSTALL PROGRAM for software. This file can be run from DOS or from WINDOWS, and Microsoft WINDOWS 95 onwards will search for a file called SETUP or INSTALL and run it when new software is to be installed.

set-up option a choice of MODE or of characteristics. The choice is made early on in the use of a program and will remain in use until specifically changed. For example, a short menu could be used to establish set-up options for a WORD PROCESSOR. These might include the choice of left-hand MARGIN size, characters per printed line, lines per page, HEADER (sense 1), FOOTER, and so on. See also DEFAULT.

set-up program see INSTALL PROGRAM.

set-up string a set of characters that can be sent to a PRINTER to produce a required effect. The user is very seldom nowadays required to type a set-up string because this can be done automatically when a choice is made in the controlling software, such as clicking (see CLICK, sense 1) a BUTTON.

seven layer model see ISO/OSI.

sex changer see GENDER MENDER.

SGML a form of MARK-UP language for documents that has become a standard for business use, allowing documents to be exchanged among different computer systems. See also HTML.

shadow 1. a style that can be applied to text or graphics in which each line appears with a shadow effect. **2.** see SHADOW PAGING.

shadowing the action of copying the contents of a ROM into RAM because RAM is faster than ROM.

shadow paging a method used in large DATABASE systems for securing data against a system CRASH (sense 1). Data that is being worked on is held in units called PAGES (sense 2), and when a page is selected, a copy (the *shadow*) is made. This copy is held until the page contents have been processed and returned to the disk.

shadow RAM see SHADOWING.

shadows colour a colour used in a PRESENTATION GRAPHICS display to create a shadowed appearance to an object.

shareware computer programs that are distributed at low cost on the understanding that a fee will be paid directly to the authors if the programs are found useful. Many users confuse shareware with PUBLIC DOMAIN programs and make no contribution. See also FREEWARE.

sharp see HASHMARK.

sheet feed the delivery of paper in single sheets to a printer. If a printer needs to use single sheets rather than roll or FANFOLD paper, the sheets have to be fed to the printer on demand. Most examples of WORD PROCESSOR allow the computer to deliver a PROMPT and then hang up until a new sheet has been inserted and a KEY (sense 1) pressed. For unattended operation, automatic sheet feeders can be bought for most DOT-MATRIX printers, but they are expensive, particularly in comparison with the prices of most small printers. LASER PRINTERS and INKJET PRINTERS normally incorporate sheet feed as standard, and some allow the use of TWIN-BIN feeders.

shelfware SOFTWARE that is never used, such as the GAMES and other software that are packaged with a computer and said to be worth as much as you paid for the machine.

shell the part of an operating system (OS) that deals with the execution of direct commands. The shell for MS-DOS is contained in a file called COMMAND.COM. Many operating systems use an additional external shell as a form of FRONT END (sense 2) to the operating system to make the system more USER-FRIENDLY. Examples are the WINDOWS 3.1 system for MS-DOS and the DOSSHELL, which was built into MS-DOS 5.0 (now discontinued).

Shell sort a fast type of sorting routine that is particularly advantageous for large lists that can be held in memory. See also BUBBLE SORT; QUICK-SORT; SELECTIVE SORT; SORT.

shield a metal screen used to protect a circuit from incoming interference (either electric or magnetic) or to prevent outgoing signals from interfering with other equipment such as radio and TV receivers.

SHIFT the KEY (sense 1) that is used to obtain UPPER-CASE letters from the KEYBOARD when LOWER-CASE letters are obtained normally. A separate CAPS LOCK key is used to maintain upper-case letters so that lower-case letters are then obtained by using the SHIFT key.

shift-in (SI) the ASCII 15 character, once used to change a CHARACTER SET on a TELETYPE.

shift-out (SO) the ASCII 14 character, once used to reverse a change of CHARACTER SET on a TELETYPE.

short card a half-length expansion card used for fitting the old ISA BUS slots.

shortcut a LINK used in WINDOWS to start a program. The shortcut file is of a few bytes only, and deleting the shortcut has no effect on the program it triggers.

shortcut icon an ICON that can be clicked to start a program in Microsoft WINDOWS 95 onwards. The use of a shortcut removes the work of finding the PATH to the program, and in addition, some options can be built into the shortcut, such as whether to use a MAXIMIZED WINDOW or a MINIMIZED WINDOW. Shortcuts can also be used for disk drives, printers, the MODEM and other items.

shortcut key a KEY (sense 1) or KEY COMBINATION that can be used to carry out a set of instructions. The key or key combination must be assigned to the instructions and this assignment saved as a file or along with the document to which it relates.

short-haul network a NETWORK that operates over short distances, as between offices in the same building.

shouting typing an EMAIL or a NEWSGROUP message using all upper-case letters.

shovelware SOFTWARE that is added to a CD-ROM to fill up the space rather than for any merit it may have.

shrink-wrapped program a program that has completed its course of development through ALPHA TEST, beta test (see BETA SOFTWARE) and RC stages, and is now ready for commercial release.

side-by-side columns columns as used in a TABLE to compare items, as distinct from NEWSPAPER COLUMNS.

SI see SHIFT-IN.

SIG (special interest group) a NEWSGROUP or association with a special interest in some topic, such as military aircraft, microprocessor chips or genetic modification.

sign the symbol or BIT used to show the POLARITY of a number as positive or negative.

signal any method of communicating a meaning. Computers use electrical signals in a BINARY (on/off) code.

signalling rate the rate of change of any aspect of a SIGNAL, such as AMPLITUDE, FREQUENCY or PHASE SHIFT, measured in Baud (changes per second, see BAUD RATE).

signal/noise ratio a measure of SIGNAL quality. Electrical noise will always be present on any transmission system. The ratio of amplitudes of the desired signal to the noise must be above some minimum value for a system to operate successfully. If this is not attained for a digital system, data will be corrupted (see CORRUPTION). See also PARITY.

signal processing alterations made to a SIGNAL, usually by HARDWARE, to improve its readability or convert between ANALOGUE and DIGITAL form.

signature 1. a set of bytes that can be used to identify a VIRUS. **2.** a set of bytes used to check that a ROM is not corrupted or damaged. **3.** words and phrases, such as a PASSWORD, on an electronic message that identify the sender. See also DIGITAL SIGNATURE.

signature analysis a method of testing digital electronic hardware by looking for a pre-defined waveform or digital signal (see SIGNATURE, sense 2) at some point in the circuit when standard inputs are present.

sign bit the BIT in a BINARY NUMBER that is used to indicate SIGN, positive or negative. By convention, the most significant bit (MSB) is used for this purpose. If a binary number has a 1 as its MSB, the number is negative. A 0 as the MSB means that the number is positive.

signed (of a BINARY NUMBER) in which the most significant bit (MSB) is used as a SIGN BIT. See UNSIGNED.

significance the weighting of a digit, signified by its place in a number. For example, in the number 123, the 1 means 100 and is the most significant figure. The 3 means 3 units and is the least significant figure. BINARY NUMBERS use a similar system of significance but based on powers of two rather than on powers of ten. See BIT.

silicon a common element that in its pure form is a SEMICONDUCTOR. Silicon is used for the manufacture of TRANSISTORs and ICs for computers, and also for PHOTOCELLs.

silicon chip see IC.

silicon disk see RAMDISK.

silicone a form of synthetic rubber or jelly used for electrical insulation, particularly where insulation must be resistant to high temperatures.

Silicon Glen the area of central Scotland that contains the largest concentration of electronics firms outside California.

Silicon Valley part of the Santa Clara area of California that contains a huge concentration of firms with interests in data technology.

SIMM (single in-line memory module) a slim board that contains a set of memory chips making up an extension to the memory of a computer, usually 8 megabytes, 16 megabytes or more in each unit. Modern SIMM units can be dropped into a SOCKET and turned so as to lock them in place. See also DIMM; SIPP.

simple mail transfer protocol see SMTP.

simplex a data transmission system having only one transmission line for communications in both directions. It allows signals to pass in one direction only at any given time. See also DUPLEX; FULL DUPLEX; HALF-DUPLEX.

simulation the use of a system to create the appearance of another. For example, simple flying-simulation programs can give all the appearance of the cockpit display of an aircraft. More complex simulators can provide a full range of cockpit controls and a projected scene through the windscreen, even some of the physical sensations of flying. The system that is simulated does not have to be a machine-control one because items as different as the management of a large office and the behaviour of water waves on a shore can be simulated. The essential feature is that the action must be capable of being represented by some mathematical function, or 'model', and therefore by a program function. The programming is extremely complex but the technique can be very rewarding. Trying out changes on a simulation system does not incur any large costs and allows experiment at low risk. See also VIRTUAL REALITY.

sine wave the simplest pattern of wave motion, a wave whose shape is that of the graph of the sine of an angle plotted against the angle size. See also SQUARE WAVE.

single-density disk a FLOPPY DISK that uses an obsolete recording system (*FM*) and can store only a small number of kilobytes per disk. See DOUBLE DENSITY; FLOPTICAL DISK; HIGH DENSITY.

single electron tunnelling an effect that can detect single electrons and which could, in theory, be used to construct small memory chips of vast capacity with very low power dissipation.

single-ended (of any cable system) in which one wire carries a signal and a second wire (or surrounding metal) is earthed.

single in-line memory module see SIMM.

single in-line pin package see SIPP.

single-key response a way of MENU choice. For actions such as making a menu choice from a limited number of items, the old type input action (press a key and then return) is clumsy and should be replaced by a single-key response so that the choice can be made by pressing a single key, not using RETURN. Single-key response should not be used if some of the choices may have the effect of losing data or of causing a FATAL ERROR by, for example, searching for a disk file that does not exist. In any case, when single-key response is used, VALIDATION of some kind is always needed.

single precision the use of four BYTES for storing a FLOATING-POINT number, allowing a precision of up to six significant figures. See also DOUBLE PRECISION; INTEGER.

single quote or **apostrophe** the ' character, ASCII 39. Formatted text from a WORD PROCESSOR can use the correct types of opening and closing quotes (' ').

sink a software way of 'losing' data; see NUL.

SIO see SERIAL INPUT/OUTPUT.

SIPP (single in-line pin package) a system of plug-in memory that was superseded by SIMM and subsequently by DIMM. The SIPP units used a pin-plug connection and could drop out if vibrated.

site licence an agreement that allows the user of a SOFTWARE package to make as many copies as are needed for the computers on one site.

sitename see HOSTNAME.

sizing handles HANDLES that are used exclusively for altering the size of an image, with no effect on image position.

skip to ignore and pass over. A data-reading program can, for example, be arranged to skip certain items, for example any invoices for a zero sum, which are not wanted.

skip factor an option for creating graphs in a WORKSHEET or PRESENTATION GRAPHICS program. The skip factor determines the increments of graphing, such as 2, 4, 6, 8 or 5, 10, 15, 20, etc.

SL a variant of INTEL processor for LAPTOP machines that incorporates a power control system, allowing it to operate at reduced power for some tasks or to shut down almost completely when not being used.

slackware a version of the LINUX operating system.

slash the FORWARD-SLASH (/) symbol that is used in DOS commands to separate letter codes for options. For example, a program called PIXIT might use the command PIXIT /M /P to work in monochrome and to print the output.

slashed zero a zero that has a thin bar diagonally drawn across it. This makes the zero much easier to distinguish from the letter O. The use of a slashed zero was important at a time when programming home computers was popular, but modern LASER and INKJET PRINTERS do not include a slashed zero in their FONTS, and they are seldom seen now.

slave processor a MICROPROCESSOR that is under the control of the main microprocessor in a computer. See also COPROCESSOR; MATHS COPROCESSOR.

sleep (of power-consuming devices) to run on low power until required.

slide a unit of display for a PRESENTATION GRAPHICS program. The slide is usually a screen display, one of a set that makes up the presentation, but it can also be produced as a 35mm film slide, as an OVERHEAD (sense 1) or as a HANDOUT.

slide show the output of a PRESENTATION GRAPHICS program in the form of slides that can be photographic slides, MONITOR (sense 2) displays or overhead projection transparencies.

SLIP (serial line Internet protocol) the older system (now replaced by PPP) of software that allows the INTERNET to be accessed by way of a SERIAL LINE.

slot see EXPANSION SLOT.

slow scan the use of slow SCAN (sense 1) rates on a video camera to reduce the BANDWIDTH needed for video signals at the cost of making fast changes invisible. See also WEBCAM.

slug the code that generates page numbers in the HEADER (sense 1) or FOOTER of a WORD PROCESSOR or DTP document.

small caps or **small capitals** a printing style that is available in some word processor FONTS. The small capitals are of the height of LOWER-CASE characters.

small computer systems interface see SCSI.

small outline DIMM a version of DIMM for LAPTOP machines, using only 72 pins and therefore smaller than the DIMM type used for DESKTOP machines.

small-office/home-office (SoHo) a market for computers and software that does not need the large resources of a large-scale user nor the pointless fast graphics of games users.

small-scale integration see THIRD GENERATION COMPUTER.

smart card a plastic card, usually a credit card, that contains a MICROPROCESSOR and MEMORY so that it can be interrogated by an ATM (sense 1) machine and can keep a tally of transactions.

SmartCursor a WINDOWS action in which a brief explanation of an action will appear when the CURSOR or POINTER (sense 1) is placed in an ICON.

Smartdrive a disk CACHE program formerly used with MS-DOS and older versions of WINDOWS.

SmartQuotes an action in a WORD PROCESSOR or a DTP program that automatically converts the quote mark (") typed on a KEYBOARD into the correct version of opening or closing quotes (" ").

smart terminal see INTELLIGENT TERMINAL.

smiley see EMOTICON.

smoke test a simple test for HARDWARE, usually following repair, to check that nothing drastic has gone wrong. If no smoke emerges after switching on, the equipment can be passed to the customer or for further testing.

smoothing 1. the rounding of a jagged outline. Some GRAPHICS drawing programs use a smooth command to round selected outlines, and it is also possible to add dots to an image to smooth an outline. **2.** the conversion of a fluctuating current or voltage into a steady value. See also AC; DC.

SMT (surface mount technology) a method of mounting chips on a printed circuit board (PCB) with the minimum length of leads, so allowing faster operation, greater reliability and reduced size.

SMTP (simple mail transfer protocol) a system for sending EMAIL from a computer, with the POP system used for incoming mail.

snail-mail the postal service, as compared to the use of FAX or other electronic mailing system.

snaking columns see NEWSPAPER COLUMNS.

snap see GRID SNAP.

snap-on pointer a form of TRACKERBALL that can be clipped to the side of a portable computer to obviate the need for a MOUSE.

snapshot 1. a file containing a screen image (see SCREEN CAPTURE). **2.** a file that contains data on the state of a program at one particular point in time, such as a DATABASE or an accounts program.

SO see SHIFT-OUT.

soak test a TEST (sense 2) of HARDWARE by allowing the machine to RUN (sense 2) continually over a long period, checking for fault conditions.

socket a system for transferring data, particularly into or out from a NETWORK.

Socket 7 a SOCKET using 321 pins, used for Pentium-I chips and by processors from ADVANCED MICRO DEVICES, CYRIX and others. Pentium-2 and later INTEL chips use a small DAUGHTERBOARD with a slot fitting.

soft (of a part of a computer system) able to be changed easily, like a program in memory. Compare HARD.

soft boot a partial reset of a system. See also HARD BOOT.

soft copy see READOUT.

soft data data that is not stored in a ROM or as wired connections in the computer but in RAM or on disk.

soft error an error caused by software, often only under a particular set of circumstances and therefore very difficult to trace and eradicate.

soft font a FONT held as a disk file. The font information is downloaded (see DOWNLOAD) to the LASER PRINTER as required. This is much less costly than using a CARTRIDGE (sense 1) but requires adequate memory within the printer and software for a WORD PROCESSOR or DTP program that can make use of the soft font. See also TRUETYPE.

soft hyphen a character code used in a WORD PROCESSOR to indicate that a word may be hyphenated if it occurs at the end of a line. No hyphen appears unless the word has been split in this way. A HARD-HYPHEN character always appears, no matter where a word is positioned.

soft key see PROGRAMMABLE KEY.

soft page break a PAGE BREAK that is not fixed but will alter when a document is edited and repaginated. Contrast HARD PAGE BREAK.

soft reset a code instruction in a program that will cause a REBOOT. This is used when a menu choice allows some factor such as screen RESOLUTION to be changed.

soft sectoring a system in which a disk is magnetically marked out (see FORMAT, sense 4) by the computer in which it will be used rather than by the manufacturer. In a *soft-sectored* disk, a small hole near the centre acts as an indexing mark, and the sectoring is numbered, starting at the position in which a light beam passes through this hole. During formatting, a set of codes is deposited on each TRACK of the disk, using the position of the SECTORING HOLE as a starting point. Compare HARD SECTORING.

soft space a character that is used to indicate a space on the screen of a document in a WORD PROCESSOR. These spaces can be altered to JUSTIFY the text and are converted into HARD SPACEs only when the document is printed.

software instructions to the computer in any form, including instructions in ROM as well as program data on the hard drive, and supplied on CD-ROM or FLOPPY DISKs. If the instructions are on ROM or PROM, they are usually referred to as FIRMWARE. The software of a computer is by far the most valuable asset of the computer user and in the case of smaller computers is very frequently of more value than the computer itself. By far the most numerous software items are the APPLICATIONS PACKAGE type, which are the programs such as WORD PROCESSOR, SPREADSHEET, DATABASE and COMMUNICATIONS that are so extensively used. Another vital item of software is the operating system (OS), which is the INTERFACE between the computer and these applications programs. DRIVERS are a more specialized type of software that allow a program to make use of a particular printer, keyboard, mouse, and so on.

Other programs are used according to the needs of the computing system. In particular, UTILITY software will be needed to analyse the cause of faults, to defragment disks (see DEFRAGMENTATION) and to create BACK-UP files. Networked computers (see NETWORK) and computers using a MULTITASKING system will also require specialized software to control these systems where the software is not already built into the operating system.

software audit a periodic check of all SOFTWARE by a company to ensure that only licensed versions are being used and that no unauthorized software (with associated VIRUS risks) is in use.

software bloat the increase in size of a program caused by adding features of doubtful utility at the cost of the size and running speed of the program. See also CREEPING FEATURISM.

software cache a portion of RAM memory, usually of 1–2 megabytes, used as a CACHE memory to hold data that has been read from the HARD DRIVE or which is about to be written to the hard drive. This cache memory can be read and written very much faster than the hard drive, so its use greatly speeds up program actions. See also STATIC RAM; WRITE-BACK CACHE; WRITE-THROUGH CACHE.

software engineering the discipline of providing software of a high standard. This includes analysis of the problem the software is designed to solve, searching for methods that provide the minimum use of memory and the lowest running time at minimum expense to the user, programming and marketing. This is engineering in the sense that it involves the traditional engineering problems of reconciling conflicting objectives and working with a view to acceptance by the ultimate user.

software handshaking the use of ASCII characters 17 and 19 as HAND-SHAKE codes. Where additional control lines can be installed, HARDWARE HANDSHAKING, which is faster, can be used, but for communication over telephone lines the software method is unavoidable.

software house 1. a company that undertakes the writing of software. **2.** a reseller of software.

software piracy see PIRACY.

solid-font printer a PRINTER, such as a DAISYWHEEL type, that uses solid character shapes as distinct from DOT-MATRIX representation as used in other types of printers including LASER PRINTERS.

software rot problems that arise because of failure to plan software for distant eventualities. The use of 2-digit year numbers in old COBOL programs is the best-known example (see Y2K).

software theft see PIRACY.

SoH see START OF HEADER.

SoHo see SMALL OFFICE/HOME OFFICE.

solid-state an electronic system using non-moving 'solid' materials such as SEMICONDUCTOR devices in place of vacuum valves and mechanical components such as relays.

solid-state storage device see RAMDISK.

Solver an ADD-IN part of MICROSOFT EXCEL that can be used to find the optimum value for a CELL by adjusting the values of other cells. For example, the value of a *target cell* can be maximized by altering values in changing cells (*decision variables*), subject to constraints that specify the limits to values in any of the cells.

son see FILE GENERATIONS.

sort 1. to put anything into order, such as ascending number order or alphabetical order. It is possible to sort data at the time when it is being entered, but this can be slow and can cause problems when items are entered incorrectly. Data is more usually sorted after it has been entered and checked and is recorded on disk. The sorting can then be done entirely in the memory of the computer, if all the items can be accommodated, or in portions, using the disk for temporary storage. Whatever sorting method is used on DATABASE files depends on a part of the data being used as a KEY (sense 2). A LIST of single words is the exception in which each word is the key, but for most sorting actions one word in a phrase or one word in one RECORD (sense 1) of a database will be used as a key. Simple sorting systems will use the first word in each group. Filenames in a directory can also be sorted, and both DOS and WINDOWS offer several types of sort, using name, date, file size and other criteria. See also BUBBLE SORT; QUICKSORT; SELECTIVE SORT; SHELL SORT. **2. (SORT)** a UTILITY that is a FILTER program, part of the MS-DOS set, allowing files of names or numbers to be put into numerical or alphabetical order for display or printing.

sort key the item that indicates position in a sorted LIST. A RECORD (sense 1) may consist of a number of items, such as name, address and age of a number of people. These records can be sorted in several ways, such as by order of ascending age, alphabetical order of surname, and so on. The item that is chosen to be tested for sorting is the sort key. For example, if age is selected as the sort key, then the list can be sorted in order of ascending or descending age.

sound any wave motion in air that is detected by the ear. The use of a SOUND BOARD in a computer allows sound software, including MULTIMEDIA, to be used effectively. The electrical signals of sound are converted into sound waves by the LOUDSPEAKER.

Sound Blaster a brand of SOUND BOARD from Creative Labs. The Blaster name is also applied to graphics cards (VideoBlaster).

sound board or **sound card** a CIRCUIT BOARD added to the PERSONAL COMPUTER by way of an EXPANSION SLOT so as to add sound capabilities to the computer, particularly for MULTIMEDIA uses. The best-known board of this type is Creative Laboratories SOUND BLASTER, which contains an interface for a CD-ROM drive.

sound chip an IC that executes sound instructions, used in a SOUND BOARD.

soundex an ALGORITHM used for SEARCH routines that codes words by sound so that the same code is generated for all words that sound the same. This allows a search to turn up words of the same sound as well as words of the same meaning.

Sound Recorder a WINDOWS program that will allow sounds to be recorded in DIGITAL form (given a suitable microphone and SOUND BOARD) and played back.

source a file or other collection of information that is to be copied or moved to another destination.

source code commands for a computer written in text form. The text file is then used by a COMPILER or an INTERPRETER to convert the commands into MACHINE CODE.

source document see SERVER APPLICATION.

space bar the long bar-shaped KEY (sense 1) nearest to the keyboard user that generates the ASCII code of 32 and places a space into text.

space character the ASCII character 32 that represents a single space.

spam to send pointless, provocative or commercial messages to one or more NEWSGROUPS or to a large number of EMAIL addresses. Commercial *spamming* is also known as JUNK EMAIL.

span a permitted range of values.

sparse index a DATABASE indexing system in which only some RECORDS (sense 1) are indexed, with others being obtained through POINTERS from a record on the index.

special character a character that is not a normal part of text or a number such as an accented character that is not part of the normal ASCII set. This includes the SEPARATOR characters and characters such as the HASH-MARK that are used for purposes other than printing as part of text.

special interest group see SIG.

specific mark-up the use of coding to mark the LAYOUT of text, such as new paragraph, columns, text alignment. See also GENERIC MARK-UP.

speech recognition or **speech to text** a system that uses a microphone to pick up the sound of speech and a set of circuits and software to convert this speech into text. This works well with languages like Japanese, in which the sounds of speech are standardized, but less well with flexible languages like English, although its use is now well established. Each user of a speech recognition system needs to log on to the system, and a new user must go through an initial period of repeating words that are shown on the screen so that differences in accents and intonation can be accommodated.

speech synthesis or **voice synthesis** a program that can be run in a computer that has sound capabilities and which will give speech-like sounds. The text that controls the speech can be any text that is placed on the screen, so that the speech synthesis programs can be used in conjunction with a WORD PROCESSOR. A good speech synthesis program will allow poor pronunciation to be corrected and will also provide for unfamiliar words to be learned. See also PHONEME.

speech to text see SPEECH RECOGNITION.

spellcheck a program used in conjunction with a WORD PROCESSOR to compare each word in a text with words held in a dictionary on disk. Spellcheck programs are supplied with a main dictionary in the language of your choice, and all permit the user to create one or more CUSTOM DICTIONARY files that can be used for words that are not present in the main dictionary. The more advanced types allow you to choose whether or not to check words with numbers (like A22d) or words all in upper-case (like NATO). See also GRAMMAR CHECKER; THESAURUS. See Fig. 40 (overleaf).

spelling flame a NEWSGROUP message that corrects the spelling of a previous message, so starting a FLAME. Each subsequent message usually contains more spelling errors.

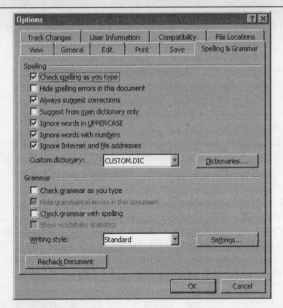

Fig. 40. **Spellcheck**. The options page for spellchecking in Word-8.

spider a SEARCH ENGINE utility that looks through the World Wide Web (WWW) finding words to index.

spike 1. a system of CUT and PASTE for a WORD PROCESSOR in which the selected text is cut and collected along with other text as if on a spike. The whole of the collected text can then be pasted in at another point. It is used mainly in MICROSOFT WORD. **2.** a brief pulse of high electrical voltage. Spikes occur in the MAINS supply during thunderstorms, when equipment is switched off or when work is being carried out on cables. A spike that affects the power supply (PSU) of the computer can wipe out data by causing a REBOOT. *Spike suppressors* can be bought and fitted into the mains supply lead to reduce this problem.

spillage the loss of data from a BUFFER or REGISTER (sense 2) because the amount of data is too large.

spindle the shaft of a DISK DRIVE.

splash screen or **banner** a screen display that contains titles and credits, used at the start of a major program or operating system (OS). WINDOWS allows you to replace the standard splash screen with one of your own making.

spline curve a curve that can be drawn, using a mathematical formula, between points that are defined by using the MOUSE. Spline curves are often used in CAD or other GRAPHICS programs, when the points that the curve must pass through are known. See also BÉZIER CURVE.

split screen a display in which two or more parts of the SCREEN (sense 1) are used for different purposes and can be cleared and scrolled independently. See also SCROLL; WINDOWS.

spoiler a phrase or message that spoils the user's enjoyment of a book, film or puzzle by revealing a plot or providing an answer. NETIQUETTE requires such spoilers to be simply coded (see ROT-13) or to be headed by a warning to sensitive readers.

spool or **background printing** or **print spooling** to RECORD (sense 2) on tape or disk to prevent a program from becoming OUTPUT-BOUND. When a program delivers a large amount of data to a PRINTER, the computer with no spooling software may have to hang up, waiting for the printer to finish before processing can resume. In a spooled system, data is sent to a disk in printer codes and fed to the printer in the gaps between processing actions. In this way, it is very often possible for the printer to operate continually during a program and for the action of the computer also to appear to be continuous. Spooling in this sense is a form of TIMESHARING of the microprocessor.

spot colour a colour printing process. The colour is applied in solid areas and any shading is done by a SCREEN (sense 2) action.

sprayer a program used in a SERVER that will organize the serving of WEB PAGES from several hosts so that the load is more evenly distributed.

spray tool an action of a PAINT type of program. Selecting the spray tool allows dots of colour to be placed on the screen as if distributed from a spray gun.

spreadsheet a type of display and forecasting system consisting of a display on the SCREEN (sense 1) in which items appear in ROWS AND COLUMNS (see Fig. 41 overleaf). Each individual position is called a CELL (sense 1). The items may be text items, but for a large number of applications they will be numbers. The number of cells can overflow the screen because the use of CURSOR-CONTROL keys or the MOUSE allows you to SCROLL the display in any direction. Some of the cells can be used to enter data, but other cells can be filled automatically by making use of relationships between items in other cells. For example, if a selling price for an item is entered in one cell, the VAT formula can be used to show the amount of tax in another cell and the price without VAT in another. In this way, a complete analysis can be built up, even if a large number of cells is needed. The advantage of using a spreadsheet of this type is that you can see at once what the effect of altering one item will be on the whole display. If, for example, the spreadsheet shows the projected costs and income for a business over a year, the effects of falling demand, additional labour costs, changes in taxation, and so on, can be seen very rapidly. If this type of action had to be carried out on paper, it would be very time-consuming and probably very inaccurate. Spreadsheet programs allow the spreadsheet display to be recorded (as a WORKSHEET file) so that it can be used again and also to be printed on paper. See also CONSOLIDATION; LOTUS 1-2-3, MICROSOFT EXCEL; SUPERCALC; VISICALC.

	1	2	3	4	5	6	7	8	9	10	11	etc.
1		Jan	Feb	Mar	Apr	May	Jun	Jul	Aug	Sep	Oct	
2												
3	Computers	2100	1300	900	800	600	200	600	800	1200	2400	
4	Peripherals	200	150	75	78	82	90	120	400	200	150	
5	Software	300	400	250	200	220	230	300	310	200	450	
6	Total Sales	2600	1850	1225	1078	902	520	1020	1510	1600	3000	
7	Direct Costs	960	1200	950	1000	1100	850	900	800	750	800	
8	Indirect	50	35	20	30	70	25	35	42	67	86	
9	Overheads	150	220	1200	450	210	120	60	75	1200	85	
etc.												

Fig. 41. **Spreadsheet**. A typical spreadsheet in the course of being filled with data – a page like this is a worksheet.

sprite a small animated image.

sprocket feed or **pin feed** a method of positioning paper in a printer. See SPROCKET HOLES.

sprocket holes the holes of square section that are punched at the edge of a continuous roll of paper that is intended to be fed through a printer by sprockets or pins. The use of *sprocketed paper* allows much more precise control of paper position and is essential if the computer is working with pre-printed forms.

spur a point in a NETWORK to which a TERMINAL can be connected.

SQL see STRUCTURED QUERY LANGUAGE.

square wave a wave shape that, when graphed, appears to be square. The AMPLITUDE of a square wave switches abruptly between two limits, and the wave is one that is used very extensively in all DIGITAL circuits. All the processing waveforms of a computer, for example, will be of this shape.

SR see SERVICE RELEASE.

SRAM see STATIC RAM.

stac compression a system of compression (see COMPRESSED FILE) devised by STAC Inc. for use with MODEMS, also used at one time for files on the HARD DRIVE. See also DRIVESPACE.

stack a data type in which the last entered data is processed first, the opposite action to that of a QUEUE (sense 1).

stacked bar graph or **stacked column graph** a form of BAR GRAPH in which more than one set of data is shown in each bar.

Stacker a COMPRESSED FILE utility that allows files to be written to and read from the HARD DISK in compressed form, increasing the number of files that can be stored. See also DRIVESPACE.

stage directions see EMOTICON.

staggered windows see CASCADE.

staircase see ALIASING.

standalone (of a part of a computer system) having the ability to work independently. The term is applied, for example, to a MICROCOMPUTER that is on line to a MAINFRAME but which can process data for itself. See also INTELLIGENT TERMINAL.

standard calculator a calculator action that provides only the basic arithmetical functions of add, subtract, multiply and divide. Percentage and EXPONENTIATION are sometimes added, also memory actions.

standard document a document, such as a letter, that is held in a WORD PROCESSOR in OUTLINE form. A standard letter, for example, would be typed with abbreviations used in all places where different versions would require different text. The name and address, for example, might be represented by NME. and ADDR., so that the SEARCH AND REPLACE facility of the word processor could be used to insert the correct names and addresses for the different versions from a MAILING LIST. With some planning, a large number of individual documents can be replaced by one standard document of this type, with the word processor inserting the changes that are needed for individual letters. If the word processor contains MAIL MERGE actions, the production of standard documents does not even need to use search and replace.

standard form the method of writing a number as a single digit and decimal fraction multiplied by a power of ten. For example, 123.45 can be written as 1.2345E2, meaning 1.2345×10^2. Most computers will accept and print REAL NUMBERs in this form. The BINARY version of this form, also called MANTISSA EXPONENT form, is used for storage and manipulation of real numbers in the computer. See also PRECISION OF NUMBER.

standard generalized mark-up language see SGML.

standard mode an obsolete WINDOWS system that allows use to be made of EXTENDED MEMORY along with the 80286 PROCESSOR.

stand-off the distance between a DTP graphics IMAGE (sense 2) and the boundary for text. Each image will be imported with its own boundary (often shown as a dotted line or SELECTION BOX), and text that is being flowed around the graphic will use the boundary as a margin line.

star network a form of NETWORK in which each TERMINAL is connected to a central SERVER. See also RING NETWORK.

start bit the opening part of a SERIAL data transmission of a BYTE. When the RS-232 system of serial transmission is used, each byte is preceded with a start BIT, which is used to prepare the receiver for the first bit of the data byte. When the start bit is received, the receiver software will count in the correct number of data bits, usually 7 or 8. Compare STOP BIT.

Start menu the main command of Microsoft WINDOWS 95 onwards. Clicking (see CLICK, sense 1) on a BUTTON marked Start (on the TOOLBAR) will reveal a pop-up menu (see PULL-DOWN MENU) that contains a set of options, and from these options any program can be started or Windows shut down.

start of header (SoH) the ASCII character 1, formerly used to signal a header on TELEPRINTER text.

start of text (STX) the ASCII character 2, used to signal the start of TELEPRINTER text.

start-up disk a FLOPPY DISK that can be created by Microsoft WINDOWS 95 onwards and used to start the machine (running DOS) in an emergency when the HARD DRIVE does not BOOT up the system or a NETWORK fault prevents booting.

Startup folder a folder in Microsoft WINDOWS 95 onwards that contains ICONS for a set of programs. These programs will be run when Windows is started, so that by placing SHORTCUT ICONS in this folder you can control what is immediately available when you run Windows.

start-up screen or **splash screen** the display of GRAPHICS (such as a logo) and text that is used to introduce a program. Many programs allow the option of suppressing the start-up screen.

state-of-the-art (of computer equipment) as up to date as possible.

static dump a printout on screen or on paper of all the parameters or settings of a system after it has completed a RUN (sense 1).

static object any OBJECT that has been pasted into a document using normal CUT and PASTE methods as distinct from linking (see LINKED OBJECT) or embedding (see EMBEDDED OBJECT). A static object cannot be edited from within the document, and editing involves starting the program that generated the object, altering the file and using cut and paste again.

static RAM (SRAM) a form of RAM that needs no REFRESH memory signals and that is very fast but prohibitively expensive and power-consuming for large-scale use in small computers. Static RAM was used in the early days of microcomputers and is now used for CACHE memory, although scarcity of chips has led to the use of EDO memory systems that allow part of the dynamic ram (DRAM) to be used for cache purposes.

station a point where signals can be received or transmitted, either in a NETWORK or in a COMMUNICATIONS LINK.

stationery 1. any paperwork used by the computer. This is usually subdivided into CONTINUOUS STATIONERY and single-sheet stationery, and may be one part or MULTIPART (see TWO-PART STATIONERY). Printers are generally set up to use the US letter size, which is 8.5 inches x 11 inches when cut, but for European use, the A4 size of 210 mm x 297 mm can be used, either for continuous or (more usually) for single sheets. The DOT-MATRIX or INKJET type of printer can make use of a wide variety of paper types, but for a LASER PRINTER the paper should be of a quality that will not curl as it is heated during the printing process. Paper specified for laser printers or photocopiers will be satisfactory. Laser printers normally use single-sheet feed from a BIN (see TWIN-BIN) rather than continuous stationery. **2.** pre-printed forms, of ten for accounts programs, that are sprocketed (see SPROCKET HOLES) and joined to form continuous stationery.

statistics the study of collections of data and the extraction of valid information from such collections.

status bar a wide bar, usually at the bottom of a screen, that contains information on the output of a program. This can range from the page and paragraph number in a WORD PROCESSOR or DTP document to a progress indicator for a slow action like downloading a file over the INTERNET.

status bit see FLAG.

status line a line of information at the top or bottom of the screen that shows choices that have been made in terms of characters per line, lines per page, etc. The status line can also show the state of progress, such as current page number, current line number, word count, etc. Several varieties of WORD PROCESSOR allow a choice of status lines according to what type of information you require.

status poll signals sent out by a central processing system to find the status of PERIPHERALS, such as the printer, keyboard and screen. A status poll might, for example, reveal that the printer is off or out of paper, the screen needs scrolling and a KEY (sense 1) is being pressed on the keyboard. See also INTERRUPT; POLLING.

steam-powered old-fashioned, with the suggestion of reliability.

stem the main vertical line in a FONT character.

stepping motor a motor that can move in precise and equal steps over a range. Each step is produced by a set of coded pulses of current to the motor, and the importance of the stepping motor lies in the fact that the pulses of current can be delivered from a suitable INTERFACE under computer control. The stepping motor is used, for example, in disk drives to control the position of the disk READ/WRITE HEAD and in printers to control the movement of a DAISYWHEEL. It also has considerable applications in PLOTTERS and for ROBOTICS. The use of stepping motors in HARD DRIVES has now been superseded by the VOICE-COIL form of drive because it has lower inertia and is faster. Such drives are also SELF-PARKING.

stereoscopy the simulation of three-dimensional images by using a pair of separate images, one for each eye. Now used in VIRTUAL REALITY displays.

sticky key action one of the ACCESSIBILITY OPTIONS of Microsoft WINDOWS

95 onwards that helps disabled users by allowing the effect of simultaneously struck keys to be simulated by pressing keys in sequence.

stop bit the BIT that follows the last bit of a BYTE in SERIAL data transmission and is used as a signal to the receiver that all the byte has been transmitted. Many PROTOCOLS (sense 1) make use of two stop bits. On reception of a stop bit, the microprocessor of the receiver will place the assembled byte into memory and set up ready for another START BIT.

stop code an EMBEDDED COMMAND code that is used to stop the PRINTER. This might be used, for example, to take a piece of headed paper out and put in plain paper. Most WORD PROCESSOR programs can set options so that the stop action is automatic at the end of a page, thus enabling single sheets to be used with the printer.

stop list a LIST of words that are not to be used. An automatic indexing program, for example, must be provided with a list of words such as 'and', 'but', and so on, that will not be indexed. A stop list can also be used along with a SPELLCHECK program to ensure that some words are never queried, and it is also possible to use the reverse action to ensure that some words are always queried even if spelled correctly; see EXCLUDE DICTIONARY.

storage the retention of data in MEMORY or in BACKING STORE. The main memory of a computer will hold the current part of the program that is being executed along with the data on which this program is working and will take other program sections from backing store as needed. Data will also be copied from the backing store, altered and re-recorded. Small amounts of data are also held in various BUFFERs, but these can be considered along with the main memory. Early MAINFRAME computers used memory of surprisingly small capacity, mainly because of the cost, unreliability and cooling requirements of memory systems of the time. A figure of 10 kilobytes was typical of many early computers, although the word size could be 24–40 bits long. Even a modest PERSONAL COMPUTER today uses 8 megabytes and many can make use of 16 megabytes or more, with large machines able to use main memory sizes of 120 megabytes or more, all of which is needed by some very elaborate operating systems (OS). There has been a comparable increase in the sizes of backing stores, for which the larger machines always provided large capacity. Backing stores of 500 megabytes for small machines and several gigabytes for large machines are now normal. Main memory uses RAM chips, which permit RANDOM ACCESS to store data along with very fast operation. Access times of 70 nanoseconds or less are common, even on small machines, and can be as low as 1 nanosecond on large machines. The reliability of ICs is very much better than could ever be achieved in the past, and the low power consumption requires much less attention to cooling. The small size of ICs also provides a large amount of memory in a small space.

The backing store for small machines will use HARD DRIVE systems, possibly augmented by CD-ROM. Larger machines can use removable disks and magnetic drum systems, sometimes with TAPE used for ARCHIVE storage.

storage allocation the method of using memory to hold different forms of data, such as RESIDENT programs, TRANSIENT programs and data created by these programs, so that there is no confusion.

storage density the amount of data stored per unit of length, area or volume of the storage MEDIUM (sense 1).

storage system any system of MEMORY or DISK that allows data to be retained.

store a memory LOCATION (sense 1) or REGISTER (sense 2).

stored program computer a modern type of DIGITAL COMPUTER that stores both PROGRAM and DATA in the same CORE MEMORY. This allows great flexibility of program use. For instance, a modern APPLICATIONS program keeps a portion of itself in memory and moves sections to and from the hard drive as required. See also VON NEUMANN.

story all the text in a single file imported into a DTP or PRESENTATION GRAPHICS program, or any coherent BLOCK (sense 2) of text treated as a single unit.

stream see CHANNEL (sense 1).

streamer or **tape drive** a TAPE mechanism using a DIGITAL tape drive and intended for carrying out the BACKUP of a complete HARD DRIVE. See also DAT.

streaming the continuous action of a TAPE BACKUP drive. This indicates the most efficient mode of operation and is normal when each HARD DRIVE DIRECTORY (sense 1) holds only a few large files. When directories contain a large number of short files, the tape will start and stop at frequent intervals.

strikethrough a text STYLE used in DTP work and in editing on a WORD PROCESSOR in which each letter is struck through by a horizontal line. This is used to indicate text that might be deleted subsequently.

string or **character string** a data type that consists of a set of characters, such as a piece of text.

string area a part of memory that is used for storing STRING data.

string formula a FORMULA used in a WORKSHEET that carries out an action on a STRING of characters, such as counting the number of characters.

string operator any OPERATOR that acts on STRINGS rather than on numbers.

stroke to press a single KEY (sense 1) on the computer keyboard. The term can also denote one side of a character shape.

stroke font a FONT created by vector drawing but with the characters drawn with thin lines, not in OUTLINE FONT form. Stroke fonts are commonly used in CAD programs.

structured language a PROGRAMMING LANGUAGE that encourages or forces the user to write self-contained units (*procedures*) of code.

structured query language (SQL or SEQUEL) a standardized form of QUERY LANGUAGE used on several DATABASE packages.

STX see START OF TEXT.

style 1. a variation in FONT pattern. The usual styles offered in each font are normal (or ROMAN), BOLD, ITALIC and UNDERLINE, together with combinations of these. Some fonts also offer STRIKETHROUGH and OUTLINE (SHADOW) styles. **2.** a collection of specifications for a PARAGRAPH, including FONT, margins, type styles, that are held as a file and can be assigned so as to create a FORMAT (sense 2) for a document quickly and easily with less risk of inconsistency in the document.

stylesheet a file used in DTP and WORD PROCESSOR actions. The stylesheet stores a particular FORMAT (sense 2) of page, allowing the user to specify what type of page is to be produced by picking a name or number. The size and shape of lettering for headings, subheadings and BODY text are then fixed by the stylesheet.

stylus a form of pen used along with a GRAPHICS TABLET or with a PEN-BASED COMPUTER.

subband encoding a method of compressing digital audio signals by removing the components that the ear cannot detect. This is used in MPEG coding and also for MINI DISC recording.

subdirectory or **branch** a form of file, held in another subdirectory or in the ROOT DIRECTORY (sense 1) of a HARD DRIVE, that will itself act as a directory, storing other files. This enables files to be kept in hierarchical groups rather than as a large list on the root directory.

submenu a MENU that appears when you CLICK (sense 1) on a main menu item.

subscribe to add one's name to a NEWSGROUP or a EMAIL list. This is usually free of charge.

subscript text lettering placed under the normal BASE LINE of a WORD PROCESSOR or DTP document. Subscript lettering is also normally of a smaller POINT size and is used mainly in mathematical and other scientific typesetting work. Contrast SUPERSCRIPT TEXT.

subset a set of items that is itself part of a larger set. For example, a demonstration program might be a subset of a program, using only a few of the facilities of that program.

substitution table 1. a list of characters from one WORD PROCESSOR document that will be substituted by other characters when the document is edited by another word processor program. **2.** a table in a WORD PROCESSOR showing which keys or key combinations are needed to obtain accented letters, Greek letters, mathematical symbols, etc. See also CHARACTER MAP.

successive approximations a method of solving a problem by applying a formula that acts on a guessed number. The result obtained from the formula is then used as a more precise guess, and the process continues until the result is the same as the number that is being used as the guess. See also ITERATION.

suicideware SOFTWARE that will cease to function after a prescribed date. This is usually a trial version or a BETA SOFTWARE copy.

suite of programs a set of interacting programs. These are generally arranged so that they can be called into use as required, working on the same data. See also PACKAGE (sense 1).

summary a brief outline of a DOCUMENT or image that can be saved along with the file. When summaries have been prepared, you can search through summary information to find a document rather than through the documents themselves. This is considerably quicker, particularly for long documents or elaborate drawings.

summation check a method of checking INTEGRITY of data by adding the code numbers (see CHECKSUM).

Supercalc™ a SPREADSHEET program. Supercalc was one of the first good spreadsheets (see also LOTUS 1-2-3; MICROSOFT EXCEL; VISICALC).

supercomputer a computer intended for performing a very large number of operations (see FLOP) per second so that it can be used for large amounts of rapidly changing data such as is required for weather forecasting. See also CRAY.

superhighway see INFORMATION SUPERHIGHWAY.

superkey an INDEX KEY for a DATABASE that allows an ENTITY to be uniquely located. A surname would not be a superkey, since two or more people might have the same surname. A social security number, however, would be a superkey since one social security number is unique to one person.

superscript text lettering placed above the normal BASE LINE of a DTP document. Superscript lettering is also normally of a smaller POINT size and is used mainly in mathematical and other scientific typesetting work. Contrast SUBSCRIPT.

Super VGA see SVGA.

supervisor the part of an operating system (OS), particularly in a MULTI-ACCESS SYSTEM, that will allocate and control the use of the MICROPROCESSOR and PERIPHERALS so as to avoid conflicts.

support 1. assistance for SOFTWARE or HARDWARE use in the form of technical advice, usually by telephone or fax. **2.** to be able to work with a device. **3.** help with a SOFTWARE package that is misbehaving. All too often telephone help is overloaded (a clue to the reliability of the software) and is inadequate. Sometimes a PATCH is available on the World Wide Web (WWW) but not by any other method.

support chip an IC that is designed to work along with a specific MICROPROCESSOR, either to extend the action or to make an action more efficient. Support chips are used typically for supplying CLOCK pulses, for carrying out DMA and for controlling BUS allocation.

suppress to prevent the use of something in computing. WORD PROCESSOR programs may suppress the printing of some characters because of undesirable effects on the printer. Other codes have to be suppressed before text is displayed on the screen for the same reasons. See NON-PRINTING CODES.

surface mount technology see SMT.

surfing searching the INTERNET, moving from one WEB PAGE to another. This also implies that the searcher will often be diverted from an initial objective because of the fascination of looking at other pages.

surge a transient increase in MAINS voltage, slower than a SPIKE (sense 2), that can be destructive to computer circuits if it persists. The power supplies of most computers can cope with most mains surges without any risk of a REBOOT.

surge protector an electrical component inserted into the power line to prevent a computer from being affected by sudden changes of supply voltage.

SVGA (Super VGA) a graphics interface that permits RESOLUTION beyond the 640 x 480 level, such as 800 x 600, 1024 x 768 or 1280 x 1024. SVGA boards also offer larger numbers of colours, up to 16.7 million, using 24 bits to code each PIXEL. The higher resolutions are slower in use, and the screen images of objects are smaller. They appear to advantage on a large MONITOR (sense 2) of 17 inches or more and on a machine that uses a GRAPHICS ACCELERATOR for the highest possible speed. Additional VIDEO MEMORY will be needed if the larger numbers of colours are being used.

S-video a VIDEO signal transmitting system that uses separate LUMINANCE and CHROMA signals rather than COMPOSITE VIDEO or RGB.

swap a switch of data between memory and disk, used in a MULTITASKING SYSTEM so that the limits of memory are not exceeded at any time.

swap file a file used to contain TASK-SWITCHING material. When an operating system (OS) allows task-switching, the whole of a program along with its data will be placed in a swap file so that it can be replaced in the memory by another program. When the program is to be resumed, the swap file is read and the program can continue from where it left off. See PERMANENT SWAP FILE.

swarf dust created from drilling or filing actions that can cause problems on floppy disks and other mechanical parts.

swash a character, usually in a DISPLAY FONT, that has a portion passing over or under adjacent characters.

swimming display a display of text or graphics in which the items move up and down or from side to side. This is usually because of the too close presence of another MONITOR (sense 2), an unsuitable video system or possible software faults.

switch 1. a program action that can be turned on or off. A switch action will remain as it has been set until altered again. In some programs, the switch setting is retained only for as long as the program is in use; in others the setting will be held in a file and used each time the program is started. See also TOGGLE. **2.** a character added to a DOS command, following a SLASHMARK, to modify the action. For example, the command DIR /W has the effect of displaying the directory in wide (80-column) form.

SX chip originally a form of INTEL MICROPROCESSOR in which the internal data paths are wider than the external paths (i.e. 32-bit data internally and 16-bit data externally), as on the 80386SX. On the 80486 chips, SX was used to mean a chip with no internal floating-point coprocessor (see MATHS COPROCESSOR). The full-scale chip was labelled as 80386DX or 80486DX. The later PENTIUM chips were available only with its built-in coprocessor.

symbolic inference the deduction of new facts using existing facts along with inference (see INFERENCE ENGINE), used in ARTIFICIAL INTELLIGENCE.

symmetric key cryptography an ENCRYPTION and DECRYPTION scheme in which both sender and receiver use the same secret KEY (sense 3). See also PUBLIC-KEY ENCRYPTION.

sync 1. to synchronize actions. **2.** (of a signal) intended to enforce SYNCHRONIZATION.

synchronization the arranging of an action to take place at the same time as another. This is a common problem in fast-action graphics because the TV display repeats at a rate of 25 times a second and screen movement can appear to be jerky unless the movement is synchronized to the screen repetition rate. Another synchronization problem concerns SERIAL transmission of data. Unless the receiver can assemble the bits that are transmitted into the correct bytes, the transmission will be hopelessly corrupted. The RS-232 PROTOCOLS (sense 1) ensure synchronizing by using standard BAUD RATES, number of START BITS, number of STOP BITS, number of data bits, and so on. Providing that both transmitter and receiver are set up to the same protocols, synchronization is automatic. See also USRT.

synchronize pages to ensure that files of WEB PAGES that are stored locally have the same content as those available on the World Wide Web (WWW).

synchronous (of two or more devices or systems) operating together in step at the same rate.

synchronous communication a system of transmitting data in which a master CLOCK pulse determines the timing of each transmitted bit. SERIAL communications with the PERSONAL COMPUTER generally use ASYNCHRONOUS TRANSMISSION.

synchronous dynamic random access memory see SDRAM.

synchronous key encryption an ENCRYPTION and DECRYPTION system that uses two keys, one of which can be public, the other private. Anything encrypted using one KEY (sense 3) can be decrypted using the other. See also PUBLIC-KEY ENCRYPTION; SYMMETRIC KEY ENCRYPTION.

synonym ring a file of a set of words that have related meanings. The file is used to assist a word SEARCH so as to produce related words, particularly for technical words.

syntax the 'grammar' of a command, as applied, for example, to a DATA-BASE QUERY, a WORKSHEET FORMULA or a DOS command. These items must take a fixed form, the syntax, and any departure from this form will cause an error message. Important points of syntax include the correct spelling of command words and the correct use of BRACKETS, PUNCTUATION MARKS and spaces.

synthesizer the portion of a sound card for a computer that allows the sounds of musical instruments to be simulated. A synthesizer will also allow sound effects, and a SPEECH SYNTHESIS facility is also obtainable for most types of sound card. Another option is the use of the MIDI interface, a way of linking synthesizers together, which is available on a few modern computers. The provision of the MIDI interface allows a computer to be linked to a full-scale music synthesizer system.

sysop (system operator) the operator of a BULLETIN BOARD.

system the computer and all its attachments, its actions, inputs and outputs, considered as a whole.

System Agent a UTILITY provided with WINDOWS 98 and available as an extra (Microsoft Plus) for WINDOWS 95. When System Agent is activated, it will carry out monitoring and remedial actions at intervals determined by the user. You can, for example, check the HARD DRIVE condition, defragment (see DEFRAGMENTATION) files and compress (see COMPRESS DISK) the hard drive by using the System Agent options.

system attribute a BIT used to mark a file in the MS-DOS operating system (OS) as one that is essential to the operation of the computer, such as the IO.SYS or MSDOS.SYS files.

system backup see FULL BACKUP.

system check a routine used to check that a system is correctly set up, such as checking for the presence and operation of PORTS.

system clock a CLOCK, as distinct from REAL-TIME CLOCK.

system crash a failure of one of the main system files on a computer, often caused by CORRUPTION of the SYSTEM TRACK on the BOOT DISK.

system date the date as maintained by the REAL-TIME CLOCK of the PERSONAL COMPUTER.

system disk a disk that contains the operating system (OS) for the computer. This usually refers to a BACKUP of the system files on a FLOPPY DISK because the main system files will be held on the HARD DRIVE.

System Monitor a utility that is part of Microsoft WINDOWS 95 onwards. When System Monitor is running, a set of graphs will appear in a WINDOW. These graphs describe system performance in terms of such items as the rate of using disk READ actions, the use of memory, the use of the SWAP FILE, etc.

system operator see SYSOP.

system prompt see PROMPT.

system resources the portion of MEMORY used by WINDOWS to hold information about how Windows is being used. This area was too limited in Windows 3.1, causing programs like MICROSOFT WORD to halt because of lack of resources even when adequate memory was present. Microsoft WINDOWS 95 onwards can allocate memory to system resources as required.

systems analysis the task of learning how a complicated system (which can be commercial or natural, an office, a power station, a river, etc.) works so that a program can be written to control it or simulate its action. Systems analysis of a business calls not only for a considerable knowledge of the computer system (which may not yet be fully specified at the time when analysis starts) but also of the business that is being analysed. It is this latter requirement that presents the greater difficulties because in large businesses the systems that have evolved may bear little resemblance to the systems that managers fondly believe exist.

system tracks the tracks, usually at the outermost part of a disk, that are used to hold the main files for the operating system (OS).

system variables the quantities that are stored into RAM by the operating system (OS) so as to RUN (sense 2) a program. In the event of a CRASH (sense 1), the program can be continued only if the values of the system variables are uncorrupted. See also REGISTRY.

T

tab character the ASCII code 9, used to cause the CURSOR to move to the next TABULATION position in a line.

tab-delimited file a DATABASE file in which the FIELDS (sense 2) are separated by TAB CHARACTERS. See also COMMA-DELIMITED FILE.

tab key (tabulation stop key) a KEY (sense 1) that will move a CURSOR in a WORD PROCESSOR to the next TAB STOP position in a line. The key is marked with two arrows and positioned on the left-hand side of the KEYBOARD next to the Q key. The tab key can be used in creating tables, but the more advanced word processors can use specialized commands for this purpose.

table a LIST of data organized into lines and columns. This can be displayed on the SCREEN (sense 1), printed or stored in the memory and on the hard drive. See also LOOK-UP TABLE; TEXT TO TABLE.

table menu see TABLE UTILITY.

table of authorities see TOA.

table of contents 1. (TOC) a table drawn up from marked portions of text in a document, such as drawing captions. The table can be created automatically, either from marked text or from chapter headings and subheadings. **2.** a file created by a CD-R or CD-RW writer when a disc is finalized (see FINALIZED DISC) so that any CD-ROM drive or music drive can read the disc correctly.

table to text a WORD PROCESSOR action that will convert a table which was created by that word processor into lines of text. Typically, you can opt for the SEPARATOR that you want to use between table items, such as a comma or a TAB CHARACTER. See also TEXT TO TABLE.

table utility or **table menu** a part of a WORD PROCESSOR program that deals with the creation and editing of tabular material. This is preferable to using tabs (see TAB CHARACTER) or spaces to tabulate material because a table utility will align proportionally spaced text in a more satisfactory way.

tab memory memory that is devoted to storing TABULATION settings. The position and type of the TAB STOP is recorded in this memory and is saved with the document. In many WORD PROCESSOR types, the tab stop settings apply for one paragraph only.

tab stop each preset or fixed tab position of the CURSOR in a line of a WORD PROCESSOR document. See also CENTRE TAB; DECIMAL TAB; LEFT TAB; RIGHT TAB.

tabular columns columns in a WORD PROCESSOR document that are set up like a TABLE so the reader is expected to view a line at a time. See also NEWSPAPER COLUMNS.

tabulation the action of moving the CURSOR to a pre-set place, a TAB STOP, by using the TAB KEY.

tabulation stop key see TAB KEY.

tactile keyboard a KEYBOARD whose KEY (sense 1) action incorporates a CLICK (sense 2) that can be felt by the user to indicate that the key has been pressed. In addition, most tactile keyboards use F and J keys which incorporate raised bars that can be used as locating points by a visually impaired user.

tag any CODE (sense 1) embedded in a text DOCUMENT, particularly formatting code that is part of an HTML document.

tag bit see METABIT.

tagged image file format see TIFF.

tape or **magnetic tape** a MEDIUM for storing data as magnetic signals, using a long narrow strip of plastic tape with magnetic material. The tape for backup purposes is normally contained in a CARTRIDGE (sense 1) or CASSETTE (sense 2), with two small reels that are enclosed in a case. When a cassette is used, the cassette also contains the PRESSURE PAD, which presses the tape against the TAPEHEAD, and there are two HUBS that are used to drive the reels for forward and reverse winding. A cartridge uses heavier construction with a metal base, with no external mechanical drive to the hubs and no pressure pads. Several sizes of cassettes and cartridges can be used, allowing storage of about 300 megabytes to several gigabytes. The backup system uses software so that the whole drive is under computer control. Microsoft WINDOWS 95 onwards incorporates software for the popular QIC80 tape systems in its BACKUP UTILITY. The main disadvantage of using tape is that it is a SERIAL system, and to gain access to any required part of the tape may require fast winding in either direction. This is less of a problem when the action is software-controlled. See also DAT.

tape archive a COMPRESSED FILE recorded on TAPE and intended as a last-resort BACKUP or a way of preserving material for which there is no foreseeable need but which may one day be of use.

tape cartridge an enclosed pair of reels wound with TAPE in the style of a videocassette. The standard tape width of quarter inch is often used (see QIC). The cartridge is used in a tape drive (see STREAMER) for BACKUP.

tape drive see STREAMER.

tape guide a smooth bar, roller or plastic cylinder that acts to guide TAPE past a TAPEHEAD. The tape guide normally uses shoulders to prevent the tape from moving sideways. Any side movement of the tape will cause incorrect placing of tracks, leading to crosstalk or BABBLE. A tape cassette or cartridge contains some plastic tape guides, but the tapehead also has its own guides.

tapehead a magnetic READ/WRITE HEAD that works on the same principles as a read/write head of a FLOPPY DISK. The main difference is that a tapehead does not move across the width of the tape but is fixed while the tape moves past it.

TAPI (telephony application program interface) the WINDOWS software that allows communication between computers linked by MODEMs.

target 1. the destination of a HYPERLINK. **2.** the destination of a file copying (see COPY, sense 1) or moving (see MOVE) action.

Targa graphics adapter see TGA.

target printer the PRINTER for which a file of text or graphics is intended. Because EMBEDDED CODEs have been used, such a file may not be printable, without conversion, on any other printer.

task any action or process to be carried out.

taskbar the bar of ICONs that appears at the foot of the WINDOWS screen, containing the Start button.

task list a list of programs that are available for use in a MULTITASKING system, some of which may be contained in a SWAP FILE rather than in MEMORY.

task management the SOFTWARE that determines how the resources of a computer system are allocated to the use of a program.

task manager the part of the WINDOWS MULTITASKING system, Version 3.1, that controls switching from one program to another.

task scheduling assignment of time or other conditions for running a scheduled program, such as disk checking.

task switching the action of exchanging one program in memory for another. This is not a multitasking action if only one program is active, so that if the memory space is insufficient a program complete with data can use a SWAP FILE, so that it is held on the HARD DRIVE in suspended animation, ready to resume when it is replaced in memory. If both programs are active then this will be a MULTITASKING action.

task tree a breakdown of a task into a HIERARCHY of simpler tasks (*subtasks*).

TCP/IP (transmission control protocol/Internet protocol) a standard system for communications between computers. At one time, the IP part of the abbreviation was used to mean *Information Provider*, because TCP/IP was formerly mainly used for DATABASE applications.

TDM see TIME DIVISION MULTIPLEX.

teaching machine a device, preferably but not necessarily computer-based, that can be used by a student for unassisted study. The machine can display text and then follow up with questions that test comprehension and reasoning. The responses to these questions determine whether another step can be taken or if further reinforcement is needed.

The use of a computer as a teaching machine, particularly in association with INTERACTIVE VIDEO, expands the capabilities of the system since software can replace the hardware methods (slides, tapes, etc.) used in the older machines.

telecommuting the use of computer, EMAIL, FAX and other office tools at home rather than in an office. This is becoming more common as a way of cutting office overheads, reducing dependence on transport and obtaining more flexible working hours.

teleconferencing or **conferencing** the use of computer, TV and sound links between widely separated users as a way of arranging a meeting without the wasted time resulting from travelling.

telemetry the transmission of data to and from a REMOTE piece of equipment which is used for measuring purposes, such as a weather satellite or spacecraft.

telephony application program interface see TAPI.

teleprinter the old-fashioned electromechanical type of keyboard and printer that uses the principles first laid down by Baudot and improved by Murray in 1903. In computing, these devices formed the only link between operator and computer until DEC introduced the interactive video TERMINAL. See also BAUD RATE.

teletext a system of transmitting information, using spare capacity of the ANALOGUE TV signal. In the time when the receiver is executing the FRAME FLYBACK, no picture information can be sent. This time can, however, be used to transmit data, which can be stored and assembled as needed. Teletext is designed to make use of this spare capacity in a standardized data-transmitting system, which can also allow the use of low-resolution colour graphics. The BBC system is termed CEEFAX; the ITV version is called Oracle. The systems are technically identical, and they also use the same methods for transmitting computer programs.

teletype a REMOTE-operated typewriter. The main difference between this and a TELEPRINTER is that the teletype uses larger diameter rolls of paper.

teletype roll a paper roll with a diameter of 127 mm.

television see TV.

telnet a standard INTERNET PROTOCOL, using TCP/IP, for REMOTE LOGIN.

template or **master page** a standard form or document that can be used by altering some details. Examples are a standard letter in a WORD PROCESSOR, a standard DTP page (a MASTER PAGE) or a data entry form in a DATABASE program.

temporal database a DATABASE that works with time-dependent data, such as diary or scheduling information.

temporary storage or **intermediate storage** or **working storage** STORAGE in computer memory that is used only momentarily. During calculations, for example, intermediate results may have to be stored, and this is done in temporary storage with the date being erased after the operation is completed. See also SCRATCHPAD.

temporary swap file a SWAP FILE for WINDOWS that is opened for a specific program and closed again when that program is closed. Microsoft Windows 95 onwards does not use temporary swap files and maintains a PERMANENT SWAP FILE on the main HARD DRIVE.

ten-finger interface the use of a human being to read text from the SCREEN (sense 1) of one computer and type it into the KEYBOARD of another. This provides the ultimate form of security against spreading a VIRUS.

tera- a prefix denoting 1012, a million million.

terminal a REMOTE DISPLAY and KEYBOARD that are connected to a computer by a data link, often a SERIAL link. See also DUMB TERMINAL; INTELLIGENT TERMINAL.

terminal block a set of connections that can be broken. In computing, this is normally a set of connectors for cables that allows the connections to be changed.

terminal emulation the use of SOFTWARE to make the computer act like a well-known type of TERMINAL when it is being used for receiving SERIAL data by way of a MODEM. Commonly used emulation standards are ANSI, VT52 and VT100.

terminate and stay resident see TSR PROGRAM.

terminator 1. a BYTE or other piece of data that indicates that a process is to be ended. For example, entering a 0 in a number-summing program could cause the program to halt. The zero byte or the carriage return (CR) code of ASCII 13 are often used as terminators in data entry forms. **2.** a resistor connected across two lines to prevent signals from being reflected from either open or closed lines. This is used in SCSI connections and NETWORK cables.

test to run a program with dummy data to find if the action is correct. See also ALPHA TEST; BETA SOFTWARE.

test coverage the extent to which a testing UTILITY probes the potential weaknesses of a program.

test data artificial data that has been prepared to TEST a system and for which the correct results are known. Test data should use values that test the extremes of the system – the highest and the lowest numbers that can be used – and should also contain data that will trigger error conditions so as to test the response of the system to such errors. See also BLACK-BOX TESTING; WHITE-BOX TESTING.

test run the use of a program with TEST DATA to check that it is operating correctly before it is used with real data.

TeX a vast and complex text-formatting and typesetting system. Although FREEWARE and still used, TeX has declined because so much of the work can be done much more simply using MICROSOFT WORD for WINDOWS.

text any non-graphics display of alphabetical or numeric characters on the SCREEN (sense 1), including punctuation and other marks.

text-based running under a command operating system (OS) such as MS-DOS or LINUX, as distinct from using a GUI like WINDOWS.

text box a box within a WINDOW that contains text, usually a message, or into which text, such as a filename, can be typed.

text chart a SLIDE in a PRESENTATION GRAPHICS program that contains mainly text rather than the usual captioned picture.

text compression the compressing of ASCII text so as to take up the minimum amount of memory.

text editor a program that will allow the entry of text appearing on the SCREEN (sense 1) into MEMORY. The text is written in lines, without WORD WRAP or other WORD PROCESSOR actions, and saved as an ASCII file. This is intended to be used by programmers for writing instruction lines in a PROGRAMMING LANGUAGE. The text can then be amended, deleted and enlarged as necessary (see ECHO CHECK). A text editor combined with a PRINT FORMATTER constitutes a word processor program.

textfile a FILE that consists of only ASCII codes. Such a file can be imported by any DTP or WORD PROCESSOR package.

text formatter see PRINT FORMATTER.

text mode see CHARACTER MODE.

text processor see WORD PROCESSOR.

text retrieval program a DATA system that allows a complete document to be examined, as distinct from a synopsis of the contents or an edit. For example, Microsoft WINDOWS 95 onwards contains a Quick Document action for reading text files but with no editing action.

text screen a display mode for text only that needs much less memory than a graphics display.

text to speech the automatic conversion of text (usually ASCII text) on SCREEN (sense 1) into spoken words.

text to table a WORD PROCESSOR action that converts text into a TABLE. Typically the words and phrases of text are separated by commas or tab characters with a carriage return at the end of each line. When the text is selected and the table to text action is used, each delimited item (see COMMA-DELIMITED FILE; TAB-DELIMITED FILE) will appear in a table cell. See also TABLE TO TEXT.

texture the surface irregularity in a colour, applied to a graphics image. Typical texture options in a paint program include brick, earth, wood, tile, and so on.

TFT (thin-film transistor) a form of LCD screen design in which each PIXEL is controlled by a separate TRANSISTOR fabricated in a set of thin film layers.

TGA (Targa graphics adapter) a graphics file format that uses 24 bits per PIXEL.

thermal paper printing paper that discolours on heating. Thermal paper was at one time used by some types of printers because it allows silent printing.

thermal printer a PRINTER that uses THERMAL PAPER. This is a form of DOT-MATRIX printer in which the needles of the printer are hot. Where each needle touches the paper, it will leave a mark caused by the chemical reaction in the paper. The advantage of thermal printing is that the needles do not have to strike the paper hard, so a thermal printer can be very quiet. Another advantage is that no inked ribbon is needed, so the print is easily kept clean. The disadvantages include high paper costs, the printing of one copy only and little choice of print colours. INKJET PRINTERs have replaced thermal printers for most applications, even in FAX machines.

thermionic valve an electronic device, almost obsolete, that controls electron flow in a vacuum. The valve has been almost completely superseded by the TRANSISTOR, which controls electron flow in a solid crystal, and the IC, which is a set of miniature connected transistors.

thesaurus a system that searches for synonyms. A thesaurus program is usually packaged (see PACKAGE, sense 1) along with a WORD PROCESSOR and a spell checker (see SPELLCHECK). The thesaurus action allows the text to be scanned and selected words with similar meanings to be used to replace marked words in the text. In addition, the thesaurus can be used to suggest antonyms, words with the opposite meaning to the selected word.

thick Ethernet a NETWORK connecting system that uses COAXIAL CABLE of 1 cm diameter. This cable permits efficient networking up to distances of about one kilometre.

thin Ethernet a NETWORK connecting system that uses COAXIAL CABLE of 0.5 cm diameter. This cable permits efficient networking up to distances of about 300 metres.

thin-film transistor see TFT.

thin space a size of space used in DTP work. The thin space is half the width of the EN SPACE.

thin window a form of LCD display used by a few computers to display information on a small subsidiary SCREEN (sense 1) on the KEYBOARD.

third generation computer the type of early computers that were the first to use small ICs (*small-scale integration*) around 1965. Such machines also used SEMICONDUCTOR memory rather than magnetic CORE MEMORY.

thrashing excessive HARD DRIVE activity when a large number of short data items are being retrieved from different parts of the disk.

thread a posting that forms a continuation of a NEWSGROUP message and supplies information relevant to the original message.

threading a DTP facility that allows text to remain connected despite editing actions.

three-dimensional graphics or **3D graphics** the use of images that simulate three dimensions by using perspective and shadows. Genuine three-dimensional images are obtained when each eye sees a slightly different view, and this can be achieved by using a headset, as in VIRTU-AL REALITY.

three-dimensional worksheet or **3D worksheet** a WORKSHEET for which several sets of ROWS AND COLUMNS can be displayed in sequence and summation or other arithmetical actions conducted through sheets as well as down columns and across rows. When several PAGES (sense 1) of such a worksheet are being used, call names can be prefixed with a page letter, such as D:A5 or B:C7. A straight slice through a set of pages (such as A:G7..Y7 to K:G7..Y7) is termed a COOKIE-CUTTER SLICE.

throughput a measure of computer performance in terms of work done per unit of time. This is measured for typical use, which involves read-ing, processing, displaying and writing data. This is often more useful than RAW DATA such as CLOCK rate, or a BENCHMARK, which measures only one aspect of performance.

thumbnail a miniature image, often used as a way of indexing a set of images.

thunk an action used by Microsoft WINDOWS 95 onwards when a program running 32-bit code has to make use of a piece of code (such as a DLL) that has been written in 16-bit code format. This slows down the pro-gram as compared to one that uses exclusively 32-bit code.

tick-list features features within a program that are never used but which must be present so that the program does not seem inferior to its competitors.

TIF a file EXTENSION denoting that the file is of graphics using the tagged image file format (TIFF) pattern.

TIFF (tagged image file format) a popular type of BITMAP graphics format for colour, grey-scale or monochrome images with RESOLUTION of up to 300 dots per inch. Many varieties of TIFF file are in use, some com-pressed (see COMPRESSED FILE), so a graphics program that saves or loads files with the TIF EXTENSION should provide for more than one format.

tilde the ~ character. This is used as part of an ALIAS (sense 1) FILENAME in DOS when a long filename has been used in a program running under Microsoft WINDOWS 95 onwards.

tiling or **tiled windows** the arrangement of SCREEN (sense 1) WINDOWS so that they do not overlap (see Fig. 42, overleaf). See also CASCADE.

tilt and swivel the action of a stand for a MONITOR (sense 2), allowing the monitor to be tilted up or down or swivelled round with little effort.

time bomb a form of BOMB (sense 1) that acts at some pre-set time.

timed backup an automatic BACKUP system used in WORD PROCESSOR, DTP and other programs. The data file is backed up at a set interval, such as every ten minutes, so that the data can be retrieved automatically in the

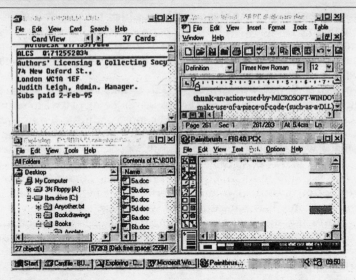

Fig. 42. **Tiling**. In this screen view, four active windows have been tiled so that all four are seen together. This is best used on large high-definition displays.

event of a system failure. The backup file is usually deleted or over-written when a new file is started. See also AUTOSAVE.

time division multiple access see TIME DIVISION MULTIPLEX.

time division multiplex (TDM) a system of communications in which several messages are transmitted simultaneously by sending small samples from each in turn along with synchronizing signals. The signals are reconstituted at the receiving end by using memory stores.

timeout a cancellation action that will take place if the user waits. This is applied usually to a PRINTER, so that a timeout message is delivered if the printer does not respond.

timesharing the use of a computer by several users, apparently all at the same time. This is done using TIME-SLICING techniques.

time-slice multitasking see PRE-EMPTIVE MULTITASKING.

time-slicing a method of allocating the use of a MICROPROCESSOR to several actions. This involves switching the microprocessor from one program to another at short intervals, particularly when the microprocessor would otherwise be idling. Time-slicing is easy when all the actions make use of KEYBOARDS because the time that is needed for a microprocessor to service a keyboard is very small compared to the time that a human operator takes to press a KEY (sense 1). Time-slicing is less easy when all the uses involve running active programs (calculating or backing up data, for example), and the method becomes cumbersome if all the uses require frequent disk ACCESS (sense 2).

time zone a geographical area in which all clocks show the same time. This should be approximately 15 degrees of longitude wide, but the boundaries are often varied for political reasons.

Tip of the Day a message system used in constituent programs of MICROSOFT OFFICE. When this facility is enabled, text will appear in a PANE each time a program is started, offering a hint about the use of the program. A few Tips are jokes; most others are very useful.

title bar the strip at the top of a WINDOW that carries the name of the program that is running in that window.

title of disk a word used as an identifying name or LABEL for a complete disk. Some disk systems allow each disk to carry a title which is stored on the disk and which appears in the disk DIRECTORY (sense 2). This is very useful for quick identification.

TOA (table of authorities) a table drawn up using a WORD PROCESSOR that contains references to sources of data, particularly to precedents for legal decisions. Each quotation can be marked in the document and the table of authorities automatically created.

TOC see TABLE OF CONTENTS (sense 1).

toggle a switch action. A KEY (sense 1) is said to be used as a toggle or to have a toggle action if pressing the key switches an action on and pressing again switches the action off. For example, the CAPS LOCK key has a toggle action. The advantage of using toggle action is that fewer KEY COMBINATIONS have to be remembered. The disadvantage is that it is not always possible to know whether an action is, at any given time, on or off. Microsoft WINDOWS 95 onwards ACCESSIBILITY OPTIONS allow you to turn on a sound option so that a BEEP sounds each time a toggle key is used – the note for turning an action off is not the same as that for turning the action on.

token-ring network a NETWORK in which a set of BITS, the *token*, circulates. Any message following the token will be transmitted throughout the system.

toner a finely powdered ink used in a LASER PRINTER. The powder must be capable of being electrostatically charged so as to adhere to the DRUM and must also have a low melting point so that it can be fixed to the paper. A magnetic 'carrier' powder is also used to pick up the toner from its cartridge. Great care must be taken in handling toner because if it is spilled it can be difficult to remove; vacuum-cleaning is not recommended because of the risk of damage to the motor and the likelihood that the toner will pass through out of the bag. Cold water should be used to remove toner from clothes; hot water will melt it into place.

toner cartridge a sealed container of TONER for a LASER PRINTER. Some toner cartridges (for example, Canon and Hewlett Packard) also contain the items that are subject to wear or fouling, such as the DRUM and the CORONA wire, so that the life of the printer itself can be very long, although cartridge replacements are expensive. Recycled cartridges for such machines should be avoided unless the source is known to be reputable.

tool any program that is used to analyse or modify another program.

toolbar or **button bar** a strip of ICON buttons that can be used to start commands or programs. Microsoft WINDOWS 95 onwards uses a toolbar at the foot of the screen for TASK SWITCHING.

toolbox a type of program that adds useful programming facilities to a computer. See also UTILITY. It is also used of the facilities available in a DTP, CAD or PAINT type of program.

ToolTip a short piece of explanatory text that appears when the POINTER is placed over an ICON.

top-down design a software design system that starts with an overall outline of what the program is intended to achieve and gradually expands to levels of greater detail.

topic drift a NEWSGROUP problem in which each THREAD tends to deviate from the original message topic until some entirely different subject is being discussed.

topic group see FORUM.

top-level domain the portion of a full INTERNET DOMAIN NAME that identifies the country of origin and type of site (academic, commercial, military, government, etc.).

top of form the position of the first printable line of a sheet of paper held in a printer. This is not necessarily at the top edge of the paper because the printer may need to run about one inch of paper through in order to grip the paper.

topology the geometrical study of NETWORK relationships, not necessarily related to computing.

touch pad an INPUT device that uses switch contacts placed under a plastic pad that may be inscribed with symbols. The device is sometimes used as a KEYBOARD substitute and is also used as a way of controlling a program, with specialized inscriptions on each of the pads. The system also has applications in GRAPHICS as a method of transferring diagrams to the SCREEN (sense 1). See also GRAPHICS TABLET.

touch screen a system of making computer inputs without using the KEYBOARD. When a finger interrupts a pair of infrared beams that cross the SCREEN (sense 1), the position of the finger can be digitized (see DIGITIZE) into X and Y COORDINATE numbers and used by the operating system (OS). The method is particularly useful for MENU choice and is an alternative to the more popular and much less expensive MOUSE. Touch screens are used mainly for displays that are open for public use.

tower case a casing that is used for a computer of high specification, such as a SERVER. The tower case is tall and narrow, taking up less space on a desk, and is often placed on the floor beside a desk. Typical tower cases offer much more internal space than the DESKTOP variety and are ideal when a system uses more than one HARD DRIVE, FLOPPY DISK drive, CD-ROM and other internal devices.

tpi (tracks per inch) the packing of TRACKs on a disk. Modern 3.5-inch floppy disks use a track density of 135 tracks per inch and closer packing can be achieved; see FLOPTICAL DISK.

track a circle on the surface of a disk that stores data. This is not a physically identifiable circle in the way that the track of a conventional gramophone disc can be identified. The track of a disk is determined by the construction of the disk drive and not by any marking on the disk itself. A track is usually subdivided into SECTORS. See also CYLINDER.

track at once a system for writing a CD-R or CD-RW disc that writes the SESSION as a set of complete TRACKs; compare DISC AT ONCE.

trackerball or **trackball** a form of inverted MOUSE, with a ball surface facing uppermost, mounted in a box, which can be rotated by the fingers or the palm of the hand in any direction so as to control the movement of the SCREEN (sense 1) CURSOR.

tracking the spacing between characters in a text. A WORD PROCESSOR will allow the tracking to be changed by whatever percentage figure is required. See also KERNING.

tracking file a file used to RECORD (sense 2) the disk locations of other files; see DELETION TRACKING.

tracks per inch see TPI.

track-to-track access time the time, measured in MILLISECONDS, needed to move the READ/WRITE HEAD of a HARD DRIVE from one TRACK to the next. This is one measure of hard drive speed.

tractor feed a method of feeding perforated or sprocketed paper into a printer. This allows the paper to be precisely positioned and is essential if continuous forms are to be used. See also FRICTION FEED; SPROCKET HOLES.

traffic computer signals passing by means of a data link.

trailer a final RECORD (sense 1) in a data file that may consist only of TERMINATOR (sense 1) bytes or that may carry information on the rest of the file.

transaction any updating work on a DATABASE FILE. This can include entry of a new RECORD (sense 1), amending a record, deleting a record, etc. Any transaction on a SERIAL file, apart from adding a record at the end of the file, normally requires the whole of the file to be read and rewritten.

transceiver a device that can transmit and receive data, such as a MODEM.

transcribe to convert from one FORMAT (sense 3) to another, such as from one disk format to another or from tape to disk.

transducer a device that converts one type of signal into another, for example, magnetic to electrical, light to electrical, and so on. A disk or tape READ/WRITE HEAD is a transducer, as is a LOUDSPEAKER, microphone or a cathode ray tube (CRT). A transducer is often an essential part of a DIGITIZER.

transfer rate the rate at which data can be moved to and from disk or the rate at which data can be moved along a SERIAL link to other computers. The rate is often expressed in BAUD, meaning for computing purposes BITS PER SECOND.

transient (of a disturbance) short-term, usually applied to a power surge (PSU) or electrical interference or NOISE pulse.

transistor the simplest SEMICONDUCTOR amplifying device. A transistor can be of bipolar or FIELD EFFECT TRANSISTOR (FET) construction. The FETs form the basis of most of the ICs used in small computers, but for larger computers in which high speed is an overriding factor, bipolar principles are used.

transistor-transistor logic see TTL.

transition see BRIDGE.

translate utility a UTILITY used by a WORD PROCESSOR, DATABASE or SPREADSHEET that will allow a document created by another program to be read. The converse action is often possible, allowing a program to create a file that is of the FORMAT (sense 2) used by another program. The translate action may be built into the word processor, database or spreadsheet.

translation program a program that will translate the language of a document into another language. The action is reasonably satisfactory when the document contains standard business phrases, but it can be ludicrously incorrect when colloquial language is used.

transmission control protocol/Internet protocol see TCP/IP.

transmit to send out data.

transparent action anything in computing that is not obvious to the user, i.e. any complicated action that is dealt with entirely by the operating system (OS) and needs no effort on the part of the user. For example, the user may specify a filename and a disk drive number, but the action of checking DIRECTORY, selecting a TRACK and SECTOR and recording a file is done 'transparently' by the disk-operating system. Another example is the refreshing of DRAM memory.

transport layer the portion of the ISO/OSI NETWORK system that defines the PROTOCOLS.

transputer a PARALLEL PROCESSING element designed as a single-CHIP computer, consisting of the MICROPROCESSOR, ROM and RAM memory and PORTS all constructed onto one single chip. Transputers are designed to link with each other to provide any size of parallel computing machine. See also OCCAM.

trash can see RECYCLE BIN.

Travan™ a form of TAPE CARTRIDGE drive, developed by COLORADO, that accepts QIC-40 or QIC-80 tapes, covering both older 120-megabyte tapes and the more recent 800-megabyte size. This allows the tape BACKUP system to be upgraded without losing the backup information in the older tapes.

trawl to look through large amounts of data for something of interest that is not indexed.

tree 1. the DIRECTORY (sense 1) or folder structure for a HARD DRIVE in which files are grouped into directories that are in turn listed along with files in a ROOT DIRECTORY. **2.** a data structure in the form of a simple HIERARCHY in which each piece of data can lead to (at least) two more. Trees are used extensively in DATABASEs, particularly in large databases. You might, for example, look up 'travel' and be given the choice of 'air', 'road', 'sea' or 'rail'. When you select 'air', you are given a list of airlines. When you select an airline, you are given a list of airports. When you select an airport, you are given a list of destinations, and when you select a destination, you are given a list of flight times. It can be fascinating to browse through but infuriating if you just want to find if there is a 1300 flight to Geneva on a Tuesday. For such an application, the type of database that accepts the KEY (sense 2) words 'flight', 'Geneva' and 'Tuesday' to find an entry that contains each word is better. See also BINARY TREE.

tree-and-branch network a form of NETWORK in which the file SERVER feeds several TERMINALs which in turn each feed several more terminals, arranged like the roots or the branches (upside-down) of a tree.

treeware printed material, particularly MANUALs.

triangle a symbol used on a MENU to indicate that a SUBMENU is available. Clicking (see CLICK, sense 1) the triangle will open the submenu.

Trojan horse a program that is apparently innocent but will carry out destructive actions when running, such as deleting or altering files. See also CRACKER; VIRUS.

troll an EMAIL or NEWSGROUP message that is deliberately incorrect, aimed at provoking a response. A troll is not as obvious as a FLAME BAIT.

trouble-shooting the detection and repair of faults, either in HARDWARE or in SOFTWARE.

TRUE one of the two BOOLEAN conditions of TRUE or FALSE, corresponding to the two possible BINARY digits. True/False actions are used in DATABASE forms, such as in Yes/No entries.

true colour the use of 24 bits per PIXEL of colour information, giving images that are very close to natural colour. See PHOTOREALISM.

TrueType a form of FONT used in WINDOWS. TrueType is a SCALEABLE FONT that can be used both for SCREEN (sense 1) display and PRINTER, requiring no expensive additions to a printer. See also POSTSCRIPT.

truncation the transforming of a REAL NUMBER into an INTEGER by omitting the fractions or the shortening of a number by omitting digits from the LEAST SIGNIFICANT end.

truncation error an error in number size that arises because a portion of a number has been omitted, often because the allocated storage space is not adequate. This is not necessarily serious, and programs can often compensate for the errors. For example, the number 4.33333333 can usually be truncated to 4.3333 without significant loss of precision.

TSR program (terminate and stay resident program) or **memory-resident program** a type of program used in a PERSONAL COMPUTER that can cease to run but remains in its reserved memory space. Such a program can be called back into operation by using a HOT KEY or called from another program.

TTL (transistor-transistor logic) a design method used for older ICs in which the signals used a voltage level from zero to +0.8V to represent logic 0 and levels 3.5V to 5.0V to represent logic 1.

TTL monitor an old type of MONITOR (sense 1) in which the VIDEO signals are digital, either on or off. This makes the monitor suitable for monochrome, or a limited range of colour signals, only. The other type of monitor, now almost universal, is the ANALOGUE MONITOR.

tune to optimize hardware and software for the best possible performance.

Turing, Alan Mathison (1912–54) the English mathematician who in 1937 proved that any problem having a logical solution could be reduced to a set of simple instruction steps, thus laying the foundation for the design of practicable computers. Turing was also responsible for the design of the ENIGMA code-breaking machine. See also BLETCHLEY PARK.

Turing test a test that can be applied to ARTIFICIAL INTELLIGENCE systems. It consists of arranging for a human operator to communicate with a computer from a remote terminal. If, from the machine's responses, the operator is unable to tell whether there is a human being or a machine at the other end, then the machine is exhibiting artificial intelligence. No machine has ever satisfied this test.

turnkey a COMPUTER SYSTEM requiring initially little or no user participation. A turnkey system of installation means that the supplier of a (large) computer system will see to its installation, wiring of peripherals, including any changes to buildings, provision of software and training or provision of operators. The name comes from the phrase that the owner only has to 'turn the key'. Turnkey is also applied to hardware or software that requires no understanding of the computer on the part of the user, and this is the direction in which microcomputers and their software are rapidly moving.

tutorial a PROGRAM that is intended to guide a learner in the use of a program. Early versions used text only, but tutorials now can show animated illustrations (see VIDEO CLIP) and simulations of program action. The price of this improved capability is the large files that need to be stored.

TV (television) the transmission by means of electrical signals of a series of transient visible images to a distant SCREEN (sense 1). At one time, small computers made use of a domestic TV receiver as a MONITOR (sense 2), but this use of a TV receiver fell into disuse with the introduction of VGA monitors. In order to make use of a TV receiver, the video signals from the computer must be modulated on to a UHF CARRIER (sense 2) signal; see MODULATION. This causes complications if the computer has to be exported because three different colour standards exist and many minor differences in specifications and in frequency ranges. A much more satisfactory system is to use a SCART connector with a suitable interface at the computer. This can be used to show PRESENTATION GRAPHICS on a large-screen TV receiver. A few types of computers designed for mainly INTERNET use are sold without a monitor but with provision for connection to a TV receiver.

TWAIN an interfacing code standard used to allow any GRAPHICS program to obtain image data from a SCANNER or DIGITAL CAMERA. The name is claimed to be an acronym of 'technology without an interesting name'.

tweak a minor adjustment intended to improve performance, applied to HARDWARE or SOFTWARE.

tweening a graphics animation method that uses the computer to insert additional frames between the frames (*key frames*) that the creator has drawn, so providing smoother animation at lower cost.

tweeter a small LOUDSPEAKER intended for reproducing the highest notes in music. See also WOOFER.

twin-bin a PRINTER that can use two paper stores, often one for A4 paper and the other for envelopes, and feed from either under software instructions.

twisted-pair cable a low-cost form of cable in which pairs of wires are twisted together to neutralize the effect of external interference to some extent. Such cable has been used in SERIAL links and for some low-cost NETWORK wiring. See also COAXIAL CABLE.

two-part stationery paper in continuous form, consisting of a top sheet, a carbon and a copy sheet.

twos complement a method of forming the BINARY equivalent of a negative number. See also NEGATION.

two-valued logic see BOOLEAN OPERATION.

TYPE the MS-DOS command to print a file to the VDU. This should be used only with text files, and a long file will 0 at a high speed. A better use of the command is TYPE | MORE, which will page the output, moving to the next PAGE (sense 1) when any KEY (sense 1) is pressed.

type code the portion of a DOMAIN NAME that indicates the type of site, such as *gov* for *government*, *ac* for *academic*, etc.

typeface or **face** the design of a complete FONT set of characters. Each design is named, and many of the names are of ancient origin.

typematic action the repeating action of the keys of a computer KEYBOARD, obtained when a KEY (sense 1) is held down for more than half a second or so.

typeover the action of replacing one character by another. See INSERT MODE; OVERTYPE MODE.

typesetting bureau an agency that will accept DTP files on disk and produce masters for printing machines. See also BROMIDE OUTPUT.

typesetting the production of a paper COPY (sense 3) that can be reproduced by photographic methods; see CAMERA-READY. At one time, a DTP program was required for typesetting, but HIGH-END WORD PROCESSOR programs such as MICROSOFT WORD or WORDPERFECT can set type for book production. See also BROMIDE OUTPUT.

type size the height of the UPPER-CASE letters of a FONT, usually measured in POINT units.

type style the form of a FONT in terms of normal (or ROMAN), BOLD, ITALIC or underlined (see UNDERLINE). See also POSTURE; WEIGHT.

typo or **typographical error** a misspelling, for example, or any other error made at the KEYBOARD.

typography the study of printing, particularly of FONT design and use.

UAE (unrecoverable application error) a problem encountered in early versions of WINDOWS. The effect of a UAE was to stop the offending program running and as often as not to stop Windows (particularly Windows 3.0) from running. Windows 3.1 suffered less from such effects, and the corresponding fault was labelled as general protection fault (GPF), which would affect only the current program. Microsoft WINDOWS 95 onwards delivers a longer message to the effect that an error has occurred, and you have the option of ignoring the error and saving your files or cancelling the use of the program. In many cases, ignoring the error and continuing working is possible.

UART (universal asynchronous receiver transmitter) a type of PORT chip that allows communication to and from the computer using SERIAL links. 'Asynchronous' means that the serial signals do not have to be transmitted continuously, only when data is being sent. Many serial port chips are manufactured so that they can be used either in synchronous or asynchronous form. Compare USART; USRT.

UCSD (University College of San Diego) a college of the University of California that has specialized in computing languages, and several versions of HIGH-LEVEL LANGUAGES bear the UCSD prefix.

UHF (ultra-high frequency) the range of radio frequencies that is used for transmitting TV signals in Britain and in many other countries.

ULA (uncommitted logic array) a CHIP in which the signal paths are left unconnected and on the surface after the main manufacturing processes. This particular feature allows a manufacturer to specify what he wants, so that a chip can be made at low cost but yet custom-designed to fit a specialized purpose. This is done by making surface connections between various points. The extensive use of ULAs was the design method by which computer prices were forced down so spectacularly in the early 1980s.

Ultra DMA or **ATA-4** a system developed by Quantum Corporation for very fast transfer of data between memory and the hard drive.

ultra-high frequency see UHF.

Ultra-SCSI a faster version of SCSI based on SCSI-2.

umb see UPPER MEMORY BLOCK.

unallowable digit a BIT that makes a BYTE or WORD (sense 2) unacceptable, not part of the set allowed for the system. For example, in the 7-bit ASCII set, setting the 8th bit would make a code unallowable.

unary operation an action on one VARIABLE, which may be a number,

BYTE or WORD (sense 2). For example, NEGATION and INCREMENT (sense 1) are operations on just one number. Compare BINARY OPERATION.

unbundled software SOFTWARE that is not provided along with a computer or other HARDWARE but has to be purchased separately.

uncommitted logic array see ULA.

uncompression see DECOMPRESSING FILES.

unconditional format a FORMAT (sense 4) action that will destroy any data on the disk and cannot be reversed by using an UNFORMAT UTILITY. Unconditional format is used for new disks and for disks whose files must be destroyed – the equivalent of using a file shredder on paper.

undelete an operating system (OS), UTILITY or TOOLBOX action that allows a 'deleted' file to be recovered. A file is deleted from disk by removing its directory entries, and providing nothing else has been recorded on the disk, the file can be recovered by replacing these entries. Microsoft WINDOWS 95 onwards shows 'deleted' files in a RECYCLE BIN from which they can be either recovered or irrevocably deleted.

underflow a number result that is too small to represent.

underline to draw a line under text on paper or on the SCREEN (sense 1). This action is useful in WORD PROCESSOR programs, particularly if the underline can be shown on the screen. Underlining is usually achieved by using EMBEDDED COMMANDS to the PRINTER, but each make of printer generally requires a different code sequence. The normal action is to use one code for the start of underlining and another for the end. In some systems, underlining automatically stops at the end of a line, in others it always continues until cancelled.

underscore the _ character, ASCII 95, used to UNDERLINE and to separate portions of a FILENAME or INTERNET USER NAME.

undo button a TOOLBAR button that can be clicked to undo the last action. Modern programs use multilevel undo, so that each time the undo button is clicked, another action in the sequence will be reversed. The undo action uses memory, and a large number of changes can result in running out of memory unless the undo action is suspended.

undo command a command used in WORD PROCESSOR, GRAPHICS and DTP programs that will reverse the most recent action. In CAD programs, the undo action can be used many times in succession, reversing earlier steps, but in some other types of programs only the most recent action can be undone. A multiple undo action can require a large amount of memory, so that on a word processor that is using a SEARCH AND REPLACE action on a long document, you may be warned that undo cannot be used without running out of memory. See also REDO COMMAND.

undocumented feature any action of a program that is not dealt with in the MANUAL or in a HELP (sense 1) file but often simply a BUG.

unexpected halt the ending of a program brought about by a fault condition.

unformat utility a UTILITY that will reverse the action of a QUICKFORMAT, allowing data to be read from a disk. See also UNCONDITIONAL FORMAT.

unformatted capacity the capacity in kilobytes of an UNFORMATTED DISK. This is of no importance for ordinary data storage since the disk must be formatted to be useful, but it indicates how much more the disk can store if used with unorthodox formatting methods, such as are used by BACKUP systems.

unformatted disk a disk in its natural state, following manufacture and before being formatted (see FORMAT, sense 3). An unformatted disk is normally unusable, but some forms of BACKUP programs can store data on such disks in compressed form.

unfreeze to remove LOCKING on a DATABASE record or a WORKSHEET row or column.

Unicode a 16-bit code for alphabetical characters, intended to cover all major world languages. This has become an extended form of ASCII in order to maintain compatibility.

uniform resource locator see URL.

uninstall an operating system (OS) or PROGRAM action that will remove a program from the HARD DRIVE and also any links that exist between the program and other SOFTWARE. This is particularly important for WINDOWS programs because of the way that dynamic link libraries (DLL) are shared among programs.

uninstaller a program that reverses the action of installing a software package, removing all references and LINKS (sense 2) and tidying up the HARD DRIVE. Many large programs now come with an uninstaller, such as InstallShield, built in.

uninterruptible power supply see UPS.

unique ID listing a method of identifying an EMAIL message, used by a POP3 SERVER.

unique key a DATABASE KEY (sense 2) that leads to one item of data only.

unit separator (US) the ASCII character 31.

universal asynchronous receiver transmitter see UART.

universal serial bus see USB.

universal synchronous/asynchronous receiver transmitter see USART.

universal synchronous receiver transmitter see USRT.

universal thunk a software routine that allows a program written for WINDOWS 3.1 to call a 32-bit dynamic link library (DLL). See also THUNK.

Unix an operating system (OS) that permits MULTI-ACCESS and MULTITASK-ING actions, originally developed for MAINFRAME computers. Unix, in the hands of a programmer, permits immense control over a computer, but it requires huge resources of RAM and disk space. Despite efforts at standardization it exists in a bewildering variety of versions. See also LINUX; XENIX.

unjustified text text of uneven line length. See JUSTIFY.

unlinking the action of removing a LINK between a file and a document. If you unlink a graphics file in a WORD PROCESSOR or DTP document, the image will disappear if it has not been saved with the document. If the image is a part of the document, it will remain visible but it will not be automatically updated when the original graphics file is altered.

unlock to remove WRITE PROTECTION from a document so that it can be modified and users on a NETWORK can edit the document.

unmoderated newsgroup a NEWSGROUP in which no attempt is made to restrain users, who may engage in fruitless and often pointless arguments, using up computer time.

unpack to extract data from a compressed form (see COMPRESSING) back into a state that allows it to be used in other programs.

unprotected field the part of a RECORD (sense 1) that can be changed. See FIELD (sense 2); RANDOM-ACCESS FILE.

unprotected software software that can be copied by making use of the normal BACKUP features of the operating system (OS). Unprotected software allows the user to take the normal precaution of working with backups, retaining the original software for emergencies. The use for business purposes of software that cannot be backed up is extremely risky.

unrecoverable application error see UAE.

unrecoverable error an error in a program that causes a CRASH (sense 1) so that data in the memory cannot be used when the program is restarted.

unshielded twisted pair the standard US telephone wire, sometimes used for small NETWORK connections on cost grounds.

unsigned (of a BINARY NUMBER) in which the most significant bit (MSB) is used as a value bit rather than as a SIGN BIT. Compare SIGNED.

unzip a decompressing utility used to extract files in ZIP form. See also PKZIP.

UPC see BAR CODE.

update to amend a file with recent data. Files often have to be updated daily, weekly or monthly, according to how rapidly the data becomes out of date. Easy updating requires the use of RANDOM-ACCESS FILES rather than SERIAL files. A file update action consists of locating the file to update and displaying it on the SCREEN (sense 1) so that the file can be edited. Finally the file must be resaved on the disk because until this is done the updating does not become effective. The effort required in updating is one reason for preferring the RELATIONAL DATABASE, as compared to simpler types, because this will ensure that updating an item such as a name and address will be effective for all the users of that file. On a simpler system, the same updating might have been required on several files.

upgrade an addition or replacement to a computer HARDWARE or SOFT-

WARE that allows better operation, such as greater speed, better use of memory, more memory, etc.

upload to transfer files from a computer over an INTERNET connection to a WEB SITE, or any transfer of files from a local system to a large central system. See also DOWNLOAD.

upper-case relating to the capital letters, as distinct from 'small' letters. Contrast LOWER-CASE.

upper memory block (UMB) or **reserved memory** or **upper memory area (UMA)** part of the MEMORY that lies between 640 kilobytes and 1 megabyte on a PERSONAL COMPUTER. This portion of memory can be used for short DOS programs if a suitable DRIVER (such as EMM386) is running. The use of UMB memory was important for DOS applications but is of little or no interest for users of Microsoft WINDOWS 95 onwards.

UPS (uninterruptible power supply) an attachment to the power line of a computer that will maintain the power supply when the MAINS power fails. This is done using batteries so that the time for which the UPS will run the computer is limited. When mains power fails, the UPS should issue a warning, and the user should save files and shut down the system in an orderly way until mains power is restored.

upthread an item that comes earlier in a THREAD of NEWSGROUP messages.

upward compatibility the ability of a simple computing system to work along with more advanced equipment. A computer is upward-compatible if a program written for it can also be used on a more advanced machine. The reverse is not necessarily true (compare DOWNWARD COMPATIBILITY). It is also used of software so that, for example, MICROSOFT WORD 6 can read and write files created by Word 2, but Word 2 cannot use the files of Word 6. Closer compatibility exists between the files of Word 6 and the later versions.

URL (uniform resource locator) the standard method of finding a site on the INTERNET. The URL uses a text phrase consisting of sections separated by FORWARD SLASH signs, with a format that allows the name to be converted easily into a numerical INTERNET ADDRESS.

USART (universal synchronous/asynchronous receiver transmitter) a type of PORT chip that can send or receive signals along SERIAL links with either synchronous or asynchronous PROTOCOLS (sense 1). Compare UART; USRT.

US-ASCII the 7-bit original ASCII code that is incorporated into later 8-bit codes and also into UNICODE.

USB (universal serial BUS) a fast type of SERIAL port connection for PERIPHERALS. USB support is built into Windows 98 and later versions. Cables are inexpensive and can be up to 5 metres long. Up to a total of 127 devices can be daisy-chained (see DAISY-CHAIN) from one outlet.

Usenet the original (1979) NEWSGROUP BULLETIN BOARD which has set standards for all others.

user area an area used for storage of data that is available for the computer user. The term applies to storage space either in RAM or on disk on which the user can store data. In RAM, the operating system (OS) will take up some memory space even if the main operating system is in ROM. Space will also be required for SCREEN (sense 1) use, and what is left is user space. Similarly, on a disk, two TRACKS may be needed for DIRECTORY (sense 2) data, and the rest of the disk surface is available for the user.

user base the number of users of a product.

user default a program DEFAULT that can be set by the user, such as the default size of paper used by a WORD PROCESSOR.

user-definable (of a program action) able to be tailored to suit the user, such as the choice between displaying or not displaying a RULE.

user-defined character a character, not a part of the ASCII set, whose shape can be defined by the user by filling in dots on a diagram.

user-friendly (of a part of a computer system) being easy to work with. A system can be said to be truly user-friendly if the first-time user can make use of it without continual reference to a MANUAL. Unfortunately, most manuals are even less user-friendly than programs, and operating systems (OS) have in the past appeared to be designed to be user-unfriendly. Because of this problem, some software producers have devised FRONT END programs that manipulate the operating system but present a user-friendly aspect to the user. Typical of these are the GUI operating systems as used on the MACINTOSH and the PERSONAL COMPUTER.

user group a set of users of one make of MICROCOMPUTER or SOFTWARE who band together to help each other, sometimes in the hope of persuading the manufacturer to support the product better.

user ID a reference name or number for a computer user on a NETWORK.

user interface the method by which the actions of a program are controlled, such as the HARDWARE keyboard or mouse, or the SOFTWARE of a GUI system.

user name a name for a computer user that, together with a PASSWORD, establishes that user's rights to log on to the system. The user name often serves as the IDENTIFIER for EMAIL.

user port a PORT at which the main data and other signals of the computer are available for any other equipment that you wish to connect. Both inputs and outputs are available, but software will be needed to operate the port.

user profile a file of information required by a NETWORK system. Each user profile contains information, such as PASSWORDs, that are specific to that user of the network.

USRT (universal synchronous receiver transmitter) a variety of PORT for sending and receiving SERIAL signals with SYNCHRONIZATION. 'Synchronous' implies that signals are sent continually in time with a clock pulse. This is true of asynchronous transmissions only during the transmission of a byte. Synchronous transmissions send a 'sync character' byte even when there is no data to send. This ensures that the signal remains synchronized at all times. In an asynchronous system, the transmitter must send START and STOP BITS to ensure that synchronization is achieved for each byte. Compare UART; USART.

utility a program that can be used to make programming easier. For the larger type of machine, these utilities will relate to such actions as formatting disks, copying programs and setting up links to other computers. A set of these utilities will generally be included with the operating system on the SYSTEM DISK. Some utilities assume a greater knowledge of the machine than would be possessed by a casual user. The term is also used of suites of utility programs intended to recover data and manipulate disk files, such as Norton's Utilities and PC-Tools. See also TOOLBOX.

uudecode a program that reads UUENCODE ASCII files and converts back into BINARY form.

uuencode a program that converts BINARY code into ASCII characters, used mainly for sending program or graphics files by EMAIL.

V the symbol for VOLTAGE.

V.90 a MODEM PROTOCOL allowing speeds of up to 56 KBPS for downloading and up to 33.6 kbps for uploading. This assumes that a modem is used at one end only, the other computer using a digital link. This standard is intended to end competition between the X2™ and K56FLEX™ systems.

vaccine a UTILITY program that is intended to protect against VIRUS infection. The vaccine (or *immunizing*) program is resident in memory and detects any attempt to change a program file. This type of program may have to be suppressed when you wish to install new programs.

validation a method of limiting the values that can be entered into a DATABASE. For example, a validation rule can specify an expression such as <>0, meaning that a zero value is unacceptable, or 'Essex' OR 'Suffolk' OR 'Norfolk' to specify acceptable answers to the field called County. Validation systems are sometimes referred to as *mugtraps*.

value a number entry in a WORKSHEET CELL. This number may be directly entered or calculated by a FORMULA.

value-added network a NETWORK that is restricted to fee-paying members and provides information that is not publicly available.

value-added reseller a wholesaler or retailer who purchases hardware or software and adds additional components to increase, in theory, the value.

VBA (Visual Basic for applications) a form of SCRIPTING LANGUAGE common (in theory) to all the programs in the MICROSOFT OFFICE set.

vanilla plain and unmodified, with no additions, basic and simple.

vapourware SOFTWARE or HARDWARE that is much talked about, often promised but delivered late or not at all, or suffering from BUGS.

variable a quantity that is represented in a program by a name (see IDENTIFIER) and whose value can be changed by such actions as ASSIGNMENT. For example, a name can represent a set of data items in a DATABASE or a RANGE in a WORKSHEET. It helps considerably if these names can be 'meaningful' in the sense that the name will remind the user of what quantity is represented.

variable length field a DATABASE field that can be automatically altered in size to suit the data, subject to a maximum size. The use of variable length fields can be a very useful way of reducing the space required for data as compared to FIXED-LENGTH FIELD use.

variants box a display used in Microsoft POWERPOINT to offer choices of shading for a slide.

VCR (video cassette recorder) used in some interactive video systems and as a BACKUP system (if suitable software and interfacing is available) for files on a HARD DRIVE.

VDU (visual display unit) the MONITOR (sense 1), SCREEN (sense 1) or TV display unit.

vector font a file that contains a set of drawing instructions for creating the shapes of characters. The advantage of this method of creating a DTP FONT is that the sizes can be scaled up or down easily; there is no need to keep a file for each size of font. See also BITMAPPED FONT.

vector graphics or **object-specific graphics** or **object-oriented drawing** a graphics drawing system. A vector graphics system allows lines to be drawn and then manipulated by using the KEYBOARD, LIGHT PEN or MOUSE. The description of the lines is geometrical, using an equation to represent a line, so that a vector drawing can be scaled easily and precisely – a different scale simply means altering a multiplier in the equation. The alternative BITMAP scheme uses individual PIXELS and cannot be rescaled easily because it is tied to the system (usually the VDU) that created it.

vector to raster conversion utility a UTILITY program that will convert a drawing in VECTOR GRAPHICS form to one in BITMAP form. Such utilities are often packaged with drawing, particularly CAD, programs. The bitmap version is sometimes described as a *slide*.

Ventura Publisher a large and comprehensive DTP program that allows for all forms and sizes of work, from a poster to a book, to be produced. See also ADOBE PAGEMAKER; MICROSOFT PUBLISHER.

verify to check a recording. When data has been saved, particularly to a BACKUP system, it is desirable to be able to check that a file has been correctly recorded before the file is erased. The verify action should check that the saved file is identical to the file in the memory. Not all verify commands carry out this complete *verification*; some simply check that the number of bytes is the same.

Versabraille™ a Braille computer for visually impaired users that allows input in Braille only, using a Braille keyboard, but the output of which can be either to a BRAILLE TACTILE DISPLAY or to a standard printer, allowing operators to check their work in Braille and then make a printout in conventional form.

version a MICROSOFT WORD system for using a single FILENAME to refer to a document that has been changed, with each change noted and the earlier edition available. A version can also be saved with a different filename to prevent the file becoming cumbersome.

version number a number carried by SOFTWARE or FIRMWARE to identify its version and in some cases its legitimacy. Major changes are indicated by a change in the INTEGER, minor changes by a change in the fraction, so that V.5.21, for example, is similar to all the series from 5.00 onwards but has been upgraded in minor ways from the previous 5.20 version. This scheme is not always followed – for example MICROSOFT WORD for WINDOWS changed from V.2.0 to V.6.0 so as to stay in line with the numbering of the version for the Mac.

verso the left-hand page in a pair of document pages, which will by convention carry an even number. See also RECTO.

vertical application a PROGRAM or SUITE OF PROGRAMS designed for use by a specific type of user, such as a dentist, an architect, etc.

vertical bar the | character, ASCII 124, or the ¦ broken vertical bar, ASCII 166. The broken bar is obtained on many UK keyboards by using the Alt Gr key in combination with the ` key to the left of the 1-key.

vertical blanking interval the suppression of video signal in the time of FRAME FLYBACK. See RASTER.

vertical centring the action of a WORD PROCESSOR that can move text or graphics so that the upper and lower size of white space is equal.

vertical justification or **feathering** (sense 2) the automatic justification of newspaper columns that avoids the effect of a ragged bottom margin by adjusting the spacing between lines. The use of vertical justification ensures that all columns end evenly at the bottom margin.

vertical resolution the ability of a MONITOR (sense 1) to display fine detail in the vertical direction. This is determined by the number of LINES (sense 2) per FRAME (sense 2). TV receivers using PAL or SECAM have a lower vertical resolution for colour than for MONOCHROME.

vertical refresh rate see REFRESH CRT.

vertical scanning frequency the rate in terms of FRAMES (sense 2) per second at which a MONITOR (sense 1) completes scanning a picture.

very large scale integration see VLSI.

very low frequency see VLF.

VESA local bus see VLB.

VGA (video graphics array) the standard graphics board system for the PERSONAL COMPUTER. This is a BITMAP, using a standard resolution of 640 PIXELS horizontally and 480 pixels vertically, with up to 16 colours on a SCREEN (sense 1). The MONITOR (sense 1) that is used for VGA is of the ANALOGUE type, permitting a much larger range of colours to be displayed as compared to the DIGITAL or TTL MONITOR. The VGA board allows the use of older graphics systems such as CGA and EGA. See also SVGA.

video (of an electrical signal) carrying picture information. The video signals from a computer are the signals that a MONITOR (sense 1) will use to form a picture, whether of text or of graphics. See also COMPOSITE VIDEO; MODULATOR (sense 1); RGB; VIDEO SIGNAL.

video adapter the circuit card, usually plugged into an EXPANSION SLOT or a LOCAL BUS slot, that provides the output to the MONITOR (sense 1). On some computers, the video adapter is part of the MOTHERBOARD but can be disabled if another board is used in an expansion slot.

video bandwidth the range of frequencies that is needed for VIDEO SIGNALS. The video bandwidth is measured in MHz and implies that any frequency from zero up to this limit will be present in a signal. For HIGH-RESOLUTION GRAPHICS and 80-column text, a video bandwidth of at least 18 MHz is desirable. This contrasts with the 5 MHz that is normally available on a domestic TV receiver. Most good quality MONITORs (sense 1) can achieve a bandwidth of 18 MHz and some more than 24 MHz.

video capture camera a video camera that will capture images as digital files. In practice, a normal camcorder can be used with its video output plugged into a video capture board in the computer.

video cassette recorder see VCR.

video CD see DVD.

video clip a file that can be used to provide an animated picture, usually of a small size, within a document in a WORD PROCESSOR or a PRESENTATION GRAPHICS program. Although compression (see COMPRESSED FILE) is used on these video files, they are very large compared to the usual size of the text document into which they can be inserted. A large number of video clips can be stored on a video COMPACT DISC.

video compression a form of compression (see COMPRESSED FILE) for video data that depends on the small differences between one FRAME (sense 2) and the next in a sequence. This allows a complete sequence to be coded using little more than is needed to describe the first frame. The best-known video compression standards are due to MPEG.

video conference a virtual meeting in which the participants can see each other as well as talk to each other. Because of BANDWIDTH restrictions, VIDEO COMPRESSION is needed.

video disc a disc that is written on by means of a LASER with a BIT pattern that represents a VIDEO SIGNAL. The information is stored in digital form, as on a COMPACT DISC, and can be read using a low-power laser. By using compression techniques, a disc of audio CD size can carry a reasonable time of VIDEO SIGNAL which can be used in MULTIMEDIA and interactive video displays. See also DVD.

video graphics array see VGA.

video memory the memory used for storing signals for the VDU display, located on the graphics adapter. The minimum is 256 kilobytes, but video memory of 2 megabytes or more is needed for high resolution and photographic colour displays.

video RAM (VRAM) the amount of RAM memory used as VIDEO MEMORY on a VIDEO ADAPTER board.

video signal a signal that can be used by a MONITOR (sense 1) or TV unit to produce a picture on the SCREEN (sense 1). This signal is not a purely

DIGITAL signal, hence the need for interface chips to generate the signals. Colour monitors for the PC require three sets of video signals, one for red, one for green and one for blue. This system is known as red-green-blue (RGB) and provides the best quality colour displays. The method used for video cassette units is COMPOSITE VIDEO, in which these three colour signals are coded into one signal along with synchronization signals.

viewer a short program for reading DOCUMENTS or GRAPHICS produced by larger applications. Viewers are often distributed as FREEWARE.

virgin tape TAPE for BACKUP purposes that has never been recorded on – the next best option is bulk-erased tape (see BULK ERASE).

virtual not real, simulated.

virtual 8086 or **virtual machine (VM)** a mode of action of chips such as the INTEL 80386 or 80486 in which a piece of memory 640 kilobytes in size is used to RUN (sense 2) a program (usually an MS-DOS program) independently of other similar pieces of memory. Each 640 kilobytes of RAM behaves as if it were controlled by a separate 8086 chip in a PC-XT type of machine. This action also allows different programs to be run in different SCREEN (sense 1) WINDOWS.

virtual 86 mode a way of using the later type of processors, such as the PENTIUM class, to run MS-DOS applications in a reserved area of memory.

virtual address an address number that is beyond the range that can be used in physically present CORE MEMORY and which refers to a LOCATION (sense 2) in a simulated (virtual) memory map that is usually implemented by using PERIPHERAL MEMORY, normally HARD DRIVE space.

virtual cache a CACHE connected between the PROCESSOR and the MEMORY MANAGEMENT system so that it cannot share its memory with other units.

virtual community a group of computer users who are in contact by EMAIL or INTERNET and who share and discuss common interests.

virtual device any simulated device, such as the use of a HARD DRIVE to simulate memory.

virtual device driver (VxD or **VXD)** a WINDOWS DEVICE DRIVER that, although a separate file with a VXD EXTENSION, is used as part of the main program code for Windows.

virtual drive see RAMDISK.

virtual host an INTERNET SERVER that can respond to more than one INTERNET ADDRESS so that it appears as a separate host machine for each address.

virtual LAN a networking system in which several NETWORKS are connected and used as if they were a single network.

virtual machine (VM) see VIRTUAL 8086.

virtual memory the use of a HARD DRIVE as if it were part of the main RAM memory of the computer. Since the capacity of a disk can be much larger than the memory of a small microcomputer, this can allow very large programs to operate in small machines, just as if the machine had a very much larger memory than is physically present. See also PERMANENT SWAP FILE.

virtual path the path to a FILE location on a remote machine as viewed by a BROWSER. The virtual part of the name is prefixed by the TILDE sign (~), and this virtual name is automatically replaced by the SERVER with the true path to the file. These virtual paths are often found in WEB SITE names where a web space is allocated to a non-commercial user.

virtual point of presence or **virtual PoP** a location used as a relay to an INTERNET PROVIDER, usually by way of a local telephone call.

virtual private network the use of ENCRYPTION to make an insecure NETWORK (usually the INTERNET) usable for secure communications. For the highest level of security, a FIREWALL may be needed at each end.

virtual reality the use of a COMPUTER SYSTEM to simulate a realistic set of conditions, after the fashion of a flight simulator (see SIMULATION) and using techniques from computer games. The most valuable applications are in the design of buildings (a prospective buyer can simulate walking through the building before it is constructed), working in dangerous spaces using a robot and in medical teaching. The user of a virtual reality system needs to wear a helmet so that stereoscopic images (see STEREOSCOPY) can be presented to the eyes, providing a three-dimensional effect, and in some systems sensors are fitted to the hands so that images of arms in the picture can be realistically moved. See also DATA GLOVE.

virtual storage the use of a HARD DRIVE as if it were memory, using a range of ADDRESS (sense 1) numbers that are reserved for this purpose.

virus a program (which can include a MACRO written for a WORD PROCESSOR or SPREADSHEET) that attaches to other program files and replicates itself so that it will be spread when programs are passed from one user to another. A virus can also be attached to a document TEMPLATE for a word processor. The effects of a virus can range from a message to CORRUPTION of a HARD DRIVE and destruction of files. Antivirus software (see VACCINE) can be of limited use, but the only certain way of avoiding a virus is to be certain that all programs loaded into the computer are from legitimate sources. A disk that has passed among several users must always be suspect.

visible bell or **visual bell** a flashing display used as an ALERT, particularly for users with hearing difficulties.

Visicalc™ the pioneer SPREADSHEET program. This was written for the APPLE-2 MICROCOMPUTER in 1979, after the idea had been rejected as impracticable by the SOFTWARE HOUSES (sense 1) for MAINFRAMES. One mainframe manufacturer went as far as to proclaim that the program was a hoax. The subsequent reaction was to find as many ways as possible around the copyright and to invent new names. The program is now obsolete, although many modern spreadsheets are closely modelled on it.

Visual Basic a PROGRAMMING LANGUAGE used with MICROSOFT WINDOWS that allows the user to make use of the Windows system and create Windows programs. The MACRO LANGUAGE used for MACROS in Microsoft applications such as WORD (sense 1), EXCEL and ACCESS (sense 4) is a form of Visual Basic known as Visual Basic for Applications (VBA).

Visual Basic for Applications see VBA.

visual bell see VISIBLE BELL.

visual display unit see VDU.

visual programming a system of programming for MACROS in which activating a LEARN instruction allows every following action to be coded into a program file until LEARN is selected again. This program file can then be replayed to reproduce the sequence of actions.

VLB (VESA local bus) a BUS with better performance than the older ISA bus, used on computers with the 80486 processor then replaced on PENTIUM machines by PCI.

VLF (very low frequency) the FREQUENCY range that is much lower than the 100 kHz used for long-wave radio broadcasts, in particular the range from 50 Hz to 50 kHz that is emitted by domestic electrical equipment. MONITORS (sense 1) radiate in the range 50 Hz to 500 kHz, as do domestic TV receivers, and some reports claim that working too close to an unshielded monitor can cause cell damage over a long period. This once sparked a lucrative market in low-emission monitors, despite the fact that radiation from the front of a monitor is much weaker than from the sides or the rear.

VLSI (very large scale integration) the construction of circuits containing millions of components on a single silicon chip.

VM see VIRTUAL 8086.

V number see V SERIES.

voice-coil drive a method of moving the READ/WRITE HEAD of a HARD DRIVE that uses a coil and magnet construction similar to that of a LOUDSPEAKER. The advantage of such a drive is that it is quiet, fast and self-parking. The older STEPPING MOTOR drive is now obsolete.

voice grade channel a signal-transmitting system that can use only a very limited BANDWIDTH, about 100 Hz to 2000 Hz. This is the range that is used by telephone systems for speech. In order to make use of voice grade channels, which include telephone lines and cassette recorders, the computer signals must be encoded as tones, using one frequency to represent digital 0 and another frequency to represent digital 1. The rate at which data can be sent using this coding is very slow unless data compression and advanced coding systems are used.

voice input see DIRECT VOICE INPUT.

voice mail or **phone mail** a computer-based system that performs the actions of a telephone answering machine at much greater cost and complexity.

voice modem a fast MODEM with a loudspeaker output and microphone input that can be used for VOICE MAIL and usually for FAX as well.

voice recognition see DIRECT VOICE INPUT.

voice synthesis see SPEECH SYNTHESIS.

volatile memory a MEMORY system that loses data when power is switched off. RAM memory is volatile, ROM is not. Some varieties of RAM, notably CMOS RAM, can make use of a backup battery that maintains data storage when the mains power supply is removed. This allows programs or data to be retained for as long as the battery can provide power, which may be up to five years. The memory is still volatile, however, in the sense that disconnecting the backup battery will clear the memory at once. See also EPROM; PROM.

volatile storage memory such as DRAM that loses all information when the power supply is shut down.

volatility the measure of how volatile a data storage system is. See VOLATILE MEMORY.

voltage (V) the measure of electrical potential difference in a circuit. The amount of voltage expresses the driving force for electric current, analogous to the pressure of water causing flow in a pipe.

volume 1. loudness, or sound AMPLITUDE. **2.** a measurable quantity of anything, such as volume of sales.

volume control a Microsoft WINDOWS 95 onwards UTILITY that places a CONTROL PANEL like an AUDIO MIXER on screen. This allows you to set the master VOLUME (sense 1) control level and also the levels of individual inputs (from compact disc, tape, microphone and other sources) so that no change in volume will occur when you switch from one source to another. See Fig. 43.

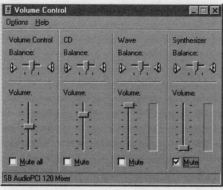

Fig. 43. **Volume control**. A typical form of mixer panel containing volume controls for sound output and for various inputs.

volume label a name used to identify a FLOPPY DISK and saved in the DIRECTORY (sense 2) of the disk.

von Neumann, John a mathematician who set out the basic tenets of the sequential STORED PROGRAM COMPUTER in 1946, building on work carried out from 1944 onwards at Los Alamos. His concept of a PROGRAM consisted of splitting a task into a sequence of small logical steps leading to the solution of a problem. Computers that employ this approach are called von Neumann machines, and this group includes most modern computers. Compare NEURAL NETWORK.

VRAM see VIDEO RAM.

V series or **V number** the standards for SERIAL links using a MODEM. The most important at the moment are those used for faster speeds, such as V32 for 9,600 bits per second and V90 for 56,000 bits per second. Other V numbers refer to standards such as V24, the signal definitions, V25, automatic answer sequence, V25bis, command language for automatic dialling, V42, error correction methods, and V42bis for data compression. See also CCITT PROTOCOL.

VT-52 a type number for a terminal whose characteristics are defined. Another common type is VT 100.

VxD or **VXD** see VIRTUAL DEVICE DRIVER.

wait state a CLOCK cycle in which a MICROPROCESSOR does nothing, waiting for memory to respond. Wait states had to be programmed into computers to slow down memory access before the use of memory banking and CACHE memory on the processor.

wall follower anyone who uses a simple procedure to solve a problem on the basis of previous success.

wallpaper see DESKTOP PATTERN.

wake up to make a remote system respond to data signals by sending a suitable code or PASSWORD.

WAN (wide area network) any NETWORK that uses SERIAL links extending over large distances (more than 1 kilometre, typically). See LAN.

wand a form of reader for a BAR CODE that need only be moved across the bar code.

want list see WISH LIST.

warm boot or **warm start** a machine restart in which memory is cleared and the operating system reloaded but without switching off the power supply unit (PSU) or the HARD DRIVE. Compare COLD BOOT.

warm link a link (see LINKED OBJECT) between a SERVER APPLICATION and a CLIENT APPLICATION that is updated only when the user opts to do so, not automatically. See also HOT LINK.

warm start see WARM BOOT.

warning a visual and/or audible message to the operator to indicate potential danger, such as overwriting of data or destruction of a disk file. Audible warnings are often more useful than visual ones, although FLASHING messages can also be useful.

watermark an image that appears, often in faint print, on each page of a DOCUMENT. For example, MICROSOFT WORD can create a watermark as part of a HEADER or FOOTER and specifying a light colour for text and graphics in the frame.

wave editor a program that allows digitized (see DIGITIZE) sound patterns to be viewed and edited, cutting out unwanted silences and even altering the sounds themselves.

waveform the shape of a graph that plots wave AMPLITUDE against time.

waveform digitization the representation of an electrical WAVEFORM by a set of numbers, usually carried out by an A TO D converter. For control and measurement, virtually every quantity that can be measured can be expressed as an electrical signal. The numbers represent the value of the AMPLITUDE of the wave at regular intervals. The interval size has to be chosen so that the waveform can be reasonably well reproduced and a rule, formulated by Shannon, is that the SAMPLING RATE at which measurements are made should be at least two times the highest FREQUENCY present in the waveform. Waveform digitization is required mainly for REAL TIME analysis of waveforms and requires fast computing speeds.

wavelength the distance between adjacent peaks of a wave.

wavelet any non-finite wave that has starting and ending times and also FREQUENCY limits.

wavetable a set of digitized (see DIGITIZE) samples of sounds of musical instruments. A SOUND CARD that features a wavetable can be used as a sound synthesizer, with or without MIDI control.

wax-ribbon printer a form of THERMAL PRINTER used mainly for high-quality colour printing in which hot needles strike a wax-impregnated ribbon and transfer some coloured wax to the paper. Such printers are very quiet in operation, comparable to INKJET in quality.

Web see WWW.

web browser a BROWSER that can connect to the World Wide Web (WWW).

webcam a SLOW-SCAN VIDEO CAPTURE CAMERA whose output in compressed form (see COMPRESSED FILE) is available on a WEB SITE.

webcasting the transmission of compressed (see COMPRESSED FILE) VIDEO pictures from one site to many others on the World Wide Web (WWW).

WebCrawler one of the many SEARCH ENGINE sites on the World Wide Web (WWW).

webmaster or **webmistress** a person responsible for the creation and maintenance of WEB PAGES at a particular WEB SITE.

web page a document that can contain text, graphics and sound, identified by its URL and available to any BROWSER on the World Wide Web (WWW).

web site a computer that acts as a SERVER for WEB PAGES. The computer may act as a virtual server, containing several WEB SITES.

web trading buying and selling conducted over the World Wide Web (WWW). This will require some form of secure connection if personal details and credit card information are exchanged.

weight see LINE WEIGHT.

weighting the assigning of more importance to some computing items than to others, used in data processing to indicate that some terms used in a search may be more significant than others.

well-behaved program a PROGRAM, of which there are few examples, that makes use only of operating system (OS) routines. Most programs bypass the operating system and take direct control of the video system in order to achieve higher speeds.

whale song see MODEM MANTRA.

what-if analysis a SPREADSHEET action in which important data items can be changed and the effects of the change displayed on the WORKSHEET.

What's This an action, indicated by a question-mark ICON, that provides HELP (sense 1) for Microsoft WINDOWS 95 onwards. When the icon is clicked, a POINTER (sense 1) appears and can be moved to any part of a WINDOW on the screen. Clicking at this point will then produce a short help item on the contents of that part of the window.

what you see is what you get see WORD PROCESSOR.

Whetstone a form of BENCHMARK for processing numerical work, named from the Leicestershire town where it was designed in 1976. Other names for benchmarks have subsequently used the second letter 'h' as a humorous gesture to this origin; see DHRYSTONE; KHORNERSTONE.

White Book 1. the ADOBE SYSTEMS POSTSCRIPT manual that describes the FONTS. **2.** one of the set of books that describes the CD-ROM system.

white-box testing or **glass-box testing** or **logical testing** testing by using selected data. The internal structure of the program is examined so that TEST (sense 2) data can be chosen that will reveal any possible weaknesses. Compare BLACK-BOX TESTING.

White Pages an INTERNET directory service for finding EMAIL addresses for named persons.

white space unused space in a DTP page. Excessive white space is undesirable and indicates inadequate planning of the document.

Whois an INTERNET directory service for finding information on named persons.

wide area network see WAN.

wide SCSI a form of SCSI connection using a 16-bit BUS.

widget any imaginary and not particularly useful contraption.

widow the last line of a DTP or WORD PROCESSOR paragraph that occurs as the first line on a new page, separating it from the rest of the paragraph. Word processors can be set up so that they will automatically move text so as to avoid creating widows or ORPHANS.

width the number of columns that can be printed on SCREEN (sense 1) or on paper.

wild card a symbol that can represent one or any group of other characters. The term is used particularly of disk filenames, but it is also used in specifying DATABASE searches. A common wild-card character is the asterisk (*). For example, the disk command DELETE L* would cause deletion of files LONG, LAME, LIMB, L123, or any other file whose name starts with the letter L. The ? character is often used as a single wild card, meaning that it can be substituted for any single character.

WIMP see GUI.

Win32 the common core of code that is used on all the MICROSOFT 32-bit operating systems (OS) from WINDOWS 95 onwards.

Win 95, Win 98 see WINDOWS 95, WINDOWS 98.

Win 2000 see WINDOWS 2000.

Winchester disk see HARD DRIVE.

window a section of the SCREEN (sense 1) that can be defined by the coordinates of its corners and used as an independent screen. This allows a set of HELP (sense 1) instructions, for example, to be displayed independently of displays on the rest of the screen because the window is unaffected by the clear screen command or by scrolling on the main screen. Some form of window control has been a feature of small computers for some time and is normally handled by commands to the operating system (OS). Most window systems allow multiple windows, which can be in different colours and feature actions such as sideways and backwards scrolling. Different windows can also be moved about on screen. Windows are used extensively along with ICONs and the MOUSE in the GUI system first employed commercially on the Apple Lisa and Macintosh.

Windows see MICROSOFT WINDOWS.

Windows 95 the operating system (OS) for PERSONAL COMPUTERs released in August 1995 as the successor to Windows 3.1. Windows 95 uses much more 32-bit code than the older versions and is faster and more reliable in use, particularly when running applications that have been written to match its characteristics (such as MICROSOFT OFFICE 95). The MS-DOS system is still used by Windows 95, but this is less apparent to the user. Subsequent versions have steadily moved away from support for older applications and towards total 32-bit working. See also THUNK.

Windows 98 an update to WINDOWS 95, incorporating the changes made in SERVICE RELEASEs and with changes in LOOK-AND-FEEL, such as extensive use of single rather than double CLICK (sense 1) actions. A revised version was released in 1999.

Windows 2000 the version of the MICROSOFT WINDOWS operating system (OS) that followed WINDOWS 98. Windows 2000 is also WINDOWS NT-5, combining what had previously been different (although basically related) operating systems.

Windows accelerator a form of GRAPHICS ACCELERATOR BOARD specifically designed to speed up the SCREEN (sense 1) handling of MICROSOFT WINDOWS programs.

Windows CE a version of MICROSOFT WINDOWS designed for PALMTOP COMPUTERs and other small-scale applications.

Windows for Workgroups a version of MICROSOFT WINDOWS 3.1 that supports the use of NETWORK connections. This was originally version 3.1, later extended to 3.11 before being replaced by WINDOWS 95.

Windows Messaging the EMAIL application for MICROSOFT WINDOWS, replaced by OUTLOOK.

Windows metafile format see WMF.

Windows NT a 32-bit PRE-EMPTIVE MULTITASKING operating system (OS) from Microsoft that was released earlier than Microsoft WINDOWS 95 but which requires much larger memory and HARD DRIVE resources. Windows and NT have now merged as WINDOWS 2000 or NT-5.

Windows socket (**winsock**) a method for interfacing MICROSOFT WINDOWS applications with NETWORK signals.

Windows Write or **Write** a simple WORD PROCESSOR that was packaged with MICROSOFT Windows 3.1. Write used its own format, creating document files with a WRI EXTENSION. In Microsoft WINDOWS 95 onwards it has been replaced by WORDPAD, which creates DOC files compatible with those of MICROSOFT WORD. Nevertheless, Wordpad lacks some features of Write, particularly the ability to read corrupted text files.

WIN.INI the initialization file for MICROSOFT Windows 3.1, not used by WINDOWS 95 onwards. See INI FILE; REGISTRY.

winsock see WINDOWS SOCKET.

Wintel the HARDWARE and SOFTWARE combination of an INTEL processor in a machine running MICROSOFT WINDOWS.

WINzip a WINDOWS version of the PKZIP compression (see COMPRESSED FILE) software.

wipe file to erase a file. This may mean erase from memory or erase from disk. In most cases the file stored on the disk is not actually erased, only its memory POINTERS or its disk DIRECTORY (sense 2) entry. The file will be destroyed when it is overwritten or, in the case of a file in memory, when the computer is switched off. See also UNDELETE; RECYCLE BIN.

wireless LAN a form of local area NETWORK (LAN) that uses a radio link as part of its networking connections.

Wirth, Niklaus the inventor of PASCAL, who has been a great influence on the progress of PROGRAMMING LANGUAGES since 1970.

wish list or **want list** a list of features that users would like to see on SOFTWARE but seldom obtain. One item high on all wish lists is a way to make a keyboard ignore key combinations other than the use of the shift key.

Wizard a MICROSOFT technique, used in the MICROSOFT OFFICE programs and in WINDOWS 95 onwards, to lead the user through what would otherwise be a tedious set of actions. The Wizard reduces such actions to a set of steps, each simple, in which the choices are clear, and on completion of the Wizard actions the desired objective, for example, the installation of a MODEM, is carried out.

wizzywig see WORD PROCESSOR.

WMF (Windows metafile format) a VECTOR GRAPHICS format used extensively in WINDOWS and for WORD PROCESSOR illustrations.

woofer a large LOUDSPEAKER intended for optimum reproduction of bass notes. See also TWEETER.

word 1. two BYTES of data. 2. (**Word**) see MICROSOFT WORD.

WordArt an ADD-IN program for MICROSOFT WORD or Microsoft POWERPOINT that allows text to be manipulated into patterns. For example, a name can be made to appear as if wrapped around a cylinder.

word break the splitting of a word at the end of a line. Most WORD

PROCESSORS do not do this, preferring to take the whole word into the next line. See also WRAP AROUND.

word count a WORD PROCESSOR action that counts words in a document. In fact, most word counts operate by counting the number of times that the space bar has been pressed, but a few make a count of the actual words. This feature is often omitted in word processors, even very expensive types, but it is very important for many authors and journalists. Many word processors do not show a word count on SCREEN (sense 1), and some will display a word count only after some other action, such as a SPELLCHECK, has been completed. MICROSOFT WORD 6.0 onwards will show a count of pages, words, characters, lines and paragraphs.

Word for Windows see MICROSOFT WORD.

WordPad a text editor for Microsoft WINDOWS 95 onwards. WordPad can produce files that are compatible with those of MICROSOFT WORD or it can save work as plain ASCII files.

WORDPERFECT™ a successful WORD PROCESSOR that is fast in use, available in both DOS and MICROSOFT WINDOWS versions and incorporates a large number of writing accessories. A junior version for DOS only was called *LetterPerfect* and was once widely used on PORTABLE machines.

word processor or **text processor** a combination of TEXT EDITOR and PRINT FORMATTER that is used for typing letters, documents or books. Because the system is computer-based, it is much easier to edit, so text can be made perfect before being printed. Modern word processors are all of the WYSIWYG (pronounced *wizziwig*) type, meaning that what is seen on the screen represents the text almost exactly as it will appear on paper. This requires the use of a HIGH-RESOLUTION GRAPHICS display on the screen. In some programs, there is also a PRINT PREVIEW facility to show exactly what the text will look like on paper. Any type of word processor allows the user to enter text, RECORD (sense 2) it, replay recorded text, merge text and format text for printing. For many authors and journalists, a word count is essential, yet surprisingly few programs provide one. See also BOILERPLATE; BLOCK OPERATION; CENTRING; FOOTER; HEADER (sense 1); INDENT; JUSTIFY; LINE LENGTH; LINE SPACING; MARKER; MICROSOFT WORD; PAGE BREAK; PRINT PAUSE; PROPORTIONAL SPACING; RULE; SEARCH AND REPLACE; SPELLCHECK; STANDARD FORM; TABULATION; THESAURUS; UNDERLINE; WORD COUNT; WORDPERFECT; WORDSTAR; WORD WRAP; WRITE-PROTECT.

word size the number of BITS that a CPU can deal with in one operation. As microcomputers have developed, the word size that can be used has increased from 8 through 16 to 32 and now to 64 bits.

word spamming the constant repetition of a word in a WEB PAGE in the hope that this will increase the likelihood of the page being presented at the top of a search list.

WORDSTAR™ an early and very successful WORD PROCESSOR program for DOS. Wordstar became a standard for business use despite the need to learn very complicated KEY (sense 1) sequences for control. Wordstar was later challenged by WORDPERFECT and MICROSOFT WORD but clung to its methods for a considerable time before bringing out a MICROSOFT WINDOWS version. The later Windows versions were outstandingly good value for money.

word wrap a WORD PROCESSOR action to move a word from the end of one line to the start of the next so that it is not split between lines. See also WORD BREAK.

workaround a way of avoiding a BUG or other software problem. The need for the workaround should be eliminated by a SERVICE RELEASE or in the next version of the software.

workbook a set of WORKSHEETs in a SPREADSHEET program that belong together, either because they form a multidimensional worksheet or because more than one sheet is needed to carry different types of information.

work disk a disk used for temporary storage of data during the running of a program. Some languages demand the use of a work disk for keeping files, even if the files are never permanently recorded. See also TEMPORARY STORAGE.

work file a file created for temporary use (such as holding data in the course of sorting) which will be deleted after use.

workgroup a set of users whose computers are connected by a NETWORK. Version 3.11 of WINDOWS was designated as *Windows for Workgroups* because it incorporated networking abilities into the familiar Windows 3.1 scheme, but the addition to the name was dropped for WINDOWS 95 onwards although the same facilities exist.

working storage see TEMPORARY STORAGE.

worksheet the form of SCREEN (sense 1) display and printed output from a SPREADSHEET, consisting of ROWS AND COLUMNS. The worksheet is the document produced by a spreadsheet program, and several worksheets in a set are referred to as a WORKBOOK. See also CELL (sense 1); CONSOLIDATION (sense 2).

workstation 1. a microcomputer system with communications facilities, usually part of a NETWORK. **2.** a complete system that can offer all the business applications of a microcomputer in one PACKAGE (sense 1). **3.** a computer stand, with all the computer peripherals kept in one place.

World Wide Web see WWW.

World Wide Web Consortium the standards-setting organization for the World Wide Web (WWW).

worm 1. a piece of code inserted by a CRACKER into a program that will cause faulty or eccentric operation. **2. (WORM)** (write once read many times) a form of OPTICAL drive that the user can write and read. The written data cannot, however, be erased.

wormhole see BACK DOOR.

wow slow fluctuations of FREQUENCY on a signal replayed from tape. Compare FLUTTER.

wrap around 1. a system of displaying text in which words are never split. See WORD WRAP. **2.** in SCREEN (sense 1) GRAPHICS, the term signifies that the CURSOR is never off-screen. If the cursor is moved too far to the left of the screen, it appears at the right-hand side, and so on.

wraparound text text that is distorted so as to appear wrapped around an object such as a cylinder.

wrap text an action that is used when a FRAME (sense 1) is inserted into a document. You can opt whether or not to wrap text around the frame, so that the text appears on each side, or to let text cover the frame.

Write see WINDOWS WRITE.

write 1. to store on disk or backup tape. **2.** to cause graphics shapes, in SCREEN (sense 1) GRAPHICS, to appear on screen.

write-back cache a CACHE memory that is organized to delay writing to a HARD DRIVE until forced to, such as when the cache is full or when data has to be read or after a set maximum time interval. Data can be lost if a machine that uses a write-back cache is switched off before the data has been written, so Microsoft WINDOWS 95 onwards requires the user to shut down, using a command that will save essential files and empty the cache before printing a message on the SCREEN (sense 1) to indicate that the computer can be switched off.

write once read many times see WORM (sense 2).

write-only language a PROGRAMMING LANGUAGE that is so complex that once written it cannot be understood by anyone reading it – including the author.

write-protect to protect data on an individual file or complete disk. A file can be write-protected by setting its READ-ONLY ATTRIBUTE. A complete FLOPPY DISK can be write-protected by using a LABEL or shutter. The older type of 5.25-inch disk required a label to be placed over a notch at the side of the disk; the 3.5-inch type of disk requires the shutter to be opened.

write-through cache a form of CACHE memory that is effective for reading data only. All written data is sent directly to the HARD DRIVE without using the cache. The improvement in speed provided by this type of cache is less than for a WRITE-BACK CACHE, but saved data is more secure against power failure or a deliberate switch-off.

WWW (World Wide Web) an INTERNET information service invented by Tim BERNERS-LEE, using HYPERTEXT documents. A CLIENT-SERVER system is used, with the client employing a BROWSER to interrogate the web and download documents.

WYSIWYG see WORD PROCESSOR.

X25 a set of standards for long-distance dialling and LONG-HAUL NET-WORKS using PSS methods.

x86 a way of referring to the older INTEL processors, the 8086, 80286, 80386 and 80486.

X-coordinate a number representing the distance measured in a horizontal direction along the SCREEN (sense 1). See also Y-COORDINATE.

XCOPY a DOS command that will COPY (sense 2) data in a way that can be programmed by the user, such as saving only files that have just been edited. XCOPY makes use of the ARCHIVE ATTRIBUTE.

X-direction the horizontal dimension of the SCREEN (sense 1). See also Y-DIRECTION.

X-distance a distance measured in a horizontal direction. On SCREEN (sense 1), the X-distance is measured horizontally starting at the left-hand side of the screen. The units of distance are screen PIXELS or column widths, depending on the screen MODE. See also Y-DISTANCE.

Xenix™ a variety of UNIX developed by the Microsoft Corporation for commercial, as distinct from academic, use.

Xeon™ see PENTIUM II.

xerography a copying system that depends on an 'image' formed from electrostatic charges. Powdered ink is attracted to the charged parts of a surface and can then be pressed on to paper. The method is the basis of most forms of office copiers and also of the LASER PRINTER for computer systems.

XGA (extended graphics array) a higher-resolution version of VGA.

x-height the height of the LOWER-CASE letters of a FONT, measured from the BASE LINE.

Xmodem a set of PROTOCOLs (sense 1) for file transfers that will correct transmission errors by requesting retransmission of a block of data when an error is detected. See also ZMODEM.

XOFF a signal sent to a remote computer along a communications link to indicate that no transfer should be made.

XON a signal sent to a remote computer along a communications link to indicate that a transfer can be made.

XOR the logical action of exclusive OR, meaning one or the other but not both.

XT bus architecture the type of 8-bit BUS used on the early IBM PERSONAL COMPUTERs, replaced by ISA in 1982.

XT disk a 5.25-inch-diameter 360-kilobyte disk, also known as double-sided double-density (DDDS), as used in the PC-XT type of computer.

XT keyboard the older style of 82-key KEYBOARD as used on the original IBM PC-XT machines. See also AT KEYBOARD.

XVGA an extended form of VGA, with higher resolution available.

XY graph any GRAPH using conventional X-Y axes but often used to mean a SCATTER GRAPH.

X-Y plotter an automatic graph PLOTTER, fed with X and Y position signals, that will plot the point at the corresponding position on a piece of paper. It is particularly useful in scientific and engineering applications. See also CHART RECORDER; FLATBED PLOTTER.

Y2K or **Year 2000** the problem that is caused by systems that store year data as two figures only, so that 00 might mean 1900 or 2000. This has been a minor problem for home computers, most of which were updated in adequate time, but caused considerable work for old systems, particularly those using COBOL. Another aspect to the problem is that some systems will not recognize Year 2000 as a leap year.

Yahoo a vast index and SEARCH ENGINE on the World Wide Web (WWW). A version intended for younger users is called *Yahooligans*.

Y-coordinate a number representing the distance measured on the SCREEN (sense 1) in a vertical direction. See also X-COORDINATE.

Y-direction a vertical direction, at right angles to the X-DIRECTION.

Y-distance a distance measured in the Y-DIRECTION. On a SCREEN (sense 1) the term often denotes a distance measured from the top of the screen downwards. The unit of distance will be the vertical size of the screen PIXEL or the width of a text row, depending on the screen MODE that is used.

Year 2000 see Y2K.

Yellow Book the set of standards applicable to CD-ROM design; see also RED BOOK.

Yellow Pages an information service on the World Wide Web (WWW).

Ymodem a development of XMODEM that speeds up transfer by using larger blocks of data.

Z

zap to remove something. For example, 'zap memory' means to clear the memory of data.

Zapf dingbats or **dingbats** a FONT that is composed of a set of symbols rather than ALPHANUMERIC characters.

Z-axis the third axis on a three-dimensional graph, used for depth.

zero the digit 0. This should not be confused with the ASCII code for zero, which is 48. Files that use ASCII codes can therefore use the number zero as a TERMINATOR (sense 1) without any risk of confusion with the ASCII-coded zero.

zero compression the removal of unnecessary leading or trailing zeros from a number. A number that was entered into the computer as 001.120 would, for example, appear as 1.12 after zero compression.

zero insertion force socket (ZIF) a SOCKET intended to allow easy insertion and removal of an IC. The ZIF socket allows the chip to be dropped into place and the connections made by clamping the pins after insertion. The clamp can be loosened to allow the chip to be pulled out. ZIF sockets have been used to allow for upgrading a computer, particularly for the earlier Pentium type of chip and all others using the SOCKET-7 connection. Later Intel processors have been permanently mounted on subboards and these are fitted into a slot rather than a socket.

zeroize to set memory or number variables to ZERO, thus ensuring that the memory will contain zero bytes and number quantities will all be assigned with the number zero.

zeroth the first item in a list that starts with a counter at zero.

zero wait state the use of a processor with no WAIT STATE pauses because of the implementation of BANKED MEMORY and internal CACHE memory.

ZIF see ZERO INSERTION FORCE SOCKET.

Zip™ drive a type of removable media drive using 100- and 150-megabyte disks of FLOPPY size, manufactured by Iomega. See also JAZ DRIVE.

zip file a compressed file created using a utility such as PKZIP.

Zmodem another variation of XMODEM, which achieves higher speed. See also YMODEM.

zone a part of the SCREEN (sense 1) used in a DTP program as composing space or for some particular purpose such as entering text.

zoom a magnified or diminished view of an IMAGE (sense 2), particularly in CAD programs.